Social Issues Primary Sources Collection

Government, Politics, and Protest

Essential Primary Sources

Social Issues Primary Sources Collection

Government, Politics, and Protest

Essential Primary Sources

K. Lee Lerner, Brenda Wilmoth Lerner, and
Adrienne Wilmoth Lerner, Editors

THOMSON

GALE

Detroit • New York • San Francisco • New Haven, Conn. • Waterville, Maine • London

Government, Politics, and Protest: Essential Primary Sources

K. Lee Lerner, Brenda Wilmoth Lerner, and Adrienne Wilmoth Lerner, Editors

Project Editors
Dwayne D. Hayes and John McCoy

Editorial
Luann Brennan, Grant Eldridge, Anne Marie Hacht, Joshua Kondek, Andy Malonis, Mark Milne, Rebecca Parks, Mark Springer, Jennifer Stock

Permissions
Lisa Kincade, Margaret Chamberlain-Gaston, Jacqueline Key

Imaging and Multimedia
Dean Dauphinais, Leitha Etheridge-Sims, Lezlie Light, Michael Logusz, Dan Newell, Christine O'Bryan, Kelly A. Quin, Denay Wilding, Robyn Young

Product Design
Pamela A. Galbreath

Composition and Electronic Capture
Evi Seoud

Manufacturing
Rita Wimberley

Product Manager
Carol Nagel

LIBRARY OF CONGRESS CATALOGING-IN-PUBLICATION DATA

Government, politics, and protest : essential primary sources / K. Lee Lerner, Brenda Wilmoth Lerner, and Adrienne Wilmoth Lerner, editors.
  p. cm. – (Social issues primary sources collection)
  Includes bibliographical references and index.
  ISBN-13: 978-1-4144-0327-4
  ISBN-10: 1-4144-0327-5 (alk. paper)
  1. Social problems--Sources. 2. Social history--Sources. 3. World politics--Sources. I. Lerner, K. Lee. II. Lerner, Brenda Wilmoth. III. Lerner, Adrienne Wilmoth.

  HN13.G68 2006
  320.9--dc22   2006023438

This title is also available as an e-book.
ISBN-13: 978-1-4144-1263-4
ISBN-10: 1-4144-1263-0
Contact your Thomson Gale sales representative for ordering information.

Printed in the United States of America
10 9 8 7 6 5 4 3 2

Table of Contents

1 PROTESTERS AND PROTEST RIGHTS

2 CIVIL AND HUMAN RIGHTS

4   CIVIL LIBERTIES AND SOCIAL ISSUES

6 LABOR, TRADE, AND GLOBALIZATION

Advisors and Contributors

While compiling this volume, the editors relied upon the expertise and contributions of the following scholars, journalists, and researchers who served as advisors and/or contributors for *Government, Politics, and Protest: Essential Primary Sources*:

Annessa Babic, Instructor and Ph.D. Candidate
SUNY at Stony Brook
Stony Brook, NY

Alicia Cafferty
University College
Dublin, Ireland

James Anthony Charles Corbett
Journalist
London, UK

Bryan Davies, J.D.
Ontario, Canada

Sandra Dunavan, M.S.
Saline, Michigan

Larry Gilman, Ph.D.
Sharon, Vermont

Amit Gupta, Ph.D.
Ahmedabad, India

Stacey N. Hannem
Journalist
Quebec, Canada

Alexander Ioffe, Ph.D.
Russian Academy of Sciences
Moscow, Russia

S. Layman, M.A.
Abingdon, MD

Adrienne Wilmoth Lerner (J.D. Candidate)
University of Tennessee College of Law
Knoxville, Tennessee

Pamela V. Michaels, M.A.
Forensic Psychologist
Santa Fe, New Mexico

Caryn Neumann, Ph.D.
Ohio State University
Columbus, Ohio

Mark Phillips, Ph.D.
Abilene Christian University
Abilene, Texas

Nephele Tempest
Los Angeles, California

Melanie Barton Zoltán, M.S.
Amherst, Massachusetts

Government, Politics, and Protest: Essential Primary Sources is the product of a global group of multi-lingual scholars, researchers, and writers. The editors are grateful to Christine Jeryan, Amy Loerch Strumolo, Kate Kretschmann, Judy Galens, and John Krol for their dedication and skill in copyediting both text and translations. Their efforts added significant accuracy and readability to this book. The editors also wish to acknowledge and thank Adrienne Wilmoth Lerner and Alicia Cafferty for their tenacious research efforts.

The editors gratefully acknowledge and extend thanks to Peter Gareffa, Carol Nagel, and Ellen McGeagh at Thomson Gale for their faith in the project and for their sound content advice. Special thanks go to the Thomson Gale copyright research and imaging teams for their patience, good advice, and skilled research into sometimes vexing copyright issues. The editors offer profound thanks to project managers Dwayne Hayes and John McCoy. Their clear thoughts, insights and trusted editorial judgment added significantly to the quality of *Government, Politics, and Protest: Essential Primary Sources*.

Acknowledgements

Copyrighted excerpts in *Government, Politics, and Protest: Essential Primary Sources*, were reproduced from the following periodicals:

AFP newswire, November 20, 2001. Copyright 2001 Agence France Press. Republished with permission of Agence France Press, conveyed through Copyright Clearance Center, Inc.—*AP Newswire*, March 11, 1988; June 16, 2005; September 25, 2005. Copyright 1988, 2005 Associated Press. All rights reserved. All reproduced by permission.—*Associated Press*, September 8, 1977. Copyright © 1977 by Reprint Management Services. Reprinted with permission of the Associated Press.—*Boston Globe*, May 2, 2005. © Copyright 2005 Globe Newspaper Company. Reproduced by permission.—*Economist*, April 7, 1979. Copyright © 1979 The Economist Newspaper Ltd. All rights reserved. Further reproduction prohibited. www.economist.com. Reprinted with permission.—*The First Twenty Years of the People's Association*, December, 1980. Reproduced by permission.—*Guardian*, January 5, 2000 for "A Bitter Pill For the World's Poor" by Isabel Hilton. Copyright Guardian Newspapers Limited 2000. Reproduced by permission of the author.—*Labour Party Conference Report 1994*, 1994. Reproduced by permission.—*Mother Jones.com*, November 24, 1999. Copyright 1999 Foundation for National Progress. Reproduced by permission.—*The Nation.com*, August 16, 2004. Copyright © 2004 by The Nation Magazine/The Nation Company, Inc. Reproduced by permission.

New Statesman, March 15, 1968; May 10, 1968. Copyright © 1968 New Statesman, Ltd. Both reproduced by permission.—*New York Times*, December 25, 1959. Copyright © 1959, renewed 1967 by United Press International. Reproduced by permission.—*New York Times*, January 16, 1968; March 28, 1973; March 8, 1992; April 17, 1993; December 12, 2004; January 14, 2006; January 21, 2006; January 28, 2006 Copyright © 1968, 1973, 1992, 1993, 2004, 2006 by The New York Times Company. All reproduced by permission.—*Oxfam Briefing Paper*, November, 2003. Reproduced with the permission of Oxfam GB, Oxfam House, John Smith Drive, Cowley, Oxford OX4 2JY UK. www.oxfam.org.uk Oxfam GB does not necessarily endorse any text or activities that accompany the materials.—*Presbyterian News Service*, February 4, 2003. Reproduced by permission.—*Psychology Today*, July 18, 2003. Reproduced by permission.—*Seattle Post-Intelligencer (online)*, December 3, 1999. Reproduced by permission.—*Time Magazine*, April 18, 1969. Copyright © 1969 Time, Inc. All rights reserved. Reproduced by permission.—*Toronto Star*, June 26, 2005. Copyright 2005 Toronto Star Newspapers, Ltd. Reproduced by permission of Torstar Syndication Services.—*Washington Post and washingtonpost.com*, December 15, 2005. Copyright © 2005, Washington Post. Reprinted with permission.

Copyrighted excerpts in *Government, Politics, and Protest: Essential Primary Sources*, were reproduced from the following books:

From *Searchlight*. CARF/Campaign against racism and fascism, 1981. Reproduced by permission.—From "Draft of the Declaration of the Establishment of the State of Israel," in *Major Knesset Debates: 1948-1981*. Edited by Netanel Lorch. University Press of America, 1993. Copyright © 1993 by The Jerusalem Center for Public Affairs. All rights reserved. Reproduced by permission.—From *The*

Party That Isn't: North Korea's Unification-Revolution Party. Research Center for Peace and Unification, 1980. Reproduced by permission.—Adams, Gerry. From *Selected Writings.* Brandon Book Publishers, 1997. © Gerry Adams 1982,1983, 1986, 1988, 1990, 1992, 1993, 1994, 1995, 1996. Reproduced by permission.—Adams, Gerry. From *A Farther Shore: Ireland's Long Road to Peace.* Random House, 2003. Copyright © 2003 by Gerry Adams. All rights reserved. Used by permission of Random House, Inc. In the UK by permission of the author.—Cook, Alistair. From *Letter From America: 1946-2004.* Allen Lane, Penguin, 2004. Copyright © 2004 the Estate of Allistair Cooke 2004. Reproduced by permission of Penguin Books, Ltd. In the rest of the world by permission of Palazzo Editions Limited.—Fogerty, John. From *Willy and the Poorboys (Creedence Clearwater Revival Album).* Jondora Music, 1969. Reproduced by permission of Concord Music Group, Inc.—Schwartz, David. From *Circle of Protest: Political Ritual in the Tibetan Uprising.* Hurst 1994 Ronald David Schwartz Reproduced by permission.—Sharp, Gene. From *The Politics of Nonviolent Action.* Porter Sargent Publishers, 1973. Reproduced by permission.—Wituska, Krystyna. From "Letters From Halle-Salle Prison," in *Wall Tappings.* Edited by Judith A. Scheffler. Feminist Press, 2002. Copyright © 1986, 2002 by Judith A. Scheffler. All rights reserved. Reproduced by permission.

Illustrations appearing in *Government, Politics, and Protest: Essential Primary Sources*, were received from the following sources:

A crane lifts up a huge solar panel on the Kyoselas new head office building on Monday, December 1, 1997 in Kyoto, Japan, photograph. AP Images.—A Soviet soldier sticks his head up out of his armored personnel carrier in Vilnius, Lithuania, during a 1991 crackdown by the USSR, photograph. Igor Gavrilov/ Time Life Pictures/Getty Images.—African immigrants sing and dance, photograph. AP Images.—AIDS activists stage a die-in on the road leading to President Bush's vacation home in Kennebunkport, Maine, photograph. AP Images.—AIDS treatment drug Saquinavir. AP Images.—American school children, photograph. © Bettmann/Corbis.—Animal rights demonstrators gather near Oxford University medical laboratory science site, Oxford, England, Thursday August 25, 2005, photograph. AP Images.—Anti-draft protesters meet a wall of police in front of the Clay Street Induction Center, Oakland, California, photograph. Oakland Tribune AP Images.—Anti-nuclear activists flash the victory sign, photograph. Sean Gallup/Newsmakers.—Anti-war protester burns US flag with small group demonstrate,

CNN Center in Atlanta, photograph. AP Images.—Archbishop Henry Edward Manning administering the temperance pledge to crowds gathered at Clerkenwell Green, London, photograph. Hulton Archive/Getty Images.—Barricades made of overturned cars block Gay Lussac Street in Paris after rioting and demonstrations by students, photograph. © Bettmann/ Corbis.—Boston Tea Party, photograph. © Bettmann/ Corbis.

Boy searches for food in a garbage pile on the side of a downtown Port-au-Prince, photograph. AP Images.—British troops, photograph.© Bettmann/ Corbis.—Brooklyn Federal Court Judge Jack B. Weinstein, photograph. © Bettmann/Corbis.—Bulter, Ruby, joins an anti-war protest, photograph. AP Images.—Bush supporter Abigail Bennett of Manchester, NH, in front of Manchester City Hal, photograph. AP Images.—Catholic children playing with toy guns under and Irish Republican Army mural in the mainly Catholic, photograph by Peter Morrison. © AP Images.—Chartist riot at Newport, Isle of Wight, Britain, photograph. © Bettmann/ Corbis.—Chavez, Cesar, photograph. AP Images.—Chinese man stands alone to block a line of tanks heading east on Beijings Cangan Blvd In Tiananmen Square, photograph. AP Images.—Churchill, Winston, Former British Prime Minister, photograph. AP Images.—Civil rights leaders sing a protest song, We Shall Overcome, photograph. © Bettmann/Corbis. —Cojti, Doris,4, holds her vaccination certificate, photograph. AP Images.—College students carrying pro-American signs, photograph. AP Images.—Counter demonstrators Ruben Israel, Stephen James, heckle anti-war demonstrators as they march in Washington to protest the US troops presence in Iraq, photograph. AP Images.—Crowd of single women protests at Boston Emergency Relief Headquarters, photograph. © Corbis/Bettmann.—Cruikshank, George, illustrator. From an illustration in Uncle Tom's Cabin, by Harriet Beecher Stowe. © Bettmann/Corbis. — Czech Republic soldiers raise their national flag during ceremony at NATO headquarters, Brussels, Belgium, photograph. AP Photo Dusan Vranic/AP Images.

Czech, photograph. Photo by Three Lions/Getty Images.—Demonstrators applaud as a man burns his draft card during a Vietnam War protest in New York Central Park, photograph. © Bettmann/Corbis.—Demonstrators from the People for the Ethical Treatment of Animals (PETA) rally partially naked as they protest the fur industry, photograph. Mike Theiler/Getty Images.—Demonstrators march in Belfast, Northern Ireland, Great Britain, photograph. © Michel Philippot/Sygma/Corbis.—Demonstrators protest against the layoff of WPA workers in San Francisco, California, photograph. © Horace Bristol/ Corbis.—Demonstrators protesting the Reagan policy on AIDS hold a sign that says Money for Condoms, Not for Contras Washington, DC, photograph. © JP Laffont/Sygma/Corbis.—Deportees, arrive at Pier 3, in Hoboken, New Jersey, photograph. AP Images.— Disabled protesters from the group Not Dead Yet block the driveway of the Woodside Hospice House, photograph. © Tom Fox/Corbis.—Drama students stage a die-in in front of the Strehler theatre in Milan, Italy, photograph. AP Images.—East German citizens help each other climb the Berlin Wall, photo- graph. © Reuters/Corbis.—Federal troops escort Black students as they arrive in a US Army stationwa- gon at Central High School in Little Rock, Arkansas, photograph. AP Images.—Filipinos light candles to commemorate AIDS victims and mark World AIDS Day, photograph © ERIK DE CASTRO/Reuters/ Corbis.—First Woolworths lunch counter sit-in, con- ducted by Joseph McNeill, Franklin McCain, Billy Smith, and Clarence Henderson, photograph. © Jack Moebes/Corbis.

Former South African President Nelson Mandela casts his vote for his country's third democratic general election, photograph. ALEXANDER JOE/ AFP/Getty Images.—Free speech protestor Danielle White holds a sign while in the Free Speech Zone outside the FleetCenter at the Democratic National Convention in Boston, photograph. © Marc Serota/Reuters/ Corbis.—Free Tibet graffiti stands on a wall in a street in Darjeeling, India, photograph. © Alison Wright/ Corbis.—French Navy Commando, photograph. AP Images.—French revolution of 1848, photograph. © Bettmann/Corbis.—Gandhi, Mahatma, photograph. © Bettmann/Corbis.—Gannett, Frank playing horse- shoes while campaigning for President, photograph. Hans Knopf/Pix Inc./Time Life Pictures/Getty Images.—Gingrich, Newt, photograph. AP Images.— Global Business Coalition President and CEO Richard Holbrooke, Secretary of State Condoleezza Rice and Senator Hillary Clinton, D-NY speak during Global Business Coalition Gala Awards, photograph. AP Images.—Goldman, Emma, photograph. The Library of Congress.—Government doctors and nurses stage a picket outside the hospital, Quezon City, north of Manila, photograph. AP Images.—Governor George C. Wallace, surrounded by Alabama state troopers, photograph. © Bettmann/Corbis.—Greenpeace acti- vists in gas masks protest the Republican policy agenda Contract With America, photograph. Terry Ashe/ Time Life Pictures/Getty Images.—Guard looks out from a tower at Guantanamo Bay in Cuba, photograph. AP Images.—Guthrie, Woody, photograph. AP

Images.—Harvard University student, photograph. © Bettmann/Corbis.—Hasiba, sits with Afghan woman protesters clad in burqas in front of the presidential palace in Kabul, photograph. AP Images.

Hawaii's annexation ceremony, Iolani Palace in Honolulu, photograph. AP Images.—Hillel, Abba, Dr., photograph. AP Images.—Hoffman, Abbie Hoffman,photograph. AP Images.—Homeless child on a protest march to the home of British Health Minister Kenneth Robinson, photograph. M. McKeown/Express/Getty Images.—Indian school girl Nivedita, 8, takes part in a protest urging people to drink natural healthy drinks, photograph, INDRANIL MUKHERJEE/AFP/Getty Images.— Indonesian local village chiefs from Toba Samosir, North Sumatra, hold pickets reading STOP VIOLATION IN OUR LAND, photograph. BAY ISMOYO/AFP/Getty Images.—Indonesian protes- ters hold banners during a White Band Day demon- stration in Jakarta, Friday, photograph. AP Images.— Iranian women in burqas show their identity cards to a soldier as they line up to vote, photograph. © Christine Spengler/Sygma/Corbis.—Jews are rounded up by the Nazis in Warsaw, Poland during the German invasion in World War II, photograph. AP Images.—Katangais students in their premises at La Sorbonne University in Paris, France during the student riots, photograph. Alain Nogues/Corbis.—Kent State University, photo- graph. © Reuters/Corbis.—King, Martin Jr., Dr. and his demonstrators stream over an Alabama River bridge at the city limits of Selma, Alabama, photo- graph. AP Images.—King, Martin Luther, Jr., staring out of the window of a jail cell, in the Jefferson County Courthouse in Birmingham, Alabama, photograph. © Bettmann/Corbis.—King, Martin Luther Jr., photograph. AP Images.—Kuhn, Maggie, photo- graph. © David Turnley/Corbis.—League of Nations in the Salle de Reforme in Geneva, photograph. Hulton Archive/Getty Images.—Leary, Timothy, Abbie Hoffman, Jerry Rubin at a news conference, photograph. AP Images.—Left-wing demonstrators celebrate in front of a water cannon during May Day demonstrations, Berlin, photograph. © Arnd Wiegmann/Reuters/Corbis.

Lindbergh, Charles, photograph. © Bettmann/ Corbis.—Liverpool, England, photograph. © Hulton- Deutsch Collection Corbis.—Lorena Pizarro and Mireya Garcia, activists of the Relatives of Missing People Association, photograph. MARTIN BERNETTI/ AFP/ Getty Images.—Love, Ken, photograph. AP Images.— Male student climbs on a Soviet tank during a protest against the Soviet crackdown in Prague, Czechoslovakia, photograph. © Bettmann/Corbis.—Man hammers away at the Berlin Wall, photograph. AP Images.—Marchers carry a casket along a section of the US-Mexico border fence in Tijuana, Mexico, Friday, October 1, 2004 to mark 10th anniversary of Operation Gatekeeper, photograph. AP Images.—May Day Parade in Moscow's Red Square, on May 1, 1928 , photograph. AP Images.—McCarthy, Joseph R., photograph. Michael Rougier/Time Life Pictures/Getty Images. —Members of Bonus Army gather with an American flag, in a shantytown at US Capitol, June 21, 1932, photograph. MPI/Getty Images.—Members of Code Pink, gather outside the gates of National Cemetery in Los Angeles, photograph. AP Images.—Members of National Womens Liberation Party hold protest signs at Miss America Pageant, Atlantic City, New Jersey on September 7, 1968, photograph. AP Images.— Members of the pro-life organization Operation Rescue block the door to a San Diego abortion clinic, photograph. © Mark Peterson/Corbis.—Men line up at their voting station in St Paul, Minnesota, to register for the draft under the newly passed Selective Service Act of 1940. photograph. © Minnesota Historical Society/Corbis.—Migrant activists protesting nightly patrols by citizen volunteers who search for people crossing US-Mexico border, photograph. David McNew/Getty Images.

Millions of paper clips are shown on display in a train car outside at Whitwell Middle School in Whitwell, Tennessee, photograph. AP Images.— Miners reading pro-union slogans on a board, before voting on the issue of staying in the Miners Federation, Bedwas, Wales, photograph. © Hulton-Deutsch Collection/Corbis.—"Misguided Lady Putting up Poster," anti-isolationist political cartoon, illustration. © Corbis.—Nader, Ralph, photograph. © Mark Constantini/San Francisco Chronicle/Corbis.— Nassau, New Providence, The Principal Rendezvous of the Anglo-Confederate Blockade-Runners An illustration shows a paddlewheel steam ship sailing into harbor. © Corbis.—National Guardsmen (rifles pointed), photograph. UPI/Corbis-Bettmann.— Native American Indians, part of the Indians of All Tribes Inc., occupying the former prison at Alcatraz Island, photograph. AP Images.—Nazi war propaganda publication, photograph. Walter Sanders/ Time Life Pictures/Getty Images.—Nazi-era images, Israeli settlers protest Israeli withdraw from Gaza, photograph. Marco Di Lauro/Getty Images.—Nepalese political activists shout slogans as they brandish banners and placards during a protest rally in Kathmandu, photograph. DEVENDRA M SINGHAFP/AFP/Getty Images.—New Orleans, Louisiana- A small boy kicks a can onto the heap of garbage on the fourth day of a strike by Sanitation Department workers, photograph.

© Bettmann/Corbis.—Newton, Massachusetts, Vice President Spiro Agnew, photograph. © Bettmann/ Corbis.—North Korean government, reporting convention in Pyongyang, photograph AP Photo Xinhua, Ji Xinlong/AP Images.

Norway, 1942 A child stands next to anti-Nazi graffiti showing support for the deposed Norwegian king, photograph. © Bettmann/Corbis.—Office employees make the thumbs down outside the French embassy at Makati in Manila, the Philippines, photograph. AP Images.—Page 6 of Mens Petition Against Annexation of Hawaii, photograph. Courtesy of the National Archives and Records Administration—Pakistani students run away from teargas fired by police, photograph. AP Images.—Pakistanis rally in Karachi, Pakistan, photograph. © Akhtar Soomroepa/Corbis.—Palestinian workers return home from Israel through Eraz crossing in Gaza Strip, photograph. © SUHAIB SALEM/Reuters/ Corbis.—Palestinians spray paint on a Danish flag, during a protest Masked gunmen demonstrated outside of the European Union office to protest, photograph. © Shawn Baldwin/Corbis.—Parade float calling for an end to the Prohibition on alcohol, photograph. © Hulton-Deutsch Collection/Corbis.—Participants in a pro choice march in Washington, DC , photograph. © Viviane Moos/Corbis.—Patriot Act, photograph. © Shaul Schwarz/Corbis.—Pedestrian studies a sign in the window of Arundel Books in Seattle, photograph. AP Images.—People march down a street in Moscow, during a May Day parade, photograph. Keystone/Getty Images.—Pitt, William, photograph. Getty Images.— Poles march in the streets with Solidarity banners during Pope John-Paul IIs 1987 visit to Poland, photograph. © Bernard Bisson/Sigma Corbis.—Police arrest an anti-globalization protester, November 20, 2003, photograph. Spencer Platt/Getty Images.

Police officer, directs a protester during a demonstration outside Loews Santa Monica Beach Hotel in Santa Monica, California, photograph. AP Images.— Police wearing riot gear forming human barricade against anti-Nuclear demonstrators, photograph. © Regis Bossu/Corbis Sygma. —Political Cartoon from Puck, 1886. © Corbis.—Poster advertising a mass-meeting of workers on the evening after the Haymarket Square riot of May 4, 1886. © Bettmann/ Corbis.—President Bush, photograph. AP Images.— President Franklin Roosevelt delivering his first inaugural address, 1933, photograph. © Underwood and Underwood/Corbis.—President Lyndon B. Johnson celebrates with Martin Luther King, Jr, Ralph Abernathy, and Clarence Mitchell after signing the Voting Rights bill into law, photograph. © Corbis.— President of the EU Commission Jaques Santer, left, shakes hands with Microsoft chairman Bill Gates, photograph. AP Images.—Prince Emmanuel Filibert of Savoy carries the Olympic torch in the streets of Turin, northern Italy, photograph. AP Images.—Pro choice demonstrators Courtney Davis, Katherine Schwartz and Nickie Ittner hold a banner that says Keep Your Laws off my Body, photograph © Reuters/Corbis.—Pro-Bush demonstrators heckled the participants of an anti-War, anti-Bush, and anti-RNC march in NYC, photograph. © Benjamin Lowy/Corbis.

Pro-choice demonstrators, photograph. Robert Sherbow/ Time Life Pictures/Getty Images.—Pro-Tibet demonstrators protest against the Beijing 2008 Olympic bid, Toronto, Canada, Sunday, March 11, 2001, photograph. AP Images.—Protest poster from Vilnius, Lithuania, caricaturing and demonizing Soviet leader Mikhail Gorbachev, photograph. Igor Gavrilov/Time Life Pictures/Getty Images.—Protester outside site of the Organization of American States foreign ministers meeting in Windsor, Ontario, Canada, photograph. AP Images.—Protester waves a multicolor flag with a Star of David during a gay rights demonstration in Warsaw, photograph. AP Images.—Protesters burn an American flag during an anti-war demonstration in Washington, DC, photograph. Hulton Archive/Getty Images.—Protesters holding up signs critical of USA Patriot Act during a demonstration, New York Stock Exchange, photograph. AP Images.—Protesters march to the Statehouse in Montpelier, Vermont, photograph. AP Images.—Protesters Rallying Against NAFTA, holding banners and a Mexican flag, in San Francisco, California, photograph. © Reuters Corbis.—Protestors smash windows of a McDonalds restaurant in downtown Gothenburg during clashes between Swedish police and anti European Union demonstrators, photograph. © Pontus Lundahlepa/Corbis.—Pulver, Bruce, photograph. AP Images.—Quang Duc, Buddhist monk, protesting, photograph. AP Images. —Randolph, Philip, photograph. Copyright © Bettmann/Corbis. —Riots on the opening day of the meeting of IMF and World Bank in Prague, photograph. AP Images.—Robinson, Jackie, photograph. Mike Smith/Pix Inc./Time Life Pictures/Getty Images.

Rosa Parks riding on newly integrated bus following Supreme Court ruling ending successful 381 day boycott of segregated buses Boycott, photograph. Don Cravens/Time Life Pictures/Getty Images.—Rosa Parks, left, with Coretta Scott King, center, and Myles Horton, photograph. AP Images.— Russian special police officer stands by the portrait of Bolshevik leader Vladimir Lenin, Gudermes, Chechnya, photograph. © Reuters/Corbis.—Senator Joseph R. McCarthy, photograph. © Bettmann/

Corbis.—Sheehan, Cindy, photograph. AP Images.—Signs confiscated from Wal-Mart protestors entering a meeting of the Chicago City Council lie on the floor outside the council chambers, photograph. Scott Olson/Getty Images.—Silhouettes of parade goers and policemen are seen in front of a display Singapore, celebrations of Singapores 40th anniversary of independence AP Images.—Smith, Tommie (center), John Carlos (fists raised), and Peter Norman (left), having received medals, 1968 Olympics, Mexico City, photograph. AP Images.—Smith, Tommie, photograph © Bettmann/Corbis.—Soldiers of the Polish Home Army man a barricade in a suburb of Warsaw, photograph. Hulton Archive/Getty Images.—South African man holds up a flag for the Afrikaner Resistance Movement (AWB), South Africa, photograph. © Megan Patricia Carter Trust/Sygma/Corbis.—South Korean protester dressed as a Chinese policeman at a rally in Athens, photograph. KIM KYUNG-HOON/Reuters/Corbis.

South Korean protesters in Seoul brandish bamboo sticks at riot police during rally, photograph. © Rhee Dong-Min/Reuters/Corbis.—Stamps attached by the British Government to goods sold in the American colonies, photograph. © Bettmann/Corbis.—Stowe, Harriet Beecher, illustration. —Striking silk workers at Turn Hall, Paterson, New Jersey, photograph. © Bettmann/Corbis.—Students march against top-ups, central London, photograph. AP Images.—Suffragette being force-fed, photograph, 1912. © Bettmann/Corbis.—Television showing Bill Gates, photograph. AP Images.—Temperance crusaders praying outside a New York tavern, illustration. MPI/Getty Images.—The Atlantic Charter, photograph. Illinois Digital Archives—The Bonus Army, stage a massed vigil on the lawn of the US Capital, Washington DC, while the Senate debate their case, photograph. MPI/Getty Images.—The Boston Boys dressed as Indians throwing tea chests from English ships into Boston harbor in historic tax protest (also known as the Boston Tea Party), photograph. Time Life Pictures/Mansell/Time Life Pictures/Getty Images.—The Declaration of the United Nations, photograph. © Hulton-Deutsch Collection/Corbis.—The first Earth Day conservation awareness celebration, New York, New York, photograph. Hulton Archive/ Getty Images.—Thin woman carrying a bundle followed by a child, photograph. © Hulton-Deutsch Collection/Corbis.—Thoreau, Henry, David, photograph. Hulton Archive/Getty Images.—Three white police officers arresting African American man during riots in Los Angeles, California, 1992 photograph. © Peter Turnley/Corbis.—Travis and naked protesters perform at the MTV Europe

About the Set

Essential Primary Source titles are part of a ten-volume set of books in the Social Issues Primary Sources Collection designed to provide primary source documents on leading social issues of the nineteenth, twentieth, and twenty-first centuries. International in scope, each volume is devoted to one topic and contains approximately 150 to 175 documents that include and discuss speeches, legislation, magazine and newspaper articles, memoirs, letters, interviews, novels, essays, songs, and works of art essential to understanding the complexity of the topic.

Each entry includes standard subheads: key facts about the author; an introduction placing the piece in context; the full or excerpted document; a discussion of the significance of the document and related event; and a listing of further resources (books, periodicals, Web sites, and audio and visual media).

Each volume contains a topic-specific introduction, topic-specific chronology of major events, an index especially prepared to coordinate with the volume topic, and approximately 150 images.

Volumes are intended to be sold individually or as a set.

THE ESSENTIAL PRIMARY SOURCE SERIES

- *Terrorism: Essential Primary Sources*
- *Medicine, Health, and Bioethics: Essential Primary Sources*
- *Environmental Issues: Essential Primary Sources*
- *Crime and Punishment: Essential Primary Sources*
- *Gender Issues and Sexuality: Essential Primary Sources*
- *Human and Civil Rights: Essential Primary Sources*
- *Government, Politics, and Protest: Essential Primary Sources*
- *Social Policy: Essential Primary Sources*
- *Immigration and Multiculturalism: Essential Primary Sources*
- *Family in Society: Essential Primary Sources*

Introduction

The right to protest, especially the actions of government, is among the most cherished rights. Such right of protest is a signatory mark of civil society. It is in the nature of protest, however, to challenge authority and law, for it is sometimes the law that is the subject of protest. From the illegal protests of colonial rebels to longstanding cultural traditions of the French *manifestation* protest often provides the tectonic force that drives the landscape of political and societal change.

Government, Politics, and Protest: Essential Primary Sources provides sources from the nineteenth century to the present, with an emphasis on the global diversity of both the cause and nature of protest, and provides abundant evidence that the right to protest often comes to blows with a governmental concern to preserve order. In the United States, the legal pillars of protest are grounded in the freedom of speech protected in the First Amendment of the Bill of Rights. Other countries that offer such guarantees express and enshrine the right to protest in various bills, laws, and declarations. Yet, the primary sources selected show that civil protest is often at odds with the law, constantly pushing and probing the limits of speech and assembly. Arrests of protestors, even those engaged in peaceful protest, are not uncommon. Critics of erosions of civil liberties further argue that globally the right of protest is subject to slow systematic erosion by governments. This historical tension between protest and government, independent of the underlying cause, is also explored in the entries selected.

Protests often arouse passions on both sides of an issue because protests can be very effective. Tidal waves of protest can force rapid political and social change. Steady protest may weather and transform politics and society more slowly, but just as surely. Protest also provides some of the most poignant moments and images in human history, and the editors of *Government, Politics, and Protest: Essential Primary Sources* have attempted to include a number of historically significant primary source images that compliment the readings provided. Many of the images stand as primary sources in their own right.

Although it is beyond the scope of this collection to cover all protest movements, and all facets of those movements and their underlying issues, *Government, Politics, and Protest: Essential Primary Sources* provides a wide-ranging and readable collection of sources designed to stimulate interest and critical thinking.

The editors sincerely hope that this book helps to foster a deeper understanding of the nature of protest, and inspires citizens to utilize the right of peaceful protest to continue the far from finished struggles for human rights, peace, and dignity—most especially on behalf of those least able to affect action themselves.

K. Lee Lerner, Brenda Wilmoth Lerner, &
Adrienne Wilmoth Lerner, editors
London, U.K. and Jacksonville, Florida
August, 2006

About the Entry

The primary source is the centerpiece and main focus of each entry in *Government, Politics, and Protest: Essential Primary Sources*. In keeping with the philosophy that much of the benefit from using primary sources derives from the reader's own process of inquiry, the contextual material surrounding each entry provides access and ease of use, as well as giving the reader a springboard for delving into the primary source. Rubrics identify each section and enable the reader to navigate entries with ease.

ENTRY STRUCTURE

- Primary Source/Entry Title, Subtitle, Primary Source Type
- Key Facts—essential information about the primary source, including creator, date, source citation, and notes about the creator.
- Introduction—historical background and contributing factors for the primary source.
- Primary Source—in text, text facsimile, or image format; full or excerpted.
- Significance—importance and impact of the primary source related events.
- Further Resources—books, periodicals, websites, and audio and visual material.

NAVIGATING AN ENTRY

Entry elements are numbered and reproduced here, with an explanation of the data contained in these elements explained immediately thereafter according to the corresponding numeral.

Primary Source/Entry Title, Subtitle, Primary Source Type

[1] **An Urgent Appeal From Our Anguished Hearts**

[2] Tibetan Protest Against Chinese Rule, 1989

[3] **Letter**

[1] **Primary Source/Entry Title:** The entry title is usually the primary source title. In some cases where long titles must be shortened, or more generalized topic titles are needed for clarity primary source titles are generally depicted as subtitles. Entry titles appear as catchwords at the top outer margin of each page.

[2] **Subtitle:** Some entries contain subtitles.

[3] **Primary Source Type:** The type of primary source is listed just below the title. When assigning source types, great weight was given to how the author of the primary source categorized the source.

Key Facts

[4] **Author:** Friends in the Struggle of the Lhasa Tiger-Leopard Group

[5] **Date:** September 27, 1989

[6] **Source:** Schwartz, Ronald David. *Circle of Protest: Political Ritual in the Tibetan Uprising.* New York; Columbia University Press, 1994.

[7] **About the Author:** The Lhasa Tiger-Leopard Group was one of the groups of political activists who opposed the Chinese occupation of Tibet. A prominent member of this group was Lhakpa Tsering, whose

death while in Chinese custody in 1989 focused international attention on the treatment of the Tibetan people under Chinese rule.

[4] **Author, Artist, or Organization:** The name of the author, artist, or organization responsible for the creation of the primary source begins the Key Facts section.

[5] **Date of Origin:** The date of origin of the primary source appears in this field, and may differ from the date of publication in the source citation below it; for example, speeches are often delivered before they are published.

[6] **Source Citation:** The source citation is a full bibliographic citation, giving original publication data as well as reprint and/or online availability.

[7] **About the Author:** A brief bio of the author or originator of the primary source gives birth and death dates and a quick overview of the person's work. This rubric has been customized in some cases. If the primary source written document, the term "author" appears; however, if the primary source is a work of art, the term "artist" is used, showing the person's direct relationship to the primary source. For primary sources created by a group, "organization" may have been used instead of "author." Other terms may also be used to describe the creator or originator of the primary source. If an author is anonymous or unknown, a brief "About the Publication" sketch may appear.

Introduction Essay

[8] **INTRODUCTION**

Until 1950, Tibet was a sovereign nation, a remote and rugged land situated in the Himalayan Mountains. Tibet had been a sanctuary for the Buddhist faith since A.D 700. For many centuries, Tibetan political leadership and religious direction were linked to the authority of the Buddhist spiritual leader, the Dalai Lama. The current Dalai Lama is the fourteenth to hold this title. In 1950, Buddhist monks comprised approximately one sixth of the population of the capital city of Lhasa.

In 1950, China invaded Tibet and took control of all government institutions. Chinese rulers claimed Tibet as a part of their empire at various times in the previous five hundred years, and the newly founded People's Republic of China relied upon this historical connection as a basis to occupy the country. Years of unrest first boiled into an armed uprising against the Chinese occupiers in 1959. The Tibetan opposition to the Chinese occupation was brutally suppressed, as numerous Tibetan leaders were summarily executed

by the Chinese. The Dalai Lama and other prominent religious leaders fled to India, where they established a government-in-exile.

In the years that followed the 1959 uprising, there were repeated allegations of atrocities committed by the Chinese against the local population. Numerous Buddhist monasteries in Lhasa and throughout Tibet were destroyed and their contents sold. The Chinese government placed significant restrictions on the observance of the Buddhist faith in Tibet. Tibetan nationals were the subjects of discrimination by the Chinese. The Dalai Lama petitioned numerous world leaders to come to the aid of the Tibetan people against the Chinese occupation, with little success. Tibet was now ruled by China as the Tibetan Autonomous Region, a component part of the greater People's Republic of China.

Another popular uprising occurred in various parts of Tibet in 1987. This revolt was spearheaded by young political dissidents, and it attracted a vigorous armed response from the Chinese military. Demonstrations continued in Lhasa into 1988, as the Dalai Lama and the Tibetan government-in-exile renewed their efforts to secure international support for the Tibetan nationalist cause. Martial law was imposed by China in March 1989, and a series of prison terms in excess of fifteen years were imposed upon the various leaders of the insurgency.

In 1989, one of the Tibetan dissident leaders, twenty year old Lhakpa Tsering, died in Chinese custody at the notorious Drapchi Prison in Lhasa. Tsering was a member of the Tiger-Leopard Group whose members and supporters authored the letter of September 27, 1989.

[8] **Introduction:** The introduction is a brief essay on the contributing factors and historical context of the primary source. Intended to promote understanding and equip the reader with essential facts to understand the context of the primary source.

To maintain ease of reference to the primary source, spellings of names and places are used in accord with their use in the primary source. Accordingly names and places may have different spellings in different articles. Whenever possible, alternative spellings are provided to provide clarity.

To the greatest extent possible we have attempted to use Arabic names instead of their Latinized versions. Where required for clarity we have included Latinized names in parentheses after the Arabic version. Alas, we could not retain some diacritical marks (e.g. bars over vowels, dots under consonants). Because there is no generally accepted rule or consensus regarding the format of translated Arabic names, we have adopted the straightforward, and we hope sensitive, policy of using names as they are used or cited in their region of origin.

Primary Source

[9] PRIMARY SOURCE

The great Protector Deities long ago commanded by Padmasambhava have not lost their power.

Though we have brought this fate upon ourselves, it is not time for the end of the aeon.

Are we not under the domination of misfortune and demonic hindrances?

Look with your eye of wisdom and see if it is time now for the forces of power to rise up.

One deity of this land of snow mountains incarnates the compassion of all the Buddhas and Bodhisattvas.

A pure unmistaken line of incarnations has come to Tibet.

Now, when the melodious sound of the wheel of Dharma is spoken, everywhere in foreign lands,

Look with your eye of wisdom on those who have stayed behind, like the corpse of a dead lion.

In the midst of the ruins of the great monasteries, magnificent places of pilgrimage, blades of grass sing a sad song.

The disputations of the monks arguing the five bundles of Sutras are not heard; a foreign song is sung.

Wild animals dwell in the hermitages and caves of practitioners of Tantra and Mantra.

Look with your eye of wisdom, you gods, how have we erred to make this happen?

Although the Buddha's wisdom is always as close to the faithful as a body and its smell,

Because of the two obstructions, I and those like me are deprived of the Buddha's words, and commentaries.

Like the agony of a baby bird whose training is not yet complete,

Look soon with your eye of wisdom upon the suffering of those sentient beings so we may see his face.

Because Tibetans are a people with great compassion and faith in Dharma,

The precious life and warm blood of our heroes and heroines is flowing in the streets of Lhasa.

Look soon with your eye of wisdom upon the torment of our friends in the struggle,

Held in the court of the Lord of Death, brought by inhuman foreign enemies to the land of men.

Unexcelled, most powerful Protectors of Tibet,

Were we not like mother and child, we could not ask this of you.

This is the anguished appeal of a child separated from its mother.

Though unbidden, we are powerless not to speak out, please be patient.

Though the ripening of our sins is relentless, there must be and end.

The Dalai Lama has said the great star of the dawn has already risen.

If we hold fast to the words of truth of the Tibetans,

There is no doubt we will soon be victorious.

From all the friends in the struggle of the Lhasa Tiger-Leopard Group

27 September 1989

[9]   **Primary Source:** The majority of primary sources are reproduced as plain text. The primary source may appear excerpted or in full, and may appear as text, text facsimile (photographic reproduction of the original text), image, or graphic display (such as a table, chart, or graph).

The font and leading of the primary sources are distinct from that of the context—to provide a visual clue to the change, as well as to facilitate ease of reading. As needed, the original formatting of the text is preserved in order to more accurately represent the original (screenplays, for example). In order to respect the integrity of the primary sources, content some readers may consider sensitive (for example, the use of slang, ethnic or racial slurs, etc.) is retained when deemed to be integral to understanding the source and the context of its creation.

Primary source images (whether photographs, text facsimiles, or graphic displays) are bordered with a distinctive double rule. Most images have brief captions.

The term "narrative break" appears where there is a significant amount of elided (omitted) material with the text provided (for example, excerpts from a work's first and fifth chapters, selections from a journal article abstract and summary, or dialogue from two acts of a play).

Significance Essay

[10] SIGNIFICANCE

Contemporaneous to the mobilization of Tibetan opposition against the Chinese, the national government of China was engaged in the suppression of the dissident movement that instigated the public demonstrations held at Tiananmen Square in Beijing between April 1 and June 4, 1989. Hundreds of protestors were killed or injured when the Chinese troops ended the demonstrations, events that touched off world-wide condemnation of Chinese tactics and attitudes toward apparently peaceful forms of protest.

The letter (in the form of a poem) written by the Friends of the Lhasa Tiger-Leopard Group does not mention China or the occupation of Tibet by name. However, the authors employ a mix of traditional Tibetan images, such as the mountains and the lion, against the context of death, blood, and foreign intervention. It is apparent that the passion for Tibetan nationalism had not faded in the almost forty years between the writing of the poem and the occupation of Tibet by China. The reference in the poem to blood flowing in the streets is with respect to the imposition of martial law by the Chinese in March, 1989, and the further repressive steps taken to quell political protests in Lhasa.

At the time of the publication of the letter by the Lhasa Group, the Dalai Lama had advanced his work to engage Western governments to support Tibetan nationalism. The Dalai Lama was awarded the Nobel Peace Prize on December 10, 1989, in recognition of his efforts to promote a peaceful resolution to the Chinese occupation of Tibet.

The award of the Peace Prize to the Dalai Lama is significant on a number of levels, as it appeared to stimulate a greater international interest in the Tibetan conflict. Between 1990 and 1993, there was a massive exodus of Buddhist monks from Tibet to India. At the same time, a number of nations passed resolutions that condemned the actions of the Chinese government as taken against the Tibetan population to limit their religious practices and cultural traditions. In 1991, the United States Senate passed a resolution declaring that Tibet was an occupied country, and that the Dalai Lama headed a government in exile. A similar resolution was passed by the Australian Senate in the same year.

The weight of international political opinion continued to favor the Tibetan nationalist cause in August of 1991, when the United Nations passed a resolution in support of Tibet as a national entity, as did the European Parliament in 1992. In the United States, President Bill Clinton signed legislation that supported the efforts of the Dalai Lama and Tibetan nationalists to preserve their identity.

It is clear that the various political pronouncements made on behalf of the Tibetan nationalists had a limited impact upon the conduct of the Chinese in Tibet. It is also clear that little or no effort was made by any nations to compel change in Tibet through the direction of economic pressure upon China. Shortly after signing the Tibetan legislation in 1994, the United States re-affirmed China's 'Most Favored Nation' trading status; this designation confirmed China's desirability as an American economic partner. The apparently contradictory signals of the United States in 1994 regarding China, in contrast to the 1991 Senate resolution can only interpreted as a belief on the part of the United States that the fostering of Chinese trade was of greater national importance that the use of trade sanctions to pursue a resolution in Tibet.

The Chinese actions against Tibetan national symbols continued in 1996 when the public display of photographs of the Dalai Lama was banned.

In recent years there has been a status quo maintained with respect to the Chinese governance of Tibet and the resolution of the human rights concerns raised by Tibetans. The Dalai Lama has persisted in his worldwide efforts to pursue a solution to the dispute with China. It is significant that while the government-in-exile continues to work from its base in northern India, the Dalai Lama has now advanced a desire to negotiate a resolution with China where Tibet would not be an independent nation, but an autonomous area within China where Tibetan religious and cultural practices can be preserved. Current American policy with respect to Tibet mirrors this attitude; In September, 2002, the Foreign Relations Authorizations' Act as signed by President George W. Bush affirmed American support for the preservation of Tibetan language and culture.

[10] Significance: The significance discusses the importance and impact of the primary source and the event it describes.

[11] FURTHER RESOURCES

Books

Dreyer, June Teufel and Barry Sautman, ed. *Contemporary Tibet; Politics, Development, and Society in a Disputed Region.* Armonk, New York; M.E. Sharpe, 2005.

Goldstein, Melvyn C. *The Snow Lion and the Dragon: China, Tibet, and the Dalai Lama*. Berkley; University of California Press, 1997.

Periodicals

Faison, Seth. "Dissident Monk Said to Die in Prison in Chinese-Controlled Tibet." *New York Times* (July 28, 1996): section 1, page 11.

Web sites

Nobel Prize Committee. "Nobel Peace Prize, 1989." April 1, 2005. <http://www.nobelprize.org/peace/laureates/1989/index.html> (accessed May 26, 2006).

[11] **Further Resources:** A brief list of resources categorized as Books, Periodicals, Web sites, and Audio and Visual Media provides a stepping stone to further study.

SECONDARY SOURCE CITATION FORMATS (HOW TO CITE ARTICLES AND SOURCES)

Alternative forms of citations exist and examples of how to cite articles from this book are provided below:

APA Style

Books: Stowe, Harriet Beecher. (1852). *Uncle Tom's Cabin*. London: John Cassell. Excerpted in K. Lee Lerner and Brenda Wilmoth Lerner, eds., (2006). *Government, Politics, and Protest: Essential Primary Sources*, Farmington Hills, Mich.: Thomson Gale.

Periodicals: Selbourne, Maud. (1915). The Suffragette Dilemma in World War One. *The Conservative and Unionist Women's Franchise Review*. 22 Excerpted in K. Lee Lerner and Brenda Wilmoth Lerner, eds., (2006). *Government, Politics, and Protest: Essential Primary Sources*, Farmington Hills, Mich.: Thomson Gale.

Web sites: *City and County of San Francisco; Department of Elections*. "No Military Recruiters in Public Schools, Scholarships for Education and Job Training." Retrieved May 29, 2006 from http://www.sfgov.org/site/election_index.asp?id=33918. Excerpted in K. Lee Lerner and Brenda Wilmoth Lerner, eds., (2006). *Government, Politics, and Protest: Essential Primary Sources*, Farmington Hills, Mich.: Thomson Gale.

Chicago Style

Books: Stowe, Harriet Beecher. *Uncle Tom's Cabin*. London: John Cassell, 1852. Excerpted in K. Lee Lerner and Brenda Wilmoth Lerner, eds., *Government, Politics, and Protest: Essential Primary Sources*, Farmington Hills, Mich.: Thomson Gale, 2006.

Periodicals: Selbourne, Maud. "The Suffragette Dilemma in World War One." *The Conservative and Unionist Women's Franchise Review*. 22 (1915). Excerpted in K. Lee Lerner and Brenda Wilmoth Lerner, eds., *Government, Politics, and Protest: Essential Primary Sources*, Farmington Hills, Mich.: Thomson Gale, 2006.

Web sites: *City and County of San Francisco; Department of Elections*. "No Military Recruiters in Public Schools, Scholarships for Education and Job Training." <http://www.sfgov.org/site/election_index.asp?id=33918> (accessed May 29, 2006). Excerpted in K. Lee Lerner and Brenda Wilmoth Lerner, eds., *Government, Politics, and Protest: Essential Primary Sources*, Farmington Hills, Mich.: Thomson Gale, 2006.

MLA Style

Books: Stowe, Harriet Beecher. *Uncle Tom's Cabin*, London: John Cassell, 1852. Excerpted in K. Lee Lerner and Brenda Wilmoth Lerner, eds., *Government, Politics, and Protest: Essential Primary Sources*, Farmington Hills, Mich.: Thomson Gale, 2006.

Periodicals: Selbourne, Maud. "The Suffragette Dilemma in World War One." *The Conservative and Unionist Women's Franchise Review*. 22, 1915. Excerpted in K. Lee Lerner and Brenda Wilmoth Lerner, eds., *Government, Politics, and Protest: Essential Primary Sources*, Farmington Hills, Mich.: Thomson Gale, 2006.

Web sites: "No Military Recruiters in Public Schools, Scholarships for Education and Job Training." *City and County of San Francisco Department of Elections*. 29 May 2006. <http://www.sfgov.org/site/election_index.asp?id=33918>. Excerpted in K. Lee Lerner and Brenda Wilmoth Lerner, eds., *Government, Politics, and Protest: Essential Primary Sources*, Farmington Hills, Mich.: Thomson Gale, 2006.

Turabian Style

Books: Stowe, Harriet Beecher. *Uncle Tom's Cabin* (London: John Cassell, 1852). Excerpted in K. Lee Lerner and Brenda Wilmoth Lerner, eds., *Government, Politics, and Protest: Essential Primary Sources* (Farmington Hills, Mich.: Thomson Gale, 2006).

Periodicals: Selbourne, Maud. "The Suffragette Dilemma in World War One." *The Conservative and Unionist Women's Franchise Review*. 22, 1915.

Excerpted in K. Lee Lerner and Brenda Wilmoth Lerner, eds., *Government, Politics, and Protest: Essential Primary Sources* (Farmington Hills, Mich.: Thomson Gale, 2006).

Web sites: *City and County of San Francisco Department of Elections.* "No Military Recruiters in Public Schools, Scholarships for Education and Job Training." available from http://www.sfgov.org/site/election_index.asp?id=33918; accessed 29 May, 2006.

Excerpted in K. Lee Lerner and Brenda Wilmoth Lerner, eds., *Government, Politics, and Protest: Essential Primary Sources* (Farmington Hills, Mich.: Thomson Gale, 2006).

Using Primary Sources

The definition of what constitutes a primary source is often the subject of scholarly debate and interpretation. Although primary sources come from a wide spectrum of resources, they are united by the fact that they individually provide insight into the historical *milieu* (context and environment) during which they were produced. Primary sources include materials such as newspaper articles, press dispatches, autobiographies, essays, letters, diaries, speeches, song lyrics, posters, works of art—and in the twenty-first century, web logs—that offer direct, first-hand insight or witness to events of their day.

Categories of primary sources include:

- Documents containing firsthand accounts of historic events by witnesses and participants. This category includes diary or journal entries, letters, email, newspaper articles, interviews, memoirs, and testimony in legal proceedings.
- Documents or works representing the official views of both government leaders and leaders of terrorist organizations. These include primary sources such as policy statements, speeches, interviews, press releases, government reports, and legislation.
- Works of art, including (but certainly not limited to) photographs, poems, and songs, including advertisements and reviews of those works that help establish an understanding of the cultural milieu (the cultural environment with regard to attitudes and perceptions of events).
- Secondary sources. In some cases, secondary sources or tertiary sources may be treated as primary sources. In some cases articles and sources are created many years after an event. Ordinarily, a

historical retrospective published after the initial event is not be considered a primary source. If, however, a resource contains statement or recollections of participants or witnesses to the original event, the source may be considered primary with regard to those statements and recollections.

ANALYSIS OF PRIMARY SOURCES

The material collected in this volume is not intended to provide a comprehensive overview of a topic or event. Rather, the primary sources are intended to generate interest and lay a foundation for further inquiry and study.

In order to properly analyze a primary source, readers should remain skeptical and develop probing questions about the source. As in reading a chemistry or algebra textbook, historical documents require readers to analyze them carefully and extract specific information. However, readers must also read "beyond the text" to garner larger clues about the social impact of the primary source.

In addition to providing information about their topics, primary sources may also supply a wealth of insight into their creator's viewpoint. For example, when reading a news article about an outbreak of disease, consider whether the reporter's words also indicate something about his or her origin, bias (an irrational disposition in favor of someone or something), prejudices (an irrational disposition against someone or something), or intended audience.

Students should remember that primary sources often contain information later proven to be false, or contain viewpoints and terms unacceptable to future generations. It is important to view the primary source within the historical and social context existing at its creation. If for example, a newspaper article is written within hours or days of an event, later developments may reveal some assertions in the original article as false or misleading.

TEST NEW CONCLUSIONS AND IDEAS

Whatever opinion or working hypothesis the reader forms, it is critical that they then test that hypothesis against other facts and sources related to the incident. For example, it might be wrong to conclude that factual mistakes are deliberate unless evidence can be produced of a pattern and practice of such mistakes with an intent to promote a false idea.

The difference between sound reasoning and preposterous conspiracy theories (or the birth of urban legends) lies in the willingness to test new ideas against other sources, rather than rest on one piece of evidence such as a single primary source that may contain errors. Sound reasoning requires that arguments and assertions guard against argument fallacies that utilize the following:

- false dilemmas (only two choices are given when in fact there are three or more options)
- arguments from ignorance (*argumentum ad ignorantiam*; because something is not known to be true, it is assumed to be false)
- possibilist fallacies (a favorite among conspiracy theorists who attempt to demonstrate that a factual statement is true or false by establishing the possibility of its truth or falsity. An argument

where "it could be" is usually followed by an unearned "therefore, it is.")
- slippery slope arguments or fallacies (a series of increasingly dramatic consequences is drawn from an initial fact or idea)
- begging the question (the truth of the conclusion is assumed by the premises)
- straw man arguments (the arguer mischaracterizes an argument or theory and then attacks the merits of their own false representations)
- appeals to pity or force (the argument attempts to persuade people to agree by sympathy or force)
- prejudicial language (values or moral judgments are attached to certain arguments or facts)
- personal attacks (*ad hominem*; an attack on a person's character or circumstances)
- anecdotal or testimonial evidence (stories that are unsupported by impartial or data that is not reproducible)
- *post hoc* (after the fact) fallacies (because one thing follows another, it is assumed to have been caused by it.)
- the fallacy of the appeal to authority (the argument rests upon the credentials of a person, not the evidence).

Despite the fact that some primary sources can contain false information or lead readers to false conclusions based on the "facts" presented, they remain an invaluable resource regarding past events. Primary sources allow readers and researchers to come as close as possible to understanding the perceptions and context of events and thus, to more fully appreciate how and why misconceptions occur.

Chronology

So that the events in this volume may be placed in a larger historical context, the following is a general chronology of important historical and social events along with specific events related to the subject of this volume.

1700s

1773: Boston Tea Party.

1774: First Continental Congress meets in Philadelphia.

1775: British and American forces clash at the battles of Lexington and Concord, igniting the American Revolution.

1775: James Watt invents the steam engine. The invention marks the start of the Industrial Revolution.

1776: Declaration of Independence asserts American colonies' independence from the British Empire and proclaims that "all men are created equal."

1781: The thirteenth state ratifies the Articles of Confederation, creating the United States.

1783: American Revolutionary War ends with the signing of the Treaty of Paris.

1785: The Daily Universal Register, later known as The Times (London), publishes its first issue.

1786: Britain establishes its first colony in Southeast Asia, beginning an age of European colonial expansion in Asia.

1787: The Constitutional Convention in Philadelphia adopts the U.S. Constitution.

1787: The "Society for the Abolition of the Slave Trade" is established in Britain.

1789: First nationwide election in the United States.

1789: Citizens of Paris storm the Bastille prison. The event ignites the French Revolution.

1789: Declaration of the Rights of Man is issued in France.

1790: First U.S. census is taken.

1791: The states ratify the Bill of Rights, the first ten amendments to the U.S. Constitution.

1793: Louis XVI, King of France, is guillotined by revolutionaries.

1793: "Reign of Terror" begins in France. Almost 40,000 people face execution.

1794: The French Republic abolishes slavery.

1796: Edward Jenner administers the first vaccination for smallpox.

1798: Irish tenant farmers rebel against British landowners in the Irish Rebellion of 1798.

1798: The United States enacts the Alien and Sedition Acts making it a federal crime to "write, publish, or utter false or malicious statements" about the United States government.

1800–1849

1800: World population reaches 1 billion.

1801: Union of Great Britain and Ireland.

1803: Napoleonic Wars begin. Napoleon's army conquers much of Europe before Napoleon is defeated at Waterloo in 1815.

1803: The United States pays France $15 million for the Louisiana Territory extending from the Mississippi River to the Rocky Mountains.

1807: The importation of slaves is outlawed in the United States, but the institution of African slavery continues until 1864.

1812: The North American War of 1812 between the United States and the United Kingdom of Great

Britain and Ireland. The war lasted until the beginning of 1815.

1814: The Congress of Vienna redraws the map of Europe after the defeat of Napoleon.

1819: South American colonial revolutions begin when Columbia declares its independence from Spain in 1819.

1820: Temperance movement begins in United States.

1822: American Colonization Society advocates the repatriation of freed African slaves to the Colony of Liberia.

1829: Lambert-Adolphe-Jacques Quetelet (1796–1874), Belgian statistician and astronomer, gives the first statistical breakdown of a national census. He correlates death with age, sex, occupation, and economic status in the Belgian census.

1830: Indian Removal Act forces the removal of Native Americans living in the eastern part of the United States.

1838: More than 15,000 Cherokee Indians are forced to march from Georgia to present-day Oklahoma on the "Trail of Tears."

1838: Samuel Finley Breese Morse (1791–1872) and Alfred Vail (1807–1859) unveil their telegraph system.

1840: John William Draper (1811–1882), American chemist, takes a daguerreotype portrait of his sister, Dorothy. This is the oldest surviving photograph of a person.

1840: Pierre-Charles-Alexandre Louis (1787–1872), French physician, pioneers medical statistics, being the first to compile systematically records of diseases and treatments.

1841: Horace Greeley (1811–1872), American editor and publisher, founds the *New York Tribune* which eventually becomes the *Herald Tribune* after a merger in 1924.

1842: The first shipment of milk by rail in the U. S. is successfully accomplished.

1845: The potato famine begins in Ireland. Crop failures and high rents on tenant farms cause a three-year famine. Millions of Irish immigrate to flee starvation.

1846: Mexican War begins as U.S. attempts to expand its territory in the Southwest.

1847: John Collins Warren (1778–1856), American surgeon, introduces ether anesthesia for general surgery. It is soon taken up worldwide as an essential part of surgery.

1847: Richard March Hoe (1812–1886), American inventor and manufacturer, patents what proves

to be the first successful rotary printing press. He discards the old flatbed press and places the type on a revolving cylinder. This revolutionary system is first used by the *Philadelphia Public Ledger* this same year, and it produces 8,000 sheets per hour printed on one side.

1848: Karl Marx publishes The Communist Manifesto.

1848: Delegates at the Seneca Falls Convention on Woman Rights advocate equal property and voting rights for women.

1848: Series of political conflicts and violent revolts erupt in several European nations. The conflicts are collectively known as the Revolution of 1848.

1848: A group of six New York newspapers form an association or news agency to share telegraph costs. It is later called the Associated Press.

1848: The first large-scale department store opens in the U.S. The Marble Dry Goods Palace in New York occupies an entire city block.

1849: John Snow (1813–1858), English physician, first states the theory that cholera is a water-borne disease and that it is usually contracted by drinking. During a cholera epidemic in London in 1854, Snow breaks the handle of the Broad Street Pump, thereby shutting down what he considered to be the main public source of the epidemic.

1850–1899

1852: Harriet Beecher Stowe's novel *Uncle Tom's Cabin* is published. It becomes one of the most influential works to stir anti-slavery sentiments.

1854: Crimean War begins between Russia and allied forces of Great Britain, Sardinia, France, and the Ottoman Empire.

1854: Violent conflicts erupt between pro-and anti-slavery settlers in Kansas Territory. The "Bleeding Kansas" violence lasts five years.

1854: Florence Nightingale (1823–1910), English nurse, takes charge of a barracks hospital when the Crimean War breaks out. Through dedication and hard work, she goes on to create a female nursing service and a nursing school at St. Thomas' Hospital (1860). Her compassion and common sense approach to nursing set new standards and create a new era in the history of the sick and wounded.

1854: Cyrus West Field (1819–1892), American financier, forms the New York, Newfoundland and

London telegraph Company and proposes to lay a transatlantic telegraph cable.

1856: *Illustrated London News* becomes the first periodical to include regular color plates.

1857: Supreme Court of the United States decision in *Dred Scott v. Sanford* holds that slaves are not citizens and that Congress cannot prohibit slavery in the individual states.

1857: The Indian Mutiny revolt against British colonial rule in India begins.

1859: Charles Robert Darwin (1809–1882), English naturalist, publishes his landmark work *On the Origin of Species by Means of Natural Selection*. This classic of science establishes the mechanism of natural selection of favorable, inherited traits or variations as the mechanism of his theory of evolution.

1860: The U. S. Congress institutes the U. S. Government Printing Office in Washington, D. C.

1861: The Civil War begins in the United States.

1861: The popular press begins in England with the publication of the *Daily Telegraph*.

1864: U.S. President Abraham Lincoln issues the Emancipation Proclamation, freeing the slaved in Union-occupied lands.

1865: The Civil War ends with the surrender of the secession states. The United States is reunified.

1865: President Lincoln is assassinated by John Wilkes Booth.

1865: The Thirteenth and Fourteenth Amendments to the U.S. Constitution are ratified. The Thirteenth Amendment outlaws slavery; the Fourteenth Amendment establishes that all persons born or naturalized in the United States as U.S. citizens and extends equal protection under the law.

1867: Britain grants Canada home rule.

1869: The first transcontinental railroad across the United States is completed.

1870: The Franco-Prussian War (1870–1871) begins.

1871: The era of New Imperialism, or "empire for empire's sake," starts a multinational competition for colonies in Africa, Asia, and the Middle East.

1876: Alexander Bell files for a patent for the telephone.

1876: The American Library Association is founded in Philadelphia, Pennsylvania by American librarian, Melvil Dewey (1851–1931), the founder of the decimal system of library classification.

1877: Reconstruction, the period of rebuilding and reunification following the U.S. Civil War, ends.

1884: International conference is held at Washington, D. C., at which Greenwich, England, is chosen as the common prime meridian for the entire world.

1885: Karl Benz invents the automobile in Germany.

1885: Louis Pasteur (1822–1895), French chemist, inoculates a boy, Joseph Meister, against rabies. He had been bitten by a mad dog and the treatment saves his life. This is the first case of Pasteur's use of an attenuated germ on a human being.

1886: Richard von Krafft-Ebing (1840–1902), German neurologist, publishes his landmark case history study of sexual abnormalities, *Psychopathia Sexualis*, and helps found the scientific consideration of human sexuality.

1890: The U.S. Census Bureau announces that the American frontier is closed.

1890: Herman Hollerith (1860–1929), American inventor, puts his electric sorting and tabulating machines to work on the U. S. Census. He wins this contract after a trial "run-off" with two other rival systems and his system performs in one year what would have taken eight years of hand tabulating. This marks the beginning of modern data processing.

1892: Ellis Island becomes chief immigration station of the eastern U.S.

1893: Panic of 1893 triggers a three-year economic depression in the United States.

1893: Sigmund Freud (1856–1939), Austrian psychiatrist, describes paralysis originating from purely mental conditions and distinguishes it from that of organic origin.

1894: Thomas Alva Edison (1847–1931), American inventor, first displays his peep-show Kinetoscopes in New York. These demonstrations serve to stimulate research on the screen projection of motion pictures as well as entertain.

1896: Landmark Supreme Court of the United States decision, *Plessy v. Ferguson*, upholds racial segregation laws.

1897: Havelock Ellis (1859–1939), English physician, publishes the first of his seven-volume work *Studies in the Psychology of Sex*. This contributes to the more open discussion of human sexuality and supports sex education.

1898: USS Maine sinks in harbor in Havana, Cuba; Spanish-American War begins.

1900–1949

1901: Guglielmo Marconi (1874–1937), Italian electrical engineer, successfully sends a radio signal from England to Newfoundland. This is the first transatlantic telegraphic radio transmission.

1903: Wright brothers make first successful flight of a controlled, powered airplane that is heavier than air.

1903: The Great Train Robbery, the first modern movie, debuts.

1904: Russo-Japanese War (1904–1905): Japan gains territory on the Asian mainland and becomes a world power.

1905: Albert Einstein (1879–1955), German-Swiss-American physicist, submits his first paper on the special theory of relativity titled "Zur Elektro-dynamik bewegter Korpen." It states that the speed of light is constant for all conditions and that time is relative or passes at different rates for objects in constant relative motion. This is a fundamentally new and revolutionary way to look at the universe and it soon replaces the old Newtonian system.

1908: A. A. Campbell-Swinton of England first suggests the use of a cathode ray tube as both the transmitter (camera) and receiver. This is the first description of the modern, all-electronic television system.

1914: Assassination of Archduke Franz Ferdinand of Austria-Hungary and his wife Sophie; World War I begins.

1914: Panama Canal is completed.

1914: The beginning of the massacre of 1.5 million Armenians by the Turkish government, later known as the Armenian Genocide.

1915: German U-boats sink the British passenger steamer RMS Lusitania.

1916: Easter Rising in Ireland begins fight for Irish independence.

1917: U.S. enters World War I, declaring war on Germany.

1917: The Russian Revolution begins as Bolsheviks overthrow the Russian monarchy.

1918: World War I ends.

1918: The Great Flu; nearly 20 million perish during the two-year pandemic.

1918: The Red Terror in Russia: Thousands of political dissidents are tried and imprisoned; 5 million die of famine as Communists collectivize agriculture and transform the Soviet economy.

1919: The ratification of the Nineteenth Amendment to the U.S. constitution gives women the right to vote.

1919: Mahatma Gandhi initiates satyagraha (truth force) campaigns, beginning his nonviolent resistance movement against British rule in India.

1920: Red Scare (1920–1922) in the United States leads to the arrest, trial, and imprisonment of suspected communist, socialist, and anarchist "radicals."

1920: KDKA, a Pittsburgh Westinghouse station, transmits the first commercial radio broadcast.

1922: 26 of Ireland's counties gain independence, the remaining six become Northern Ireland and remain under British rule.

1922: Mussolini forms Fascist government in Italy.

1925: Geneva Protocol, signed by sixteen nations, outlaws the use of poisonous gas as an agent of warfare.

1925: The Scopes Monkey Trial (July 10-25) in Tennessee debates the state's ban on the teaching of evolution.

1927: Charles Lindbergh makes the first solo nonstop transatlantic flight.

1928: Alexander Fleming discovers penicillin.

1929: Black Tuesday. The U.S. stock market crashes, beginning the Great Depression.

1930: Rubber condoms made of a thin latex are introduced.

1932: Hattie Wyatt Caraway of Arkansas is the first woman elected to the U.S. Senate.

1932: The Nazi party capture 230 seats in the German Reichstag during national elections.

1932: RCA (Radio Corporation of America) makes experimental television broadcasts from the Empire State Building in New York.

1933: Adolf Hitler named German chancellor.

1933: President Franklin D. Roosevelt announces the New Deal, a plan to revitalize the U.S. economy and provide relief in during the Great Depression. The U.S. unemployment rate reaches twenty-five percent.

1933: U. S. President Franklin Delano Roosevelt (1882–1945) makes the first of his "fireside chats" to the American people. He is the first national leader to use the radio medium comfortably and regularly to explain his programs and to garner popular support.

1935: Germany's Nuremburg Laws codify discrimination and denaturalization of the nation's Jews.

1938: Anti-Jewish riots across Germany. The destruction and looting of Jewish-owned businesses is know as *Kristalnacht*, "Night of the Broken Glass."

1938: Hitler marches into Austria; political and geographical union of Germany and Austria proclaimed. Munich Pact—Britain, France, and Italy agree to let Germany partition Czechoslovakia.

1939: Germany invades Poland. Britain and France go to war against Germany in response, beginning World War II.

1939: U.S. declares its neutrality in World War II.

1939: The Holocaust (Shoah) begins in German-occupied Europe. Jews are removed from their homes and relocated to ghettos or concentration camps. The *Einsatzgruppen*, or mobile killing squads, begin the execution of one million Jews, Poles, Russians, Gypsies, and others.

1939: Television debuts to the public at the World's Fair.

1941: The U.S. Naval base at Pearl Harbor, Hawaii is bombed by Japanese Air Force. Soon after, the United States enters World War II, declaring war on Germany and Japan.

1941: The first Nazi death camp, Chelmno, opens. Victims, mainly Jews, are executed by carbon monoxide poisoning in specially designed killing vans.

1942: Executive Order 9066 orders the internment of Japanese immigrants and Japanese-American citizens for the duration of World War II.

1942: Enrico Fermi (1901–1954), Italian-American physicist, heads a Manhattan Project team at the University of Chicago that produces the first controlled chain reaction in an atomic pile of uranium and graphite. With this first self-sustaining chain reaction, the atomic age begins.

1943: Penicillin is first used on a large scale by the U. S. Army in the North African campaigns. Data obtained from these studies show that early expectations for the new drug are correct, and the groundwork is laid for the massive introduction of penicillin into civilian medical practice after the war.

1945: Auschwitz death camp is liberated by allied forces.

1945: World War II and the Holocaust end in Europe.

1945: Trials of Nazi War criminals begin in Nuremberg, Germany.

1945: United Nations is established.

1945: Displaced Persons (DP) camps established throughout Europe to aid Holocaust survivors. In the three years following the end of World War II, many DPs immigrate to Israel and the United States.

1945: United States destroys the Japanese city of Hiroshima with a nuclear fission bomb based on uranium-235. Three days later a plutonium-based bomb destroys the city of Nagasaki. Japan surrenders on August 14 and World War II ends. This is the first use of nuclear power as a weapon.

1948: Gandhi assassinated in New Delhi.

1948: Soviets blockade of Berlin. U.S. and Great Britain begin airlift of fuel, food and necessities to West Berlin. The event, the first conflict of the Cold War, became known as the Berlin Airlift (June 26-Sept 30, 1949).

1948: United Nations issues the Universal Declaration of Human Rights.

1948: Israel is established as an independent nation.

1948: American zoologist and student of sexual behavior, Alfred C. Kinsey (1894–1956) first publishes his *Sexual Behavior in the Human Male*.

1949: South Africa codifies apartheid.

1949: Soviets test their first atomic device.

1950–1999

1950: President Truman commits U.S. troops to aid anti-Communist forces on the Korean Peninsula. The Korean War lasts from 1950–1953.

1951: First successful oral contraceptive drug is introduced. Gregory Pincus (1903–1967), American biologist, discovers a synthetic hormone that renders a woman infertile without altering her capacity for sexual pleasure. It soon is marketed in pill form and effects a social revolution with its ability to divorce the sex act from the consequences of impregnation.

1952: First hydrogen bomb is detonated by the U.S. on an atoll in the Marshall Islands.

1954: Sen. Joseph R. McCarthy begins hearings of the Senate Permanent Subcommittee on Investigations, publicly accusing military officials, politicians, media, and others of Communist involvement.

1954: Landmark decision of the United States Supreme Court, *Brown v. Board of Education*, end of segregation of schools in the United States.

1955: Emmett Till, age 14, is brutally murdered for allegedly whistling at a white woman. The event galvanizes the civil rights movement.

1955: Rosa Parks refuses to give up her seat on a Montgomery, Alabama, bus to a white passenger, defying segregation.

1955: Warsaw Pact solidifies relationship between the Soviet Union and it communist satellite nations in Eastern Europe.

1957: President Eisenhower sends federal troops to Central High School in Little Rock, Ark., to enforce integration.

1957: Soviet Union launches the first satellite, Sputnik, into space. The Space Race between the USSR and the United States begins.

1958: Explorer I, first American satellite, is launched.

1960: African-American students in North Carolina begin a sit-in at a segregated Woolworth's lunch counter; the sit-in spread throughout the South.

1961: Soviet Cosmonaut Yuri Gagarin becomes first human in space.

1961: Berlin Wall is built.

1961: Bay of Pigs Invasion: the United States sponsors an attempt to overthrow Cuba's socialist government but fails.

1962: *Silent Spring* published; environmental movement begins.

1962: Cuban Missile Crisis.

1963: Rev. Martin Luther King, Jr., delivers his "I Have a Dream" speech at a civil rights march on Washington, D.C.

1963: The U. S. and the Soviet Union establish a direct telephone link called the "hot line" between the White House and the Kremlin. It is intended to permit the leaders of both countries to be able to speak directly and immediately to each other in times of crisis.

1964: U.S. President Lyndon Johnson announces ambitious social reform programs known as the Great Society.

1964: President Johnson signs the Civil Rights Act of 1964.

1965: March from Selma: state troopers and local police fight a crowd of peaceful civil rights demonstrators, including the Rev. Martin Luther King, Jr., as the group attempted to cross a bridge into the city of Selma.

1965: First U.S. combat troops arrive in South Vietnam.

1965: Voting Rights Act prohibits discriminatory voting practices in the United States.

1965: Watts Riots: 35 people are killed and 883 injured in six days of riots in Los Angeles.

1966: Betty Friedan and other leaders of the feminist movement found the National Organization for Women (NOW).

1968: Rev. Martin Luther King, Jr., is assassinated in Memphis, Tennessee.

1968: Cesar Chavez leads a national boycott of California table grape growers, which becomes known as "La Causa."

1969: Stonewall Riots in New York City spark the gay rights movement.

1969: U.S. successfully lands a manned mission, Apollo 11, on the moon.

1972: Arab terrorists massacre Israeli athletes at Olympic Games in Munich, Germany.

1973: *Roe v. Wade*: Landmark Supreme Court decision legalizes abortion on demand during the first trimester of pregnancy.

1973: The American Psychiatric Association removes the classification of homosexuality as a mental disorder.

1976: Steve Jobs and Steve Wozniak invent personal computer.

1977: International human rights advocacy group Amnesty International awarded the Noble Peace Prize.

1978: The Camp David Accord ends a three-decade long conflict between Israel and Egypt.

1979: Iran hostage crisis begins when Iranian students storm the U.S. embassy in Teheran. They hold 66 people hostage who are not released until 1981, after 444 days in captivity.

1980: President Carter announces that U.S. athletes will boycott Summer Olympics in Moscow to protest Soviet involvement in Afghanistan (Jan. 20).

1981: Urban riots breakout in several British cities, protesting lack of opportunity for minorities and police brutality.

1981: AIDS identified.

1986: U.S. space shuttle Challenger explodes 73 seconds after liftoff.

1987: U.S. President Ronald Reagan challenges Soviet leader Mikhail Gorbachev to open Eastern Europe and the Soviet Union to political and economic reform.

1989: Fall of the Berlin Wall.

1989: Tiananmen Square protest in Beijing, China.

1989: The Internet revolution begins with the invention of the World Wide Web.

1991: Soviet Union dissolves.

1991: Persian Gulf War (January 16 -February 28): U.S. leads "Operation Desert Storm" to push Iraqi occupying forces out of Kuwait.

1992: U.S. and Russian leaders formally declare an end to the Cold War.

1992: L.A. Riots: The acquittal of four white police officers charged with police brutality in the beating of black motorist Rodney King sparks days of widespread rioting in Los Angeles.

1992: WHO (World Health Organization) predicts that by the year 2000, 30 to 40 million people will be infected with the AIDS-causing HIV. A Harvard University group argues the that the number could reach more than 100 million.

1993: A terrorist bomb explodes in basement parking garage of World Trade Center, killing six.

1994: First all-race elections in South Africa; Nelson Mandela elected President.

1998: Torture and murder of gay college student Matthew Shepherd.

1999: NATO forces in former Yugoslavia attempt to end mass killings of ethnic Albanians by Serbian forces in Kosovo.

2000–

2001: Terrorists attacks on the World Trade Center in New York and the Pentagon in Washington, D.C. kill 2,752.

2001: Controversial Patriot Act passed in the United States.

2001: United States and coalition forces begin War on Terror by invading Afghanistan (Operation Enduring Freedom), overthrowing the nation's Islamist Taliban regime in December of 2001.

2002: Slobodan Milosevic begins his war crimes trial at the UN International Criminal Tribunal on charges of genocide and crimes against humanity. He is the first head of state to stand trial in an international war-crimes court, but died before the trial concluded.

2002: After United States and coalition forces depose Islamist Taliban regime in Afghanistan, girls are allowed to return to school and women's rights are partially restored in areas controlled by U.S. and coalition forces.

2003: U.S. space shuttle Columbia breaks apart upon re-entry, killing all seven crew members.

2003: United States and coalition forces invade Iraq.

2003: The U.S. declares an end to major combat operations in Iraq. As of June 2006, U.S. fighting forces remain engaged in Iraq.

2003: November 18, the Massachusetts Supreme Judicial court rules denying same-sex couples marriage rights violates the state constitution, legalizing same-sex marriages.

2004: Islamist terrorist bombing of commuter rail network in Madrid, Spain.

2005: Islamist terrorist bombings in London. Bombs simultaneously detonate in on the Underground and city busses.

1 Protesters and Protest Rights

Protesters and Protest Rights

This book is based on the assumption that freedoms of thought, conscience, political association, assembly, and speech are essential human rights. Accordingly, this volume begins with the definitive statement of protest rights in the United States, the First Amendment to the U.S. Constitution. The editors intend this chapter to spark discussion on several fundamental questions about policy and protest. What makes an individual an activist? When is protest useful or necessary? Are there any places or occasions inappropriate for protest? What forms of protest can, or should, individuals use? When, if ever, are illegal acts an acceptable form of protest? What does protest achieve?

Examples of protests against government policy span the ages and the globe. While the most modern protests may look strikingly different from the (often violent) protests throughout history, the act of protest itself is almost timeless. Today, protest actions take many forms, from marches to music ("This Land is Your Land"). Protest imagery is often poignant ("Buddhist Monk Sets Himself on Fire"), sometimes controversial ("Burning the American Flag in Protest"), and occasionally absurd ("Pie in the Eye").

Introduced in this chapter are the modern philosophical and practical underpinnings of protest, with an editor-chosen emphasis on non-violence. Highlighted here are Henry David Thoreau's classic ode to civil disobedience, a thoughtful compilation of *Methods of Non-Violent Protest and Persuasion*, and the pamphlet "Your Rights to Demonstrate and Protest." "Direct Action", alternatively, argues that violence and property damage are sometimes necessary or justified means of protest. The tension between policy makers and protesters is briefly addressed, both through claims of media bias in the coverage of protests, and controversial laws that corral protesters into "Free Speech Zones."

Finally, the themes and protests forms presented in this introductory chapter are raised throughout this volume. For example, most of the 198 "Methods of Non-Violent Protest and Persuasion" appear at least once throughout the book. Often, one protest movement or assembly combines several methods. Subsequent chapters are divided based on the motivations and issues that drive various protests. Whether a non-violent protest for civil rights or direct action to promote environmental justice, the fundamental questions posed here are equally vital to understanding the protesters and protests.

U.S. Constitution, Amendment I

Legislation

By: James Madison

Date: 1789

Source: "Amendment I." *The Constitution of the United States of America*, 1789.

About the Author: James Madison crafted much of the text of what would become the Bill of Rights for the United States Constitution. Madison helped to create the Democratic party in the 1790s and went on to become the fourth president of the United States.

INTRODUCTION

The First Amendment to the United States Constitution was written as part of the Bill of Rights, the first ten amendments to the Constitution. The First Amendment is best known for addressing freedom of religion, free speech, a free press, the right of people to assemble, and the right to appeal to the government with grievances. In drafting the initial version of the Bill of rights in 1789, James Madison was influenced by the 1689 English Bill of Rights and the 1776 Virginia Bill of Rights, written by delegate George Mason. The inclusion of a Bill of Rights patterned after the two previous documents was the source of agreement and argument for the founding fathers.

The Revolutionary War against the colonial power of Britain had been sparked in large part by decisions made by King George III and the British Parliament, decisions which the colonists could not readily influence through any legal or political process. A Bill of Rights, proponents argued, would strip any future leader of the United States of absolute power; granting the people human liberties in the founding documents themselves would preserve the republic being formed and shaped in the late 1780s and early 1790s. The drafters were not unanimous in support of a Bill of Rights; Alexander Hamilton argued that ratification of the Constitution without a Bill of Rights was appropriate and just, for the people did not relinquish their natural rights by entering into a contract with a government; codifying those rights was unnecessary, in Hamilton's opinion, because the government had no inherent right or power to abridge natural rights.

A pro-choice march in Washington, D.C., April 9, 1989. © VIVIANE MOOS/CORBIS.

The First Amendment incorporated rights that had been abridged directly by the British power in previous decades; the amendment protects these rights from legislation by Congress, and the court system interprets the Constitution based on these enumerated rights. The First Amendment, crafted to protect a wide array of rights, has become a cornerstone in American democracy and in shaping civil society.

PRIMARY SOURCE

Congress shall make no law respecting an establishment of religion, or prohibiting the free exercise thereof; or abridging the freedom of speech, or of the press; or the right of the people peaceably to assemble, and to petition the Government for a redress of grievances.

SIGNIFICANCE

The First Amendment, in U.S. society, is associated with the concept of freedom of expression, be it in the form of religion, speech, the press, or through physical or media protests. The "establishment clause" in the First Amendment prohibits Congress from establishing a state religion or showing preference for one religion over another. The "separation of church and state" concept stretched into public schools in the 1963 Supreme Court case *Murray v. Curlett*, which found that mandatory prayer in public schools was unconstitutional, in violation of the First Amendment. Eight years later, in 1971, the Supreme Court ruled in *Lemon v. Kurtzman* that public school systems funds could not be spent to send students to religious schools. Public schools, as a government institution, must remain secular and funds must be spent on secular interests. The freedom of religion in the First Amendment is often interpreted as freedom from religion; the establishment clause prevents the government from creating a state religion, while individuals are free to worship in their religion of choice as long as their actions related to religion do not violate the rights of others or established law.

Freedom of speech and of the press faced an early challenge: the Alien and Sedition Acts of 1798. Signed into law by President John Adams, the Sedition Act included a provision that made it a crime to publish "false, scandalous, and malicious writing" against the federal government or any elected or appointed official. The Acts angered colonists, who viewed such moves as an encroachment on the new rights guaranteed by the Constitution, and Thomas Jefferson won election to the presidency in 1800 in part because of anger at Adams for signing the acts into law. While courts have limited some speech, such as hate speech or sexually explicit conversation in the workplace, free speech protections have shaped a society that permits a wide range of opinions to be expressed and published—even those opinions that run counter to the political party in charge in the White House or Congress.

Historically, the Supreme Court has interpreted the extent to which individuals can exercise the rights expressed in the First Amendment. In addition, while the amendment states that Congress cannot abridge the rights of the people, the Supreme Court has interpreted the amendment to include the federal government as a whole. Supreme Court cases addressing various aspects of the First Amendment include the 1963 case *Edwards v. South Carolina*, which protected the rights of African-American high school students to peacefully assemble and protest; the 1966 case *A Book Named "John Cleland's Memoirs of a Woman of Pleasure"*

v. Attorney General of Massachusetts, which examined questions of obscenity in printed material versus free speech; and the 2006 decision *Garcetti v. Ceballos*, which restricts the First Amendment rights of all federal employees when notifying managers about wrongdoing or problems on the job.

In crafting the First Amendment, James Madison and his colleagues worked to create a society in which free expression would be guaranteed for all citizens, with a judicial mechanism for weighing the rights of the individual against the rights of society. As this eighteenth-century document is applied to twenty-first-century norms, the First Amendment continues to provide guidance in shaping the personal, the political, and the public in American society.

FURTHER RESOURCES
Books

Abrams, Floyd. *Speaking Freely: Trials of the First Amendment*. New York: Viking Adult, 2005.

Breyer, Stephen. *Active Liberty: Interpreting Our Democratic Constitution*. New York: Knopf, 2005.

Nelson, Samuel P. *Beyond the First Amendment: The Politics of Free Speech and Pluralism*. Baltimore, MD: Johns Hopkins University Press, 2005.

Stone, Geoffrey R. *Perilous Times: Free Speech in Wartime: From the Sedition Act of 1798 to the War on Terrorism*. New York: W.W. Norton, 2005.

Civil Disobedience

Essay

By: Henry David Thoreau

Date: 1849

Source: Thoreau, Henry David. "Civil Disobedience" in Blackwood, R. T. and A. L. Herma, eds. *Problems in Philosophy*. Englewood Cliffs, NJ: Prentice Hall, 1975.

About the Author: Henry David Thoreau was a naturalist and writer who lived in Massachusetts in the mid-nineteenth century. His writings, especially the book *Walden* and the essay *Civil Disobedience*, had little influence during his lifetime but became world-famous during the twentieth century.

INTRODUCTION

Henry David Thoreau (1817–1862) was an essayist and naturalist who lived in Concord, Massachusetts. He was a member of an informal group of New

Henry David Thoreau, in 1856. GETTY IMAGES.

England thinkers known as Transcendentalists, who shared a belief that the life of the spirit went beyond or transcended the truths available from science or organized religion. He wrote a number of books and essays, including, most famously, *Walden* (1854) and the essay "Civil Disobedience."

In 1842, Thoreau began to refuse paying his poll tax. The poll tax was an annual sum demanded of every adult Massachusetts male between the ages of twenty and seventy. Thoreau's intention was straightforward: he was an ardent Abolitionist or opponent of slavery, and, as he explains in "Civil Disobedience," wished to dissociate himself from any government that either actively enabled slavery or acquiesced in its existence.

In May, 1846, the United States went to war with Mexico. The result of the war was the forced cession by Mexico to the United States of about half its territory, an area including the present-day states of Arizona, California, Nevada, and New Mexico—almost a quarter of the United States' present area. (Mexico was forced to accept $15,000,000 for the territory, about $300,000,000 in 2005 dollars.) The war was viewed by some Americans, including virtually all Abolitionists, as aggressive and unjust. Thoreau mentions the Mexican War several times in "Civil Disobedience" as an exemplary reason for refusing to cooperate with government.

By 1846, when the Mexican War began, the Concord tax collector had been asking Thoreau to pay his poll tax for years. Two months after the start of the war, however, he accosted Thoreau in the street and asked again for the money. Thoreau refused to pay and was escorted politely to the town jail, where he was imprisoned for refusal to pay the tax.

Thoreau was not the first Transcendentalist to be jailed for refusal to pay the poll tax: Bronson Alcott (1799–1888) and Charles Lane (1800–1870) had both been arrested in 1842 for Abolitionism-inspired tax resistance. In both cases, a third party paid off their debt against the protestor's will, rather than allow a town scandal to occur. In Thoreau's case, too, an anonymous third party—probably an aunt—paid the tax. He was released after spending only one night in jail. Thoreau was annoyed by this outcome, since he had wished his imprisonment to be longer in order to have greater political impact.

In 1848, he gave a public lecture based on his experiences and on his philosophy of resistance to the State. The next year, an essay version of the lecture was published under the title "Resistance to Civil Government." The phrase "civil disobedience," which is today a basic term of the political vocabulary, was never actually used by Thoreau, but was attached to the essay when it was published in book form four years after his death. The identity of the editor who devised the famous phrase is not known.

PRIMARY SOURCE

Unjust laws exist: shall we be content to obey them, or shall we endeavor to amend them, and obey them until we have succeeded, or shall we transgress them at once? Men generally, under such a government as this, think that they ought to wait until they have persuaded the majority to alter them. They think that, if they should resist, the remedy would be worse than the evil. But it is the fault of the government itself that the remedy *is* worse than the evil. *It* makes it worse. Why is it not more apt to anticipate and provide for reform? Why does it not cherish its wise minority? Why does it cry and resist before it is hurt? Why does it not encourage its citizens to be on the alert to point out its faults, and do better than it would have them? Why does it always crucify Christ, and excommunicate Copernicus and Luther, and pronounce Washington and Franklin rebels?

One would think, that a deliberate and practical denial of its authority was the only offence never contemplated by government; else, why has it not assigned its definite, its suitable and proportionate penalty? If a man who has no property refuses but once to earn nine shillings for the State, he is put in prison for a period unlimited by any law that I know, and determined only by the discretion of those who placed him there; but if he should steal ninety times nine shillings from the State, he is soon permitted to go at large again.

If the injustice is part of the necessary friction of the machine of government, let it go, let it go: perchance it will wear smooth—certainly the machine will wear out. If the injustice has a spring, or a pulley, or a rope, or a crank, exclusively for itself, then perhaps you may consider whether the remedy will not be worse than the evil; but if it is of such a nature that it requires you to be the agent of injustice to another, then I say, break the law. Let your life be a counter friction to stop the machine. What I have to do is to see, at any rate, that I do not lend myself to the wrong which I condemn.

As for adopting the ways in which the State has provided for remedying the evil, I know not of such ways. They take too much time, and a man's life will be gone. I have other affairs to attend to. I came into this world, not chiefly to make this a good place to lie in, but to live in it, be it good or bad. A man has not everything to do, but something; and because he cannot do *everything*, it is not necessary that he should do *something* wrong. It is not my business to be petitioning the Governor or the Legislature any more than it is theirs to petition me; and if they should not hear my petition, what should I do then? But in this case the State has provided no way: its very Constitution is the evil. This may seem to be harsh and stubborn and unconciliatory; but it is to treat with the utmost kindness and consideration the only spirit that can appreciate or deserves it. So is all change for the better, like birth and death, which convulse the body.

I do not hesitate to say, that those who call themselves Abolitionists should at once effectually withdraw their support, both in person and property, from the government of Massachusetts, and not wait till they constitute a majority of one, before they suffer the right to prevail through them. I think that it is enough if they have God on their side, without waiting for that other one. Moreover, any man more right than his neighbors constitutes a majority of one already.

SIGNIFICANCE

The number of persons who have been moved to political action partly by Thoreau's essay is in the many thousands or possibly millions, and includes a number of world-famous activists. Indian independence leader Mahatma Gandhi (1869–1948) read "Civil Disobedience" in 1906, when he was living in South Africa and fighting racist laws in that country. He often cited it as basic to his own theory of nonviolent resistance, which eventually won India its independence from the British Empire in 1947. Thoreau himself, it should be noted, was not a pacifist; although he does not advocate violence in "Civil Disobedience," in later essays he approved of violent resistance against slavery.

Emma Goldman and Martin Buber both cited Thoreau's essay as a key influence. An unnamed member of the Danish resistance to Nazi occupation during World War II later wrote, "Thoreau's 'Civil Disobedience' stood for me, and for my first leader in the resistance movement, as a shining light with which we could examine the policy of complete passivity which our government had ordered for the whole Danish population... I lent Thoreau's books to friends, told them about him, and our circle grew. Railroads, bridges, and factories that worked for the Germans were blown up" (quoted by Thoreau scholar Lawrence Rosenwald). Martin Luther King (1929–1968), leader of the American movement for civil rights and racial equality in the 1950s and 1960s, read Thoreau as a young man in college and in his autobiography said that "I remembered how, as a college student, I had been moved when I first read this work. I became convinced that what we were preparing to do in Montgomery was related to what Thoreau had expressed. We were simply saying to the white community, 'We can no longer lend our cooperation to an evil system.'" "Civil Disobedience" is also cited today by the war-tax resistance movement, which refuses to pay taxes to governments that are waging wars the protestors consider unjust.

Thoreau's influence on the modern world has been great in other areas as well. He has profoundly shaped the environmental movement, for example, through such works as *Walden* and the essay "Walking." Thoreau is one of the few philosophers of the nineteenth century who is read today not only by students and scholars but by millions of ordinary people who are moved—often to action—by what he had to say.

FURTHER RESOURCES
Books
Harding, Walter. *The Days of Henry Thoreau: A Biography*. New York: Dover, 1962.

Periodicals

Hendrick, G. "The Influence of Thoreau's 'Civil Disobedience' on Gandhi's Satyagraha." *The New England Quarterly*. 29,4(1956): 462-71.

Herr, William A. "Thoreau: A Civil Disobedient?" *Ethics*. 85,1(1974): 87-9.

Web sites

Oxford University Press. "The Theory, Practice, and Influence of Thoreau's Civil Disobedience." August 7, 2003. <http://www.wellesley.edu/Peace/Rosenwald/thoreau.html> (accessed May 15, 2006).

Direct Action

Essay

By: Voltairine de Cleyre

Date: 1912

Source: de Cleyre, Voltairine. "Direct Action," 1912.

About the Author: Voltairine de Cleyre (1866–1912), once was one of the best-known anarchist women in the United States. A freethinker who was unwilling to accept a rigid definition of anarchism, she created her own style of anarchy that incorporated tolerance and feminism.

INTRODUCTION

The theory of anarchism gained some popularity in the United States in the late nineteenth and early twentieth centuries. It arose partly in response to federal, state, and local government support for business at the expense of workers who demanded better working conditions and improved wages. Anarchists believed that formal government of any type was unnecessary and wrong in principle. Although largely forgotten today, Voltairine de Cleyre gained considerable fame for her writings in support of anarchism and the oppressed American workers.

De Cleyre, born into poverty in Michigan, became a freethinker in early adulthood. After a brief flirtation with socialism, she embraced and then abandoned many varieties of anarchism. Individualist anarchism first attracted de Cleyre because it promised that the essential institutions of commerce were good but were made bad by state interference. De Cleyre later disagreed with the economic views of the individualists and became a mutualist anarchist. She saw mutualism, under which organizations of workers would remove the need for an employer, as a combination

of socialism and individualism. However, De Cleyre's pacifism prompted her to reject mutualism because it included self-policing. Finally, she decided to simply embrace anarchism without adjectives. She became an anarchist because she loved liberty and saw anarchism as the political philosophy that allowed the most freedom. To de Cleyre, anarchism was freedom from compulsion.

It was not freedom from violence. De Cleyre encouraged tolerance of a variety of methods of achieving liberty, including violent methods. The anarchists of her era argued passionately about peaceful methods versus confrontational tactics. While de Cleyre would not engage in violence, she excused workers who did, such as the McNamara brothers. In October 1910, the *Los Angeles Times* building was bombed because its owner, Harrison Gray Otis, opposed unions. Twenty-one people were killed by the explosion and fire. The McNamara brothers, J.J. and J.B., were arrested for the crime. Both men pleaded guilty. De Cleyre argued that each individual should choose the method that best expresses his or her self and condemn no one who chooses a different method.

■ PRIMARY SOURCE

From the standpoint of one who thinks himself capable of discerning an undeviating route for human progress to pursue, if it is to be progress at all, who, having such a route on his mind's map, has endeavored to point it out to others; to make them see it as he sees it; who in so doing has chosen what appeared to him clear and simple expressions to convey his thoughts to others,—to such a one it appears matter for regret and confusion of spirit that the phrase "Direct Action" has suddenly acquired in the general mind a circumscribed meaning, not at all implied in the words themselves, and certainly never attached to it by himself or his co-thinkers.

However, this is one of the common jests which Progress plays on those who think themselves able to set metes and bounds for it. Over and over again, names, phrases, mottoes, watchwords, have been turned inside out, and upside down, and hindside before, and sideways, by occurrences out of the control of those who used the expressions in their proper sense; and still, those who sturdily held their ground, and insisted on being heard, have in the end found that the period of misunderstanding and prejudice has been but the prelude to wider inquiry and understanding.

I rather think this will be the case with the present misconception of the term Direct Action, which through the misapprehension, or else the deliberate misrepresentation, of certain journalists in Los Angeles, at the time the

The Boston Tea Party, an example of what Voltairine de Cleyre calls direct action. PHOTO BY TIME LIFE PICTURES/MANSELL/TIME LIFE PICTURES/ GETTY IMAGES.

McNamaras pleaded guilty, suddenly acquired in the popular mind the interpretation, "Forcible Attacks on Life and Property." This was either very ignorant or very dishonest of the journalists; but it has had the effect of making a good many people curious to know all about Direct Action.

As a matter of fact, those who are so lustily and so inordinately condemning it, will find on examination that they themselves have on many occasion practised direct action, and will do so again.

Every person who ever thought he had a right to assert, and went boldly and asserted it, himself, or jointly with others that shared his convictions, was a direct actionist. Some thirty years ago I recall that the Salvation Army was vigorously practising direct action in the maintenance of the freedom of its members to speak, assemble, and pray. Over and over they were arrested, fined, and imprisoned; but they kept right on singing, praying, and marching, till they finally compelled their persecutors to let them alone. The Industrial Workers are now conducting the same fight, and have, in a number of cases, compelled the officials to let them alone by the same direct tactics.

Every person who ever had a plan to do anything, and went and did it, or who laid his plan before others, and won their co-operation to do it with him, without going to external authorities to please do the thing for them, was a direct actionist. All co-operative experiments are essentially direct action.

Every person who ever in his life had a difference with anyone to settle, and went straight to the other persons involved to settle it, either by a peaceable plan or otherwise, was a direct actionist. Examples of such action are strikes and boycotts; many persons will recall the action of the housewives of New York who boycotted the butchers, and lowered the price of meat; at the present moment a butter boycott seems looming up, as a direct reply to the price-makers for butter.

These actions are generally not due to any one's reasoning overmuch on the respective merits of directness or indirectness, but are the spontaneous retorts of those who feel oppressed by a situation. In other words, all people are, most of the time, believers in the principle of direct action, and practices of it. However, most people are also indirect or political actionists. And they are both these things at the same time, without making much of an analysis of either. There are only a limited number of persons who eschew political action under any and all circumstances; but there is nobody, nobody at all, who has ever been so "impossible" as to eschew direct action altogether.

Those who, by the essence of their belief, are committed to Direct Action only are—just who? Why, the non-resistants; precisely those who do not believe in violence at all! Now do not make the mistake of inferring that I say direct action means non-resistance; not by any means. Direct action may be the extreme of violence, or it may be as peaceful as the waters of the Brook of Shiloa that go softly. What I say is, that the real non-resistants can believe in direct action only, never in political action. For the basis of all political action is coercion; even when the State does good things, it finally rests on a club, a gun, or a prison, for its power to carry them through.

Now every school child in the United States has had the direct action of certain non-resistants brought to his notice by his school history.

In the period of agitation and excitement preceding the revolution, there were all sorts and kinds of direct action from the most peaceable to the most violent; and I believe that almost everybody who studies United States history finds the account of these performances the most interesting part of the story, the part which dents into the memory most easily.

Among the peaceable moves made, were the non-importation agreements, the leagues for wearing home-spun clothing and the "committees of correspondence." As the inevitable growth of hostility progressed, violent direct action developed; e.g., in the matter of destroying the revenue stamps, or the action concerning the tea-ships, either by not permitting the tea to be landed, or by putting it in damp storage, or by throwing it into the harbor, as in Boston, or by compelling a tea-ship owner to set fire to his own ship, as at Annapolis. These are all actions which our commonest textbooks record, certainly not in a condemnatory way, not even in an apologetic way, though they are all cases of direct action against legally constituted authority and property rights. If I draw attention to them, and others of like nature, it is to prove to unreflecting repeaters of words that direct action has always been used, and has the historical sanction of the very people now reprobating it.

George Washington is said to have been the leader of the Virginia planters' non-importation league; he would now be "enjoined," probably by a court, from forming any such league; and if he persisted, he would be fined for contempt....

Among the various expressions of direct rebellion was the organization of the "underground railroad." Most of the people who belonged to it believed in both sorts of action; but however much they theoretically subscribed to the right of the majority to enact and enforce laws, they didn't believe in it on that point. My grandfather was a member of the "underground;" many a fugitive slave he helped on his way to Canada. He was a very patient, law-abiding man in most respects, though I have often thought that he respected it because he didn't have much to do with it; always leading a pioneer life, law was generally far from him, and direct action imperative. Be that as it may, and law-respecting as he was, he had no respect whatever for slave laws, no matter if made by ten times of a majority; and he conscientiously broke every one that came in his way to be broken.

There were times when in the operation of the "underground" that violence was required, and was used. I recollect one old friend relating to me how she and her mother kept watch all night at the door, while a slave for whom a posse was searching hid in the cellar; and though they were of Quaker descent and sympathies, there was a shotgun on the table. Fortunately it did not have to be used that night....

The other day I read a communication in the Chicago *Daily Socialist* from the secretary of the Louisville local Socialist Party to the national secretary, requesting that some safe and sane speaker be substituted for Bohn, who had been announced to speak there. In explaining why, Mr. Dobbs makes this quotation from Bohn's lecture: "Had the McNamaras been successful in defending the interests of the working class, they would have been right, just as John Brown would have been right, had he been successful in freeing the slaves. Ignorance was the only crime of John Brown, and ignorance was the only crime of the McNamaras."

Upon this Mr. Dobbs comments as follows: "We dispute emphatically the statements here made. The attempt to draw a parallel between the open—if mistaken—revolt of John Brown on the one hand, and the secret and murderous methods of the McNamaras on the other, is not only indicative of shallow reasoning, but highly mischievous in the logical conclusions which may be drawn from such statements.

Evidently Mr. Dobbs is very ignorant of the life and work of John Brown. John Brown was a man of violence; he would have scorned anybody's attempt to make him out anything else. And once a person is a believer in violence, it is with him only a question of the most effective way of applying it, which can be determined only by a knowledge of conditions and means at his disposal. John Brown did not shrink at all from conspiratorial methods. Those who have read the autobiography of Frederick Douglas and the Reminiscences of Lucy Colman, will recall that one of the plans laid by John Brown was to organize a chain of armed camps in the mountains of West Virginia, North Carolina, and Tennessee, send secret emissaries among the slaves inciting them to flee to these camps, and there concert such measures as times and conditions made possible for further arousing revolt among the negroes....

...And yet history has not failed to understand John Brown. Mankind knows that though he was a violent man, with human blood upon his hands, who was guilty of high treason and hanged for it, yet his soul was a great, strong, unselfish soul, unable to bear the frightful crime which kept 4,000,000 people like dumb beasts, and thought that making war against it was a sacred, a God-called duty, (for John Brown was a very religious man—a Presbyterian).

It is by and because of the direct acts of the forerunners of social change, whether they be of peaceful or warlike nature, that the Human Conscience, the conscience of the mass, becomes aroused to the need for change. It would be very stupid to say that no good results are ever brought about by political action; sometimes good things do come about that way. But never until individual rebellion, followed by mass rebellion, has forced it. Direct action is always the clamorer, the initiator, through which the great sum of indifferentists become aware that oppression is getting intolerable.

SIGNIFICANCE

Most of the anarchists in the U.S. in the early twentieth century were either individualist or revolutionary. De Cleyre is unusual in that she combined the two forms. She was part of a long libertarian tradition in the nation. As de Cleyre occasionally noted in her writings, she joined the founding fathers in stressing the sanctity of the individual. The majority of anarchists, though, did not have deep American roots. Although de Cleyre was native-born, anarchism particularly appealed to immigrants from Eastern and Southern Europe. These Italians and Russians tended toward revolutionary anarchism and they are the ones who engaged in campaigns of bombings and shootings against industrialists and political leaders. The anarchists, as de Cleyre did, argued passionately about peaceful methods versus confrontational tactics.

The assassination of President William McKinley by anarchist Leon Czolgosz in 1901 was a confrontational tactic that ultimately doomed the anarchist movement. The murder confirmed the public image of anarchism as a foreign menace. While anarchists continued to write and organize, the audience for anarchist thought declined. Many anarchists were

deported in 1919 as dangerous aliens. The Red Scare of the 1920s effectively halted all anarchist activity. By this time, de Cleyre was dead. The short span of her life is generally blamed as the reason why she has been overlooked in histories of the anarchist movement in the U.S., unlike her far-better-known contemporary Emma Goldman.

FURTHER RESOURCES
Books

Avrich, Paul. *An American Anarchist: The Life of Voltairine de Cleyre*. Princeton, NJ: Princeton University Press, 1978.

DeLamott, Eugenia C. *Gates of Freedom: Voltairine de Cleyre and the Revolution of the Mind*. Ann Arbor, MI: University of Michigan Press, 2004.

Marsh, Margaret S. *Anarchist Women, 1870–1920*. Philadelphia, PA: Temple University Press, 1981.

Buddhist Monk Sets Himself on Fire

Photograph

By: Malcolm Browne

Date: June 11, 1963

Source: AP/Wide World Photos. Reproduced by permission.

About the Author: Malcolm Browne began his career as a chemist before being drafted during the Korean War and working as a reporter for *Pacific Stars and Stripes* newspaper. A war correspondent and Pulitzer Prize winner, Browne worked as an editor for *Discover* magazine.

INTRODUCTION

While civil rights protests in the southern United States gained intensity in 1963, during President John F. Kennedy's administration, political events halfway around the world in South Vietnam soon gained worldwide attention via a very different form of political protest.

In 1954, France was forced out of Vietnam after nearly one hundred years as the colonial power in Indochina. At the Geneva Accords, France and Vietnam agreed to split the area along the seventeenth parallel temporarily; elections would be held in 1956 to reunite the country. United States President Dwight D. Eisenhower and Secretary of State John

Foster Dulles disagreed with the results of the Geneva Accords, concerned that too much power was relegated to the Communist Party in Vietnam; with communist China and the U.S.S.R. as close neighbors to Vietnam, the Americans saw the possibility of a completely communist Asia as an unacceptable potential result of the Geneva Accords.

In 1955, the Eisenhower administration backed the formation of the Government of the Republic of Vietnam, or South Vietnam; an unofficial vote led to the election of Ngo Dinh Diem, a Catholic anti-communist. American economic, military, and political aid created Diem's regime as a counterbalance to communism. In November 1955, Eisenhower sent military support to train the South Vietnam army, marking the official beginning of American military involvement in Vietnam.

Diem claimed that the Democratic Republic of Vietnam, or North Vietnam, led by communist Ho Chi Minh, planned to invade South Vietnam. Nearly one million people from North Vietnam poured into South Vietnam between 1955 and 1956; Diem became suspicious that many were sent by Ho Chi Minh as spies. In 1957, with American aid and Central Intelligence Agency assistance, Diem attacked North Vietnam. At the same time he passed Law 10/59, which allowed Diem's government to detain any person suspected of being a communist sympathizer without formal charges and without a trial.

Public protests over Law 10/59 erupted throughout South Vietnam; many of the protestors were Buddhist nuns and monks. Joining peasants and others who fought against the perceived corruption and hegemony of Diem's rule, the Buddhist nuns and monks staged public protests and in some cases actively fought against police forces. In 1961, President Eisenhower's administration and President John F. Kennedy inherited the South Vietnam issue; Diem was viewed as an important ally but also unstable in many ways. Kennedy offered Diem limited military, technical, and financial support,

PRIMARY SOURCE

Buddhist Monk Sets Himself on Fire Thich Quang Duc, a Buddhist monk, burns himself to death on the streets of Saigon, South Vietnam, June 11, 1963. He is protesting the persecution of Buddhists by the government. AP/WIDE WORLD PHOTOS. REPRODUCED BY PERMISSION.

but refused to commit troops. In 1963, Diem's brother, Ngo Dinh Nhu, attacked Buddhist pagodas throughout South Vietnam, invading sacred religious orders. Nhu accused the monks of harboring communists or being communists themselves; the monks and their supporters filled the streets of Saigon in protest. Self-immolation, or intentional suicide by setting oneself on fire, became an act of political protest for Buddhist monks and nuns in South Vietnam.

In the picture below Thich Quang Duc, a sixty-seven year old monk from the Linh-Mu religious order in South Vietnam, arrived on a busy street corner in Saigon by car. He stepped out of the car and was accompanied by two fellow monks. Thich Quang Duc assumed the lotus meditation position and the two monks poured gasoline on him. He then lit a match and set himself on fire.

PRIMARY SOURCE

BUDDHIST MONK SETS HIMSELF ON FIRE
See primary source image.

SIGNIFICANCE

According to Vietnamese Buddhist tradition, self-immolation as a practice is a centuries-old tradition. Viewed as the ultimate sacrifice, self-immolation is believed to be a method or a plea for ending suffering in the world. Thich Quang Duc's dramatic choice of a busy corner in Saigon caught international attention; David Halberstam, a reporter for the *New York Times* in 1963, as well as Malcolm Browne, an Associated Press photographer, captured the scene in print and film as eyewitnesses to the self-immolation. According to Browne hundreds of nuns and monks lined the streets, prepared to stop anyone who interfered with the self-immolation; the protest was organized as a message to Diem concerning his interference in religious life in South Vietnam and the attacks on pagodas.

The news story and photograph reached an international audience within days and provoked shock and outrage; U.S. President John F. Kennedy reportedly told the U.S. ambassador to South Vietnam, Henry Cabot Lodge, that the Diem regime's mistreatment of Buddhist nuns and monks and conditions leading to self-immolations had to end. On November 1, 1963, both Diem and his brother Nhu were captured and assassinated.

Malcolm Browne's photograph won the Pulitzer Prize, and Thich Quang Duc's dramatic suicide brought attention to the abuses of the Diem regime. Two months after Thich Quang Duc's self-immolation another monk set himself on fire in Phanthiet, approximately one hundred miles from Saigon. In May 1966 Thich Nu Thanh Quang, a Buddhist nun, set herself on fire in Hue, the town where Thich Quang Duc's pagoda was located.

In 1965, four Americans set themselves on fire to protest U.S. involvement in the Vietnam War, in cities ranging from Detroit to New York City to San Diego. Basque nationalists self-immolated during Franco's regime in Spain, while Chinese protestors used self-immolation during student uprisings in 1989. The pattern of self-immolation as a form of protest persists in the twenty-first century; on December 26, 2003 a Buddhist monk set himself on fire in Charlotte, North Carolina to protest human rights abuses in his home country of Vietnam.

FURTHER RESOURCES
Books
Halberstam, David. *The Best and the Brightest*. Ballantine Books, 1993.

Topmiller, Robert J. *The Lotus Unleashed: The Buddhist Peace Movement in South Vietnam, 1964–1966*. University of Kentucky Press, 2002.

Periodicals
King, Sallie B. "They Who Burned Themselves for Peace: Quaker and Buddhist Self-Immolators during the Vietnam War." *Buddhist-Christian Studies*. (2000): 127.

Web sites
News 14 Carolina. "Monk Sets Himself on Fire in Protest." December 26, 2003. <http://www.news14charlotte.com/content/local_news/> (accessed May 20, 2006).

Burning the American Flag in Protest

Photograph

By: Anonymous

Date: c. 1969

Source: Photo by Hulton Archive/Getty Images.

About the Photographer: This photograph is part of the collection at Getty Images, a worldwide provider of visual content materials to such communications groups as advertisers, broadcasters, designers, magazines, news media organizations, newspapers, and producers. The identity of the photographer is not known.

INTRODUCTION

France added the Southeast Asian country of Vietnam to its empire in the late nineteenth century. After World War II, Vietnamese nationalism (the desire for an independent nation-state) and Communism led to increasing military resistance to the French colonial presence, which was gradually withdrawn. The United States, motivated by fear of what it called a "domino effect" on other Asian countries if Vietnam were to go Communist, became entangled in Vietnam in the 1950s and early 1960s. In 1965, the United States invaded South Vietnam on a large scale; the number of U.S. troops in Vietnam peaked at over 540,000 in March 1969, a few months after this photograph was taken.

Protest against U.S. involvement in the Vietnam War began slowly, but, by the end of the war, it was a major factor in the U.S. decision to withdraw. Millions participated in various protest actions, including writing, speaking, teaching, marches, leaving the country to avoid being drafted, refusal to respond to draft orders, burning of draft cards, the return of military medals to the government, and—rarely but famously—the burning of American flags. In regard to the character of the protest tactics employed by the antiwar movement, it should be noted that, contrary to a myth that has achieved wide currency in U.S. society, there is no contemporaneous historical evidence—no news reports, photographs, films, written testimonials, or audio recordings dating to the war period—to show that antiwar protestors spat on returning Vietnam veterans. If this form of protest occurred, it was rare rather than typical; indeed, anti-war Vietnam veterans were themselves an important vanguard of the protest movement. Flag-burning was also an atypical action, adoption of the flag as a peace-movement symbol being far more common. Nevertheless, as this photograph shows, flag-burning did occur. Such gestures were generally made by the most radical factions of the anti-war movement.

PRIMARY SOURCE

BURNING THE AMERICAN FLAG IN PROTEST
See primary source image.

PRIMARY SOURCE

Burning the American Flag in Protest: Protesters burn an American flag during an aniti-war demonstration in Washington, D.C., 1969. PHOTO BY HULTON ARCHIVE/GETTY IMAGES.

SIGNIFICANCE

Burning of the flag is a symbolic act designed to shock observers. As philosopher Paul Tillich (1886–1965) has written, "the flag participates in the power and dignity of the nation for which it stands.... An attack on the flag is felt as an attack on the majesty of the group in which it is acknowledged. Such an attack is considered blasphemy." Starting in the late nineteenth century, the offensive nature of flag burning—or, indeed, of any treatment of the flag perceived as insulting—has resulted in the passage of a number of flag-protection laws, several U.S. Supreme Court decisions, and much debate about the nature of free speech.

Between 1897 and 1919, most U.S. states adopted laws banning flag desecration. Early concern centered on uses of the flag in commercial advertising rather than on its immolation in political protests. In

An anti-war protester burns a U.S. flag in front of the CNN Center in Atlanta, March 20, 2003. AP IMAGES.

1890, a bill was approved by the U.S. House of Representatives (but not the Senate) that would have made it a crime to "deface, disfigure, or prostitute [the flag] for purposes of advertising." In *Halter v. Nebraska* (1907), the U.S. Supreme Court upheld the constitutionality of a state law under which a beer company was fined for including an image of the flag on its label.

The first federal anti-flag-desecration law was passed in 1968 in response to flag burnings such as the one shown in this photograph. (Burning is also the traditional method of disposing of a worn flag; anti-desecration laws always declare such burning non-criminal.) The new law specified up to a year in jail for anyone who "knowingly casts contempt upon any flag of the United States by publicly mutilating, defiling, burning or trampling upon it." A number of challenges to the law were brought in court. In *Street v. New York* (1968), the Court struck down the conviction

of a flag-burning protestor and stated that "the freedom to express publicly one's opinions about our flag, including those opinions which are defiant or contemptuous," is guaranteed by the First Amendment to the Constitution, which states, in part, that "Congress shall make no law...abridging the freedom of speech." In *Smith v. Goguen* (1974), the Court also raised questions about what constitutes an actual flag. These questions would also arise in later cases before the Court, and continue to be raised by opponents of anti-flag-desecration laws: is a piece of colored cloth with thirteen stripes and thirty-nine stars a flag for the purposes of the legislation? What about twelve stripes and fifty stars? What about a red, white, and green flag, or a pencil sketch of a flag, or a piece of white paper with the words "This Is An American Flag" written on it? If symbolic acts or statements other than flag desecration are found to be equally offensive, can they be banned as well?

In 1989, the latest phase of political pressure for federal anti-desecration action began after the U.S. Supreme Court struck down a Texas flag-desecration law in *Texas v. Johnson*. The Court said that flag-burning, regardless of how offensive it might be to some persons, was symbolic speech, therefore protected by the First Amendment. In less than a month, Senator Robert Dole (Republican, Kansas) introduced a bill that would amend the Constitution to ban flag desecration. The amendment did not pass the U.S. Senate, but other senators introduced the Flag Protection Act of 1989, which quickly passed both houses of Congress. In 1990, in *United States v. Eichman*, the U.S. Supreme Court overturned the Act.

Since 1990, the U.S. House of Representatives has voted by large majorities six times to approve a flag-desecration amendment, but in every case the bill has failed to pass in the U.S. Senate by a small margin (or has not made it to a vote). The proposed amendment would read, "The Congress shall have power to prohibit the physical desecration of the flag of the United States." The U.S. House approved a flag-desecration amendment employing this wording in 2005, and the U.S. Senate will vote on the measure in 2006. If such an amendment ever passes, it must still be ratified by three-fourths of U.S. state legislatures to become the Twenty-Eighth Amendment

FURTHER RESOURCES
Books
Goldstein, Robert Justin. *Flag Burning and Free Speech: The Case of Texas v. Johnson*. Lawrence: University Press of Kansas, 2000.

Periodicals
Allen, Mike. "House Passes Constitutional Amendment to Ban Flag Burning." *Washington Post* (June 23, 2005).

Kellman, Laurie. "House Approves Move to Outlaw Flag Burning." *San Francisco Chronicle* (June 22, 2005).

Vice President Spiro T. Agnew's Claims Television News Is Biased

Speech excerpt

By: Spiro T. Agnew

Date: November 13, 1969

Source: Agnew, Spiro. Remarks delivered in Des Moines, Iowa, November 13, 1969. Available online at *American Rhetoric* <http://www.americanrhetoric. com/speeches/ spiroagnew.htm> (accessed May 26, 2006).

About the Author: Spiro T. Agnew (1918–1996) served as vice-president of the United States under Richard Nixon from 1969 to 1973. Known for his combative style, Agnew resigned from the vice-presidency after being charged with accepting bribes when he served as governor of Maryland.

INTRODUCTION

Spiro T. Agnew gained fame for his verbal attacks against liberals and the media during the Nixon administration. As a centrist who lacked the star power to outshine Nixon, Agnew became the Republican choice for vice-president in 1968 and was sworn into office on January 20, 1969. He often said what Nixon felt but could not publicly express.

Agnew was known for his candor but was also notoriously thin-skinned and insensitive to the inflammatory impact of his words. As governor of Maryland from 1966 to 1968, he initiated tax reform, increased aid to antipoverty programs, established the strictest state law in the country against water pollution, repealed the state law against interracial marriage, supported open housing, and pushed for the liberalization of abortion laws. He also showed a talent for making enemies.

Agnew took a strong stand for law and order and categorized peaceful demonstrations as "militant pushing." In 1968, he ordered the arrest of 227 trespassing Bowie State University students who were holding a sit-in to protest dilapidated buildings at the predominantly black campus. "I refuse to knuckle under to the demands of students no matter how justified they are," he explained. When Baltimore erupted in flames after the assassination of Martin Luther King in 1968, Agnew arranged a meeting with 100 moderate black leaders who had tried to restore calm by walking the streets during the violence. Demanding that they repudiate Black Power radicals, he then gave a speech that prompted 70 of the attendees to walk out.

Agnew also had no patience for those who criticized the Vietnam War and the Nixon administration. On November 3, 1969, Nixon told the American people in a televised address that antiwar protesters would not dictate American policy and that his new Vietnamization policy would bring peace by withdrawing American ground combat forces from the country. Continuing the counteroffensive against the antiwar movement, on November 13, Agnew vehemently denounced television news broadcasters as

Vice President Spiro Agnew meets with the press on March 19, 1971, after his speech criticizing the news media as being biased.
© BETTMANN/CORBIS.

a hostile, unelected, elite who subjected Nixon's speeches to "instant analysis" because their "minds were made up in advance."

PRIMARY SOURCE

I think it's obvious from the cameras here that I didn't come to discuss the ban on cyclamates or DDT. I have a subject which I think if of great importance to the American people. Tonight I want to discuss the importance of the television news medium to the American people. No nation depends more on the intelligent judgment of its citizens. No medium has a more profound influence over public opinion. Nowhere in our system are there fewer checks on vast power. So, nowhere should there be more conscientious responsibility exercised than by the news media. The question is, "Are we demanding enough of our television news presentations?" "And are the men of this medium demanding enough of themselves?"

Monday night a week ago, President Nixon delivered the most important address of his Administration, one of the most important of our decade. His subject was Vietnam. My hope, as his at that time, was to rally the American people to see the conflict through to a lasting and just peace in the Pacific. For 32 minutes, he reasoned with a nation that has suffered almost a third of a million casualties in the longest war in its history.

When the President completed his address—an address, incidentally, that he spent weeks in the preparation of—his words and policies were subjected to instant analysis and querulous criticism. The audience of 70 million Americans gathered to hear the President of the United States was inherited by a small band of network commentators and self-appointed analysts, the majority of whom expressed in one way or another their hostility to what he had to say.

It was obvious that their minds were made up in advance. Those who recall the fumbling and groping that followed President Johnson's dramatic disclosure of his intention not to seek another term have seen these men in a genuine state of nonpreparedness. This was not it.

One commentator twice contradicted the President's statement about the exchange of correspondence with Ho Chi Minh. Another challenged the President's abilities as a politician. A third asserted that the President was following a Pentagon line. Others, by the expressions on their faces, the tone of their questions, and the sarcasm of their responses, made clear their sharp disapproval.

To guarantee in advance that the President's plea for national unity would be challenged, one network trotted out Averell Harriman for the occasion. Throughout the President's address, he waited in the wings. When the President concluded, Mr. Harriman recited perfectly. He attacked the Thieu Government as unrepresentative; he criticized the President's speech for various deficiencies; he twice issued a call to the Senate Foreign Relations Committee to debate Vietnam once again; he stated his belief that the Vietcong or North Vietnamese did not really want military take-over of South Vietnam; and he told a little anecdote about a "very, very responsible" fellow he had met in the North Vietnamese delegation.

All in all, Mr. Harrison offered a broad range of gratuitous advice challenging and contradicting the policies outlined by the President of the United States. Where the President had issued a call for unity, Mr. Harriman was encouraging the country not to listen to him. . . .

Now every American has a right to disagree with the President of the United States and to express publicly that disagreement. But the President of the United States has a right to communicate directly with the people who elected him, and the people of this country have the right to make up their own minds and form their own opinions about a Presidential address without having a President's words and thoughts characterized through the prejudices of hostile critics before they can even be digested. . . .

The purpose of my remarks tonight is to focus your attention on this little group of men who not only enjoy a right of instant rebuttal to every Presidential address, but, more importantly, wield a free hand in selecting, presenting, and interpreting the great issues in our nation. First, let's define that power.

At least 40 million Americans every night, it's estimated, watch the network news. Seven million of them view ABC, the remainder being divided between NBC and CBS According to Harris polls and other studies, for millions of Americans the networks are the sole source of national and world news. In Will Rogers' observation, what you knew was what you read in the newspaper. Today for growing millions of Americans, it's what they see and hear on their television sets.

Now how is this network news determined? A small group of men, numbering perhaps no more than a dozen anchormen, commentators, and executive producers, settle upon the 20 minutes or so of film and commentary that's to reach the public. This selection is made from the 90 to 180 minutes that may be available. Their powers of choice are broad.

They decide what 40 to 50 million Americans will learn of the day's events in the nation and in the world. We cannot measure this power and influence by the traditional democratic standards, for these men can create national issues overnight. They can make or break by their coverage and commentary a moratorium on the war. They can elevate men from obscurity to national prominence within a week. They can reward some politicians with national exposure and ignore others.

For millions of Americans the network reporter who covers a continuing issue—like the ABM or civil rights—becomes, in effect, the presiding judge in a national trial by jury. . . .

Now what do Americans know of the men who wield this power? Of the men who produce and direct the network news, the nation knows practically nothing. Of the commentators, most Americans know little other than that they reflect an urbane and assured presence seemingly well-informed on every important matter. We do know that to a man these commentators and producers live and work in the geographical and intellectual confines of Washington, DC, or New York City, the latter of which James Reston terms the most unrepresentative community in the entire United States.

Both communities bask in their own provincialism, their own parochialism.

We can deduce that these men read the same newspapers. They draw their political and social views from the same sources. Worse, they talk constantly to one another, thereby providing artificial reinforcement to their shared viewpoints. Do they allow their biases to influence the selection and presentation of the news? David Brinkley states objectivity is impossible to normal human behavior. Rather, he says, we should strive for fairness.

Another anchorman on a network news show contends, and I quote: "You can't expunge all your private convictions just because you sit in a seat like this and a camera starts to stare at you. I think your program has to reflect what your basic feelings are. I'll plead guilty to that. . . ."

The views of the majority of this fraternity do not—and I repeat, not—represent the views of America. That is why such a great gulf existed between how the nation received the President's address and how the networks reviewed it. Not only did the country receive the

President's speech more warmly than the networks, but so also did the Congress of the United States. . . .

Now I want to make myself perfectly clear. I'm not asking for Government censorship or any other kind of censorship. I am asking whether a form of censorship already exists when the news that 40 million Americans receive each night is determined by a handful of men responsible only to their corporate employers and is filtered through a handful of commentators who admit to their own set of biases. . . .

Now a virtual monopoly of a whole medium of communication is not something that democratic people should blindly ignore. And we are not going to cut off our television sets and listen to the phonograph just because the airways belong to the networks. They don't. They belong to the people. As Justice Byron wrote in his landmark opinion six months ago, "It's the right of the viewers and listeners, not the right of the broadcasters, which is paramount."

Now it's argued that this power presents no danger in the hands of those who have used it responsibly. But as to whether or not the networks have abused the power they enjoy, let us call as our first witness, former Vice-President Humphrey and the city of Chicago. According to Theodore White, television's intercutting of the film from the streets of Chicago with the "current proceedings on the floor of the convention created the most striking and false political picture of 1968—the nomination of a man for the American Presidency by the brutality and violence of merciless police."

If we are to believe a recent report of the House of Representative Commerce Committee, then television's presentation of the violence in the streets worked an injustice on the reputation of the Chicago police. According to the committee findings, one network in particular presented, and I quote, "a one-sided picture which in large measure exonerates the demonstrators and protestors." Film of provocations of police that was available never saw the light of day, while the film of a police response which the protestors provoked was shown to millions.

Another network showed virtually the same scene of violence from three separate angles without making clear it was the same scene. And, while the full report is reticent in drawing conclusions, it is not a document to inspire confidence in the fairness of the network news. Our knowledge of the impact of network news on the national mind is far from complete, but some early returns are available. Again, we have enough information to raise serious questions about its effect on a democratic society.

Several years ago Fred Friendly, one of the pioneers of network news, wrote that its missing ingredients were conviction, controversy, and a point of view. The networks have compensated with a vengeance.

And in the networks' endless pursuit of controversy, we should ask: What is the end value—to enlighten or to profit? What is the end result—to inform or to confuse? How does the ongoing exploration for more action, more excitement, more drama serve our national search for internal peace and stability?

Gresham's Law seems to be operating in the network news. Bad news drives out good news. The irrational is more controversial than the rational. Concurrence can no longer compete with dissent. One minute of Eldridge Cleaver is worth 10 minutes of Roy Wilkins. The labor crisis settled at the negotiating table is nothing compared to the confrontation that results in a strike—or better yet, violence along the picket lines. Normality has become the nemesis of the network news.

Now the upshot of all this controversy is that a narrow and distorted picture of America often emerges from the televised news. A single, dramatic piece of the mosaic becomes in the minds of millions the entire picture. The American who relies upon television for his news might conclude that the majority of American students are embittered radicals; that the majority of black Americans feel no regard for their country; that violence and lawlessness are the rule rather than the exception on the American campus.

We know that none of these conclusions is true.

Perhaps the place to start looking for a credibility gap is not in the offices of the Government in Washington but in the studios of the networks in New York! Television may have destroyed the old stereotypes, but has it not created new ones in their places? What has this "passionate" pursuit of controversy done to the politics of progress through logical compromise essential to the functioning of a democratic society?

The members of Congress or the Senate who follow their principles and philosophy quietly in a spirit of compromise are unknown to many Americans, while the loudest and most extreme dissenters on every issue are known to every man in the street. How many marches and demonstrations would we have if the marchers did not know that the ever-faithful TV cameras would be there to record their antics for the next news show . . .?

In this search for excitement and controversy, has more than equal time gone to the minority of Americans who specialize in attacking the United States—its institutions and its citizens?

Tonight I've raised questions. I've made no attempt to suggest the answers. The answers must come from the media men. They are challenged to turn their critical powers on themselves, to direct their energy, their talent, and their conviction toward improving the quality and objectivity of news presentation. They are challenged to structure their own civic ethics to relate to the great responsibilities they hold.

And the people of America are challenged, too—challenged to press for responsible news presentation. The people can let the networks know that they want their news straight and objective. The people can register their complaints on bias through mail to the networks and phone calls to local stations. This is one case where the people must defend themselves, where the citizen, not the Government, must be the reformer; where the consumer can be the most effective crusader....

Now, my friends, we'd never trust such power, as I've described, over public opinion in the hands of an elected Government. It's time we questioned it in the hands of a small unelected elite. The great networks have dominated America's airwaves for decades. The people are entitled to a full accounting of their stewardship.

SIGNIFICANCE

The American public overwhelmingly supported Nixon's Vietnamization program. Meanwhile, the administration's counteroffensive against antiwar activists paid dividends. Many of the peace activists in Congress decided that it was wise to lay low for awhile. However, the administration's public relations campaign against the antiwar movement suffered a serious setback at the end of November when Seymour Hersh filed the first of a series of reports in more than 30 newspapers that American troops had massacred 350 to 500 unarmed South Vietnamese civilians in the hamlet of My Lai. The subsequent discovery that the military had covered up the killings for over a year would further fuel antiwar sentiments.

It took Nixon four years to end American involvement in Vietnam, during which time the conflict expanded into Cambodia and Laos. A 1971 opinion poll indicated that more than 60 percent of respondents considered it a mistake to have sent American troops into Vietnam. Many supporters of the war blamed the media for creating this antiwar sentiment through biased reporting. Subsequent reporting from war zones was closely controlled by the government in an effort to avoid a repeat. The war, the longest ever fought by the U.S., shattered consensus and contributed to severe internal disorder at home.

FURTHER RESOURCES
Books
Agnew, Spiro T. *Go Quietly ... Or Else*. New York: Morrow, 1980.

Coyne, John R, Jr. *The Impudent Snobs: Agnew vs. the Intellectual Establishment*. New York: Arlington House, 1972.

Wells, Tom. *The War Within: America's Battle Over Vietnam*. New York: Henry Holt, 1994.

Jimi Hendrix Playing at Woodstock

Photograph

By: Henry Diltz

Date: August 18, 1969

Source: Diltz, Henry. "Jimi Hendrix Playing at Woodstock." Corbis Corporation.

About the Photographer: Henry Diltz began his career in 1963 as a musician, playing banjo and clarinet for the Modern Folk Quartet, a band he co-founded. After the group disbanded, he began focusing on music photography, working with groups including The Lovin' Spoonful and Crosby, Stills, and Nash. Diltz remains an active photographer and by 2006 had provided photos for more than 200 album covers.

INTRODUCTION
In 1969, the youth movement of the 1960s was in full swing. Rock music had taken America by storm, the Vietnam War provided a rallying point for anti-government protests, and Timothy Leary's admonition to "Turn on, tune in, drop out" was being taken literally by thousands of young people. Sensing an opportunity, four young men decided to organize what they hoped would be the largest rock concert ever, surpassing the previous record of 20,000. They chose a location near Bethel, New York, naming their planned event The Woodstock Art and Music Fair.

The fair organizers leased 600 acres of alfalfa fields from Max Yasgur, a dairy farmer, and began signing bands. Some of the biggest names in 1960s pop music were contracted, including the Who and Jimi Hendrix. Advance ticket sales soon outgrew the original plans, topping 75,000 and causing Yasgur to consider breaking his lease. He decided to honor the lease when an angry neighbor put up a sign reading "Local People Speak Out/Stop Max's Music Festival/No 150,000 Hippies Here/Buy No Milk."

So many people came to that field in New York that the organizers stopped trying to charge admission partway through the event. Estimates of attendance vary from 300,000 to 500,000. Depending on the number chosen, Woodstock was, for several days, either the second or third largest settlement in the state of New York. The New York Thruway was so clogged with cars attempting to reach the concert that it was closed down by the state police. The festival, scheduled for three days, stretched to four.

During those four days, rainshowers turned portions of the huge alfalfa field into mud. Thousands of people bathed nude in a nearby pond. Alcohol, marijuana, and other recreational drugs were freely consumed. The event became a massive celebration of what has been called the counterculture, a set of cultural choices made in conscious opposition to the traditional symbols of American adulthood, including neatly-coiffed hair, and unquestioning support for the U.S. government. Much of the music emanating from the stage was overtly political. Thousands sang along with Country Joe's anthem, "Feel Like I'm Fixin' to Die Rag," with its chorus "And it's one, two, three, what are we fightin' for?/Don't ask me I don't give a damn/Next stop is Vietnam." There was one death from a drug overdose and another person died after being run over by a tractor, but given the large number of people and the inadequate facilities, the gathering was notably peaceful.

As the concert stretched past the weekend into Monday morning, performer Jimi Hendrix faced an unenviable task. Originally scheduled to close the event the previous night, Hendrix took the stage on Monday morning with a poorly rehearsed band and a lethargic audience exhausted from the previous three days. Once on stage, Hendrix delivered what is today considered one of history's most important rock performances, combining personal hits with improvised numbers and even a heavily reworked rendition of the "Star Spangled Banner." By its conclusion, the set became one of the most memorable events at Woodstock.

PRIMARY SOURCE

JIMI HENDRIX PLAYING AT WOODSTOCK
See primary source image.

SIGNIFICANCE

Woodstock has achieved such mythic significance—helped by the best-selling Woodstock record and epic three-hour movie, which eventually enabled the concert project to turn a profit—that Americans

PRIMARY SOURCE

Jimi Hendrix Playing at Woodstock Renowned rock guitarist Jimi Hendrix performing live at Woodstock. © HENRY DILTZ/ CORBIS.

who were young adults at the time of Woodstock have often been referred to as the Woodstock Generation or Woodstock Nation. Yet the significance of Woodstock is debatable. Political protest and popular music were already defining 1960s youth culture before the concert took place.

Nevertheless, Woodstock has become a powerful symbol, both positive and negative, of the youth culture of the 1960s. Conservative commentators have derided the event as exposing the emptiness of the pleasure-driven values expressed by the music and literature of the time. In 2003, *Wall Street Journal* editor Daniel Henninger wrote an essay, "Anti-Woodstock," in which he suggested that "youth culture in America is a lifestyle, emphasizing the thing that youth tend to be very good at: thinking about themselves.... Some say the youth culture began at Woodstock, the celebration of song, self and mud in 1969." Henninger went on to suggest that the U.S. invasion and occupation of Iraq in 2003 is an anti-Woodstock that is teaching young men and women "commitment to the military's culture of selflessness." As an example of "remarkably well-spoken, courteous and other-directed" youth reliably produced by Marine training on Parris Island, he cited an incident where a reporter in Iraq offered to let four Marines use his satellite cell phone to call home. One Marine, Henninger said, "ran off to get his sergeant who hadn't talked to his pregnant wife in three months" and the others offered to call the parents of a dead comrade rather than their own families. Unfortunately, the cell-phone incident turned out to be mythical; the *Wall Street Journal* later appended a notice to the essay identifying the anecdote as a "false tale" that had been "circulating widely on the Web."

The stereotyped image of the 1960s that has formed around Woodstock is almost equally mythical: a contemptible (or glorious) vacation from history during which flowers, beads, drugs, and electric guitars displaced reality. The actual period was far more complex. Arnold Skolnick offered his own modest summary of Woodstock: "Something was tapped, a nerve in this country, and everybody just came."

Jimi Hendrix is considered one of the most creative and influential guitarists in history. He died in 1970 while on tour in London, England.

FURTHER RESOURCES
Books
Bennett, Andy, ed. *Remembering Woodstock*. Burlington, VT: Ashgate, 2004.

Cross, Charles. *Room Full of Mirrors: A Biography of Jimi Hendrix*. New York: Hyperion, 2005.

Spitz, Robert Stephen. *Barefoot in Babylon: The Creation of the Woodstock Music Festival*. New York: Viking Press, 1979.

Periodicals
Anonymous. "Pushing the button." *The Economist* (December 16, 1995).

Norman, Michael. "The 'Holy Ground' of the Woodstock Generation." *New York Times* (August 16, 1984).

Sierz, Aleks. "Read your roots." *New Statesman* (December 6, 2004).

Web sites
Google Video. "Jimi Hendrix - Woodstock Improv 1969." January 20, 2006. <http://video.google.com/videoplay?docid=2460058168987804953> (accessed July 5, 2006).

Woodstock Preservation Archives. "Statement on the Historical and Cultural Significance of the 1969 Woodstock Festival Site." September 25, 2001. <http://www.woodstockpreservation.org:81/archmat/FinalSigState.pdf> (accessed May 26, 2006).

Two Judges Decline Drug Cases, Protesting Sentencing Rules

Newspaper article

By: Joseph B. Treaster

Date: April 17, 1993

Source: *New York Times*

About the Author: Joseph B. Treaster has been a reporter for the *New York Times* for more than thirty years, working from many different countries. Treaster is currently posted in New York, reporting on financial news, and has written several books, including a biography of American economist Paul Volcker, former chairman of the Federal Reserve and a book on *New York Times* coverage of the Middle East hostage crisis. Most recently, Treaster was the *New York Times* lead reporter in covering Hurricane Katrina.

INTRODUCTION

The Sentencing Reform Act of 1984 mandated the creation of the U.S. Sentencing Commission, which was established in 1985. The stated purpose of the commission was to put forward sentencing policies and practices that would 1) ensure that the goals of just punishment, deterrence, incapacitation, and rehabilitation are being met; 2) eliminate sentencing disparity—the phenomenon of defendants receiving vastly different sentences for similar offences; 3) allow mitigating or aggravating factors to be considered in determining the appropriate penalty. The result of the commission's study was Federal Sentencing Guidelines; a formulaic prescription for judges to use in calculating a fitting sentence that accounted for the type and severity of the offence, in combination with the offender's prior convictions. The intersection of the various factors tells the judge what the range of the sentence should be, within a very narrow window.

At the same time, political concern about the growing drug problem in the United States prompted the passage of the Anti-Drug Abuse Act in 1986. This act, and its 1988 amendments, set a variety of mandatory minimum sentences for drug possession and trafficking. In combination with the existing Federal Sentencing Guidelines, this legislation severely limited judicial discretion in determining sentences for drug offences and contributed to an increase in lengthy prison terms, designed to be a weapon in the 'war on drugs.' Some federal judges, dissatisfied with

Judge Jack B. Weinstein. © BETTMANN/CORBIS.

their inability to act on conscience and to account for mitigating factors in sentencing, have revolted against the concept of mandatory minimums and sentencing guidelines by refusing to preside over drug-related cases.

PRIMARY SOURCE

Two of New York City's most prominent Federal judges said yesterday that they would no longer preside over drug cases, going public with a protest that calls attention to what dozens of Federal judges are doing quietly across the country.

The decisions, by Jack B. Weinstein of Brooklyn and Whitman Knapp of Manhattan, were made in protest against national drug policies and Federal sentencing guidelines. They said that the emphasis on arrests and imprisonment, rather than prevention and treatment, had been a failure, and that they were withdrawing from the effort.

Federal court officials estimated that about 50 of the 680 Federal District judges are refusing to take drug cases. The protest is confined to senior judges, a category of judges eligible for retirement who are given wide latitude in choosing their cases.

NOT A BLANKET REFUSAL

The two judges, who have not spoken out against drug policies in the past, said that on special request they would be willing to preside over a drug case to help an overloaded colleague. But they said they would insist that the sentencing be done by others.

A handful of Federal judges have called for the legalization of drugs, and a few judges have resigned rather than apply what they regarded as overly harsh sentences.

"The present policy of trying to prohibit drugs through the use of criminal law is a mistake," said Robert W. Sweet, a Federal judge in Manhattan who began advocating legalization of drugs four years ago. "It's a policy that's not working. It's not cutting down drug use. The best way to do this is through education and treatment."

Judge Knapp and Judge Weinstein both said they were not calling for legalization of drugs, nor did they offer any specific solutions to the drug problem. Both said the change in administrations in Washington had not been a factor in their decisions, but Judge Knapp said that "Clinton has not committed himself to the war on drugs in such a way as the Republican Administration had," and he hoped his action might influence the President.

The decisions of Judge Knapp and Judge Weinstein are likely to have little impact on the flow of cases through the Federal courts. But a top Federal administrative judge said that the actions would probably have a great symbolic effect.

"A lot of judges feel the present system breeds injustice," said Federal District Judge William W. Schwarzer, the director of the Federal Judicial Center, the educational and research agency in Washington for the Federal courts.

He said many judges feel that sentencing rules enacted by Congress that provide for little or no judicial discretion "load up the prisons but have not done much else to improve the drug situation."

"People think they can stop the drug traffic by putting people in jail and by having terribly long sentences," said Judge Knapp, who is 82 years old and rose to prominence in the 1970's when he headed the Knapp Commission, which investigated police corruption in New York City.

"But," Judge Knapp said, "of course it doesn't do any good."

AVAILABILITY CITED

Both he and Judge Weinstein, who is 72 years old, said that while the number of people arrested and imprisoned on drug charges has risen sharply over the last decade, drugs remained easily available in New York and other cities.

"The penalties have been increased enormously," said Judge Weinstein, "without having any impact. It's just a futile endeavor, a waste of taxpayers' money.":

Judge Thomas C. Platt, the chief Federal judge in Brooklyn, would not comment on the actions of the two judges. But Judge Thomas P. Griesa, the chief Federal judge in Manhattan, said: "I believe the enforcement of the anti-narcotics laws serves a very important purpose."

"Even though it is far from successful in any ideal sense," he continued, "it is society's way of doing the best it can to combat this deadly plague of a criminal nature. Beyond any statistical or tangible results there is a moral value in having society take a stand against this."

Robert C. Bonner, the administrator of the Drug Enforcement Administration and a former federal district judge and prosecutor, said that "no matter how well intended, unfortunately, no one judge in no one courtroom is in a very good position to judge the overall effectiveness of drug prosecutions."

Mr. Bonner said that the ability to prosecute drug cases in the Federal courts "plays a critical role in the D.E.A.'s global strategy to incapacitate major trafficking organizations."

"While cocaine is far more available than any of us would like to see it be," he said, "it is less readily available in New York and other major urban areas than it was five years ago."

According to the latest Federal estimates, 1.9 million Americans used cocaine in 1991 compared with 5.8 million in 1985. The reasons for the decline are not entirely clear. But many drug experts say a heightened awareness of the harm cocaine can do along with a shift toward healthier living has contributed more to the decline than has law enforcement.

Dr. Herbert D. Kleber, a former senior drug adviser to President George Bush and now an official of the Center on Addiction and Substance Abuse at Columbia University, said that while he favored such alternatives to prison as mandatory treatment programs for nonviolent convicts, he did not feel that judges should refuse to preside over cases.

"They shouldn't be able to pick which laws they feel like upholding." Dr. Kleber said. "Just enforcing the criminal law is inadequate, but it is one important component.

We need not just criminal law but increased treatment and prevention programs."

Judge Knapp said he had been considering the effectiveness of drug policy for years but did not decide to speak out until he was asked to address a lunch meeting last month.

He said he had quietly stopped handling drug cases about a year ago, but he had not told anyone outside the courts until a reporter asked him about Judge Weinstein's decision.

Judge Weinstein announced his intentions in a memo to colleagues last Monday and again in a speech Wednesday night at Benjamin N. Cardozo School of Law. His speech and the decision to stop handling drug cases was first reported by the *New York Law Journal* on Thursday.

Judge Weinstein said he had decided to act after being forced by sentencing guidelines to send a peasant woman from West Africa to prison for 46 months on a smuggling charge and to give a man 30 years in jail for his second drug offense.

"These two cases," he said, "confirm my sense of depression about much of the cruelty I have been party to in connection with the war on drugs."

Vincent L. Broderick, a former New York City Police Commissioner now serving as a Federal district judge in Manhattan, said that in more than a decade of the latest drug war, "We haven't dealt at all with why people go to drugs. Why aren't we spending more money in this area?"

SIGNIFICANCE

In addition to severely curtailing the discretion exercised by federal judges, the restrictive Federal Sentencing Guidelines and the Anti-Drug Abuse Laws have resulted in more and lengthier custodial sentences for drug offences in the United States. Many judges, like Justices Knapp and Weinstein, lawyers, and criminologists are opposed to the notion of mandatory minimum sentences and statutory rulings, arguing that the guidelines fail to serve the need for rehabilitation and don't leave room for the consideration of mitigating factors in sentencing, resulting in a trend toward more punitive and generalized sentencing. Although the sentencing commission's original directive allowed for the consideration of the defendant's individual situation and potential for rehabilitation in deviating from the guidelines, later amendments determined that personal factors related to the defendant were "not ordinarily relevant" to sentencing. Despite popular protest and evidence that lengthier sentences for drug convictions were contributing to an overall rise in the prison population—but not resulting in lower rates of drug offending—the sentencing guidelines remained in force until a landmark U.S. Supreme Court decision in January 2005.

In 2003, Freddie Booker was convicted by a jury of possession of at least 50 grams of cocaine with intent to distribute. According to the Federal Sentencing Guidelines, this offence carries a mandatory minimum sentence of ten years with the maximum sentence being life imprisonment. During the sentencing hearing, the judge determined by a preponderance of evidence that Booker had also been in possession of more cocaine than the jury had convicted him of trafficking and had obstructed justice by providing false information to the authorities. Taking these findings into consideration and applying the Federal Sentencing Guidelines, the judge ruled that the sentencing range for Booker was increased to a minimum of thirty years to life and gave him the minimum thirty year sentence.

Booker's lawyers appealed the ruling on the grounds that the additional factors taken into account at sentencing were beyond the scope of the jury's conviction and were subject to a much lower burden of proof—a 'preponderance of evidence' instead of 'beyond reasonable doubt.' At appeal, Booker's lawyers argued that the sentencing guidelines' allowance of factors not proven before a jury and not contained in his criminal history violated the defendant's Sixth Amendment right to a trial by jury and that the sentencing guidelines were therefore unconstitutional. While Booker's conviction was upheld by the court of appeals, his sentence was overturned and the government appealed this ruling to the U.S. Supreme Court.

On January 12, 2005, the U.S. Supreme Court ruled in favor of Booker, noting that the Sixth Amendment does indeed apply to the sentencing guidelines and that the statutory maximum sentence must be applied by the judge on the basis of facts admitted by the defendant or found before a jury. Because the facts applied in Booker's sentencing were not found before a jury, he in fact had a right to the lower sentence of a ten year minimum. The court also noted that if the sentencing guidelines were merely advisory, rather than mandatory, the Sixth Amendment would not apply. However, because the sentencing guidelines are mandated by law, they must conform to constitutional standards. On the application of the guidelines themselves, the Supreme Court ruled that the mandatory application

of the sentencing guidelines was unconstitutional, and found that the clause that judges be required to apply the guidelines unequivocally should be removed from the legislation, effectively rendering the sentencing guidelines as suggestive rather than binding and restoring the power of judicial discretion in sentencing.

In the wake of the Booker decision, a report by the U.S. Sentencing Commission in March 2006 revealed that the majority of federal judges continue to sentence in accordance with the advisory guidelines. While judges are giving out an increased number of sentences that fall below the guideline minimums (from nine percent to fifteen percent), the average sentence for drug trafficking has actually increased from eighty-three to eighty-five months. The reintroduction of judicial discretion into drug sentencing has not resulted in significantly more lenient penalties, nor has it led to a stark departure from the sentencing guidelines in practice. The value of judicial discretion is most significant when judges are faced with exceptional situations and cases in which justice is not adequately served by a formulaic prescription and more humane and practical responses are necessary. The outcry of federal justices and the constitutional challenge of the Booker case have restored decision-making power to the hands of judges who are in the best position to consider the relevant factors of each case and make sentencing decisions tailored to the situation of individual defendants. The outcome of the Booker decision resulted in amendments to the Federal Sentencing Guidelines in May 2006.

FURTHER RESOURCES

Periodicals

Clarke, Judy. "The Sentencing Guidelines: What a Mess." *Federal Probation* 55 (1991): 45–49.

Mauer, Marc. "The Causes and Consequences of Prison Growth in the United States." *Punishment and Society* 3 (2001): 9–20.

Sabet, Kevin A. "Making It Happen: The Case for Compromise in the Federal Cocaine Law Debate." *Social Policy & Administration* 39 (2005): 181–191.

Web sites

U.S. Sentencing Commission. "Final Report on the Impact of United States V. Booker on Federal Sentencing." March 2006. <http://www.ussc.gov/booker_report/Booker_Report.pdf> (accessed May 21, 2006).

U.S. Sentencing Commission. "United States v. Booker:" January 12, 2005. <http://www.ussc.gov/Blakely/04-104.pdf> (accessed May 15, 2006).

Your Rights to Demonstrate and Protest

Pamphlet

By: National Lawyers Guild

Date: 2000

Source: *Your Rights to Demonstrate and Protest: A Guide for Demonstrators, Marchers, Speakers and Others Who Seek to Exercise Their First Amendment Rights.* New York: National Lawyers Guild, 2000.

About the Author: The National Lawyers Guild, a membership organization made up of lawyers, professors of law, law students, and legal system workers, is an advocacy group devoted to fighting racism, expanding rights for women and minorities, and protecting civil liberties in the United States.

INTRODUCTION

The First Amendment to the U.S. Constitution guarantees the right to assemble and the right to free speech. The amendment states that "Congress shall make no law respecting an establishment of religion, or prohibiting the free exercise thereof; or abridging the freedom of speech, or of the press; or the right of the people peaceably to assemble, and to petition the Government for a redress of grievances." Since its ratification in 1791, the First Amendment—part of the first ten amendments to the Constitution that make up the Bill of Rights—has been interpreted via the court system and the U.S. Supreme Court to include the right to protest peacefully in the United States.

U.S. Supreme Court cases such as the 1963 *Edwards v. South Carolina* case, which stated that African American high schools students engaged in protests were protected by the First Amendment, and the 1966 case *Brown v. Louisiana*, which held that

Pro-choice demonstrators Courtney Davis, Katherine Schwartz and Nickie Ittner show their support for abortion rights at a National Organization for Women rally outside the Houston Astrodome on August 15, 1992. © REUTERS/CORBIS

protestors have protest rights under the First and Fourteenth Amendments, historically protect protest rights. The rulings in other cases placed some limits upon protest rights. For example, the 1977 *National Socialist Party of America v. Village of Skokie* ruling created requirements for procedures for rejecting groups who wish to stage protests, while the 1994 Supreme Court case *Madsen v. Women's Health Center* placed limits on anti-choice groups who wished to protest in front of women's reproductive health centers where abortions are performed. The ruling in this case created a thirty-six-foot "buffer zone" around clinic entrances and prohibited protestors from approaching the clinic or any person within that limited space.

While the right to protest is guaranteed in the Constitution and has been defined through case law, limits have also been placed on protestors through government regulation as well as state and local laws. In this pamphlet from the National Lawyers Guild, an organization devoted to civil liberties and rights protection, the right to demonstrate and protest is defined, explained, and presented as a call to engage.

PRIMARY SOURCE

GENERAL GUIDELINES

Q. Can my free speech rights be restricted because of what I want to say—even if it's controversial?
A. No. The First Amendment prohibits restrictions based on the content of speech. However, this does not mean that the Constitution completely protects all types of free speech activity in every circumstance. Police and government officials are allowed to place certain non-discriminatory and narrowly drawn "time, place and manner" restrictions on the exercise of First Amendment rights.

Q. Where can I engage in free speech activity?
A. Generally, all types of expression are constitutionally protected in traditional "public forums" such as public sidewalks and parks. Public streets can be used for marches subject to reasonable permit conditions. In addition, speech activity may be permitted at other public locations such as the plazas in front of government buildings which the government has opened up to similar speech activities.

Q. What about free speech activities on private property?
A. The general rule is that free speech activity cannot take place on private property without the consent of the property owner. However, in California, the courts have recognized an exception for large shopping centers and have permitted leafleting and petitioning to take place in the public areas of large shopping centers. The shopping center owners, however, are entitled to impose regulations that, for example, limit the number of activists on the property and restrict their activities to designated "free speech areas." Most large shopping centers have enacted detailed free speech regulations that require obtaining a permit in advance. Recent court decisions have found that the "shopping center exception" does not apply to single, free-standing stores, such as a Wal-Mart or Trader Joe's.

Q. Do I need a permit before I engage in free speech activity?
A. Not usually. However, certain types of events require permits. Generally, these events include: (1) a march or parade that does not stay on the sidewalk and other events that require blocking traffic or street closures; (2) a large rally requiring the use of sound amplifying devices; or (3) a rally at certain designated parks or plazas, such as federal property managed by the General Services Administration. Many permit procedures require that the application be filed several weeks in advance of the event. However, the First Amendment prohibits such advance notice requirements from being used to prevent rallies or demonstrations that are rapid responses to unforeseeable and recent events. Also, many permit ordinances give a lot of discretion to the police or city officials to impose conditions on the event, such as the route of a march or the sound levels of amplification equipment. Such restrictions may violate the First Amendment if they are unnecessary for traffic control or public safety, or if they interfere significantly with effective communication with the intended audience. A permit cannot be denied because the event is controversial or will express unpopular views.

SPECIFIC PROBLEMS

Q. If organizers have not obtained a permit, where can a march take place?
A. If marchers stay on the sidewalk and obey traffic and pedestrian signals, their activity is constitutionally protected even without a permit. Marchers may be required to allow enough space on the sidewalk for normal pedestrian traffic and not unreasonably obstruct or detain passers-by.

Q. May I distribute leaflets and other literature on public sidewalks?
A. Yes. Pedestrians on public sidewalks may be approached with leaflets, newspapers, petitions and solicitations for donations. Tables may also be set up on sidewalks for these purposes if sufficient room is left for pedestrians to pass. These types of free speech activity are legal as long as entrances to building are not blocked and passers-by are not physically or unreasonably detained. No permits should be required.

Q. Do I have a right to picket on public sidewalks?
A. Yes. This is an activity for which a permit is not required. However, picketing must be done in an orderly, non-disruptive fashion so that pedestrians can pass by and entrances to buildings are not blocked. Contrary to the belief of some law enforcement officials, picketers are not required to keep

moving, but may remain in one place as long as they leave room on the sidewalk for others to pass.

Q. Can the government impose a financial charge on exercising free speech rights?
A. Increasingly, local governments are imposing financial costs as a condition of exercising free speech rights. These include application fees, security deposits for clean-up, or charges to cover overtime police costs. Unfortunately, such charges that cover actual administrative costs or the actual costs of re-routing traffic have been permitted by some courts so long as they are uniformly imposed on all groups. However, if the costs are greater because an event is controversial (or a hostile crowd is expected)—the courts will not allow such costs to be imposed. Also, regulations with financial requirements should include a waiver for groups that cannot afford the charge, so that even grassroots organizations can exercise their free speech rights. Therefore, a group without significant financial resources should not be prevented from engaging in a march simply because it cannot afford the charges the City would like to impose.

Q. Can a speaker be silenced for provoking a crowd?
A. Generally, no. Even the most inflammatory speaker cannot be punished for merely arousing the audience. A speaker can be arrested and convicted for incitement only if he or she specifically advocates violence or illegal actions and only if those illegalities are imminently likely to occur.

Q. Do counter-demonstrators have free speech rights?
A. Yes. Although counter-demonstrators should not be allowed to physically disrupt the event they are protesting, they do have the right to be present and to voice their views. Police are permitted to keep two antagonistic groups separated but should allow them to be within the general vicinity of one another.

Q. Is heckling protected by the First Amendment?
A. Although the law is not settled, heckling should be protected, unless hecklers are attempting to physically disrupt an event, or unless they are drowning out the other speakers.

Q. Does it matter if other speech activities have taken place at the same location in the past?
A. Yes. The government cannot discriminate against activists because of the controversial content of their message. Thus, if you can show that events similar to ours have been permitted in the past (such as a Veterans or Memorial Day parade), then the denial of your permit application is an indication that the government is involved in selective enforcement.

Q. What other types of free speech activity are constitutionally protected?
A. The First Amendment covers all forms of communication including music, theater, film and dance. The Constitution also protects actions that symbolically express a viewpoint. Examples of such symbolic forms of speech include wearing masks and costumes or holding a candlelight vigil. However, symbolic acts and civil disobedience that involve illegal conduct may be outside the realm of constitutional protections and can sometimes lead to arrest and conviction. Therefore, while the act of sitting in a road may be expressing a political opinion, the act of blocking traffic may lead to criminal punishment.

Q. What should I do if my rights are being violated by a police officer?
A. It rarely does any good to argue with a street patrol officer. Ask to talk to a superior and explain your position to her or him. Point out that you are not disrupting anyone else's activity and that your actions are protected by the First Amendment. If you do not obey an officer, you might be arrested and taken from the scene. You should not be convicted if a court concludes that your First Amendment rights have been violated.

SIGNIFICANCE

Freedom of protest in the United States stretches back to colonial times. During World War I women's rights activists famously protested and picketed in front of the White House gates, demanding the vote for women from President Woodrow Wilson and the U.S. Congress. Union and labor protestors in the 1920s and 1930s, anti-war activists in the 1960s and early 1970s, and anti-globalization activists in the 1990s, all are part of the waves of protest protected by the First Amendment. The National Lawyers Guild outlines the intricacies of protest rights.

The 2001 USA PATRIOT Act included a provision making it a felony to breach a security barrier at an official government event. Even if the President or Vice President is not at the event, Secret Service agents would have the power to arrest protestors or any individual who crossed a security line. Civil liberties groups condemned the provision as a violation of free speech and a tactic aimed at dampening dissent.

In the spring of 2006, millions of protestors in all major cities in the United States engaged in immigration protests. These protestors were demonstrating their opposition to a Republican-sponsored immigration bill that would make the presence of an undocumented worker in the United States a felony. These peaceful protests—by millions of individuals across the length and breadth of the United States—were hailed as an effective use of protest and free speech for political purposes. While "Police and government officials are allowed to place certain non-discriminatory and narrowly drawn "time, place and manner' restrictions on the exercise of First Amendment rights," and while protestors can be charged administrative fees to cover costs to local, state, and federal governments, the First Amendment right to exercise free speech as part of a physical, public protest remains a strong component of civil society in the United States.

FURTHER RESOURCES
Books

Abrams, Floyd. *Speaking Freely: Trials of the First Amendment.* New York: Viking Adult, 2005.

Breyer, Stephen. *Active Liberty: Interpreting Our Democratic Constitution.* New York: Knopf, 2005.

Nelson, Samuel P. *Beyond the First Amendment: The Politics of Free Speech and Pluralism.* Baltimore, MD: Johns Hopkins University Press, 2005.

Stone, Geoffrey R. *Perilous Times: Free Speech in Wartime: From the Sedition Act of 1798 to the War on Terrorism.* New York: W. W. Norton, 2005.

Pie in the Eye

The Cream Tart in Modern Politics

News article

By: Paul Sussman

Date: November 23, 2000

Source: *CNN*. "Pie in the Eye—the Cream Tart in Modern Politics." <http://archives.cnn.com/2000/WORLD/europe/11/23/pie.protest/> (accessed May 22, 2006).

About the Author: Paul Sussman is a freelance journalist. He lives in London ten months each year and spends the remaining months excavating in Egypt. He has authored fiction and non-fiction books, including the novel *The Last Secret of the Temple* (2005).

INTRODUCTION

Political protests take many forms, ranging from the merely startling to the potentially deadly. For example, protesters frequently gather a crowd to publicize their cause; the 1963 Civil Rights march in Washington D.C., drew over 200,000 people to hear Martin Luther King Jr. make his famous "I have a dream" speech. Some protests consist of little more than staying home from work; many large American cities have endured the discomfort of work stoppages by city garbage collectors, resulting in mountains of rubbish in the streets and immense political pressure to reach a settlement.

Some protests are more dramatic. As Coca-Cola CEO Douglas Daft spoke at Yale University in 2004, protesters calmly walked onto the stage, removed jackets to reveal shirts splattered with fake blood, and fell to the ground in a so-called die-in. Daft continued his speech, surrounded by the bodies.

Some political protesters use force. Animal rights activists frequently encourage violence against property and personnel involved in animal testing, while political extremists in many parts of the world resort to kidnapping, murder, and terrorism to influence local, national, and international politics.

Against this backdrop of bloodshed and violence, one form of political protest remains both relatively harmless and strikingly effective, at least in terms of attracting attention. While angry crowds down through history have pelted opponents with a variety of missiles including stones, rotten fruit, and dead animals, one object remains the weapon of choice for those wishing to humiliate a public figure: a pie in the face.

The act of shoving a cream-filled pie into another person's face (or a tart in his eye, as the Europeans put it) has a long and rich history. Silent films of the early twentieth century often employed the pie gag as part of slapstick routines, and countless television shows and movies have staged pie fights. The Three Stooges were well known for hitting each other with anything handy, which frequently seemed to be several large cream pies. The 1964 film *Dr. Strangelove*, which told the story of an accidental nuclear war, was originally scripted to conclude with an enormous pie fight between U.S. and Soviet representatives, though the director scrapped the scene after shooting it. By the late twentieth century, the term "pie in the face" came into use as a general term for any publicly humiliating experience.

Pieing (the common verb form for the act of hitting someone in the face with a pie) appears to have been adopted as a political weapon during the 1970's. Well-known victims span the gamut of political views and positions, and include Microsoft CEO Bill Gates, Star Trek legend William Shatner, Canadian politician Jacques Duchesneau, and conservative writer Ann Coulter, whose pieing experience can be viewed online. Shatner's appearance in this list suggests that a pie in the face is no longer reserved for the political and economic elite.

■ PRIMARY SOURCE

The attacker mingles with the crowd, weapon in hand, waiting to pounce. As his victim approaches he edges

While meeting with the press to endorse Peter Camejo for governor, Ralph Nader is hit in the face with a pie by an unidentified man. San Francisco, California, August 12, 2003. © MARK CONSTANTINI/SAN FRANCISCO CHRONICLE/CORBIS.

forward slightly, body tense, one eye on the security guards, the other on his victim's face.

Now his target is alongside and, with a defiant yell, the attacker strikes, lunging forward, arm raised. For a moment the world seems to stand still, then the weapon makes contact and . . . splat!

Whipped cream showers everywhere, there is a strong smell of vanilla, another world leader falls prey to a cream tart.

Over the last few years an increasing number of politicians, celebrities and industrialists have been subjected to cream pie attacks.

The attacks have taken place throughout the world, and claimed such illustrious victims as Microsoft's Bill Gates, Canadian Prime Minister Jean Chretien, former European Commission President Jacques Delors and Dutch Finance Minister Gerrit Zalm, who was last year felled by an organic banana pie at the opening of the Amsterdam Stock Exchange.

Most recently Frank Loy, the United States' chief negotiator at the U.N. conference on climate change in The Hague, the Netherlands, had a pastry pushed into his face by an environmental campaigner protesting at U.S. reluctance to reduce its greenhouse gas emissions.

"It's essentially a form of democratic anarcho-populist politics," explains Dr. Rodney Barker, Reader in Government at the London School of Economics. "What it's doing is saying that those who are taken incredibly seriously both by themselves and the media deserve to be knocked down a peg or two.

"It's about pointing out to the general public that the emperor doesn't have as many clothes as he thinks he does." Among the most active are The Biotic Baking Brigade and Mad Anarchist Bakers' League in the U.S., The Meringue Marauders in Canada, T.A.A.R.T. in Holland and People Insurgent Everywhere (PIE) in the UK.

Eggs and rotten cats Although history records numerous incidents of objects being thrown at public figures—as early as the 1st century AD Roman chroniclers were describing how the Emperor Nero was pelted with onions in the Colosseum—the use of the cream pie as a means of political protest is a relatively recent phenomenon.

A whole network of mainly left-wing pie-wielding activist organizations now exists around the globe, intent on "flanning" those in positions of power and influence.

"In the past people have tended to express themselves by throwing eggs, vegetables or rotten cats," says Barker. "That can be harmful, however. The whole thing about cream pies is that allows you to make your point without actually hurting anybody."

Two figures have been especially prominent in the rise of confectionery as an instrument of political protest.

In the U.S. left-wing activist Aron Kay has been dubbed "The Pieman" for a whole series of attacks stretching across almost three decades, and including such victims as right-wing political commentator William F. Buckley, former CIA director William Colby and former New York Mayor Abe Beame.

In Belgium, meanwhile, Noel Godin, the "Godfather of the Cream Pie,"has, since 1969, been engaged in what he describes as a "cream crusade" against "the great and the wicked."

During that time his International Patisserie Brigade has "entarted" everyone from New Wave film director Jean-Luc Godard to Bill Gates.

"There are a thousand forms of subversion," he commented in a 1995 interview with the Observer magazine, "But few, in my opinion, can equal the convenience and immediacy of a cream pie." Godin and his fellow pie-throwers plan their attacks meticulously, exchanging information on the movement of prominent figures via the Internet and employing sophisticated diversionary tactics to outwit security guards.

A rudimentary "pie-wielders' code" has developed, with activists adhering to certain basic rules of engagement: the pie must be "deposited lovingly" rather than simply thrown, attackers should try to wear some sort of silly costume, the attack should humiliate, but not injure.

"We only use the finest patisserie," Godin told Britain's Observer newspaper, "Ordered at the last minute from small local bakers. Quality is everything." Whether such attacks actually have any effect on the world's decision makers, other than adding to their dry cleaning bill, is doubtful.

An increasing number of people, however, are seeing the cream pie as a useful means of venting their frustration and making a political point.

"It might not have any direct effect on a politician's policies," admitted a spokesmen for Dutch flan activists T.A.A.R.T. "What it does do is bring issues to the notice of the general public.

"There are few better ways of getting your voice heard than by slapping a big soggy pie in someone's face."

SIGNIFICANCE

The popularity of pieing is somewhat difficult to explain. Pie throwers often appear to invest numerous hours tracking their intended target, planning the attack, and documenting the encounter online for others to view. Despite these efforts, pieing appears far more entertaining than effective, since few serious politicians would revise their policies in response to a pastry assault. Instead, pie throwers appear to be motivated by a general desire to draw attention to a particular cause, and for this purpose, the act seems quite effective. Few other actions allow a common citizen to stand toe-to-toe with a wealthy business leader or powerful political figure and for a brief moment appear to have gained the upper hand.

Does pieing have a future as a tool of political change? It seems ironic that the simple act of throwing a cream pie remains popular almost a century after its first appearance; the fact that the act is still humorous so long after its initial appearance suggests that it taps into something most people find at least slightly amusing. Whether it makes for good politics or not, pie throwing is funny, suggesting that it will continue to occur. And for those not yet bold enough to fling the actual article, several web sites allow users to throw virtual pies at a variety of well-known figures, suggesting that today's young web surfers may well become tomorrow's pie throwing protestors.

FURTHER RESOURCES
Books

Chaffee, Lyman G. *Political Protest and Street Art: Popular Tools for Democratization in Hispanic Countries.* Greenwood Press, 1993.

Epstein, Barbara. *Political Protest and Cultural Revolution : Nonviolent Direct Action in the 1970s and 1980s.* University of California Press, 1991.

Pierce, Richard B. *Polite Protest: The Political Economy Of Race In Indianapolis, 1920–1970.* Indiana University Press, 2005.

Periodicals

Anderson, Christopher J. and Silvia M. Mendes. "Learning to Lose: Election Outcomes, Democratic Experience and Political Protest Potential." *British Journal of Political Science.* 36 (2006): 91–111.

Barovick, Harriet. "Ma Power!" *Time.* 167(2006): 16.

Moorer, Talise D. "Seven Hampton U students tried for 'Drive Out Bush' Protest." *New York Amsterdam News.* 96(2005): 4.

Web sites

Bitstorm. "Bill Gates hit with cream pie." <http://www.bitstorm.org/gates/> (accessed May 23, 2006).

Shane Jensen. "Classic Pie in the Face Humor." July 10, 2004. <http://www.piesintheface.com> (accessed May 23, 2006).

What Makes an Activist?

Magazine article

By: Anne Becker

Date: July 18, 2003

Source: Becker, Anne. "What Makes an Activist?" *Psychology Today* (July 18, 2003).

About the Author: Freelance writer Anne Becker is a regular contributor to *Psychology Today*.

INTRODUCTION

Activists are people who participate in some form of action to enact social or political change. These actions can range from simple things, such as letter-writing campaigns or boycotts of certain products, to participation in public protests, to, in extreme cases, terrorist acts. Some activists seek to confront their opposition, either in an attempt to sway their opinion or to gain support from others and thereby put their opinion in the majority, while others seek merely to educate the public regarding their opinions.

British schoolchildren protest against a potential war with Iraq in Edinburgh, Scotland, on March 17, 2003. © REUTERS/CORBIS.

PRIMARY SOURCE

We all recognize the protestors among us: neighbors who circulate petitions for clean-air bills, animal-rights groups in the subway harassing elderly women in fur coats, students calling for peace. We often share their convictions, but voice them in a whisper. So what distinguishes the demonstrators from the do-nothings?

The fact is, activists choose to take up causes for a wide variety of reasons—some not as straightforward as they might seem.

To start, take a look at Mom and Dad. Parental modeling can play a significant role in shaping future activists, according to Lauren Duncan, Ph.D., an assistant professor of psychology at Smith College who has studied activism. She found that students with a parent who fought in Vietnam were much more likely to protest against the 1991 Gulf War than those whose parents were not war veterans. "Parents teach their kids [what they believe are] appropriate ways to respond to particular situations," explains Duncan.

Personality also helps prime protesters. Those who find personal meaning in current events are inclined to speak out for a cause, according to Duncan. She is currently researching why some people feel emotionally drained after a newscast while others can turn off the TV set without qualms.

Individuals are more likely to feel a personal connection if they see themselves as part of the community affected by an issue, says Debra Mashek, Ph.D., a research fellow at George Mason University, who specializes in "moral" emotions. Millions of women embraced this sense of collective identity during the women's rights movement, for example.

Some psychologists say that most acts of altruism—defined as devotion to the interests of others—actually spring from a desire to help oneself. Jeffrey Kottler, Ph.D., chair of the department of counseling at California State University at Fullerton and author of *Doing Good: Passion and Commitment for Helping Others*, states that altruism can be reciprocal: Humans act benevolently for conscious or unconscious gain.

"Theorists talk about it in terms of cost-benefit analysis, as if it's a rational thing," he says. "We don't do anything selflessly; we do it because it'll come back to us later—someone will owe us something down the line or it will increase our status in the community."

Does that mean altruistic acts are inherently selfish?

"Selfish is one way to say it, but it takes on such a negative connotation," says Mashek. "If I am an anti-war protestor, then by standing up for what I think is right I'm helping the world, because the world is my community, and in so doing, I help myself."

We would all be better off today if we could broaden our sense of community, according to Kottler. He recently returned from researching bushmen in the African nation of Namibia, where tribe members consider all material possessions communal. "They don't understand 'this is mine,' because they have such a strong sense of community," he says. "In America, our kin live all over the place and this leads to a lack of responsibility for taking care of other people."

Kottler subscribes to a theory of empathic arousal, which explains good acts as motivated by the intrinsic psychological and physiological rewards they provide the doer. "There's a helper's high: When you extend yourself to someone else, it produces an altered state of consciousness. You feel aroused, you feel wonderful, you float on air."

Actively speaking out for others can generate this feeling, says Kottler. "People are totally preoccupied with themselves to the exclusion of the rest of the world," he says. "The more you can get out of yourself and reach out to others, the more meaningful and satisfying life can be."

SIGNIFICANCE

Activism can take many forms based on a person's interests, and participation can occur on a variety of levels. People who become activists at a young age are often reacting to their upbringing or some strong belief held by their family. For example, someone vocal for women's rights might be the product of a feminist household, or might as easily have come from a household where women were considered second class citizens. In the first case, the person mimics the behavior he or she witnessed as a child, standing up for the rights of women as equals in the family setting, in the workplace, and in society at large. In the second instance, the person rebels against his or her upbringing, deciding that women deserve better treatment and greater respect. As a result, the individual may become active in the struggle for women's rights on a more global scale. Likewise, a person's ideas might be influenced by growing up with a relative who fought in a war, giving them incentive to work toward peace, or with a family member in a wheelchair, providing them with the motivation to work for better handicapped access in public locations.

But other influences toward activism can come from an individual's peers or mentors, as well. Young people often become active for a particular cause during their college years, when campus life introduces them to new political agendas at a time when they are finally old enough to vote and to serve in the armed forces. This new ability to have a say in the nation's political life and to live with the consequences of political decisions can be a strong motivating factor in a person's desire to learn about the government and to take a stand regarding issues of concern. Also, the college experience introduces students to varied cultures and beliefs, some of which might inspire an interest in a cause, such as poor living conditions in a developing nation or the treatment of prisoners of war in different parts of the world.

Historically, activism appears to increase and decrease in waves, with the trends being linked to both the political and economic climate and, often, to whether or not the country is at war. In the late 1960s and early 1970s, protestors were vocal in their opposition to the continued U.S. presence in Vietnam. Students on campuses across the country protested in an effort to convince the government to pull out of the war, and some of the demonstrations became violent. Campus protests spilled over to the general public, precipitating a variety of events, including a march on the U.S. Capitol and synchronized rallies around the country. While it is difficult to know whether the protests led to an earlier withdrawal from Vietnam, they did affect U.S. policy through the elimination of the draft in favor of a voluntary armed forces in 1973. Additional war-related protests include the more recent demonstrations against the war in Iraq, which began as U.S. confidence in the purpose of the conflict started to wane, leading to a drop in public support.

Political activism extends well beyond support or demonstration against a war. For over a century, women have rallied to fight for their rights, including the right to vote in political elections, the right to receive equal wages for the equal work, or the right to control their own medical decisions. Environmental protests encompass a broad range of topics, from global warming and the systematic destruction of the ozone layer, to endangered species, to the deforestation of the planet and the pollution of land and water. Religious groups protest certain types of scientific research, maintaining that scientists are interfering with aspects of life and death that are not in the human domain and demanding legislation to reinforce the boundary between science and religion. Health care, free speech, affirmative action, tax dollars contributed to education, and censorship of the

media—there is an ever-growing list of subjects in which activists involve themselves, depending on their interests, their backgrounds, and the issues that affect their lives.

FURTHER RESOURCES
Books

Kush, Christopher. *The One-Hour Activist: The 15 Most Powerful Actions You Can Take to Fight for the Issues and Candidates You Care About.* Jossey-Bass, 2004.

McDarrah, Fred. *Anarchy, Protest, and Rebellion: And the Counterculture that Changed America.* New York: Thunder's Mouth Press, 2003.

Reed, T. V. *The Art of Protest.* Minneapolis: University of Minnesota Press, 2005.

Web sites

SpeakOut.com. <http://speakout.com/index.html> (accessed June 1, 2006).

Working Assets. "Act for Change." <http://www. workingforchange.com/activism/index.cfm> (accessed June 1, 2006).

Bush Zones Go National

The Creation of "Free-Speech Zones"

Magazine article

By: Jim Hightower

Date: August 16, 2004

Source: Hightower, Jim. "Bush Zones Go National." *The Nation.* August 16, 2004.

About the Author: Jim Hightower (1943–) is a columnist, political commentator, and former Texas Agriculture Commissioner.

INTRODUCTION

The term "free-speech zone" (or "protest zone" or similar terms) refers to a fenced-in or otherwise restricted area in which people are required to stay if they wish to speak critically of an event or person, display signs, and the like. Usually, a free-speech zone is remote from travel routes, convention centers, or other locations where protestors congregate to be seen and heard. Proponents of such zones argue that they are necessary to protect prominent persons from possible attack, or (in the case of university-campus zones) to enable speakers to express themselves without interruption. Critics argue that the real goal of

Danielle White protests the policy of restricting demonstrators to "Free Speech Zones" outside the Democratic National Convention in Boston, July 27, 2004. © MARC SEROTA/REUTERS/CORBIS

establishing free-speech zones is to shield controversial persons from dissent. If enforced selectively against those expressing negative rather than positive ideas, free-speech zones may also be used to create, for the benefit of television cameras, the appearance of uniformly enthusiastic crowds greeting a political figure such as the President; only welcoming signs will be visible.

When a free-speech zone is designated by a law enforcement agency, protesting outside the zone can result in arrest, fine, and imprisonment. When they are designated by a university, protest may result in institutional disciplinary action.

Free-speech zones appear to have first been designated on university campuses in the late 1980s. These early zones were not physically caged or fenced, but consisted of officially designated protest areas outside which protestors were asked not to stray. In the 1990s, selective permit issuing was used by the administration of President Bill Clinton on at least one occasion; members of the Christian Defense Coalition, a pro-life group, were denied permits to picket during the 1996 Clinton inaugural parade, although Clinton supporters were allowed to demonstrate. The practice of physically fenced-in or caged holding areas for free speech appeared after 2001, when designation of free-speech zones during public appearances became routine during the administration of President George W. Bush.

PRIMARY SOURCE

Bush Zones Go National At the 2000 GOP nominating convention in Philadelphia, candidate Bush created a fenced-in, out-of-sight protest zone that could only hold barely 1,500 people at a time. So citizens who wished to give voice to their many grievances with the Powers That Be had to:

(1) Schedule their exercise of First Amendment rights with the decidedly unsympathetic authorities.

(2) Report like cattle to the protest pen at their designated time, and only in the numbers authorized.

(3) Then, under the recorded surveillance of the authorities, feel free to let loose with all the speech they could utter within their allotted minutes (although no one—not Bush, not convention delegates, not the preening members of Congress, not the limousine-gliding corporate sponsors, and certainly not the mass media—would be anywhere nearby to hear a single word of what they had to say).

Imagine how proud the Founders would be of this interpretation of their revolutionary work. The Democrats, always willing to learn useful tricks from the opposition, created their own "free-speech zone" when they gathered in Los Angeles that year for their convention.

Once ensconced in the White House, the Bushites institutionalized the art of dissing dissent, routinely dispatching the Secret Service to order local police to set up FSZs to quarantine protesters wherever Bush goes. The embedded media trooping dutifully behind him almost never cover this fascinating and truly newsworthy phenomenon, instead focusing almost entirely on spoon-fed soundbites from the President's press office.

An independent libertarian writer, however, James Bovard, chronicled George's splendid isolation from citizen protest in last December's issue of The American Conservative (www.amconmag.com). He wrote about Bill Neel, a retired steelworker who dared to raise his humble head at a 2002 Labor Day picnic in Pittsburgh, where Bush had gone to be photographed with worker-type people. Bill definitely did not fit the message of the day, for this sixty-five-year-old was sporting a sign that said: The Bush Family Must Surely Love the Poor, They Made so Many of Us.

Ouch! Negative! Not acceptable! Must go!

Bill was standing in a crowd of pro-Bush people who were standing along the street where Bush's motorcade would pass. The Bush backers had all sorts of Hooray George-type signs. Those were totally okey-dokey with the Secret Service, but Neel's . . . well, it simply had to be removed.

He was told by the Pittsburgh cops to depart to the designated FSZ, a ballpark encased in a chain-link fence a third of a mile from Bush's (and the media's) path. Bill, that rambunctious rebel, refused to budge. So they arrested him for disorderly conduct, dispatched him to the luxury of a Pittsburgh jail, and confiscated his offending sign.

At Bill's trial, a Pittsburgh detective testified that the Secret Service had instructed local police to confine "people that were making a statement pretty much against the President and his views." The district court judge not only tossed out the silly charges against Neel but scolded the prosecution: "I believe this is America. Whatever

happened to 'I don't agree with you, but I'll defend to the death your right to say it?"

This was no isolated incident. Bovard also takes us to St. Louis, where George appeared last year. About 150 sign-toting protesters were shunted off to a zone where they could not be seen from the street, and—get ready to spin in your grave, Jimmy Madison—the media were not allowed to talk to them, and protesters were not allowed out of the protest zone to talk to the media.

Now meet Brett Bursey. He committed the crime of holding up a No War for Oil sign when sensitive George visited Columbia, South Carolina, last year. Standing amid a sea of pro-Bush signs in a public area, Bursey was commanded by local police to remove himself forthwith to the FSZ half a mile away from the action, even though he was already two football fields from where Bush was to speak. No, said Brett. So, naturally, they arrested him. Asked why, the officer said, "It's the content of your sign that's the problem."

Five months later, Brett's trespassing charge was tossed on the rather obvious grounds that—yoo-hoo!—there's no such thing as a member of the public trespassing on public property at a public event. But John Ashcroft is oblivious to the obvious, so the Justice Department of the United States of America (represented in this case by—can you stand it?—U.S. Attorney Strom Thurmond Jr.) inserted itself into this local misdemeanor case, charging our man Brett with a federal violation of "entering a restricted area around the president." Great Goofy in the Sky—he was two hundred yards away, surrounded by cheering Bushcalytes who were also in the "restricted area."

Ashcroft/Thurmond/Bush attempted to deny Bursey's lawyers access to Secret Service documents setting forth official policy on who gets stopped for criticizing the President, where, when and why. But Bursey finally obtained the documents and posted them on the South Carolina Progressive Network website, www.scpronet.com; they reveal that what the Secret Service did goes against official policy.

Then there's the "Crawford Contretemps." In May of 2003, a troupe of about one hundred antiwar Texans were on their way by car to George W's Little Ponderosa, located about five miles outside the tiny town of Crawford. To get to Bush's place, one drives through the town—but the traveling protesters were greeted by a police blockade. They got out of their cars to find out what was up, only to be told by Police Chief Donnie Tidmore that they were violating a town ordinance requiring a permit to protest within the city limits.

But wait, they said, we're on our way to Bush's ranchette—we have no intention of protesting here. Logic was a stranger that day in Crawford, however, and Chief Tidmore warned them that they had three minutes to turn around and go back from whence they came, or else they'd be considered a demonstration, and, he reminded them, they had no permit for that. (Tidmore later said that he actually gave them seven minutes to depart, in order to be "as fair as possible.").

Five of the group tried to talk sense with Tidmore, but that was not possible. Their reward for even trying was to be arrested for refusing to disperse and given a night in the nearby McLennan County jail. The chief said he could've just given them a ticket, but he judged that arresting them was the only way to get them to move, claiming that they were causing a danger because of the traffic.

This February, the five were brought to trial in Crawford. Their lawyer asked Tidmore if someone who simply wore a political button reading "Peace" could be found in violation of Crawford's ordinance against protesting without a permit. Yes, said the chief. "It could be a sign of demonstration."

The five were convicted.

The Bushites are using federal, state, and local police to conduct an undeclared war against dissent, literally incarcerating Americans who publicly express their disagreements with him and his policies. The ACLU and others have now sued Bush's Secret Service for its ongoing pattern of repressing legitimate, made-in-America protest, citing cases in Arizona, California, Virginia, Michigan, New Jersey, New Mexico, Texas—and coming soon to a theater near you!

If incarceration is not enough to deter dissenters, how about some old-fashioned goon-squad tactics like infiltration and intimidation of protesters? In May of 2002, Ashcroft issued a decree terminating a quarter-century-old policy that bans FBI agents from spying on Americans in their political meetings and churches.

Not only were federal agents "freed" by Bush and his attack dog Ashcroft to violate the freedoms (assembly, speech, privacy) of any and all citizens, but they were encouraged to do so. This unleashing of the FBI was done in the name of combating foreign terrorists. The Bushites loudly scoffed at complaints that agents would also be used to spy on American citizens for political purposes having nothing to do with terrorism. While officials scoffed publicly, however, an internal FBI newsletter quietly encouraged agents to increase surveillance of antiwar groups, saying that there were "plenty of reasons" for doing so, "chief of which it will enhance the paranoia endemic in such circles and will further service to get the point across that there is an FBI agent behind every mailbox."

Likewise, in May of last year, the Homeland Security Department waded butt-deep into the murky waters of political suppression, issuing a terrorist advisory to local law enforcement agencies. It urged all police officials to keep a hawk-eyed watch on any homelanders who [Warning: Do not read the rest of this sentence if it will shock you to learn that there are people like this in your country!] have "expressed dislike of attitudes and decisions of the U.S. government."

MEMO TO TOM RIDGE, SECRETARY OF HSD: Sir, that's everyone. All 280 million of us, minus George Bush, you and the handful of others actually making the decisions. You've just branded every red-blooded American a terrorist. Maybe you should stick to playing with your color codes.

Last November, Ashcroft weighed back in with new federal guidelines allowing the FBI to make what amount to pre-emptive spying assaults on people. Much like the nifty Bush-Rumsfeld doctrine of attacking countries to preempt the possibility that maybe, someday, some way, those countries might pose a threat to the United States, the Bush-Ashcroft doctrine allows government gumshoes to spy on citizens and noncitizens alike without any indication that the spied-upon people are doing anything illegal. The executive directive gives the FBI authority to collect "information on individuals, groups, and organizations of possible investigative interest."

The language used by Ashcroft mouthpiece Mark Corallo to explain this directive is meant to be reassuring, but it is Orwell-level scary: What it means, says Corallo, is that agents "can do more research." "It emphasizes early intervention" and "allows them to be more proactive." Yeah, they get to do all that without opening a formal investigation (which sets limits on the snooping), much less bothering to get any court approval for their snooping. A proactive secret police is rarely a positive for people.

With the FBI on the loose, other police powers now feel free to join in the all-season sport of intimidating people. In Austin, even the Army was caught snooping on us. At a small University of Texas conference in February to discuss Islam in Muslim countries, two Army officers were discovered to be posing as participants. The next week, two agents from the Army Intelligence and Security Command appeared on campus demanding a list of participants and trying to grill Sahar Aziz, the conference organizer. Alarmed by these intimidating tactics, Aziz got the help of a lawyer, and the local newspaper ran a story. The Army quickly went away—but a spokeswoman for the intelligence command refused even to confirm that the agents had been on campus, much less discuss why the U.S. Army is involved in domestic surveillance and intimidation.

In California, an antiwar group called Peace Fresno included in its ranks a nice young man named Aaron Stokes, who was always willing to be helpful. Unfortunately, Aaron died in a motorcycle wreck, and when his picture ran in the paper, Peace Fresno learned that he was really Aaron Kilner, a deputy with the sheriff's department. The sheriff said he could not discuss the specifics of Kilner's infiltration role, but that there was no formal investigation of Peace Fresno under way. He did insist, however, that there is potential for terrorism in Fresno County. "We believe that there is," the sheriff said ominously (and vaguely). "I'm not going to expand on it."

If the authorities think there is terrorist potential in Fresno (probably not real high on Osama's target list), then there is potential everywhere, and under the Bush regime, this is plenty enough reason for any and all police agencies to launch secret campaigns to infiltrate, investigate, and intimidate any and all people and groups with politics that they find even mildly suspicious . . . or distasteful.

The attitude of police authorities was summed up by Mike van Winkle, a spokesperson for the California Anti-Terrorism Information Center (another spinoff of the Homeland Security Department—your tax dollars at work). After peaceful antiwar protesters in Oakland were gassed and shot by local police, van Winkle [Note: I do not make up these names] explained the prevailing thinking of America's new, vast network of antiterrorist forces: You can make an easy kind of link that, if you have a protest group protesting a war where the cause that's being fought against is international terrorism, you might have terrorism at that protest. You can almost argue that a protest against that is a terrorist act. I've heard terrorism described as anything that is violent or has an economic impact. Terrorism isn't just bombs going off and killing people.

SIGNIFICANCE

Today, free-speech zones arranged for political events or figures usually consist of small, fenced-in—sometimes completely caged-in—areas located distantly from the activity or person to be shielded. Organizers of the event or, in the case of a Presidential or Vice-Presidential visit, the Secret Service (charged with protecting the President and Vice President) contact local police forces, usually city police, who then build and primarily enforce the free-speech zone. Alternatively, Secret Service personnel may enforce the Zone directly.

The American Civil Liberties Union has alleged a large number of cases involving the selective herding of negative demonstrators into free-speech zones, or away from the President or other powerful persons. In one case (partly described in the primary source), a protestor named Brett Bursey was arrested in Columbia, South Carolina in October, 2002 for refusing to leave a rally for President Bush at a public airport and go to a fenced protest zone or free-speech zone half a mile away. "I told the police that I was in a free-speech zone called the United States of America," Bursey said. He was found guilty by a Federal judge and fined $500 (although he could have received six months in jail and a $5,000 fine).

Bursey's case was heard in the Fourth Circuit Federal Appeals court by a three-judge panel, but in May 2005, that court upheld his conviction. In January 2006, the Supreme Court refused to hear the case, allowing Bursey's conviction to stand.

Not all free-speech zones have been created to protect Republican political figures; one of the most notorious zones was created for the Democratic National Convention in Boston in July, 2004. The city police created a free-speech zone under an abandoned elevated train line, made from chain-link fencing, razor wire, black plastic sheeting, and concrete highway barriers. The zone contained no sanitary facilities, tables and chairs were not allowed inside, and the area was only large enough for about one thousand protestors. It was not only fenced in, but also roofed over with plastic netting and razor wire.

The American Civil Liberties Union and the Massachusetts chapter of the National Lawyers Guild filed suit against the legality of the zone. The Federal judge in the case declared that the fenced-in area was a "festering boil," and after a tour of the site said, "I at first thought, before taking a view, that the characterization of the space as being like a concentration camp was litigation hyperbole. I now believe that it's an understatement. One cannot conceive of what other elements you would put in place to make a space more of an affront to the idea of free expression." Nevertheless, the judge refused to order any changes in the arrangement. According to the *Chicago Tribune* newspaper, convention organizers argued that the free-speech zone was "necessary to prevent protesters from hurling objects at delegates arriving at the Fleet Center."

Despite repugnance across the political spectrum for the idea of restricting free speech, no major legal victories have been won against the practice of confining protestors to free-speech zones.

FURTHER RESOURCES
Periodicals

Bovard, James. "Free-Speech Zone": The Administration Quarantines Dissent." *The American Conservative*. December 15, 2003.

Eaton, Leslie. "Aftereffects: Questions of Security and Free Speech." *The New York Times*. April 27, 2003.

Jones, Tim. "Free-speech zone" Far From It, Protestors Say." *The Chicago Tribune*. July 25, 2004.

Web sites

American Civil Liberties Union. "Free Speech Under Fire: The ACLU Challenge to 'Protest Zones.'" September 23, 2003. <http://www.aclu.org/freespeech/protest/11419res20030923.html> (accessed May 23, 2006).

2 Civil and Human Rights

Civil and Human Rights

Civil rights and liberties are those rights and protections granted to all individuals through the law. Most accepted definitions differentiate civil rights from human rights, which are rights that are universal to all individuals regardless of nation, government, or system of law. The editors of this volume appreciate the distinction between universal, natural rights and privileges granted by law, but further assert that civil rights and liberties are often the legal expression or guarantee of human rights. Freedom from slavery is a human right. Voting rights may be civil rights, but when those rights are abridged on account of race, that arbitrary distinction violates an individual's human rights of dignity and security of person, equality, and political expression. Therefore, as in the context of the American civil rights movement, the struggle for civil rights is often the fight for human rights.

Included in this chapter are a number of articles highlighting human rights issues, such as the treatment of women under the former Taliban regime in Afghanistan and government oppression of political dissidents in China. A march in support of gay rights is part of the movement for privileges enumerated in the United Nations Universal Declaration of Human Rights—the rights to marry and found a family. Lastly, the article "Two Prosecutors at Guantanamo Quit in Protest" further illustrates the melding of civil and human rights concerns in the actions of two unlikely activists.

The African-American struggle for civil rights from slavery to segregation is featured in this chapter.

From 1954–1968 most of the leaders of the civil rights movement adopted a consistent protest creed of non-violence. Acts of civil disobedience and nonviolent action, from sit-ins to boycotts, protested racial segregation, voter discrimination, and violence against black Americans. Non-violent protest was not always met with peaceful reaction. Equally as iconic as images of protest are images of police brutality, mob violence, and riots.

Highlighted here are some of the most famous and successful protests of the civil rights movement. Martin Luther King, Jr.'s "Letter from a Birmingham Jail" stands among the most powerful testaments of the movement. Though a book cannot fully convey the power of protest music, "We Shall Overcome" was a popular civil rights anthem that like many others was adopted from an old religious melody.

The protests of the civil rights era were largely confined to the South; riots rocked mainly northern and midwestern cities. However, the civil rights movement captured public attention across the United States and abroad. It was the first great protest movement captured on television. The sights and sounds of protest buzzed in households far remote from the events of the day. Fully contemplating the civil rights movement is impossible without viewing its poignant images. In this chapter are photographs of Rosa Parks and the Montgomery Bus Boycott, the march from Selma, and Alabama Governor George Wallace's infamous "stand in the school house door" in protest of the enrollment of African-American students at the Univeristy of Alabama.

Uncle Tom's Cabin

Illustration

By: George Cruikshank

Date: ca. 1862

Source: Stowe, Harriet Beecher. *Uncle Tom's Cabin.* London: John Cassell, 1852. Image © Bettmann/Corbis. Reproduced by permission.

About the Illustrator: George Cruikshank (1792–1878) was a popular English artist and illustrator. After many years of contributing political cartoons to periodicals, he became a well-known illustrator of children's literature and other works. Cruikshank illustrated more than 850 books.

INTRODUCTION

During the 1830s and 1840s, the abolitionist movement, centered in New England, gained prominence throughout the northern United States. A number of national abolitionist organizations, several magazines and newspapers, and an anti-slavery political party known as the Liberty Party emerged during this period, and the movement became respectable and attracted many new followers. A controversial 1850 law, the Fugitive Slave Act, galvanized the abolitionists and drew to the anti-slavery movement many who had formerly been reluctant to get involved. The law made it easier for southern slaveowners to retrieve escaped slaves in the North and issued stiff penalties for anyone helping runaway slaves. With the passage of this law, even free blacks who had lived in the North for many years were at risk of being sent back into slavery. Many free blacks left the northern United States and found safe haven in Canada, as did slaves escaping through the Underground Railroad.

American writer Harriet Beecher Stowe (1811–1896) was raised in a prominent family of social reformers and abolitionists. Her father, Lyman Beecher, was a highly regarded minister, and her sister, Catherine Beecher, became a proponent of education for women. In 1852 Stowe released her novel *Uncle Tom's Cabin* in an attempt to persuade readers of the evils of slavery. The novel depicts the lives of several slaves, including Uncle Tom, a strong, gentle, and faithful man who bears his miserable life because he's certain of redemption after death; and George and Eliza Harris, who risk their lives to escape their bonds and preserve their family. Stowe dramatized

An 1859 advertisement for Harriet Beecher Stowe's *Uncle Tom's Cabin.* The novel sold extremely well. PUBLIC DOMAIN.

the humiliation, misery, and desperation of the slaves, and, most significantly, she illustrated their humanity, highlighting their familial connections and their desire for dignity and freedom.

PRIMARY SOURCE

UNCLE TOM'S CABIN

See primary source image.

SIGNIFICANCE

Uncle Tom's Cabin rapidly became a best seller; within a year more than 300,000 copies had been purchased in the United States, and many more were sold abroad. The novel's influence was felt throughout the northeastern United States, and many historians cite the work as a factor in the rising tensions between the North and the South that led to the American Civil War (1861–65). Stowe's dramatic writing style, coupled with illustrations like those of George Cruikshank, proved intensely persuasive to some readers and extremely offensive to others. Some southern states banned the

THE SEPARATION OF THE MOTHER AND CHILD.

"The old men of the company, partly by persuasion and partly by force, loosed the poor creature's last despairing hold, and, as they led her off to her new master's waggon, strove to comfort her."—Page 105.

PRIMARY SOURCE

Uncle Tom's Cabin: In a scene from *Uncle Tom's Cabin*, a mother is separated from her child as the two are sold to different owners.
© BETTMANN/CORBIS. REPRODUCED BY PERMISSION.

book, and a number of predominantly southern authors wrote competing works that portrayed slaveowners as compassionate and gentle caregivers to their slaves.

In the years following the publication of *Uncle Tom's Cabin*, the issue of slavery rose to the top of the national agenda, becoming a focal point of the surmounting hostility between the North and the South. Abraham Lincoln (1809–1865), a northerner, was elected president in 1860. Lincoln had asserted that holding together a divided nation was his top priority and that he would not interfere with the southern states' slaveholding practices, but southern leaders nonetheless perceived Lincoln as a threat to their way of life. A number of southern states seceded from the union after the 1860 election. When southern forces took control of South Carolina's Fort Sumter in April 1861, Lincoln called out the Union troops and the Civil War began.

On January 1, 1863, Lincoln signed the Emancipation Proclamation, a document that declared the freedom of all slaves living in states that were at war with the Union. The Emancipation Proclamation did not fully abolish slavery, however. Other laws freed slaves in most border states and lands occupied by Union forces. In some regions—such as parts of Virginia, Kentucky, and the city of New Orleans—slavery persisted until the end of the Civil War. In early 1865, Congress passed the Thirteenth Amendment to the U.S. Constitution, outlawing slavery throughout the United States.

FURTHER RESOURCES
Books
Hedrick, Joan D. *Harriet Beecher Stowe: A Life*. New York and Oxford: Oxford University Press, 1994.

Stewart, James Brewer. *Holy Warriors: The Abolitionists and American Slavery*. New York: Hill and Wang, 1976.

Tackach, James. *Uncle Tom's Cabin: Indictment of Slavery*. San Diego: Lucent Books, 2000.

Web sites

Harriet Beecher Stowe Center. <http://www.harrietbeecherstowecenter.org/index_home.shtml> (accessed June 4, 2006).

PBS. "Africans in America." <http://www.pbs.org/wgbh/aia/home.html> (accessed June 4, 2006).

The Jim Crow Car

Book excerpt

By: Frederick Douglass

Date: 1855

Source: Douglass, Frederick. "The Jim Crow Car." In *My Bondage and My Freedom*. New York: Miller, Orton & Mulligan, 1855.

About the Author: In 1817 or 1818, Frederick Augustus Washington Bailey was born into slavery at Holme Hill Farm in Talbot County, Maryland. Raised on plantations and then in Baltimore, Frederick taught himself to read, worked as a ship caulker, and then escaped to New York in September 1838. After marrying and changing his surname to Douglass, he settled in New Bedford, Massachusetts, where he met abolitionist William Lloyd Garrison and began speaking at the meetings of the Massachusetts Anti-Slavery Society. His public lectures on slavery, abolition, and racial prejudice soon made him a celebrity as well as an immensely popular public speaker. In 1845, Douglass wrote the autobiographical *Narrative of the Life of Frederick Douglass, An American Slave*, which became a best-seller. In 1847, Douglass moved to Rochester, N.Y., where he published and edited his own newspaper, *The North Star*. In 1851, *The North Star* merged with the *Liberty Party Paper* to form the *Frederick Douglass' Paper*, and then from 1859–1863, the *Douglass Monthly*. Douglass's other well-known books include *My Bondage and My Freedom* (1855) and *Life and Times of Frederick Douglass* (1881). Many of his essays and speeches have been collected and republished. Douglass also served as the U.S. marshal and recorder of deeds for Washington, D.C., in the late 1870s and early 1880s; was the minister to Haiti and Charge d'Affaires for Santo Domingo in 1889; and campaigned against lynching and for women's suffrage before his death in 1895.

INTRODUCTION

Although this account of Frederick Douglass's forcible removal from an Eastern Railroad Company car in Massachusetts was published in *My Bondage and My Freedom* in 1855, the incident that he describes took place between 1841 and 1843, when Douglass traveled through a number of New England states, speaking almost nightly at the meetings of several different anti-slavery and abolitionist groups. Historians have actually found evidence for Douglass's eviction from segregated railroad cars on many different occasions during these years. Douglass also describes how he made a practice of resisting removal to the "mean, dirty, and uncomfortable car set apart for colored travelers" that he saw as incontrovertible evidence for "slaveholding prejudice" in the north in his 1881 autobiography, the *Life and Times of Frederick Douglass*.

Although Douglass is most well known for his abolitionist writing, *The Jim Crow Car* is an interesting example of his influential work on racial prejudice and segregation in the northern United States. *The Jim Crow Car* is also notable for its description of early Jim Crow regulations, and as an example of resistance to Jim Crow—both physically and through the later publication of this account—by the first widely recognized African American activist.

PRIMARY SOURCE

I will now ask the kind reader to go back a little in my story, while I bring up a thread left behind for convenience sake, but which, small as it is, cannot be properly omitted altogether; and that thread is American prejudice against color, and its varied illustrations in my own experience.

When I first went among the abolitionists of New England, and began to travel, I found this prejudice very strong and very annoying. The abolitionists themselves were not entirely free from it, and I could see that they were nobly struggling against it. In their eagerness, sometimes, to show their contempt for the feeling, they proved that they had not entirely recovered from it; often illustrating the saying, in their conduct, that a man may "stand up so straight as to lean backward." When it was said to me, "Mr. Douglass, I will walk to meeting with you; I am not afraid of a black man," I could not help thinking—seeing nothing very frightful in my appearance— "And why should you be?" The children at the north had all been educated to believe that if they were bad, the old black man—not the old devil—would get them; and it was evidence of some courage, for any so educated to get the better of their fears.

The custom of providing separate cars for the accommodation of colored travelers, was established on nearly all the railroads of New England, a dozen years ago. Regarding this custom as fostering the spirit of caste,

African-American union leader A. Philip Randolph (left) leads picketers outside the Democratic National Convention in Philadelphia, July 12, 1948. They are demanding the Democrats adopt an anti-Jim Crow plank in their party platform. © BETTMANN/CORBIS. REPRODUCED BY PERMISSION.

I made it a rule to seat myself in the cars for the accommodation of passengers generally. Thus seated, I was sure to be called upon to betake myself to the "Jim Crow car." Refusing to obey, I was often dragged out of my seat, beaten, and severely bruised, by conductors and brakemen. Attempting to start from Lynn, one day, for Newburyport, on the Eastern railroad, I went, as my custom was, into one of the best railroad carriages on the road. The seats were very luxuriant and beautiful. I was soon waited upon by the conductor, and ordered out; whereupon I demanded the reason for my invidious removal. After a good deal of parleying, I was told that it was because I was black. This I denied, and appealed to the company to sustain my denial; but they were evidently unwilling to commit themselves, on a point so delicate, and requiring such nice powers of discrimination, for they remained as dumb as death. I was soon waited on by half a dozen fellows of the baser sort (just such as would volunteer to take a bull-dog out of a meeting-house in time of public worship), and told that I must move out of that seat, and if I did not, they would drag me out. I refused to move, and they clutched me, head, neck, and shoulders. But, in anticipation of the stretching to which I was about to be subjected, I had interwoven myself among the seats. In dragging me out, on this occasion, it must have cost the company twenty-five or thirty dollars, for I tore up seats and all. So great was the excitement in Lynn, on the subject, that the superintendent, Mr. Stephen A. Chase, ordered the trains to run through Lynn without stopping, while I remained in that town; and this ridiculous farce was enacted. For several days the trains went dashing through Lynn without stopping. At the same time that they excluded a free colored man from their cars, this same company allowed slaves, in company with their masters and mistresses, to ride unmolested.

After many battles with the railroad conductors, and being roughly handled in not a few instances, proscription was at last abandoned; and the "Jim Crow car"—set up for the degradation of colored people—is nowhere found in New England. This result was not brought about without the intervention of the people, and the threatened enactment of a law compelling railroad companies to respect the rights of travelers. Hon. Charles Francis Adams performed signal service in the Massachusetts legislature, in bringing this reformation; and to him the colored citizens of that state are deeply indebted.

Although often annoyed, and sometimes outraged, by this prejudice against color, I am indebted to it for many passages of quiet amusement. A half-cured subject of it is sometimes driven into awkward straits, especially if he happens to get a genuine specimen of the race into his house.

SIGNIFICANCE

Jim Crow is best described as a system of customs and laws that reinforced racial segregation and subordination in the United States. Jim Crow laws became increasingly pervasive in southern states in the years following post-Civil War Reconstruction. The legality of these laws was upheld by the U.S. Supreme Court in 1896 by the *Plessy v. Ferguson* decision. Jim Crow laws covered countless different aspects of African-American life. They regulated everything from marriage, access to health care, voting, education, and sports activities, to the use of public accommodation, facilities, and transportation, mainly from the 1870s until the last of the laws were struck down in the 1950s and 1960s. Few people, however, realize that Jim Crow laws were not uncommon in the northern U.S., particularly in the years before the Civil War. In fact, the term Jim Crow (taken from a minstrel show character popular in the 1830s) was first used to describe racial segregation as it was applied to northern railroad cars, like the one in Massachusetts that Douglass describes here.

In 1843, following fierce campaigns by Frederick Douglass and other abolitionists, Massachusetts passed a law forbidding discrimination by color on all public railroads. Charles Francis Adams, the anti-slavery Massachusetts state representative (1840–1843) and state senator (1843–1845) whom Douglass mentions in *The Jim Crow Car*, was instrumental in promoting this groundbreaking legislation on equal rights. Massachusetts and many other northern states passed additional anti-segregation statutes in the following years, although legislation supporting segregation, especially in regard to intermarriage and voting, was

also ratified in some northern states. These laws were relatively few in number compared to those in the south, however.

Unfortunately, as Douglass notes in *The Jim Crow Car* and his other writings, racial prejudice existed independent from laws or even moral aspirations, and was much harder to eradicate. In fact, in 1872, Frederick Douglass's home in Rochester, N.Y., was destroyed, probably by arson, less than a month after he was nominated in the presidential campaign for Vice President on Victoria C. Woodhull's Equal Rights Party ticket. After the death of his first wife, Anna Murray, in 1882, in 1884 Douglass married his secretary, the white reformer and activist Helen Pitts. The resulting scandal indicates the depths of Jim Crow custom, if not legislature, in the north. Douglass continued to speak out against prejudice, Jim Crow laws, and lynching until his death eleven years later.

FURTHER RESOURCES
Books
Douglass, Frederick. *Life and Times of Frederick Douglass*. Hartford, Conn.: Park Publishing, 1881.

Lampe, Gregory P. *Frederick Douglass, Freedom's Voice, 1818–1845*. East Lansing, Mich.: Michigan State University Press, 1998.

The Oxford Frederick Douglass Reader, edited by William L. Andrews. New York: Oxford University Press, 1996.

Periodicals
Ruchames, Louis. "Jim Crow Railroads in Massachusetts." *American Quarterly* 8, 1 (1956): 61–75.

The Suffragette Dilemma in World War One

Journal article

By: Maud Selbourne

Date: 1915

Source: Selbourne, Maud. "The Suffragette Dilemma in World War One." *The Conservative and Unionist Women's Franchise Review* 22 (1915).

About the Author: Lady Maud Selbourne was married to William Waldegrave Palmer, the second earl of Selbourne. The couple lived in South Africa, where the earl was stationed as High Commissioner of South Africa; Lady Selbourne Township is named for her. An active suffragette in early twentieth-century in Britain,

Lady Selbourne was the treasurer of the Consultative Committee of Constitutional Women's Suffrage Societies and a founder of the Conservative and Unionist Women's Franchise Association.

INTRODUCTION

Although Swedish women had been granted limited franchise by 1862, New Zealand led the women's suffrage (also known as "woman suffrage") effort by giving all women of majority status the right to vote in 1893. Starting with Wyoming in 1869, American women in individual states gradually gained the vote in the 1870s, 1880s, and 1890s. During this same period, however, British women could only watch as male suffrage rights were expanded in their country. Although the philosopher John Stuart Mill had advocated for women's suffrage in 1867, Parliament considered, then passed, a bill permitting wider voting rights for working class men. In 1885 Parliament extended the vote to most men over the age of 21.

The fight for British female suffrage began in the 1860s, roughly parallel to its sister movement in the

Suffragettes and anti-war protestors in New York City, August 29, 1914. © BETTMANN/CORBIS.

United States. Highly educated, often aristocratic women such as Emmaline Pankhurst, her daughters Christabel and Sylvia, Millicent Garrett Fawcett helped organize and lead the movement to enfranchise women in Britain.

By 1903, when these women formed the Women's Political and Social Union (WPSU), suffrage activists had been working for nearly four decades. The WPSU was a more radical organization than the National Union of Women's Suffrage Societies, which had fought for suffrage and other social issues since 1887. Despite minor victories, such as the right to run for council or vote in local elections in some areas of Britain, suffragettes saw other nations extend the vote to some—if not all—women. Pankhurst and her daughters were convinced that more militant action was needed to bring attention to their cause.

By 1905 the WPSU was well known for disrupting political party gatherings and fighting against any party that did not work toward female suffrage. When the Liberal Party gained control of the government the following year, more than 400 of the 650 Ministers of Parliament were sympathetic to female enfranchisement. The Women's Suffrage Bill, introduced in March 1907, timed out before passage, however. Over the next seven years various bills for women's suffrage were introduced, timed out, or dropped because of new elections. In the meantime, WPSU members were jailed for protests and disruptions and force-fed during hunger strikes; the latter tactic gained them sympathy from the British public. By the beginning of World War I in 1914, suffragettes struggled with the dual issues of the war effort and gaining the vote.

■ PRIMARY SOURCE

It may be useful at the beginning of a New Year just to take stock, as it were, of the reasons which lead us Conservative women to be in favour of the change which is involved in cutting away the sex basis of the parliamentary franchise.

For it is implied in our profession of Conservatism that we require every proposal of change to be abundantly justified. Our natural prepossessions are against change. On the other hand, common sense teaches us that some change is necessary. "Time is the great innovator," as Lord Bacon says, "and a forward retention of custom is as turbulent a thing as an innovation." So that the *Conservative* avoids change until it becomes necessary, but does not delay it, when delay is deleterious.

The grounds on which we think the granting of votes to women is a timely reform may be divided into two groups, under the heads of reason and experience. Reason teaches us that women are naturally as fit to vote as men. Their intellectual capacity differs to certain extent from that of the other sex. There are fewer people of genius among women than among men; but in practical common sense there is no such inferiority, and in conduct more men fail than women. These are reasonable grounds for expecting that women will make as good voters as men.

Experience emphatically confirms the deductions of reason. The weight of testimony in all countries which have made the experiment is overwhelmingly that it has worked for good.

And now when we see how much misery has been caused by the failure of the men of peace to restrain the lovers of war in the German nation, we may justly think that in the male sex the lovers of war are too numerous. The addition of women to the electorate will always strengthen the forces that make for peace. We know that some wars are rendered inevitable, but to women war brings nothing but sorrow. To some men it also brings glory, so that they do not always fairly weight the evil side of it.

Maud Selbourne.

SIGNIFICANCE

Lady Maud Selbourne, wife of the second earl of Selbourne, helped found the Conservative and Unionist Women's Franchise Association, a group of upper-class British women who favored suffrage for "qualified" women. The Conservative and Unionist Women's Franchise Association (CUWFA) produced the *Conservative and Unionist Women's Franchise Review* from 1910 to 1916.

In sharp contrast to the WPSU, the hunger strikes from suffragettes, and the WPSU's interest in the Labor party, the CUWFA advocated a more restrained approach. Continuing to work for the women's vote during World War I was frowned upon by many, including some women's voting rights activists. Women were expected to support the troops and their country during the war, and to continue to clamor for the vote was often viewed as unpatriotic.

At the same time, as Lady Selbourne notes, "we see how much misery has been caused by the failure of the men of peace to restrain the lovers of war.... The addition of women to the electorate will always strengthen the forces that make for peace." By using the war as a platform, Selbourne capitalized on British

patriotism and used the war effort to her advantage without appearing to be opportunistic.

By war's end in 1918, women's efforts during the war and a sympathetic public paved the way for the enfranchisement of many women: Parliament granted women 30 and older (and men over 21) the right to vote. Ten years later, in 1928, universal suffrage was granted to any citizen 21 or older.

FURTHER RESOURCES
Books

Buele, Mary Jo, and Paul Buehle. *The Concise History of Woman Suffrage: Selections from History of Woman Suffrage.* Urbana and Chicago: University of Illinois Press, 2005.

Felder, Deborah G. *A Century of Women: The Most Influential Events in Twentieth-Century Women's History.* Kensington Publishing Corp., 1999.

Fletcher, Ian Christopher, and Laura E. Nym Mayhall, et al. *Women's Suffrage in the British Empire; Citizenship, Nation and Race.* London: Routledge, 2000.

Holton, Sandra Stanley. *Feminism and Democracy: Women's Suffrage and Reform Politics in Britain, 1900–1918.* Cambridge, UK: Cambridge University Press, 2003.

Suffragette Lady Constance Lytton Goes on Hunger Strike

Book excerpt

By: Constance Lytton

Date: 1914

Source: Scheffler, Judith A., ed. *Wall Tappings: Women's Prison Writings, 200 A.D. to the Present.* New York: The Feminist Press at CUNY, 2002.

About the Author: Constance Lytton was the daughter of Robert, Earl of Lytton and Viceroy to India, where Constance Lytton lived for the first eleven years of her life. Angered by her mother's refusal to permit her to marry a man beneath her social status, Constance Lytton devoted herself to women's suffrage and birth control rights campaigns. Lytton wrote the book *Prison and Prisoners*, describing her experience as a member of the Women's Social and Political Union and her work for suffrage.

INTRODUCTION

The issue of female suffrage in Britain gained the attention of many women from the upper classes, well-educated and financially stable women who watched as women's suffrage efforts in the United States, Sweden, New Zealand, Australia, and the Netherlands gained steam throughout the last few decades of the 19th century and the first decade of the 20th century. An 1885 British law gave most men over the age of twenty-one the right to vote; in 1887, seventeen smaller women's rights societies merged to form the National Union of Women's Suffrage Societies (NUWSS). The NUWSS organized women for letter campaigns, appeals to Parliament, the creation of publications on the issue of female suffrage, and focused on other social issues as well. Part of NUWSS's goal was to demonstrate female political engagement while arguing that women deserved the right to vote.

In 1903, Emmaline Pankhurst and five other women joined to form the Women's Social and Political Union (WSPU), a suffrage organization that used more radical means to gain attention for the issue of the female vote. Like the clash between the more conservative National American Women's Suffrage

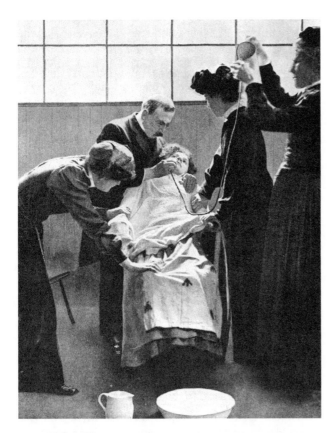

A propaganda piece published by woman suffragists in London, 1912. It depicts a suffragist on a hunger strike while in prison. Prison officials are inserting a tube into her nose so she can be forcibly fed. © BETTMANN/CORBIS

Association and the radical National Women's Party in the United States, NUWSS and the WSPU argued over the best approach to gain women the vote. The WSPU broke windows in government buildings, shouted down government officials during public speeches, and held large demonstrations which deteriorated into violence, leading to the suffragettes' arrest.

In 1909, one of the imprisoned WSPU members, Marion Dunlop, refused to eat while imprisoned. Prison officials released her as her hunger strike gained media attention. Other suffragettes joined in organized hunger strikes; as law enforcement officials struggled to balance the women's safety with the creation of these women as political martyrs, prison officials settled on a policy of force-feeding. Suffragettes such as Emmaline Pankhurst and American Alice Paul endured such force-feedings; the press covered the events and the public clamored for the women's release. WSPU continued to use violence against personal and government property, hunger strikes, and public intimidation against politicians and government officials who blocked women's right to vote.

Constance Lytton joined WSPU in 1908 or 1909; a young woman of privilege forbidden to marry a man of lower social status whom she loved, Lytton joined the WSPU with a commitment to helping forward the cause of female suffrage and women's rights in general. In 1909, Lytton was arrested during a WSPU protest in the House of Commons; British officials released her when they learned she was the daughter of the Earl of Lytton, Viceroy to India. Angered by her special treatment, Constance Lytton adopted the pseudonym "Jane Warton" for future protests.

■ PRIMARY SOURCE

Disguised as Jane Warton.

From Prisons and Prisoners, *1914.*

Under a Government which imprisons any unjustly, the true place for a just man (or woman) is also a prison. [—Henry David Thoreau]

I was sent to Liverpool and Manchester to join in working an Anti-Government campaign during a General Election in January, 1910. Just before I went, there came the news of the barbarous ill-treatment of Miss Selina Martin and Miss Leslie Hall, while on remand in Walton Gaol. They had been refused bail, and, while awaiting their trial, their friends were not allowed to communicate with them. This is contrary to law and precedent for prisoners on remand. As a protest they had started a hunger strike. They were fed by force, in answer to which they broke the windows of their cells. They were put in irons for days and nights together, and one of them was frog-marched in the most brutal fashion to and from the room where the forcible feeding was performed. These facts they made known to their friends at the police court on the day of their trial.

I heard, too, of another prisoner in Liverpool, Miss Bertha Brewster, who had been re-arrested after her release from prison, and charged with breaking the windows of her prison cell, which she had done as a protest against being fed by force. She had been punished for this offence while in prison. She did not respond to the summons, and when arrested on a warrant, three and a half months later, she was sentenced to six weeks' hard labour for this offence.

I felt a great wish to be in Liverpool, if possible, to get public opinion in that town to protest against such treatment of women political prisoners. If I failed in this, I determined myself to share the fate of these women.

When I was in Manchester, Mary Gawthorpe was ill with the internal complaint which has since obliged her to give up work. She saw me in her room one day. We had been distressed beyond words to hear of the sufferings of Selina Martin and Leslie Hall. Mary Gawthorpe said, with tears in her eyes, as she threw her arms round me: "Oh, and these are women quite unknown—nobody knows or cares about them except their own friends. They go to prison again and again to be treated like this, until it kills them!" That was enough. My mind was made up. The altogether shameless way I had been preferred against the others at Newcastle, except Mrs. Brailsford who shared with me the special treatment, made me determine to try whether they would recognise my need for exceptional favours without my name. . . .

I joined the W.S.P.U. *(1)* again, filling up the membership card as Miss Jane Warton. The choice of a name had been easy. When I came out of Holloway Prison, a distant relative, by name Mr. F. Warburton, wrote me an appreciative letter, thanking me for having been a prisoner in this cause. I should take the name of Warburton. When I went to Newcastle, my family raised no objection. Now nobody was to know of my disguise, but Warburton was too distinguished a name; that would at once attract attention. I must leave out the "bur" and make it "Warton." "Jane" was the name of Joan of Arc (for Jeanne is more often translated into "Jane" than "Joan") and would bring me comfort in distress. A family sympathetic to our cause, who lived in the suburb near Walton Gaol, were informed that a keen member, Miss Warton, would call at their house in the afternoon before the protest meeting to investigate the outside of the gaol and the governor's house by daylight, and that she was ready to be arrested if she could not obtain the release of the prisoners. . . .

At last the longed-for moment had arrived, and I was taken off to my cell. To my joy there was a window which opened a little bit; at night it was lit by a gas jet that was set in the depth of the wall behind the door, the passage side, and covered in by a thick glass. I was ever so tired—I laid down and slept.

The next day was Sunday (January 16), but they did not ask us to go to chapel. For several days I did not wear my cap and apron in my cell, but did not in other ways continue my protest against the clothes. The cold seemed to me intense, and I wore the skirt of my dress fastened round my neck for warmth. The Governor, accompanied by the Matron, came to see me, but he was in a temper about our having broken his windows, so I said nothing. He was in a fury at the way I had fastened my skirt. I answered that it was for warmth and that I would gladly put on more clothes and warmer ones if he gave them to me. Later on the Senior Medical Officer came in. He was a short, fat, little man, with a long waxed moustache. I should have said he disliked being unkind; he liked the chaff over things; but as I looked at him I thought I would rather be forcibly fed by anyone in the world than by him, the coarse doctors at Newcastle and the cross little doctor I had seen the night before. I said I had not asked to see him, but he made no examination and asked no questions.

I lay on my bed most of the day, for they did not disturb me, and I tried to keep warm, as I felt the cold fearfully. They brought me all my meals the same as usual, porridge in the morning at 7, meat and potatoes mid-day at twelve, porridge at 4:30. When they were hot I fed on the smell of them, which seemed quite delicious; I said "I don't want any, thank you," to each meal, as they brought it in. I had made up my mind that this time I would not drink any water, and would only rinse out my mouth morning and evening without swallowing any. I wrote on the walls of my cell with my slate pencil and soap mixed with the dirt of the floor for ink, "Votes for Women," and the saying from Thoreau's *Duty of Civil Disobedience*— "Under a Government which imprisons any unjustly, the true place for a just man (or woman) is also a prison". . . . [I dreamt] of a moonlit balcony that was hung with sweetest smelling flowers, honeysuckle and Jessamine, apple-blossom and sweet scented verbena; thee was only the sound of night birds throbbing over the hills that ranged themselves below the balcony. On it there slept my sister-in-law, and on the balustrade, but making no noise, was a figure awake and alert, which was my brother. My dream was of a land which was seen by my father in his poem of "King Poppy," where the princess and the shepherd boy are the types etherealized. I woke suddenly. I could sleep a little in detached moments, but this dream had made the prison cell beautiful to me; it had a way out.

The strain was great of having to put on my shoes, which were too small, every time I was taken out of my cell to empty slops or to see the Governor. The Matron was shocked that I did not put the right heel in at all and every day I was given another pair, but they were all alike in being too small for my right foot.

The next day, Monday (January 17) the wardress took my bed and bedding away because I would not make it up, but lay on it in the daytime. I told her if she wished she must roll me off, but that I did not intend voluntarily to give it up. She was quite amiable, but rolled me towards the wall and took the bed and bedding from underneath me. There was a little table in my cell which was not fastened to the wall. I turned it upside down and was able to sit in it with my body resting against one of the legs. It was very uncomfortable, but I felt too ill to sit up in the chair, and the concrete floor was much too cold without the bed. Every now and then I got up and walked backwards and forwards in the cell to get a little warmth into me. The Chaplain came in for a moment. He was a tall, good-looking man, of the burly, healthy sort. It seemed to me, from his talk, that he would be very well suited to be a cricket match or football parson, if there were such a thing, but he was totally unsuited to be the Chaplain of a prison, or anyhow of a woman's prison. He thought it wise to speak to me as a "Suffragette." "Look here, it's no good your thinking that there's anything to be done with the women here—the men sometimes are not such bad fellows, and there are many who write to me after they've left here, but the women, they're all as bad as bad can be, there's absolutely no good in them." I did not answer, but I felt inclined to say "Then good-bye to you, since you say you can do no good with the women here."

Presently an officer came and led me out. The manner of nearly all the officers was severe; one or two were friends but most of them treated me like dirt. I was shown along the gangway of the ward, which seemed to me very large, much larger than the D X at Holloway, and went into various directions like a star. It was warm, there were hot pipes against which I was made to stand with my back to the wall, and for a moment, as I put my feet to rest on the pipes, I could think of nothing else but the delight of their heat. The Governor was very cross. I had decided not to do the days on bread and water. He would not let me speak to him at all and I was led out, but, before I had got to my cell, I was called back into his presence. "I hear you are refusing to take your food, so it's three days in a special cell." I was taken out and down a staircase till we reached the ground floor. I think my cell was two stories above, but I am not sure; then down again and into a short passage that looked as if it was underground, with a window at the top seemingly only just level with the ground. The door of a cell was opened, I was put inside and the door locked. It was larger than the cell upstairs, and the jug, basin, etc., were all made

of black gutta-percha, not of tin, placed on the floor. This would have been bad for the ordinary prisoner, as it was quite impossible to tell whether the eating things were clean or not and, in any case, it smelt fairly strong of gutta-percha; but as the rule for me was neither to eat nor drink, I was able to put up with it well. The bed was wider than an ordinary plank bed and nailed to the ground, so that I was able to lie on it without being disturbed. Best of all was the fact that it was nearer to the heating apparatus and so seemed quite warm when I was led in. I did not notice at first that the window did not open, but when I had been there six or seven hours it became wonderfully airless. I only left my cell for minutes at a time, when I was allowed to draw water, and the air of the corridor then seemed fresh as mountain air by comparison. I had an idea that Elsie Howey or some of the others would have been put into a punishment cell too. I called, but in vain, my voice had grown weak and my tongue and throat felt thick as a carpet, probably from not drinking anything. I tried signaling with raps on the wall, "No surrender—no surrender," Mrs. Leigh's favourite motto, but I was never sure of corresponding raps, though sometimes I thought I heard them. I could not sleep for more than about an hour at a time, my legs drew up into a cramped position whenever I went off and the choking thickness in my mouth woke me.

Tuesday, January 18, I was visited again by the Senior Medical Officer, who asked me how long I had been without food. I said I had eaten a buttered scone and banana sent in by friends to the police station on Friday at about midnight. He said "Oh, then, this is the fourth day; that is too long, I shall have to feed you, I must feed you at once," but he went out and nothing happened till about six o'clock in the evening when he returned with, I think, five wardresses and the feeding apparatus. He urged me to take food voluntarily. I told him that was absolutely out of the question, that when our legislators ceased to resist enfranchising women then I should cease to resist taking food in prison. He did not examine my heart nor feel my pulse; he did not ask to do so, nor did I say anything which could possibly induce him to think I would refuse to be examined. I offered no resistance to being placed in position, but lay down voluntarily on the plank bed. Two of the wardresses took hold of my arms, one held my head and one my feet. One wardress helped to pour the food.... The sense of being overpowered by more force than I could possibly resist was complete, but I resisted nothing except with my mouth. The doctor offered me the choice of a wooden or steel gag; he explained elaborately, as he did on most subsequent occasions, that the steel gag would hurt and the wooden one not, and he urged me not to force him to use the steel gag. But I did not speak nor open my mouth, so after playing about for a moment or two with the wooden one he finally had to recourse to the steel. He seemed annoyed at my resistance and he broke into a temper as he plied my teeth with the steel implement. He found that on either side at the back I had false teeth mounted on a bridge which [he] did not take out. The superintending wardress asked if I had any false teeth, if so, that they must be taken out; I made no answer and the process went on. He dug his instrument down on to the sham tooth, it pressed fearfully on the gum. He said if I resisted so much with my teeth, he would have to feed me through the nose. The pain of it was intense and at last I must have given way for he got the gag between my teeth, when he proceeded to turn it much more than necessary until my jaws were fastened wide apart, far more than they cold go naturally. Then he put down my throat a tube which seemed to me much too wide and was something like four feet in length. The irritation of the tube was excessive. I choked the moment it touched my throat until it had got down. Then the food was poured in quickly; it made me sick a few seconds after it was down and the action of the sickness made my body and legs double up, but the wardresses instantly pressed back my head and the doctor leant on my knees. The horror of it was more than I can describe. I was sick over the doctor and wardresses, and it seemed a long time before they took the tube out. As the doctor left he gave me slap on the cheek, not violently, but, as it were, to express his contemptuous disapproval and he seemed to take for granted that my distress was assumed. At first it seemed such an utterly contemptible thing to have done that I could only laugh in my mind. Then suddenly I saw Jane Warton lying before me, and it seemed as if I were outside of her. She was the most despised, ignorant and helpless prisoner that I had seen. When she had served her time and was out of the prison, no one would believe anything she said, and the doctor when he had fed her by force and tortured her body, struck her on the cheek to show how he despised her! That was Jane Warton, and I had come to help her.

When the doctor had gone out of the cell, I lay quite helpless. The wardresses were kind and knelt round to comfort me, but there was nothing to be done, I could not move, and remained there in what, under different conditions, would have been an intolerable mess. I had been sick over my hair, which, though short, hung on either side of my face, all over the wall near my bed, and my clothes seemed saturated with it, but the wardresses told me they could not get me a change that night as it was too late, the office was shut. I lay quite motionless, it seemed paradise to be without the suffocating tube, without the liquid food going in and out of my body and without the gag between my teeth. Presently the wardresses all left me, they had orders to go, which were carried out with the usual promptness. Before long I heard the sounds of the forced feeding in the cell next to mine. It was almost more than I could bear, it was Elsie Howey, I was sure. When the ghastly process was over and all quiet, I tapped on the wall and called out at the top of my voice, which wasn't much just then, "No surrender," and there came the answer past any doubt in Elsie's voice, "No surrender." After this I fell back and lay as I fell. It was not very long before the wardress came and announced that I was to go back upstairs as, because of the feeding, my time in the punishment cell was over. I was taken into the same cell which I had before; the long hours till morning were a nightmare of agonized dread for a repetition of the process.

The next day, Wednesday, January 19, they brought me clean clothes. When the wardresses were away at breakfast I determined to break the thick glass of my gas jet to show what I thought of the forcible feeding, it seemed the last time I should have the strength required. I took one of my shoes, which always lay at my side except when I moved from my cell, let it get a good swing by holding it at the back of my shoulder and then hurled it against the glass with all the strength that I had. The glass broke in pieces with a great smashing sound. The two wardresses, who were in charge of the whole ward while the others were away, came into my cell together; I was already back in my bed. They were young, new to the work, and look rather frightened. I told them I had done it with a shoe, and why. "But that is enough," I said, "I am not going to do any more now." This reassured them and they both laughed. They took away the shoes as "dangerous," and brought me the slippers instead, and, to my intense relief, I never saw them again. As the morning wore on, one after the other of the officials proclaimed that I had done a shameful thing. On being changed to the cell next door, one of the head wardresses—I never made out exactly who she was—was in a great temper. I had told her, as I did every one of the officials, why I had broken my gas jet. "Broken it, yes, I should just think you had, indeed. And all that writing scribbled over your cell; can't keep the place decent." "I'm so sorry," I said; "I assure you there was nothing indecent in what I wrote on the wall." "No, not indecent, but—" she hesitated and, as the words would not come to her assistance, the remark remained unfinished.

I had not been long in the other cell before the doctor and four or five wardresses appeared. He was apparently angry because I had broken the jet glass; he seized one of the tin vessels and began waiving it about. 'I suppose you want to smash me with one of these?" he exclaimed. I said to him, so that all the wardresses with him could hear, "Unless you consider it part of your duty, would you please not strike me when you have finished your odious job" (or I may have said "slap me," I do not remember). He did not answer, but, after a little pause, he signed me to lie down on the bed. Again the choice of the wooden or steel implement, again the force, which after a time I could not withstand, in the same place as yesterday where the gum was sore and aching. Then the feeling of the suffocating tube thrust down and the gate of life seemed shut. The tube was pressed down much too far, it seemed to me, causing me at times great pain in my side. The sickness was worse than the time before. As the tube was removed I was unavoidably sick over the doctor. He flew away from me and out of the cell, exclaiming angrily, "If you do that again next time I shall feed you twice." I had removed my serge jacket and taken several precautions for my bed, but I am afraid one or two of the officers and the floor and wall were drenched. I shut my eyes and lay back quite helpless for a while. They presently brought in fresh clothes, and a woman, another prisoner, came and washed the floor. It seemed terrible that another prisoner should do this, it was altogether a revolting business. Two wardresses came and overlooked her work, one of them said, in a voice of displeased authority: "Look at her! Just look at her! The *way* she's doing it!" The woman washed on and took no notice; her face was intensely sad. I roused myself and said, "Well at any rate, she's doing what I should be doing myself and I am very grateful to her." The wardresses looked surprised at me but they said nothing. . . .

That day I thought I would clean my window. . . .Though the day was generally spent in loneliness, I knew that I might be visited at any hour, so I put off till about 3:30, when the ward was generally quiet for a time. All the furniture in the cell was movable, so I placed the table in front of the window and the chair on the top, then I climbed up. Through the small part of the window that opened I looked down, and in a beautiful red glow of the sinking sun I saw a sight that filled my very soul with joy, In the gloaming light—it was an exercise ground that I looked down upon—I saw walking round, all alone, a woman in her prisoner's dress, and in her arms she carried another little prisoner, a baby done up in a blanket. I was too high up to hear her, but I could see distinctly that she cooed and laughed to her little companion, and perhaps she sang to it too. I never saw maternal love more naturally displayed. The worlds of the Chaplain came back to my mind— "The woman, they're all as bad as bad can be, there's absolutely no good in them." No good in them! And yet amongst them there was this little woman who, at least, loved her child and played with it as only a motherheart can!

I got down and put the table and chair in their place; I felt amazed, having seen a sight as beautiful as the most beautiful picture in the world.

(1) Women's Social and Political Union.—Ed.

SIGNIFICANCE

Constance Lytton's two experiences in prison stand in stark contrast to each other. As Lady Lytton she was released immediately, while as "Jane Warton" her lack of noble identity led to her experiences being force fed, treated poorly by doctors, and to an understanding of how fellow suffragettes suffered in prison.

Once prison officials learned that "Jane Warton" was really Constance Lytton, she was released immediately. Lytton had been sickly as a child, and her health was compromised by her fourteen days in prison. In spite of her health problems, Lytton toured the country, lecturing on her prison experiences; her wealth, connections, and status as the daughter of an Earl gained her an audience of peers with influence and power. The practice of force-feeding hunger strikers ended soon after her lecture tours began.

Within a year of her prison experience Lytton was arrested once more for breaking windows during a suffragette protest; her poor health led authorities to release her, and in 1912, she suffered a stroke that included partial paralysis on her right side. In spite of the paralysis she wrote the book *Prison and Prisoners*. In 1918, Britain granted the vote to all women aged thirty and above. Constance Lytton died in 1923, five years before the minimum age for female voters was changed to twenty-one, the same qualification for male voters.

FURTHER RESOURCES
Books

Buele, Mary Jo and Paul Buehle. *The Concise History of Woman Suffrage: Selections from History of Woman Suffrage*. University of Illinois Press, 2005.

Felder, Deborah G. *A Century of Women: The Most Influential Events in Twentieth-Century Women's History*. Kensington Publishing Corp., 1999.

Fletcher, Ian Christopher and Laura E. Nym Mayhall et al. *Women's Suffrage in the British Empire; Citizenship, Nation and Race*. Routledge, 2000.

Holton, Sandra Stanley. *Feminism and Democracy: Women's Suffrage and Reform Politics in Britain, 1900–1918*. Cambridge University Press, 2003.

Highlights from the First Session of the League of Nations

Magazine article excerpt

By: Anonymous

Date: January 1921

Source: "Highlights from the First Session of the League of Nations." *Current History*. 13 (1921): 2, 1–14.

About the Author: *Current History* is the oldest periodical in the United States that deals with world political affairs. It is owned by the New York Times Company, and began publication in 1914 to analyze issues relating to World War I.

INTRODUCTION

World War I (1914–1918), which killed as many as ten million people and wounded twenty-one million others, was seen by some as "the war to end all wars." Seeking an end to war as conflict resolution, the victorious Allied powers met outside Paris in the spring of 1919. The Treaty of Versailles, drafted largely by Great Britain's David Lloyd George, France's Georges Clemenceau, Italy's Vittorio Orlando, and United States President Woodrow Wilson, included the covenant of the League of Nations, intended to be a forum in which states could resolve disputes peacefully.

While the Europeans wanted a congress system, Wilson pushed for a standing international body, outlined in his Fourteen Points as a "general association of nations ... for the purpose of affording mutual guarantees of political independence and territorial integrity to great and small states alike." The league

promoted national self-determination to replace old monarchical structures, and urged the replacement of secret diplomacy and alliances with "open covenants of peace, openly arrived at."

On January 10, 1920, the League of Nations was established to promote international cooperation, peace, and security. By December 1920, forty-eight states had signed the covenant and by doing so agreed to the league's goals, which include rejecting war as a response to disputes, open relations between nations, the rule of international law, and respect for treaty obligations. League members were also expected to acknowledge that peace relied on the reduction of armaments.

The league was to reside in Geneva and use both French and English as its working languages. Its organization included an assembly, comprised of member representatives; a council, consisting of representatives from the Allies—the United States, Great Britain, and France, plus four members chosen from the assembly. The secretary general and his staff comprised the secretariat. The covenant also established a

Hundreds gather during the first session of the League of Nations in the Salle de Reforme in Geneva, Switzerland, on November 15, 1920. PHOTO BY HULTON ARCHIVE/GETTY IMAGES.

permanent Court of International Justice and the International Labor Organization.

PRIMARY SOURCE

The League Assembly
What the Delegates of Forty-one Nations Accomplished in the First Session at Geneva.

The beginning of a new epoch in history, as many believe, was marked by the first meeting of the Assembly of the League of Nations at Geneva, Switzerland, on Nov. 15, 1920, when representatives of forty-one nations came together to contrive new means and methods for the peaceful settlement of international disputes. In human history there exists no parallel to this assemblage of white, black, brown, and yellow men of almost every religion and tongue, all united by a common desire—to reduce the world's wars and promote the welfare of mankind.

Vast and bristling with difficulties was the task that confronted these men. Among the disconcerting factors were the failure of America's 100,000,000 people to join the League of Nations, and the uncertainty as to what the President-elect would do after his inauguration next March; the exclusion of Germany and Russia from present membership [Germany joined in 1926; Russia in 1934] the heritage of wars which the World War has left, especially in Turkey and Eastern Europe, and, last but not least, the maze of international jealousies, conflicting aims, and smoldering enmities represented on the floor of the Assembly itself. In the minds of the French delegates lurked the spectre of a fear that the Versailles Treaty would be revised to their injury; they went to Geneva resolved that no part of the treaty should be altered. The small nations feared the monopoly of power by the great. Burning questions of racial equality, notably in respect to the Japanese, lay all too near the outwardly calm surface. Yet the general mood was hopeful, and when the Assembly adjourned, after a month of earnest labor and debate, that feeling was justified by the results.

For days before the opening session a stream of delegates, visitors, and journalists poured into Geneva, overtaking the beautiful little city's resources, though not its spirit of hospitality. The streets looked like a vast fair where all the races of mankind had met. On every building fluttered the colors of many nations. The humblest dwelling, the stately tower of St. Peter's Cathedral, even the streamers on the placid blue waters of Lake Leman, were bedecked with flags and bunting. Dense throngs were in constant motion over the stately Bridge of Mont Blanc, by which the marching delegates, escorted by white-cloaked Swiss officials, crossed the Rhone to the Salle de Reformation, where the Assembly was to meet. This plain, prim building, reminiscent of Calvinism, was guarded by Swiss gendarmes in blue cloaks and cocked hats.

The Opening Ceremony

Dr. Motta, the Swiss President, who was to be honorary Chairman, led a procession of the Swiss Federal Council and the State Council of the Canton of Geneva to the place of meeting on the morning of the 15th. This procession, with its modest military display, was cheered as it passed through the crowded rue de Rhone and reached the Salle de Reformation at 11 o'clock. With Paul Hymans (Belgium), Acting President of the Assembly, Dr. Motta took the seat reserved for him on the dais.

M. Hymans rang his bell at 11:16 and opened the proceedings. He looked down upon a sea of faces—Caucasian, Indian, Mongolian—representing almost every racial type. On the left, toward the middle, sat the Japanese delegates; on the right, nearer the front, the Chinese sat, bespectacled and serious. All forty-one nations were there, except Honduras, whose delegates had not yet reached Geneva. There were 241 delegates in all, and the forty-one nations were these:

Argentina,
Australia,
Belgium,
Bolivia,
Brazil,
Canada,
Chile,
China,
Colombia,
Cuba,
Czechoslovakia,
Denmark,
France,
Great Britain,
Japan,
Haiti,
India,
Honduras,
Greece,
Guatemala,
Jugoslavia,
Liberia,
Netherlands,
New Zealand,
Norway,
Panama,
Paraguay,
Persia,
Peru,
Poland,

Portugal,
Rumania,
Salvador,
Siam,
South Africa,
Spain,
Sweden,
Switzerland,
Uruguay,
Venezuela.

Impressively M. Hymans declared the first session of the Assembly of the League of Nations to be in session. The covenant, he explained, had provided that this meeting should be summoned by the President of the United States; accordingly, the League Council, on May 20, had asked President Wilson to issue the call, and on July 17 he had set this hour and place for the meeting.

Dr. Motta, speaking in French, next welcomed the delegates in the name of the Swiss people and Government. In acknowledging the honor that had been conferred upon Geneva he paid a graceful tribute to Belgium, declaring that if the choice had depended upon new-won glory and sacrifice, Brussels, instead of Geneva, would have been chosen. He then asked permission to send a message of gratitude to President Wilson, and expressed the earnest hope that the United States would soon take its rightful place in the League. The land of Washington and Lincoln, he declared, would not turn its face away from a plan to co-operate for the peace and prosperity of the world. The spirit of Dr. Motta's tribute to President Wilson was crystallized later into this special message, which M. Hymans sent:

> The Assembly of the League of Nations has by unanimous vote instructed me to send you its warmest greetings and to express its earnest wishes that you may speedily be restored to complete health. The Assembly recognizes that you have done perhaps more than any other man to lay the foundations of the League. It feels confident that the present meetings will greatly advance those principles of cooperation between all nations which you have done so much to promote.

The reply of President Wilson was:

> The greeting so graciously sent me by the Assembly of the League of Nations through you has gratified me very deeply indeed. I am indeed proud to be considered to have played any part in promoting the concord of nations with the establishment of such an instrumentality as the League, to whose increasing usefulness and success I look forward with perfect confidence. Permit me to extend my personal greetings to the Assembly, if they will be gracious enough to receive them, together with an expression of my hope and belief that their labors will be of immense value to the whole civilized world.

On motion of Dr. Motta, M. Hymans was made permanent President of the Assembly by a vote of 35 to 6, and took the chair amid applause.

Dispute over New Members

At the afternoon session the work of arranging rules of procedure was begun. It was decided to appoint six committees—or commissions, as the French say—each to report to the Assembly on an important subject. While these were getting under way a general debate began on certain points that were highly charged with electricity. One of these was the admission of new members. Albania, Austria, Azerbaijan, and Bulgaria had applied for membership, and when the President made technical objections to their admission a heated dispute, led by Signor Tittoni and Lord Robert Cecil, was precipitated. Lord Robert said a refusal would create a bad impression. Bourgeois and Viviani spring to their feet, demanding to know whether this implied the admission of Germany. The British delegate answered with an emphatic No. Tittoni then declared in a vigorous speech that public opinion would refuse to exclude any State on a mere technicality. The debate waxed stormy, and the President was compelled to make frequent use of his gavel. In the end the four applications were referred to the Commission on New Memberships, and the question was postponed to a later session. One important result of this preliminary tilt was that the way was left open for Germany to make her application at any future time she deemed propitious. As France had threatened to leave the Assembly if Germany were admitted, even by a two-thirds vote, the Berlin Government had no present intention of pushing the matter to an issue.

Later Sessions

The official language to be used was a problem that had to be solved a few days later. French and English developed almost equal claims to predominance, and it was finally decided that both languages should be used, all speeches and documents being translated from one into the other. On Nov. 20, however, various Spanish-speaking nations presented a motion that their language also be given an official status. Eighteen nations, including Belgium and Great Britain, supported this request, on the ground that Spanish countries represented at least 40 per cent of the League's membership. But, because even two languages were found to make the proceedings slow and cumbersome, the motion was rejected, much to the chagrin of the Spanish-speaking delegates. Already the smaller nations were beginning to feel that they were being dominated by the larger powers.

Rules intended to operate for the next five years were adopted on Nov. 30. They filled a document of seven pages and set up the whole machinery for future meetings of the Assembly. The first rule decreed that it should meet every year on the first Monday in September. . . .

Admission of New Members

Though the Assembly had set its face against the scheme of wholesale admission of all sovereign States, proposed by the departing delegation, and though, at its very first session, it had shown clearly that it had no present intention of admitting Germany, it was quite ready to consider proposals for the admission of other enemy nations that had made a sincere attempt to fulfill their treaty obligations. The admission of Austria, which made its application and appointed M. Mensdorff, former Austrian Ambassador to London, to speak on its behalf in the Assembly, was favorably considered on Dec. 15. Bulgaria was admitted to the League at the session of Dec. 9, despite the opposition of France, after the Membership Commission had reported in her favor. A factor which influenced this result was the receipt of a report from Marshal Foch declaring that Bulgaria had done more than any other of the Central Powers to fulfill the terms of the treaty.

Finland, Luxemburg, and Costa Rica were admitted on Dec. 16, and Albania was admitted on Dec. 17 after some debate, in which Delegate Inman of India dwelt upon the excellent impression which this act would have upon Mohammedans throughout the world. The six nations above named were all the new ones admitted; they brought the total membership to forty-seven. The application of Azerbaijan, Georgia, the Ukraine, Esthonia, Latvia, Lithuania, Montenegro and Lichtenstein were rejected for the present, most of them on the ground maintained by President Wilson that former Russian territory should not be disposed of until a responsible Russian government had given its consent.

Armenia almost won admission. Dr. Nansen of the sub-committee had handed in a favorable report, and the movement, led by M. Viviani, the "silver-tongued" orator of France, bade fair to be successful. The turn of the wheel of history, however, produced a volte-face [about-face] on the part of the Assembly. Delegate Fisher of England had received advance news that Armenia had abandoned her resistance to the Turks and gone Bolshevist; he therefore moved for postponement, and before the next meeting the whole story of Armenia's capitulation had been published in the papers. The Premiers decided against recognition, and on Nov. 25 the Assembly decided instead, to ask President Wilson to mediate between the Armenians and the Nationalist forces of Mustapha Kemal. Mr. Wilson accepted the task and appointed Henry W. Morgenthau,

former United States Ambassador to Turkey, to act as his representative. . . .

Establishment of World Court

One positive action taken by the Assembly, considered to be of the greatest importance in its bearing on future international disputes, was the adoption of the project of an International Tribunal, drawn up at The Hague not long ago by eminent jurists, led by Elihu Root.

After an all-day debate, on Dec. 13, the plan was adopted, subject to its signing and ratification by a majority of the nations. Provision was made for ratification by the United States. The court is to sit at The Hague. It will have eleven judges, elected by the League. Debate arose over the much-disputed question of whether or not the new world tribunal should have compulsory jurisdiction. The smaller nations wished this, the large powers did not. Great Britain, France, Italy and Japan were strong in their opposition. The other thirty-six nations fought for it obstinately. The big nations stood fast in their decision that they would not engage themselves to submit all disputes to the court. Vigorous speeches marked the debate throughout, and one delegate, Senator Lafontaine of Belgium, made a powerful and moving appeal. It was repeatedly pointed out, however, by the opposers that Austria would never have agreed to submit the Serbian dispute to such a court, had it existed, before going to war. The debate assumed at times an aspect of considerable acrimony. Leon Bourgeois of France, recipient of the Nobel Peace Prize of 1919, who had fought nearly all his life for the establishment of a world court with compulsory jurisdiction, and was now compelled, under orders from his Government, to oppose it, was, to many, a tragic figure.

The draft of the court plan provided for compulsory jurisdiction on the ground that if the court had power only when the parties agreed to it the world would see a repetition of the fiasco of The Hague tribunal. But the League Council, controlled by the large powers, refused to admit this proposal, and carried the day in committee. The world tribunal, however, was established as a great international body, empowered to arbitrate in all disputes threatening future war; the importance of this fact could not be gainsaid [denied]. One dream of the workers for future peace had become a reality.

SIGNIFICANCE

The League of Nations enjoyed several diplomatic successes before its demise. In 1921 the issue of the Åland Islands was brought to arbitration by Finland and Sweden. Historically the islands belonged to

Finland. The Swedish-speaking residents, however, wanted Swedish control. The league determined that the island should remain under Finnish rule but that no weapons would be kept on the island. All parties agreed to the ruling. In 1922 the league settled a dispute between Germany and Poland over Upper Silesia, when a referendum on which country the region should join led to rioting. The league split the territory between the two nations. In 1923, the League decided the issue of the Lithuanian port of Memel. Initially under league jurisdiction, Lithuania sought its control. The league declared the port an international zone under Lithuanian direction. In 1925, after a Greek soldier was shot and killed by a Bulgarian sentry on the border between the two nations, Greece invaded Bulgaria. The League ordered both nations to stop fighting, and demanded that Greece withdraw its troops and pay a fine.

Despite these and other preliminary successes, the organization was disbanded by 1946. One factor leading to its demise was a lack of significant membership. Although Wilson had been instrumental in the league's creation, the Senate refused to ratify the Treaty of Versailles, which contained the league covenant. Other nations left the league, as Japan and Germany did in 1933. Many nations never joined at all. Perhaps most importantly, the league lacked any effective leverage or deterrent; the Allies in particular were often unwilling to enforce economic or military sanctions. The organization's lack of political will to denounce Japanese and German aggression in the 1930s helped pave the way for World War II.

Despite its limitations, the league's legacy lives on in the United Nations, which retains much of the original organizational structure and goals. As an outgrowth of the league, the new organization continued much of its predecessor's work, including the creation of an international world health body and work in developing nations.

FURTHER RESOURCES
Books
Knock, Thomas J. *To End All Wars: Woodrow Wilson and the Quest for a New World Order*. Princeton: Princeton University, 1995.

Web sites
Yale University. "The Covenant of the League of Nations." <http://www.yale.edu/lawweb/avalon/leagcov.htm> (accessed May 10, 2006).

BBC. "The League of Nations and the United Nations." <http://www.bbc.co.uk/history/state/nations/league_nations_01.shtml> (accessed May 10, 2006).

Letters from Halle-Salle Prison

Letter

By: Krystyna Wituska

Date: September 18, 1943

Source: Scheffler, Judith A., ed. *Wall Tappings (2nd edition)*. New York; Feminist Press, City University of New York, 2002.

About the Author: Krystyna Wituska was a member of the Polish resistance movement that fought against the occupying German army after Poland was invaded in 1939. In 1942, Wituska was captured. During the period between her capture and her execution in 1944, Wituska wrote over ninety letters from prison that described her imprisonment and her outlook towards both her life and her inevitable death in custody.

INTRODUCTION

The Second World War began with the German invasion of Poland on September 1, 1939. The Soviet Union invaded eastern Poland on September 17, 1939, in furtherance of a secret pact made between Germany and the Soviet Union earlier that year known as the Molotov-Von Ribbentrop agreement. Poland was defeated on October 6, 1939; its government never formally surrendered and instead it established itself as a government-in-exile in London.

By 1941, the Polish resistance, or underground, was organized around the ZWZ (the Union of Armed Resistance), the forerunner to the Polish Home Army. The ZWZ engaged primarily in acts of sabotage against rail lines and German armed forces transportation. The ZWZ also undertook military intelligence gathering operations regarding German troop, tank, and aircraft movements that the ZWZ passed along to British military commanders. In the course of the war, the Polish underground enjoyed a number of notable intelligence successes, including the discovery of the location of the German V-1 rocket manufacturing plant.

Wituska joined the ZWZ in 1941. Fluent in German, Wituska was assigned to observe and report on German troop movements in the Warsaw region. She acted in this capacity until 1942, when her name was discovered among those listed in the papers of her fiancé, who was also a ZWZ member. Wituska was arrested by the Gestapo, the German secret police, and forcefully interrogated. Wituska was then transported to Germany, where she was incarcerated in a series of prisons, most

Soliders of the Polish Home Army man a barricade in a suburb of Warsaw, 1944. PHOTO BY HULTON ARCHIVE/GETTY IMGAES.

notably the Alt-Moabit prison in Berlin, and the Halle-Salle prison in the city of Halle, in eastern Germany.

The two letters excerpted here are a part of a ninety-six letter collection, one that includes both letters to Wituska's parents and to the daughter of the German prison guard, Hedwig Grimpe, who risked her own life to smuggle the Wituska letters out of Alt-Moabit.

▋ PRIMARY SOURCE

Alt-Moabit, Berlin
18 September 1943

[This letter was given to *Sonnenschein* to keep and then forward to the Wituska family after Krystyna's death. Mrs. Grimpe did this after the war.]

Dearest parents,

You will receive this letter after my death. It will be sent to you by a person to whom we are immeasurably indebted. She has been our friend, and our guardian. At great personal risk, she tried as much as possible to ease our difficult fate; she shared with us whatever she could, never asking for anything in return. We called her our "Ray of Sunshine," because whenever she came into our

cell, she brought her joy and laughter. We became friends with her daughter. You saw her once, Daddy; do you remember?

I only regret that I will never be able to repay her for everything that she did for us, for her dear heart of gold. She was especially fond of me and I loved her as one can only love one who offers a hand when you are truly in need and never thinks of this as charity, but only as something normal. Please don't forget her.

Dearest parents, writing this letter, I still don't know what will be the outcome of my application for clemency, but believe me that I am completely ready for death and I don't entertain any false hopes. Our long separation has deepened my feelings for you, and it pains me to leave you in such sorrow. But believe me, I am prepared to go to my death with head held high, without fear. This is my last obligation to you and to my country. Prison was for me a good, often difficult school of life, but there were nevertheless joyful, sunny days. My friendship with Mimi will remain with me, an unforgettable and wonderful memory until the end. She taught me to never lose my humour, to laugh at "them," and to die bravely. We will die on the eve of our victory knowing that we did not resist in vain against injustice and brute force.

Don't despair beloved parents, be brave dearest Mummy. Remember that I watch over you and grieve over every one of your tears. But when you smile, I smile with you.

May God reward you for the love and care with which you have enveloped me. Farewell, dearest parents, farewell....

Halinka.

Halle/Saale,
26 June 44.

Beloved parents,

How hard it is to write this last letter. But you must believe me—I am not afraid of death, I do no regret my life. I only think how much sorrow I give you, how you will grieve during the last hours of my life. I want to thank you again for your care and your love, for your unconditional dedication, my dearest Mummy! I can never thank you enough for everything you have done for me, for my joyful, carefree childhood. Don't cry,

Mummy, may God ease your pain. I know that you long ago forgave me all the trouble and worry I caused you. I am looking for words that would help me cheer you but I can only think of one sentence that *Pani* Wanda said when she lost Lolek: "God's best-loved die young."

I am completely at peace, believe me, and I will remain serene to the end. My last obligation to Poland and to you—is to die bravely.

Beloved Daddy, dearest Mummy, I feel you are with me today and I am so conscious of my great love for you. I dedicate my last thoughts to you.

Be brave! Bid me farewell.

Your Tina.

SIGNIFICANCE

The letters of Krystyna Wituska are remarkable both for their insights into the character of their author, as well illustrating the considerable sensitivity possessed by Wituska regarding the relationship between her life and her pending death.

Wituska was not treated as a prisoner of war by the Germans, as might otherwise have been the case for a captured enemy combatant. She was imprisoned and the subject of an execution order for her work with respect to gathering military intelligence. For reasons that are unclear, Wituska's execution did not take place until late June 1944, over fifteen months after the order to do so was issued.

At the time of her letter from Alt-Moabit prison in Berlin dated September 18, 1943, Wituska had been imprisoned for approximately nine months. She was awaiting her application for clemency from her execution order in good spirits; Wituska plainly believes that her request will be rejected by the German authorities. The tone of the letter is one of resolution regarding her likely fate; Wituska employs language that echoes the sentiments expressed by all freedom and resistance fighters in the course of history—she is prepared to die an honorable death and one that will occur in advance of her country's ultimate victory over the enemy.

Wituska also describes the actions of the Alt-Moabit prison guard (later identified as Hedwig Grimpe) in bringing an element of humanity into her life in prison. It is plain from the attitude demonstrated by her captors towards Wituska, had Grimpe been discovered assisting Wituska with the sending of her letters, it is certain that she would have suffered harsh consequences or death.

In her letter of June 28, 1944, Wituska is preparing for the death that she now knows to be inevitable. She has spent a further nine months in harsh and unremitting prison conditions, and yet the tone of her final farewell to her family as expressed in this letter is as cheerful and as resolute as the words written the year before. It is evident that the period of eighteen months imprisonment has not broken Wituska's resolve to be brave and steadfast in the face of her execution. Much of Wituska's sentiment about her death is directed to her understanding of the concept of personal responsibility, to both her family and her country.

The Nazi regime in all of the countries occupied by the German army throughout the course of the Second World War was as repressive and as determined as any in recorded history. The actions of Grimpe underscore the basic notion that at its essence, humanity and a sympathetic consideration for the plight of another human being will occasionally conquer oppression and brutal treatment. As Wituska noted in her letter, Grimpe received no benefit and she took significant risks to provide comfort to Wituska.

It is of interest that the sentiments of Wituska concerning her imprisonment and her execution were apparently unknown to her comrades in the Polish underground after her capture. Wituska was not an important member of the ZWZ and there was no effort made to rescue her; thousands of Polish resistance fighters were captured and executed by German authorities between 1939 and the retreat of the German army in 1945. Unlike many romanticized figures in history who were imprisoned as a result of their participation in the advancing of a cause or political objective, the capture and the subsequent execution of Wituska was an accepted consequence of the war against the Germans. Her words of hope and her uplifted spirit were never used as propaganda to boost the resolve of the Polish fighters.

Wituska's letters have a historical impact similar to that of the *Diary of Anne Frank*, the renowned writings of the thirteen-year-old Jewish girl who hid with her family from the German authorities in occupied Amsterdam in 1942. It is an irony of history that the Frank diaries and the Wituska letters span the same general period, from 1942 to 1944. Both Wituska and Frank write with an immediacy and a poignancy that provide a historical coloring that is not present in other contemporary sources.

FURTHER RESOURCES
Books

Frank, Anne. *Anne Frank; Diary of a Young Girl*. New York; Doubelday, 1995.

Tomaszewski, Irene, ed. *I am First a Human Being: The Letters of Krystyna Wituska*. Quebec City; Vehicule Press, 1997.

Tomaszewski, Irene, ed. *Inside a Gestapo Prison: The Letters of Krystyna Wituska 1942–1944*. Detroit, Michigan; Wayne State University Press, 2006.

Web sites

National Film Board of Canada. "Web of War." July 1, 2005. <http://www.nfb.ca/trouverunfilm/> (accessed May 20, 2006).

Montgomery Bus Boycott

Photograph

By: Don Cravens

Date: December 26, 1956

Source: Photo by Don Cravens//Time Life Pictures/ Getty Images.

About the Photographer: Don Cravens began his career as a combat photographer in the U.S. Army. While working for Time-Life, Craven captured numerous significant moments of the civil rights movement.

INTRODUCTION

Like most southern American cities at that time, Montgomery, Alabama, was thoroughly racially segregated in the mid–1950s. After the 1954 U.S. Supreme Court decision *Brown v. Board of Education* outlawed segregation in schools, civil rights workers everywhere saw an opportunity for change. In Montgomery,

activists focused on the city bus system, a source of frustration and humiliation for black riders. African Americans, who constituted three-quarters of the bus line's riders, were forced to sit in the back rows of the bus. Furthermore, they had to enter in the front of the bus to pay, then step back down to the sidewalk and re-enter the bus through the rear door. Occasionally, after a black rider had paid but before he or she could get back on the bus, the bus driver would simply drive away. If a white person entered the bus and could not find a seat, a seated black person was ordered by the bus driver to stand.

In 1955, civil rights workers in Montgomery began to plan for a citywide bus boycott. To implement their plan, they needed a model citizen to defy the segregationist policy and to get arrested for that action. On December 1, 1955, Rosa Parks (1913–2005), a forty-three-year-old seamstress and civil rights worker, fulfilled that role. After refusing to give up her seat to a white passenger on that Thursday evening, Parks was arrested. The following Monday, after a weekend of intense planning by civil rights activists, the black citizens of Montgomery held a one-day boycott of the bus lines. Organizers were unsure whether the black community would unite for the boycott and risk harassment for challenging the system of segregation known as Jim Crow. The boycott was an overwhelming success, however, and community leaders decided to extend it.

The city's black leaders formed the Montgomery Improvement Association (MIA) to organize the boycott, and they elected as the MIA's leader a young, educated, charismatic minister who had recently moved to Montgomery and who would become the civil rights movement's most visible leader: Martin Luther King Jr. (1929–1968). As the boycott stretched on, black citizens found other ways to travel through the city. Some walked or rode bicycles, others benefited from the network of carpools organized by the MIA. They endured threats and sometimes beatings from white segregationists, and the leaders of the MIA faced particularly intense pressure. The boycott persisted, however, and at the same time the segregationist policies of the bus line were challenged in court. More than a year after the boycott had begun, the U.S. Supreme Court upheld a lower court's order to end segregation on Montgomery's city buses. The day after the ruling reached Montgomery, on December 21, 1956, black citizens once again began riding the buses.

PRIMARY SOURCE

Montgomery Bus Boycott: Rosa Parks rides on a newly integrated bus in Montgomery, Alabama, following the end of the Montgomery Bus Boycott. December 26, 1956. PHOTO BY DON CRAVENS//TIME LIFE PICTURES/GETTY IMAGES.

PRIMARY SOURCE

MONTGOMERY BUS BOYCOTT
See primary source image.

SIGNIFICANCE

The success of the Montgomery bus boycott marked an early and significant victory for the civil rights movement. It demonstrated that ordinary citizens, when united and determined, could make a difference. Rosa Parks became an inspiring symbol of courage and dignity. And Martin Luther King Jr. achieved international recognition for his leadership of the boycott, earning particular admiration for his advocacy of nonviolent resistance. A group of southern black religious leaders who had given their support to the boycott met a few weeks after the boycott had ended and decided to establish a formal organization to coordinate civil rights efforts throughout the South. They formed the Southern Christian Leadership Conference (SCLC), which went on to become one of the movement's most visible and effective organizations. The SCLC elected King as its first president.

The strategies employed during the Montgomery bus boycott were emulated elsewhere, including boycotts in the Alabama cities of Birmingham and Mobile and in Tallahassee, Florida. Throughout the next several years, campaigns were launched to end segregation in cities all across the South. While the setbacks were numerous and the obstacles substantial, the civil rights movement achieved many notable victories, ultimately bringing an end to legal segregation in the South.

FURTHER RESOURCES
Books
Brinkley, Douglas. *Rosa Parks*. New York: Viking Penguin, 2000.

Martin Luther King Jr. is cheered by supporters as he announces that the Montgomery bus boycott will continue, on April 26, 1956. AP IMAGES.

Wexler, Sanford. *The Civil Rights Movement*. New York: Facts on File, 1999.

Williams, Juan. *Eyes on the Prize: America's Civil Rights Years, 1954–1965*. New York: Viking, 1987.

Winters, Paul A., editor. *The Civil Rights Movement*. San Diego, Calif.: Greenhaven, 2000.

Web sites

Montgomery Bus Boycott. "They Changed the World: The Story of the Montgomery Bus Boycott." <http://www.montgomeryboycott.com/> (accessed June 5, 2006).

Time Magazine. "The Time 100: Rosa Parks." June 14, 1999. <http://www.time.com/time/time100/heroes/profile/parks01.html> (accessed June 5, 2006).

Mob Rule Cannot Be Allowed to Override the Decisions of Our Courts

Speech

By: Dwight D. Eisenhower

Date: September 24, 1957

Source: Eisenhower, Dwight D. "Mob Rule Cannot Be Allowed to Override the Decisions of Our Courts." September 24, 1957. Available online at <http://historymatters.gmu.edu/d/6335> (accessed May 22, 2006).

About the Author: Dwight D. Eisenhower (1890–1969) served as president of the United States between 1953 and 1961. Prior to his election, Eisenhower was the Supreme Commander of the Allied forces in Europe until the conclusion of the Second World War in 1945. He was also appointed the first Supreme Commander of the North Atlantic Treaty Organization (NATO) in 1949.

INTRODUCTION

The legal foundation for public school desegregation in Little Rock (and throughout the United States) was the Supreme Court decision *Brown v. Board of Education of Topeka*, decided on May 17, 1954. The Court ruled that racial segregation in public schools, even where such practices created "separate but equal" educational institutions, was discriminatory and unconstitutional. To redress this, the Court declared that school desegregation should be accomplished 'with all deliberate speed.'

The *Brown* ruling was a watershed in American racial relations, igniting strong passions, particularly in Southern states, where desegregation efforts often met with stiff resistance and even violent confrontations. In Arkansas, the Little Rock school board had complied with *Brown* grudgingly, establishing a foot-dragging desegregation timetable in which full integration of all-white Central High School would not be complete until 1963. In September 1957, however, three years after *Brown*, a federal court ordered Little Rock's Central High School to admit black students immediately.

The events that unfolded were not entirely anticipated. Since Governor Orval Faubus's election in 1954, the city of Little Rock had desegregated its public transportation systems without significant difficulty. Arkansas was actually regarded as one of the southern states most receptive to integration. But when nine black students attempted to enroll at Central on September 3, 1957, a large and unruly mob of white protestors refused to let them enter the building. Despite the court mandate, Faubus cited fears of violence and called in the Arkansas National Guard to keep the black students out. He declared that "blood would run in the streets" if the black students were allowed into the school.

Eisenhower was determined to enforce the Supreme Court decision, and he met with Faubus in Rhode Island on September 14, 1957. Press releases were then issued that appeared to represent an understanding between the governor and the president that the court order would be enforced. The protestors at Central High School, however, continued their demonstrations in the week that followed, and Faubus continued to order the National Guard to prevent the students from entering the school.

A September 20 court ruling ordered Faubus to stop using National Guard troops to defy *Brown*, and the nine were finally admitted to Central on September 23. Violence continued both inside and outside the school, and by mid-morning, they were forced to leave.

In response, Eisenhower issued the first of two presidential proclamations unique in American peacetime history. In the first, issued September 23, 1957, "Obstruction of Justice in the State of Arkansas," Eisenhower directed anyone not complying with the Supreme Court order to desist. When it became apparent that the protests would continue, however, Eisenhower issued a second proclamation the following day that brought the confrontation to its peak. Federal troops were deployed to enforce the Court order and to ensure the nine students safe passage into the school. Later the same day, Eisenhower made the following television and radio address to the American people.

PRIMARY SOURCE

Good Evening, My Fellow Citizens: For a few minutes this evening I want to speak to you about the serious situation that has arisen in Little Rock. To make this talk I have come to the President's office in the White House. I could have spoken from Rhode Island, where I have been staying recently, but I felt that, in speaking from the house of Lincoln, of Jackson, and of Wilson, my words would better convey both the sadness I feel in the action I was compelled today to take and the firmness with which I intend to pursue this course until the orders of the Federal Court at Little Rock can be executed without unlawful interference.

In that city, under the leadership of demagogic extremists, disorderly mobs have deliberately prevented the carrying out of proper orders from a Federal Court. Local authorities have not eliminated that violent opposition and, under the law, I yesterday issued a Proclamation calling upon the mob to disperse.

This morning the mob again gathered in front of the Central High School of Little Rock, obviously for the purpose of again preventing the carrying out of the Court's order relating to the admission of Negro children to that school.

Whenever normal agencies prove inadequate to the task and it becomes necessary for the Executive Branch of the Federal Government to use its powers and authority to uphold Federal Courts, the President's responsibility is inescapable. In accordance with that responsibility, I have

Federal troops escort African American students as they arrive in a U.S. Army station wagon at Central High School in Little Rock, Arkansas, during the first week of integration, September 1957. AP IMAGES.

today issued an Executive Order directing the use of troops under Federal authority to aid in the execution of Federal law at Little Rock, Arkansas. This became necessary when my Proclamation of yesterday was not observed, and the obstruction of justice still continues.

It is important that the reasons for my action be understood by all our citizens. As you know, the Supreme Court of the United States has decided that separate public educational facilities for the races are inherently unequal and therefore compulsory school segregation laws are unconstitutional.

Our personal opinions about the decision have no bearing on the matter of enforcement; the responsibility and authority of the Supreme Court to interpret the Constitution are very clear. Local Federal Courts were instructed by the Supreme Court to issue such orders and decrees as might be necessary to achieve admission to public schools without regard to race—and with all deliberate speed.

During the past several years, many communities in our Southern States have instituted public school plans for gradual progress in the enrollment and attendance of school children of all races in order to bring themselves into compliance with the law of the land.

They thus demonstrated to the world that we are a nation in which laws, not men, are supreme.

I regret to say that this truth—the cornerstone of our liberties—was not observed in this instance.

It was my hope that this localized situation would be brought under control by city and State authorities. If the use of local police powers had been sufficient, our traditional method of leaving the problems in those hands would have been pursued. But when large gatherings of obstructionists made it impossible for the decrees of the Court to be carried out, both the law and the national interest demanded that the President take action.

Here is the sequence of events in the development of the Little Rock school case.

In May of 1955, the Little Rock School Board approved a moderate plan for the gradual desegregation of the public schools in that city. It provided that a start toward integration would be made at the present term in the high school, and that the plan would be in full operation by 1963. Here I might say that in a number of communities in Arkansas integration in the schools has already started and without violence of any kind. Now this Little Rock plan was challenged in the courts by some who believed that the period of time as proposed in the plan was too long.

The United States Court at Little Rock, which has supervisory responsibility under the law for the plan of desegregation in the public schools, dismissed the challenge, thus approving a gradual rather than an abrupt change from the existing system. The court found that the school board had acted in good faith in planning for a public school system free from racial discrimination.

Since that time, the court has on three separate occasions issued orders directing that the plan be carried out. All persons were instructed to refrain from interfering with the efforts of the school board to comply with the law.

Proper and sensible observance of the law then demanded the respectful obedience which the nation has a right to expect from all its people. This, unfortunately, has not been the case at Little Rock. Certain misguided persons, many of them imported into Little Rock by agitators, have insisted upon defying the law and have sought to bring it into disrepute. The orders of the court have thus been frustrated.

The very basis of our individual rights and freedoms rests upon the certainty that the President and the Executive Branch of Government will support and insure the carrying out of the decisions of the Federal Courts, even, when necessary with all the means at the President's command.

Unless the President did so, anarchy would result.

There would be no security for any except that which each one of us could provide for himself.

The interest of the nation in the proper fulfillment of the law's requirements cannot yield to opposition and demonstrations by some few persons.

Mob rule cannot be allowed to override the decisions of our courts.

Now, let me make it very clear that Federal troops are not being used to relieve local and state authorities of their primary duty to preserve the peace and order of the community. Nor are the troops there for the purpose of taking over the responsibility of the School Board and the other responsible local officials in running Central High School. The running of our school system and the maintenance of peace and order in each of our States are strictly local affairs and the Federal Government does not interfere except in a very few special cases and when requested by one of the several States. In the present case the troops are there, pursuant to law, solely for the purpose of preventing interference with the orders of the Court.

The proper use of the powers of the Executive Branch to enforce the orders of a Federal Court is limited to extraordinary and compelling circumstances. Manifestly, such an extreme situation has been created in Little Rock. This challenge must be met and with such measures as will preserve to the people as a whole their lawfully protected rights in a climate permitting their free and fair exercise. The overwhelming majority of our people in every section of the country are united in their respect for observance of the law—even in those cases where they may disagree with that law.

They deplore the call of extremists to violence.

The decision of the Supreme Court concerning school integration, of course, affects the South more seriously than it does other sections of the country. In that region I have many warm friends, some of them in the city of Little Rock. I have deemed it a great personal privilege to spend in our Southland tours of duty while in the military service and enjoyable recreational periods since that time.

So from intimate personal knowledge, I know that the overwhelming majority of the people in the South—including those of Arkansas and of Little Rock—are of good will, united in their efforts to preserve and respect the law even when they disagree with it.

They do not sympathize with mob rule. They, like the rest of our nation, have proved in two great wars their readiness to sacrifice for America.

A foundation of our American way of life is our national respect for law.

In the South, as elsewhere, citizens are keenly aware of the tremendous disservice that has been done to the people of Arkansas in the eyes of the nation, and that has been done to the nation in the eyes of the world.

At a time when we face grave situations abroad because of the hatred that Communism bears toward a system of government based on human rights, it would be difficult to exaggerate the harm that is being done to the prestige and influence, and indeed to the safety, of our nation and the world.

Our enemies are gloating over this incident and using it everywhere to misrepresent our whole nation. We are portrayed as a violator of those standards of conduct which the peoples of the world united to proclaim in the Charter of the United Nations. There they affirmed "faith in fundamental human rights" and "in the dignity and worth of the human person" and they did so "without distinction as to race, sex, language or religion."

And so, with deep confidence, I call upon the citizens of the State of Arkansas to assist in bringing to an immediate end all interference with the law and its processes. If resistance to the Federal Court orders ceases at once, the further presence of Federal troops will be unnecessary and the City of Little Rock will return to its normal habits of peace and order and a blot upon the fair name and high honor of our nation in the world will be removed.

Thus will be restored the image of America and of all its parts as one nation, indivisible, with liberty and justice for all.

Good night, and thank you very much.

SIGNIFICANCE

The federal troops arrived in Little Rock the next day. Eisenhower's intervention was bitterly attacked by forces on both sides. By late September 1957, however, the tensions in Little Rock had cooled to the point where eight of the nine black students who sought to enroll at Central High School had done so.

The Little Rock schools crisis began as a rearguard action by segregationists against the inevitability of school integration; the threatening and vociferous mobs that assembled at Central High School represented a large segment of the population in the South. Its primary significance, however, became subsumed in the larger question of state versus federal power.

When federal troops arrived in Little Rock after Eisenhower's second proclamation, cities and states throughout the South were galvanized into protest. The army was described variously as an invasion, an occupation, and an encroachment on local affairs. In light of other outstanding federal court rulings to integrate southern public high schools, fear was rife in many regions of the South that sending the army to Little Rock might be the first of many such federal acts against local governments to impose integration, instead of permitting it to occur at a pace determined by local government.

The legal issues at play in Little Rock continued to percolate for another year. The local school board sought a ruling to suspend further integration of the schools until the expression 'deliberate speed' had been further defined. A United States District Court in Little Rock granted the school board a two-and-one-half year delay to continue with integration. This ruling was ultimately overturned on appeal; the Supreme Court ultimately ruled that integration continue in Little Rock schools without delay.

In response, Faubus closed all four Little Rock high schools in August 1959, on the premise that he wished to avoid further violence. City high school students were absorbed into the county school system. When the Little Rock schools reopened in 1959, the facilities were integrated. Protests that accompanied the reopening were visible and initially disruptive, but the situation gradually settled by 1960.

Faubus's central role is particularly significant in light of his political background. A liberal Democrat (his middle name, Eugene, was given to him in honor of Eugene Debs, an early leader of American socialism), Faubus had overseen the integration of Little Rock transportation services after his election as governor in 1954. It's likely, however, that he had a powerful motive to side with the segregationists; he feared that the local Democratic Party would not support his renomination as gubernatorial candidate in the 1958 elections. Faubus's popularity, however, remained undiminished, and he was reelected in successive terms until 1966.

Eisenhower's address on September 24 linked the rule of law and the supremacy of a federal court order. By using such terms as anarchy, mob rule, and extremism to characterize the actions of the Little Rock protestors, he indicated clearly that the debate about integration was over, settled beyond question by the nation's highest court, and to continue that debate in the form of violent protest violated the rule of law. Eisenhower also advanced his case in a remarkably nonpartisan fashion. As a Republican, however, he did not politicize the issue or mention Governor Faubus by name or deed, nor did he suggest that any partisan political forces were at work in Little Rock.

Eisenhower's suggestion that America's international image had been tarnished by the protestors' lawless actions linked the battle over school integration to the threat posed by America's Communist enemies, another key national concern of the Cold War (1946-1991) years. This is a clear appeal to those with no direct interest in the Little Rock crisis to side with the federal government as an act of patriotism.

FURTHER RESOURCES
Books
Bates, Daisy. *The Long Shadow of Little Rock: A Memoir*. Fayetteville: University of Arkansas Press, 1986.

Duram, James C. *A Moderate among Extremists: Dwight D. Eisenhower and the School Desegregation Crisis*. Chicago; Nelson-Hall, 1981.

Reed, Roy. *Faubus: The Life and Times of an American Prodigal.* Fayetteville: University of Arkansas Press, 1997.

Web sites

Dwight D. Eisenhower Presidential Library and Museum. "Little Rock School Integration Crisis." <http://www.eisenhower.archives.gov/dl/LittleRock/littlerockdocuments.html> (accessed May 23, 2006).

University of Oregon. "Little Rock, 1957: An Overview." <http://www.uoregon.edu/~jbloom/race/overview.htm> (accessed May 21, 2006).

Negroes Plan Protest

Newspaper article

By: Anonymous

Date: December 25, 1959

Source: The *New York Times*, December 25, 1959.

About the Author: The *New York Times* is one of the most respected and widely circulated newspapers in the United States.

INTRODUCTION

Jackie Robinson (1919–1972) became the first black athlete to play in major league baseball in 1947 when he joined the Brooklyn Dodgers. As the man who broke the color line in baseball, Robinson became a hero to many African Americans. He used his fame to promote civil rights.

The Georgia-born Robinson played for the Kansas City Monarchs, a club in the Negro American Baseball League. While playing for the Monarchs in 1945, he was signed by Dodgers' president Branch Rickey and assigned to the Dodgers' Montreal farm team. He was heralded as the first black athlete to be under contract to a major league baseball team. After spending a season in Montreal, Robinson joined the Dodgers in 1947. He led the team to a National League pennant, batting .297 and playing mostly at second base, and was voted Rookie of the Year. Noted for his hitting, fielding, and baserunning, Robinson helped the Dodgers win five more pennants as well as the 1955 World Series championship. He was traded to the New York Giants in the beginning of the 1957 season and retired from baseball with a lifetime average of .311. Robinson was elected to the Hall of Fame in 1962.

A civil rights activist, Robinson used his fame and popularity to promote black business ventures. He also served as chair of the National Association for the Advancement of Colored People Fight for Freedom fund. Robinson worked for passage of the Civil Rights Act of 1964, which prohibited discrimination in public accommodations such as airport waiting rooms.

PRIMARY SOURCE

Carolina March to Cite Incident Involving Jackie Robinson
Greenville, S.C., Dec. 24 (UPI)—Some 5,000 Negroes will march to the Greenville Airport on New Year's Day to protest a racial incident involving Jackie Robinson, the former baseball star.

The plan was announced by the Rev. J.S. Hall, spokesman for the two groups sponsoring the demonstration—the Committee on Racial Equality and the Greenville Ministerial Alliance.

Mr. Hall said that when Mr. Robinson visited Greenville last Oct. 25 he was asked to move to the air terminal's waiting room for Negroes. Mr. Robinson was here to address a meeting of the South Carolina chapter of the National Association for the Advancement of Colored People.

Mr. Robinson reportedly refused to leave the white waiting room. He later told the 1,700 persons at the N.A.A.C.P. meeting that he "hoped that by 1963 all of the group could use the white facilities at the airport."

SIGNIFICANCE

Robinson's pioneering efforts made it possible for other black men to play professional sports. By 1960, every baseball team had some black players, if only in the farm clubs. This speedy process ended segregated baseball and also destroyed the separatist black major leagues while converting thousands of African Americans into major-league fans. Not everyone welcomed this change. Some white owners, fearful of a tidal wave of black players, established quotas while black militants saw the death of black leagues as a concession to white racism.

Robinson was a moderate integrationist who did not hesitate to assert his rights. As he realized, sports were an area in which black men could combat racial prejudice. Several black athletes became heroes, particularly to African Americans, by becoming models of black manhood and outperforming whites. Track star Jesse Owens in the 1930s and boxer Muhammad Ali (formerly Cassius Clay) in the 1960s and 1970s demonstrated that race had nothing to do with ability to succeed. Black athletes challenged white supremacist beliefs and, by doing so, gave support to the civil rights movement.

FURTHER RESOURCES
Books

Falkner, David. *Great Time Coming: The Life of Jackie Robinson, from Baseball to Birmingham*. New York: Simon and Schuster, 1995.

Meier, August, and Elliott M. Rudwick. *CORE: A Study in the Civil Rights Movement, 1942–1968*. New York: Oxford University Press, 1973.

Tygiel, Jules. *Baseball's Great Experiment: Jackie Robinson and His Legacy*. New York: Oxford University Press, 1997.

Civil Rights Workers Sing "We Shall Overcome"

Photograph

By: Anonymous

Date: c.1962

Source: © Bettmann/Corbis.

About the Photographer: This photograph resides in the Bettmann archives of the Corbis Corporation, a Seattle-based company with a collection of over seventy million curent and historical photographs and moving images.

INTRODUCTION

Religious leaders were key organizers and leaders of the Civil Rights movement of the 1960s and infused the movement with a sense of spirituality. Mixed into the movement seeking political rights and humanitarian reforms were the rhetoric and songs of churches historically and centrally important to African Americans. Songs such as, "We Shall Overcome," became popular with both activists and sympathizers, each interpreting lyrics in light of their own particular struggles. For example, African American labor unions using it as an anthem representing the struggle for racial freedom. The famous singer and activist, Joan Baez, performed the song during the March on Washington in 1963, which had an estimated attendance of up to 500,000 people. At the same event, speakers urged the U.S. Congress to pass an anti-discrimination bill, and civil rights leader, Martin Luther King Jr., delivered his now famous "I Have a Dream" speech.

Songs have historically been an important part of African American communities, with African slaves bringing a diverse polyphonic style in which several voices sing simultaneously in harmony. Slaves commonly sang while working in the fields, and sometimes used songs as codes for planning escapes or slave rebellions. In African American churches, traditional hymns sung in the polyphonic manner became known as gospel music. In the twentieth century, African Americans used new songs, and adapted older well-known songs, to build camaraderie and commitment in the struggle for equal rights and an end to racism.

The lyrics of "We Shall Overcome" were adapted from a gospel song entitled "I Will Overcome Some Day," written in 1900 by Charles Tindley. The melody was taken from a pre-Civil War song, "No More Auction Block for Me," which referred to the African American slave trade in the southern United States. Many African American Baptist and Methodist church congregations used Tindley's song during their services in the early 1900s.

It began to be used as a freedom song by tobacco workers in Charleston, South Carolina, who were pushing for more equal labor rights. The song was also shared with members of a white chapter of the Charleston Food, Tobacco, and Agricultural Workers Union at a Highlander Folk School workshop.

Founded in 1932, the Highlander Folk School near Knoxville, Tennessee, was a unique place, since it allowed the meeting of both black and white workers struggling to organize labor unions. Still in existence today, the Highlander Education and Research Center has brought together community organizers, grassroots leaders, educators, and researchers to address social, economic, and environmental issues facing people of the southern states. The Center has been involved in historically significant social justice movements, including the southern labor movement, the Civil Rights movement between the 1940s and the 1960s, and the Appalachian people's movements in the 1970s and 1980s.

The music director at the Highlander Center, Zilphia Horton, incorporated "We Shall Overcome" into all of her workshops during the 1940s and 1950s. Horton taught the song to folk singer, Pete Seeger, who added new verses to produce the version most commonly perfomed today. Guy Carawan, Horton's successor at the Highlander Center, taught the song to student protestors in Nashville, Tennessee, in 1960. Shortly after that, Carawan led the song at a meeting of student sit-in leaders at Shaw University in Raleigh, North Carolina. It is reported that the wide acceptance of the song at this meeting led to its nationwide use as the anthem of the Civil Rights movement.

PRIMARY SOURCE

Civil Rights Workers Sing "We Shall Overcome": Civil rights leaders, including Martin Luther King Jr., sing "We Shall Overcome" together. © BETTMANN/CORBIS.

PRIMARY SOURCE

CIVIL RIGHTS WORKERS SING "WE SHALL OVERCOME"
See primary source image.

SIGNIFICANCE

As evidenced by the news photo taken from era of the Civil Rights struggle, the singing of "We Shall Overcome" united races and denominations struggling for racial and social justice. Singing became a way to express both passion and protest.

Since 1966, royalties from the commercial use of "We Shall Overcome" have gone to support the Highlander Center through the We Shall Overcome Fund. The fund supports the use of art and activism to challenge injustice within African American communities throughout the South. The fund encourages proposals from diverse communities focusing on ending racism, sexism, and homophobia, and working to end economic and environmental injustice. The center funds performance and visual arts projects, workshops and conferences, and the preservation of Civil Rights movement documents.

The National Park Service and other U.S. federal agencies have created "We Shall Overcome: Historic Places of the Civil Rights Movement," a travel itinerary highlighting over fifty significant sites involved with the African American Civil Rights movement. The Civil Rights movement counts as its successes the Civil Rights Act of 1964 and the Voting Rights Act of 1965. The 1964 Act, signed by President Lyndon Johnson the year after the March on Washington, outlawed discrimination at workplaces, and required equal access to public facilities. The Voting Rights Act took down barriers for all African Americans to participate equally in elections.

FURTHER RESOURCES

Books

Albert, Peter, and Ronald Hoffman. *We Shall Overcome: Martin Luther King, Jr., and the Black Freedom Struggle*. Philadelphia, Penn.: Da Capo, 1990.

Hansen, Drew. *The Dream: Martin Luther King, Jr., and the Speech that Inspired a Nation*. New York: HarperCollins, 2003.

Southern, Eileen. *The Music of Black Americans: A History*. New York: W. W. Norton, 1997.

Periodicals

Baker, Robert E. "200,000 Jam Mall in Mammoth Rally in Solemn, Orderly Plea for Equality." *Washington Post* (August 29, 1963).

Web sites

Highlander Research and Education Center. <http://www.highlandercenter.org> (accessed May 20, 2006).

U.S. National Park Service. "Historic Places of the Civil Rights Movement: We Shall Overcome." <http://www.cr.nps.gov/nR/travel/civilrights/index.htm> (accessed May 20, 2006).

Letter From a Birmingham Jail

Letter

By: Martin Luther King Jr.

Date: April 16, 1963

Source: Estate of Martin Luther King Jr.

About the Author: Martin Luther King Jr. (1929–1968) was a Baptist minister and civil rights leader who, as president of the Southern Christian Leadership Council, spearheaded the struggle for racial equality throughout the late 1950s and 1960s.

INTRODUCTION

Of all the inspiring words that came out of the civil rights movement of the 1960s, few are as famous as those contained in Martin Luther King's "Letter from a Birmingham Jail." Written in response to eight white local clergy who criticized his work and ideas as unwise and wrong, the letter is King's explanation of the importance of civil rights protesting. It is one of the most famous documents in American history.

By the 1950s, Birmingham, Alabama, a steel city that had once represented the best of the New South, had become symbolic of a South determined to maintain the old racial ways. Eugene "Bull" Connor, Birmingham's notorious Commissioner of Public Safety, maintained white supremacy with a ferocious combination of arrests, harassment, and violence. Since founding the Alabama Christian Movement in 1956, Reverend Fred Shuttlesworth had doggedly battled Birmingham's white leadership. For his efforts, Shuttlesworth was blown out of bed by an explosion on Christmas night in 1956, hauled off to jail for trying to desegregate a bus in 1957, and saw his church turned into rubble by dynamite in 1958. In 1962, Shuttlesworth persuaded the Southern Christian Leadership Council (SCLC), led by King to target its protests at segregation in Birmingham.

King had a good chance of getting killed in Birmingham. Yet the city's business leaders were also worried. SCLC had scheduled its protests to begin in the fall, with the aim of disrupting the central business district when it was most vulnerable during the Christmas shopping season. The chamber of commerce stopped the protests by agreeing to integrate

Martin Luther King Jr. in his jail cell at the Jefferson County Courthouse in Birmingham, Alabama, November 3, 1967.
© BETTMANN/CORBIS. REPRODUCED BY PERMISSION.

the public facilities in five downtown stores. The agreement collapsed when Connor threatened to prosecute the stores. With Christmas too close for an effective boycott, King and Shuttlesworth rescheduled the protests to coincide with the Easter shopping season.

On April 3, 1963, SCLC began its Birmingham protest. However, by this time, Connor had lost his reelection bid to a racial moderate and many of the black middle class in Birmingham opposed the protests because they feared such demonstrations might jeopardize the slow but steady progress on race relations in the city. Many local blacks also were angry about being kept out of the planning for the demonstrations, while Birmingham's black newspaper criticized King for being a mere publicity seeker. Confronted by widespread opposition and resentment, King decided to go to jail to inspire support. He wanted to stiffen the resolve of his backers, get national publicity for the protests, and pressure the federal government to take some sort of positive action. King entered Birmingham Jail on Good Friday for violating an injunction against protesting. He finished "Letter from a Birmingham Jail," composed in the margins of a newspaper with a stubby pencil, before being released on bail on April 20.

■ PRIMARY SOURCE

MY DEAR FELLOW CLERGYMEN:

While confined here in the Birmingham City Jail, I came across your recent statement calling our present activities "unwise and untimely." Seldom, if ever, do I pause to answer criticism of my work and ideas. If I sought to answer all the criticisms that cross my desk, my secretaries would be engaged in little else in the course of the day, and I would have no time for constructive work. But since I feel that you are men of genuine goodwill and your criticisms are sincerely set forth, I would like to answer your statement in what I hope will be patient and reasonable terms.

I think I should give the reason for my being in Birmingham, since you have been influenced by the argument of "outsiders coming in." I have the honor of serving as president of the Southern Christian Leadership Conference, an organization operating in every Southern state, with headquarters in Atlanta, Georgia. We have some eighty-five affiliate organizations all across the South—one being the Alabama Christian Movement for Human Rights. Whenever necessary and possible we share staff, educational and financial resources with our affiliates. Several months ago our local affiliate here in Birmingham invited us to be on call to engage in a nonviolent

direct action program if such were deemed necessary. We readily consented and when the hour came we lived up to our promises. So I am here, along with several members of my staff, because I have basic organizational ties here.

Beyond this, I am in Birmingham because injustice is here. Just as the eighth century prophets left their little villages and carried their "thus saith the Lord" far beyond the boundaries of their home towns; and just as the Apostle Paul left his little village of Tarsus and carried the gospel of Jesus Christ to practically every hamlet and city of the Graeco-Roman world, I too am compelled to carry the gospel of freedom beyond my particular home town. Like Paul, I must constantly respond to the Macedonian call for aid.

Moreover, I am cognizant of the interrelatedness of all communities and states. I cannot sit idly by in Atlanta and not be concerned about what happens in Birmingham. Injustice anywhere is a threat to justice everywhere. We are caught in an inescapable network of mutuality, tied in a single garment of destiny. Whatever affects one directly affects all indirectly. Never again can we afford to live with the narrow, provincial "outside agitator" idea. Anyone who lives inside the United States can never be considered an outsider anywhere in this country.

You deplore the demonstrations that are presently taking place in Birmingham. But I am sorry that your statement did not express a similar concern for the conditions that brought the demonstrations into being. I am sure that each of you would want to go beyond the superficial social analyst who looks merely at effects, and does not grapple with underlying causes. I would not hesitate to say that it is unfortunate that so-called demonstrations are taking place in Birmingham at this time, but I would say in more emphatic terms that it is even more unfortunate that the white power structure of this city left the Negro community with no other alternative.

In any nonviolent campaign there are four basic steps: 1) Collection of the facts to determine whether injustices are alive. 2) Negotiation. 3) Self-purification and 4) Direct action. We have gone through all of these steps in Birmingham. There can be no gainsaying of the fact that racial injustice engulfs this community.

Birmingham is probably the most thoroughly segregated city in the United States. Its ugly record of police brutality is known in every section of this country. Its unjust treatment of Negroes in the courts is a notorious reality. There have been more unsolved bombings of Negro homes and churches in Birmingham than any city in this nation. These are the hard, brutal and unbelievable facts. On the basis of these conditions, Negro leaders sought to negotiate with the city fathers. But the political leaders consistently refused to engage in good faith negotiation. . . .

You may well ask: "Why direct action? Why sit-ins, marches, etc.? Isn't negotiation a better path?" You are exactly right in your call for negotiation. Indeed, this is the purpose of direct action. Nonviolent direct action seeks to create such a crisis and establish such creative tension that a community that has constantly refused to negotiate is forced to confront the issue. It seeks so to dramatize the issue that it can no longer be ignored. I just referred to the creation of tension as a part of the work of the nonviolent resister. This may sound rather shocking. But I must confess that I am not afraid of the word tension. I have earnestly worked and preached against violent tension, but there is a type of constructive nonviolent tension that is necessary for growth.... So the purpose of the direct action is to create a situation so crisis-packed that it will inevitably open the door to negotiation. We, therefore, concur with you in your call for negotiation. Too long has our beloved Southland been bogged down in the tragic attempt to live in monologue rather than dialogue.

One of the basic points in your statement is that our acts are untimely....

We have waited for more than three hundred and forty years for our constitutional and God-given rights.... But when you have seen vicious mobs lynch your mothers and fathers at will and drown your sisters and brothers at whim; when you have seen hate filled policemen curse, kick, brutalize and even kill your black brothers and sisters with impunity; when you see the vast majority of your twenty million Negro brothers smothering in an airtight cage of poverty in the midst of an affluent society; when you suddenly find your tongue twisted and your speech stammering as you seek to explain to your six-year-old daughter why she can't go to the public amusement park that has just been advertised on television, and see tears welling up in her eyes when she is told that Funtown is closed to colored children, and see the depressing clouds of inferiority begin to form in her little mental sky, and see her begin to distort her little personality by unconsciously developing a bitterness toward white people; when you have to concoct an answer for a five-year-old son asking in agonizing pathos: "Daddy, why do white people treat colored people so mean?"; when you take a cross-country drive and find it necessary to sleep night after night in the uncomfortable corners of your automobile because no motel will accept you; when you are humiliated day in and day out by nagging signs reading "white" and "colored"; when your first name becomes "nigger," your middle name becomes "boy" (however old you are) and your last name becomes "John," and your wife and mother are never given the respected title "Mrs."; when you are harried by day and haunted by night by the fact that you are a Negro, living constantly at tip-toe stance never quite knowing what to expect next, and plagued with inner fears and outer resentments; when you are forever fighting a degenerating sense of "nobodiness"; then you will understand why we find it difficult to wait. There comes a time when the cup of endurance runs over, and men are no longer willing to be plunged into an abyss of despair. I hope, sirs, you can understand our legitimate and unavoidable impatience.

You express a great deal of anxiety over our willingness to break laws. This is certainly a legitimate concern. Since we so diligently urge people to obey the Supreme Court's decision of 1954 outlawing segregation in the public schools, it is rather strange and paradoxical to find us consciously breaking laws. One may well ask: "How can you advocate breaking some laws and obeying others?" The answer is found in the fact that there are two types of laws: There are *just* and there are *unjust* laws. I would agree with Saint Augustine that "An unjust law is no law at all."...

I hope you can see the distinction I am trying to point out. In no sense do I advocate evading or defying the law as the rabid segregationist would do. This would lead to anarchy. One who breaks an unjust law must do it *openly, lovingly,* (not hatefully as the white mothers did in New Orleans when they were seen on television screaming "nigger, nigger, nigger") and with a willingness to accept the penalty. I submit that an individual who breaks a law that conscience tells him is unjust, and willingly accepts the penalty by staying in jail to arouse the conscience of the community over its injustice, is in reality expressing the very highest respect for law....

If I have said anything in this letter that is an overstatement of the truth and is indicative of an unreasonable impatience, I beg you to forgive me. If I have said anything in this letter that is an understatement of the truth and is indicative of my having a patience that makes me patient with anything less than brotherhood, I beg God to forgive me.

I hope this letter finds you strong in the faith. I also hope that circumstances will soon make it possible for me to meet each of you, not as an integrationist or a civil rights leader, but as a fellow clergyman and a Christian brother. Let us all hope that the dark clouds of racial prejudice will soon pass away and the deep fog of misunderstanding will be lifted from our fear-drenched communities and in some not too distant tomorrow the radiant stars of love and brotherhood will shine over our great nation with all their scintillating beauty.

Yours for the cause of Peace and Brotherhood,
Martin Luther King, Jr.

SIGNIFICANCE

"Letter from a Birmingham Jail" can be seen as one of the best justifications of nonviolence as a political strategy ever articulated. Influenced by Indian leader Mahatma Gandhi's concept of *satyagraha*, King used love as the instrument to overthrow the violent hatred of white racists. In Birmingham, Connor was the violent racist. On May 2, hundreds of black schoolchildren, at the urging of the SCLC, marched from the Sixteenth Street Baptist Church into the arms of arresting officers. Within a week, more than 2,000 children were in police custody. Connor could not control his anger any longer. Under his command, the police turned German shepherds upon the protesters, in a scene that reminded many observers of Nazi Germany. The marchers who failed to disperse were than assaulted with high-pressure water hoses.

The scenes of racial brutality drew international condemnation, at a time when the United States sought to win the Cold War by winning the hearts and minds of the people in Africa, Latin America, Asia, and Europe. The Soviet Union quickly capitalized on the incident by ridiculing the failure of the federal government to fulfill the ideals of American democracy in its own territory. A deeply embarrassed President John F. Kennedy, who had always displayed more interest in foreign policy than domestic matters, announced his intention to present a comprehensive civil rights bill to the U.S. Congress. This legislation, passed after Kennedy's 1963 murder, is the landmark Civil Rights Act of 1964 that banned discrimination on account of race.

The Birmingham campaign sealed King's reputation as the outstanding moral and political leader of the Civil Rights Movement. His strategy of nonviolence had succeeded dramatically. He had turned civil rights into a national security concern. Although not the first black leader to advocate the philosophy of nonviolence, King was the first to implement it on a mass scale with revolutionary consequences.

FURTHER RESOURCES
Books

Bass, S. Jonathan. *Blessed Are the Peacemakers: Martin Luther King, Jr., Eight White Religious Leaders, and the Letter from Birmingham Jail*. Baton Rouge: Louisiana State University Press, 2001.

Branch, Taylor. *Parting the Waters: America in the King Years, 1954–63*. New York: Simon & Schuster, 1988.

Fairclough, Adam. *To Redeem the Soul of America: The Southern Christian Leadership Conference and Martin Luther King, Jr.* Athens: University of Georgia Press, 1987.

Oates, Stephen. *Let the Trumpet Sound: The Life of Martin Luther King, Jr.* New York: New American Library, 1985.

The Stand in the Schoolhouse Door

Photograph

By: Anonymous

Date: June 11, 1963

Source: Photo by MPI/Getty Images.

About the Photographer: This photograph is part of the collection at Getty Images, a worldwide provider of visual content materials to such communications groups as advertisers, broadcasters, designers, magazines, new media organizations, newspapers, and producers. The photographer is not known.

INTRODUCTION

In May 1954, the U.S. Supreme Court, through *Brown v. Board of Education*, decided that any state statute that allowed for segregation with regard to race within public schools was unconstitutional. Members of the Supreme Court ruled in favor of outlawing racial segregation based on the rationale that the "separate but equal" doctrine for public education would never provide African-American students with the same educational opportunities as those available to white students.

While campaigning for governor of Alabama as a pro-states' rights/pro-segregation candidate, U.S. politician George Wallace (1919–1998) promised that, if elected, he would physically block any attempts to integrate Alabama's all-white public school system. Upon being elected in 1962, Wallace made his inaugural speech as governor of Alabama. According to the Alabama Department of Archives and History, Wallace stated: "In the name of the greatest people that have ever trod this earth, I draw a line in the dust and toss the gauntlet before the feet of tyranny ... and I say ... segregation now ... segregation tomorrow ... segregation forever."

Early in 1963, a federal judge ordered that Vivian Malone and James Hood, two Alabama black students, be admitted to the University of Alabama at Tuscaloosa beginning the summer session of 1963. Knowing the importance of the federal order, President John F. Kennedy and Attorney General Robert F. Kennedy personally negotiated how the process would be performed in order to ensure that the two black students were successfully enrolled, including the procedure to counter the likelihood that Wallace would not allow the representatives of the federal government to carry out the intended order.

PRIMARY SOURCE

The Stand in the Schoolhouse Door: George Wallace, the governor of Alabama, stands in the doorway of the administrative building of the University of Alabama in Tuscaloosa, June 11, 1963, in order to prevent two Afican-American students from entering. PHOTO BY MPI/ GETTY IMAGES.

On June 11, 1963, Wallace personally blocked the entrance door to Foster Auditorium on the main campus of the University of Alabama in order to prevent Malone and Hood from enrolling as undergraduates. A large group of national, state, and local media correspondents and photographers were present to record the historic event. State police surrounded the building and Alabama National Guard soldiers were prepared to remove Wallace physically if he refused to step aside peacefully. Standing next to federal marshals, Deputy Attorney General Nicholas Katzenbach (1922–), who was sent on behalf of the Kennedy administration, asked Wallace to abide by the federal court order to accept court-ordered desegregation. Wallace refused the directive by countering with the constitutional right of states to operate public schools, universities, and colleges. When Katzenbach called the president to inform him of the situation, Kennedy immediately federalized the Alabama National Guard so they could legally remove Wallace with force if necessary.

PRIMARY SOURCE

THE STAND IN THE SCHOOLHOUSE DOOR
See primary source image.

SIGNIFICANCE

With the governor now facing federal troops, a tense confrontation was created as Wallace continued his barricade. After a few moments, however, Wallace retreated from the entrance and allowed the two students to register for classes. The deep-seated moral division within the country over desegregation was apparent that day on the campus of the University of Alabama. The incident between Wallace and Katzenbach became known as the Stand in the Schoolhouse Door. The scene on the morning of June 11, 1963, was an important event in the U.S. civil rights movement of the 1960s.

Because of the publicity the incident caused, Wallace was catapulted into the national focus. He completed his term as governor but, at that time, Alabama law prevented a governor from serving two consecutive terms. (The law has since been revoked.) Wallace, therefore, had his wife, Lurleen Burns Wallace, run for the gubernatorial office. She was elected governor in 1968, while Wallace himself ran unsuccessfully for the presidency. Wallace was re-elected governor of Alabama again in 1970. In 1972, he was shot and paralyzed while campaigning for the Democratic Party presidential nomination. Wallace was again re-elected Alabama governor in 1974. In 1976, he unsuccessfully campaigned for a third time for the presidency. Leaving the governor's post in 1979, Wallace accepted a position at the University of Alabama. He was re-elected governor of Alabama in 1982, and retired in 1987. In the 1980s, Wallace publicly reversed his earlier racial views and asked to work with black leaders.

President Kennedy appeared on national television the night of June 11, 1963 to state that the civil rights of all citizens was an important moral issue. Before this day, Kennedy was only tentatively in support of enforcing civil rights. However, the conflict in Alabama pushed Kennedy to commit his administration to enforce civil rights. Kennedy told the people of the United States that it was the obligation of all persons to guarantee equal rights and equal opportunities to all citizens. Because of the forceful way he dealt with Wallace, Kennedy became a leader within the civil rights movement. Actively guiding the

Governor George C. Wallace of Alabama (left) meets with reporters at the University of Alabama, on his way to "stand in the schoolhouse door" and prevent desegregation. © BETTMANN/CORBIS.

country to end segregation, in June 1963, Kennedy proposed civil rights legislation.

The Civil Rights Act of 1964 was enacted by Congress and signed into law by President Lyndon B. Johnson on July 2, 1964, less than eight months after President Kennedy was assassinated. The Act prohibited discrimination in public accommodations and employment and specifically authorized the U.S. Attorney General to file lawsuits to force school desegregation. With the federal government actively enforcing *Brown v. Board of Education*, the end of school segregation was moving steadily forward. At the beginning of the twenty-first century, no public school in the United States was legally allowed to segregate its students.

Vivian Juanita Malone Jones (1942–2005), a transfer student from an all-black college, became the first African-American to graduate from the University of Alabama. In 1965, she received a Bachelor of Arts degree in business management and, subsequently, joined the civil rights division of the U.S. Department of Justice. In 1996, Jones retired as the director of civil rights and urban affairs and director of environmental justice for the U.S. Environmental Protection Agency.

James Hood left the University of Alabama after only two months in attendance, and transferred to Wayne State University in Detroit, Michigan. He earned his Bachelor of Arts degree in political science and police administration and a master's degree in criminal justice administration, both from Michigan State University in Lansing. Hood worked four years as a deputy police chief in Detroit and then joined the administration of a technical college in Madison, Wisconsin. Hood returned to the University of Alabama in 1995 to work on his doctorate degree in higher education administration, which he was awarded on May 17, 1997.

Vivian Jones and George Wallace met again in October 1996 when the Wallace Family Foundation selected Jones to be the first recipient of the Lurleen B. Wallace Award for Courage. Wallace apologized to both Hood and Jones before he died for his actions on that day of June 11, 1963.

FURTHER RESOURCES
Books

Carter, Dan T. *The Politics of Rage: George Wallace, the Origin of the New Conservatism, and the Transformation of American Politics*. New York: Simon and Schuster, 1995.

Clark, E. Culpepper. *The Schoolhouse Door: Segregation's Last Stand at the University of Alabama*. New York: Oxford University Press, 1993.

Frady, Marshall. *Wallace*. New York: Random House, 1996.

Gaillard, Frye. *The Cradle of Freedom: Alabama and the Movement that Changed America*. Tuscaloosa, Ala.: University of Alabama Press, 2004.

Web sites

Alabama Department of Archives and History. "The 1963 Inaugural Address of Governor George C. Wallace." January 14, 1963. <http://www.archives.state.al.us/govs_list/inauguralspeech.html> (accessed May 31, 2006).

Alabama Department of Archives and History. "Statement and Proclamation of Governor George C. Wallace, University of Alabama, June 11, 1963." <http://www.archives.state.al.us/govs_list/schooldoor.html> (accessed May 31, 2006).

Allison Carter, The University of Alabama. "James Hood: Still Working for Equality." <http://www.ccom.ua.edu/od/article_hood.shtml> (accessed May 31, 2006).

Debbie Elliott, National Public Radio. "Wallace in the Schoolhouse Door: Marking the 40th Anniversary of Alabama's Civil Rights Standoff." <http://www.npr.org/templates/story/story.php?storyId=1294680> (accessed May 31, 2006).

March from Selma

Photograph

By: Anonymous

Date: March 10, 1965

Source: AP Images.

About the Author: This photograph was taken by a contributor to the Associated Press, a worldwide news agency based in New York.

INTRODUCTION

In 1965, Martin Luther King Jr. chose Selma, Alabama as the site of a renewed voting rights campaign. The growing militancy of the civil rights movement made it essential that he score a quick victory in order to restore confidence in his non-violent approach. When segregationist police attacked the peaceful marchers, King had his victory. The Voting Rights Act of 1965 passed through Congress shortly thereafter.

Selma was home to 14,400 whites and 15,100 blacks, but the city's voting rolls were ninety-nine percent white. Every time that an African American attempted to register to vote, Sheriff Jim Clark and his deputies, many of whom were Ku Klux Klan members, turned the would-be voter away. During one week, more than three thousand black protesters were arrested for protesting this voting ban. In February 1965, a mob of state troopers assaulted a group of blacks, fatally shooting a young man, Jimmie Lee Jackson, as he tried to protect his mother and grandmother.

Jackson's death inspired black leaders to organize a fifty-four-mile (eighty-seven-kilometer) march from Selma to Montgomery to petition Governor George Wallace for protection of blacks registering to vote. On March 7, the march began. King was absent, having returned to Atlanta because of pressure from White

House officials. He missed the sixty helmeted state troopers and local police with gas masks who lined up opposite the six hundred marchers at the foot of the Edmund Pettus Bridge. While white spectators cheered and Sheriff Clark ordered them to attack, the troopers moved on the protesters, swinging bullwhips and rubber tubing wrapped in barbed wire. The marchers stumbled over each other in retreat and seventeen went to the hospital with injuries. That evening, horrified viewers throughout the nation watched the images from the Pettus Bridge on television.

This incident, known as Bloody Sunday, pushed the administration of President Lyndon B. Johnson

■ PRIMARY SOURCE

March from Selma Dr. Martin Luther King, Jr., and supporters march over the Edmund Pettus Bridge during the second of their three attempted marches from Selma to Montgomery, Alabama, on March 9, 1965. The marches brought attention to the struggle for Afircan American voting rights. AP IMAGES.

into action to protect the voting rights of African Americans. To keep the pressure on, King led a second march on March 9th. A federal injunction had forbidden the marchers to proceed to Montgomery while their case was investigated, but as a comrpomise King and his marchers were allowed to cross the Edmund Pettus ridge, pray and demonstrate, and then return to Selma voluntarily. Later, the federal courts ruled that the protest should be allowed to take place, and King led a third and final march from Selma to Montgomery, starting on March 21 and ending March 25th in front of the state capitol.

PRIMARY SOURCE

MARCH FROM SELMA

See primary source image.

SIGNIFICANCE

The Selma marches kept public attention focused on the injustices African Americans faced in the South, despite the recent passage of the Civil Rights Act of 1964. They played a major role in encouraging President Johnson and other political leaders to move forward with another landmark civil rights bill, which would become the Voting Rights Act of 1965.

Lyndon Johnson made greater and more effective efforts on behalf of civil rights than any other politician of his era. Both the Civil Rights Act of 1964 and the Voting Rights Act of 1965 are part of Johnson's legacy, though both pieces of legislation passed largely because of the efforts of King. His strategy of nonviolence posed against the violence of the segregationists made civil rights activists look reasonable and sympathetic.

The Voting Rights Act made possible by Selma allowed millions of African Americans in the South to cast ballots without being intimidated. The legislation removed artificial barriers such as poll taxes and literacy tests that served to bar blacks from the voting booths. For the first time, the Constitution applied to all of the people as blacks were permitted to enjoy all of the rights and privileges of citizenship that they had been granted by the Fourteenth Amendment in 1868. The Voting Rights Act is set to expire in 2007. While it is expected to be renewed, some legislators have argued that it is no longer needed.

FURTHER RESOURCES

Books

Fager, Charles. *Selma, 1965*. New York: Scribner, 1974.

Garrow, David J. *Protest at Selma: Martin Luther King, Jr. and the Voting Rights Act of 1965*. New Haven, Conn.: Yale University Press, 1978.

Stanton, Mary. *From Selma to Sorrow: The Life and Death of Viola Liuzzo*. Athens, Ga.: University of Georgia Press, 1998.

We Shall Overcome

Speech

By: Lyndon Baines Johnson

Date: March 15, 1965

Source: Johnson, Lyndon Baines. "We Shall Overcome." Address on voting legislation to the Joint Session of Congress, Washington, D.C., March 15, 1965.

About the Author: Lyndon Baines Johnson (1908–1973) was the thirty-sixth president of the United States. He served in the U.S. House of Representatives and the U.S. Senate before becoming John F. Kennedy's vice president in 1960. When Kennedy was assassinated in November 1963, Johnson became president and held that office for six years.

INTRODUCTION

During the summer of 1964, the U.S. Congress passed a landmark law, the Civil Rights Act of 1964, that had been initiated by President John F. Kennedy (1917–1963) and supported by his successor, President Lyndon Baines Johnson. With its prohibition of racial discrimination in public places and on public transportation, the Civil Rights Act marked the end of Jim Crow segregationist laws in the South.

While the Civil Rights Act brought about significant changes, it failed to guarantee the right of all citizens to vote, a fundamental goal of the civil rights movement. The Fifteenth Amendment to the U.S. Constitution, passed after the Civil War (1861–1865), secured the right of black men to vote, but southern states had erected a number of obstacles that effectively barred African Americans from the polls. For example, in some southern states voters had to pass a complicated literacy test, while in others they had to pay a poll tax, which many blacks could not afford. Throughout the South, blacks were intimidated, threatened, and sometimes attacked when they attempted to register to vote.

In early 1965, civil rights leader Martin Luther King Jr. (1929–1968) traveled to the deeply segregated city of Selma, Alabama, with other leaders of the Southern Christian Leadership Conference (SCLC) as well as members of the Student Nonviolent Coordinating Committee (SNCC). They staged a series of demonstrations to draw attention to the need for voting rights legislation. Civil rights leaders organized a fifty-four-mile march from Selma to Montgomery, Alabama's capital, to present a list of complaints to Governor George Wallace. On March 7, hundreds of peaceful marchers started for Montgomery, only to be attacked by Selma police and state troopers wielding batons, cattle prods, and tear gas. Many marchers were injured, and the day came to be known as "Bloody Sunday." The police violence was captured by news photographers and made the front pages of newspapers across the country, arousing tremendous sympathy for the civil rights workers. After another repelled attempt to march out of Selma on March 9, three white ministers who supported the civil rights movement were attacked by white segregationists in Selma. One of the ministers, James Reeb, was beaten with a club and later died of his injuries.

In the months prior to the attempted march from Selma to Montgomery, President Johnson had expressed his view that the Civil Rights Act of 1964, as well as judgments by the courts, would be sufficient to secure the right to vote for African Americans. He and others in his administration had stated that Congress might not pass a voting rights law, which would be strongly opposed by southern lawmakers. However, the events in early March, particularly on "Bloody Sunday," persuaded Johnson that the time was right to send a voting rights bill to Congress. Rather than simply send the proposed legislation to Congress, he decided to personally address the lawmakers and the nation, using the authority of his office to convey the historical and moral importance of this law. On March 15, 1965, President Johnson appeared before Congress to urge lawmakers to pass the Voting Rights Act, a law that would guarantee African Americans the right to vote.

■ PRIMARY SOURCE

Mr. Speaker, Mr. President, Members of the Congress:

I speak tonight for the dignity of man and the destiny of democracy. I urge every member of both parties, Americans of all religions and of all colors, from every section of this country, to join me in that cause.

At times history and fate meet at a single time in a single place to shape a turning point in man's unending search for freedom. So it was at Lexington and Concord. So it was a century ago at Appomattox. So it was last week in Selma, Alabama. There, long-suffering men and women peacefully protested the denial of their rights as Americans. Many were brutally assaulted. One good man, a man of God, was killed.

There is no cause for pride in what has happened in Selma. There is no cause for self-satisfaction in the long denial of equal rights of millions of Americans. But there is cause for hope and for faith in our democracy in what is happening here tonight. For the cries of pain and the hymns and protests of oppressed people have summoned into convocation all the majesty of this great government—the government of the greatest nation on earth. Our mission is at once the oldest and the most basic of this country: to right wrong, to do justice, to serve man.

In our time we have come to live with the moments of great crisis. Our lives have been marked with debate about great issues—issues of war and peace, issues of prosperity and depression. But rarely in any time does an issue lay bare the secret heart of America itself. Rarely are we met with a challenge, not to our growth or abundance, or our welfare or our security, but rather to the values, and the purposes, and the meaning of our beloved nation.

The issue of equal rights for American Negroes is such an issue.

And should we defeat every enemy, and should we double our wealth and conquer the stars, and still be unequal to this issue, then we will have failed as a people and as a nation. For with a country as with a person, "What is a man profited, if he shall gain the whole world, and lose his own soul?"

There is no Negro problem. There is no Southern problem. There is no Northern problem. There is only an American problem. And we are met here tonight as Americans—not as Democrats or Republicans. We are met here as Americans to solve that problem.

This was the first nation in the history of the world to be founded with a purpose. The great phrases of that purpose still sound in every American heart, North and South: "All men are created equal," "government by consent of the governed," "give me liberty or give me death." Well, those are not just clever words, or those are not just empty theories. In their name Americans have fought and died for two centuries, and tonight around the world they stand there as guardians of our liberty, risking their lives.

Those words are a promise to every citizen that he shall share in the dignity of man. This dignity cannot be found in a man's possessions; it cannot be found in his power, or in his position. It really rests on his right to be treated as a man equal in opportunity to all others. It says that he shall share in freedom, he shall choose his leaders, educate his children, provide for his family according to his ability and his merits as a human being. To apply any other test—to deny a man his hopes because of his color, or race, or his religion, or the place of his birth is not only to do injustice, it is to deny America and to dishonor the dead who gave their lives for American freedom.

Our fathers believed that if this noble view of the rights of man was to flourish, it must be rooted in democracy. The most basic right of all was the right to choose your own leaders. The history of this country, in large measure, is the history of the expansion of that right to all of our people. Many of the issues of civil rights are very complex and most difficult. But about this there can and should be no argument.

Every American citizen must have an equal right to vote.

There is no reason which can excuse the denial of that right. There is no duty which weighs more heavily on us than the duty we have to ensure that right.

Yet the harsh fact is that in many places in this country men and women are kept from voting simply because they are Negroes. Every device of which human ingenuity is capable has been used to deny this right. The Negro citizen may go to register only to be told that the day is wrong, or the hour is late, or the official in charge is absent. And if he persists, and if he manages to present himself to the registrar, he may be disqualified because he did not spell out his middle name or because he abbreviated a word on the application. And if he manages to fill out an application, he is given a test. The registrar is the sole judge of whether he passes this test. He may be asked to recite the entire Constitution, or explain the most complex provisions of State law. And even a college degree cannot be used to prove that he can read and write.

For the fact is that the only way to pass these barriers is to show a white skin. Experience has clearly shown that the existing process of law cannot overcome systematic and ingenious discrimination. No law that we now have on the books—and I have helped to put three of them there— can ensure the right to vote when local officials are determined to deny it. In such a case our duty must be clear to all of us. The Constitution says that no person shall be kept from voting because of his race or his color. We have all sworn an oath before God to support and to defend that Constitution. We must now act in obedience to that oath.

Wednesday, I will send to Congress a law designed to eliminate illegal barriers to the right to vote. . . .

I want to really discuss with you now, briefly, the main proposals of this legislation.

This bill will strike down restrictions to voting in all elections—Federal, State, and local—which have been used to deny Negroes the right to vote. This bill will establish a simple, uniform standard which cannot be used, however ingenious the effort, to flout our Constitution. It will provide for citizens to be registered by officials of the United States Government, if the State officials refuse to register them. It will eliminate tedious, unnecessary lawsuits which delay the right to vote. Finally, this legislation will ensure that properly registered individuals are not prohibited from voting. . . .

To those who seek to avoid action by their National Government in their own communities, who want to and who seek to maintain purely local control over elections, the answer is simple: open your polling places to all your people.

Allow men and women to register and vote whatever the color of their skin.

Extend the rights of citizenship to every citizen of this land.

There is no constitutional issue here. The command of the Constitution is plain. There is no moral issue. It is wrong—deadly wrong—to deny any of your fellow Americans the right to vote in this country. There is no issue of States' rights or national rights. There is only the struggle for human rights. I have not the slightest doubt what will be your answer. . . .

I recognize that from outside this chamber is the outraged conscience of a nation, the grave concern of many nations, and the harsh judgment of history on our acts.

But even if we pass this bill, the battle will not be over. What happened in Selma is part of a far larger movement which reaches into every section and State of America. It is the effort of American Negroes to secure for themselves the full blessings of American life. Their cause must be our cause too. Because it's not just Negroes, but really it's all of us, who must overcome the crippling legacy of bigotry and injustice.

And we shall overcome.

As a man whose roots go deeply into Southern soil, I know how agonizing racial feelings are. I know how difficult it is to reshape the attitudes and the structure of our society. But a century has passed, more than a hundred years since the Negro was freed. And he is not fully free tonight.

It was more than a hundred years ago that Abraham Lincoln, a great President of another party, signed the Emancipation Proclamation; but emancipation is a proclamation, and not a fact. A century has passed, more than a hundred years, since equality was promised. And yet the Negro is not equal. A century has passed since the day of promise. And the promise is un-kept.

The time of justice has now come. I tell you that I believe sincerely that no force can hold it back. It is right in the eyes of man and God that it should come. And when it does, I think that day will brighten the lives of every American. For Negroes are not the only victims. How many white children have gone uneducated? How many white families have lived in stark poverty? How many white lives have been scarred by fear, because we've wasted our energy and our substance to maintain the barriers of hatred and terror?

And so I say to all of you here, and to all in the nation tonight, that those who appeal to you to hold on to the past do so at the cost of denying you your future.

This great, rich, restless country can offer opportunity and education and hope to all, all black and white, all North and South, sharecropper and city dweller. These are the enemies: poverty, ignorance, disease. They're our enemies, not our fellow man, not our neighbor. And these enemies too—poverty, disease, and ignorance: we shall overcome.

Now let none of us in any section look with prideful righteousness on the troubles in another section, or the problems of our neighbors. There's really no part of America where the promise of equality has been fully kept. In Buffalo as well as in Birmingham, in Philadelphia as well as Selma, Americans are struggling for the fruits of freedom. This is one nation. What happens in Selma or in Cincinnati is a matter of legitimate concern to every American. But let each of us look within our own hearts and our own communities, and let each of us put our shoulder to the wheel to root out injustice wherever it exists. . . .

And I have not the slightest doubt that good men from everywhere in this country, from the Great Lakes to the Gulf of Mexico, from the Golden Gate to the harbors along the Atlantic, will rally now together in this cause to vindicate the freedom of all Americans.

For all of us owe this duty; and I believe that all of us will respond to it. Your President makes that request of every American.

The real hero of this struggle is the American Negro. His actions and protests, his courage to risk safety and even to risk his life, have awakened the conscience of this nation. His demonstrations have been designed to call attention to injustice, designed to provoke change, designed to stir reform. He has called upon us to make good the promise of America. And who among us can say that we would have made the same progress were it not for his persistent bravery, and his faith in American democracy.

For at the real heart of battle for equality is a deep seated belief in the democratic process. Equality depends not on the force of arms or tear gas but depends upon the force of moral right; not on recourse to violence but on respect for law and order.

And there have been many pressures upon your President and there will be others as the days come and go. But I pledge you tonight that we intend to fight this battle where it should be fought—in the courts, and in the Congress, and in the hearts of men.

We must preserve the right of free speech and the right of free assembly. But the right of free speech does not carry with it, as has been said, the right to holler fire in a crowded theater. We must preserve the right to free assembly. But free assembly does not carry with it the right to block public thoroughfares to traffic.

We do have a right to protest, and a right to march under conditions that do not infringe the constitutional rights of our neighbors. And I intend to protect all those rights as long as I am permitted to serve in this office.

We will guard against violence, knowing it strikes from our hands the very weapons which we seek: progress, obedience to law, and belief in American values.

In Selma, as elsewhere, we seek and pray for peace. We seek order. We seek unity. But we will not accept the peace of stifled rights, or the order imposed by fear, or the unity that stifles protest. For peace cannot be purchased at the cost of liberty. . . .

The bill that I am presenting to you will be known as a civil rights bill. But, in a larger sense, most of the program I am recommending is a civil rights program. Its object is to open the city of hope to all people of all races.

Because all Americans must have the right to vote. And we are going to give them that right. All Americans must have the privileges of citizenship—regardless of race. And they are going to have those privileges of citizenship—regardless of race.

But I would like to caution you and remind you that to exercise these privileges takes much more than just legal right. It requires a trained mind and a healthy body. It requires a decent home, and the chance to find a job, and the opportunity to escape from the clutches of poverty.

Of course, people cannot contribute to the nation if they are never taught to read or write, if their bodies are stunted from hunger, if their sickness goes untended, if their life is spent in hopeless poverty just drawing a welfare check. So we want to open the gates to opportunity. But we're also going to give all our people, black and white, the help that they need to walk through those gates. . . .

Beyond this great chamber, out yonder in fifty States, are the people that we serve. Who can tell what deep and unspoken hopes are in their hearts tonight as they sit there and listen. We all can guess, from our own lives, how difficult they often find their own pursuit of happiness, how many problems each little family has. They look most of all to themselves for their futures. But I think that they also look to each of us.

Above the pyramid on the great seal of the United States it says in Latin: "God has favored our undertaking." God will not favor everything that we do. It is rather our duty to divine His will.

But I cannot help believing that He truly understands and that He really favors the undertaking that we begin here tonight.

SIGNIFICANCE

The title of President Johnson's address, "We Shall Overcome," refers to the song that had become the anthem of the civil rights movement. Johnson's use of the phrase in his speech emphasized his point that the quest for social justice should not simply be a goal of the African American community, but of the entire nation. According to Robert Dallek in his book *Flawed Giant*, after Johnson uttered those words, numerous lawmakers stood up and cheered: "Tears rolled down the cheeks of senators, congressmen, and observers in the gallery, moved by joy, elation, a sense that the victor, for a change, was human decency...." Dallek goes on to describe the address as "Johnson's greatest speech."

A few days after Johnson's speech, on March 21, 1965, more than 3,000 marchers headed once again from Selma to Montgomery. Governor Wallace had refused to grant the marchers police protection against angry mobs, so President Johnson placed the Alabama National Guard under federal control, ordering the troops to protect the marchers. He also called in 2,000 soldiers from the U.S. Army and hundreds of other federal agents. Five days later, on March 25, the marchers reached Montgomery, their numbers having swelled to approximately 25,000. The Selma-to-Montgomery march became one of the most significant events of the civil rights movement. A few months later, on August 6, President Johnson signed into law the Voting Rights Act of 1965. The impact of this law was felt within a short period: registration of black voters increased rapidly over the next few years, and the number of African Americans elected to public office began a steady climb not just in the South but throughout the United States.

FURTHER RESOURCES
Books

Bernstein, Irving. *Guns or Butter: The Presidency of Lyndon Johnson*. New York: Oxford University Press, 1996.

Dallek, Robert. *Flawed Giant: Lyndon Johnson and His Times, 1961–1973*. New York: Oxford University Press, 1998.

Wexler, Sanford. *The Civil Rights Movement*. New York: Facts on File, 1999.

Williams, Juan. *Eyes on the Prize: America's Civil Rights Years, 1954–1965*. New York: Viking, 1987.

Winters, Paul A. *The Civil Rights Movement*. San Diego, Calif.: Greenhaven Press, 2000.

Web sites

We Shall Overcome: Historic Places of the Civil Rights Movement. "Selma-to-Montgomery March." <http://www.cr.nps.gov/nr/travel/civilrights/sitelist1.htm> (accessed June 3, 2006).

Have Sanitation Workers a Future?

Flyer

By: Anonymous

Date: 1968

Source: *U.S. National Archives and Records Administration.* "Teaching With Documents: Court Documents Related to Martin Luther King Jr., and Memphis Sanitation Workers." <http://www.archives.gov/education/lessons/memphis-v-mlk/> (accessed June 2, 2006).

About the Author: The author of the flyer is anonymous but Martin Luther King Jr. was involved in the organization of marches to support the rights of the sanitation workers. King Jr., (1929–1968) was a U.S. civil rights pioneer. He is probably best known for his "I Have a Dream" speech delivered in Washington, D.C., in 1963. He was assassinated in Memphis, Tennessee, in 1968 at the age of thirty-nine.

INTRODUCTION

The 1960s were an unsettled period in U.S. history, with conflict raging over the Vietnam War, generational differences, and civil rights. The South, with its long history of discrimination and segregation, remained particularly volatile. By the mid–1960s, Dr. Martin Luther King Jr.'s "I Have a Dream" speech still reverberated in the ears of activists, and slow headway was being made.

In Memphis, Tennessee, in 1968, racial tensions were running high. Most of Memphis's garbage collectors and sewer department workers were African Americans, and on a rainy day in February,

These New Orleans's dumpsters are filled to overflowing on January 23, 1969, the fourth day of a strike by Sanitation Department workers. © BETTMANN/CORBIS.

two otherwise unrelated events occurred that led to one of the largest civil rights actions of the 1960s.

Memphis garbage collectors endured deplorable working conditions, hoisting leaky garbage cans into dilapidated trucks in all types of weather. The city paid sanitation workers $1.80 per hour with no benefits, vacation, or pension; many of the workers qualified for welfare. The garbage collectors were so fouled by their daily work that other city workers labeled them walking buzzards.

On a rainy February afternoon, two of these workers climbed inside the back of their truck to escape the rain. While they sat inside, an electrical short activated the truck's hydraulic compactor, trapping the men inside and crushing them. The city responded by paying funeral expenses and one month's salary to the men's families.

The second event involved more than twenty workers in the city's sewage department. These black employees were sent home without pay due to the rain, while their white supervisors were allowed to remain at work, drawing their usual salary. While such treatment was hardly unusual, when combined with the deaths of the two sanitation workers, it threw fuel on a racial fire that had been smoldering in Memphis for decades.

With the help of a local labor organizer, the garbage and sewer workers began making plans to form a labor union. In response, the city fired any worker involved in the organizing plans. This action proved to be the final insult, and on February 12, more than three-quarters of the city's sanitation workers went on strike. Over the following weeks, garbage piled up in the city's streets, and local ministers called on their members to boycott city services and march in support of the strike.

PRIMARY SOURCE

Have Sanitation Workers a Future?

Yes. If You Will Help Us Build It.
Now? That's Simple—

WE NEED YOU!

1. Do not shop downtown, or in the downtown branch stores anywhere in the city or any enterprise named Loeb.
2. Stop your subscriptions to the daily newspapers. Get news about the Movement from radio or television and by joining the mass meetings. Be sure to pay your newspaper carrier this commission.
3. Do not buy new things for Easter. Let our Lent be one of sacrifices. What better way to remember Jesus' work for us and the world?
4. Support the workers with letters and telegrams to the Mayor and City Council.
5. Join us in the daily marches downtown.
6. Call others each day and remind them of the movement.
7. Attend nightly mass meetings Monday through Friday.
8. Do not place your garbage at the curb. Handle it the best way you can without helping the city and the Mayor's efforts to break the strike.
9. Whenever you associate with white people, let them know what the issues are and why you support this cause.
10. Support the relief efforts for the workers and their families with gifts of money and food. Checks can be made out to "C.O.M.E." and food taken to Clayborn Temple A.M.E. Church, 280 Hernando.

SIGNIFICANCE

As the strike dragged into March, garbage fires began to spread through the city's south side and hundreds of protestors were arrested, often on trumped-up charges. On March 18, thousands gathered to hear Dr. King speak about the effort, and a citywide march was scheduled for March 22. The march, postponed six days due to snow, began peacefully, but quickly turned violent; police intervened using mace and nightsticks. By its end, hundreds had been arrested and one sixteen-year-old boy was dead. National Guard troops were quickly dispatched to patrol the city and a 7:00 p.m. curfew was instituted.

As April began, tensions cooled somewhat as the city curfew was lifted and National Guard troops were withdrawn. On April 3, King spoke once again, delivering a message in which he alluded to the Biblical leader Moses, who glimpsed the Promised Land but was not permitted to enter it. King's words were strangely prophetic: "I may not get there with you, but I want you to know tonight that we as a people will get to the Promised Land." The following day, after stepping onto his hotel balcony, King was shot dead.

In the aftermath of the killing, riots and marches spread across the country. Protestors from throughout the United States gathered in Memphis, and city residents, many of them white, joined in the peaceful protests. President Lyndon Johnson, whose earlier attempts to mediate the dispute had been rebuffed, quickly dispatched Undersecretary of Labor James Reynolds to Memphis. Following days of intense mediation effort, and in the face of mounting pressure from both President Johnson and Governor Buford Ellington, a settlement was reached on April 16. Under the deal's terms, the city recognized the sanitation workers' union and allowed a dues check-off on worker paychecks.

In the years following the strike, the American Federation of State, County, and Municipal Employees (AFSCME) became the largest labor union in Memphis. Other city workers, including police and firefighters, also organized, and African Americans became more vocal and active in city politics. Safety and working conditions improved significantly in many blue-collar city jobs.

In the twenty-first century, Memphis remains a racially diverse city, with more than 1.2 million residents in the city and surrounding areas split almost equally between white and black. A 1998 survey found that a majority of white residents and two-thirds of black residents rate the city's race relations either average or good, though a second poll conducted around the same time found somewhat lower satisfaction levels. In 1991, Willie W. Herenton became the city's first African American mayor, and, in 2003, was elected to a city-record fourth consecutive term.

FURTHER RESOURCES
Books
Brecher, Jeremy. *Strike!* Revised and updated edition. Cambridge, Mass.: South End Press, 1997.

Estes, Steve S. *I Am a Man!: Race, Manhood, and the Civil Rights Movement*. Chapel Hill: University of North Carolina Press, 2006.

Lacey, Fred. *Memphis Workers Fight: The City Sanitation Workers' Strike*. Boston: New England Free Press, 1969.

Periodicals
Berbier, Mitch, and Elaine Pruette. "When Is Inequality a Problem?" *Journal of Contemporary Ethnography* 35 (2006): 257–284.

Green, Laurie B. "Race, Gender, and Labor in 1960s Memphis: 'I am a man' and the Meaning of Freedom." *Journal of Urban History* 30 (2004): 465–489.

Isaac, Larry. "I Am a Man!" *Southern Cultures* 12 (2006): 96–98.

Web sites

American Rhetoric. "Dr. Martin Luther King, Jr.: 'I Have a Dream.'" <http://www.americanrhetoric.com/speeches/Ihaveadream.htm> (accessed June 2, 2006).

Wayne State University, Walter P. Reuther Library. "Walking Buzzards." <http://www.reuther.wayne.edu/MAN/2Memphis.htm> (accessed June 5, 2006).

Tennessee Halted in School Inquiry

Newspaper article

By: The New York Times

Date: January 15, 1968

Source: "Court Enjoins Legislature on Highlander Study." *The New York Times*, January 15, 1968.

About the Author: *The New York Times* is an American daily newspaper that was first published in 1851, with a circulation of over one million copies.

INTRODUCTION

In 1968, the Highlander Research and Education Center and its predecessor institution had been in operation for more than thirty-five years when Highlander advanced a legal challenge to a renewed attempt by the state legislature of Tennessee to disrupt its operations. The Highlander facility was founded in Tennessee in 1932 by Myles Horton (1905–1990) as the Highland Folk School, a training center for labor organizers and other social and community activists.

Horton had established Highlander in furtherance of his belief that to truly advance the prospects of the poor people of the southern states, both black and white, ordinary people must have access to education. The Highland methods of delivering educational programming were controversial from the time of the school's inception. Highlander did not grant diplomas or degrees for the successful completion of its courses. Instead, the Highlander programs were primarily modeled on the concept of educational workshops, where the accumulation of

knowledge was a collective experience between instructors and students.

By the late 1930s, the Highlander Folk School was active in the training of labor leaders working with the newly established Congress of Industrial Organizations (CIO). At that time, the CIO was endeavoring to organize large segments of the textiles and clothing industries; a nonviolent demonstration technique developed through the relationship between the CIO and the Highlander school during this period was the sit down strike.

Eleanor Roosevelt (1884–1962), wife of U.S. president Franklin Roosevelt, was a strong supporter of the Highland Folk School until her death, an affiliation that was one of many that caused her to be characterized as a 'Red' and a communist sympathizer in American conservative political circles.

The Highlander School became a catalyst to other elements of social activism in the 1950s. Horton was a strong proponent of the aims of the desegregation movements in southern public schools and a number of these activists received both training and support at Highland. In 1957, Highland teachers established a series of programs that became popularly known as the Citizenship Schools. In these programs, uneducated blacks were provided with language and writing instruction to assist them in passing the literacy tests that were a prerequisite to voter registration in southern states such as North and South Carolina. The literacy tests had presented a significant bar to black voter registration in these states.

The Highlander School attracted bitter opposition to both its programs and its very existence from the state establishment in Tennessee. Highlander was depicted in conservative circles as a communist training school and generally un-American in its outlook. The state commenced legal action against Highlander in 1959 to revoke its school charter; after a lengthy legal contest, the state was successful in both closing the school and in securing a forfeiture of the school property. Myles Horton re-established the school as the Highland Research and Education Center in 1962 under a new state charter.

The new Highlander facility continued to operate in much the same fashion as the original school. With the growth of the civil rights movement throughout the South in the years following 1963, Highlander played an important role in the education of many social activists. The backlash against the segregation of institutions such as the University of Alabama in 1963 was directed by some white political forces in

Rosa Parks, Coretta Scott King and Myles Horton sing while Parks has a room in the Martin Luther King Center in Atlanta dedicated in her name, on October 13, 1988. AP IMAGES.

Tennessee into a renewed effort to close Highlander in 1967. This action resulted in the Tennessee state legislature resolution to investigate the school for subversive activities.

PRIMARY SOURCE

Court Enjoins Legislature on Highlander Study

Special to The New York Times

Nashville, Jan 15—A Federal court has ordered the Tennessee Legislature to drop a proposed investigating of "subversive" activities at the Highlander Educational and Research Center.

The court said that legislatures had undisputed authority to investigate, but that the resolution ordering the Highlander study was "void on its face for vagueness and over-breadth."

The ruling was handed down here Thursday by District Judge William E. Miller. Copies of the order were made available today by the American Civil Liberties Union.

The Highlander center and its forerunner, the Highlander folk School, have been in a running battle with Tennessee authorities for 30 years. Critics have linked the institutions with communism and integration.

The folk school was established in 1934 and was initially active in training labor organizers. After World War II, it began promoting the advance of Southern Negroes. The school had many supporters, including Mrs. Franklin D. Roosevelt.

In 1959, the Legislature investigated the school, then located at Monteagle, Tenn. Subsequently, the Legislature ordered local authorities to move for an evocation of the school's charter. That action was successful.

In 1961, the Highlander center was established at Knoxville, Tenn., under a new charter. Myles Horton, who had headed the folk school, became president of the new institution. The civil rights activities were continued.

Last year, the Legislature established a joint committee to investigate a second time and to determine if the center was engaged in "activities subversive of the government of the state."

"While admittedly the states have a legitimate concern in this area," Judge Miller said, "such investigations are fraught with constitutional dangers."

"The term 'subversion' is capable of multiple meanings," he said, adding:

"Without exception the term connotes unpopular words or deeds. Too often, 'subversion' takes on the meaning of any activity which is not in tune with prevailing social, political, economic, or religious values of the community."

Legal authorities believed it was the first time a Federal court had enjoined a state legislative investigation. The ruling is also important, they said, because it touches on first Amendment issues that have been raised elsewhere.

Judge Miller found the proposed investigation a "threat to protected liberties" on two grounds.

He said that the Highlander center could not determine what information the committee would seek and that the resolution did not provide the "requisite guidance . . .to insure that the inquiry is within constitutional boundaries."

The Federal injunction was obtained by a group of lawyers led by Charles Morgan Jr., the Civil Liberties Union counsel in Atlanta, and by I.T. Creswell Jr., Reber F. Boult Jr., Whitworth Stokes Jr., and George E. Barrett, all of Nashville.

SIGNIFICANCE

The attempt by the Tennessee legislature to investigate the alleged subversion practiced at the Highlander school and the subsequent grant of a federal injunction to prevent the state investigation in January 1968 is an episode in the larger civil rights movement in the United States that is significant from legal, political and social perspectives.

In the traditional distribution of constitutional powers between the courts and the state, legislatures enact laws and the investigative agencies of the state, typically sworn law enforcement personnel, further the objects of the legislation in a manner consistent with the scope of the law. The power of a court to review a particular legislative enactment as being within the state's constitutional power is traditionally available after the statute in question has been passed. The inherent judicial power to review any actions taken by an investigative agency may be invoked to quash a search warrant or to suppress the introduction into

evidence in any subsequent proceeding the product of an unlawful search.

The order of the Federal Court to enjoin the Tennessee legislature from acting upon a resolution is unique in American jurisprudence, as the injunction remedy issued in favor of the Highlander school was something of a hybrid of the two traditional injunctive powers of the court. At the time of the issuance of the federal injunction, no investigation had yet been initiated and no evidence had been gathered by an official agency—the resolution of the state legislature could be characterized as a declaration of intent to take a future investigative action. The decision of the Federal Court, in its finding that the legislative resolution was too broadly worded, is akin to the judicial branch of government telling the elected legislators of Tennessee that they are limited in what they may consider for legislative action.

In considering the true intent in the Tennessee resolution to investigate Highlander, it is clear that the initiative was a part of the backlash against the entire civil rights movement that had resulted in significant gains by the black community of the South. For the conservative aspects of Tennessee society and elsewhere in the South, Highlander school represented an ongoing subversive influence in society, particularly in labor relations and in the effort to empower black citizens through voter registration.

The decision of the Tennessee legislature to mount a second attack in less than ten years upon the existence of the Highlander school is as remarkable as the grant of the injunction in Federal court. While Highlander was unquestionably a bastion of left-wing political sympathies, it was supported by a broad coalition of civil rights leaders, including Martin Luther King (1929–1968). Having re-established itself after the first battle with the state in 1961, it seems that the 1967 resolution against Highland was doomed to failure.

The efforts of the Highlander school to promote its Citizenship programs to extend the literacy of black persons in the Carolinas in the late 1950s had contributed to the abolition of literacy testing in the voter registration process mandated by the *Voting Rights Act of 1965*. By 1968, demographic shifts attributable to a greater number of black persons being registered and voting were beginning to be observed in many states, including Tennessee.

The injunction granted in the federal Court was never appealed by the state of Tennessee, and the decision remains a startling precedent as to the breadth of the judicial powers claimed against a state legislature. The actions of the state and the grant of the injunction provided both Highlander and the causes with which it was identified significant favorable publicity. Highlander became a key player in the social activism known as the *Poor People's Campaign* in 1968. In subsequent years, programs assisting in the alleviation of poverty in the Appalachian region became a training focus at the Highlander center. The school ran a number of ongoing workshops and other long-term initiatives to publicize the economic and environmental problems caused to the people of Appalachia through strip mining in the coal fields and related occupational health and safety issues. Highlander also provided ongoing support to community groups throughout the Appalachian region to provide better community medical education.

In recent years, Highlander has expanded its educational activism to embrace global issues, particularly those related to the environment and immigration. Since 1967, the Highlander facility has prospered as a provider of education and training on a wide array of social issues.

FURTHER RESOURCES

Books

Glen, John. *Highlander: No Ordinary School*. Knoxville: University of Tennessee Press, 1996.

Horton, Aimee Isgrig. *The Highlander Folk School, 1932–1961*. Toronto: Catalyst Centre, 2002.

Horton, Myles, and Dale Jacobs, ed. *Myles Horton Reader: Education for Social Change*. Knoxville: University of Tennessee Press, 2003.

Periodicals

Levine, Daniel P. "The Birth of Citizenship Schools: Entwining the Struggles for Literacy and Freedom." *The History of Education Quarterly* 44, 3, (2004): 388–414.

Web sites

PBS. "The American Experience: Eleanor Roosevelt." 1999 <http://www.pbs.org/wgbh/amex/eleanor/sfeature/fbi_rp_01.html> (accessed June 25, 2006).

Olympic Athletes on Podium

Photograph

By: Anonymous

Date: October 17, 1968

Source: AP/Wide World Photos. Reproduced by permission.

About the Photographer: This photograph is a part of the photographic archive maintained by the Associated Press, an international news media organization.

INTRODUCTION

During the summer of 1968, American race relations were a more persistent and contentious social issue than at any time since the end of the Civil War. Ironically, black athletes had established themselves as elite performers in every major team sport in the United States: In the National Football League, players such as Jim Brown, Gale Sayers, and David (Deacon) Jones were stars. NBA centers Wilt Chamberlain and Bill Russell were basketball icons. The major league baseball color barrier had fallen only 20 years before; black players such as Willie Mays and Henry Aaron were stars generally accepted on an equal footing with the best white players.

The performance of the United States Summer Olympic team in 1968 corresponded with the success enjoyed by black athletes in American professional sports. One hundred meter sprinter Jim Hines and long jumper Bob Beamon both established world records in their events. The world record set by 400-meter runner Lee Evans in Mexico remained unbroken for almost 25 years.

The ascendancy of so many athletes, however, stood in stark contrast to the social dilemmas created by desegregation and the problems faced by ordinary black Americans. Issues such as school integration, voter registration laws, and initiatives to help blacks secure better employment opportunities all spurred protracted national debate.

By 1968, discontent within the black communities of the United States had spawned a variety of organizations and individuals dedicated to social change. Some, such as Dr. Martin Luther King (1929–1968), advocated nonviolent means to accomplish their goals. Others, such as Malcolm X (1925–1965) and groups such as the Black Panthers, advocated more violent measures to achieve equality. "Black power" became a catchphrase that described any organization or attitude that sought to advance black interests.

Against this backdrop of American success and social upheaval, sprinters Tommie Smith and John Carlos, gold and bronze medalists respectively in the 200-meter sprint final, ascended the Olympic podium.

PRIMARY SOURCE

OLYMPIC ATHLETES ON PODIUM
See primary source image.

PRIMARY SOURCE

Olympic Athletes on Podium: Tommie Smith (center) and John Carlos (right) at the 1968 Mexico City Olympics. The two men used the international spotlight of the medal ceremony honoring their first and third place finishes in the 200-meter sprint to deliver a protest against racism in the United States. AP/WIDE WORLD PHOTOS. REPRODUCED BY PERMISSION.

SIGNIFICANCE

The photograph of sprinters Tommie Smith and John Carlos is one of the most famous in the history of sport. Their clenched fists and bowed heads remain the most enduring image of the 1968 Summer Olympics.

The gesture was not entirely a surprise to other members of the United States Olympic Team. In the period leading up to the Olympics in October 1968, Smith and other black athletes had been encouraged to boycott the Games by an American organization, the Olympic Project for Human Rights (OPHR) which believed that so long as blacks generally occupied second-class status in America, they should not support its national Olympic team. After much discussion, however, Smith decided to compete.

Smith and Carlos used symbolism to send a political message to the world. Both men wore black socks, without shoes, to symbolize poverty and racist oppression. Smith clenched his right fist, to symbolize the power and Carlos raised his left as an example of the unity of the black people, respectively. Smith wore a scarf around his neck to signify black pride; Carlos wore beads to honor those who had died in lynchings and other violent acts. Neither man sang the American anthem as it was played. Each wore an OPHR badge, as did silver medalist Peter Newman of Australia, a white athlete who acted in solidarity at their request.

Repercussions for the two were immediate; the crowd at the stadium booed them. Within a few hours, both were removed from the American Olympic team and were expelled from the Games by the International Olympic Committee. On their return to the United States, both Carlos and Smith received death threats and their personal lives became difficult. Carlos had significant difficulty finding employment of any kind, particularly within the athletic community, while Smith eventually played professional football for three years, then went on to become a sports educator and coach in track and field events.

Smith and Carlos saw little financial benefit from their actions. Neither man entered into a book contract or endorsement agreement of any sort, as might have been the case today. Smith stated that his intention was to stand up for black America, however, and there can be little doubt that he achieved that objective to a considerable extent. There is no question that their Black Power salute was the first such demonstration in a world sports forum; it spurred debate about the position of blacks in American society, but whether Smith and Carlos moved or persuaded anyone was also debatable.

That debate may have been settled in October 2005, when Smith and Carlos's alma mater, San Jose State University in California, dedicated a statute on its campus to honor their actions in Mexico City, as a symbol of the struggle in the advancement of black people in America.

FURTHER RESOURCES
Books

McCartney, John T. *Black Power Ideologies: An Essay in African-American Political Thought.* Philadelphia; Temple University Press, 2006.

Ogban, Jeffrey Ogbonna Green. *Black Power: Radical Politics and African American Identity.* Baltimore; Johns Hopkins University Press, 2004.

Tommie Smith throws up his hands in celebration after winning the 200-meter dash at the Mexico City Olympics, October 16, 1968. Silver medalist Peter Norman is behind Smith, bronze medalist John Carlos is left of Smith. © BETTMANN/CORBIS.

Web sites

British Broadcasting Corporation. "On This Day: October 17." <http://news.bbc.co.uk/onthisday/hi/dates/stories/october/17/newsid_3535000/3535348.stm> (accessed May 19, 2006).

Godfather Wins Oscar As Best Film

Newspaper article

By: Steven V. Roberts

Date: March 28, 1973

Source: Roberts, Steven V. "Godfather Wins Oscar As Best Film." The *New York Times* (March 28, 1973).

About the Author: American writer, journalist, and commentator Steven V. Roberts (1943–) writes for several

publications such as the *New York Times* and the *U.S. News & World Report*. Roberts also appears regularly as a guest on such radio and television stations as ABC Radio, CNN, and PBS, and on such programs as "Washington Week in Review" and "Hardball with Chris Matthews." In addition, he and his wife, Cokie Roberts, write a nationally syndicated newspaper column and are contributing writers for the magazine *USA Weekend*.

INTRODUCTION

Oscar-winning American actor Marlon Brando (1924–2004) is widely considered one of the greatest film actors in modern times. Brando is probably best remembered for his portrayals of Stanley Kowalski in the movie "A Streetcar Named Desire" (1951), a rebellious motorcyclist named Johnny in *The Wild One* (1953), Terry Malloy in *On the Waterfront* (1954), Don Vito Corleone in *The Godfather* (1972), and Colonel Kurtz in *Apocalypse Now* (1979).

Sashim Littlefeather informs the audience at the Academy Awards that Marlon Brando will decline to accept his Oscar as best actor for his role in "The Godfather", to protest the treatment of American Indians in motion pictures and on television. AP IMAGES.

In the gangster movie *The Godfather*, Brando was awarded the Academy Award for Best Actor in 1972 (his second and last Oscar) for his captivating portrayal of the head of a Mafia crime family. Brando, however, refused to attend the Academy Award ceremony. Instead, he boycotted it on March 27, 1973, by sending Sacheen Littlefeather, who wore a traditional Apache deerskin dress and turquoise jewelry to decline the award on Brando's behalf.

Littlefeather was about to deliver a political speech written by Brando about the plight of Native Americans when a high-ranking representative for the Academy told her that she would be forcibly removed from the stage if she talked for more than forty-five seconds. Thus, the woman was forced to paraphrase the content of Brando's intended speech. The abbreviated speech and the original speech, which Littlefeather gave to the media afterwards, involved a blistering criticism about how poorly the Native

Americans have been treated and depicted within the film industry and by government policy. Littlefeather also stated that Brando was angry with the U.S. government concerning its history of crimes against Native Americans, particularly the 1890 massacre by U.S. troops of Native Americans at Wounded Knee in South Dakota.

Upon finishing the speech, Littlefeather was applauded by some people but was also booed by others in the audience who did not appreciate her criticizing how Hollywood portrayed Native Americans. It was later publicized that Littlefeather was born Maria Cruz (1947–) and was not a Native American but a minor actress and activist of Mexican descent. It was still later learned that Littlefeather was indeed part Native American with bloodlines of Apache, Yaqui, Pueblo, and Caucasian. At this time, she primarily worked as a public service director for a San Francisco Bay-area radio station and participated in the American Indian Movement (AIM), which included the November 1969–June 1971 occupation by Native Americans at Alcatraz Island, the site of the former prison in San Francisco Bay. The protest was intended to popularize poor conditions under which many Native Americans lived while on reservations throughout the United States.

PRIMARY SOURCE

Hollywood, Calif, March 27—the Oscar awards were a cabaret—and sometimes a political platform.

"The Godfather," the legend of an aging Mafia chieftain, won the award as best picture of the year, but it won only two others out of a total of 10 nominations.

Marlon Brando received the Oscar for his portrayal of the title role in "The Godfather," but he refused to accept it as a protest against the movie industry's treatment of the American Indian.

In place of Mr. Brando, a young Apache named Shasheen Little Feather surprised the star-laden audience by taking the sage and delivering an emotional diatribe against the film community.

That community, she told the press conference later, has "been responsible for making a mockery of Indians" and "injuring the minds of Indian children."

Mr. Brando, she said, thought he could be "of more use" by journeying to Wounded Knee, S D., where a group of militant Indians have been protesting for the last month.

Afterwards, Clint Eastwood, one of tonight's masters of ceremonies, came on and asked whether someone would say a word on behalf of all the cowboys killed in those Western films.

It was the second time in two years that an Oscar for best actor had been turned down. In 1971 George C. Scott announced that he did not want to be considered for an Oscar for his performance in "Patton," but the Academy gave it to him anyway. His Oscar remains unclaimed.

SIGNIFICANCE

Beginning in the early 1960s, Marlon Brando was actively involved with the rights of the Native Americans. In fact, he was arrested on March 2, 1964 in Washington State while supporting the fishing rights of Native Americans on the Puyallup River after the state government attempted to regulate their fishing on the river.

During the mid–1970s, Brando was concerned about the future of Native Americans. During the 1973 Academy Awards ceremony, he indicated through Littlefeather that he would not attend the festivities so that he could help at the incident occurring at Wounded Knee. At the time, AIM members were occupying the town of Wounded Knee, which is located on the Pine Ridge Oglala Sioux Reservation in South Dakota. During the 71-day standoff at Wounded Knee in 1973, two Native Americans were killed and a U.S. marshal was paralyzed in the fighting that occurred between members of AIM and local supporters and members of the Federal Bureau of Investigation (FBI), U.S. marshals, and the Bureau of Indian Affairs. Although a committee was later appointed to investigate the grievances levied by AIM leaders, no official response was ever given. Brando never made it inside Wounded Knee, stating in his autobiography that he arrived too late to gain entrance. Brando also contributed to many Native American organizations and fundraisers in support for the rights of Native Americans.

By turning down the Oscar at the Academy Awards ceremony, Brando caused a large controversy in the Hollywood actor's community. At the time, the Brando/Littlefeather incident was considered an offensive and embarrassing event for the film industry. Brando considered the award ceremony trivial when compared to the discrimination, poverty, and misrepresentations that were being forced upon the Native Americans. The incident was talked about across the United States for quite a while. Today, the incident is considered another of a long list of bizarre incidents that happen in Hollywood. After the incident, Brando told reporters that his act of refusing the Oscar was not meant to show disrespect for the award.

Brando was well known as an activist for Native American rights. He adopted and identified with many of their religious and spiritual traditions. In his autobiography *Songs My Mother Taught Me*, Brando discusses in two chapters his thoughts about Native Americans and relates some of his experiences with them. The incident at the Academy Awards ceremony helped to create additional motivation for Native Americans and positive public relations for their movement. Primarily, Brando lent his celebrity status and provided monetary funds to help promote the rights of Native Americans.

FURTHER RESOURCES
Books

Bosworth, Patricia. *Marlon Brando*. New York: Viking, 2001.

Brando, Marlon, with Robert Lindsey. *Brando: Songs My Mother Taught Me*. New York: Random House, 1994.

Carey, Gary. *Marlon Brando: The Only Contender*. New York: St. Martin's Press, 1985.

Grobel, Lawrence. *Conversations with Brando*. New York: Cooper Square Press, 1999.

Manso, Peter. *Brando: The Biography*. New York: Hyperion, 1994.

Thomson, David. *Marlon Brando*. New York: DK, 2003.

Web sites

American Movie Classics (AMC). "Marlon Brando." <http://www.amctv.com/person/detail?CID=1642-1-EST> (accessed May 27, 2006).

New York Times. "That Unfinished Oscar Speech." <http://www.nytimes.com/packages/html/movies/bestpictures/godfather-ar3.html> (accessed June 3, 2006).

Britain's 1981 Urban Riots

Magazine article

By: Anonymous

Date: September 1981

Source: "Britain's 1981 Urban Riots." *Searchlight* (September 1981): 16–20.

About the Author: *Searchlight* magazine is a British publication focusing on the movement against racism and fascism.

INTRODUCTION

In April 1981, riots broke out Brixton, a district in south London whose population is largely black. These riots followed the stabbing death of a black youth and were generalized as a protest against racial discrimination. However, as the year progressed, additional riots erupted in other parts of England and brought attention to the plight of nonwhites, as well as to oppression and institutionalized racism on the part of the police. To better understand the circumstances that fueled the riots, the British government commissioned Lord Scarman to investigate the causes of the riots. The Scarman report cited the racial disadvantage of the Brixton residents as a catalyst for the violence. Following the July riots in Southall, a district in western London, and Liverpool, the scope of Lord Scarman's report was expanded to investigate these riots as well. In these riots, however, whites joined the violent demonstrations along with the nonwhites, suggesting that the catalyst was more than racial discrimination.

In 1981, Brixton was almost entirely populated by descendents of black West Indian immigrants. Approximately half of this population was unemployed at the time that the riots broke out. During this period, the police were engaged in "Operation Swamp," which

involved stopping and searching youths. Employing the broad "sus" laws that allowed police to stop and search anyone suspected of planning a crime, the police mainly targeted the black youths in Brixton. On April 10, 1981, the crowd that gathered suggested that the officers were antagonizing an injured man. Unemployment, the economic depression of the district, and distrust of the police heightened tensions and set off these first riots. These riots left 300 people injured, eighty-three buildings burned, and twenty-three vehicles damaged.

More riots occurred in other parts of London. In Southall, a predominantly Asian suburb, tensions were ripe for violence following a 1979 confrontation between Asian youths and the police. The confrontation was provoked by the death of Blair Peach, an Asian anti-racism activist, who was allegedly killed by the National Front, a right-wing white supremacy organization. The Asian community harbored resentment toward the police, believing that Peach's death had not been adequately investigated. When a right-wing neo-Nazis planned a concert at the Hambrough

Wrecked buildings and cars in Brixton, London, following the 1981 riots. © RICHARD OLIVIER/CORBIS.

Tavern in Southall in July 1981, the scene was set for conflict to occur. The skinheads who converged on the district passed out flyers to the local residents and displayed white supremacy paraphernalia. This provoked the youths in this largely Pakistani population to respond by burning down the tavern. This act touched off several days of confrontations between the Asian youths and police.

In Liverpool, nine days of riots followed the heavy-handed arrest of a black motorcyclist. The motorcyclist escaped arrest when a crowd surrounded the officers. Tensions between residents and the police had been strained by widespread police detention, particularly of black youths. In addition, the police were accused of oppressive tactics such as harassing and planting drugs on youths and beating suspects. As a result, when the motorcyclist was stopped, a crowd gathered and allowed him to escape. During this episode, several police officers were injured. Although this appeared at first to be a racially motivated response by blacks to police oppression, subsequent reports have found that whites and blacks acted together against the police during these nine days. Crowds of black and white men used overturned cars to create barricades, while youths threw rocks and petrol bombs at the police. By the end of these riots, over 500 people had been arrested and seventy buildings had been demolished.

◼ PRIMARY SOURCE

The July 'riots' marked a turning point in British politics. They showed us that the anger of black youth, condemned to permanent unemployment and harassment, knows no bounds. Their actions on the streets destroyed at a stroke the myth that the police are invincible—a lesson not lost on the dispossessed white youth. For if the April 'riot' in Brixton demonstrated the pent-up anger of the black youth, the July 'riots' showed us that the malaise went deeper still. In Merseyside and many other cities it was the youth of the working class—black and white side by side—petrol bombing the police, their vehicles and their police stations.

SOUTHALL

The 'riots' began over the weekend of July 3–5. As dusk fell on Friday July 3, coachloads of skinheads arrived in Southall for a concert at the notoriously racist Hambrough Tavern in the Broadway.

The "coaches had a National Front banner and they (the youths) were all wearing National Front medallions" (*Guardian* 4.7.81). Trouble started quickly. A group of skinheads attacked the wife of the owner of an Asian shop, the Maharajah general stores. Later, her husband, Darshanlal Kalhan said: "Whatever our boys did was purely in self-

defence. It was an unprovoked attack. There will be no foolish action from our people, but if anyone comes again and tries the same thing, God help them. We can control our children so far, but no further." (*Sunday Times* 5.7.81).

Immediately after the attack, hundreds of Asian youth came onto the streets and besieged the pub. Only 30 police were on the spot and by 10pm the pub had been set ablaze with petrol bombs. Police reinforcements, 600 were there by 11pm, fought a pitched battle with the Asian youth. One of the injured Asians, 35 year old Narotam Lal who had been knocked unconscious by police said: "One of the policemen told me: 'You will be another Blair Peach'" (*News of the World* 5.7.81).

. . . Even as the television was carrying pictures of the street fighting and fires in Southall, and Eldon Griffiths, Tory MP and adviser to the Police Federation, was calling for the introduction of water cannon on the radio news, no one realized that within hours Toxteth in Liverpool would be in flames.

LIVERPOOL

Over four nights of 'rioting', starting on the Friday, 150 buildings were burnt down, 258 police needed hospital treatment, and 160 people were arrested. In the now familiar pattern a small incident provided the 'spark' for the weekend. At 9pm a black motorcyclist was stopped by the police, a crowd gathered, the motorcyclist was handcuffed, put in a blue transit, and police reinforcements called for. The crowd stoned the police and the motorcyclist jumped from the van and was dragged away by the crowd. Masses of police arrived, with truncheons drawn, a battle ensued. The one person arrested was Leroy Cooper, who happened to be nearest to the police van. He was charged with two counts of GBH to two officers and actual bodily harm to another (*Daily Post* 6.7.81).

. . . On the Friday, police vehicles in Toxteth were repeatedly stoned by roaming gangs until 1pm in the morning. On the Saturday, shortly after 10pm, youth stoned police cars and started setting fire to derelict buildings. By 12.30 barricades had been thrown up and police with riot shields were rushed in to be met with petrol bombs, bricks and chunks of concrete. By 5am buildings were still blazing. At 6am 90 reinforcements arrived from Greater Manchester and charged the black and white youth: "They were banging their batons on their riot shields. It was like something from the film *Zulu*, commented one youth" (*Sun* 6.7.81).

'Order' was restored by 7.30am on the Sunday morning. . . .

On the Sunday and through to early Monday morning "all hell" was to break loose in the words of one policeman. The scale of the 'riot' is hard to convey. Building after building was set on fire. A black community worker said: "It was obvious why people went for the police, but there were exact reasons why each of those buildings was hit. The bank for obvious reasons, the Racquets Club because the judges use it, Swainbanks furniture store because people felt he was ripping off the community." . . .

With 800 police in the area, with reinforcements from Cheshire, Lancashire and Greater Manchester the police totally lost control of Toxteth. The ferocity of the 'rioters' completely smashed the ranks of the police who retreated from the area at 11pm. Unigate milk floats were set on fire and directed at the police lines; scaffolding poles were used to charge the pockets of riot-shielded police and petrol bombs rained down. At 1am the Press Association reported that looting was widespread with not a policeman in sight. In one incident the police brought out an old fire engine and tried to hose down the 'rioters' but it was "seized" and "set alight" (*Press Association* 1.17am). At 2.15am the police started firing CS gas. It later emerged that several of the gas cartridges were intended for use only in a siege when cars or the walls of buildings had to be penetrated (*New Statesman* 1.7.81). At least four people were badly injured: one 21 year old black footballer, Phil Robbins, was hit in the chest and back by one of the gas canisters which should not have been used.

Oxford claimed on the Sunday that: 'It is exclusively a crowd of black hooligans intent on making life unbearable and indulging in criminal activities" (*Guardian* 6.7.81). This matched his remark in 1978 when he described black Liverpudlians as "the product of liaisons between white prostitutes and African sailors" (*New Statesman* 17.7.81). But it is clear from every report that it was the black and white youth together who fought the police, and more than that, middle-aged white women were reportedly helping to make petrol bombs for the kids to throw.

Pictures in the press also belied this interpretation. There were orderly queues outside shops while people— young, old, and middle-aged—waited their turn to take their pickings from the shops. This is not the first time that this has happened in Liverpool; it occurred in 1911 and again in 1919 during the police strike. What happened in Toxteth was not a 'raceriot', it was the working class of the area rising up against the police and the symbols of a society whose fruits are denied to them.

The Deputy Chief Constable, Peter Wright, could find no comprehension for what happened. "These people are destroying their own neighbourhood" (*New Standard* 6.7.81). In sharp contrast was the article by a black woman journalist on the *Daily Post*, June Henfrey: "The people of Toxteth have long been dissatisfied with the type of policing they get. Some months ago a young white woman told me that she thought people in Liverpool 8 should be paid danger money for living there,

not because of crime but because of the level of police activity . . . At least no one so far has suggested that the youngsters of Toxteth should be sent home. They are at home, and bitter though it may be not to find the promised land in a strange country, it is infinitely more so to be dispossessed in one's own." (6.7.81.).

"REPRESSION . . . THE ONLY ANSWER"

Mrs Thatcher, who appeared on the television news opening the Royal Agricultural Show in Warwickshire, commented: "I am very concerned about what has happened. It is terrible." A debate in the commons on the Monday was described in a *Guardian* editorial: "As with Northern Ireland, the political mood in the House of Commons yesterday was overwhelmingly one of bafflement. . . . Suddenly, forces appear to have been unleashed which nobody knows how to control" (Guardian 7.81.) . . . What was already becoming clear from the government, the state and the media was that the only response was going to be one of greater repression. . . .

MANCHESTER

The major 'rioting' of the week occurred in Manchester. 'Rioting' broke out in three separate areas of Moss Side in the early hours of Wednesday morning when 300 black and white youths petrol bombed and stoned police, and set fire to shops. . . .

On the Thursday night: "24 police wagons each manned by 10 steel-helmeted riot police roared around the shopping and housing area pinning black and white youths to walls and arresting them. Several youths were knocked to the ground by the wagons . . . The rioters moved on to take up positions in high rise flats and flyovers to hurl down rocks on the wagons. Later snatch squads of police moved into the flats. Youths—black and white— were kicked to the ground before being taken away." (Daily Mirror 10.7.81).

On July 21 a white local GP and deacon of the Moss Side Baptist church, Donald Bodey said that he injuries inflicted on people by the police were "terrifying ", and published his case notes (*Times* 22.7.81).

BRITAIN ABLAZE

The 'riots' of the weekend of July 10–12 took place in over 30 towns and cities, and in many cities 'rioting' took place in several different areas. The police national plan for providing mutual aid to neighbouring forces was in tatters. The places affected were: Bradford, Halifax, Blackburn, Preston, Liverpool, Birkenhead, Ellesemere Port, Chester, Stoke Shrewsbury, Wolverhampton, Birmingham, High Wycombe, Southampton, Newcastle, Knaresborough, Leeds, Hull, Huddersfield, Sheffield, Stockport, Nottingham,

Derby, Leicester, Luton, London, Maidstone, Aldershot and Portsmouth.

The Sunday papers, unable to keep up with the events of the weekend, contained many diverse comments. Three in particular are worth recording; in the *Observer* regular columnist Alan Watkins wrote: "For myself, I should support the shooting of petrol bombers on sight" (12.7.81). Over the page author James McClure recorded what happened in Toxteth in the bar of the central Liverpool police station. One of the stories he overheard was: "There was this one young bobby in the line ... and he's taking a batterin' for five hours and his bottle goes— he's away, shield, the lot, down a side street, cryin'—gets into a doorway with his shield over him. He's sobbin' away, y'know, and there's this voice behind him: 'Come on lad! On yer feet! Let's see you back up there.' 'I can't sarge', he says. 'I'm not your sergeant', the voice says, 'I'm a super-intendent.' The bobby jumps up: 'bloody hell', he says, 'I didn't realise I'd run that far.'"

While in the *Sunday Telegraph*, a lone voice, John Alderson, the Chief Constable for Devon and Cornwall, said in an interview that the police had already over-reacted. Asked if a hardline police response was now inevitable, he replied: "Emphatically not. There has to be a better way than blind repression." And asked if he would approve of the use of CS gas, water cannon and rubber-bullets ... replied: " ... and guns, and machine guns, mobs with guns and cells of gunmen and bombs under cars? Where does the escalation stop? We are at a critical watershed" (12.7.81).

SIGNIFICANCE

Lord Scarman released his report in November 1981 and identified racial discrimination and economic deprivation to be the culprits in creating the fertile ground for the discontent displayed during the riots. The report was the first recognition that police practiced discrimination. The report further encouraged Britons to embrace ethnic diversity and employ policies to end discrimination. As a result, the British government began to recognize its poor treatment of minority groups. The government initiated policies giving support to cultural centers and ethnic festivals. In addition, "sus" laws were amended to require police have reasonable suspicion before they could stop and search individuals. Since the 1981 riots, some progress has been made toward racial diversity as displayed through the presence of nonwhite members of parliament. In addition, the number of nonwhite police in London has risen to seven percent.

FURTHER RESOURCES
Periodicals
Cowell, Alan. "What Britain Can Tell France About Rioters." *New York Times* (November 11, 2005).

"Learning from Lawrence." *Economist* (February 27, 1999).

Moody, John. "Europe Street Wars: Youths Vent Their Rage." *Time* (October 14, 1985).

Web sites
BBC. "Brixton and Toxteth Riots 1981." <http://www.bbc.co.uk/history/timelines/england/pwar_brixton_toxteth_riots.shtml> (accessed May 10, 2006).

Afghan Women Tear off Burqas

News article

By: Pierre Celerier

Date: November 20, 2001

Source: Celerier, Pierre. "Afghan Women Tear off Burqas." Agence France Presse, November 20, 2001.

About the Author: Pierre Celerier works as a correspondent for the Agence France Presse, a worldwide news agency based in Paris.

INTRODUCTION

In 1992, the Soviet backed government ruling in Afghanistan dissolved leading to the outbreak of civil war among warlords rivaling for power. By 1994, the Taliban emerged as a group of mullahs, or Islamic scholars, with a tremendous arsenal and following. Led by Mullah Mohammad Omar, the Taliban began to seize power throughout Afghanistan through policies of aggressively attacking opponents and successfully neutralized the rivaling warlords. In 1996, the Taliban captured Kabul, the capital, and established the Islamic Emirate of Afghanistan. The Taliban successfully instituted Sharia or Islamic law and the government was led by Islamic scholars. The foundation of the social policies of the Taliban was found in both the Deobandi interpretation of Islamic law and in the traditions of Pashtunwali, or the tribal code of the Pashtuns. Policies dictating social behavior were enforced by the Ministry for the Enforcement of

Afghan women clad in burqas are part of a group of protestors gathered in front of the presidential palace in Kabul, Afghanistan, on May 8, 2004. They are there to demand the government protect the rights of the disabled. AP IMAGES.

Virtue and Suppression of Vice, or the Amr bil-Maroof wa Nahi An il-Munkir.

Edicts which governed social behavior under the Taliban encompassed aspects of everyday life. The Taliban imposed a ban on the watching of movies, television and videos. In addition, listening to music was banned. Men were ordered not to shave or trim their beards, mandating that the facial hair should protrude from the chin. Those people with non-Islamic names were ordered to change the names to Islamic ones. All people were ordered to attend prayers in mosques five times a day. Certain sports deemed to be un-Islamic were banned. In addition, the wearing of white shoes or white socks was prohibited because the Taliban flag was white.

As a result of these oppressive policies, many nations refused to recognize the Taliban as the government of Afghanistan. However, United Arab Emirates, Pakistan, and Saudi Arabia were the few countries that recognized the Taliban.

In addition to the strict social polices that encumbered the general population, the Taliban placed additional restrictions on women. One of the first acts by the Taliban was to close girl's schools. In addition, women were prohibited from working outside their homes. Hospitals were segregated and only fully clothed women and girls could only be examined by a male doctor. Women were not allowed to laugh in public, let ankles or wrists show, or wear nail polish. In addition, women could not move outside their homes without a mahram (a close male relative such as a father, brother or husband) to escort her. Those women who broke the restrictions placed upon them could be publicly beaten by the religious police under the Department for the Propagation of Virtue and the Suppression of Vice. As a result of the strict social policies under the Taliban, ninety percent of women and sixty percent of men were illiterate. No elections or political debates were held. The policies regarding medical treatment resulted in Afghanistan having the second highest maternity mortality rate in the world.

The Taliban also required women moving outside of their homes to wear a burqa. A full burqa covers the entire face and body of the woman, in addition to a net curtain which conceals the woman's eyes. The burqa existed in Afghanistan before the Taliban's rise to power but was not required by law, until they came to power. The policy was enforced by threats and beating by the religious police. The burqa became a metaphor for the oppression felt by women under the Taliban's policies. However, the policy was also economically oppressive. The cost of purchasing a burqa prevented many women from owning their own. Neighborhoods shared a single burqa and women not in possession of the dressing could not leave their homes.

■ PRIMARY SOURCE

Around 200 Afghan women threw off their burqa veils in the Afghan capital Tuesday in a symbolic protest to demand respect for women's rights after the collapse of the Taliban regime. They included former politicians, academics, activists and teachers who had been confined indoors or forced to wear the hated burqa, which covered them from head to foot, in public for the past five years.

"You are the heroic women of Kabul," organiser Soraya Parlika told the group, members of the newly formed Union of Women in Afghanistan. "You have been imprisoned in your own homes, you have been beaten, you have been deprived of work and forced to beg, but you stood firm and you should be called heroes. Now it's time to fight for your rights."

But the group was forced to cancel its planned protest march from a residential suburb to the main United Nations compound due to security concerns. "They told me they could not provide an assurance of security on the route because they don't have enough police," Parlika said, referring to the anti-Taliban opposition forces who now control the city.

Even so the women, who wore light head-scarves covering their hair, were among the first to show their faces in public here since the Taliban captured the city in 1996. The Taliban evacuated Kabul a week ago in the face of heavy U.S. air strikes and opposition ground attacks, ending their hardline Islamic rule condemned around the world for its treatment of women.

To uphold a misguided notion of women's "honor," females were denied education and banned from all work except in the health sector. They could not leave their homes without a burqa—which covered even their faces

in a cloth mesh—and could not travel without a close male relative.

In the last months of the Taliban's radical Islamic regime here, leader Mullah Mohammad Omar even issued a decree banning women from attending picnics, deemed a sinful pleasure with no place in Islam. But hopes are high that with the collapse of the Taliban a new constitution guaranteeing equal rights for women will be drawn up ahead of the creation of a broad-based, multi-ethnic government.

Parlika, a former communist and secretary general of the Afghan Red Crescent, said the first priority for the women of Kabul was the right to work. Many have lost husbands in the past twenty years of war, but under the Taliban, widows were reduced to begging to support their families. Thousands of others relied on foreign food aid.

The opposition Northern Alliance, which is not as hardline as the Taliban but has a far from spotless record on women's rights, has urged women to go back to work.

In a symbolic gesture a few hours after they marched into the city last Tuesday, a woman's voice was heard reading the news on Radio Afghanistan. "I did not expect that I would ever be back on the radio," said newsreader Jamila Mujahed. "Now I sit here at the microphone and think that I am dreaming."

United Nations Human Rights Commissioner Mary Robinson on Monday said a post-Taliban government in Afghanistan must include women. "With regard to the future of Afghanistan it is crucial that strong government institutions be established with the full participation of women," Robinson said in New Delhi. "They should have the capacity to promote and protect all human rights in a non-discriminatory and effective manner."

■

SIGNIFICANCE

Prior to the Taliban's rise to power in Afghanistan, women's rights were protected under the Afghan constitution. In the 1920s, Afghan women were granted the right to vote and the 1960s constitution provides for gender equality under the law. By 1977, women occupied positions in the highest legislative body. In the 1990s, seventy percent of schoolteachers were women, fifty percent of government workers were women and forty percent of doctors in Kabul were women. The 1996 edict that prevented women from working reduced many women to poverty after losing their jobs.

With the overthrow of the Taliban by the U.S. backed Northern Alliance, the prospects for women have improved. Following the overthrow, women were invited to participate in talks to form the new Afghan government. The new constitution provides for gender equality, grants women the right to vote, allows women to run for office, and permits women to own and inherit property. In addition, at the December 2003 elections, sixty-four of the 500 seats at the National Council went to women.

FURTHER RESOURCES

Periodicals

Kim, Lucian. "Tenacity under Afghan Burqas." *Christian Science Monitor*. July 19, 2000.

Thrupkaew, Noy. "Behind the Burqa." *American Prospect*. November 5, 2001.

Web sites

U.S. Department of State. "Report on the Taliban's war on women." November 17, 2001. <http://www.state.gov/g/drl/rls/6185.htm> (accessed May 15, 2006).

Boycott Beijing 2008

Editorial

By: Reporters Sans Frontières

Date: 2001

Source: *Reporters sans frontières.* "Why We Are Boycotting Beijing 2008?" 2001. <http://www.rsf.org/rubrique.php3?id_rubrique=174> (accessed May 17, 2006).

About the Author: *Reporters sans frontières* is an independent international organization that works to eliminate censorship laws that restrict freedom of press. The organization has branches in Germany, Austria, Belgium, Canada, Spain, France, Italy, Sweden, and Switzerland, and offices in Abidjan (Côte d'Ivoire), Bangkok, New York, Tokyo, and Washington, and maintains a trilingual (French, English, and Spanish) website also known as Reporters without Borders and *Reporteros sin fronteras.*

INTRODUCTION

The Olympic Charter states that "the goal of the Olympic movement is to contribute to building a peaceful and better world by educating youth through sport practiced without discrimination of any kind." Ideally, pure athletic talent, and not race, gender, religious belief, or politics, should determine an athletes' participation. Unfortunately, Olympic Games

have been used as a propaganda tool and a political instrument, threatening the Olympic ideal.

The Nazis appropriated the Games in Berlin, Germany, in 1936, despite public protests about the regime and its racist policies. During the 1956 Games in Melbourne, Australia, the Suez crisis and Soviet oppression in Hungary prompted some countries to withdraw from the competition. The International Olympic Committee (IOC) voted to expel the Republic of South Africa in 1964 for its apartheid policies [laws that permitted discrimination against people of color]. The ban ended in 1992, after South Africa renounced its repressive and racist policies. At the 1968 Mexico City Games, African American athletes protested racial discrimination in the United States. In 1972, Rhodesia, another white-ruled African nation known for its apartheid policies, was banned from the Games just four days before their start.

The most tragic intrusion of politics into the Olympic Games occurred during the Munich Games in 1972, when eight Palestinian terrorists murdered two Israeli athletes and kidnapped nine others in an attempt to gain the release of Palestinian prisoners held in Israel. When an ill-prepared German rescue attempt failed, the Palestinians murdered the remaining hostages.

Several countries have declined participation in the Games as a means of political protest. More than twenty African and Arab nations boycotted the 1976 Montreal Games. They demanded that New Zealand, a country with ties to South Africa, be expelled. The IOC refused. Four years later, as many as sixty countries, led by the United States, boycotted the 1980 Moscow Games to protest that country's invasion of Afghanistan. Subsequently, the USSR led a thirteen-nation boycott of the 1984 Los Angeles Games, citing "security concerns."

The 2008 Olympic Games scheduled to be held in Beijing, have also been threatened with a boycott. Protestors cite China's human rights violations, invasion and occupation of Tibet, environmental concerns, and other issues. Human rights organizations and other opponents of the Chinese government call the decision to allow China to host the 2008 Games "historical misjudgment" and "reward for a corrupt regime." The European Parliament has urged the IOC to revoke China's host status and to reconsider their application "when the authorities of the PRC have made a fundamental change in their policy on human rights, and the promotion of democracy and the rule of law."

Pro-Tibet demonstrators protest against the Beijing 2008 Olympics bid outside a hotel where International Olympic Committee Evaluation Commission were holding a news conference in Toronto, Canada, on March 11, 2001. AP IMAGES.

The following article, published on the *Reporters sans frontières* website, accuses the Chinese Government of several human rights violations.

■ **PRIMARY SOURCE**

Why We Are Boycotting Beijing 2008?
A New Wave of Repression Justified by the Olympics

Moscow 1980: The Positive Effect of the Boycott

No Olympics without Democracy !

A New Wave of Repression Justified by the Olympics

While a wide majority of International Olympic Committee (IOC) members were voting, on July 13, 2001, to attribute the 2008 Summer Olympics to Beijing, Chinese police received an order to step up their executions of delinquents and intensify repression against "subversive Internet users." IOC members, encouraged by

their president, Juan Antonio Samaranch, who personally supported China's bid, paid no attention to the repeated calls against the Beijing bid.

Internet Users, Tibetans and Falungong Members Repressed

Chinese authorities, satisfied by this decision, reinforced repression against Internet users, Tibetans, members of the Falungong spiritual movement, foreign scholars, the Muslim Uigur minority, democrats, foreign journalists and delinquents, all "in the name of the Chinese Olympics." Vice-Prime minister Li Lanqing stated, four days after the IOC's vote, that "China's Olympic victory" should incite the country to preserve its "healthy life," especially by fighting against the Falungong movement which "foments insecurity." It should be reminded that at least 100 Falungong followers have died in detention since the movement was banned, and at least 10,000 others are in Chinese jails. On July 19, Hu Jintao stated that after Beijing's "triumph," it was "essential to fight strongly against separatist activities orchestrated by the Dalai Lama and anti-Chinese forces around the world."

At Least 35 Cyber Dissidents Arrested

In July also, former President Jiang Zemin defended the idea of a "healthy" Chinese Internet. In concrete terms, 35 cyber-dissidents are in jail, and more than 8,000 Internet cafés have been closed; dozens of web sites and forums were censored in July. In western China, authorities in Xinjiang province, where the country's Muslim minority lives, sentenced four Uigurs accused of "separatism" to death, Meanwhile, two German journalists, who were investigating a case of contaminated blood in Henan province, were arrested and accused of "working illegally." Finally, police and judicial authorities received orders to continue the "Strike Hard" campaign against delinquency. Between 3,000 and 4,000 Chinese have already been executed this year, either shot in the neck or by lethal injection, and this is often done in public, in stadiums.

The idea that granting China the Olympics would incite the Chinese authorities to improve human rights has been swept away by recent events. We can look forward to seven years of repression, especially against Tibetans and Uigurs, and all those considered to be "subversive elements." The IOC has, in fact, invested the Chinese regime with a task it will carry out zealously: host safe Olympics. This means arrests of dissidents, social "cleansing," and censorship against "critical" elements, especially journalists.

Balance of Power

Unfortunately, the reactions from democratic governments—"we hope the Olympics will lead to improvements in human rights"—have no effect on the Chinese regime. History has shown that totalitarian regimes are more sensitive to a balance of power than to "constructive dialogue." A boycott therefore seems the only strategy to force Chinese authorities to respect human rights before 2008.

The Olympic movement was discredited in 1936, when it allowed the Nazis to make the Games a spectacle to glorify the Third Reich. In 1980, in Moscow, the IOC suffered a terrible defeat when more than 50 countries boycotted the Olympics. The Netherlands, Germany, the United States, Egypt and so many others refused to countenance the Soviet regime. In 2008, the international sporting movement must refuse to tolerate one of the world's bloodiest dictatorships.

SIGNIFICANCE

The modern Olympics were established with the highest ideals, including fostering international cooperation. Yet the Olympics are exploited by powerful interest groups, especially governments and corporations. Issues such as commercialization, bidding wars, blood doping [the illegal practice of increasing an athlete's red blood cell supply to improve performance], racism, and gender inequality have clouded the Olympics for decades.

The privilege of hosting the Games is a source of national and civic pride, with the opportunity to showcase a host country and city. Unfortunately, repressive regimes often find international sport a convenient avenue for good publicity. In fact, the 1936 Berlin Olympics were an obvious ploy to demonstrate the prowess of Nazi Germany. According to California Republican Congressman Tom Lantos, "Hitler benefited enormously from the 1936 Olympics in Berlin.

A South Korean protester dressed as a Chinese policeman pretends to beat his colleague, who is playing the role of a North Korean defector, at a rally in Athens, August 12, 2004. North Korean refugee activists rallied on Thursday criticizing North Korea and China for their treatment of North Korean refugees and calling for a boycott of the Beijing 2008 Olympic Games. KIM KYUNG-HOON/REUTERS/CORBIS.

And we know what happened in the years following. The Soviet Union had the Olympics in 1980, and there came nine years of Soviet suppression."

Whether or not the Olympics should be used as a means of political protest, however, is still debated. Opponents argue that boycotting works against a country's political interests. Others believe that the Olympics give totalitarian regimes an opportunity to improve. Soon after China's bid to host the 2008 Olympics was accepted, for example, Human Rights Watch stated that "the human rights record of a country should be taken into serious consideration by the International Olympic Committee in selecting the site for the 2008 Olympics, but we are not opposed a priori to China getting the Games. Experience with the 1995 UN Women's Conference in Beijing has shown that having thousands of people from around the world in China can focus attention on the country, including on the degree of state control and fear of political protest."

The IOC maintains that international sporting competitions foster goodwill between countries. In January 2006 the United Nations and IOC chiefs pledged to use them as a tool to promote peace in war-torn countries. IOC chief Jacques Rogge, in a joint statement with UN Secretary General Kofi Annan, said that through sport "what we are doing is trying to bring the athletes together not necessarily only in matches, also in training camps, so they can live together longer than just a matter than one or two hours." He also added that "we believe that this is a very important symbol that people can live together, that people respect each other and that sport is a uniting factor."

FURTHER RESOURCES
Books
Hulme, Derick. *The Political Olympics: Moscow, Afghanistan, and the 1980 U.S. Boycott.* New York: Praeger Publishers, December 30, 1990.

Periodicals
Hargreaves, John. "Olympism and Nationalism: Some Preliminary Consideration." *International Review for the Sociology of Sport.* 27, no. 2 (1992): 119–137.

Web sites
Chinaorbit.com. "Positions within the IOC Concerning the Question of Human Rights." May 17, 2006. <http://www.chinaorbit.com/Olympic_Games_2008_and_Human_R.1229.0.html> (accessed May 17, 2006).

CNN. "Olympic Boycotts." <http://edition.cnn.com/SPECIALS/cold.war/episodes/20/spotlight> (accessed May 17, 2006).

Daily Times. "UN and Olympic Chiefs Pledge to Use Sports against War." January 25, 2006. < http://www.dailytimes.com.pk/default.asp?page=2006%5C01%5C25%5Cstory_25-1-2006_pg2_9 > (accessed May 17, 2006).

International Olympic Committee. "Montreal 1976." <http://www.olympic.org/uk/games/past/index_uk/> (accessed May 17, 2006).

International Olympic Committee. "Olympic Charter." August 2004. <http://multimedia.olympic.org/pdf/en_report_122.pdf> (accessed May 17, 2006).

Los Angeles 1992 Riots

Book excerpt

By: Alistair Cooke

Date: 2004

Source: Alistair Cooke. *Letters From America: 1946–2004.* New York: Penguin, 2004.

About the Author: Alistair Cooke (1908–2004), a British journalist and broadcaster, started his career as a film critic with the British Broadcasting Corporation (BBC) in 1934. The following year, he was appointed London correspondent for the National Broadcasting Corporation (NBC) In 1937, he moved to the United States as a commentator on American affairs, for BBC.

Cooke's most notable contribution to the media came as a commentator for American Letter (later renamed to *Letter from America*), a fifteen-minute weekly radio broadcast that discussed news and issues in the United States from a British perspective. The series began in 1946 and continued uninterrupted every week until Cooke's death in 2004. In June 2005, Penguin Books published *Letter from America: 1946–2004*—a selection of transcripts of the radio program.

INTRODUCTION
Historically, police brutality and discrimination against minorities has often caused riots in the United States. In 1919, law enforcement authorities in Chicago failed to apprehend a few white youths on charges of beating up a black male. Subsequently, the city witnessed wide-spread rioting by many men from the African American community.

In the United States, most incidents of rioting have occurred in communally sensitive neighborhoods. For instance, in 1935, a minor shoplifting episode triggered large-scale violence in Harlem,

Three white police officers arrest an African American man during the 1992 riots in Los Angeles, California. © PETER TURNLEY/CORBIS.

New York. The cause of the violence was a rumor that a black woman was manhandled by the Harlem Police—an entity known for discrimination against blacks. Rumors of the arrest and subsequent shooting of a black youth caused severe rioting in Watts, California, in 1965. There have been many other similar instances of unrest in the past few decades.

In most cases, the U.S. Government has formed official commissions to determine the causes of riots. According to these commissions, the main reasons, apart from police discrimination, are low level of education and few job opportunities for minorities. While investigating the Watt riots of 1965, the McCone Commission concluded that poverty, inequality, and racial discrimination were the root causes. In this case, the successful implementation of Proposition 14, in November 1964, also acted as a catalyst in provoking the black community. Proposition 14 had invalidated the Rumford Fair Housing Act—an initiative establishing equal opportunity for African American home buyers by prohibiting racial discrimination by sellers and landlords.

In the past, vindication of those accused of brutality against minorities has also incited rioting. In March 1991, an eighty-one second video tape caught four police officers beating up a black motorist relentlessly. Followed by months of investigation, this incident, which took place in Los Angeles, received extensive media coverage. More than ten years later, in April 1992, a twelve-member jury consisting mainly of white jurors absolved the police officers of any wrong doing—a verdict that was strongly condemned by most. Subsequently, the city witnessed one of its worst cases of communal violence that included looting, arson, and widespread rioting. The primary source is a transcript of popular BBC commentator Alistair Cooke's account of this incident on his radio broadcast, *Letter from America*.

PRIMARY SOURCE

And then home, and, as I always do just before turning in, to flip through thirty-two television channels—it's now fifty—and light briefly on Channel 24, which is Atlanta's

CNN, the television world news station that is most often there, as the general said, "fastest with the mostest." I see a helicopter shot of a street intersection and stalled truck, and what looks like a man sprawled on the ground—one or two other men running around, making gestures. They are all so tiny, seen from the air. It's probably a random shooting somewhere, most likely in Harlem or Los Angeles, maybe. We see at least one every night. Something's hurriedly spoken about a verdict. So to bed, to read a new book which claims, and for once maybe rightly, to have solved after a hundred and four years the identity of Jack the Ripper. So to sleep.

Thursday morning, and—the first words I heard from an announcer in Los Angeles, were, 'worse, much worse, than Watts'. Because we can now see it was historically the forerunner of dreadful things to come two, three years later, we had better look back to Watts. Watts was that frowsy but not slummy suburb of Los Angeles where a while policeman's arrest of a black youth started a rumour that the black man had been shot. The rumour grew: he'd been wounded, no, killed, in cold blood. Within an hour, a full-scale riot was thriving in that black neighbourhood, and within twenty-four hours the whole suburb was ablaze, loud with guns and happy looters. There was a time when it appeared the chaos might not be controlled by the ten thousand men of the National Guard, who'd been ordered in by the Governor of California. The National Guard is the civilian reserve militia which every state has on call, and which can, in a war or other emergency, be mobilized as regular army under the regular military command. I try to clarify the function of the misleadingly named National Guard because we'll come to look at their part in this week's riots. By the end of that dreadful week in 1965, Watts was a large, gutted suburb. And it was mentioned the other night that after twenty-seven years, it is not wholly recovered or rebuilt.

Well, if the horror of Watts was triggered by a tiny casual arrest and a ballooning false rumour, what triggered the rage of south central Los Angeles last Wednesday night? Let's go back as calmly as we can and look at what started it all.

On the night of 3 March 1991, a black motorist was seen by a police car whizzing along a boulevard at a breakneck pace and the police pursued him. It took quite a time to catch up with him, by which time other police cars and many other policemen had come to form almost an impromptu posse, twenty-three in all. When they did catch him, two other men in the car gave themselves up without resistance; they were handcuffed and taken off into custody. The driver remained defiant and aggressive, so freewheeling with arms and legs that one of the policemen said he assumed the man was high on some drug.

Anyway, what came next would doubtless have been buried in the police records but for a unique accident that made what happened on that night-time street something for all the world to see. A man who lived in an apartment overlooking what was now a scene on the street was aroused by the noise of the police siren and the following scuffle. He picked up his video camera, stood (on his porch, I imagine) and cranked away. His film lasted for eighty-one seconds, and horrified everybody who subsequently saw it, and saw it, and saw it, on television. Four police officers were flailing their batons and flogging the driver, writhing and squirming on the ground. It's true he wasn't going to lie down and take it—he wriggled, but his body also jerked in reflexes, of pain, surely from the beating he was taking. In eighty-one seconds, almost a minute and a half, there were fifty-six counted beatings.

Eleven days later, a Los Angeles grand jury indicted one police sergeant and three police officers. They pleaded not guilty. The Attorney General of the United States responded by ordering an immediate review of complaints of brutality against the Los Angeles police. The review expanded to cover the whole nation—that was thirteen months ago—and the report has not been published. The Mayor of Los Angeles, a black man who's been in office for an unprecedented twenty years, appointed a commission to investigate the Los Angeles police department. There was for a time a wrangle over the chief of police, a white man, who was charged with insensitivity and condoning bad police behaviour. A month or two later, he promised to retire this spring. He was still there this week. A month or so after the beating, the driver, Rodney King, and his wife, filed a federal civil rights suit against the city of Los Angeles. Three weeks later, Mr. King was discovered in a parked car with a transvestite prostitute. He failed to get away but after two months all charges were dropped.

Meanwhile, the grand jury brought no charges against the nineteen police officers who were bystanders. But the four men who were seen to do the beating eventually, after many legal manoeuvres, came to trial a year to the day after the event. By the way, on the motion of the defence which maintained that the four policemen could not get a fair trial in the black-dominated quarter where the incident took place, the trial was moved to another suburb (which, it's important to remark, is almost entirely white and is called home by about two thousand policemen and their families). Although one or two blacks were called for jury duty, they were quizzed and excused by the defence, which is its privilege. The sitting jury consisted of ten whites, one Hispanic, one Asian. On 23 April the case went to the jury. We gather from the jurors themselves that their verdict was arrived at within an hour or two (an astonishing feat for an American jury, which can battle it out for days and weeks) but took another three days to argue, and was eventually hung, on one count against one officer.

So it was this past Wednesday evening when the stunning verdict came—actually over the television, for the trail was televised throughout. The four had been found not guilty, of brutality and of excessive force (that is, going beyond the needs of the cause). In interviews after the result, the jurors willing to speak said the amateur motion picture was crude (so it was, it was filming a very crude event), did not express the physical threat Mr King posed, and that much of the flailing was into the thin night air.

It's fair to say that a vast majority of the country will refuse to believe a word of it. The first shot I saw, of a stalled truck and a prone man and one or two running around, was the beginning: a white truck driver dragged to the pavement and beaten up by blacks. I'd better say at once that in all the following burnings and lootings were done by blacks and poor whites, who now had what everybody told them was just cause to vent their longsuppressed rage and disillusion in the equality that wasn't there, and the jobs that weren't forthcoming.

In the beginning, what we saw were the flaming suburbs by night, and black people complaining that it had taken the fire department twenty minutes to answer their call. On any night, the average calls to the Los Angeles fire department are ten. Last Wednesday night, over a hundred and twenty fires blazed in central and south central Los Angeles, and then beyond. And the firemen were being attacked, along with the police and the paramedics. Los Angeles is not a skyscraper city but a huge collection, connection, of ninety suburbs over five hundred and fifty square miles. Sunset Boulevard alone runs for twenty-two miles—through sections that could be in Hong Kong, in Mexico, in Korea, in Kansas City. On Thursday night forty fires burned, out beyond by miles, up into the rich and by now—I should guess—terrified habitat of the film and television folk; the designers, the yuppies, who mean no harm.

By Friday noon, the President had sent a light infantry battalion into a 'staging area' near Los Angeles, to be used if the National Guard and the police cannot control things. By Friday, the worst we feared had happened: the rioting, looting contagion had spread to San Francisco, to Atlanta, to Seattle, and in a smaller way to other towns thousands of miles apart. There were peaceable black demonstrations in Kansas City and on the campus of a college in Baton Rouge, Louisiana.

In Watts, before the end, there was the awful fear that ten thousand of the National Guard might not be enough. If the violence from the poor and the hoodlum packs and the juvenile gangs takes over many cities, the President and his generals may have to worry whether there'll be enough troops to contain what could become a race rebellion.

There's one discernible piece of good news in all this. Now that the State of California has exhausted its legal procedure (the verdict is the end), the federal government can move in, and it could institute a new trial but not on the same grounds. That would run the risk of double jeopardy. The Justice Department, through the Attorney General, has revived a criminal investigation in to the incident of the beating to see if the constitutional civil rights of Mr. King were violated. It's the ground on which, just a year ago, the Kings filed their suit against the city of Los Angeles.

SIGNIFICANCE

Set up soon after the Los Angeles riots in 1991, the Christopher Commission headed by attorney Warren Christopher, investigated the operations and structure of the Los Angeles Police Department (LAPD). The commission's report concluded that many officers in the LAPD ignored written guidelines of the department by frequently using excessive force against the public. The use of excessive force is also a direct violation of the Fifth and Fourteenth Amendments of the U.S. Constitution.

The Los Angeles riots, and other similar incidents, have assumed significance as they highlight the issue of racial discrimination in the United States. It also fueled increasing public concern with racial profiling in the United States. Racial profiling is the practice of targeting racial minorities for special scrutiny under the assumption that they are more likely to be criminals. A July 2001 Gallup poll reported that out of those surveyed, fifty-five percent of whites and eighty-three percent of blacks felt that racial profiling, especially by law enforcement officials, was widespread in the United States.

Critics of racial profiling argue that racial profiling does not serve any purpose. According to the American Civil Liberties Union (ACLU), in addition to being discriminatory, such practices are mostly ineffective and biased. Moreover, the ACLU states that racial profiling can cause resentment amongst minorities, which in turn incites hostile behavior and non-cooperation.

Widespread opinion that the majority of crimes are committed by African Americans augments racial discrimination and profiling. Police drug interdiction programs conclude that a majority of drug sellers and users are people of color—a claim refuted by government agencies. Some government studies state that the number of people using and selling drugs from each race is actually in proportion to their population. Human rights activists state that race-based assumptions of law enforcement officials perpetuate negative racial stereotypes and lead to violent incidents such as the Los Angeles riots.

In the past few decades, there has been a growing concern in the international community about discriminatory practices prevalent in law enforcement agencies in United States. International human-rights groups, Amnesty International and Human Rights Watch, have authored studies that severely condemn some police actions against minorities. Entities such as the European Union have become increasingly vocal in their condemnation of racial bias in the United States, especially after the terrorist attack on the World Trade Center in September 2001.

The U.S. Government is also known to be a critic of racial discrimination and profiling. While addressing a Joint Session of Congress on February 27, 2001, President George W. Bush declared that racial profiling was wrong and his government intended to put an end to it. At a news conference in March 2001, U.S. Attorney General John Ashcroft mentioned that racial profiling creates a "lose-lose" situation because it destroys the potential for underlying trust that "should support the administration of justice as a societal objective, not just as a law enforcement objective."

Various initiatives have been undertaken by the government to prevent unfair racial profiling. In June 2003, the Civil Rights Division of the U.S. Department of Justice issued several guidelines to law enforcement agencies on racial profiling. These guidelines explicitly prohibit profiling in routine or spontaneous activities. They further emphasize that stereotyping specific races as having a greater propensity to commit crimes is completely prohibited. Although the Civil Rights Division recognizes the need for racial profiling in cases of terrorism, it maintains that such practices should be in accordance to the nation's constitution. Consequently, even in the context of national security, law enforcement authorities have to maintain constitutional restriction on the use of generalized stereotypes.

Independent commissions claim that despite preventive measures taken by the government, racial discrimination and police brutality is on the rise. These commissions advocate frequent psychological testing of officers and a system of tracking citizen complaints to ensure fair and unbiased policies. Reports suggest that most cities in the United States have a high likelihood of racial violence. According to a 2001 study published by the National Organization of Black

Law Enforcement Executives, a stray racially motivated incident could again instigate large-scale riots.

FURTHER RESOURCES
Books
Nelson, Jill. *Police Brutality: An Anthology*. New York: W. W. Norton, 2001.

Web sites
American Civil Liberties Union. "Racial Profiling: Old and New." <http://www.aclu.org/racialjustice/racialprofiling/index.html> (accessed May 10, 2006).

Chicago Tribune. "The Global Costs of Police Brutality in the US." May 28, 2001. <http://www.commondreams.org/views01/0528-06.htm> (accessed May 10, 2006).

CNN.com. "Rodney King reluctant symbol of police brutality." March 3, 2001. <http://archives.cnn.com/2001/LAW/03/02/beating.anniversity.king.02> (accessed May 10, 2006).

Human Rights Watch. "The Christopher Commission Report." <http://www.hrw.org/reports98/police/uspo73.htm> (accessed May 10, 2006).

Slate Magazine. "Riot Act." April 20, 2001. <http://www.slate.com/id/104699> (accessed May 10, 2006).

U.S. Department of Justice. "GUIDANCE REGARDING THE USE OF RACE BY FEDERAL LAW ENFORCEMENT AGENCIES." June 2003. <http://www.usdoj.gov/crt/split/documents/guidance_on_race.htm> (accessed May 10, 2006).

U.S. Legal Forms, Inc. "Police Brutality Law and Legal Definition." <http://www.uslegalforms.com/legaldefinitions/police-brutality> (accessed May 10, 2006).

Marching with a Message

Newspaper article

By: Scott Roberts

Date: June 26, 2005

Source: Roberts, Scott. "Marching with a Message." *Toronto Star*. June 26, 2005.

About the Author: Scott Roberts is a staff writer for the *Toronto Star*.

INTRODUCTION

The United States and Canada share both a continent and a similar lesbian rights history. Until the 1960s, Canadian lesbians stayed in the shadows, fearful of persecution for their sexual orientation. In the late 1960s, a series of social and political developments pushed lesbians to leave the closet in search of greater personal and political freedoms.

In the 1960s, both Quebec nationalists and Native American activists began to agitate against the oppression that had been directed at them by the Anglo majority. At the same time, New Left student activists and the militant wing of the New Democratic Party provided training for the largely white, middle class women who started the women's liberation movement in English Canada. Many of these women, now conscious of oppression, then proceeded to found the lesbian rights movement in the early 1970s. This lesbian activism was prompted by the high-profile arrests of four lesbians at a Toronto bar for disorderly behavior in 1974, a raid by an official Toronto anti-pornography and morality squad on a gay news journal; and the firings of lesbian workers and soldiers.

A protester waves a multicolor flag with a Star of David during a gay rights demonstration in Warsaw, November 27, 2005. Protesters rallied against the banning of a gay rights march the week before, and to demand tolerence and freedom of speech from Poland's new conservative leaders. AP IMAGES.

Mass protests against these injustices galvanized forces and politicized thousands.

In subsequent years, the lesbian rights movement has gotten stronger in Canada and has come to include a cultural element. Lesbians across the country launched their own newsletters and periodicals, formed all-female musical groups, started record companies, and set up large-scale lesbian musical festivals. The building of a strong lesbian community removed the sense of isolation that had long plagued lesbians. By 1998, Toronto had the second largest Lesbian and Gay Pride Day Parade worldwide after San Francisco's. Lesbians, however, worried about the loss of women-only spaces. The annual Dyke March serves as a way to show pride in lesbian culture and to reinforce the need for lesbian spaces.

■ PRIMARY SOURCE

It was not your typical wedding. There were no brides-maids, no cake—not even a familiar face in the crowd. And that's just how Paula Kruse and Ann Hudson wanted it.

The lesbian couple from Denver, Colo., were married in a quickie ceremony yesterday in the thick of Pride Week festivities. At an altar lined with white roses, the two read their vows in front of hundreds of strangers in a ceremony they could not have south of the border.

When they sealed the deal with a kiss, onlookers showered the couple with bubbles and a rainbow of confetti in a show of support.

For these newlyweds, the first stop as a married couple was not a honeymoon suite or a catered reception. It was the Dyke March.

"We just thought it would be great to get married and then hop right into the Dyke March," said Kruse, dressed in her white wedding gown. "It's such a great event and we're happy to be part of it."

Celebrating its 10th year in Toronto, the Dyke March is a women-only affair, born out of a movement to give lesbians a distinct voice in the community. Each year the march precedes the massive Pride Parade by a day— a warm-up routine for the big show, if you will. But make no mistake, the Dyke March has an identity all its own.

For starters, it's not a parade. There are no floats, no marching bands, no clowns throwing candy. It's a march; a friendly protest that supporters say brings lesbian and women's issues into the limelight.

"This is an opportunity for women to come together for one day of the year and be a member of the majority and walk together," said Natasha Garda, co-chair of Pride

Toronto. "It's a safe and positive space for women to voice their advocacy."

And that's where it differs from today's parade. Where the Pride Parade has become mainly celebratory, the Dyke March continues to be activist and grassroots. Student groups, AIDS activists and even church leaders marched in support of the lesbian community. Placards praising same-sex marriage legislation and gender equality were prevalent.

"Both of these events are celebrations but the Dyke March is also about empowerment," said Garda. "It's about solidarity and acceptance. It sends the message that we're here, we're queer and we're women."

Though the Dyke March has historically been more reserved than the flamboyant Pride Parade, several participants tried to spice it up yesterday.

One woman dressed as a butterfly weaved in and out of marchers while a drag queen handed out homemade cookies to pedestrians lining Church St.

The march began, as it always has, with members of the women-only Amazon Biker Club revving up their engines and leading the way north on Church St., west on Bloor St., then south along Yonge St.

Lisa Wunch and Edit Farun have marched in the event for the past seven years. This time they brought their three-year-old daughter Carly.

"She's very proud of the fact she has two moms," said Wunch. "We're here celebrating the diversity of our family."

The Dyke March has come a long way since being launched in 1996 by Lesha Van Der Bij and Lisa Hayes. With a budget of fifty dollars and a staff of four volunteers, the two managed to draw about 5,000 supporters to the city's inaugural march despite heavy rain and some disapproving hecklers.

Since then, the march has grown into a mainstream event, drawing tens of thousands of participants from across North America. But it hasn't been without its hardships.

In 1999, the event was nearly cancelled when interest in organizing the march faded. Hayes and Van Der Bij had put together three marches and were looking to pass on the responsibility.

Eventually community members volunteered to take up the torch and the march continued.

The Dyke March has been criticized for being exclusionary. Some go as far as saying it divides the gay community.

"Having a Dyke March promotes segregation not unity," said Dave McKee, who attended the march. "I think there should only be one Pride march."

Supporters of the Dyke March disagree with the argument and believe it helps instill equality.

"Men still dominate this world and the gay and lesbian community is no different than that," said Van Der Bij. "Women don't have the same kind of visibility in the gay community as men do. This is one single event dominated by women. And we think that's empowering."

Van Der Bij believes that lesbians have different interests and goals than gay men and it's important to acknowledge that.

"There's an assumption that the gay community is all one big group but we're not," she said. "There are differing issues and concerns for women that men don't have and vice versa."

For Kruse and Hudson, the only pressing concern may be getting used to married life.

The two are heading to Niagara Falls today before flying back to Denver tomorrow. It's not much of a honeymoon, but they don't seem to mind.

"It's just so exciting to be legally married," said Kruse, who got engaged to Hudson at a drag queen bingo.

"It's finally official. This is an opportunity for women to come together for one day of the year...."

Natasha Garda, co-chair of Pride Toronto: "This is one single event dominated by women. And we think that's empowering?"

SIGNIFICANCE

In 2003, Canadian Prime Minister Jean Chrétien proposed legalizing same-sex marriage throughout the country. After many delays and much discussion, Bill C-38, the authorizing legislation, eventually passed on July 19, 2005 and became law the next day. The vote for passage of Bill C-38 was relatively close in the House of Commons—158 to 133—but overwhelming in the Senate, which affirmed the legislation 47 to 21 with three abstentions. By the time of the victory all of the provinces and territories except Alberta, Prince Edward Island, the Northwest Territories, and Nunavut had already adopted laws enabling gay men and lesbians to marry. Chrétien's successor, Stephen Harper, has promised to revisit the vote with the aim of overturning it, but has yet to do so.

Some lesbians have criticized the pro-assimilation goals of the lesbian rights movement. However, there is agreement among Canadian activists that Canada is among the most progressive countries in the world on gay and lesbian rights. Legal gains in Canada have been more numerous than in the United States. Activists argue that this difference between the neighbors can be attributed to a much less powerful Christian fundamentalist right wing in Canada; the pro-gay efforts of the liberal New Democratic Party to redefine family and spouse both provincially and federally; cross-provincial organizing of gay and lesbian rights groups; and a long tradition of welfare-state provisions. The gains are not cemented though, as conservative groups continue to seek to overturn them.

FURTHER RESOURCES

Books

Herman, Didi. *Rites of Passage: Struggles for Lesbian and Gay Legal Equality*. Toronto: University of Toronto Press, 1994.

Kinsman, Gary. *The Regulation of Desire: Homo and Hetero Sexualities in Canada*. Montreal: Black Rose Books, 1996.

Ross, Becki. *The House that Jill Built: A Lesbian Nation in Formation*. Toronto: University of Toronto Press, 1995.

Relatives of the "Disappeared" Protest

Photograph

By: Martin Bernetti

Date: September 11, 2005

Source: MARTIN BERNETTI/AFP/Getty Images.

About the Author: Martin Bernetti's photographs have been published by the Associated Press, Reuters, and Agence France-Presse. Based in Quito, Ecuador, Bernetti travels internationally, teaching photography in addition to working as a photojournalist.

INTRODUCTION

On September 11, 1973, the government of Chile was taken over in a military coup staged by the army's commander in chief, 57-year-old General Augusto Pinochet. The elected president, Salvador Allende Gossens, was attacked in *La Moneda*, the presidential palace in Santiago; air strikes against the building led to its quick capture by Pinochet's forces. Allende either committed suicide or was killed that day, and Pinochet took control of the country.

Allende, a Socialist elected in 1970, had angered social and economic conservatives with policies that included "land reform," in which he intended to seize all land holdings larger than 80 hectares [100 acres]; nationalization of industries such as copper mining, steel, and banking; and gender equality reform. Allende had nationalized more than 90% of all industry by the end of his first year in office, angering foreign investors

and triggering intense interest from the United States. U.S. military forces had helped train Chilean military officers, with CIA support; by the time Pinochet staged his coup President Richard Nixon and Secretary of State Henry Kissinger were firmly behind him.

During Pinochet's first 8 years in power, from 1973 to 1989, more than 40,000 citizens were rounded up in anti-leftist campaigns and held in the National Stadium or other torture centers. Reports from Amnesty International and Human Rights Watch document cases of electroshock applied to genitals, rape of women by trained police dogs, beating, mutilations, and attacks on small villages in which every able-bodied man was rounded up and executed. Up to 4,000 people disappeared; most of the *desaparecidos* were former Socialist party workers, leftist sympathizers, university professors, labor organizers, and family members.

During Pinochet's rule two forms of silent, but public, protest emerged. Women, largely from the lower economic classes, used *arpilleras* (tapestries that show scenes of daily life), to tell stories of disappeared persons, violence against villages, and oppression. These were a silent protest against Pinochet, and women gathered in churches, meeting halls, and private homes to weave these works of dissent.

Mothers and wives also performed traditional dances such as "La cueca," the Chilean national dance, in public squares; they danced alone as a form of protest, and to remember the *desaparecidos*. In 1987 Sting recorded the song "They Dance Alone," with lyrics that included: "It's the only form of protest they're allowed / I've seen their silent faces scream so loud." The song brought worldwide attention to the missing and their families' struggle to find answers about their loved ones' fate. In 1989, following increasingly violent and public opposition, a plebescite intended to rubber stamp another eight-year term for Pinochet returned a majority of "No" votes. Free national elections followed, and an overwhelming majority chose Christian Democrat Patricio Aylwin, who became president in 1990.

PRIMARY SOURCE

RELATIVES OF THE "DISAPPEARED" PROTEST
See primary source image.

SIGNIFICANCE

Following Aylwin's ascent to the presidency, Pinochet made himself senator for life, and remained commander in chief of the armed forces until 1998.

Relatives of the "Disappeared" Protest Lorenza Pizarro and Mireya Garcia, activists for the Relatives of Missing People Association, march during a demonstration marking the 32nd anniversary of the coup that put General Augusto Pinochet in power, September 11, 2005. MARTIN BERNETTI/AFP/GETTY IMAGES.

Although requests for information about torture victims and *desaparecidos* had been constant throughout Pinochet's rule, the demand increased with Aylwin's election. In 1998, when Pinochet traveled to England for medical care, international cries for his arrest led to a Spanish court's ruling that he could be tried for war crimes against Spanish citizens caught up in the 1973 coup.

On October 17, 1998, Pinochet was arrested in London. The following August the Chilean minister of defense created a commission to investigate human rights abuses in Chile during his rule. In January 2001 the commission revealed the fate of approximately 180 of the *desaparecidos;* little or no information was available for the rest. Another investigatory body, the National Commission on Political Imprisonment and Torture identified more than 27,000 torture victims. In 2004 the Chilean government announced a reparations payment plan, giving torture victims

approximately $2,500 and children born in or detained in prison up to $6,800 in a lump sum.

Between 1998 and 2004 Pinochet's status in Spanish, English, and Chilean courts bounced from "medically unfit" to "adequate to stand trial"; in 2005 he was indicted once more in Chile. As of this writing he is nearly 90 and being held under house arrest; his trial is still pending.

FURTHER RESOURCES
Books

Agosin, Marjorie. *Tapestries of Hope, Threads of Love: The Arpillera Movement in Chile, 1974–1994*. Albuquerque: University of New Mexico Press, 1996.

Kornbluh, Peter. *The Pinochet File: A Declassified Dossier on Atrocity and Accountability*. New York: New Press, 2004.

Timerman, Jacobo. *Chile: Death in the South*. New York: Knopf, 1987.

Websites

Amnesty International. "Chile—Torture: An International Crime." <http://web.amnesty.org/library/index/engamr220101999> (accessed May 8, 2006).

Two Prosecutors at Guantanamo Quit in Protest

Newspaper article

By: Jess Bravin

Date: August 1, 2005

Source: Bravin, Jess. "Two Prosecutors at Guantanamo Quit in Protest." *The Wall Street Journal* (August 1, 2005).

About the Author: Jess Bravin is a staff reporter for the *Wall Street Journal*, an international business and finance news publication based in New York.

INTRODUCTION

Since the Spanish-American War of 1898, the United States has controlled the territory on both sides of Guantanamo Bay, Cuba, an area of about 45 square miles (116 square kilometers). The U.S. Navy has used the inholding as a military base, but since 2002, camps at the facility have also been used to hold between five hundred and seven hundred persons captured in various countries, primarily Afghanistan and Iraq. The prisoners are alleged by the United States to be "the worst of the worst" (Defense Secretary Donald Rumsfeld, 2002), the most

A guard looks out from a tower at the U.S. Naval Station Guantanamo Bay in Cuba, April 13, 2005. AP IMAGES.

dangerous persons captured in what the United States and many media outlets term "the war on terror." Said Secretary Rumsfeld on June 27, 2005, "If you think of the people down there, these are people, all of whom were captured on a battlefield. They're terrorists, trainers, bomb makers, recruiters, financiers, [Osama bin Laden's] bodyguards, would-be suicide bombers, probably the twentieth 9/11 hijacker."

In 2001, President George W. Bush ordered that military commissions would be created to try select Guantanamo detainees for war crimes. These commissions are superficially court-like: there are judges, lawyers for the defense, and lawyers for the prosecution. However, in the Guantanamo tribunals evidence for the prosecution can be kept secret from the defense and the accused can only use lawyers approved by the Defense Department (i.e., in effect, the prosecution).

In 2005, while preparing the case against four alleged war criminals, two military officers resigned from the prosecution team in protest. The *Wall Street Journal* and *New York Times* broke the story simultaneously on August 1, 2005, reporting that internal e-mails from the two officers had accused the military commission trial process of being "rigged" to produce

convictions. They accused colleagues of withholding or destroying evidence, such as documents detailing charges that one of the accused had confessed under torture. (Confessions given under torture are notoriously unreliable because a torture victim will say anything to make the torture stop.)

The Defense Department vigorously denied all the charges brought by the two officers. The chief prosecutor, who had been repeatedly criticized by one of the resigning officers, said that the accusations against him were "monstrous lies."

PRIMARY SOURCE

Two Air Force prosecutors quit last year rather than take part in military trials they considered rigged against alleged terrorists held at Guantanamo Bay, Cuba.

Maj. John Carr, then a captain, and Maj. Robert Preston accused fellow prosecutors of ignoring torture allegations, failing to protect exculpatory evidence and withholding information from superiors. Altogether, the actions "may constitute dereliction of duty, false official statements or other criminal conduct," Maj. Carr wrote in a

March 15, 2004, email summarizing his complaints to the then-chief prosecutor, Army Col. Fred Borch.

The email is one of several made available by officials in the Defense Department office that provides legal counsel to individuals charged under the military commission system President Bush created in 2001. The officials said defense lawyers obtained the emails last week from Col. Will Gunn, the departing head of the office, who is retiring from the Air Force. He couldn't be reached for comment.

Maj. Carr and Maj. Preston requested that they be reassigned rather than participate in the proceedings. Maj. Carr now handles civil litigation at the Pentagon, according to a colleague, and Maj. Preston is an instructor at the Air Force Judge Advocate General's School at Maxwell Air Force Base in Montgomery, Ala. Neither returned calls seeking comment.

The Defense Department says the allegations were investigated and found to be without merit, although they did prompt some management changes at the prosecution office.

The Bush administration hopes to restart the military commissions trying Guantanamo prisoners as soon as next month, after a federal appeals court in July found the proceedings lawful. The ruling, by a three-judge panel that included Supreme Court nominee John G. Roberts Jr., reversed a lower court that halted the proceedings in November on the grounds that they violated due process and U.S. obligations under the Geneva Conventions.

Lawyers for the Guantanamo defendants say they are pursuing appeals and other court action to declare the proceedings illegal. On Capitol Hill several lawmakers are considering possible legislation to regulate the military commissions and review detainee treatment. The Bush administration argues that congressional action would interfere with counterterrorism efforts.

Defense Department officials say several reviews, including one by a Pentagon inspector general, found nothing to substantiate the Carr and Preston allegations. "We found absolutely no evidence of ethical violations, no evidence of any criminal misconduct," says Air Force Brig. Gen. Thomas Hemingway, legal adviser to the military commissions' appointing authority, as the administrative arm of the trials is called.

Gen. Hemingway acknowledges personality differences and "an awful lot of miscommunications" in the prosecution office, but says organizational problems have since been corrected.

Still, military lawyers assigned to defend accused terrorists say the emails buttress longstanding complaints about the proceedings' fairness. They say they want to review the investigations of the former prosecutors' allegations but haven't been given access to the findings. "It's real concerning," says Air Force Lt. Col. Sharon Shaffer, who is defending alleged al Qaeda accountant Ibrahim Ahmed Mahmoud al Qosi, who was captured in Afghanistan. "I know both of these Air Force prosecutors, they are very ethical, highly respected individuals."

The emails detail events in the preparation of cases against three of the four Guantanamo prisoners currently facing charges of war crimes.

In his email to Col. Borch, Maj. Carr describes "an environment of secrecy, deceit and dishonesty" in the prosecution office and suggests that despite lack of evidence, officials initially planned to tie the defendants to the most notorious al Qaeda attacks: the U.S. Embassy bombings in Africa, the USS Cole, and the Sept. 11, 2001, strikes on New York and Washington. Such charges were scaled back, he wrote, after Justice Department officials "appeared less than totally comfortable with our theory."

Col. Borch distributed the Carr and Preston emails throughout his office on March 15, 2004, with a cover note calling the allegations "monstrous lies."

The next month, Col. Borch was reassigned to the Army's Judge Advocate General's School in Charlottesville, Va., and later retired from the military. He now is court clerk at the U.S. District Court in Raleigh, N.C. "I've moved on with my life and don't care to discuss the case any more," Mr. Borch said.

Maj. Carr wrote that three prosecutors had suppressed "FBI allegations of abuse at Bagram" by failing to forward to superiors information they learned from Federal Bureau of Investigation agents "over dinner and drinks." Bagram is a military interrogation center in Afghanistan where many prisoners were held before being taken to Guantanamo. Maj. Carr singled out another superior officer for criticism, Navy Cmdr. Scott Lang, accusing him of misrepresentations regarding evidence. "Either he consciously lied to the office or does not know the facts of his case after 18 months of working on it," Maj. Carr wrote.

Specifically, he accused Cmdr. Lang of suppressing statements by defendant Ali Hamza Ahmad Sulayman al Bahlul that he had been tortured. Prosecutors say Mr. Bahlul, who was captured in Afghanistan, made al Qaeda propaganda videos. He is charged with conspiracy to commit war crimes.

Maj. Carr suggested that Mr. Bahlul told his interrogators that he had been tortured at a detention center after his capture. But Cmdr. Lang denied that there was any evidence of mistreatment during a November 2003 mock trial conducted by prosecutors to prepare for the real trial. Moreover, Maj. Carr wrote, his copy of Cmdr. Lang's notes detailing the torture allegations "is now missing from my notebook."

Maj. Carr added that an FBI agent "related last week that he called and spoke to Cmdr. Lang about the systematic destruction of statements of the detainees, and CDR Lang said that this did not raise any issues."

Cmdr. Lang has since retired from the Navy. He didn't return a telephone call seeking comment.

In his email, Maj. Carr suggests that prosecutors took steps to avoid putting comments or concerns about the proceedings in writing. He contends that prosecutors were providing advice to the appointing authority, the entity that oversees the proceedings and that may rule on defense motions and requests. After Maj. Preston told Col. Borch that advising the authority could create "a potential appearance of partiality, you advised him not to stop giving advice, but to only give advice orally," Maj. Carr wrote to Col. Borch.

Maj. Michael Mori, a Marine Corps lawyer defending another one of the detainees charged with war crimes, David Hicks of Australia, says the emails suggest the prosecution and appointing authority are "all living together, just one big, happy family."

Maj. Carr writes that Col. Borch "repeatedly said to the office that the military panel will be handpicked and will not acquit these detainees, and we only needed to worry about building a record for the review panel."

Criticisms of the prosecution's professionalism are sprinkled throughout the emails. Instead of "at least a minimal effort to establish a fair process and diligently prepare cases against significant accused," Maj. Carr wrote, he found an amateurish attempt "to prosecute fairly low level accused [terrorists] in a process that appears to be rigged. It is difficult to believe that the White House has approved this situation, and I fully expect that one day, soon, someone will be called to answer for what our office has been doing for the last 14 months."

President Bush authorized the military commissions to try non-U.S. citizens alleged to be engaged in terrorism for war crimes. The president directed that the trials be "full and fair" but said they need not offer defendants the same rights required by the U.S. Constitution or afforded U.S. military defendants in courts-martial.

Maj. Preston, in an email dated March 11, 2004, wrote, "I lie awake worrying about this every night … writing a motion saying that the process will be full and fair when you don't really believe it will be is kind of hard— particularly when you want to call yourself an officer and a lawyer."

SIGNIFICANCE

The legality of the U.S. detention of prisoners at Guantanamo Bay and other prisons outside the United States, as well as at secret prisons run by the CIA in Eastern Europe and other locations, has been challenged numerous times since 2002. The United States has been accused of illegal detention, kidnapping, torture, and rigged or sham legal processes. In 2004, FBI agents reported that torture was being used at Guantanamo. The United Nations Commission on Human Rights stated in 2004 that the United States was systematically torturing and inflicting "cruel, inhuman and degrading treatment" (also illegal) on Guantanamo detainees. In February 2006, the Commission called for the United States to close down Guantanamo. In 2004, a confidential report of the International Committee of the Red Cross was leaked in which the organization concluded that officially approved U.S. interrogation practices at Guantanamo were "tantamount to torture." The United States has stated repeatedly that all detainees are held legally and treated humanely.

A number of lawsuits have been brought on behalf of Guantanamo detainees. In June 2004, the U.S. Supreme court held in *Rasul v. Bush* that U.S. courts do have jurisdiction to consider legal challenges to detentions of foreign nationals at Guantanamo. In response—though the legal adequacy of this response has itself been disputed—the U.S. government created the Combatant Status Review Tribunals in July 2004. These tribunals were held from July 2004 to March 2005 and were charged with determining whether individual detainees could be classified as illegal combatants on the basis of evidence. Each tribunal consisted of three U.S. military officers who reviewed the status of individual prisoners. Of several hundred detainees reviewed, the tribunal found that thirty-eight were not combatants, illegal or otherwise; however, only four of this group had yet been released as of May 2006.

Like the military commission conducting war trials, the status-review tribunal process has been accused of being a rigged or sham procedure. In 2005, the complete file on a German-Turkish prisoner, Murat Kurnaz, was accidentally released. Although the tribunal had concluded that that Kurnaz was a member of the terrorist organization Al Qaeda, according to the *Washington Post* (March 27, 2005) the evidence in the file almost all tended to establish Kurnaz's innocence. It showed that both U.S. military intelligence and German police had concluded that Kurnaz was not linked to Al Qaeda or any other terrorist organization. The only evidence against Kurnaz was an anonymous note alleging that he is a terrorist.

In 2005, transcripts of Combatant Status Review Tribunal proceedings (with portions censored) were released in response to a Freedom of Information Act request by the Associated Press. A review of this and other declassified information found that, despite Secretary Rumsfeld's claim that "these are people, all of whom were captured on a battlefield," the majority of Guantanamo detainees were not captured on any battlefield but were rendered into American hands by third parties, sometimes in exchange for cash bounties. Michael Scheuer, the former head of the CIA's unit dedicated to capturing Osama bin Laden, the head of Al Qaeda, resigned in 2004 and claimed publicly that less than ten percent of Guantanamo detainees were terrorists.

The Defense Department states that it has investigated the charges made by the two officers who resigned in protest at the conduct of the Guantanamo military trials, and determined, in the words of spokesperson Lawrence Di Rita, that the charges were "much ado about nothing." The U.S. government categorically denies that prisoners are mistreated at Guantanamo, that innocent persons are held there, or that the procedures used to determine their status are inadequate.

FURTHER RESOURCES
Books
Saar, Erik and Viveca Novak. *Inside the Wire: A Military Intelligence Soldier's Eyewitness Account of Life at Guantanamo.* New York: Penguin Press, 2005.

Periodicals
Eggen, Dan and Jeffery R. Smith. "FBI Agents Allege Abuse of Detainees at Guantanamo Bay." The *Washington Post* (December 21, 2004): A1.

Farley, Maggie. "Report: U.S. is Abusing Captives." The *New York Times* (February 13, 2006): A1.

Hegland, Corine. "Empty Evidence." The *National Journal* (February 4, 2006).

Leonnig, Carol D. "Panel Ignored Evidence on Detainee: U.S. Military Intelligence, German Authorities Found No Ties to Terrorists." The *Washington Post* (March 27, 2005).

Lewis, Neil A. "Two Prosecutors Faulted Trials for Detainees." The *New York Times* (August 1, 2005).

Web sites
Jurist Legal News Archiva. "Guantanamo." <http:// jurist.law.pitt.edu/currentawareness/guantanamo.php> (accessed May 16, 2006).

3 War and Peace

War and Peace

While opposition to war is not a modern phenomenon, this chapter focuses on anti-war protest in the twentieth and twenty-first centuries. Beginning in the twentieth century, advancements in transportation and communication permitted larger planned gatherings and brought home commentary on war policy and images of protest.

When World War I erupted in Europe in 1914, the United States wrestled with whether to enter the war. For three years, the United States proclaimed neutrality in the conflict, but when the United States entered the war against the German and Austrian empires, some citizens opposed the shift in policy and the revival of the draft. Opponents of the war included socialists, anarchists, German-Americans and many women's and religious groups. In response to anti-war protests, the government passed new Sedition Acts, criminalizing some public acts and speech in opposition to the government war policy. This chapter features articles on the World War I peace and anti-conscription movements, as well as the "Bonus Army" mass veterans' protest for promised benefits.

World War II was marked by relatively little anti-war protest. The citizens of the nations fighting Nazi Germany and Imperial Japan for the most part supported war as the only way to stop brutal and aggressive regimes.

Many sources in this chapter chronicle the peace movement in the United States during the Vietnam War era. The confluence of the counterculture movement and peace activism among the nation's youth sparked mass protests against the conflict in Vietnam and produced many of the last century's iconic images of antiwar protest. As reinstatement of the draft heightened antiwar sentiment, radical protesters marched, and burned flags and draft cards. When protestors and police or National Guardsmen met, the results could be tragic, such as at Kent State in 1970. The Vietnam War had its supporters as well, who turned out to counterprotest and, at least according to President Nixon, constituted the "great silent majority" of Americans.

The fighting in Afghanistan and Iraq has sparked a new round of demonstrations in the twenty-first century, with anti-war protestors and counterprotestors taking to the streets. Featured in this chapter are articles on antiwar protests in Europe and the United States, including those led by controversial activist Cindy Sheehan, whose son was killed in combat in Iraq. Also highlighted here are efforts to reduce the influence of military recruiters in schools and a rally in support of U.S. troops in Iraq.

Women Carrying Peace Banner

Photograph

By: Anonymous

Date: 1915

Source: © Bettmann/Corbis.

About the Photographer: This photograph is part of the Bettman Archives, held by the Corbis Corporation, a digital imaging and photography company with head-quarters in Seattle and offices worldwide.

INTRODUCTION

The photograph depicts members of the Women's Peace Party (WPP) demonstrating in Manhattan, New York in 1915. The WPP had been formed in January of that year in protest at the out-break the previous summer of war in Europe. By 1915, the war was rapidly becoming a worldwide conflict, although the United States remained neutral at this time. The first major demonstration against the war by women in America had been held within a month of its outbreak, when 1,500 women marched along Fifth Avenue in New York, dressed in black mourning clothes, to the sound of muffled drumbeat. The August 1914 peace parade contributed to the forma-tion of a number of influential American peace organ-izations, including the WPP and the nationwide American Union against Militarism.

The WPP, which was not a party in the political sense, owed its origins to two important social move-ments of the time: the international peace movement and the women's suffrage movement. The two main leaders of the WPP at the time of its formation, Jane Addams and Carrie Chapman Catt, were central fig-ures in these two social movements respectively.

The peace movement had been growing in impor-tance since the late nineteenth century, when the first international official Peace Conference took place in The Hague in 1898. In America there were reportedly some forty-five separate peace organizations estab-lished between 1900 and 1914. Jane Addams was prominent in the peace movement and was an active member of the Anti-Imperialist League.

The American women's suffrage movement had been actively campaigning for the political enfran-chisement of women for more than half a century, and had organized as the National American Woman Suffrage Association (NAWSA). This organization had formed strong linkages with women's groups in Europe, through the International Woman Suffrage Alliance (IWSA) and the International Council of Women (ICW). The outbreak of war was seen initially by the suffragists as a threat to the cause of women's enfranchisement, as well as a threat to the lives of their many friends and comrades in Europe.

More than 3,000 women attended the WPP's first convention in 1915 and its membership reached a peak of 40,000 in early 1916, by which time there were numerous branches across the country, and many prominent American women had joined the Party. In April 1915, the WPP sent a delegation to the conven-tion of the Women's International League for Peace and Freedom (WILPF) in The Hague, Holland. At home, they pressured President Woodrow Wilson to continue his attempts to persuade the warring nations to negotiate a peace settlement, and through the inter-national women's peace movement they attempted to influence the statements of the warring nations to cease the hostilities, but met with little success. The Party became divided internally by different political objectives, and in 1916 Catt and her NAWSA col-leagues broke away, concerned by issues of national security and becoming increasingly aware that involve-ment in war might bring greater opportunities for the emancipation of women.

PRIMARY SOURCE

WOMEN CARRYING PEACE BANNER
See primary source image.

SIGNIFICANCE

In 1916, President Wilson embarked on a prepar-edness campaign in the expectation that America might have to enter the war, which included the use of physical education classes in schools for the purpose of military training. The WPP were strongly opposed to the school program and held mass demonstrations in protest.

In 1917, America entered the war in response to Germany's renewed submarine campaign in which many U.S. vessels had been sunk with the loss of American lives. The involvement of the United States was the decisive factor in the Allied nations' victory against Germany and the other Central Powers.

Soon after the end of the war, suffrage was granted to many American women through the Nineteenth Amendment to the U.S. Constitution, which was

PRIMARY SOURCE

Women Carrying Peace Banner: Women march down Fifth Avenue, New York City, in a 1915 protest against war. They are led by (left to right): Rose Young, Alice Carpenter, Florence Woolson, and Portia Willis. © BETTMANN/CORBIS.

approved by Congress in June 1919 and ratified by thirty-six states during the following year.

The women's peace movement was one of the earliest manifestations of the politicization of women in the western world. This can be largely attributed to the major social, economic and technological changes of the late nineteenth and early twentieth centuries which were transforming women's lives and ways of thinking.

Social and political systems were changing with the extension of suffrage to all male adults in many western countries, while rapid capitalization and the creation of jobs to support the war effort were increasing the numbers of women who were in paid employment outside the home. In the family sphere, improved domestic technology was freeing many women from the drudgery of household chores that had previously

taken up much of their time, while the introduction of efficient contraceptive techniques meant that they no longer spent most of their lives rearing children. Smaller family sizes also meant that more women were able to receive an education. Under these circumstances, women started to question many of the social and political norms of their time, and began to organize themselves to fight for political objectives, even though their lack of suffrage in many countries excluded them from doing so through established mechanisms.

Within the peace movement, women put forward a female perspective on the cost of war, claiming that women suffered not only as a result of the violence against them as citizens of a society at war, but in terms of their emotional and financial loss when male partners or close relatives were killed. However, once war started, many women

"MISGUIDED LADY" PUTTING UP POSTER.

This anti-isolationist cartoon from World War I (1914–1918) portrays a thinly disguised German solider putting up a banner for the Organization of American Women for Strict Neutrality. © CORBIS. REPRODUCED BY PERMISSION.

turned away from the movement as nationalist loyalties took precedence in their emotions.

The impact of the women's peace movement is difficult to measure. Its main objective of bringing about an end to the First World War was not achieved, and while its efforts and the increased visibility of women in the political sphere may have helped to bring about the enfranchisement of American women after the War, this achievement was probably due in at least equal measure to the contributions that American women had made to the war effort.

FURTHER RESOURCES

Alonso, Harriet Hyman. *Peace as a Women's Issue: A History of the U.S. Movement for World Peace and Women's Rights.* Syracuse, N.Y.: Syracuse University Press, 1993.

Degen, Marie Louise. *The History of the Women's Peace Party.* The John Hopkins Press, 1939.

Wynn, Neil A. *From Progressivism to Prosperity: World War I and American Society.* Holmes & Meier, 1986.

No-Conscription League Manifesto

Pamphlet

By: Emma Goldman

Date: 1917

Source: Goldman, Emma. "No-Conscription League Manifesto." Records of the Department of War and Military Intelligence Division, Record Group 165, National Archives, 1917.

About the Author: Emma Goldman (1869–1940), also known as Red Emma, was one of the most famed anarchists of the early twentieth century. A speaker and writer, Goldman had immigrated to the United States from Lithuania in 1885. Imprisoned during World War I for obstructing conscription, she was deported in 1919 for being an alien radical.

INTRODUCTION

The No Conscription League only lasted for six weeks during 1917. Founded and led by anarchist Emma Goldman in New York City, the league specialized in anti-draft manifestos, mass meetings, and defiant rhetoric. The stated purpose of the organization was to simply stand by those who had already decided to refuse military service.

Shortly after its entry into World War I in April 1917, the United States instituted a draft. As had happened with the first draft during the Civil War, the issue of forcing men to put their lives and limbs at risk quickly became controversial. When Great Britain began conscription in 1916, the law created the category of conscientious objector to allow pacifists to serve their country in a noncombatant role if they could convince a tribunal of the quality of their objection. The U.S. Selective Service Act of May 1917 provided for religious conscientious objectors but had no formal mechanism for recognizing such men. In practice, the exemption did not work well. During the war about three thousand members of recognized peace churches, such as the Quakers, were granted noncombatant alternatives to military service. Those who belonged to religious sects without a traditional antiwar stance, who opposed war for political reasons, or who refused any form of compulsory service were

Emma Goldman. THE LIBRARY OF CONGRESS.

forcibly inducted. The political objectors included socialists, anarchists, members of the International Workers of the World, and radicals.

As an anarchist, Goldman did not want to tell anyone what to do. As a woman and therefore ineligible for conscription, she refused to tell men not to fight. Accordingly, the No Conscription League did not counsel anyone against compliance with the draft.

PRIMARY SOURCE

NO CONSCRIPTION! CONSCRIPTION has now become a fact in this country. It took England fully 18 months after she engaged in the war to impose compulsory military service on her people. It was left for "free" America to pass a conscription bill six weeks after she declared war against Germany.

What becomes of the patriotic boast of America to have entered the European war in behalf of the principle of democracy? But that is not all. Every country in Europe has recognized the right of conscientious objectors—of men who refuse to engage in war on the ground that they are opposed to taking life. Yet this democratic country makes

no such provision for those who will not commit murder at the behest of the war profiteers. Thus the "land of the free and the home of the brave" is ready to coerce free men into the military yoke.

No one to whom the fundamental principle of liberty and justice is more than an idle phrase, can help but realize that the patriotic clap-trap now shouted by press, pulpit and the authorities, betrays a desperate effort of the ruling class in this country to throw sand in the eyes of the masses and to blind them to the real issue confronting them. That issue is the Prussianizing of America so as to destroy whatever few liberties the people have achieved through an incessant struggle of many years.

Already all labor protective laws have been abrogated, which means that while husbands, fathers and sons are butchered on the battlefield, the women and children will be exploited in our industrial bastiles to the heart's content of the American patriots for gain and power.

Freedom of speech, of press and assembly is about to be thrown upon the dungheap of political guarantees. But crime of all crimes, the flower of the country is to be forced into murder whether or not they believe in war or in the efficacy of saving democracy in Europe by the destruction of democracy at home.

Liberty of conscience is the most fundamental of all human rights, the pivot of all progress. No man may be deprived of it without losing every vestige of freedom of thought and action. In these days when every principle and conception of democracy and individual liberty is being cast overboard under the pretext of democratizing Germany, it behooves every liberty-loving man and woman to insist on his or her right of individual choice in the ordering of his life and actions.

The NO-CONSCRIPTION LEAGUE has been formed for the purpose of encouraging conscientious objectors to affirm their liberty of conscience and to make their objection to human slaughter effective by refusing to participate in the killing of their fellow men.

The NO-CONSCRIPTION LEAGUE is to be the voice of protest against the coercion of conscientious objectors to participate in the war. Our platform may be summarized as follows:

We oppose conscription because we are internationalists, anti-militarists, and opposed to all wars waged by capitalistic governments.

We will fight for what we choose to fight for; we will never fight simply because we are ordered to fight.

We believe that the militarization of America is an evil that far outweighs, in its anti-social and anti-libertarian effects, any good that may come from America's participation in the war.

We will resist conscription by every means in our power, and we will sustain those who, for similar reasons, refuse to be conscripted.

We are not unmindful of the difficulties in our way. But we have resolved to go ahead and spare no effort to make the voice of protest a moral force in the life of this country. The initial efforts of the conscientious objectors in England were fraught with many hardships and danger, but finally the government of Great Britain was forced to give heed to the steadily increasing volume of public protest against the coercion of conscientious objectors. So we, too, in America, will doubtless meet the full severity of the government and the condemnation of the war-mad jingoes, but we are nevertheless determined to go ahead. We feel confident in arousing thousands of people who are conscientious objectors to the murder of their fellow men and to whom a principle represents the most vital thing in life.

Resist conscription. Organize meetings. Join our League. Send us money. Help us to give assistance to those who come in conflict with the government. Help us to publish literature against militarism and against conscription.

SIGNIFICANCE

After organizing two public rallies against conscription, Goldman became the subject of a government investigation. However, Goldman had immigrated to America because the country promised free choice and she would not be intimidated into silence. Having learned that federal agents had infiltrated her rallies to entrap nonregistrants, she vowed to limit her future league activities to the written word. The government had other plans. On June 15, 1917, Goldman was arrested under the Alien and Sedition Acts for obstructing the war effort and organizing anti-conscription rallies. Promptly convicted, she received a sentence of two years in prison. In 1919, Goldman was deported. She settled in Britain and continued to advocate for the rights of the working class until her death during a speaking tour in Canada.

A number of war objectors were court-martialed and sentenced to terms in military camps and prison. Of the five hundred American men who were court-martialed for resisting the draft, seventeen received death sentences and 142 received life terms. Although none of the death sentences was ever carried out, physical abuse of objectors in military camps was commonplace. Guards subjected objectors to compulsory exercise, solitary confinement, inadequate rations and cruel punishment. About twenty-five objectors died in prison. Meanwhile, more than 1,500 Mennonites,

Hutterites, and Amish fled to Canada to avoid military service. The American Union Against Militarism and the American Civil Liberties Union (then known as the National Civil Liberties Bureau) were founded in part to provide legal aid to these men.

The suppression of free speech and brutal treatment accorded objectors during World War I became a matter of public discussion and concern as the United States debated the merits of isolationism in the 1920s and 1930s. By the time of World War II, most major countries in the West had passed legislation regulating conscientious objection. The abuses of World War I would not be repeated in the United States.

FURTHER RESOURCES
Books

Harries, Meiron and Susie Harries. *The Last Days of Innocence: America at War, 1917–1918.* New York: Vintage, 1997.

McKay, Ernest A. *Against Wilson and War, 1914–1917.* Malabar, Fla.: Krieger, 1996.

Moritz, Theresa and Albert Moritz. *The World's Most Dangerous Woman: A New Biography of Emma Goldman.* Vancouver: Subway, 2001.

Schlissel, Lillian. *Conscience in America: A Documentary History of Conscientious Objection in America, 1757–1967.* New York: Dutton, 1968.

The Bonus Army

World War I Veterans Protest in Washington, D.C.

Photograph

By: Anonymous

Date: June 21, 1932

Source: Photo by MPI/Getty Images.

About the Photographer: This photograph is part of the collection at Getty Images, a worldwide provider of visual content materials to such communications groups as advertisers, broadcasters, designers, magazines, new media organizations, newspapers, and producers. The photographer is not known.

INTRODUCTION

In the days and weeks after a stock market crash set off the Great Depression in October 1929, Americans turned to every possible financial resource. Those among the unemployed who were veterans of World War I turned to the IOUs they had received from

PRIMARY SOURCE

The Bonus Army: Members of the "Bonus Army" gather around a shack with an American flag, in a shantytown within sight of the U.S. Capitol, June 21, 1932. PHOTO BY MPI/GETTY IMAGES.

the U.S. government. In the summer of 1932, they marched to Washington, D.C. to demand payment from Congress.

In 1924, during boom times, Congress had voted to pay $1000 in 1945 to each veteran of World War I to compensate each man for his military service. Those who served as privates during the war earned only one dollar a day, much less than civilians working in the war industry. Veterans' organizations had lobbied for this adjusted compensation but first President Warren G. Harding and then President Calvin Coolidge vetoed the bill. Finally, the bill became law over Coolidge's veto.

Many of the veterans feared that they and their families would starve to death before collecting the money in 1945. In a time of great distress, they considered it reasonable to ask for their money to be paid ahead of schedule. In 1929, in response to their pleas, Representative Wright Patman of Texas, a former machine gunner, introduced a bill providing for immediate payment in full. It was defeated, but Patman kept the bill before Congress. It began to act as a magnet, attracted homeless and unemployed ex-servicemen to Washington, where they lobbied for its passage.

The Bonus March was largely spontaneous. From one city after another groups of veterans began to move toward Washington. Some men brought their wives and children. While some marched in overalls, many wore parts of their military uniforms. After about 30,000 marchers set up camp in Washington, President Herbert Hoover persuaded Congress to vote down immediate payment of the bonus because its $2.4 billion cost was too expensive.

PRIMARY SOURCE

THE BONUS ARMY

See primary source image.

SIGNIFICANCE

After the defeat of the Bonus Bill, many veterans did not leave Washington because they had no homes to return to. The Treasury Department then ordered the removal of veterans who were staying in a old building that department officials wanted to demolish to provide work for the unemployed. Word of the impending expulsion spread quickly, and men from other bonus marcher camps came running to prevent the evictions. A riot ensued in which two men were killed by Treasury Police.

After this violence, the District Commissioners asked for military assistance to restore order. On July 28, 1932, Hoover sent regular army troops under the command of General Douglas MacArthur to remove the marchers. MacArthur used tanks, tear gas, and cavalry to roust the veterans from their main camp in Anacostia Flats. Residents had no time to remove any of their belongings. Women and children ran while photographers snapped pictures. The camp was then burned to the ground.

The public revulsion against the attack upon the heroes of yesteryear was so great that many involved attempted to place the blame elsewhere. Hoover ultimately accepted responsibility. When Franklin D. Roosevelt, campaigning for the presidency against Hoover, saw the photos of the burning camp in the newspaper, he knew that he had just won the election. The Bonus March placed the final nail in the coffin of Hoover's presidency.

FURTHER RESOURCES
Books

Daniels, Roger. *The Bonus March: An Episode of the Great Depression.* Westport, CT: Greenwood, 1971.

Dickson, Paul and Thomas B. Allen. *The Bonus Army: An American Epic.* New York: Walker, 2005.

The "Bonus Army", veterans of the First World War stage a massed vigil on the lawn of the U.S. Capitol, Washington DC, while the Senate debate their case. About 2000 protestors refused to leave after a demand for payment of a war bonus was not approved by the Senate. PHOTO BY MPI/GETTY IMAGES.

Lisio, Donald J. *The President and Protest: Hoover, MacArthur, and the Bonus Riot.* New York: Fordham University Press, 1994.

Norwegian Anti-Nazi Protest

German Occupation of Norway, 1940–1945

Photograph

By: Anonymous

Date: January 5, 1942

Source: © Bettmann/Corbis.

About the Photographer: This photograph is a part of the archive maintained by Corbis Corporation, an international provider of visual content materials to a wide range of consumers in the communications industries. The identity of the photographer is unknown.

PRIMARY SOURCE

Norwegian Anti-Nazi Protest: A child stands next to anti-Nazi graffiti showing support for the deposed Norwegian king, 1942.
© BETTMANN/CORBIS.

INTRODUCTION

Prior to 1905, Norway had been organized in a variety of national structures and had participated in various alliances with its Scandinavian neighbors. Norway became an independent nation once more in 1905, when its union with Sweden terminated. Shortly after Norway's independence, King Haakon VII (1872–1957) was installed as the head of Norway's constitutional monarchy, fulfilling a national referendum that selected this form of government over that of a republic. Norway was an officially neutral nation during World War I.

When World War II erupted in September 1939 with the German invasion of Poland, Norway immediately declared itself neutral, as did its Scandinavian neighbors, Sweden, Finland, and Denmark. Norway's proximity to England across the North Sea made its fjords and ice-free ports an attractive potential base for Germany from which to attack British shipping with

both surface ships and submarines. Germany also saw Norway as a useful staging ground for its air force. The Russian invasion of Finland in late 1939 reinforced for Germany the strategic importance of the entire Scandinavian region.

Germany invaded Norway in April 1940. After a two-month campaign in which the Norwegian armed forces were supported by British troops, the German army gained control of the country. King Haakon and his ministers escaped to England, where they established a government-in-exile for the duration of the war. Many Norwegians left the country shortly after the German occupation began, many of whom joined the British or Canadian armed forces. Approximately 50,000 Norwegian civilians fled to neutral Sweden, where they lived in refugee camps for the duration of the war.

The German effort to subjugate Norway was significantly aided by local sympathizers led by Vidkun

Quisling (1887–1945), a former military leader who headed a political party modeled after the German Nazi Party at the time of the German invasion. Quisling was established as the prime minister of the pro-German government that nominally led Norway until the end of the war in 1945.

PRIMARY SOURCE

NORWEGIAN ANTI-NAZI PROTEST
See primary source image.

SIGNIFICANCE

Norway represented a considerable strategic prize for the German armed forces in the spring of 1940. When France fell to the German army in June 1940, the earlier conquest of Norway meant that England was effectively surrounded on the European continent. However, the distance from Germany, the rugged terrain, and the determined efforts of the Norwegian underground resistance movement throughout the entire German occupation required Germany to maintain a very large military presence in Norway—approximately 350,000 German soldiers were stationed in Norway throughout the war. This deployment, a ratio of one German soldier for every eight Norwegian citizens, represented a significant drain on German military resources.

The sign supporting King Haakon shown in this photograph is an example of the Norwegian civil disobedience that took place throughout the German occupation. The government-in-exile headed by the king in London made regular radio broadcasts into Norway. The London exiles also produced a continual stream of leaflets and other paper propaganda in an effort to maintain a national spirit in Norway throughout the occupation.

The most subtle of the acts of civil disobedience was the "paper clip protest" conducted by Norwegians in every walk of life at various times during the German occupation. The paper clip was invented by a Norwegian, Johan Vaaler, in 1899. When the Norwegian government fled the German invasion in 1940, the German military leadership decreed that no Norwegian citizens could wear any button, image, or likeness of King Haakon on their person. The paper clip—a uniquely Norwegian invention designed to hold items together—was the popular symbol seized upon as a replacement for images of the king and as a sign of Norwegian unity.

Millions of paper clips are shown on display in a train car outside at Whitwell Middle School in Whitwell, Tennessee, September 2, 2004. The students started collecting paper clips after learning that some Norwegians wore them on clothing as an anti-Nazi protest and memorial for Holocaust victims. AP IMAGES.

The paper clips also came to have a second meaning. When the German occupiers required the Jewish residents of the capital city of Oslo to wear a yellow star to distinguish themselves from the rest of the Norwegian population, the paper clip became a symbol of solidarity with the Jewish citizens. Ultimately, the German occupiers learned of the significance of the paper clip that appeared on the lapels of Norwegians and many were jailed for this form of silent expression.

The photograph is also significant in its representation of the depth of passion that most Norwegians felt for their nation throughout the German occupation. The Norwegian resistance movement was an active and well organized force throughout the war. Given the proximity of the Norwegian coastline to England, a number of commando-style raids were conducted as joint operations by the Norwegian resistance and British operatives. The most significant military success achieved by the Norwegian resistance was directed at the German atomic research program based in Norway. A key heavy water manufacturing plant was destroyed in March 1943, followed by the sinking of a ship carrying 1,300 lb (590 kg) of heavy water in February 1944. (Heavy water contains deuterium, a heavy isotope of hydrogen, which renders the water useful in the creation of a sustained, nuclear chain reaction.) These acts slowed the German nuclear research program that, at the time of the attacks, was probably more advanced than the Allied program.

It is clear that the Norwegian sense of patriotism did not dim during the five years of occupation. Norway quickly re-established itself as a constitutional monarchy after the German surrender in Europe in May 1945. Quisling was tried and executed for treason in October 1945. However, Quisling achieved a peculiar form of immortality; a "quisling" is a recognized term for traitor in European English usage.

FURTHER RESOURCES
Books
Kersaudy, Francois. *Norway 1940*. Lincoln: University of Nebraska Press, 1998.

Mann, Chris. *Hitler's Artic War: The German Campaign in Norway, Finland and the USSR 1940–45*. New York: Thomas Dunne Books, 2003.

Web sites
BBC. "The Norway Campaign in World War Two." <http://www.bbc.co.uk/history/war/wwtwo/norway_campaign_01.shtml> (accessed June 2, 2006).

EuroDocs. "History of Norway: Primary Documents." <http://eudocs.lib.byu.edu/index.php/History_of_Norway:_Primary_Documents> (accessed June 1, 2006).

The Atlantic Charter

Declaration

By: Franklin D. Roosevelt and Winston Churchill

Date: August 12, 1941

Source: Roosevelt, Franklin D. and Winston Churchill. The Atlantic Charter. August 12, 1941. Courtesy of the Illinois Digital Archives.

About the Author: Franklin D. Roosevelt (1882–1945) was the thirty-second president of the United States of America, serving from 1933–1945. Winston Church (1874–1965) served as the Prime Minister of Britain from 1940–1945.

INTRODUCTION
Prior to Japanese attacks on the U.S. military facilities at Pearl Harbor, Hawaii, on December 6, 1941, U.S. foreign policy was often characterized as an isolationist. The senate refused to allow the U.S. to join the League of Nations, and those who developed foreign policy condemned U.S. intervention into the Western hemisphere. Following the devastation of World War I (1915–1918), most Americans were opposed to a military build up and supported the disarmament that occurred after the war. In Europe, however, Hitler began to reveal his war plans by 1938. In 1939, the U.S. had declared its neutrality in the conflict that had begun to spread across Europe. By 1940, Franklin Roosevelt had been reelected U.S. president and the U.S. Congress passed a conscription bill. In Europe, France signed an armistice with Germany, and Britain became the target of daily air raids. Without popular support to join the war, the U.S. offered its support to the allied nations in the form of the Lend-Lease Act and U.S. Naval escorts of supply convoys en route to Britain. The prime minister of Britain, Winston Churchill, needed the U.S. to become more active in the war effort, and in August of 1941, Churchill met with President Roosevelt at a secret meeting. Prior to this meeting, President Roosevelt and Prime Minister Churchill had corresponded, but had never met fact-to-face.

Both Roosevelt and Churchill went to great lengths to come to the meeting and each came with a different agenda. Roosevelt traveled aboard the presidential yacht, *Potomac*, and then aboard the USS *Augusta* to Placentia Bay, Newfoundland. Churchill crossed the Atlantic Ocean aboard the HMS *Prince of Wales* to the secret meeting weeks after the vessel engaged and sunk the German battleship *Bismarck*. Churchill arrived at the meeting with the first draft of what would become the Atlantic Charter. For Churchill, the charter would serve as a roadmap to guide the struggle against Nazi Germany. Roosevelt sought to end the colonial era. Americans mistrusted some British motives, considering them to be a continuation of the colonial Old World era. As such, the scope of the charter was expanded to encompass the principles for peace following the war.

Each leader was required to compromise on key components to the charter. Churchill was forced to

THE Atlantic Charter

THE President of THE UNITED STATES OF AMERICA and the Prime Minister, Mr. *Churchill*, representing HIS MAJESTY'S GOVERNMENT IN THE UNITED KINGDOM, being met together, deem it right to make known certain common principles in the national policies of their respective countries on which they base their hopes for a better future for the world.

1.　*Their countries seek no aggrandizement, territorial or other.*

2.　*They desire to see no territorial changes that do not accord with the freely expressed wishes of the peoples concerned.*

3.　*They respect the right of all peoples to choose the form of government under which they will live; and they wish to see sovereign rights and self-government restored to those who have been forcibly deprived of them.*

4.　*They will endeavor, with due respect for their existing obligations, to further the enjoyment by all States, great or small, victor or vanquished, of access, on equal terms, to the trade and to the raw materials of the world which are needed for their economic prosperity.*

5.　*They desire to bring about the fullest collaboration between all nations in the economic field with the object of securing, for all, improved labor standards, economic advancement and social security.*

6.　*After the final destruction of the Nazi tyranny, they hope to see established a peace which will afford to all nations the means of dwelling in safety within their own boundaries, and which will afford assurance that all the men in all the lands may live out their lives in freedom from fear and want.*

7.　*Such a peace should enable all men to traverse the high seas and oceans without hindrance.*

8.　*They believe that all of the nations of the world, for realistic as well as spiritual reasons, must come to the abandonment of the use of force. Since no future peace can be maintained if land, sea or air armaments continue to be employed by nations which threaten, or may threaten, aggression outside of their frontiers, they believe, pending the establishment of a wider and permanent system of general security, that the disarmament of such nations is essential. They will likewise aid and encourage all other practicable measures which will lighten for peace-loving peoples the crushing burden of armaments.*

August 14, 1941

FRANKLIN D. ROOSEVELT

WINSTON S. CHURCHILL

OWI Poster No. 50. Additional copies may be obtained upon request from the Division of Public Inquiries, Office of War Information, Washington, D. C.　　　U.S. GOVERNMENT PRINTING OFFICE 1943—O-517773

The Atlantic Charter, signed by Franklin Roosevelt and Winston Churchill on August 14, 1941, outlines the principles that the United States and the United Kingdom sought to achieve in fighting Nazi Germany. ILLINOIS DIGITAL ARCHIVES.

The Declaration by United Nations, signed by 26 nations on January 1, 1942. The document declared the intention of those countries to uphold the Atlantic Charter, defeat the Axis Powers, and defend jusitce for peaceful nations. © HULTON-DEUTSCH COLLECTION/CORBIS.

accept Roosevelt's goal of ensuring freedom of the seas. Churchill was also forced to broaden the scope of the charter to include language about self-determination for all peoples, fueling the movement to grant independence to British colonies. Roosevelt compromised on the goal of creating an international organization. The secret treaties in Europe that predated the World Wars led the U.S. to adopt a policy of isolationism. The League of Nations, formed after World War I, was highly unpopular within the U.S. and as such, the U.S. failed to join the organization, leading to its subsequent demise. Seeking to avoid the perception that the charter would merely revive the League of Nations, Roosevelt agreed to the establishment of a system of general global security.

PRIMARY SOURCE

THE ATLANTIC CHARTER

The President of the Untied States of America and the Prime Minister, Mr. Churchill, representing His Majesty's Government in the United Kingdom, being met together, deem it right make known certain common principles in the national policies of the respective countries on which they base their hopes for a better future for the world.

1. Their countries seek no aggrandizement, territorial or other.

2. They desire to see no territorial changes that do not accord with the freely expressed wishes of the peoples concerned.

3. They respect the right of all peoples to choose the form of government under which they will live; and they wish to see sovereign rights and self government restored to those who have been forcibly deprived of them.

4. They will endeavor, with due respect for their existing obligations, to further the enjoyment by all States, great or small, victor or vanquished, of access, on equal terms to the trade and to the raw materials of the world which are needed for their economic prosperity.

5. They desire to bring about the fullest collaboration between all nations in the economic field with the object of securing, for all, improved labor standards, economic advancement and social security.

6. After the final destruction of the Nazi tyranny, they hope to see established a peace which will afford to all nations the means of dwelling in safety within their own boundaries, and which will afford assurance that all the men in all the lands may live out their lives in freedom from fear and want.

7. Such a peace should enable all men to traverse the high seas and oceans without hindrance.

8. They believe that all of the nations of the world, for realistic as well as spiritual reasons must come to the abandonment of the use of force. Since no future peace can be maintained if land, sea or air armaments continue to be employed by nations which threaten, or may threaten, aggression outside of their frontiers, they believe, pending the establishment of a wider and permanent system of general security, that the disarmament of such nations is essential. They will likewise aid and encourage all other practicable measures which will lighten for peace-loving peoples the crushing burden of armaments.

Franklin D. Roosevelt
Winston S. Churchill

August 14, 1941

SIGNIFICANCE

The conference convened on August 9, 1941, and concluded with a press conference three days later announcing the charter. The agreement was dubbed the Atlantic Charter by the *London Daily Herald*. The main goal for Churchill was to involve the U.S. more deeply in the war. However, the signing of the treaty did not result in an immediate declaration of war on Germany by the U.S. Although the charter recognized Nazi Germany as a mutual enemy, the U.S. would not become officially involved in the war until after the attack on Pearl Harbor. Although the charter did not bring the U.S. onto the battlefield as a British ally, it did solidify the relationship between the U.S. and Britain and endorsed aims for peace. The eight points to the charter served as an affirmation of common principles held by the two nations. In addition, the charter laid the framework for the creation of the United Nations after the war. Formed in 1945, the United Nations was intended to provide a forum for international negotiation that would bring the world closer to the ideals of the charter.

FURTHER RESOURCES
Periodicals

Haskew, Michael. "The Atlantic Charter laid the foundation for the United Nations." *World War II*. September 1, 2001.

Schlesinger, Arthur. "The Atlantic Charter: Design for Tomorrow?" *New York Times*. August 11, 1991.

Promoting the Maintenance of International Peace and Security in Southeast Asia

Gulf of Tonkin Resolution

Legislation

By: Lyndon B. Johnson and U.S. Congress

Date: August 6, 1964

Source: U.S. House of Representatives. 88th Congress, Second Session. "Report No. 1708. Promoting the Maintenance of International Peace and Security in Southeast Asia" August 6, 1964.

About the Author: Lyndon B. Johnson (1908–1973) was the thirty-sixth president of the United States. Although the speeches of modern American presidents are conventionally attributed to the presidents themselves, the actual words are often composed by professional speechwriters who remain anonymous.

INTRODUCTION

On August 3, 1964, the administration of President Lyndon B. Johnson (1908–1973) claimed that North Vietnam had made an unprovoked attack on a U.S. naval vessel operating in international waters in the Gulf of Tonkin, a large inlet forming the coast of North Vietnam and the southernmost portion of mainland China. Johnson's Secretary of Defense, Robert McNamara (1916–) said that "While on routine patrol of international waters the U.S. destroyer *Maddox* underwent an unprovoked attack." Two days later, it was claimed, North Vietnamese patrol boats attacked a pair of U.S. ships in the Tonkin Gulf. Johnson asked Congress to pass a resolution that would give him the authority to use military force against Vietnam; this message is the primary source given here. The legislation, H.J. Res.

1145, also known as the Gulf of Tonkin Resolution, was passed by unanimous vote in the House of Representatives and with only two dissenting votes in the Senate. Although Johnson had said in his message that the U.S. "seeks no wider war," the following year, 1965, saw a full-scale commitment of the U.S. military to fight the North Vietnamese. By 1969 over 540,000 U.S. troops were in Vietnam, based on the authority granted in the Gulf of Tonkin Resolution.

Yet the Gulf of Tonkin Resolution was, as many historians of the period now agree, founded on inaccurate claims.

First, it was not true that the *Maddox* was on routine patrol. According to the U.S. Naval Institute, the *Maddox* was actually gathering signals intelligence to be used for U.S.-directed commando attacks on North Vietnam. Under the guidance of the U.S. Central Intelligence Agency, a covert program of intelligence-gathering and sabotage missions against North Vietnam had begun in 1961. South Vietnamese commandos in fast patrol boats bought from Norway (to conceal U.S. involvement) bombarded the North Vietnamese coast using mortars, rockets, and recoilless rifles. The operation was approved personally by U.S. General William C. Westmoreland in Saigon, capital of South Vietnam. On July 31, 1964, patrol boats in the covert fleet attacked North Vietnamese installations on the islands of Hon Me and Hon Nieu. North Vietnam quickly lodged a formal complaint, but McNamara replied, inaccurately, that "Our Navy played absolutely no part in, was not associated with, was not aware of, any South Vietnamese actions, if there were any." When the signals-intelligence ship *Maddox* approached the North Vietnamese coast on August 2, 1964, the North Vietnamese assumed that it would take part in further attacks, and dispatched five torpedo boats to confront it. The *Maddox* fired across the bow of the lead North Vietnamese vessel; the North Vietnamese fired back; the *Maddox* drove off the vessels with its superior firepower, killing at least one sailor. The only damage suffered by the *Maddox* was a hit from a single machine-gun bullet.

Moreover, there was no second attack at all. Although U.S. vessels maneuvered vigorously and fired many rounds on the night of August 4, it is now known that they were shooting at empty ocean. In December, 2005, with the release of formerly classified documents of the National Security Agency (NSA), it was learned that the NSA's own operatives had, in the words of the agency's internal historian, "mishandled" signals intelligence and given a "deliberately skewed"

version of intercepted communications to the White House. "The overwhelming body of reports, if used," the NSA's historian wrote in a secret 2001 article, "would have told the story that no attack had happened. So a conscious effort ensued to demonstrate that an attack occurred." Although critics of the Gulf of Tonkin resolution had long argued that there had been no second attack, this was the first detailed confirmation of that claim. Despite the skewed intelligence, President Johnson himself quickly suspected that there had been no second attack. Tapes made by Johnson, declassified in 2001, showed him concluding only two weeks after the Gulf of Tonkin Resolution that "they [the North Vietnamese in the supposed second incident] hadn't fired at all." In 1965 he said, "For all I know, our Navy was shooting at whales out there." Yet Johnson had told Congress that there was "unequivocal proof" of a second Vietnamese attack. Until 2005, neither the Congress nor the U.S. public was ever informed that the crucial second attack, cited by Johnson in his message to Congress, had not occurred.

▉ PRIMARY SOURCE

88th Congress, 2nd Session

House of Representatives

Report No. 1708

Promoting the Maintenance of International Peace and Security in Southeast Asia

August 6, 1964.—Committed to the Committee of the Whole House on the State of the Union and ordered to be printed

Mr. Morgan, from the Committee on Foreign Affairs, submitted the following

Report

[To accompany H.J. Res. 1145]

The Committee on Foreign Affairs, to whom was referred the joint resolution (H.J. Res. 1145), to promote the maintenance of international peace and security in southeast Asia, having considered the same, report favorably thereon without amendment and recommend that the joint resolution do pass.

Committee Action

On August 5, 1964, the President of the United States transmitted to the Congress a message (H. Doc. 333, 88th Cong,. 2d sess.) requesting the Congress to take appropriate action to carry out certain recommendations relative to preserving the peace in southeast Asia. The text of the message follows:

To the Congress of the United States:

Last night I announced to the American people that the North Vietnamese regime had conducted further deliberate attacks against U.S. naval vessels operating in international waters, and that I had therefore directed air action against gunboats and supporting facilities used in these hostile operations. This air action has now been carried out with substantial damage to the boats and facilities. Two U.S. aircraft were lost in the action.

After consultation with the leaders of both parties in the Congress, I further announced a decision to ask the Congress for a resolution expressing the unity and determination of the United States in supporting freedom and in protecting peace in southeast Asia.

These latest actions of the North Vietnamese regime have given a new and grave turn to the already serious situation in southeast Asia. Our commitments in that area are well known to the Congress. They were first made in 1954 by President Eisenhower. They were further defined in the Southeast Asia Collective Defense Treaty approved by the Senate in February 1955.

This treaty with its accompanying protocol obligates the United States and other members to act in accordance with their constitutional processes to meet Communist aggression against any of the parties or protocol states.

Our policy in southeast Asia has been consistent and unchanged since 1954. I summarized it on June 2 in four simple propositions:

1. *America keeps her word.* Here as elsewhere, we must and shall honor our commitments.
2. *The issue is the future of southeast Asia as a whole.* A threat to any nation in that region is a threat to all, and a threat to us.
3. *Our purpose is peace.* We have no military, political, or territorial ambitions in the area.
4. *This is not just a jungle war, but a struggle for freedom on every front of human activity.* Our military and economic assistance to South Vietnam and Laos in particular has the purpose of helping these countries to repel aggression and strengthen their independence.

The threat to the free nations of southeast Asia has long been clear. The North Vietnamese regime has constantly sought to take over South Vietnam and Laos. This communist regime has violated the Geneva accords for Vietnam. It has systematically conducted a campaign of subversion, which includes the direction, training, and supply of personnel and arms for the conduct of guerrilla warfare in South Vietnamese territory. In Laos, the North Vietnamese regime has maintained military forces, used Laotian territory for infiltration into South Vietnam, and most recently carried out combat operations—all in direct violation of the Geneva agreements of 1962....

As President of the United States I have concluded that I should now ask the congress, on its part, to join in affirming the national determination that all such attacks will be met, and that the United States will continue in its basic policy of assisting the free nations of the area to defend their freedom.

I have repeatedly made clear, the United States intends no rashness, and seeks no wider war. We must make it clear to all that the United States is united in its determination to bring about the end of Communist subversion and aggression in the area. We seek the full and effective restoration of the international agreements signed in Geneva in 1954, with respect to South Vietnam, and again in Geneva in 1962, with respect to Laos.

I recommend a resolution expressing the support of the Congress for all necessary action to protect our Armed Forces and to assist nations covered by the SEATO Treaty. At the same time, I assure the Congress that we shall continue readily to explore any avenues of political solution that will effectively guarantee the removal of Communist subversion and the preservation of the independence of the nations of the area....

I urge the congress to enact such a resolution promptly and thus to give convincing evidence to the aggressive communist nations, and to the world as a whole, that our policy in southeast Asia will be carried forward—and that the peace and security of the area will be preserved.

The events of this week would in any event have made the passage of a congressional resolution essential. But there is an additional reason for doing so at a time when we are entering on 3 months of political campaigning. Hostile nations must understand that in such a period the United States will continue to protect its national interests, and that in these matters there is no division among us.

Lyndon B. Johnson.

The White House, *August 5, 1964*

SIGNIFICANCE

The Gulf of Tonkin Resolution is generally viewed as a key step in the escalation of the Vietnam War, which ended in 1975 with final U.S. withdrawal and the eventual victory for North Vietnam and the Communist rebels of South Vietnam.

In recent years, the Gulf of Tonkin incident has been repeatedly compared to the lead-up to the Iraq war. As with Vietnam, an imminent military threat against the United States was cited by the U.S.

government in the months before the U.S. invasion of Iraq. Special emphasis was placed on stockpiles of chemical, biological, and possibly nuclear weapons allegedly possessed by Iraq. On the basis of such claims, Congress approved the 2002 Authorization for Use of Military Force Against Iraq with relatively little dissent. However, when U.S. military inspection teams arrived in Iraq, they repeated the earlier failure of U.N. inspection teams to find any stockpiles of weapons of mass destruction. In December 2005, President George W. Bush admitted that "It is true that much of the intelligence turned out to be wrong."

According to the *New York Times* (Oct. 31, 2005) the National Security Agency (NSA) delayed release of its secret conclusion that there had been no second Gulf of Tonkin attack because "higher-level agency [NSA] policymakers ... were fearful that it might prompt uncomfortable comparisons with the flawed intelligence used to justify the war in Iraq." An agency spokesperson denied that "any political consideration was involved," but such comparisons were nevertheless drawn; in 2005, the National Security Archive at George Washington University stated that "the parallels between the faulty intelligence on Tonkin Gulf and the manipulated intelligence used to justify the Iraq War make it all the more worthwhile to re-examine the events of August 1964 in light of new evidence."

FURTHER RESOURCES

Books

Alterman, Eric. *When Presidents Lie: A History of Official Deception and its Consequences*. New York: Viking, 2004.

Moïse, Edwin E. *Tonkin Gulf and the Escalation of the Vietnam War*. Chapel Hill: University of North Carolina Press, 1996.

Periodicals

Lewis, Neil A. "A Nation Challenged: The Resolution: Measure Backing Bush's Use of Force Is as Broad as a Declaration of War, Experts Say." *The New York Times*. September 17, 2001.

Shane, Scott. "Vietnam Study, Casting Doubts, Remains Secret." *The New York Times*. October 31, 2005.

Shane, Scott. "Vietnam War Intelligence "Deliberately Skewed," Secret Study Says." *The New York Times*. December 2, 2005.

Web sites

CNN.com. "Bush Takes Responsibility for Invasion Intelligence." December 14, 2005. <http://edition.cnn.com/2005/POLITICS/12/14/bush.iraq/> (accessed May 18, 2006).

The National Security Archive, George Washington University. "Tonkin Gulf Intelligence "Skewed" According to Official History and Intercepts." December 1, 2005. <http://www.gwu.edu/~nsarchiv/NSAEBB/NSAEBB132/press20051201.htm> (accessed May 18, 2006).

U.S. Naval Institute. "The Secret Side of the Tonkin Gulf Incident (by Dale Andradé and Kenneth Conboy)." August, 1999. <http://www.usni.org/navalhistory/articles99/nhandrade.htm> (accessed May 18, 2006).

Counterprotesters Heckle Anti-War Demonstrators

Photograph

By: The Associated Press

Date: October 16, 1965

Source: AP Images.

About the Photographer: The Associated Press is a worldwide news agency based in New York.

INTRODUCTION

In the first mass organized protest against the Vietnam War, about 100,000 Americans in several dozen cities throughout the nation marched together on March 15 and 16, 1965 in the International Days of Protest. Organized by the Vietnam Day Committee (VDC), the marchers mostly did not seek withdrawal from Vietnam but instead advocated for negotiations with the North Vietnamese.

The Vietnam War had its roots in American support for the French governance of the country in the years immediately following World War II. In these years of the Cold War, the United States fought to stop the spread of communism from North Vietnam into South Vietnam. By the mid–1950s, the United States covered eighty-five percent of France's costs for men and materials to battle communist insurgents from the North. Supposed attacks by North Vietnamese patrol boats on U.S. Navy destroyers gave President Lyndon Johnson the justification in August 1964 to request permission from Congress to increase U.S. participation in Vietnam. Given a blank check to do whatever was necessary to protect American forces, Johnson began sending ground combat troops to Vietnam. On March 8, 1965, the ninth Marine Expeditionary Brigade stormed ashore onto the beaches of Da Nang as the first combat troops to

PRIMARY SOURCE

Counterprotestors Heckle Anti-War Demonstrators: College students carrying pro-American signs heckle anti-war student demonstrators protesting U.S. involvement in Vietnam at Boston Common in Boston, Massachusetts, October 16, 1965. AP IMAGES.

arrive. They were purportedly sent there to guard American installations, but the Marines soon began operating offensively.

The antiwar movement, led by students, formed in response to the commitment of combat troops to Vietnam as well as the escalating draft calls. Student activism usually met with strong resistance and criticism in these early days of the war. Students for a Democratic Society (SDS) was one of the few national student organizations to devote considerable energy to antiwar activism in the mid–1960s. SDS, founded in 1960 as a liberal multi-issue group, conducted research through its Peace Research and Education Project to build a strong case against U.S. involvement in Vietnam. SDS members formed VDC and organized the March 1965 protests in response to the arrival of combat troops. Portrayed as Communist dupes and spoiled young rich kids who used outrageous tactics to rebel against their parents, the students found it difficult to gain respect. In Seattle and New York City, marchers scuffled with hostile spectators. Passing motorists shouted and spit on the protesters. In Oakland, Hell's Angels motorcycle club members

attacked marchers while spectators drowned out protesters in Los Angeles by singing the theme from "The Mickey Mouse Club" television show. During the New York City march, in one of the best known episodes of draft resistance during the Vietnam War, a young Catholic pacifist David Miller burned his draft card in defiance of a recently enacted federal law. The remains of the card were quickly snatched up by an FBI agent and later used to send Miller to prison for two years.

PRIMARY SOURCE

COUNTERPROTESTERS HECKLE ANTI-WAR DEMONSTRATORS

See primary source image.

SIGNIFICANCE

In many cities, the International Days of Protest marches were the first local protests against the

Opponents of the anti-war movement heckle anti-war demonstrators who are marching in Washington to protest the U.S. presence in Iraq, October 25, 2003. AP IMAGES.

Vietnam War. Supporters of the war immediately responded to the marches. FBI director J. Edgar Hoover testified before Congress that the Communists had orchestrated the antiwar protests, despite the lack of any evidence to substantiate this claim. Most members of Congress believed Hoover and the government began large-scale investigations of the antiwar movement. Meanwhile, members of the American Legion, Veterans of Foreign Wars, and other pro-war groups planned a pro-war demonstration for October 30 in New York City. On that day, more than 20,000 people marched down Fifth Avenue in support of the government's policies. However, neither the government nor the pro-war organizations succeeded in mustering massive public support for U.S. policy in Vietnam. The antiwar movement continued to grow.

A majority of Americans turned against the war following the Tet Offensive in January 1968. Despite a nearly unlimited supply of air planes and artillery, rifles and mortars, napalm and night scopes, the draft and a massive defense budget, the United States could not impose control over one of the poorest countries in the world. Upon taking office in 1969, President Richard Nixon proposed to "Vietnamize" the war by turning all of the fighting over to the South Vietnamese. Nixon viewed this strategy as a honorable way of withdrawing. The last American ground forces left Vietnam in 1973 with the remaining U.S. military personnel exiting in 1975. The war officially ended on

April 30, 1975 when the South Vietnamese capital of Saigon fell to North Vietnamese forces.

FURTHER RESOURCES
Books
DeBenedetti, Charles. *An American Ordeal: The Antiwar Movement of the Vietnam Era*. Syracuse, NY: Syracuse University Press, 1997.

Olson, James S. and Randy Roberts. *Where the Domino Fell: America and Vietnam, 1945–1995*. New York: St. Martin's Press, 1996.

Wells, Tom. *The War Within: America's Battle Over Vietnam*. New York: Henry Holt, 1994.

Fortunate Son

Song lyrics

By: John Fogarty

Date: 1969

Source: Creedence Clearwater Revival. "Fortunate Son." *Willy and the Poorboys*. Jondora Music, 1969.

About the Author: John Fogarty founded Creedence Clearwater Revival, the leading American rock band from 1969 to 1971. The album *Willy and the Poor Boys* with the song, "Fortunate Son," came out in November 1969 and quickly became platinum-selling.

INTRODUCTION

John Fogarty of the 1960s rock group, Creedence Clearwater Revival (CCR), expressed something rare in American rock music. Unlike his peers, Fogarty showed a keen awareness of class differences. "Fortunate Son" (1969) was the only popular antiwar song of the 1960s to observe that the sons of the working class were more likely to be drafted than the sons of the privileged.

The United States had drafted men to serve in World War II and then resumed conscription in 1948 during the earliest years of the Cold War. Draft resistance was rare until the late 1960s when public opinion began to turn against American involvement in the Vietnam War. While public perception and subsequent public memory held that most Vietnam soldiers were drafted, in reality about half of soldiers were drafted. However, many draft-age males found it more prudent to enlist before their numbers came up because they thought they would be drafted anyway and they wanted to pick their branch of service. Many men chose to join the Air Force or Navy, as opposed to the Army or Marine Corps, to lessen their chances of going to Vietnam.

The image of a poor boy forced to fight while a rich man dodges the draft, popularized in Fogarty's song, is not quite accurate. A Massachusetts Institute of Technology study in 1992 found that while thirty percent of those killed in action came from the lowest third of the income range, twenty-six percent of combat deaths came from families earning in the highest third. Of all combat deaths in Vietnam, seventy-three percent of those killed were volunteers. The perception that blacks fought in disproportionate numbers is also not accurate. African American males made up 13.1 percent of the draft-age males and 12.6 percent of the military, showing that they served in numbers representative of their percentage of the population. Black servicemen also tended to volunteer for combat units at rates higher than whites.

Much of the anger about the draft came because of the number of deferments that allowed "fortunate sons" to avoid or delay service. Unlike the era of World War II, college students during Vietnam could obtain deferments because their education was deemed to be in the national interest by the federal government. Initially, college students were eligible for II-S deferments until they fulfilled their degree requirements or reached their twenty-fourth birthday, whichever came first. However, in early 1966, the Selective Service System initiated the Selective Service College Qualification Test. Any student ranking in the lower levels of his class became eligible for the draft.

PRIMARY SOURCE

Fortunate Son

Some folks are born made to wave the flag,
Ooh, they're red, white and blue.
And when the band plays hail to the chief,
Ooh, they point the cannon at you, lord.

It ain't me; it ain't me; I ain't no senator's son, son.
It ain't me; it ain't me; I ain't no fortunate one, no.

Yeah!

Some folks are born silver spoon in hand,
Lord, don't they help themselves, oh.
But when the taxman comes to the door,
Lord, the house looks like a rummage sale, yes.

It ain't me; it ain't me; I ain't no millionaire's son, no.
It ain't me; it ain't me; I ain't no fortunate one, no.

Some folks inherit star spangled eyes,
Ooh, they send you down to war, lord,

Anti-draft and anti-Vietnam War protest marchers are confronted by a wall of police officers in front of the Clay Street induction center in Oakland, California, on October 21, 1967. THE OAKLAND TRIBUNE/AP IMAGES.

And when you ask them, how much should we give?
Ooh, they only answer more! more! more! yeah,

It ain't me; it ain't me; I ain't no military son, son.
It ain't me; it ain't me; I ain't no fortunate one, one.

It ain't me; it ain't me; I ain't no fortunate one, no no no.
It ain't me; it ain't me; I ain't no fortunate son, no no no,

SIGNIFICANCE

CCR disbanded in October 1972 after its seventh album, *Mardi Gras* sold poorly. In subsequent years, Fogarty became bitterly estranged from the other band members. He released several solo albums and won a Grammy in 1997. CCR was inducted into the Rock and Roll Hall of Fame in 1993.

In December 1969, President Richard Nixon announced a draft lottery system that eliminated many of the inequities of the older system. However,

as the war continued and antiwar sentiment became more widespread, more young men began to resist the draft. The most popular way of beating the draft involved failing the preinduction physical. Once a young man became eligible for the draft, he was required to have an examination to determine his physical, mental, and moral fitness for military service. While some men pretended to be gay to get rejected for service, other men aggravated old sports injuries or artificially raised their blood pressure. A man who failed the examination would be classified as IV-F, permanently exempting him from all military service or I-Y, making him available only in time of declared war or national emergency.

By 1973, ground combat troop withdrawals allowed the president to end the draft as of July 1973 and create an all-volunteer army. The last American troops left Vietnam in 1975. The military has since remained an all-volunteer service.

FURTHER RESOURCES

Books

Herring, George C. *America's Longest War: The United States and Vietnam, 1950–1975*. New York: Alfred A. Knopf, 1986.

Krepinevich, Andrew F., Jr. *The Army and Vietnam*. Baltimore: Johns Hopkins University Press, 1986.

Olson, James S. and Randy Roberts. *Where the Domino Fell: America and Vietnam, 1945–1995*. New York: St. Martin's Press, 1996.

Draft Card Burning Protest

Photograph

By: Anonymous

Date: June 20, 1969

Source: AP/Wide World Photos. Reproduced by permission.

About the Photographer: This photograph is a part of the archive maintained by the Associated Press, a worldwide news agency based in New York. The photographer is not known.

INTRODUCTION

The Viet Nam era draft card is also known by its legal description, the status card. The draft card was an aspect of the Selective Service Act, the federal legislation that legalized the conscription of eligible males into the American armed services during the Viet Nam war (1962–1973).

In the early days of the military involvement of the United States in the Viet Nam conflict, the effects of the draft were not widely felt throughout the American population, as the number of American military personnel deployed in Viet Nam was less than 25,000 persons. After the Congress and the Senate passed the legislation known as the Gulf of Tonkin Resolution in August, 1964, President Lyndon Johnson (1908–1973) was empowered to take whatever military steps were deemed necessary to preserve American interests in Viet Nam and the greater South East Asia region. The American military presence and its corresponding exposure to casualties increased after 1965.

Between 1965 and 1969, the Selective Service Act provided various means whereby eligible males could be declared exempt from the draft. The most common exemptions were those extended to persons enrolled in a college or university, members of the National Guard, or members of the Peace Corps.

The American university campuses became prominent aspects of the growing anti-war movement that began to attract national attention after 1965. The burning of draft cards became such a popular method of protest against the war in Viet Nam that President Johnson signed into law an amendment to the federal legislation in August of 1965 that rendered the burning of a draft card to be a criminal act, punishable by up to five years in prison or a 10,000 dollar fine.

The constitutionality of the draft card prosecutions was tested in the Supreme Court of the United States in May, 1968, in the case of *United States v. O'Brien*. The Court upheld the law, ruling that the burning of a draft card interfered with the smooth and effective function of the Selective Service system. The court indicated that there were other means available to a person who wished to freely express their views concerning the war without destroying the government issued card.

As the involvement of the United States military in Viet Nam increased between 1966 and 1969, the forms of protest against the war broadened. In addition to the burning of draft cards, the well publicized refusal of boxer Cassius Clay (later Muhammad Ali) in 1966 to respond to his draft notice and the 'March on the Pentagon' as organized by various peace groups in 1967 brought further focus to the issues concerning the American involvement in Viet Nam.

As American military casualties mounted through 1968, chants such as 'Hey, hey, LBJ, how many kids did you kill today?' were directed at President Johnson at public gatherings by protestors. The anti-war movement was a significant factor in the decision of Johnson not to seek a further term in the 1968 presidential election.

Thousands of eligible young men under the draft fled the United States to Canada or Europe to avoid the prospect of being compelled into service in Viet Nam. When the peace talks involving representatives of the United States, North Viet Nam, and South Viet Nam did not produce an agreement to end the conflict, the war continued and the domestic protests took on an increased urgency through 1969. The protestor depicted burning his draft card in June, 1969 is representative of the sentiment expressed by a significant segment of the American population that the war was no longer worth the cost.

PRIMARY SOURCE

Draft Card Burning Protest: Protestor Ken Love burns his draft card in Chicago, June 20, 1969. AP/WIDE WORLD PHOTOS. REPRODUCED BY PERMISSION.

PRIMARY SOURCE

DRAFT CARD BURNING PROTEST

See primary source image.

SIGNIFICANCE

The primary significance of a draft eligible American male burning his draft card in the summer of 1969 is in the powerful symbolism that this simple act represents. The symbolic burning of the draft card was not an act that reflected the attitudes of much of the American population at that time. In a Gallup public opinion poll taken in July of 1969, a time roughly contemporaneous with that of the photograph, fifty-three percent of Americans surveyed approved of the manner in which President Richard Nixon was handling the Viet Nam war, with thirty percent who disapproved and the balance undecided. While the anti-war movement had an undeniable resonance with the young and the liberal elements of American society, in June 1969 there was not yet a broad consensus that the involvement in Viet Nam should end.

By 1969, the burning of a draft card did not defeat the subject's eligibility to be drafted; the American government had a data bank that operated independently of the paper card to record the identity of all persons liable to be drafted.

By the end of the American involvement in Viet Nam in 1973, over 170,000 eligible males were excused from active military service on the basis of being declared conscientious objectors. The protestors who demonstrated by burning their draft cards or evading service by leaving the United States are not included in this total.

Prosecution was not a common consequence of draft card burning. After the O'Brien ruling from the Supreme Court, there appears to have been an implicit desire on the part of law enforcement to avoid directing further attention at a visible example of the anti-war protest movement. Persons who burned their draft cards were often classified as 'delinquent' for the purposes of Selective Service and liable to be drafted in priority to the other eligible persons.

The Nixon administration was successful in temporarily solidifying a reasonably solid base of public support for its war management and direction when Nixon referred to his pro-war constituency in a speech made in November 1969, as the "Silent Majority" in the midst of a demonstrative anti-war movement.

Shortly after the Silent Majority speech, however, the protest movement picked up further momentum with the organizing of the National Moratorium, held November 15, 1969, involving protests held throughout the country, including a march on Washington by between 250,000 and 500,000 persons. With the revisions to the Selective Service process in December 1969 that placed an emphasis upon the random selection of males between the ages of nineteen and twenty years, the pace of the anti-war protests symbolized by the draft card burning photograph of June, 1969 accelerated.

The draft card burnings as a form of protest became obsolete in 1973 when the federal government suspended the military draft and any requirement on the part of otherwise eligible male to register for military service. The registration component was reinstituted in 1980, but the return to a conscripted military

Demonstrators applaud as a man burns his draft card during a Vietnam War protest in New York's Central Park on April 15, 1967. © BETTMANN/CORBIS.

service will require an act of Congress of the United States. Registration now has significant civil consequences, as a failure to register will prohibit a person from obtaining federal employment, admission to most state sponsored universities, and other forms of government programs.

FURTHER RESOURCES

Books

Bailey, Beth, William H. Chafe and Howard Sitkoff, ed. *A History of Our Time: Readings on Post-War America*. New York; Oxford University Press, 2002.

Elmer, Jerry. *Felon for Peace: The Memoir of a Viet Nam-era Draft Resister*. Nashville, Tennessee; Vanderbilt University Press, 2005.

Web sites

Washington Post. "The Viet Nam Protests: When Worlds Collided." 2000 <http://www.washingtonpost.com/wp-srv/local/2000/vietnam092799.htm> (accessed June 2, 2006).

UC Berkeley Library. "Anti Viet Nam War Protests, 1969." <http://lib.berkeley.edu.MRC/pacificaviet/#1969> (accessed June 2, 2006).

The Great Silent Majority

Speech

By: Richard M. Nixon

Date: November 3, 1969

Source: Nixon, Richard. Remarks delivered November 3, 1969. Available online at *American Rhetoric*. <http://www.americanrhetoric.com/speeches/richardnixon-greatsilentmajority.html> (accessed may 26, 2006).

About the Author: Richard M. Nixon (1913–1994) served as the 37th president of the United States from 1969 to 1974. Nixon had numerous foreign policy successes,

President Richard Nixon poses for pictures after his "silent majority" speech. © BETTMANN/CORBIS.

including the removal of U.S. combat troops from Vietnam, but ultimately resigned the presidency in the wake of the Watergate scandal.

INTRODUCTION

Richard M. Nixon entered the White House in 1969 determined not to allow the Vietnam War to destroy his presidency, as it had impaired the previous administration of Lyndon B. Johnson. On November 3, 1969, Nixon delivered a speech that he regarded as the most important of his career. He outlined his strategy for victory in Vietnam and declared that he would not allow policy to be dictated by antiwar protesters. He famously named his supporters as the Great Silent Majority.

By the fall of 1969, discontent with the Vietnam War was mounting in the United States. By September, only thirty-five percent of Americans supported Nixon's war policies. On October 15 of the same year, in towns and cities across the nation, opponents of the war participated in a massive moratorium protest. More than two million people held candlelight vigils, engaged in discussions, and attended church

services as part of the largest antiwar demonstration in American history. The media, which provided live coverage of the rallies, highlighted the moderate tone of the moratorium and its middle-class constituency.

Nixon assumed that the moratorium would undercut his efforts to negotiate with the North Vietnamese. He decided to take the offensive against the peace protesters by orchestrating a campaign of pro-Americanism that focused public attention on the critics of the war rather than the war itself. The centerpiece of his offensive was the speech he gave on November 3, 1969.

PRIMARY SOURCE

Good evening, my fellow Americans.

Tonight I want to talk to you on a subject of deep concern to all Americans and to many people in all parts of the world, the war in Vietnam.

I believe that one of the reasons for the deep division about Vietnam is that many Americans have lost confidence in what their Government has told them about our policy. The American people cannot and should not be asked to support a policy which involves the overriding issues of war and peace unless they know the truth about that policy.

Tonight, therefore, I would like to answer some of the questions that I know are on the minds of many of you listening to me.

How and why did America get involved in Vietnam in the first place?

How has this administration changed the policy of the previous Administration?

What has really happened in the negotiations in Paris and on the battlefront in Vietnam?

What choices do we have if we are to end the war?

What are the prospects for peace?

Now let me begin by describing the situation I found when I was inaugurated on January 20: The war had been going on for four years. Thirty-one thousand Americans had been killed in action. The training program for the South Vietnamese was beyond [behind] schedule. Five hundred and forty-thousand Americans were in Vietnam with no plans to reduce the number. No progress had been made at the negotiations in Paris and the United States had not put forth a comprehensive peace proposal.

The war was causing deep division at home and criticism from many of our friends, as well as our enemies, abroad.

In view of these circumstances, there were some who urged that I end the war at once by ordering the immediate withdrawal of all American forces. From a political standpoint, this would have been a popular and easy course to follow. After all, we became involved in the war while my predecessor was in office. I could blame the defeat, which would be the result of my action, on him—and come out as the peacemaker. Some put it to me quite bluntly: This was the only way to avoid allowing Johnson's war to become Nixon's war.

But I had a greater obligation than to think only of the years of my Administration, and of the next election. I had to think of the effect of my decision on the next generation, and on the future of peace and freedom in America, and in the world.

Let us all understand that the question before us is not whether some Americans are for peace and some Americans are against peace. The question at issue is not whether Johnson's war becomes Nixon's war. The great question is: How can we win America's peace?

Well, let us turn now to the fundamental issue: Why and how did the United States become involved in Vietnam in the first place? Fifteen years ago North Vietnam, with the logistical support of Communist China and the Soviet Union, launched a campaign to impose a Communist government on South Vietnam by instigating and supporting a revolution....

Now many believe that President Johnson's decision to send American combat forces to South Vietnam was wrong. And many others, I among them, have been strongly critical of the way the war has been conducted.

But the question facing us today is: Now that we are in the war, what is the best way to end it?

In January I could only conclude that the precipitate withdrawal of all American forces from Vietnam would be a disaster not only for South Vietnam but for the United States and for the cause of peace.

For the South Vietnamese, our precipitate withdrawal would inevitably allow the Communists to repeat the massacres which followed their takeover in the North fifteen years before. They then murdered more than 50,000 people and hundreds of thousands more died in slave labor camps.

We saw a prelude of what would happen in South Vietnam when the Communists entered the city of Hue last year. During their brief rule there, there was a bloody reign of terror in which 3,000 civilians were clubbed, shot to death, and buried in mass graves.

With the sudden collapse of our support, these atrocities at Hue would become the nightmare of the entire nation and particularly for the million-and-a half Catholic refugees who fled to South Vietnam when the Communists took over in the North.

For the United States this first defeat in our nation's history would result in a collapse of confidence in American leadership not only in Asia but throughout the world....

For these reasons I rejected the recommendation that I should end the war by immediately withdrawing all of our forces. I chose instead to change American policy on both the negotiating front and the battle front in order to end the war fought on many fronts....

We have offered the complete withdrawal of all outside forces within one year. We have proposed a cease fire under international supervision. We have offered free elections under international supervision with the Communists participating in the organization and conduct of the elections as an organized political force. And the Saigon government has pledged to accept the result of the election.

We have not put forth our proposals on a take-it-or-leave-it basis. We have indicated that we're willing to discuss the proposals that have been put forth by the other side. We have declared that anything is negotiable, except the right of the people of South Vietnam to determine their own future....

The defense of freedom is everybody's business—not just America's business. And it is particularly the responsibility of the people whose freedom is threatened. In the previous Administration, we Americanized the war in Vietnam. In this Administration, we are Vietnamizing the search for peace.

The policy of the previous Administration not only resulted in our assuming the primary responsibility for fighting the war, but even more significant did not adequately stress the goal of strengthening the South Vietnamese so that they could defend themselves when we left....

And now we have begun to see the results of this long-overdue change in American policy in Vietnam. After five years of Americans going into Vietnam we are finally bringing American men home. By December 15 over 60,000 men will have been withdrawn from South Vietnam, including twenty percent of all of our combat forces. The South Vietnamese have continued to gain in strength. As a result, they've been able to take over combat responsibilities from our American troops.

Two other significant developments have occurred since this Administration took office. Enemy infiltration, infiltration which is essential if they are to launch a major attack over the last three months, is less than twenty percent of what it was over the same period last year. And most important, United States casualties have declined during the last two months to the lowest point in three years.

Let me now turn to our program for the future. We have adopted a plan which we have worked out in cooperation with the South Vietnamese for the complete withdrawal of all U.S. combat ground forces and their replacement by

South Vietnamese forces on an orderly scheduled time-table. This withdrawal will be made from strength and not from weakness. As South Vietnamese forces become stronger, the rate of American withdrawal can become greater. . . .

My fellow Americans, I am sure you can recognize from what I have said that we really only have two choices open to us if we want to end this war. I can order an immediate precipitate withdrawal of all Americans from Vietnam without regard to the effects of that action. Or we can persist in our search for a just peace through a negotiated settlement, if possible, or through continued implementation of our plan for Vietnamization, if necessary—a plan in which we will withdraw all of our forces from Vietnam on a schedule in accordance with our program as the South Vietnamese become strong enough to defend their own freedom.

I have chosen this second course. It is not the easy way. It is the right way. It is a plan which will end the war and serve the cause of peace, not just in Vietnam but in the Pacific and in the world.

In speaking of the consequences of a precipitous withdrawal, I mentioned that our allies would lose confidence in America. Far more dangerous, we would lose confidence in ourselves. Oh, the immediate reaction would be a sense of relief that our men were coming home. But as we saw the consequences of what we had done, inevitable remorse and divisive recrimination would scar our spirit as a people.

We have faced other crises in our history and we have become stronger by rejecting the easy way out and taking the right way in meeting our challenges. Our greatness as a nation has been our capacity to do what has to be done when we knew our course was right. I recognize that some of my fellow citizens disagree with the plan for peace I have chosen. Honest and patriotic Americans have reached different conclusions as to how peace should be achieved. In San Francisco a few weeks ago, I saw demonstrators carrying signs reading, "Lose in Vietnam, bring the boys home." Well, one of the strengths of our free society is that any American has a right to reach that conclusion and to advocate that point of view.

But as President of the United States, I would be untrue to my oath of office if I allowed the policy of this nation to be dictated by the minority who hold that point of view and who try to impose it on the nation by mounting demonstrations in the street. For almost 200 years, the policy of this nation has been made under our Constitution by those leaders in the Congress and the White House elected by all the people. If a vocal minority, however fervent its cause, prevails over reason and the will of the majority, this nation has no future as a free society.

And now, I would like to address a word, if I may, to the young people of this nation who are particularly concerned, and I understand why they are concerned, about this war. I respect your idealism. I share your concern for peace. I want peace as much as you do. There are powerful personal reasons I want to end this war. This week I will have to sign eighty-three letters to mothers, fathers, wives, and loved ones of men who have given their lives for America in Vietnam. It's very little satisfaction to me that this is only one-third as many letters as I signed the first week in office. There is nothing I want more than to see the day come when I do not have to write any of those letters.

I want to end the war to save the lives of those brave young men in Vietnam. But I want to end it in a way which will increase the chance that their younger brothers and their sons will not have to fight in some future Vietnam some place in the world.

And I want to end the war for another reason. I want to end it so that the energy and dedication of you, our young people, now too often directed into bitter hatred against those responsible for the war, can be turned to the great challenges of peace, a better life for all Americans, a better life for all people on this earth.

I have chosen a plan for peace. I believe it will succeed. If it does not succeed, what the critics say now won't matter. Or if it does succeed, what the critics say now won't matter. If it does not succeed, anything I say then won't matter.

I know it may not be fashionable to speak of patriotism or national destiny these days, but I feel it is appropriate to do so on this occasion. Two hundred years ago this nation was weak and poor. But even then, America was the hope of millions in the world. Today we have become the strongest and richest nation in the world, and the wheel of destiny has turned so that any hope the world has for the survival of peace and freedom will be determined by whether the American people have the moral stamina and the courage to meet the challenge of free-world leadership.

Let historians not record that, when America was the most powerful nation in the world, we passed on the other side of the road and allowed the last hopes for peace and freedom of millions of people to be suffocated by the forces of totalitarianism.

So tonight, to you, the great silent majority of my fellow Americans, I ask for your support. I pledged in my campaign for the Presidency to end the war in a way that we could win the peace. I have initiated a plan of action which will enable me to keep that pledge. The more support I can have from the American people, the sooner that pledge can be redeemed. For the more divided we are at home, the less likely the enemy is to negotiate at Paris.

Let us be united for peace. Let us also be united against defeat. Because let us understand—North Vietnam cannot defeat or humiliate the United States. Only Americans can do that.

Fifty years ago, in this room, and at this very desk, President Woodrow Wilson spoke words which caught the imagination of a war-weary world. He said: "This is the war to end wars." His dream for peace after World War I was shattered on the hard reality of great power politics. And Woodrow Wilson died a broken man.

Tonight, I do not tell you that the war in Vietnam is the war to end wars, but I do say this: I have initiated a plan which will end this war in a way that will bring us closer to that great goal to which—to which Woodrow Wilson and every American President in our history has been dedicated—the goal of a just and lasting peace.

As President I hold the responsibility for choosing the best path for that goal and then leading the nation along it.

I pledge to you tonight that I shall meet this responsibility with all of the strength and wisdom I can command, in accordance with your hopes, mindful of your concerns, sustained by your prayers.

Thank you and good night.

SIGNIFICANCE

Nixon's speech was an effective tactical move that undercut public support for the organized antiwar movement. Polls conducted after the speech showed that nearly seventy-five percent of the public considered themselves to be part of the silent majority. By a margin of sixty-five percent to twenty-five percent, the public agreed with Nixon's claim that antiwar activists were giving aid and comfort to the enemy.

Nixon's appeal to the silent majority tapped into the deep class resentment that shaped attitudes toward the war and toward antiwar protesters. By 1969, many white, middle-class Americans were convinced that a willful minority of violent youth, militant blacks, and arrogant intellectuals had seized control of the public debate, showing contempt for mainstream values and threatening social stability. Nixon's speech intensified the cultural clash. Middle class Americans viewed the antiwar movement as an elitist attack on American troops by privileged students who had avoided the war. More importantly, Nixon had managed to transform himself into a cultural populist fighting for mainstream values. By withdrawing troops while channeling popular resentment against his critics, Nixon had grabbed control over the politics of war.

Nixon's mastery of the Vietnam War would not last for long. At the same time that he announced the Vietnamization policy, he authorized the covert bombing of neutral Cambodia in the areas used by North Vietnam as part of a supply line. When a journalist ran a story about the covert bombing, Nixon ordered illegal wiretapping to find the person responsible for leaking the information. The wiretapping became the first of many such surveillance operations that became part of the scandal that led to Nixon's later resignation from office.

FURTHER RESOURCES
Books

Ambrose, Stephen. *Nixon*. New York: Simon and Schuster, 1987.

Morgan, Iwan W. *Nixon*. London: Oxford University Press, 2002.

Small, Melvin. *The Presidency of Richard Nixon*. Lawrence: University Press of Kansas, 1999.

Kent State Shootings

Photograph

By: John Filo

Date: May 4, 1970

Source: Photo by John Filo/Getty Images.

About the Photographer: Photographer John Filo was an undergraduate photojournalism major at Kent State University in 1970. His photograph, sent to the Associated Press the evening of the Kent State shootings, won a Pulitzer Prize. Filo went on to join the staff of *Newsweek* and currently works for CBS.

INTRODUCTION

By the late 1960s student protests against the Vietnam war and the military draft had become part of university life on college campuses. On December 1, 1969, the United States reinstated the draft lottery for men between the ages of 19 and 25 for the first time since World War II, fueling further student protests, although all full-time students received draft deferments at that time. On April 30, 1970 President Nixon announced a military incursion into Cambodia, igniting still more demonstrations.

Kent State University in Kent, Ohio, was a mid-sized midwestern university attended by mostly middle- and working-class students. On May 1, 1970,

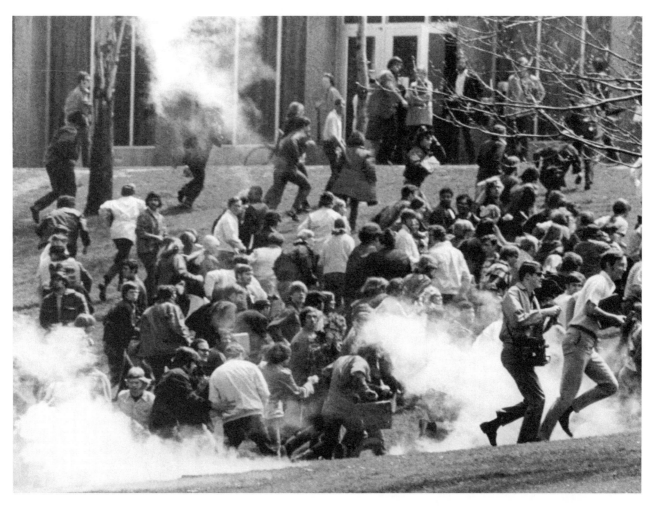

Kent State University students scatter away from tear gas dispensed by the National Guard during the clash between anti-war protestors and the Guard that led to the death of four students, May 4, 1970. © REUTERS/CORBIS.

a campus-wide demonstration against the war began on the Commons. That evening vandals broke storefront windows in town; conflicting reports attributed the vandalism to both bikers and students. Bars and businesses closed, but not before a crowd of close to 100 protestors lit a bonfire; when police arrived, marauding bikers and students threw beer bottles at them. The disruption angered local businesses, the mayor, and area residents, many of them farmers and workers who were not affiliated with the university, and some of whom were members of the local Army National Guard unit stationed in Canton.

On May 2 Mayor Leroy Satrom asked Ohio Governor James Rhodes to send the National Guard to help maintain order. Troops had arrived that evening to find the Reserve Officers Training Corps (ROTC) building on the Kent State campus ablaze;

local and state officials, as well as townspeople, attributed the fire to protestors, although the arsonists were never identified. A large crowd of over 500 gathered around the burning building to cheer; the crowd slashed the fire fighters' hoses, temporarily preventing them from extinguishing the blaze. By evenings' end, law enforcement officials had arrested a number of protestors, the National Guard was on campus, and tear gas had been used against the crowds.

By May 3 nearly 1,000 National Guard troops were in town and on campus. Governor Rhodes held a press conference declaring the use of stones or other projectiles against law enforcement would be treated as a crime, and that the campus would face a curfew enforced by National Guard troops. Demonstrators marched to the east edge of campus, next to town businesses, and requested a meeting with Mayor

PRIMARY SOURCE

Kent State Shootings: Mary Ann Vecchio screams as she kneels over the body of fellow student Jeffrey Miller, after National Guard troops opened fire on anti-war protestors at Kent State University, May 4, 1970. PHOTO BY JOHN FILO/GETTY IMAGES.

Satrom and Kent State University President Robert White. Initially told that such a meeting would occur, by 11:00 that night the crowd learned that neither Satrom nor White would appear; the National Guard used tear gas, helicopters, and bayonets to disperse the protestors, injuring some of them.

Students planned a rally on the Commons for May 4; although university officials had printed more than 12,000 flyers to declare that gatherings and protests were prohibited, few students got them. By noon nearly 200 students gathered, ringing the campus bell to protest the military presence. Under orders to disperse the crowd, National Guardsmen began to march across the Commons. Protestors threw rocks and lobbed tear gas. By 12:20 some soldiers knelt and pointed rifles directly at protestors, but did not fire.

At 12:25 the situation appeared to be improving and the crowd appeared to be dispersing; General Robert Canterbury ordered the troops to leave. As some troops and students walked away, a group of more than 20 soldiers, standing atop a small hill above the Commons but facing a parking lot near residence halls, opened fire. Between sixty-one and sixty-seven shots were fired; four students were killed and nine others wounded, one paralyzed for life.

PRIMARY SOURCE

KENT STATE SHOOTINGS
See primary source image.

A group of students gather around an individual who was injured during the Kent State Shootings, May 4, 1970. © REUTERS/CORBIS.

SIGNIFICANCE

This photograph, taken by a photojournalism student who worked in the photo lab at Kent State, was snapped seconds after the Guardsmen fired on the students. Jeffrey Miller, whose body is shown in the photo, was one of the protestors; fellow protestor and student Alison Krause died from a gunshot wound as well. The two other students were killed that day, Sandra Sheuer and William Schroeder, were caught in the line of fire as they walked across campus as part of their day's routine.

The approximate distance of gunshot victims from the National Guard troops remains the source of much debate concerning the actual threat protestors posed to National Guard troops; the closest gunshot victim was approximately 70 feet away, while the furthest was 750 feet away. General Canterbury initially told reporters that a sniper had opened fire and Guardsmen were shooting in response, but investigations found no evidence for this claim.

Faculty marshals convinced students to leave and medical professionals attended to the dead and wounded. Kent State was shut down for six weeks, and as news of the shootings spread, millions of students across the country protested, closing more than 800 campuses in the United States. Ten days after the Kent State shootings, Jackson State University in Jackson, Mississippi, experienced a similar incident: Police shot and killed two students and wounded twelve during protests while National Guardsmen were present on campus. The Jackson State shootings, however, garnered little press compared to Kent State, prompting charges of racism; Jackson State's student population is largely African-American. When Kent State marked the twentieth anniversary of the shootings in 1990, the Jackson State incident gained more retrospective coverage. In many historical monographs and popular articles on student protests Jackson State's experience receives thorough coverage.

No Guardsman was ever tried for the shootings. In September 1970, twenty-four students and one faculty member were charged in connection with the burning of the ROTC building and the May 4 protests, though charges were later dismissed. Three others were also charged in connection to the protests.

The Kent State shootings prompted a change in National Guard protocol. Many Guardsmen claim that their role has been distorted; as Chief Warrant Officer John Listman Jr. noted, "National Guardsmen have long been the villains of the tragic events... at Kent State. But violent demonstrators injured 60 Guardsmen and burned buildings in four days of mayhem prior to the shootings. It is a part of the saga that often goes untold." (Other sources state that only one Guardsman sustained injuries severe enough for treatment.) More than thirty-five years later, the conflict still generates heated discussion in the Kent area; many residents remain convinced that the Guardsmen's actions were justified, given the level of violence and rioting at the time.

In 1971 Kent State established the Center for Peaceful Change and developed one of the first conflict-management degrees in the United States. In 1990 and 1999, Kent State erected memorials to the events of May 4 and those injured and killed that day.

FURTHER RESOURCES

Books

Caputo, Philip. *13 Seconds: A Look Back at the Kent State Shootings*. New York: Chamberlain Brothers, 2005.

Hensley, Thomas R., with James A. Best. *The Kent State Incident: Impact of Judicial Process on Public Attitudes*. Westport, CT: Greenwood Press, 1981.

Morrison, Joan, and Robert K. Morrison. *From Camelot to Kent State: The Sixties Experience in the Words of Those Who Lived It*. Oxford University Press, U.S.A., 2001.

Periodicals

Adamek, Ramond J., and Jerry M. Lewis. "Social Control Violence and Radicalization: The Kent State Case." *Social Forces*. 51 (1973): 342–347.

Listman, John W. Jr. "Kent's Other Casualties." *National Guard*. (May 2002).

Websites

Lewis, Jerry M., and Thomas R. Hensley. *Kent State University Department of Sociology*. "The May 4 Shootings at Kent State University: The Search for Historical Accuracy." <http://dept.kent.edu/sociology/lewis/LEWIHEN.htm> (accessed May 8, 2006).

Proclamation 4483

Granting Pardon for Violations of the Selective Service Act, August 4, 1964 to March 28, 1973

Proclamation

By: Jimmy Carter

Date: January 21, 1977

Source: *U.S. Department of Justice.* "Granting Pardon for Violations of the Selective Service Act, August 4, 1964 to March 28, 1973." January 21, 1977. <http://www.usdoj.gov/pardon/carter_proclamation.htm> (accessed May 31, 2006).

About the Author: James Earl Carter, who always signed his name as Jimmy Carter, served as the thirty-ninth president of the United States from 1977 to 1981.

INTRODUCTION

On January 21, 1977, his first day as President of the United States, Jimmy Carter issued a pardon to all Americans convicted of or still sought for draft violations in the Vietnam War. With this action, he met a larger campaign pledge to speed the nation's healing from the tumultuous Vietnam era. The American people split almost evenly on support for the pardon, however, demonstrating that Vietnam still divided the nation.

The Vietnam War had begun almost unnoticed by most Americans, but by the mid-1960s, it had become the dominating fact of American political life. American views of the war conflicted profoundly. While many Americans viewed the war as a noble effort to stop the spread of Communism, an equal number of Americans viewed U.S. involvement as unjustifiable. The last Americans left Vietnam in 1975, but the war remained extremely fresh in American memory in 1977.

Carter expected that his proclamation would anger or disappoint more than half of all Americans. He was correct. The pardon covered the 2,393 draft evaders who were under indictment, about 9,000 who were convicted or pleaded guilty and who now have their records cleared, and about 1,200 who were under investigation for alleged violations. It also covered all the young men, estimated at hundreds of thousands, who simply never registered for the draft.

Men line up to register for the draft under the newly passed Selective Sericec Act of 1940, in St. Paul, Minnesota. © MINNESOTA HISTORICAL SOCIETY/CORBIS.

PRIMARY SOURCE

Acting pursuant to the grant of authority in Article II, Section 2, of the Constitution of the United States, I, Jimmy Carter, President of the United States, do hereby grant a full, complete and unconditional pardon to: (1) all persons who may have committed any offense between August 4, 1964 and March 28, 1973 in violation of the Military Selective Service Act or any rule or regulation promulgated thereunder; and (2) all persons heretofore convicted, irrespective of the date of conviction, of any offense committed between August 4, 1964 and March 28, 1973 in violation of the Military Selective Service Act, or any rule or regulation promulgated thereunder, restoring to them full political, civil and other rights.

This pardon does not apply to the following who are specifically excluded therefrom:

1. All persons convicted of or who may have committed any offense in violation of the Military Selective Service Act, or any rule or regulation promulgated thereunder, involving force or violence; and

2. All persons convicted of or who may have committed any offense in violation of the Military Selective Service Act, or any rule or regulation promulgated thereunder, in connection with duties or responsibilities arising out of employment as agents, officers or employees of the Military Selective Service system.

IN WITNESS WHEREOF, I have hereunto set my hand this 21st day of January, in the year of our Lord nineteen hundred and seventy-seven, and of the Independence of the United States of America the two hundred and first.

SIGNIFICANCE

Shortly after the amnesty announcement a poll showed that the American people opposed the pardon by a forty-six percent to forty-two percent plurality. Opponents of his proclamation argued that Carter did too much by allowing those who evaded the draft to come home without fear of prosecution. Meanwhile, many groups that supported a general amnesty viewed the pardon as doing too little because it did not include deserters or soldiers who had received a less-than-honorable discharge. Civilian protesters, selective service employees, and those who initiated any act of violence also were not covered in the pardon. To remedy this gap, Carter subsequently offered a short window of amnesty for deserters and an opportunity for former service members to upgrade undesirable or general discharges. During the Vietnam era, 2,600 men deserted and 432,000 service members received undesirable or general discharges. Only a small portion eventually upgraded their discharges. Carter's program did not affect the 1,903 dishonorable and 28,759 bad conduct discharges issued to servicemen after court-martial.

On June 24, 1977, the U.S. Senate voted forty-four to thirty-eight to block the funds that permitted the implementation of the amnesty program. The cut-off of funding aimed to keep federal employees from processing dismissals of draft-evasion charges and from acting to end investigations of alleged evasion. However, U.S. Justice Department officials announced that the cutoff would have little practical effect, since virtually all investigations and all draft evasion indictments had been dropped.

Only 283 draft evaders took advantage of the amnesty. About 7,500 American draft resisters in Canada had renounced their American citizenship and they had no intention of returning to the U.S. The U.S. Justice Department had prosecuted 9,042 persons for Selective Service violations and the Senate action had no effect on the processing of pardons for these men. However, only a small number of the former soldiers sought pardons.

FURTHER RESOURCES
Books

Baskir, Lawrence M., and William A. Strauss. *Chance and Circumstance: The Draft, the War, and the Vietnam Generation*. New York: Vintage, 1978.

Foley, Michael S. *Confronting the War Machine: Draft Resistance During the Vietnam War*. Chapel Hill: University of North Carolina Press, 2006.

Kaufman, Burton I. *The Presidency of James Earl Carter, Jr.* Lawrence: University Press of Kansas, 1993.

NATO London Declaration

Declaration

By: Heads of State and Government participating in the meeting of the North Atlantic Council

Date: July 6, 1990

Source: *North Atlantic Treaty Organization (NATO).* "London Declaration." <http://www.nato.int/docu/basictxt/b900706a.htm> (accessed May 25, 2006).

About the Author: The North Atlantic Treaty Organization (NATO) is a military alliance formed in 1949 by the United States, Great Britain, Canada, France, and other northern European nations. NATO was constituted as a defensive alliance, primarily concerned with threats posed by the Soviet Union and its allies. The North Atlantic Council is the body constituted from representatives of each NATO member nation. It determines and coordinates NATO policy.

INTRODUCTION

The North Atlantic Treaty Organization (NATO) is a military alliance established in 1949. NATO was created as a response to the threat to Western stability posed by the rise of the Eastern European bloc of Communist nations headed by the Soviet Union. The Soviet-led alliance became known as the Warsaw Pact nations. The original membership of NATO included the Allied nations of World War II, the United States, Great Britain, Canada, and France. NATO's other charter members included Belgium, Denmark, the Netherlands, Iceland, Portugal, Norway, and Italy. The United States in particular was anxious to reinforce its military treaties after the Soviet Union successfully detonated an atomic bomb for the first time in 1949, thereby establishing a nuclear weapon capability. As tensions between East and West deepened into the 1950s, Greece and Turkey were admitted to NATO in 1952, with West Germany joining the alliance in 1955.

During the course of the Cold War, there were a number of occasions when it appeared that the NATO nations would be engaged in a "hot" war with the Soviet Union and its allies. In each case, the threat was diffused. In May 1960, a United States spy plane flown by Gary Powers was captured after flying over Soviet airspace, an event that triggered an escalation in tensions between the two nations. The hostilities between the Soviet Union and the United States reached a fever pitch in October 1962, when it became

Czech Republic soldiers raise their national flag during a ceremony, as Hungary, Poland and the Czech Republic officially joined NATO, in Brussels, Begium on March 16, 1999. AP IMAGES.

apparent that the Soviet Union was prepared to use a military base built in Cuba, a Soviet ally, located 90 miles (150 km) from the Florida coastline. This dispute, known as the Cuban Missile Crisis, was resolved when the Soviet Union withdrew its missiles from Cuba in November 1962.

Reform-minded forces rose to prominence in the Warsaw Pact nations during the 1980s. The Berlin Wall, an iconic symbol of the division between the Eastern and Western nations, was constructed as the division between East and West Berlin in 1961. The wall was torn down in November 1989, and with the end of the wall came a rapid movement towards the liberalization of East Germany and its Eastern Bloc neighbors that continued for several years. The NATO London Declaration was made as those developments were consuming Eastern Europe.

PRIMARY SOURCE

1. Europe has entered a new, promising era. Central and Eastern Europe is liberating itself. The Soviet Union has embarked on the long journey towards a free society. The walls that once confined people and ideas are collapsing. Europeans are determining their own destiny. They are choosing freedom. They are choosing economic liberty. They are choosing peace. They are choosing a Europe whole and free. As a consequence, this Alliance must and will adapt.

2. The North Atlantic Alliance has been the most successful defensive alliance in history. As our Alliance enters its fifth decade and looks ahead to a new century, it must continue to provide for the common defence. This Alliance has done much to bring about the new Europe. No-one, however, can be certain of the future. We need to keep

standing together, to extend the long peace we have enjoyed these past four decades. Yet our Alliance must be even more an agent of change. It can help build the structures of a more united continent, supporting security and stability with the strength of our shared faith in democracy, the rights of the individual, and the peaceful resolution of disputes. We reaffirm that security and stability do not lie solely in the military dimension, and we intend to enhance the political component of our Alliance as provided for by Article 2 of our Treaty.

3. The unification of Germany means that the division of Europe is also being overcome. A united Germany in the Atlantic Alliance of free democracies and part of the growing political and economic integration of the European Community will be an indispensable factor of stability, which is needed in the heart of Europe. The move within the European Community towards political union, including the development of a European identity in the domain of security, will also contribute to Atlantic solidarity and to the establishment of a just and lasting order of peace throughout the whole of Europe.

4. We recognise that, in the new Europe, the security of every state is inseparably linked to the security of its neighbours. NATO must become an institution where Europeans, Canadians and Americans work together not only for the common defence, but to build new partnerships with all the nations of Europe. The Atlantic Community must reach out to the countries of the East which were our adversaries in the Cold War, and extend to them the hand of friendship.

5. We will remain a defensive alliance and will continue to defend all the territory of all our members. We have no aggressive intentions and we commit ourselves to the peaceful resolution of all disputes. We will never in any circumstance be the first to use force.

6. The member states of the North Atlantic Alliance propose to the member states of the Warsaw Treaty Organisation a joint declaration in which we solemnly state that we are no longer adversaries and reaffirm our intention to refrain from the threat or use of force against the territorial integrity or political independence of any state, or from acting in any other manner inconsistent with the purposes and principles of the United Nations Charter and with the CSCE Final Act. We invite all other CSCE member states to join us in this commitment to non-aggression.

7. In that spirit, and to reflect the changing political role of the Alliance, we today invite President Gorbachev on behalf of the Soviet Union, and representatives of the other Central and Eastern European countries to come to Brussels and address the North Atlantic Council. We today also invite the governments of the Union of Soviet Socialist Republics, the Czech and Slovak Federal Republic, the Hungarian Republic, the Republic of Poland, the People's Republic of Bulgaria and Romania to come to NATO, not just to visit, but to establish regular diplomatic liaison with NATO. This will make it possible for us to share with them our thinking and deliberations in this historic period of change.

8. Our Alliance will do its share to overcome the legacy of decades of suspicion. We are ready to intensify military contacts, including those of NATO Military Commanders, with Moscow and other Central and Eastern European capitals.

9. We welcome the invitation to NATO Secretary General Manfred Woèrner to visit Moscow and meet with Soviet leaders.

10. Military leaders from throughout Europe gathered earlier this year in Vienna to talk about their forces and doctrine. NATO proposes another such meeting this Autumn to promote common understanding. We intend to establish an entirely different quality of openness in Europe, including an agreement on "Open Skies".

11. The significant presence of North American conventional and US nuclear forces in Europe demonstrates the underlying political compact that binds North America's fate to Europe's democracies. But, as Europe changes, we must profoundly alter the way we think about defence.

12. To reduce our military requirements, sound arms control agreements are essential. That is why we put the highest priority on completing this year the first treaty to reduce and limit conventional armed forces in Europe (CFE) along with the completion of a meaningful CSBM package. These talks should remain in continuous session until the work is done. Yet we hope to go further. We propose that, once a CFE Treaty is signed, follow-on talks should begin with the same membership and mandate, with the goal of building on the current agreement with additional measures, including measures to limit manpower in Europe. With this goal in mind, a commitment will be given at the time of signature of the CFE Treaty concerning the manpower levels of a unified Germany.

13. Our objective will be to conclude the negotiations on the follow-on to CFE and CSBMs as soon as possible and looking to the follow-up meeting of the CSCE to be held in Helsinki in 1992. We will seek through new conventional arms control negotiations, within the CSCE framework, further far-reaching measures in the 1990s to limit the offensive capability of conventional armed forces in Europe, so as to prevent any nation from maintaining disproportionate military power on the continent. NATO's High Level Task Force will formulate a detailed position for these follow-on conventional arms control talks. We will make provisions as needed for different regions to redress disparities and to ensure that no one's security is

harmed at any stage. Furthermore, we will continue to explore broader arms control and confidence-building opportunities. This is an ambitious agenda, but it matches our goal: enduring peace in Europe.

14. As Soviet troops leave Eastern Europe and a treaty limiting conventional armed forces is implemented, the Alliance's integrated force structure and its strategy will change fundamentally to include the following elements:

- NATO will field smaller and restructured active forces. These forces will be highly mobile and versatile so that Allied leaders will have maximum flexibility in deciding how to respond to a crisis. It will rely increasingly on multinational corps made up of national units.
- NATO will scale back the readiness of its active units, reducing training requirements and the number of exercises.
- NATO will rely more heavily on the ability to build up larger forces if and when they might be needed.

15. To keep the peace, the Alliance must maintain for the foreseeable future an appropriate mix of nuclear and conventional forces, based in Europe, and kept up to date where necessary. But, as a defensive Alliance, NATO has always stressed that none of its weapons will ever be used except in self-defence and that we seek the lowest and most stable level of nuclear forces needed to secure the prevention of war.

16. The political and military changes in Europe, and the prospects of further changes, now allow the Allies concerned to go further. They will thus modify the size and adapt the tasks of their nuclear deterrent forces. They have concluded that, as a result of the new political and military conditions in Europe, there will be a significantly reduced role for sub-strategic nuclear systems of the shortest range. They have decided specifically that, once negotiations begin on short-range nuclear forces, the Alliance will propose, in return for reciprocal action by the Soviet Union, the elimination of all its nuclear artillery shells from Europe.

17. New negotiations between the United States and the Soviet Union on the reduction of short-range forces should begin shortly after a CFE agreement is signed. The Allies concerned will develop an arms control framework for these negotiations which takes into account our requirements for far fewer nuclear weapons, and the diminished need for sub-strategic nuclear systems of the shortest range.

18. Finally, with the total withdrawal of Soviet stationed forces and the implementation of a CFE agreement, the Allies concerned can reduce their reliance on nuclear weapons. These will continue to fulfill an essential role in the overall strategy of the Alliance to prevent war by ensuring that there are no circumstances in which nuclear retaliation in response to military action might be discounted.

However, in the transformed Europe, they will be able to adopt a new NATO strategy making nuclear forces truly weapons of last resort.

19. We approve the mandate given in Turnberry to the North Atlantic Council in Permanent Session to oversee the ongoing work on the adaptation of the Alliance to the new circumstances. It should report its conclusions as soon as possible.

20. In the context of these revised plans for defence and arms control, and with the advice of NATO Military Authorities and all member states concerned, NATO will prepare a new Allied military strategy moving away from "forward defence" where appropriate, towards a reduced forward presence and modifying "flexible response" to reflect a reduced reliance on nuclear weapons. In that connection NATO will elaborate new force plans consistent with the revolutionary changes in Europe. NATO will also provide a forum for Allied consultation on the upcoming negotiations on short-range nuclear forces.

21. The Conference on Security and Cooperation in Europe (CSCE) should become more prominent in Europe's future, bringing together the countries of Europe and North America. We support a CSCE Summit later this year in Paris which would include the signature of a CFE agreement and would set new standards for the establishment, and preservation, of free societies. It should endorse, inter alia:

- CSCE principles on the right to free and fair elections;
- CSCE commitments to respect and uphold the rule of law;
- CSCE guidelines for enhancing economic cooperation, based on the development of free and competitive market economies; and
- CSCE cooperation on environmental protection.

22. We further propose that the CSCE Summit in Paris decide how the CSCE can be institutionalised to provide a forum for wider political dialogue in a more united Europe. We recommend that CSCE governments establish:

- a programme for regular consultations among member governments at the Heads of State and Government or Ministerial level, at least once each year, with other periodic meetings of officials to prepare for and follow up on these consultations;
- a schedule of CSCE review conferences once every two years to assess progress toward a Europe whole and free;
- a small CSCE secretariat to coordinate these meetings and conferences;
- a CSCE mechanism to monitor elections in all the CSCE countries, on the basis of the Copenhagen Document;

- a CSCE Centre for the Prevention of Conflict that might serve as a forum for exchange of military information, discussion of unusual military activities, and the conciliation of disputes involving CSCE member states; and
- a CSCE parliamentary body, the Assembly of Europe, to be based on the existing parliamentary assembly of the Council of Europe in Strasbourg, and include representatives of all CSCE member states.

The sites of these new institutions should reflect the fact that the newly democratic countries of Central and Eastern Europe form part of the political structures of the new Europe.

23. Today, our Alliance begins a major transformation. Working with all the countries of Europe, we are determined to create enduring peace on this continent.

SIGNIFICANCE

The London Declaration of July 6, 1990, has a primary historical significance; it is the foundation document that initiated the transformation of NATO in a post-Cold War Europe. The declaration is a blueprint for change, describing the way in which NATO would govern itself in its future dealings with the Soviet Union and its allies.

The declaration was the first clear acknowledgement by the NATO membership that it recognized the permanent nature of the profound changes that had transpired in the former Eastern Bloc nations. Because the precise nature and extent of those changes was still unclear, the NATO members did not make wholesale commitments to arms reduction or wholesale changes in defense policies when the declaration was promulgated. However, there are clear expressions throughout the declaration that NATO and the former Warsaw Pact were no longer adversaries. In light of the political changes in Eastern Europe, NATO strategies concerning both defense and arms reduction were poised to change so that they would reflect the new face of Europe. This attitude was prescient, since former Warsaw Pact nations Hungary, Poland, and the Czech Republic were admitted into the NATO alliance within a few years of the London Declaration.

The political response to the London Declaration was mixed in the period immediately following its release. In Britain, debates in the House of Commons indicated an enthusiasm for the new European order, tempered with a recognition that, for the short term, the status quo would be maintained regarding NATO's military operations. Quite soon, however, the NATO alliance became a coalition of former adversaries. NATO

now included Italy, West Germany, and the three former Eastern Bloc nations, evidence of how the world had reconfigured itself since the end of World War II in 1945.

The London Declaration also foreshadowed the position of the United States as the one remaining global superpower. Since the founding of the United States in 1776, it had occupied a position of military and commercial strength, but not overriding supremacy. The influence of the United States had been counterbalanced by the power of other nations, first England, Germany, and Japan, and then the Soviet Union. With the fall of Communism in Europe, and the subsequent inclusion of Eastern Bloc nations in both the political and military alliances of the NATO nations, the United States became the de facto world superpower.

The expressions of intent set out in the London Declaration led to a revamping of NATO's structure, accomplished during a conference of NATO members known as the Rome Summit in November 1991. The Rome Summit laid the groundwork for significant arms reductions in Europe. The newly constituted NATO forces participated in a coordinated response to the 1999 civil war in Kosovo, in the former Yugoslavia. NATO delivered air strikes and ground attacks for three months against Serbian targets in support of the Albanian insurgency known as the KLA. The NATO deployment in Kosovo is significant because it represents a relatively straight line progression from the principles articulated in the London Declaration—that there would be a larger group of European nations making decisions concerning collective action.

The culmination of the post-Cold War world envisaged by NATO in the London Declaration of 1990 occurred in May 2002, with the creation of the NATO-Russian Council. The creation of this council brought Russia fully into the NATO orbit.

FURTHER RESOURCES

Books

Solomon, Gerald B. *The NATO Enlargement Debate, 1990–1997*. Washington, D.C.; Center for Strategic and International Studies/Praeger Publishers, 1998.

Periodicals

Baker, James A., III. "Russia in NATO." *Washington Quarterly* (Winter 2002): 95–103.

Web sites

The United Kingdom Parliament. "House of Commons Hansard Debates, July 17, 1990." <http://www.publication.parliament.uk/pa/cm198990/cmhansard/1990-07–17/Orals-1.html> (accessed May 26, 2006).

Major Combat Operations in Iraq Have Ended

Speech

By: George W. Bush

Date: May 1, 2003

Source: *The White House*. "Operation Iraqi Freedom: President Bush Announces Major Combat Operations in Iraq Have Ended." May 1, 2003. <http://www.whitehouse.gov/news/releases/2003/05/20030501-15.html> (accessed May 25, 2006).

About the Author: George W. Bush is the forty-third president of the United States.

INTRODUCTION

On March 20, 2003, a coalition of military forces composed mostly of Americans invaded Iraq. Iraqi resistance was ineffective, and U.S. troops rapidly overwhelmed the country. Widespread fears that Iraq might use chemical or biological weapons to counter the invasion proved groundless, as U.S. military search teams replicated the earlier failure of United Nations weapons inspectors to find such weapons in Iraq. Baghdad, the capital city of Iraq, fell to U.S. forces on April 9, 2003.

On May 1, 2003, U.S. president George W. Bush (1946–) gave a speech on the deck of the aircraft carrier *USS Abraham Lincoln* to proclaim victory. Every aspect of the event was carefully choreographed for maximum public-relations impact: Bush flew to the aircraft carrier, which was halted approximately 30 miles (48 kilometers) off the California coast near San Diego, in the copilot seat of a Navy S-3B Viking antisubmarine aircraft that had been re-marked with the words "Navy 1" and "George W. Bush Commander in Chief." (The aircraft that usually transports the president is named "Air Force One.") In addition to the pilot and the president, the four-seater plane carried a second pilot and a Secret Service agent. The plane made two passes by the carrier and then landed. Bush appeared wearing a flight suit and carrying a white helmet under his arm and posed for photographs in which he saluted sailors, shook hands with them, and draped his arms over their shoulders. Several hours later, in a conventional suit and tie, he delivered the speech in which he made his famous "major combat operations are over" statement. Behind him, draped from the ship's flight control tower, was a large, machine-printed banner reading "MISSION ACCOMPLISHED."

President Bush declares the end of major combat in Iraq as he speaks aboard the aircraft carrier *USS Abraham Lincoln* off the California coast, May 1, 2003. AP IMAGES.

▮ PRIMARY SOURCE

THE PRESIDENT: Thank you all very much. Admiral Kelly, Captain Card, officers and sailors of the USS Abraham Lincoln, my fellow Americans: Major combat operations in Iraq have ended. In the battle of Iraq, the United States and our allies have prevailed. (Applause.) And now our coalition is engaged in securing and reconstructing that country.

In this battle, we have fought for the cause of liberty, and for the peace of the world. Our nation and our coalition are proud of this accomplishment—yet, it is you, the members of the United States military, who achieved it. Your courage, your willingness to face danger for your country and for each other, made this day possible. Because of you, our nation is more secure. Because of you, the tyrant has fallen, and Iraq is free. (Applause.)

Operation Iraqi Freedom was carried out with a combination of precision and speed and boldness the enemy did not expect, and the world had not seen before. From distant bases or ships at sea, we sent planes and missiles that could destroy an enemy division, or strike a single bunker. Marines and soldiers charged to Baghdad across 350 miles of hostile ground, in one of the swiftest advances of heavy arms in history.

You have shown the world the skill and the might of the American Armed Forces.

This nation thanks all the members of our coalition who joined in a noble cause. We thank the Armed Forces of the United Kingdom, Australia, and Poland, who shared in the hardships of war. We thank all the citizens of Iraq who welcomed our troops and joined in the liberation of their own country. And tonight, I have a special word for Secretary Rumsfeld, for General Franks, and for all the men and women who wear the uniform of the United States: America is grateful for a job well done. (Applause.)

The character of our military through history—the daring of Normandy, the fierce courage of Iwo Jima, the decency and idealism that turned enemies into allies—is fully present in this generation. When Iraqi civilians looked into the faces of our servicemen and women, they saw strength and kindness and goodwill. When I look at the members of the United States military, I see the best of our country, and I'm honored to be your Commander-in-Chief. (Applause.)

In the images of falling statues, we have witnessed the arrival of a new era. For a hundred of years of war, culminating in the nuclear age, military technology was designed and deployed to inflict casualties on an ever-growing scale. In defeating Nazi Germany and Imperial Japan, Allied forces destroyed entire cities, while enemy leaders who started the conflict were safe until the final days. Military power was used to end a regime by breaking a nation.

Today, we have the greater power to free a nation by breaking a dangerous and aggressive regime. With new tactics and precision weapons, we can achieve military objectives without directing violence against civilians. No device of man can remove the tragedy from war; yet it is a great moral advance when the guilty have far more to fear from war than the innocent. (Applause.)

In the images of celebrating Iraqis, we have also seen the ageless appeal of human freedom. Decades of lies and intimidation could not make the Iraqi people love their oppressors or desire their own enslavement. Men and women in every culture need liberty like they need food and water and air. Everywhere that freedom arrives, humanity rejoices; and everywhere that freedom stirs, let tyrants fear. (Applause.)

We have difficult work to do in Iraq. We're bringing order to parts of that country that remain dangerous. We're pursuing and finding leaders of the old regime, who will be held to account for their crimes. We've begun the search for hidden chemical and biological weapons and already know of hundreds of sites that will be investigated. We're helping to rebuild Iraq, where the dictator built palaces for himself, instead of hospitals and schools. And we will stand with the new leaders of Iraq as they establish a government of, by, and for the Iraqi people. (Applause.)

The transition from dictatorship to democracy will take time, but it is worth every effort. Our coalition will stay until our work is done. Then we will leave, and we will leave behind a free Iraq. (Applause.)

The battle of Iraq is one victory in a war on terror that began on September the 11, 2001—and still goes on. That terrible morning, 19 evil men—the shock troops of a hateful ideology—gave America and the civilized world a glimpse of their ambitions. They imagined, in the words of one terrorist, that September the 11th would be the "beginning of the end of America." By seeking to turn our cities into killing fields, terrorists and their allies believed that they could destroy this nation's resolve, and force our retreat from the world. They have failed. (Applause.)

In the battle of Afghanistan, we destroyed the Taliban, many terrorists, and the camps where they trained. We continue to help the Afghan people lay roads, restore hospitals, and educate all of their children. Yet we also have dangerous work to complete. As I speak, a Special Operations task force, led by the 82nd Airborne, is on the trail of the terrorists and those who seek to undermine the free government of Afghanistan. America and our coalition will finish what we have begun. (Applause.)

From Pakistan to the Philippines to the Horn of Africa, we are hunting down al Qaeda killers. Nineteen months ago, I pledged that the terrorists would not escape the patient justice of the United States. And as of tonight, nearly one-half of al Qaeda's senior operatives have been captured or killed. (Applause.)

The liberation of Iraq is a crucial advance in the campaign against terror. We've removed an ally of al Qaeda, and cut off a source of terrorist funding. And this much is certain: No terrorist network will gain weapons of mass destruction from the Iraqi regime, because the regime is no more. (Applause.)

In these 19 months that changed the world, our actions have been focused and deliberate and proportionate to the offense. We have not forgotten the victims of September the 11th—the last phone calls, the cold murder of children, the searches in the rubble. With those attacks, the terrorists and their supporters declared war on the United States. And war is what they got. (Applause.)

Our war against terror is proceeding according to principles that I have made clear to all: Any person involved in committing or planning terrorist attacks against the American people becomes an enemy of this country, and a target of American justice. (Applause.)

Any person, organization, or government that supports, protects, or harbors terrorists is complicit in the murder of the innocent, and equally guilty of terrorist crimes.

Any outlaw regime that has ties to terrorist groups and seeks or possesses weapons of mass destruction is a grave danger to the civilized world—and will be confronted. (Applause.)

And anyone in the world, including the Arab world, who works and sacrifices for freedom has a loyal friend in the United States of America. (Applause.)

Our commitment to liberty is America's tradition—declared at our founding; affirmed in Franklin Roosevelt's Four Freedoms; asserted in the Truman Doctrine and in Ronald Reagan's challenge to an evil empire. We are committed to freedom in Afghanistan, in Iraq, and in a peaceful Palestine. The advance of freedom is the surest strategy to undermine the appeal of terror in the world. Where freedom takes hold, hatred gives way to hope. When freedom takes hold, men and women turn to the peaceful pursuit of a better life. American values and American interests lead in the same direction: We stand for human liberty. (Applause.)

The United States upholds these principles of security and freedom in many ways—with all the tools of diplomacy, law enforcement, intelligence, and finance. We're working with a broad coalition of nations that understand the threat and our shared responsibility to meet it. The use of force has been—and remains—our last resort. Yet all can know, friend and foe alike, that our nation has a mission: We will answer threats to our security, and we will defend the peace. (Applause.)

Our mission continues. Al Qaeda is wounded, not destroyed. The scattered cells of the terrorist network still operate in many nations, and we know from daily intelligence that they continue to plot against free people. The proliferation of deadly weapons remains a serious danger. The enemies of freedom are not idle, and neither are we. Our government has taken unprecedented measures to defend the homeland. And we will continue to hunt down the enemy before he can strike. (Applause.)

The war on terror is not over; yet it is not endless. We do not know the day of final victory, but we have seen the turning of the tide. No act of the terrorists will change our purpose, or weaken our resolve, or alter their fate. Their cause is lost. Free nations will press on to victory. (Applause.)

Other nations in history have fought in foreign lands and remained to occupy and exploit. Americans, following a battle, want nothing more than to return home. And that is your direction tonight. (Applause.)

After service in the Afghan—and Iraqi theaters of war—after 100,000 miles, on the longest carrier deployment in recent history, you are homeward bound. (Applause.) Some of you will see new family members for the first time—150 babies were born while their fathers were on the Lincoln. Your families are proud of you, and your nation will welcome you. (Applause.)

We are mindful, as well, that some good men and women are not making the journey home. One of those who fell, Corporal Jason Mileo, spoke to his parents five days before his death. Jason's father said, "He called us from the center of Baghdad, not to brag, but to tell us he loved us. Our son was a soldier."

Every name, every life is a loss to our military, to our nation, and to the loved ones who grieve. There's no homecoming for these families. Yet we pray, in God's time, their reunion will come.

Those we lost were last seen on duty. Their final act on this Earth was to fight a great evil and bring liberty to others. All of you—all in this generation of our military—have taken up the highest calling of history. You're defending your country, and protecting the innocent from harm. And wherever you go, you carry a message of hope—a message that is ancient and ever new. In the words of the prophet Isaiah, "To the captives, 'come out,'—and to those in darkness, 'be free.'"

Thank you for serving our country and our cause. May God bless you all, and may God continue to bless America. (Applause.)

SIGNIFICANCE

Bush's dramatic appearance on the *USS Abraham Lincoln* and his triumphant speech on its flight deck were hailed by many commentators as a major public-relations coup and the symbolic end of the Iraq War. However, even at the time Bush was accused by some critics of grandstanding, and his proclamation that "major combat operations are over" has been frequently turned against him by critics in the succeeding three years.

Triumph began to turn to embarrassment less than six months later, when it was revealed that the "MISSION ACCOMPLISHED" banner hanging behind the President during his speech was not produced by the sailors of the *USS Abraham Lincoln*. Bush seemed to assert that they had produced it when he said that "The 'Mission Accomplished' sign, of course, was put up by the members of the *USS Abraham Lincoln*, saying that their mission was accomplished. I know it was attributed somehow to some ingenious advance man from my staff—they weren't that ingenious, by the way." However, the White House eventually admitted that the sign had, in fact, been produced by White House staffers, though, as spokesperson Scott McClellan pointed out, it had indeed been physically "put up" by the crew of the vessel.

Far more serious was the failure of the military situation in Iraq to improve. On the day of Bush's speech, the *New York Times* reported that "The Bush administration is planning to withdrawl most United States combat forces from Iraq over the next several months…" But this did not happen, and U.S. military casualties did not cease. At the time of Bush's speech, only 139 U.S. troops had been killed in the Iraq war; a year later, the death toll was up to almost 600 and no withdrawal of combat forces had occurred. Criticized by Democrats for speaking too soon in 2003, Bush defended his speech, saying, "We're making progress, you bet."

Over the next two years, U.S. military casualties continued to mount. By May 16, 2006, they outweighed those that had occurred before the "end of major combat operations" by a factor of more than sixteen (2,449 dead; about 20,000 wounded). U.S. troop strength in Iraq was still at 132,000, while the number of insurgents fighting U.S. forces in Iraq had risen from approximately 5,000 to approximately 20,000. Iraqi civilian deaths had risen to least 35,000 as measured by verifiable media reports of specific deaths, and to 100,000 or possibly more as estimated by the peer-reviewed British medical journal *The Lancet* in 2005 (reporting on the only on-the-ground scientific survey of Iraqi civilian deaths performed to date). The third anniversary of Bush's speech was marked by renewed criticism contrasting the "Mission Accomplished" of 2003 with the grim realities of 2006. Senator Frank Lautenberg (D–NJ) said, "The mission was not accomplished then, and it is not accomplished now. Looking back on it, the president's public relations stunt on the aircraft carrier is an embarrassing symbol of the administration's naive and inept approach to Iraq."

As measured using polls, Bush's overall popularity rating had declined from seventy-one percent in 2003 to thirty-one percent by the date of the third anniversary of his "Mission Accomplished" speech. The percentage of Americans who agreed that Bush should be impeached, as measured by an April 2006 *Washington Post* poll, was actually higher (thirty-three percent) than his approval rating at the time.

FURTHER RESOURCES

Periodicals

Kamen, Al. "By Rumsfeld's Standards, Mission Accomplished." The *Washington Post* (March 27, 2006).

Web sites

CBC News. "In Depth: Casualties in the Iraq War." May 16, 2006. <http://www.cbc.ca/news/background/iraq/casualties.html> (accessed May 26, 2006).

CBS News. " 'Mission Accomplished' Anniversary: President Declared End to Major Combat Operations Three Years Ago." May 1, 2006. <http://www.cbsnews.com/stories/2006/05/01/iraq/main1562030.shtml> (accessed May 26, 2006).

No Military Recruiters in Public Schools, Scholarships for Education and Job Training

Legislation

By: Todd Chretien

Date: 2005

Source: *City and County of San Francisco Department of Elections*. "No Military Recruiters in Public Schools, Scholarships for Education and Job Training." 2005. <http://www.sfgov.org/site/election_index.asp?id=33918> (accessed May 29, 2006).

About the Author: In May 2006 Todd Chretien was the Green Party candidate for the United States Senate in the state of California. He worked as part of the group College Not Combat and authored Proposition 1.

INTRODUCTION

The 2001 No Child Left Behind (NCLB) Act improved education standards and accountability for school systems throughout the United States. Section 9528, one of its lesser-known provisions, however, requires that "each local educational agency receiving assistance under this Act shall provide, on a request made by military recruiters or an institution of higher education, access to secondary school students names, addresses, and telephone listings." According to the law, parents of students must "opt out" if they wish to restrict military recruiters' access to their children's names, addresses, and telephone numbers. In addition, any school—public or private—that receives federal funding but refuses to comply with the provision can face the loss of federal funds. Because the United States does not have compulsory national service

A Bush supporter jumps on stage in front of an anti-Bush banner after "Kerry for President" New Hampshire campaign chair, Bill Shaheen, spoke in front of the banner, May 1, 2004. AP IMAGES.

requirements; the dissemination of personal information was not, in the eyes of some parents, students, and activists, a justifiable transfer of data.

The provision escaped the attention of many secondary school administrators initially, but by 2002 a steady stream of media stories emerged as parents learned that their child's school district was providing the required information to military recruiters. Students in schools from Vermont to Utah complained that the act was an encroachment on personal rights; parents organized opt-out information campaigns, and criticized schools districts for failing to notify parents of the NCLB policy.

At the same time, some schools pointed to conflicts between the armed forces' "Don't Ask, Don't Tell" policy concerning homosexuals in the military and school policies against discrimination based on sexual orientation. Such clashes between military recruitment programs on college campuses such as Yale University led to the 2005 court case *Burt v. Rumsfeld*, in which the U.S. District Court held that Yale could continue to bar military recruiters from employment fairs, though the U.S. Department of Justice is pursuing the case on appeal.

As enrollment in the all-volunteer army and reserve units in the United States declined during the wars in Afghanistan and Iraq, military recruiters became more thorough in their approach and the government used appeals to gain access to students in high schools. The city of San Francisco put the question of military access to students to voters on November 8, 2005 in the form of Proposition 1.

A student at Youth Empowerement School in Oakland, California, joins an anti-war protest in front of San Francisco City Hall, July 11, 2005. AP IMAGES.

PRIMARY SOURCE

Proposition I

Shall it be City policy to oppose military recruiting in public schools and consider funding scholarships for education and training that could provide an alternative to military service?

Digest

by the Ballot Simplification Committee

THE WAY IT IS NOW: The San Francisco Unified School District operates the City's public schools. The District receives federal money to pay part of its operating costs. By accepting federal money, the District must permit U.S. military recruiters access to its schools. Colleges and universities that receive federal funds are subject to similar requirements.

THE PROPOSAL: Proposition I is a declaration of policy that the people of San Francisco oppose the federal government's use of public schools to recruit students for service in the military.

Proposition I is also a declaration that San Francisco should consider funding scholarships for higher education and job training that could provide an alternative to military service.

A "YES" VOTE MEANS: If you vote "yes," you want it to be City policy to oppose military recruiters' access to public schools and to consider funding scholarships for education and training that could provide an alternative to military service.

A "NO" VOTE MEANS: If you vote "no," you do not want this to be City policy.

SIGNIFICANCE

San Francisco voters approved Proposition 1, also known as "College Not Combat," by a 59% to 41% vote. Reaction to the vote ranged from elation on the part of anti-recruiter groups such as College Not Combat and Campus Anti-war Network to anger from commentator Bill O'Reilly, who responded to news of the vote by telling citizens in San Francisco: "You want to be your own country? Go right ahead. And if al Qaeda comes in here and blows you up, we're not going to do anything about it."

The group behind the push for Proposition 1, College Not Combat, called for city and county officials to create viable alternatives to military service in the form of greater job opportunities and scholarships for those targeted by military recruiters; the proposition did not call upon the city or county to act in violation of the Solomon Amendment or the No Child Left Behind Act.

The 59% win for antimilitary recruitment activists (often referred to as "counter-recruiters,") reflected the growing anti-war movement as American deaths in the Iraq War exceeded 2,000. Critics derided the measure as a symbol of San Francisco's fringe status as a highly liberal, progressive city, while supporters argued that the measure demonstrated that a major American city did not support Section 9528 of the No Child Left Behind Act or any military recruitment in higher education.

In December 2005 the United States Supreme Court heard arguments in *Rumsfeld v. FAIR*, which tests the constitutionality of the Solomon Amendment; the Solomon Amendment requires colleges and universities to permit military recruiters to engage in the same activities as other potential employers in campus recruitment drives, or the institution faces the loss of federal funds. As of this writing, the Supreme Court had not issued a decision.

FURTHER RESOURCES
Periodicals

Trotter, Andrew. "Justices Weigh Colleges' Right to Limit Military Recruiters." *Education Week*. 25, no. 14 (December 2005): 22.

Web sites

USA Today. "'Counter-recruiters' Shadowing the Military." March 7, 2005. <http://www.usatoday.com/news/nation/2005-03-07-counter-recruiters_x.htm> (accessed May 29, 2006).

United States Department of Education. "Joint Letter from Secretary Paige and Secretary Rumsfeld." October 9, 2002. <http://www.ed.gov/policy/gen/guid/fpco/hottopics/ht10-09-02c.html> (accessed May 29, 2006).

Praise Mingles with Anger as Hundreds Turn Out for Rally to Support Troops

Magazine article

By: Elisabeth Goodridge

Date: September 25, 2005

Source: AP Newswire

About the Author: Elisabeth Goodridge is a writer for the Associated Press, a worldwide news agency based in New York.

INTRODUCTION

This article highlights the declining level of public support in the U.S. for the continued presence of American troops in Iraq following the invasion of 2003. In October 2005, a rally in support of the troops in Iraq was poorly attended, while in contrast many thousands of people turned out for an anti-war demonstration held around the same time.

The views of the American public on the 2003 invasion and subsequent occupation of Iraq by U.S.-led coalition troops were mixed from the outset, with some arguing that military action against Iraq was not justified. Over time, as more and more lives have been lost in Iraq, including more than 2,400 U.S. military personnel by mid–2006, the balance of public opinion has reportedly shifted in favor of withdrawing U.S. troops from the country.

Iraq was invaded by a U.S.-led coalition in March 2003, after the Iraqi regime failed to cooperate fully with U.N. weapons inspectors searching for chemical and biological weapons and for evidence of a nuclear weapons program. Under the terms of the settlement following Iraq's defeat in the 1990–1991 Gulf War, Iraq had been required to destroy all non-conventional weapons and the facilities for their production. However, the Iraqi regime under Saddam Hussein had increasingly obstructed the access of U.N. inspectors and was believed to have concealed the existence of stockpiled weapons in reports submitted to the U.N.

Although concern about Iraq's possible possession of weapons of mass destruction (WMDs) was the precipitating factor for the coalition invasion in 2003, other reasons were also cited by the U.S. These included violations within Iraq of U.N. Security Council resolutions on human rights, and the alleged links of the Saddam Hussein regime with terrorist groups, notably Al-Qaeda, implicated in the attacks on the World Trade Center on September 11, 2001.

Following the invasion, the coalition forces quickly overpowered the Iraqi government, and took control of Baghdad. The U.S. declared the war officially over on May 1, 2003. In June, a temporary coalition government was set up in Iraq to begin the process of reconstruction and to oversee the training of a new Iraqi security force that could defend the country. A deadline for the handover of self-government to Iraq was agreed for June 2004, at which time an Iraqi caretaker government was created in advance of democratic elections. The initial tasks of this government included making arrangements for the trial of Saddam Hussein for his brutalities against the Iraqi people. Hussein had been found and captured by coalition forces in December 2003. His trial began in October 2005, with Hussein initially charged with the killing of 140 men following a failed assassination attempt against him.

The challenges facing Iraq were immense. Its economy had virtually collapsed from the effects of many years of U.N.-imposed economic sanctions, and the infrastructure of the country was in a state of severe decay. Added to this, an insurgency movement arose that embarked on a long-running terror campaign against the coalition forces and the new administration.

Reactions from the Iraqi population to the invasion and occupation were polarized between those who welcomed their liberation from the brutalities of the Saddam Hussein regime, and those who were fiercely opposed to U.S. interference and the presence of coalition troops in their country. Among the latter, an insurgency movement developed, known as the Anti-Iraqi Forces (AIF), who reportedly amassed weapons and other supplies during the widespread looting that occurred in the aftermath of the U.S. invasion and the fall of the government. The movement was initially made up of loyal followers of Saddam Hussein, but these were soon joined by other Iraqis and foreign freedom fighters, allegedly with links to Al-Qaeda.

Supporters of President Bush and the war in Iraq demonstrate in New York City, August 28, 2004. They are heckling participants in an anti-war, anti-Republican march taking place just prior to the Republican National Convention. © BENJAMIN LOWY/CORBIS.

Between 2003 and the time of writing in 2006, many Iraqis and coalition military personnel have been killed in insurgency bombing attacks, while other foreign personnel in Iraq have been kidnapped and killed by the insurgents.

In January 2006, parliamentary elections were held in Iraq, with parties organized largely along sectarian lines. The Shia-led United Iraqi Alliance gained the most votes, but failed to win an absolute majority, while Kurdish parties and the Sunni Arab bloc also gained a significant number of seats. The violence in Iraq shows no sign of abating following the establishment of the new Iraqi government.

■ PRIMARY SOURCE

Support for U.S. troops fighting abroad mixed with anger toward anti-war demonstrators at home as hundreds of people, far fewer than organizers had expected, rallied Sunday on the National Mall just a day after tens of thousands protested against the war in Iraq.

"No matter what your ideals are, our sons and daughters are fighting for our freedom," said Marilyn Faatz, who drove from New Jersey to attend the rally. "We are making a mockery out of this. And we need to stand united, but we are not."

About 400 people gathered near a stage on an eastern segment of the mall, a large patchwork American flag serving as a backdrop. Amid banners and signs proclaiming support for U.S. troops, several speakers hailed the effort to bring democracy to Iraq and Afghanistan and denounced those who protest it.

Many demonstrators focused their ire at Cindy Sheehan, the California woman whose protest near President Bush's Texas home last summer galvanized the anti-war movement. Sheehan was among the speakers at Saturday's rally near the Washington Monument on the western part of the mall, an event that attracted an estimated 100,000 people.

"The group who spoke here the other day did not represent the American ideals of freedom, liberty and spreading that around the world," Sen. Jeff Sessions, an

Alabama Republican, told the crowd. "I frankly don't know what they represent, other than to blame America first."

One sign on the mall read "Cindy Sheehan doesn't speak for me" and another "Arrest the traitors"; it listed Sheehan's name first among several people who have spoken against the war.

Melody Vigna, 44, of Linden, California, said she wants nothing to do with Sheehan and others at nearby Camp Casey, an anti-war site set up to honor her son, Casey, who was killed in Iraq.

"Our troops are over there fighting for our rights, and if she was in one of those countries she would not be able to do that," Vigna said.

The husband of Sherri Francescon, 24, of Camp Lejeune, North Carolina, serves in the Marine Corps in Iraq. One of the many military wives who spoke during the rally, Francescon said that the anti-war demonstration had left her frustrated.

"I know how much my husband does and how hard he works, and I feel like they don't even recognize that and give him the respect he deserves," Francescon said. "I want him to know and I want his unit to know that America is behind them, Cindy doesn't speak for us, and that we believe in what they are doing."

Organizers of Sunday's demonstration acknowledged that their rally would be much smaller than the anti-war protest but had hoped that as many as 20,000 people would turn out.

On Saturday, demonstrators opposed to the war in Iraq surged past the White House in the largest anti-war protest in the nation's capital since the U.S. invasion. The rally stretched through the night, a marathon of music, speechmaking and dissent on the mall.

National polls have found steadily declining support for the war in Iraq, with a majority of Americans now believing the war was a mistake.

In an AP-Ipsos poll this month, only 37 percent approved or leaned toward approval of how President George W. Bush has handled the situation in Iraq; strong disapproval outweighed strong approval by 2-1, 46 percent to 22 percent.

SIGNIFICANCE

The pre-emptive invasion and occupation of Iraq by the United States has been controversial from the outset. Some have argued that the invasion contravened international law, and that the U.S. should not have gone ahead without the support of the United Nations. Opponents of the war also highlight the fact that no firm evidence of any

WMDs was ever found in Iraq, calling into question the rationale for the invasion. On the other hand, supporters of the war point out that the coalition forces did bring an end to the undoubtedly brutal and corrupt regime of Saddam Hussein, who was found to have imprisoned and murdered many thousands of political opponents, and to have stashed huge amounts of cash.

By mid–2006 the situation in Iraq showed no real sign of improvement. Although a democratically elected parliament was in place, violence, killings, and sabotage continued to be a feature of daily life in Iraq and little progress had been made on reconstructing the country. In the U.S., the level of support for the presidency of George W. Bush and the Republican Party had become closely tied to the Iraq conflict and the issue of whether to bring the troops home.

FURTHER RESOURCES
Books
Kaplan, Lawrence, F., and W. Kristol. *The War over Iraq: Saddam's Tyranny and America's Mission*. New York: Encounter Books, 2003.

Record, Jeffrey. *Dark Victory: America's Second War Against Iraq*. Annapolis, Md.: Naval Institute Press, 2004.

Periodicals
Smith, Caroline. "Rally 'Round the Flag: Opinion in the United States Before and After the Iraq War." *Brookings Review* (June 22, 2003).

Web sites
BBC News. "The Struggle for Iraq." <http://news.bbc.co.uk/2/hi/in_depth/middle_east/2002/conflict_with_iraq/default.stm> (accessed May 31, 2006).

Cindy Sheehan Leads Protest Against the Iraq War

Photograph

By: Evan Sisley

Date: September 26, 2005

Source: AP Images.

About the Author: Evan Sisley is a photographer for the Associated Press, a worldwide news agency based in New York.

PRIMARY SOURCE

Cindy Sheehan Leads Protest Against the Iraq War: Police carry Cindy Sheehan, the California woman who used her son's death in Iraq to spur the anti-war movement, as she is arrested during a demonstration outside the White House, September 26, 2005 in Washington. AP IMAGES.

INTRODUCTION

Cindy Sheehan (1957–) is a mother and political activist who, starting in the summer of 2005, participated in a number of protests against the war in Iraq. Sheehan rapidly became a national figure in 2005 after she began camping outside the borders of President George W. Bush's ranch in Crawford, Texas, demanding a meeting with the President.

Sheehan's son, Army Specialist Casey Sheehan (1979–2004), was killed in action in Iraq. She met with President Bush in June 2004, along with several members of other military families and soon after voiced a mixture of criticism and approval in describing the meeting. By early 2005, she had become entirely critical of the president and his conduct of the war. In August 2005, speaking of her apparent change of heart regarding her first meeting, for

which she has been widely criticized by supporters of the Iraq war, she said, "The first time [I met with Bush] I was deeply in shock and grief, and I wasn't as informed as I am now. I'm not a mother in shock any more. I'm still a grieving mother, but now I'm an angry mother."

In January 2005, Sheehan loaned her son's combat boots to a traveling display organized by the American Friends Service Committee (Quakers) to call attention to the human cost of the Iraq war. In that month, she also helped found Gold Star Families for peace, an antiwar organization composed of Americans who have lost relatives serving in the military in the Iraq war. (The phrase "gold star" refers to the banner bearing a gold star, which may be displayed by any family that has lost a close relative in U.S. military service, a custom in force since World War I.) In

August 2005, she decided to camp out by the side of the road near President Bush's ranch near Crawford, Texas, until such time as he would grant her a second meeting, and, as she put it, explain to her the "noble cause" he had alleged in several speeches was served by U.S. military deaths in Iraq. Sheehan was joined by other antiwar protestors, including a number of mothers whose sons had died in Iraq, and her protest was covered widely by U.S. and international media.

The protest shown in this photograph took place on September 26, 2005. Sheehan and hundreds of other antiwar demonstrators, headed by a group of religious leaders, were arrested after marching to the White House gate and attempting to deliver to the president a list of the names of all U.S. soldiers killed in Iraq. The list also included the names of many Iraqi civilians who have died in the war. The protestors did not expect the president or his representative to actually accept delivery of the list. After making their symbolic demand, they sat down on the sidewalk in front of the White House. The U.S. Park Police, with whom the protest plan had been discussed beforehand, then arrested 370 of the demonstrators, beginning with Cindy Sheehan. All those arrested were charged with demonstrating without a permit and fined $50 each.

Members of Code Pink, a women's peace activist group, gather outside the gates of National Cemetery in Los Angeles, March 19, 2003. Protesters carry body bags and children's coffins as well as peace signs and banners in a mock funeral procession during a rally against possible war in Iraq. AP IMAGES.

PRIMARY SOURCE

CINDY SHEEHAN LEADS PROTEST AGAINST THE IRAQ WAR

See primary source image.

SIGNIFICANCE

Sheehan provoked both praise and outrage because she spoke out against the Iraq war in a cultural context that greatly reveres fallen military personnel and treats their surviving relatives with heightened respect. Traditionally, these family members are expected to be grieving but supportive of the military mission their loved ones died performing and grateful for the posthumous honors bestowed by the government. It is therefore incongruous when the mother of a dead soldier harshly criticizes the mission that the soldier died performing. Nor was the style of Sheehan's protest polite or motherly. She has repeatedly accused President Bush of being a liar and a war criminal. (The

war-criminal charge is a reference to a statement by former Supreme Court Justice Robert Jackson, U.S. prosecutor at the first round of trials of Nazi war criminals held after World War II at Nuremberg. Jackson said that aggressive war is "the supreme international crime, differing only from other war crimes in that it contains within itself the accumulated evil of the whole.") Sheehan was widely praised and widely attacked because she combined motherhood, martyrdom, and angry protest in an unusual manner and framed them dramatically by camping in a tent outside the home of the president.

Like her attempted delivery of a roster of the dead to the White House in 2005, Sheehan's demand for a Crawford interview was symbolic: no actual meeting with the President was anticipated. In fact, the granting of such an interview might have greatly diminished the political impact of the campout protest.

Sheehan has continued her activism since camping near the president' Crawford ranch. She was invited to the 2006 State of the Union Address in January, but was arrested before the speech began for wearing a t-shirt bearing the message "2,245 dead. How many more?" Also in January 2006, Sheehan traveled to Venezuela, as the guest of the government, to participate with Venezuelan President Hugo Chavez in the Caracas World Social Forum, an anti-globalization gathering.

FURTHER RESOURCES
Books

Rising-Moore, Carl and Becky Oberg. *Freedom Underground: Protesting the Iraq War in America*. New York: Chamberlain Bros., 2004.

Periodicals

Dvorak, Petula. "White House Sidewalk Protest Leads to Arrest." *The Washington Post*. September 27, 2005.

Fletcher, Michael A. "Cindy Sheehan's Pitched Battle: In a Tent Near Bush's Ranch, Antiwar Mother of Dead Soldier Gains Visibility." *The Washington Post*. August 13, 2005.

Web sites

CNN.com. "Soldier's Mom Digs In Near Bush Ranch." August 7, 2005. <http://edition.cnn.com/2005/POLITICS/08/07/mom.protest/> (accessed May 15, 2006).

4 Civil Liberties and Social Issues

Civil Liberties and Social Issues

A survey of U.S. history reveals cyclical curtailment and restoration of civil liberties. In times of conflict, civil liberties are often restricted. After the outbreak of the French Revolution, the United States passed the Sedition Act of 1798, outlawing various forms of political criticism. Though the law was in force for only a few years, it established precident. The Sedition Act was revived, in more stringent form in 1918 after the United States entered World War I. Hundreds of political radicals were jailed; many immigrants charged as radicals or subversives were deported. Both Sedition Acts are included in this chapter because both were subjects of vociferous protest—even if by a minority of citizens. At the outbreak of World War II, one of the bleakest chapters in U.S. history, Japanese and Japanese-American internment, was described at the time as a necessary national security precaution. Troublingly absent was large-scale protest of internment policies—the reason that the subject is not discussed here even though, second to African slavery, internment policies represent the most egregious abridgement of human rights and civil liberties in the history United States. Several sources in the chapter discuss the Patriot Act and protest responses to the controversial legislation. Similarly divisive issues, including limited domestic survelience of protest activities, are presented as part of a broad conversation on civil liberties after the September 11, 2001 terrorist attacks.

Two sources focus on the nadir of the House UnAmerican Activities Committee and the McCarthy hearings. "A Declaration of Conscience" features Senator Maragret Chase Smith's speech on the Senate floor in protest of the McCarthy inquests. Invoking the protections of the Constitution and the civil liberties granted in the Bill of Rights, Smith asserted that "the basic principles of Americanism [are the] right to criticize; the right to hold unpopular beliefs; the right to protest; [and] the right of independent thought."

This chapter also provides a brief look at social issues that have ignited protest. A temperance protest contrasts a demonstration in favor of ending Prohibition. "Coat Hangers Used in Abortion Protest" provides insight into the origins of one of the most recognized modern protest symbols. The long-divisive issue of abortion spawned not only full-time, dedicated protest movements on both sides of the issue but also laws protecting clinics, patients, and defining legal protest conduct near facilities that provide abortion services. Finally, two articles touch upon protests surrounding the current debate over illegal immigration and immigration law reform.

Sedition Act of 1798

Legislation

By: United States Congress

Date: July 14, 1798

Source: Sedition Act of 1798. Available at: *University of Oklahoma College of Law.* "A Chronology of U.S, Historical Documents: The Sedition Act of 1798." <http://www.law.ou.edu/ushistory/sedact.shtml> (accessed June 3, 2006).

About the Author: At the time this act was passed into law, President John Adams (1735–1826) and the Federalist Party led the U.S. government. This political party's main focus was on creating and maintaining a sense of nationalism in the newly formed United States of America.

INTRODUCTION

The Sedition Act of 1798 was written to prevent conspiracies in opposition to the American government both at home and abroad. Signed into law by Federalist John Adams during a time when relations between America and France were strained and many Americans believed war was imminent, the act was denounced by his opponents in the Virginia House of Delegates as being unconstitutional. In particular, the protest document, drawn by James Madison, accused that the Sedition Act was absolutely forbidden by the First Amendment to the U.S. Constitution.

■ PRIMARY SOURCE

An Act in addition to the act, entitled "An act for the punishment of certain crimes against the United States."

SEC. 1. Be it enacted . . ., That if any persons shall unlawfully combine or conspire together, with intent to oppose any measure or measures of the government of the United States, which are or shall be directed by proper authority, or to impede the operation of any law of the United States, or to intimidate or prevent any person holding a place or office in or under the government of the United States, from undertaking, performing or executing his trust or duty; and if any person or persons, with intent as aforesaid, shall counsel, advise or attempt to procure any insurrection, riot, unlawful assembly, or combination, whether such conspiracy, threatening, counsel, advice, or attempt shall have the proposed effect or not, he or they shall be deemed guilty of a high misdemeanor, and on conviction, before any court of the United States having jurisdiction thereof, shall be punished by a fine not exceeding five thousand dollars, and by imprisonment during a term not less than six months nor exceeding five years; and further, at the discretion of the court may be holden to find sureties for his good behaviour in such sum, and for such time, as the said court may direct.

SEC. 2. That if any person shall write, print, utter, or publish, or shall cause or procure to be written, printed, uttered or published, or shall knowingly and willingly assist or aid in writing, printing, uttering or publishing any false, scandalous and malicious writing or writings against the government of the United States, or either house of the Congress of the United States, or the President of the United States, with intent to defame the said government, or either house of the said Congress, or the said President, or to bring them, or either of them, into contempt or disrepute; or to excite against them, or either or any of them, the hatred of the good people of the United States, or to excite any unlawful combinations therein, for opposing or resisting any law of the United States, or any act of the President of the United States, done in pursuance of any such law, or of the powers in him vested by the constitution of the United States, or to resist, oppose, or defeat any such law or act, or to aid, encourage or abet any hostile designs of any foreign nation against the United States, their people or government, then such person, being thereof convicted before any court of the United States having jurisdiction thereof, shall be punished by a fine not exceeding two thousand dollars, and by imprisonment not exceeding two years.

SEC. 3. That if any person shall be prosecuted under this act, for the writing or publishing any libel aforesaid, it shall be lawful for the defendant, upon the trial of the cause, to give in evidence in his defence, the truth of the matter contained in the publication charged as a libel. And the jury who shall try the cause, shall have a right to determine the law and the fact, under the direction of the court, as in other cases.

SEC. 4. That this act shall continue to be in force until March 3, 1801, and no longer . . .

SIGNIFICANCE

Tensions developed between John Adams and Thomas Jefferson (1743–1826) for many reasons, and these tensions led to the events surrounding the Sedition Act of 1798. First, Jefferson and Adams were opponents in the election of 1796. As a result of that election, Adams was elected president, and Jefferson, through a flaw in the Electoral College system, was elected vice president instead of Adams' running mate. Jefferson supported the revolution underway in France, while Adams opposed the French conflict and did not want America to be drawn into the fray.

The Sedition Act would not only keep the French from inciting fervor for their cause in America, but it would also keep Jefferson and his supporters from stirring up wider sympathy for the French. Opponents of the Sedition Act considered the act a mechanism for silencing opposition to Federalist ideals. The Sedition Act is divided into four sections, with the first of these defining what actions could be construed as conspiracy to oppose the government. Offenses included instigating insurrections, causing riots, or opposing a government measure. It was also deemed unlawful to hinder a government official from performing his obligations in any way. The second section established as criminal any malicious words used against the United States government or its officials. This was particularly aimed at those who might defame the character of the president or Congress or injure the reputation of those offices in any way. It also made it unlawful to oppose federal laws or to conspire with foreign nations against the United States.

Thirdly, the Sedition Act provided that any person charged with a crime under the act would be entitled to defend himself. The jury by which he would be tried would be given the right to determine the law and punishment as it might apply. The fourth section of the Act pronounced the expiration date as March 3, 1801.

The protests of eminent anti-federalists such as James Madison and Thomas Jefferson could not prevent the Sedition Act from becoming law, and the U.S. Supreme Court never ruled on the constitutionality of the act. Over the next two years, several newspaper publishers were convicted and/or fined under the act. However, only two years after Adams approved the Sedition Act, Thomas Jefferson was elected president and promptly pardoned those who had been convicted and repaid those who had been fined.

Although the Sedition Act of 1798 expired in 1801, and the U.S. Supreme Court never tried its constitutionality, the act set a precedent for two similar laws enacted in subsequent centuries. In 1918, another Sedition Act was made law in reaction to World War I. Again, in 2001, the USA PATRIOT Act became law in the wake of the September 11, 2001, terrorist attacks on the World Trade Center in New York and the Pentagon in Washington, D.C. In both of these subsequent cases, the constitutionality of such a controversial act of Congress has been questioned by opponents, who maintain that such laws violate the First Amendment right to freedom of speech guaranteed by the U.S. Constitution.

FURTHER RESOURCES
Books
Stone, Geoffrey R. *Perilous Times: Free Speech in Wartime: From the Sedition Act of 1798 to the War on Terrorism.* New York: W. W. Norton, 2005.

Web sites
National Archives and Records Administration. "The Formation of Political Parties: The Alien and Sedition Acts." <http://www.archives.gov/exhibits/treasures_of_congress/page_5.html#> (accessed June 1, 2006).

Temperance Protest

Illustration

By: Anonymous

Date: 1874

Source: MPI/Getty Images.

About the Illustrator: This illustration is part of the collection at Getty Images, a worldwide provider of visual content materials to such communications groups as advertisers, broadcasters, designers, magazines, new media organizations, newspapers, and producers. The identity of the artist is not known.

INTRODUCTION

Two days before Christmas 1873, in Hillsboro, Ohio—a town of 5,000 people and thirteen liquor shops—the temperance preacher Dr. Dioclesian Lewis gave a speech to several hundred townsfolk. At the end of his address Lewis called upon the women of Hillsboro to visit the local liquor stores and saloons and provide a demonstration of prayer, persuasion, and song to dissuade their patrons from drinking the intoxicating spirits on sale. The following morning, Mrs. Eliza J. Thompson, daughter of a former governor and the town's most prominent woman, was unanimously elected president of what would be called the Committee of Visitation, and the women of Hillsboro went to work.

Lewis had specifically instructed the women on the tactics to use. They must first attempt to ask sellers of liquor to sign pledges that they would cease to sell it; if they refused, the women would begin prayer and song services in the establishment selling liquor. Lewis recognized the virtuousness of the female sex and the emotional impact women would have. As a result, he decreed that only women should participate, although male support—both financial and moral—was important, the men were to remain in the background.

Quickly the women's efforts began to meet with success. In a relatively small rural community where most people knew each other, men were shamed into avoiding the saloon. For many, the prospect of clambering over a praying friend or neighbor in order to get a drink became too daunting and the bars soon emptied. In other cases, where saloons were operating without licenses or were known to serve minors, the crusaders threatened to invoke the law unless they closed.

"After calling at all drug stores," wrote Mrs. Thompson (wrongly inferring that the results were immediate), "the pledge being signed by all save one, when counted various saloons and hotels with varied success, until by continuous daily visitations with persuasion, prayer, song, and Scripture reading, the drinking places of the town were reduced from 13 to one drugstore, one hotel, and two saloons, and they sold very cautiously." In actuality, this partial victory had required almost two months of constant hounding and special prayer meetings staged every morning and mass meetings each evening.

Lewis was a veteran campaigner, not just on temperance, but on a wide range of feminist issues. However his greatest successes came as a temperance leader. He was an inspiring and charismatic speaker, captivating audiences with the harrowing tales of his boozy father and long suffering mother, who eventually fought back. Leading other wives with drunken husbands in a praying campaign against the saloon keeper who supplied the booze to her husband, Lewis's mother had prevailed upon the saloonkeeper to seek an alternative means of earning a living. "Ladies," Lewis would conclude his lecture, "You might do the same here if you had the faith."

Within months the prayer and visitation brigades of Hillsboro had exploded into a fully fledged temperance campaign—the Woman's Crusade—that spanned America's rural Midwest. Word spread quickly around Ohio about the women of Hillsboro and there was barely a community in the state not planning a crusade of its own or awaiting the arrival of Dr. Lewis. Not only did the religious press begin to report on the work of the Ohio women, but other newspapers, such as the *New York Tribune* which sent out a reporter to follow Dr. Lewis, began to pick up on his deeds. This ignited the crusade, spreading word far beyond the rural communities where it started and beyond the borders of Ohio. Within weeks of appearing at Hillsboro, Lewis was accepting invitations to lecture and organize praying bands as far away as Columbus, Cleveland, Chicago, Cincinnati, and Pittsburgh.

Nevertheless, Lewis did not believe that the crusade could succeed in the large cities, where liquor traffic was strongly entrenched in the politics, business, and the culture of the metropolis, and he urged the women to confine their efforts to small towns and villages. As such, the depiction of temperance campaigners outside a New York saloon, shown below, is either an unusual event or springs from the imagination of the artist.

PRIMARY SOURCE

TEMPERANCE PROTEST
See primary source image.

SIGNIFICANCE

While Lewis was unquestionably an inspirational and even incendiary presence, it was ultimately the women who organized their own protests and, as he had himself envisaged, had the greatest impact on those they visited. Many embarked on their crusades without ever hearing Lewis speak. Usually the women came from the upper classes of their towns. Mark Twain characterized them as women who were "not the inferior sorts, the very best in their village communities."

The women were highly vigilant in monitoring their local liquor dealers. They were informed of their prospective shipments, and learned when deliveries would be made to incompliant saloons. Invariably, when a delivery was made, the crusaders would be waiting outside the saloon ready to point the finger of scorn at those who continued to sell liquor.

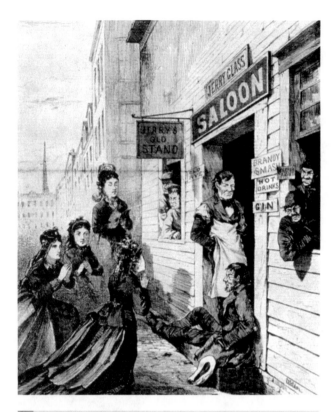

PRIMARY SOURCE

Temperance Protest: Ilustration showing temperance crusaders praying outside a New York tavern, 1874. MPI/GETTY IMAGES.

As befits what was effectively a religious crusade, a number of so-called miracles were reported. For example, in Cleveland, Ohio, a saloon keeper set fierce dogs upon a Mrs. Charles Wheeler as she knelt praying on the sidewalk. Apparently, without even ceasing her prayer, she invoked the power of God to tame the dogs. The dogs then crouched at her feet quietly and even meekly followed her home. Scores of such tales were spread by the press throughout the crusade.

Though the women accomplished a good deal less than they claimed, they were instrumental in obtaining indictments of about 1,000 liquor licensing offenders. At the height of the crusade, 17,000 small town Ohio saloons, drug stores, and other dispensers of drink by the glass went temporarily out of business, a further 1,000 closed in New York State, and throughout the country, almost 30,000 closed. Eight of Ohio's biggest distilleries suspended operations, as did 750 breweries elsewhere. There was a consequent decline in beer consumption estimated at 6,000,000 gallons, with a loss to government in liquor taxes exceeding $1 million.

The initial excitement created by the crusade began to subside by the summer of 1874 and the successes of the prayer and visitation brigades soon proved ephemeral. Within a year virtually every town that had witnessed a crusade had as many saloons and drinking establishments as before the movement.

There was, nevertheless, a significant legacy left by the temperance crusaders. The multitude of local organizations the crusade left behind united under the banner of the Woman's Christian Temperance Union (WCTU). Within a decade the WCTU became the largest political organization of women in the world. Its inspirational leader, Miss Frances Willard, like many of its members had first become involved in temperance during the crusade. She united temperance with a wider agenda of feminist issues and the alliance of the WCTU with prohibition politics in the 1910s would be instrumental in gaining American women the vote.

The women's crusade also helped revitalize the American temperance movement. The country had previously been preoccupied with the Civil War and subsequent rebuilding. As a result, the prohibition statues of the 1850s—the so-called Maine Laws, when thirteen states and two territories adopted prohibition and several others came very close—had virtually been dismantled. Within a few years of the Woman's Crusade, Kansas readopted prohibition and anti-liquor agitation had become increasingly part of the national mainstream political agenda. As a third party, the Prohibition Party had a decisive role in the 1884 presidential election and a few years later the Anti-Saloon League was created. As a lobbying group, the Anti-Saloon League had a dramatic impact on Washington politics, leading the way to a political shift against liquor interests so seismic that the sale and manufacture of alcohol was prohibited in 1919 by a constitutional amendment.

FURTHER RESOURCES
Books

Asbury, Herbert. *The Great Illusion.* New York: Doubleday, 1950.

Kobler, John. *Ardent Spirits: The Rise and Fall of Prohibition.* New York: G. P. Putnam's, 1973.

Sinclair, Andrew. *Prohibition: The Era of Excess.* Boston: Little Brown, 1962.

Illustration showing Archbishop Henry Edward Manning administering the temperance pledge to crowds gathered at Clerkenwell Green, London, 1850. PHOTO BY HULTON ARCHIVE/GETTY IMAGES.

Sedition Act of 1918

An Amendment to Section 3 of the Espionage Act of June 15, 1917

Legislation

By: U.S. Congress

Date: May 16, 1918

Source: *The World War One Document Archive*. "The Sedition Act, 1918." <http://www.gwpda.org/1918/usspy.html> (accessed May 18, 2006).

About the Author: The U.S. Senate and the U.S. House of Representatives, which enacted this legislation, are the two houses of the U.S. Congress. The U.S. Congress is the legislative or law-making branch of the American government.

INTRODUCTION

In early April 1917, the United States entered World War I, which had been raging since 1914. Nationalistic sentiment ran high, and there was little sympathy for the idea of dissident free speech. "We must have no criticism now," said a former Secretary of War, Elihu Root (1845–1937). On June 15, 1917, the Espionage Act was passed. Although ostensibly an anti-spying measure, it also contained language that could be (and was) used to prosecute anyone who criticized U.S. participation in the war. It specified penalties for anyone who, "when the United States is at war, shall willfully cause or attempt to cause insubordination, disloyalty, mutiny, or refusal of duty in the military or naval forces...." However, many citizens wanted an additional law to explicitly criminalize any form of speech critical of the war. A number of states and cities passed statewide or community anti-sedition ordinances in 1917 and 1918. Sedition is defined as any speech or act that incites discontent with or rebellion against a government.

Communities with large numbers of German immigrants were especially suspected of sedition because Germany was the nation's primary opponent in the war. In Oklahoma, for example, the state Loyalty Bureau employed secret agents to infiltrate German-American communities and expose signs of disloyalty. Oklahoma and some other states passed laws banning the speaking or teaching of the German language, and in some locales German-language books were burned. Some German words were replaced by patriotic-sounding phrases: for the word "sauerkraut," for example, pro-war Americans often substituted "victory cabbage." In May 1918, Montana's state anti-sedition law became the basis for an amendment to the Espionage Act of 1917 that was known as the Sedition Act. (The wording of the federal statute was almost identical to that of the Montana statute.) The new law included the language of the original Espionage Act about forbidding incitement to insubordination and further forbade virtually any criticism or disparagement whatsoever of the government, military, or flag.

PRIMARY SOURCE

Sec. 3 Whoever, when the United States is at war, shall willfully make or convey false reports or false statements with intent to interfere with the operation or success of the military or naval forces of the United States, or to promote the success of its enemies, or shall willfully make or convey false reports or false statements, or say or do anything except by way of bona fide and not disloyal advice to an investor or investors, with intent to obstruct the sale by the United States of bonds or other securities of the United States or the making of loans by or to the United States, and whoever when the United States is at war, shall willfully cause or attempt to cause, or incite or attempt to incite, insubordination, disloyalty, mutiny, or refusal of duty, in the military or naval forces of the United States, or shall willfully obstruct or attempt to obstruct the recruiting or enlistment services of the United States, and whoever, when the United States is at war, shall willfully utter, print, write or publish any disloyal, profane, scurrilous, or abusive language about the form of government of the United States or the Constitution of the United States, or the military or naval forces of the United States, or the flag of the United States, or the uniform of the Army or Navy of the United States into contempt, scorn, contumely, or disrepute, or shall willfully utter, print, write, or publish any language intended

to incite, provoke, or encourage resistance to the United States, or to promote the cause of its enemies, or shall willfully display the flag of any foreign enemy, or shall willfully by utterance, writing, printing, publication, or language spoken, urge, incite, or advocate any curtailment of production in this country of any thing or things, product or products, necessary or essential to the prosecution of the war in which the United States may be engaged, with intent by such curtailment to cripple or hinder the United States in the prosecution of war, and whoever shall willfully advocate, teach, defend, or suggest the doing of any of the acts or things in this section enumerated, and whoever shall by word or act support or favor the cause of any country with which the United States is at war or by word or act oppose the cause of the United States therein, shall be punished by a fine of not more than $10,000 or the imprisonment for not more than twenty years, or both: Provided, That any employee or official of the United States Government who commits any disloyal act or utters any unpatriotic or disloyal language, or who, in an abusive and violent manner criticizes the Army or Navy or the flag of the United States shall be at once dismissed from the service. . . .

Sec. 4 When the United States is at war, the Postmaster General may, upon evidence satisfactory to him that any person or concern is using the mails in violation of any of the provisions of this Act, instruct the postmaster at any post office at which mail is received addressed to such person or concern to return to the postmaster at the office at which they were originally mailed all letters or other matter so addressed, with the words 'mail to this address undeliverable under Espionage Act' plainly written or stamped upon the outside thereof, and all such letters or other matter so returned to such postmasters shall be by them returned to the senders thereof under such regulations as the Postmaster General may prescribe.

Approved, May 16, 1918.

SIGNIFICANCE

The Sedition Act targeted all forms of criticism of the government, military, or U.S. participation in the war. Both the federal and state anti-sedition statutes were used to arrest, try, and imprison pacifists, Socialists, and German-Americans. In Montana, 79 persons—more than half of whom were born in Europe—were convicted of sedition, often for casual remarks made in saloons. One man received a seven-and-one-half to twenty-year jail sentence for saying that wartime food regulations were, in his words, "a joke." All were pardoned posthumously by the governor of Montana in 2006.

Over 2,000 prosecutions were based on the federal Espionage and Sedition Acts during World War I, most of leftists. About 900 of those accused spent time in jail. Two months after the Espionage Act was passed, Charles Schenck, a Socialist, was arrested in Philadelphia for handing out leaflets criticizing the draft and American involvement in the war. Schenck's pamphlet asserted that the Thirteenth Amendment, which prohibits "involuntary servitude," made the draft unconstitutional. He also recommended peaceful acts of resistance, such as the signing of petitions. He was tried, convicted, and sentenced to six months in jail. He appealed his case to the U.S. Supreme Court, which upheld his conviction in *Schenck v. United States* (March 3, 1919). It was in arguing this case that Justice Oliver Wendell Holmes first made the oft-cited argument that the First Amendment does not protect "shouting fire in a [crowded] theatre." U.S. historian Howard Zinn replies that although "Holmes's analogy was clever and attractive...a more apt analogy for Schenck was someone getting up between the acts at a theater and declaring that there are not enough fire exits." Or, Zinn suggests, "someone shouting, not falsely, but truly, to people about to buy tickets and enter a theater, that there was a fire raging inside."

Another famous arrest under the Sedition Act was that of Eugene Debs (1855–1926), a Socialist and labor leader who ran for President five times. Debs was arrested for saying that "Wars throughout history have been waged for conquest and plunder.... And that is war in a nutshell." Since there were young men of draft age in the audience, his words were deemed seditious. The U.S. Supreme Court upheld his conviction in 1919 and Debs spent thirty-two months in jail. The remainder of his sentence was commuted when the Sedition Act and parts of the Espionage Act were repealed in 1921. However, much of the Espionage Act remains U.S. law. President John F. Kennedy sought (unsuccessfully) in 1963 to apply it to journalists in Vietnam writing articles that were critical of the U.S.-supported Diem regime and were, in the President's opinion, "likely to impede the war effort."

The Sedition Act of 1918 was not the first Sedition Act in U.S. history. Almost a century earlier, the Sedition Act of 1798 made it illegal to criticize Congress or the President. The Sedition Act of 1798 has never been repealed, but most legal experts agree that it would not withstand a challenge on First Amendment grounds today. However, U.S. courts, including the U.S. Supreme Court, have traditionally

been compliant with government desires during wartime, even when those desires openly violate the Constitution. During World War II, for example, the internment in prison camps of 110,000 Japanese-American U.S. citizens who had been accused of no crime was upheld by the Supreme Court in *Korematsu v. United States* (1944). Today, this decision is viewed by most legal scholars as a violation of basic Constitutional rights.

During the first year of the Iraq war (2003–), a number of right-wing commentators called for the imprisonment of war critics. For example, best-selling right-wing columnist Ann Coulter (1961–) wrote in 2003, "Whenever the nation is under attack, from within or without, liberals side with the enemy." She also applied the word "treason" to left and liberal criticism of U.S. actions in Iraq. (Treason is a more serious crime than sedition, punishable by death under U.S. federal law.) Even victory cabbage is not necessarily a thing of the past; during the run-up to the U.S. invasion of Iraq, when France was failing to support U.S. calls for a war, two Republican members of Congress ordered all congressional cafeterias and snack shops to stop selling French fries and French toast and begin selling Freedom fries and Freedom toast instead.

FURTHER RESOURCES

Books

Stone, Geoffrey R. *Perilous Times: Free Speech in Wartime from the Sedition Act of 1798 to the War on Terrorism.* New York: W.W. Norton, 2004.

Periodicals

Douglass, Matt. "Mont. Governor Pardons 78 in Sedition Case." *Washington Post* (May 4, 2006).

Liptak, Adam. "Sedition: It Still Rolls Off the Tongue." *New York Times* (May 7, 2006).

Anti-Prohibition Protest

Photograph

By: Anonymous

Date: c. 1925

Source: © Hulton-Deutsch Collection/Corbis.

About the Photographer: This photograph is part of the collection of the Corbis Corporation, headquartered in Seattle, with a worldwide archive of over 70 million images. The identity of the photographer is not known.

INTRODUCTION

In the early twentieth century, America's foremost political issue involved liquor and temperance. Alcohol had played a significant part in the life of America ever since the first settlers landed on its eastern seaboard more than 300 years earlier. But, the country had also, for more than a century, harbored the most powerful and militant temperance movement in the world. For a hundred years, these two diametrically opposed camps—America's drinkers and its temperance advocates—had traded blows in a phoney war before a series of stunning political reversals in the 1910s placed the momentum firmly in the hands of the dry camp. "Dry" was the name given to the coalition of religious, temperance, and prohibition organizations, while the pro-alcohol camp was known as the 'wets.' During this time, most states implemented legislation that prohibited alcohol and the Anti-Saloon League became the most powerful lobbying organization in the country, with its influence pervading every level of Washington politics.

In August 1917, the dry movement's overwhelming political strength achieved the ultimate success. The U.S. Senate passed the Eighteenth Amendment to the United States Constitution by a vote of sixty-five to twenty. The amendment prohibited the manufacture, sale, transportation, and importation of intoxicating liquors for beverage purposes. The U.S. House of Representatives subsequently passed it as well and it was sent to the individual American states for ratification. The ratification votes were almost a formality, since thirty-three states already had prohibited liquor within their borders. Mississippi became the first state to ratify national prohibition on January 8, 1918, and, on January 14, 1919, Nebraska became the thirty-sixth state to ratify the amendment. Two days later, the U.S. Secretary of State announced that the amendment had been ratified by the required number of states, and would go into effect across the United States one year from that day.

PRIMARY SOURCE

ANTI-PROHIBITION PROTEST

See primary source image.

SIGNIFICANCE

Organized crime became a major feature of the American landscape during the prohibition era. An unintended effect of the constitutional prohibition on alcohol was to push the sale of liquor underground. Alcohol consumption was hardly impacted, while gangsters such as Johnny Torrio and Al Capone accumulated fortunes worth hundreds of millions of dollars. Indeed, the consumption of alcohol became the largest collective act of civil disobedience ever witnessed in America.

During prohibition every sector of American society broke the law. The law impacted all social classes and communities, and for visitors too, prohibition was a tremendous irritation. Winston Churchill, a regular visitor to America throughout the dry years, complained bitterly about having to obtain a medical prescription to satisfy his appetite for brandy. Similarly, King George V was distinctly unimpressed, allegedly describing prohibition as an 'outrage.' The gangsters grabbed all the headlines, but the real story was the masses disobeying the law on a scale America had never previously known. For most of America's prohibition era, alcohol consumption was the most significant form of protest.

Before the passage of the Eighteenth Amendment, the liquor lobby had been almost as powerful as the dry movement, and far richer. Prohibition decimated its ranks and the forced closure of legally operating breweries and distilleries cut off its funding. As a result, the wet movement lacked a coordinated or powerful voice during the early years of the prohibition era.

However, by the mid-1920s, it was obvious to even casual observers that prohibition was not working. Newspapers published reports of prohibition violations virtually every day. Gangsters were taking hold of America's cities, and increasing levels of violence accompanied bootlegging and liquor smuggling. Scores of Americans were poisoned every week by drinking moonshine. And, in the midst of all this turmoil, prohibition had very little impact on improving the fabric of American society, as it had been intended to do.

Whatever the defects of prohibition, the dry movement could always assume the moral high ground. One of the reasons the Eighteenth Amendment had been passed in the first place was the negative social effect of the typical American saloon. Instead, the wet movement began using fiscal arguments and pointing to the benefits that liquor duties brought to the American economy. Even among those sympathetic to prohibition, many were not necessarily willing to pay higher taxes in order to

PRIMARY SOURCE

Anti-Prohibition Protest: This parade float—an oversized beer barrel—is plastered with slogans calling for an end to Prohibition. Economic justifications are featured prominently. © HULTON-DEUTSCH COLLECTION/CORBIS.

compensate for the budget deficit caused by the loss of liquor duty revenues.

These arguments became more persuasive as America was plunged into economic depression following the Stock Market Crash of 1929. Leaders of business, including fifteen of the twenty-eight directors of General Motors, the Dupont family, and Newcomb Carlton, president of Western Union (significantly, an organization that had once backed the drys), began to promote the economic benefits of repealing the Eighteenth Amendment. Economic strife dealt a fatal blow to the dry movement. As during the Civil War, before which many states had prohibition statutes in place, questions of whether a man could take a drink seemed irrelevant when the American people were afflicted by daily disasters. At a

time when federal tax revenues were dropping, the prospect of repealing prohibition offered a double benefit to the treasury—the significant amounts being spent on the futile effort to enforce the Eighteenth Amendment could be eliminated and enormous sums of revenue could be collected by taxing liquor.

Republican President Herbert Hoover was predominantly dry in conviction, and there was little indication that he would ever be swayed into the opposing camp. For another year America drifted uncertainly on, with prohibition legislation still undermined by the gangsters and the economy in dire straits. Then, at the 1932 Democratic Convention, an outright commitment to repeal from a high level politician was finally adopted. When the presidential candidate,

Women protesters march during an anti-Prohibition parade in Newark, New Jersey, October 28, 1932. More than 20,000 people took part in the mass demand for the repeal of the 18th Amendment. AP IMAGES.

Franklin D. Roosevelt, appeared on stage to accept his nomination, he told the hall—to shouts of approval—"From this day on, the Eighteenth Amendment is doomed!"

Within months Roosevelt was in the White House, and just days after his arrival he set about destroying the Eighteenth Amendment. Dramatic cuts were made to the Prohibition Bureau and Congress modified the Volstead Act (the primary prohibition legislation) to permit the sale and manufacture of beer. Within a little over a month, the U.S. Congress passed a resolution authorizing the submission of a repeal amendment (the Twenty-first Amendment) to state conventions. On April 10, 1933, Michigan became the first state to ratify the Twenty-first Amendment, and, on November 7, 1933, Utah became the thirty-sixth and deciding state to adopt it. Four weeks later, the Twenty-first Amendment, repealing the Eighteenth Amendment, became part of the U.S. Constitution.

FURTHER RESOURCES
Books

Asbury, Herbert. *The Great Illusion*. New York: Doubleday, 1950.

Kobler, John. *Ardent Spirits: The Rise and Fall of Prohibition*. New York: G. P. Putnam's, 1973.

Sinclair, Andrew. *Prohibition: The Era of Excess*. Boston: Little Brown, 1962.

A Declaration of Conscience

In Protest of the McCarthy Hearings

Speech

By: Margaret Chase Smith

Date: June 1, 1950

Source: *United States Senate*. "Margaret Chase Smith: A Declaration of Conscience, June 1, 1950." <http://www.senate.gov/artandhistory/history/common/generic/Speeches_Smith_Declaration.htm> (accessed May 22, 2006).

About the Author: U.S. Congressperson Margaret Madeline Chase Smith (1897–1995), born in Skowhegan, Maine, represented her home state as a U.S. Representative (Maine's second district) for four terms (1939–1949). During World War II, she served on the House Naval Affairs Committee. Later, in 1949, Smith was elected as U.S. Senator (Maine), and she served in this capacity for twenty-four years (1949–1973). Smith was the first woman to serve in both the House of Representatives and the Senate. In both chambers, she played important roles in the nation's foreign policy and military affairs.

As a moderate Republican, Smith was publicly critical about extremes in both the Democratic and Republican parties. She is possibly best remembered for her strong opposition to the tactics of Senator Joseph R. McCarthy (1908–1957) in a campaign he orchestrated against Communist activity in the United States in the early 1950s—a campaign often called McCarthyism. On June 1, 1950, Smith gave her now-famous fifteen-minute "Declaration of Conscience" speech on the Senate floor to oppose the crusade of McCarthy. According to the Margaret Chase Smith Library, Smith later said of her accomplishments: "If I am to be remembered in history, it will not be because of legislative accomplishments, but for an act I took as a legislator in the U.S. Senate when on June 1, 1950, I spoke…in condemnation of McCarthyism, when the junior Senator from Wisconsin had the Senate paralyzed with fear that he would purge any Senator who disagreed with him."

In 1964, Smith became the first woman to become a presidential nominee of a major U.S. political party when she was nominated at the Republican National Convention. Smith received the Presidential Medal of Freedom and the American Spirit Award, the U.S. Air Force's premier award. In 1973, Smith was one of the original inductees into the National Women's Hall of Fame.

INTRODUCTION

Senator Joseph McCarthy first gained national attention on February 9, 1950, when he began a campaign against the foreign policy of President Harry Truman, which included charges that the State Department and its Secretary, Dean Acheson, had allowed U.S. citizens who were Communists to penetrate its organization. McCarthy implied that he possessed lists of people—within such groups as the federal government, the military, broadcast and defense industries, and universities and colleges—who were Communist conspirators. He garnered power through political manipulations to defeat several important Democrats for re-election to the Senate. His accusations scared many politicians and other leaders and prominent citizens who thought they might soon appear on his lists. Consequently, his critics usually did not challenge his statements. When he was challenged, however, the accused were usually unable to defend themselves against the allegations brought in front of the federal investigative body. As a result, they were often blacklisted, which ruined their professional careers and their personal reputations.

U.S. Senator Margaret Chase Smith thought initially that Senator McCarthy was bringing important attention to a disturbing problem within the federal government. However, upon further investigation of McCarthy's documents, she found little evidence to support his claims. Smith began to feel that McCarthy was unfair and inaccurate, and that his statements were not credible. At the same time, Smith saw an atmosphere of fear sweeping through the political community of Washington D.C. due to McCarthy's actions. To counter McCarthy's campaign and to oppose his tactics, Smith delivered a speech called "Declaration of Conscience." In the speech, Smith (along with support from six other Republican senators) voiced her concern over the lack of national leadership in the United States, within both the Republican and Democratic political parties. She also expressed her concern that any citizen could be classified as a Communist or Fascist simply by expressing basic beliefs that ran counter to those of certain people in political power. Without mentioning his name, Smith implicated McCarthy for using what she thought were dishonest and immoral tactics.

PRIMARY SOURCE

Mr. President, I would like to speak briefly and simply about a serious national condition. It is a national feeling of fear and frustration that could result in national suicide and the end of everything that we Americans hold dear. It is a condition that comes from the lack of effective leadership in either the Legislative Branch or the Executive Branch of our Government.

That leadership is so lacking that serious and responsible proposals are being made that national advisory commissions be appointed to provide such critically needed leadership.

I speak as briefly as possible because too much harm has already been done with irresponsible words of bitterness and selfish political opportunism. I speak as briefly as possible because the issue is too great to be obscured by eloquence. I speak simply and briefly in the hope that my words will be taken to heart.

I speak as a Republican. I speak as a woman. I speak as a United States Senator. I speak as an American.

The United States Senate has long enjoyed worldwide respect as the greatest deliberative body in the world. But recently that deliberative character has too often been debased to the level of a forum of hate and character assassination sheltered by the shield of congressional immunity.

It is ironical that we Senators can in debate in the Senate directly or indirectly, by any form of words, impute to any American who is not a Senator any conduct or motive unworthy or unbecoming an American—and without that non-Senator American having any legal redress against us—yet if we say the same thing in the Senate about our colleagues we can be stopped on the grounds of being out of order.

It is strange that we can verbally attack anyone else without restraint and with full protection and yet we hold ourselves above the same type of criticism here on the Senate Floor. Surely the United States Senate is big enough to take self-criticism and self-appraisal. Surely we should be able to take the same kind of character attacks that we "dish out" to outsiders.

I think that it is high time for the United States Senate and its members to do some soul-searching—for us to weigh our consciences—on the manner in which we are performing our duty to the people of America—on the manner in which we are using or abusing our individual powers and privileges.

I think that it is high time that we remembered that we have sworn to uphold and defend the Constitution. I think that it is high time that we remembered that the Constitution, as amended, speaks not only of the freedom of speech but also of trial by jury instead of trial by accusation.

Whether it be a criminal prosecution in court or a character prosecution in the Senate, there is little practical distinction when the life of a person has been ruined.

Those of us who shout the loudest about Americanism in making character assassinations are all too frequently those who, by our own words and acts, ignore some of the basic principles of Americanism:

The right to criticize;
The right to hold unpopular beliefs;
The right to protest;
The right of independent thought.

The exercise of these rights should not cost one single American citizen his reputation or his right to a livelihood nor should he be in danger of losing his reputation or livelihood merely because he happens to know someone who holds unpopular beliefs. Who of us doesn't? Otherwise none of us could call our souls our own. Otherwise thought control would have set in.

The American people are sick and tired of being afraid to speak their minds lest they be politically smeared as "Communists" or "Fascists" by their opponents. Freedom of speech is not what it used to be in America. It has been so abused by some that it is not exercised by others.

. . .

As members of the minority party, we do not have the primary authority to formulate the policy of our Government. But we do have the responsibility of rendering constructive criticism, of clarifying issues, of allaying fears by acting as responsible citizens.

As a woman, I wonder how the mothers, wives, sisters, and daughters feel about the way in which members of their families have been politically mangled in the Senate debate—and I use the word "debate" advisedly.

As a United States Senator, I am not proud of the way in which the Senate has been made a publicity platform for irresponsible sensationalism. I am not proud of the reckless abandon in which unproved charges have been hurled from the side of the aisle. I am not proud of the obviously staged, undignified countercharges that have been attempted in retaliation from the other side of the aisle.

I do not like the way the Senate has been made a rendezvous for vilification, for selfish political gain at the sacrifice of individual reputations and national unity. I am not proud of the way we smear outsiders from the Floor of the Senate and hide behind the cloak of congressional immunity and still place ourselves beyond criticism on the Floor of the Senate.

. . .

It is with these thoughts that I have drafted what I call a Declaration of Conscience. I am gratified that the senator from New Hampshire [Mr. Tobey], the senator from Vermont [Mr. Aiken], the senator from Oregon [Mr. Morse], the senator from New York [Mr. Ives], the senator from Minnesota [Mr. Thye], and the senator from New Jersey [Mr. Hendrickson] have concurred in that declaration and have authorized me to announce their concurrence.

SIGNIFICANCE

Senator Margaret Chase Smith's "A Declaration of Conscience" was the first speech by a politician to criticize and challenge McCarthy. A few senators applauded Smith's speech, but the vast majority silenced their comments and opinions, fearing McCarthy's wrath. Smith's words angered McCarthy. However, the public expressed its enthusiastic support for Smith, as did many newspapers and civil liberties organizations.

Over the next four years, Smith, along with others, felt McCarthy's vengeance. Although against Senate tradition, McCarthy removed Smith immediately from an investigation committee. McCarthy also accused various political officials of subversive activities. His accusations came to a head on April 22, 1954. At this time, the Senate began to investigate McCarthy's accusations that the U.S. Army and the secretary of the Army were guilty of wrongdoing, including withholding information on foreign espionage activities, and counter-charges made by Army leaders accusing McCarthy and his staff of threatening army officials. For six weeks the hearings were shown on live television. These hearings, which became known as the Army-McCarthy hearings, were the first nationally televised congressional inquiry. They are now considered a milestone merger between television and U.S. politics.

Around this same time, McCarthy sponsored a challenger to Smith's senate seat when she ran for re-election. However, Maine voters rejected McCarthy's efforts, and soundly re-elected Smith. Although McCarthy clashed with Smith, she still was appointed to two important Senate committees: Armed Services and Appropriations.

On June 17, 1954, McCarthy was cleared of the charges leveled at him during the Senate hearings, but he received a massive amount of unfavorable press as a result of the televised proceedings. On December 2, 1954, Smith voted with a majority of other senators to approve a resolution condemning Senator McCarthy. In the end, McCarthy was censured for the underhanded tactics that he used in his investigations and for the abuses that he inflicted upon senators and members of Senate committees. His political influence quickly diminished in the Senate and throughout the United States, but McCarthy remained a member of the Senate until his death in 1957.

Although it did not produce an immediate reaction, Margaret Chase Smith's speech to members of the Senate helped to end McCarthy's political influence and his anti-Communist campaign. The speech also brought Smith to the attention of the nation, showing the American people her courage, independence, and, most importantly, her commitment to justice. According to the Margaret Chase Smith Policy Center, Smith concluded the saga of McCarthyism with her statement:

"My creed is that public service must be more than doing a job efficiently and honestly. It must be a complete dedication to the people and to the nation with full recognition that every human being is entitled to courtesy and consideration, that constructive criticism is not only to be expected but sought, that smears are not only to be expected but fought, that honor is to be earned but not bought."

FURTHER RESOURCES
Books

Herman, Arthur. *Joseph McCarthy: Reexamining the Life and Legacy of America's Most Hated Senator*. New York: Free Press, 2000.

Lewis, William C., Jr., ed. *Margaret Chase Smith: Declaration of Conscience*. (American National Biography, Scribner Encyclopedia of American Lives.) New York: Doubleday, 1972.

Morgan, Ted. *Reds: McCarthyism in Twentieth-century America*. New York: Random House, 2003.

Sherman, Janann. *No Place for a Woman: A Life of Senator Margaret Chase Smith*. New Brunswick, N.J.: Rutgers University Press, 2000.

Wallace, Patricia Ward. *Politics of Conscience: A Biography of Margaret Chase Smith*. Westport, Conn.: Praeger, 1995.

Web sites

Margaret Chase Smith Library. "Expanded Biography." <http://www.mcslibrary.org/bio/biolong.htm> (accessed May 16, 2006).

Margaret Chase Smith Policy Center, The University of Maine. "Biography: Margaret Chase Smith (1897–1995)." <http://www.umaine.edu/mcsc/AboutUs/Bio.htm> (accessed May 22, 2006).

Telegram from Joseph McCarthy to President Harry S. Truman

Telegram

By: Joseph McCarthy

Date: February 11, 1950

Source: *The National Archives.* "Teaching With Documents: Telegram from Senator Joseph McCarthy to President Harry S. Truman." <http://www.archives.gov/education/lessons/mccarthy-telegram/> (accessed May 25, 2006).

About the Author: Joseph Raymond McCarthy (1908–1957), was born in the town of Grand Chute, near Appleton, Wisconsin. He graduated with a law degree from Marquette University in Milwaukee, Wisconsin, in 1935. In 1946, he was elected as a Republican to the U.S. Senate. A staunch opponent of Communism, McCarthy worked towards exposing Communist elements in the U.S. government throughout his political career. He died at the Bethesda Naval Hospital in Maryland on May 2, 1957.

INTRODUCTION

In 1919, after the end of World War I and the Bolshevik Revolution in Russia (the first Communist revolution of the twentieth century), fear of the increased influence of Communists, Socialists, and anarchists gripped the United States. Known as the "Red Scare," during this period the government of President Woodrow Wilson was allegedly confronted with the prospect of Communists taking over the administration. To curb the influence of Communism on government policies, the U.S. Justice Department, under Attorney General A. Mitchell Palmer, initiated the General Intelligence Division of Bureau of Investigation on August 1, 1919. The Bureau arrested and detained several suspected Communists. Although, the Red Scare dissipated by the summer of 1920, concerns about Communism continued to linger.

In the 1930s, gripped by the Great Depression, the focus of the U.S. government shifted to economic

Senator Joseph R. McCarthy appears on television on April 6, 1954, to respond to criticisms leveled at him by CBS newscaster Edward R. Murrow. McCarthy told a coast to coast audience that Murrow "as far back as twenty years ago, was engaged in propaganda for Communist causes." © BETTMANN/CORBIS.

policies that could help counter the crisis. However, the administration also established several committees to control the growth of Communism in the country. Anti-Communist activities were toned down the early 1940s, when the United States and the Soviet Union were allies in the fight against Nazi Germany. World War II (1939–1945) led to the spread of Communism throughout Eastern Europe, and after the war anti-Communist sentiment in the United States rose to new heights. Many members of the U.S. Congress proposed anti-Communist measures. One of the most outspoken anti-Communist senators was Republican Joseph R. McCarthy from Wisconsin.

Owing to the mounting pressure of the Cold War, U.S. President Harry S. Truman (1884–1972) established a loyalty program for federal employees to contain Communism. Several federal employees were investigated for suspected Communist ideology. Reportedly, almost 3,000 employees resigned (or were fired) as a consequence of the investigation. The U.S. Justice Department was also instructed to compile a list of organizations engaging in Communist activities.

However, on February 9, 1950, Senator McCarthy, in a speech at Wheeling, West Virginia, attacked Truman's foreign policy by accusing the U.S. State Department of harboring Communists. McCarthy claimed that he had in his possession a list bearing the names of more than 200 State Department officials who were allegedly members of the Communist Party. This list was, however, never made public. The accusation garnered national attention at a time when fear of Communism at its peak in most Western countries.

On February 11, 1950, two days after his Wheeling Speech, Senator McCarthy sent a telegram to President Truman. In this telegram, McCarthy asserted that he had names of fifty-seven State Department officials with Communist ideologies working against the interest of the United States. He further emphasized that the President should take appropriate action to deal with Communist infiltration in the State Department.

▮ PRIMARY SOURCE

Reno, Nevada Feb 11 1139A

The President
The White House

In a Lincoln Day speech at Wheeling Thursday night I stated that the State Department harbors a nest of communists and communist sympathizers who are helping to shape our foreign policy. I further stated that I have in my possession the names of 57 communists who are in the State Department at present. A State Department spokesman flatly denied this and claimed that there is not a single communist in the department. You can convince yourself of the falsity of the State Department claim very easily. You will recall that you personally appointed a board to screen State Department employees for the purpose of weeding out fellow travelers. Your board did a pains-taking job. And named hundreds which it listed as "dangerous to the security of the nation", because of communistic connections.

While the records are not available to me, I know that of one group of approximately 300 certified to the secretary for discharge, he actually discharged only approximately 80. I understand that this was done after lengthy consultation with Alger Hiss. I would suggest therefore, Mr. President, that you simply pick up your phone and ask Mr. Acheson how many of those whom your board had labeled as dangerous, he failed to discharge. The day the House Un-American Activities Committee exposed Alger Hiss as an important link in an inter-national communist spy ring, you signed an order forbidding the State Departments giving to the Congress any information in regard to the disloyalty or the communistic connections of anyone in that department, dispite this State Department blackout, we have been able to compile a list of 57 communists in the State Department. This list is available to you, but you can get a much longer list by ordering the Secretary Acheson to give you a list of these whom your own board listed as being disloyal, and who are still working in the State Department. I believe the following is the minimum which can be expected of you in this case.

1. That you demand that Acheson give you and the proper congressional committee the names and a complete report on all of those who were placed in the department by Alger Hiss, and all of those still working in the State Department who were listed by your board as bad security risks because of the communistic connections.
2. That under no circumstances could a congressional committee obtain any information or help from the Executive Department in exposing communists.

Failure on your part will label the Democratic Party of being the bed-fellow on inter-national communism. Certainly this label is not deserved by the hundreds of thousands of loyal American Democrats throughout the nation, and by the sizable number of able loyal Democrats in both the Senate and the House.

Joe McCarthy U.S.S. Wis.

SIGNIFICANCE

McCarthy's Wheeling Speech and his subsequent telegram to President Truman came at a time when the world was witnessing the rise of Communism in China followed by the nuclear tests in the Soviet Union. In the United States, several prominent personalities, suspected of Communist ties, were arrested. These included former State Department official Alger Hiss, nuclear physicist Klaus Fuchs, who admitted to divulging critical information to the Soviet Union, and scientists Julius and Ethel Rosenberg who were suspected of espionage.

According to many, McCarthy's allegations appeared credible in the light of the above-mentioned arrests. President Truman, allegedly livid, vehemently opposed the accusations. In March 1950, he responded by stating, "I think the greatest asset that the Kremlin has is Senator McCarthy." Truman held McCarthy to be responsible for aiding Soviet interests by sabotaging the nation's bipartisan foreign policy efforts.

Nevertheless, in the following years, McCarthy's views found extensive support in the United States. Soon after Republican Dwight D. Eisenhower (1890–1969) was elected president, McCarthy was appointed chairman of the Senate Permanent Subcommittee on Investigations of the Committee on Government Operations. Under his chairmanship, the focus of the subcommittee shifted from exposing corrupt officials to eradicating Communist infiltration. In 1953, 117 executive sessions were held by the committee as compared to only six in 1952.

However, McCarthy's search for Communists in various U.S. institutions, and his anti-Communist policies—popularly known as 'McCarthyism'—soon attracted criticism. Severely condemned for his unsuccessful investigation of the Army Signal Corps, many found his behavior unconstitutional and condescending. McCarthy's reputation was further compromised after he accused General Ralph W. Zwicker, a high ranking U.S. Army officer, of being unworthy of his rank. Subsequently, in December 1954, McCarthy was censured by the Senate after it passed a resolution condemning him for abusing his power as a Senator.

Though, McCarthy is considered to be one of the most reviled Senators in U.S. history, the Wheeling speech and his telegram to President Truman are considered significant in containing Communism in the United States. The telegram was widely endorsed by the American public at the time.

FURTHER RESOURCES

Books

Fried, Albert. *McCarthyism, The Great American Red Scare: A Documentary History*. New York: Oxford University Press, 1996.

Web sites

Appleton Public Library. "Biography, Joseph McCarthy (1908–1957)." <http://www.apl.org/history/mccarthy/biography.html> (accessed May 25, 2006).

Biographical Directory of the United States Congress. "McCarthy, Joseph Raymond (1908–1957)." <http://bioguide.congress.gov/scripts/biodisplay.pl?index=M000315> (accessed May 25, 2006).

History Matters. "'Enemies from Within': Senator Joseph R. McCarthy and President Harry S. Truman Trade Accusations of Disloyalty." <http://historymatters.gmu.edu/d/6456> (accessed May 25, 2006).

MSNBC. "50 years ago, TV helped to end McCarthyism." June 8, 2004. <http://www.msnbc.msn.com/id/5165583> (accessed May 25, 2006).

U.S. Government Printing Office. "Executive Sessions of the Senate Permanent Subcommittee on Investigations of the Committee on Government Operations." January 2003. <http://a257.g.akamaitech.net/7/257/2422/06amay20030700/www.gpo.gov/congress/senate/mccarthy/83869.html> (accessed May 25, 2006).

University of Washington. "The Cold War and Red Scare in Washington State." <http://www.washington.edu/uwired/outreach/cspn/curcan/main.html> (accessed May 25, 2006).

Homeless Child on a Protest March

Photograph

By: M. McKeown

Date: December 6, 1965

Source: Photo by M. McKeown/Express/Getty Images.

About the Photographer: This photograph is part of the collection at Getty Images, a worldwide provider of visual content materials to such communications groups as advertisers, broadcasters, designers, magazines, new media organizations, newspapers, and producers. No information is available about the photographer.

INTRODUCTION

This image of a young child on a homelessness protest march in 1965 reflects the housing crisis that was taking place in the United Kingdom at that time, and which was most poignantly portrayed in the influential TV drama *Cathy Come Home* (1966). This told the story of a young London couple with three children, evicted from their flat after the father lost his job because of an industrial injury, who spiraled into poverty, with the wife and children eventually living in a hostel. The drama had a major impact on the British public and has been attributed with putting homelessness onto the British political agenda and leading to the establishment of charities for the homeless such as Shelter and Crisis.

The homelessness crisis of the United Kingdom in the 1960s was largely due to the effects of post-war urban renewal programs which were moving residential housing and industry out of inner city areas, and creating a lack of affordable housing in the cities. Some people moved willingly to the suburbs, while others who lost their homes were offered alternative public housing or forced onto the private rental market. The new public housing developments mainly consisted of flats in tower blocks, which soon earned a poor reputation because of bad design features and concerns about safety, particularly following the collapse of the Ronan Point tower block in East London from a gas explosion in 1968. In the private rental market, families were often at the mercy of unscrupulous landlords, such as the infamous Peree Rachman, who exploited their tenants ruthlessly, provided very poor quality housing for extortionate rents, and used tactics of intimidation to evict those whose rents were protected by earlier rent control legislation. These practices were investigated in the 1963 Milner Holland report on 'Housing in Greater London' produced for the House of Commons Committee on Housing in Greater London, which made recommendations for London's future housing and on the need for legislation to protect tenants.

Until the late 1960s, government policy treated homelessness as a welfare issue rather than a housing problem, in effect blaming homeless people for their own inadequacies. If homeless people had children, these were often taken into care, or families were broken up with wives and children given places in hostels where fathers were not allowed to stay with them. However, the increasing media interest in homelessness put pressure on the government to address homelessness as a housing issue rather than a welfare problem. Around the same time, a report by J. W. B. Douglas, entitled "The Home and the School" highlighted the adverse impact that poor housing conditions, among other factors, had on the health, education and general well-being of children, focusing even more attention on the important role of good housing in people's lives.

In 1974, it was recommended by central government that local authorities should transfer responsibility for dealing with the homeless from social services to housing authorities, but many councils did not act on the recommendations at that time. As the problems of homelessness continued, the squatting movement emerged. Activists who were frustrated at the failure of local authorities to provide housing for the homeless moved families into unoccupied houses which had been acquired by local councils for demolition as part of urban renewal programs. Aggressive attempts by local authorities to evict the squatters were widely covered in the media, and it has been claimed that these increased public support for the movement. The government tried to control the practice of squatting by passing the Criminal Law Act of 1977, which made entering and remaining on property without permission a criminal offence. However, some local authorities entered into housing co-operatives with groups of squatters which grew into successful long-standing social housing schemes.

The Housing (Homeless Persons) Act of 1977 required local authorities to house the most vulnerable homeless people, including families with children, but only if they could prove they had not intentionally made themselves homeless, and had a connection with the local area. This was later replaced by the 1996 Housing Act, still based on a system whereby homeless people have to meet specified criteria before they can be provided with public housing.

PRIMARY SOURCE

HOMELESS CHILD ON A PROTEST MARCH
See primary source image.

SIGNIFICANCE

The problems of homelessness and poor quality housing in Britain have not been completely resolved. In 2006, research was released by the charity Shelter

PRIMARY SOURCE

Homeless Child on a Protest March: A homeless child on a protest march to the home of British Health Minister Kenneth Robinson, December 6, 1965. PHOTO BY M. MCKEOWN/EXPRESS/GETTY IMAGES.

which claimed that the number of households living in temporary "bed and breakfast" accommodation increased dramatically from 6,400 in 1976, to more than 100,000 in 2006, while the building of public and 'social' housing for low-income income families fell by eighty-seven percent over this twenty-year period.

Since the 1980s, government policies have focused on increasing private home ownership and expanding the private rental sector through the use of tax incentives, reduced spending on public housing provision and the 'Right to Buy' scheme which enabled council house tenants to buy their properties at prices below market values. However, these policies later contributed to even more homelessness as soaring interest rates on mortgages led to many house repossessions and evictions. Home prices in many areas of the United Kingdom continue to be among the most expensive in the world.

FURTHER RESOURCES
Books
Conway, Jean. *Housing Policy.* Gildredge, 2000.

Kahn, Alfred J. *Family Change and Family Policies in Great Britain, Canada New Zealand, and the United States.* Clarendon Press, 1997.

House of Commons Committee on Housing in Greater London. *Housing in Greater London.* HMSO, 1965.

Web sites
The Guardian. "Homeless crisis deeper 40 years after landmark TV programme." February 15, 2006. <http://society.guardian.co.uk/communities/news/0,1709912,00.html> (accessed June 3, 2006).

Resource Information Service. "homelesspages." <http://www.homelesspages.org.uk/index.asp> (accessed June 3, 2006).

Sorbonne Revolt

Magazine article

By: Margot Lyon

Date: May 10, 1968

Source: Lyon, Margot. "Sorbonne Revolt." *New Statesman*, May 10, 1968.

About the Author: Margot Lyon contributes this report from Paris to the *New Statesman*, a weekly magazine featuring commentary on politics and current affairs.

INTRODUCTION

The French student riots of May, 1968, began when the ongoing conflict at the University of Paris at Nanterre led the administration to shut down the university and threaten several students with expulsion. In a display of solidarity, students at the University of the Sorbonne in Paris gathered to protest the closure. The Sorbonne's administration reacted by calling the police in to arrest protestors leaving campus. The situation continued to escalate, with additional students joining the protest in defense of those targeted by the police. When the authorities implemented tear gas in an attempt to end the protest, even more students joined the demonstration. While the police eventually cleared the area, arresting many of the protestors in the process, the use of force ultimately backfired on the administration. The following Monday, the *Union Nationale des Etudiants de France*, France's largest student trade union, joined with the union of university teachers in a march to protest

Barricades block Gay Lussac Street in Paris after rioting and demonstrations by students demanding sweeping reforms at the Sorbonne University, May 11, 1968. © BETTMANN/CORBIS.

the police involvement. When they arrived at the Sorbonne where police maintained a line of defense, the protest developed into a large-scale riot. Over the days that followed, the government's forceful reaction to the situation continued to draw sympathy for the protestors, leading various unions to strike or to join in the demonstration and resulting in a month of protests and discord throughout Paris.

■ PRIMARY SOURCE

The pitched battles that raged in the Quartier Latin between ten thousand students and the Paris police this week have left the French gasping with amazement and dismay—and General de Gaulle, it is said, fuming at the outrage to France's image just at the moment when the world's pressmen are arriving for the Vietnam peace talks. After the weekend's disturbances, when almost six hundred students were arrested and the Sorbonne closed, the real violence began at the Place St. Germain and the Rue de Rennes last Monday. In no time at all the demonstration turned into a riot; students tore up chunks of macadam and broke paving stones for missiles, not only to throw at the gendarmes but to smash shop windows. Cars and buses were immobilized with tyres slashed, and normal traffic brought to a standstill. Before nightfall Education Minister Alain Peyrefitte appealed on TV for an end to violence, and promised to talk to student representatives if rioting stopped.

His offer came months if not years, too late. What students were telling him—conscious of the world's eye on them and relishing the publicity—was that their patience was exhausted. The numbers of demonstrators involved quashing the myth, cherished up to now by the administration, that the entire quarrel has been inflated by small groups of left-wing trouble-makers led by Maoist ringleader Daniel Cohn-Bendit, a German student from the Sorbonne's arts faculty. Significantly, this is located in the red Paris suburb of Nanette—a four-year old 'model' faculty of soulless ferro-concrete, already grown dingy, set down in a muddy wasteland where there is nowhere for students to go and nothing to see. But trouble in recent weeks at Nantes, Nice, Bordeaux, Besancon and Montpellier has by no means all been stage-managed by the Nanterre activists. It may not even have been touched off by a wish to outdo the spectacular outbreaks in Berlin and Rome, Madrid or even Columbia. The grievances are real, longstanding and bitterly resented.

First of them is the failure of French postwar administrations (even Gaullism, despite its pride in national culture and grandeur) to provide decent educational opportunities for les enfants de France. In 1945, just over 123,000 students, almost all of them middle-class in origin, attended universities. Now, in 1968, there are 514,000—crowded into laboratories, libraries and lecture halls that are totally inadequate and, even worse, run on outworn disciplinary principles, like an Oxbridge controlled by little Napoleons. Twenty-year-olds, who in the lecture-room are expected to be capable of sophisticated thinking, and who outside them quite naturally discuss anything from Vietnam to race or the gold questions, are subjected to regulations in the halls of residence as if they were still children—or conscripts. 'Our faculties are run like barracks or boarding schools' is the nation-wide grievance that has driven French students wild.

Inevitably, the trouble first broke out over sex—or, let's say, the limitation on visiting between men and women students. It hit the headlines in the autumn of 1965, when the men students of Antony (part of the extended cite universitaire on the southern outskirts of Paris) manhandled workmen building a portress's lodge for the girls' dormitory. The lodge was finally built, with hundreds of police to guard the bricklayers. But repeated appeals to allow men and women students adult freedom were met only last February, when Peyrefitte decreed that students over twenty-one could invite women to their rooms until eleven p.m.! But girls of any age, whether major or minor, were denied the same right because 'by the laws of nature' they stood more risk.

That, in part, is what led to this week's street fighting. But the right to freedom between the sexes is the symbol of all the rights the students claim: essentially, the right to have their adulthood recognized, even if their maturity is precocious by traditional standards; the right to escape from paternalism. They want to democratize education, although it is an entrenched preserve of deeply traditional France. Yet at the same time the students are also fighting to preserve the old ideal of a liberal education against the encroachments of our technocratic age. One of their main complaints is that French universities are being turned into forcing-houses for the mass-produced elite that the national economy needs. In resisting this type of change, they—like student rebels throughout Europe—are questioning the university's role in society and, through this, the nature of modern society itself. Paradoxically, they may thereby be contributing to the further break-up of the university ideal that they seek to defend.

■

SIGNIFICANCE

The student riots at the Sorbonne, and even the protest that began earlier at the University of Paris at Nanterre, were about far more than the students' rights to entertain members of the opposite sex in their dormitory rooms. While this restriction provided the catalyst for the demonstrations, and the timing of the protests was very much affected by the presence of representatives of the international press for the

Vietnam peace talks, the driving force behind the events was the students' need to govern themselves and to be accepted as viable members of adult society. Due to the baby boom following World War Two, the increase in the number of students seeking a university education had put a burden on educational resources and the quality of university services had declined as a result. The students demanded a voice in their educational system and in the rules that governed their housing, as well as those that governed their society. They also stood up for better academic conditions, holding the government to their earlier promise of sufficient educational opportunities for all Frenchmen willing to apply themselves, a promise the nation had fallen short of fulfilling in the more than two decades since the end of the war when it was proposed.

As a result, the students' determination spread to other demographic groups, encouraging workers to stand up for their rights as well and promoting strikes by a number of major unions, both in sympathy with the student protests and on their own behalf. The protests spread across the country, affecting the Sud-Aviation factory in Nantes, the Renault car factory at Cleon, and shutting down the Cannes Film Festival. Planes and trains went off schedule and the newspapers deliveries became irregular. What began as a simple protest against poor conditions and a lack of rights at a branch of the University of Paris ended up affecting the majority of the nation.

The revolt at the Sorbonne created new political situations, as well. During the latter stages of the protest, when workers joined the march and the unions were on strike, demands were not limited to the need for higher wages, but in some more radical instances called for an ousting of the existing government, including then-President Charles de Gaulle. While de Gaulle refused to step down and went so far as to assure himself of the support of the French military if the rioting continued, he ultimately dissolved the National Assembly and agreed to new elections the following month. He was forced to make these announcements over the radio, as the national

Katangais students in their premises at La Sorbonne University in Paris, France, during the 1968 student riots. ALAIN NOGUES/CORBIS SYGMA.

television service was part of the strike. Ultimately, he was reelected, but the term proved to be his last.

The protests themselves, with their demands for rights for students and workers, echoed the earlier revolutionary struggles in France, as well as in other countries around the globe. New political figures rose as a result of the protests, most notably Daniel Cohn-Bendit, then a twenty-three-year-old student at the University of Nanterre, who served as spokesman there during the early days of the protest and who was arrested prior to the closing of the school. Cohn-Bendit rose through the European political arena in the years following the revolts, and eventually became co-president of the European Green party in the European Parliament. During the protests, Cohn-Bendit stood for the voice of the students, demanding the right to certain freedoms and claiming that the Sorbonne and the university system in its entirety belonged to the people. The effect of the riots on the state of the nation and the near-collapse of the French government served as a warning to other countries that were experiencing student protests, proving that small radical student groups could not be ignored.

FURTHER RESOURCES
Books
Touraine, A. *The May Movement: Revolt and Reform: May 1968—the Student Rebellion and Workers' Strikes—the Birth of a Social Movement*. Random House, 1971.

Periodicals
Barry, Skip. "Be Realistic—Demand the Impossible (Analysis of the Revolt Led by Students and Workers in Paris, France in May, 1968)." *Dollars and Sense*. (July 28, 2005).

Web sites
University of California at Davis. "Shock Wave: Part Three—All Power to the Imagination—France 1968." May 6, 1998. <http://trc.ucdavis.edu/erickson/mru/france.htm> (accessed May 21, 2006).

Victoria University Library at the University of Toronto. "Icons of Revolution." May, 1998. <http://library.vicu.utoronto.ca/exhibitions/posters/> (accessed May 21, 2006).

No More Miss America!

Manifesto

By: Robin Morgan

Date: September 7, 1968

Source: Morgan, Robin. "No More Miss America!." *New York Radical Women*, 1968

About the Author: Born in 1941, Robin Morgan is a feminist speaker, writer, and activist. Her articles have appeared in the *Atlantic*, the *Hudson Review*, the *Los Angeles Times*, the *New Republic*, the *New York Times*, *Off Our Backs*, the *Village Voice*, and in *Ms* magazine, where she was a columnist or an editor from 1974 to 1993. Morgan is also the author or editor of over sixteen non-fiction books, novels, and volumes of poetry, including *Sisterhood is Powerful* (1970), *Going Too Far* (1977), *The Demon Lover* (1989), *The Word of a Woman* (1994), *Sisterhood is Global* (1996), and *The Burning Time* (2006).

INTRODUCTION
On September 7, 1968, the New York Radical Women (NYRW), a newly formed women's liberation group, staged a colorful protest on the boardwalk outside the Atlantic City, New Jersey, Convention Center, the site of the Miss America pageant. Robin Morgan, one of the founders of the NYRW and a protest organizer, wrote "No More Miss America!" in order to explain the group's objections to the popular beauty pageant. Several hundred women from other feminist groups and cities came to New Jersey to participate in the demonstration. Many carried signs and chanted, a live sheep was crowned Miss America, and objects symbolizing female oppression, including magazines, curlers, cosmetics, girdles, and bras, were tossed into a barrel designated the Freedom Trash Can. During the pageant itself, protestors in the audience opened a banner that proclaimed "Women's Liberation" and yelled "Freedom for Women."

The Miss America demonstration is often described as the beginning of the second wave of feminism in the United States. It was certainly the first time that the mainstream media—the television news, magazines, and newspapers—covered radical feminist protest. The widespread stories on this women's protest provoked storms of controversy, introduced feminism to millions, and signaled an era of profound social change for women.

PRIMARY SOURCE

On September 7th in Atlantic City, the Annual Miss America Pageant will again crown "your ideal." But this year, reality will liberate the contest auction-block in the guise of "genyooine" de-plasticized, breathing women. Women's Liberation Groups, black women, high-school and college women, women's peace groups, women's welfare and social-work groups, women's job-equality

Members of the National Women's Liberation Party picket in front of Convention Hall in New Jersey, September 7, 1968. The Miss America Pageant would be held there later that day. AP IMAGES.

groups, pro-birth control and pro-abortion groups—women of every political persuasion—all are invited to join us in a day-long boardwalk-theater event, starting at 1:00 P.M. on the Boardwalk in front of Atlantic City's Convention Hall. We will protest the image of Miss America, an image that oppresses women in every area in which it purports to represent us.

There will be: Picket Lines; Guerrilla Theater; Leafleting; Lobbying Visits to the contestants urging our sisters to reject the Pageant Farce and join us; a huge Freedom Trash Can (into which we will throw bras, girdles, curlers, false eyelashes, wigs, and representative issues of *Cosmopolitan, Ladies' Home Journal, Family Circle*, etc.—bring any such woman-garbage you have around the house); we will also announce a Boycott of all those commercial products related to the Pageant, and the day will end with a Women's Liberation rally at midnight when

Miss America is crowned on live television. Lots of other surprises are being planned (come and add your own!) but we do not plan heavy disruptive tactics and so do not expect a bad police scene. It should be a groovy day on the Boardwalk in the sun with our sisters. In case of arrests, however, we plan to reject all male authority and demand to be busted by policewomen only. (In Atlantic City, women cops are not permitted to make arrests—dig that!).

Male chauvinist-reactionaries on this issue had best stay away, nor are male liberals welcome in the demonstrations. But sympathetic men can donate money as well as cars and drivers.

Male reporters will be refused interviews. We reject patronizing reportage. *Only newswomen will be recognized.*

The Ten Points We Protest:

1. *The Degrading Mindless-Boob-Girlie Symbol.* The Pageant contestants epitomize the roles we are all forced to play as women. The parade down the runway blares the metaphor of the 4-H Club county fair, where the nervous animals are judged for teeth, fleece, etc., and where the best "Specimen" gets the blue ribbon. So are women in our society forced daily to compete for male approval, enslaved by ludicrous "beauty" standards we ourselves are conditioned to take seriously.

2. *Racism with Roses.* Since its inception in 1921, the Pageant has not had one Black finalist, and this has not been for a lack of test-case contestants. There has never been a Puerto Rican, Alaskan, Hawaiian, or Mexican-American winner. Nor has there ever been a *true* Miss America—an American Indian.

3. *Miss America as Military Death Mascot.* The highlight of her reign each year is a cheerleader-tour of American troops abroad—last year she went to Vietnam to pep-talk our husbands, fathers, sons and boyfriends into dying and killing with a better spirit. She personifies the "unstained patriotic American womanhood our boys are fighting for." The Living Bra and the Dead Soldier. We refuse to be used as Mascots for Murder.

4. *The Consumer Con-Game.* Miss America is a walking commercial for the Pageant's sponsors. Wind her up and she plugs your product on promotion tours and TV—all in an "honest, objective" endorsement. What a shill.

5. *Competition Rigged and Unrigged.* We deplore the encouragement of an American myth that oppresses men as well as women: the win-or-you're-worthless competitive disease. The "beauty contest" creates only one winner to be "used" and forty-nine losers who are "useless."

6. *The Woman as Pop Culture Obsolescent Theme.* Spindle, mutilate, and then discard tomorrow. What is so ignored as last year's Miss America? This only reflects the gospel of our Society, according to Saint Male: women must be young, juicy, malleable—hence age discrimination and the cult of youth. And we women are brainwashed into believing this ourselves!

7. *The Unbeatable Madonna-Whore Combination.* Miss America and Playboy's centerfold are sisters over the skin. To win approval, we must be both sexy and wholesome, delicate but able to cope, demure yet titillatingly [expletive deleted]. Deviation of any sort brings, we are told, disaster: "You won't get a man!!" .

8. *The Irrelevant Crown on the Throne of Mediocrity.* Miss America represents what women are supposed to be: inoffensive, bland, apolitical. If you are tall, short, over or under what weight The Man prescribes you should be, forget it. Personality, articulateness, intelligence, and commitment—unwise. Conformity is the key to the crown—and, by extension, to success in our Society.

9. *Miss America as Dream Equivalent To-?* In this reputedly democratic society, where every little boy supposedly can grow up to be President, what can every little girl hope to grow to be? Miss America. That's where it's at. Real power to control our own lives is restricted to men, while women get patronizing pseudo-power, an ermine clock and a bunch of flowers; men are judged by their actions, women by appearance.

10. *Miss America as Big Sister Watching You.* The pageant exercises Thought Control, attempts to sear the Image onto our minds, to further make women oppressed and men oppressors; to enslave us all the more in high-heeled, low-status roles; to inculcate false values in young girls; women as beasts of buying; to seduce us to our selves before our own oppression.

NO MORE MISS AMERICA.

SIGNIFICANCE

The Miss America protest and Robin Morgan's manifesto put forward many of the issues that were, and continue to be, critically important to feminists. First and foremost, both focused national attention on the objectification of women and their status and roles in American society. Many of the protestors, including Robin Morgan, were also involved with the New Left and other liberal concerns of the day, and a critique of the pageant's relationship to race, capitalism, and the war in Vietnam, is prominent in Morgan's work.

The Miss America demonstration was not without its shortcomings, however. Despite the fact that nothing in the Freedom Trash Can was ever burned—the protestors did not have a burn permit—one journalist mentioned bra burning as the equivalent of draft card burning, a current form of anti-war protest. The media soon fastened on *New York Post* reporter Lindsy Van Gelder's phrase, and over the next few months the image of feminists as out of control, neurotic, defiant bra burners emerged. The idea that radical feminists were unattractive, bitter, or jealous of other women, and that the protestors were criticizing the Miss America contestants, rather than the pageant and the society that promoted it, came to haunt feminists. Despite the fact that thousands embraced feminism after the publicity engendered by the Miss America protest, the new stereotype of women's libbers kept many others away from the movement.

The pageant and its feminist critique have recently been used to analyze the gains and failures of feminism itself. Throughout the 1970s and 1980s, the Miss

America pageant became progressively more liberal, emphasizing scholarship, achievement, and public service over female beauty, largely as a response to feminist led changes in society. In recent years, some contestants maintain that their involvement in the now less popular pageant is a personal, feminist-empowered choice. Critics argue that the continued existence of Miss America and the enduring relevance of Morgan's manifesto highlight the limits of liberal feminism, the problems inherent in the third wave or more recent manifestations of feminism, and the unfinished business of radical feminists.

FURTHER RESOURCES
Books

Morgan, Robin. *Going Too Far: The Personal Chronicle of a Feminist*. New York: Vintage Books, 1978.

Rosen, Ruth. *The World Split Open: How the Modern Women's Movement Changed America*. New York: Viking Penguin, 2000.

Periodicals

Dow, Bonnie J. "Feminism, Miss America, and Media Mythology." *Rhetoric & Public Affairs*. 6 (1) (2003): 127–149.

Lieb, Thom. "The Emergence of a Myth: When Journalists, and Activists, Got Burned." *Clio Among the Media*. Winter (2005):3–4.

Tonn, Mari Boor. "Miss America Contesters and Contestants: Discourse about Social 'Also-Rans.'" *Rhetoric & Public Affairs*. 6 (1) (2003):150–160.

Harvard and Beyond: The University Under Siege

Magazine article excerpt

By: Anonymous

Date: April 18, 1969

Source: "Harvard and Beyond: The University Under Siege." *Time*. April 18, 1969.

About the Author: *Time* magazine is a weekly publication featuring news analysis and commentary.

INTRODUCTION

The late 1960s and early 1970s was a period of political unrest in the United States. The nation's participation in the Vietnam War was a major motivating factor and led to an increase in public demonstrations and protests, a phenomenon that extended to the student populations of many American universities. The protest movement focused on a desire to promote peace in direct opposition to wartime activities and also actively rejected the government policy of conscription, or the draft. When it became clear that broad movements against the war were unlikely to cause major changes, protestors also targeted smaller issues that were more directly linked to their personal lives yet still political in nature. University protests originated at the University of California at Berkeley in 1964, a campus known for liberal political beliefs and a tendency toward activism. However, by 1969, Harvard University joined the ranks of American universities whose students were staging protests, proving that even the more conservative, traditionally structured institutions were not immune to the growing unrest on campuses across the country. The events at Harvard also illustrated how standard administrative practices for dealing with minor uprisings were no longer practical or effective, as the students refused to be intimidated by authority figures and went on to find other methods of making their displeasure with the situation clear.

■ PRIMARY SOURCE

IT finally happened to Harvard, too. In a sequence of confrontations that has now become a deplorable custom on American campuses, a small band of student rebels seized an administration building to protest university policies and to deliberately provoke a crisis. Police were then summoned to oust the intruders; moderate students, angered at both the fact of the "bust" and what they felt was police brutality, were radicalized into organizing a strike. The three-day boycott of classes was the first in the modern history of a venerable institution that prides itself on its devotion to learning and the rational resolution of differences. It was a shock—to faculty, students and administration alike—that for a time the "Harvard way" had failed. No matter how soon the present crisis is resolved, the great temple of learning on the Charles will never be quite the same.

The conflict began at noon on Wednesday. About 250 students from Harvard and Radcliffe, most of them members of Students for a Democratic Society and the pro-Mao Progressive Labor Party, appeared outside University Hall, the three-story administration building at the center of Harvard Yard. They reiterated six "unnegotiable" demands made on the Harvard Corporation. *The issues: the abolition of ROTC and an end to what the radicals consider Harvard's "expansionist" approach to its urban surroundings.

Chanting "Fight! Fight!," the students marched into the hall, which contains the offices of the Harvard deans, though not the university president's. When one of the five deans asked the students to leave, he was jeered and shouted down. The rebels then forcibly evicted the deans and their assistants. They locked themselves inside the building, securing the doors with red bicycle chains, and proceeded to hold meetings to discuss further strategy. "The Corporation," their proclamation grandly noted, "can issue a statement when it gives in."

Initially there was widespread disapproval of their tactics: seizing a building is simply not the Harvard way. Two students in the crowd outside University Hall even burned S.D.S. in effigy, and there were cheers when Franklin L. Ford, Harvard's ranking academic dean, announced through a bullhorn that the gates of Harvard Yard would be shut at 4:30 P.M., thus locking up the lock-in. Ford also warned the radicals to vacate the premises within fifteen minutes or face charges of criminal trespass. The radicals sat tight.

The radicals were also unmoved by a scathing answer to their demands from President Nathan M. Pusey. They had charged that the university planned to tear down Negro slums in Roxbury to make room for the expanding Harvard Medical School, and that members of the Corporation had illegitimate vested interests in preserving ROTC on campus: "These businessmen want Harvard to continue producing officers for the Viet Nam war or for use against black rebellions at home for political reasons." Pusey flatly denied that the university planned to destroy the housing. He also noted that Harvard had recently taken account of student objections by stripping ROTC of course credit, but was prevented from abolishing it entirely by "contractual obligations" to the Government. He began his statement by challenging the rebels' sincerity: "Can anyone believe the Harvard S.D.S. demands are made seriously?" He ended it on the same note: "How can one respond to allegations which have no basis in fact?"

Within thirty minutes after the seizure, Pusey began a six-hour round of conferences with his deans, his administrative board and the masters of the nine Harvard houses at the presidential residence, 17 Quincy Street. "It was all very informal," said one participant in the talks. "Very simply, he sought advice, and we gave it."

Pusey eventually decided to use force. A major factor in his decision was the legitimate fear that the radicals might rifle the university's confidential files. Friday morning, in fact, the Boston underground newspaper Old Mole printed seven Harvard documents that had obviously been discovered by the invaders.

Shortly before dawn on Thursday, four hundred policemen entered the Yard. About half were state troopers; the rest were drawn from the constabularies of Cambridge,

Boston and other parts of the metropolitan area. Facing them on the south steps of University Hall were about 120 students, with wet pieces of torn bed sheets ready to put across their faces in case tear gas was used. Dean Fred L. Glimp of Harvard College gave the radicals one last chance. "You have five minutes to vacate the building," he announced over the bullhorn, but his words were drowned out by students chanting in unison "Pusey must go; ROTC must go!"

The troopers charged. In less than a minute, the students were pushed and shoved, punched and clubbed, and driven from the steps. Then, after unlimbering sledgehammers, chain cutters and a four-ft.-long iron battering ram, the troopers forced their way into the building. Screams of anger and pain were heard inside. The troopers began removing the protesters, dragging some away by their long hair and butting others with billy clubs. By 5:30 A.M., a mere twenty-five minutes after they made the initial charge, the police had cleared the building. In all, 184 persons were arrested on charges of criminal trespass; forty-five were injured seriously enough to be treated at hospitals. Four more were hospitalized: a Harvard student, a policeman and two women outsiders, one with a broken back and the other with a broken ankle.

The radicals' seizure of University Hall and their implacable demands were deliberate attempts to disrupt the good order of the university; the tactics succeeded beyond the fondest dreams of their perpetrators. Even moderate students who agreed with Pusey about the demands of the radicals were shocked that he had called in the police at all. At midday Thursday, 1,500 students assembled in Memorial Church for a heated four-hour discussion. Calling for Pusey's resignation if he refused to accept their demands, the moderates passed a resolution that students, faculty and administrators besides the president be given voting seats on the Harvard Corporation and that all those arrested be granted amnesty by the administration and the courts. They backed up their demands by calling for a three-day strike. Class attendance next day was down seventy-five percent.

Privately, a number of professors and administrators have worried for months about the possibility of "another Columbia." Like the troubled campus on Morningside Heights, Harvard, to many of its students, is a large impersonal school with a faceless administration and a brilliant faculty who are as much concerned with the demands of research as with the art of teaching. Despite its past reputation as a prim, proper school for the elite, Harvard today is undeniably hip (TIME, March 14). It has as many beards as Berkeley, as much grass as Columbia—and one of the nation's most active S.D.S. chapters.

At the same time, though, the majority of students and faculty never seriously expected that the campus really would explode in the way it did. The rights of dissent and discussion are sacred at Harvard, and in the past six months, the faculty has been alert to accommodate student requests that it recognized as legitimate. In addition to abolishing course credit for ROTC, the university readily agreed to establish a program of Afro-American studies when Negro students insisted on it. It is, moreover, in keeping with the Harvard way that basic decisions are not, as at less democratic universities, made only by a small inner circle of deans. Proposals for major changes are discussed widely among faculty members—and students too—before they are acted on. There may be tension at Harvard, but there is communication as well.

The S.D.S. radicals and their allies had clearly violated Harvard's tradition of open communication and rational discourse. Yet there was some feeling on campus that Nathan Pusey himself, in a much lesser way, might have violated the tradition by summoning the police without gaining a consensus of his community. A distant and pompous-seeming figure to undergraduates ever since he became president in 1953, Pusey rules his campus more like a guiding presence than an order-giving commander, and he has admitted to being perplexed by youthful demands for instant action. At the same time, he says that he admires the idealism of this generation of students. As he told TIME Correspondent Barry Hillenbrand recently: "Insofar as they are expressing a deep displeasure with the quality of life and want to see it changed, I am wholly sympathetic, and it is my hope that the students will continue to work for these ends."

Pusey said in a news conference that he called for the police because continued occupation of the administration building would have made it "virtually impossible" for the faculty to conduct its business and would have brought the university to an indefinite standstill. In defending the autonomy of Harvard against McCarthyism in the 1950s, and in countless speeches since then, Nathan Pusey has amply proved his deep commitment to intellectual freedom.

That he should see no alternative to the use of force in defending that freedom is symbolic of the dilemma facing the American university today.

In one sense, the Harvard drama is still an isolated phenomenon. More than 6,700,000 students attend the nation's 2,500 colleges and universities. Fewer than two percent of those millions are destructive radicals, and only a handful of campuses have erupted so far. Still, that two percent amounts to perhaps 100,000 activists, quite enough for a sizable guerrilla war. Over the past year, in fact, disorders have leaped like firebrands from campus to campus—Berkeley, Brandeis, Chicago, Columbia, and Howard, to name a few. At Duke and Wisconsin, the turmoil required the National Guard. Black militants and

striking teachers closed San Francisco State College for five months, a shutdown punctuated by police raids, arson attempts, and bomb explosions.

If perspective helps, student violence has been a recurrent problem throughout history. The college years are those of peak physical energy, a search for identity, freedom and power—all reasons to lash out at frustrating restrictions. Medieval students often scorned learning in favor of brawling and thieving; early American collegians were equally unruly. In 1825, the University of Virginia faculty requested police protection against "personal danger" from belligerent students. Professors at other Nineteenth century U.S. campuses were shouted down, pelted with refuse. Not only have students frequently rioted against one another; they have also started quite a few revolutions.

A recent poll conducted for FORTUNE showed that about forty percent of students enter college with the hope of bringing about change in the world. And that may be the crux of the problem. In hitting out at the university, the student rebels hit out at a society that they do not respect. Why don't they? Perhaps because the society does not sufficiently respect itself. It is a commonplace that today's young are raised permissively. More important, they are raised in an atmosphere in which conviction is too often asserted either apologetically or with an excessive, bullying vehemence that only masks a lack of true certainty. Increasingly, American society has failed to persuade its young that experience (hence age) counts for something, and that reasonable patience in the attainment of goals is necessary. The cry is for instant gratification, instant realization of ideals. Rosemary Park, former president of Barnard College, urges adults to "examine their judgments. We will find then that their concern with public issues off the campus is a search for absolutes, an absolute wrong to be righted, civil rights; the exploitation of an innocent society to be protected, Viet Nam."

When extremists halt classes, they kill the spirit of a university in somewhat the same way that the Nazis did in the 1930s. Seizing buildings is only slightly less dangerous. A recent Harris poll showed that eighty-nine percent of Americans wanted police to quell campus rebels, whatever the radicalizing effect on moderate students. Voters are pushing state legislators for repressive laws. California has more than one hundred such bills before its senate and assembly: One provides five-year sentences for class disrupters; another would empower a new state agency to seize a troubled campus and fire every official, from the president down.

Do extremists want that? Some do. In their view, it would ripen the U.S. for revolution. And yet the university is one of the best possible bases from which sane radicals can expect to mount sizable political support in the U.S. Only the campus is ideally equipped to analyze or attack poverty and pollution, to appeal to the ghetto as well as suburbia. How it should so use those skills is an open question, but if radicals seriously hope to change society, destroying universities is sheer lunacy. The trouble is, of course, that their goal is less reform than romance—coming alive in action. At the Sorbonne last year, one rebel happily chalked on a wall: "The more I make revolution, the more I make love, the more I make love, the more I make revolution."

The Role of the University Whatever the structural or procedural reforms, one central question remains: To what extent should universities become active participants in changing society? Even in merely training people, they change society. But activists want more. Charles Palmer, student-body president at Berkeley, argues that "the university must respond to minority needs instead of just the agricultural and business needs if it is going to be moral." Says David Kemnitzer, a twenty-two-year-old anthropology student at Berkeley: "The university should be examining this society and constructing alternative societies. It should be enshrining Black Panther Spokesman Eldridge Cleaver and [Herbert] Marcuse. It should provide an environment where people can become loving, intelligent and sentient beings. It should be finding ways to run companies so employees don't have to have the—exploited out of them. Universities should free people from labor."

Berkeley's Chancellor Roger Heyns disagrees: "We should play an advisory and consultative role, but the university should never be a political action unit. I don't think we should run things." Says Ray Heffner, president of Brown University: "The university must not be aloof from the most pressing problems of our time. And yet the university cannot be so committed to transforming society along definite lines that it loses its function as objective analyst and critic of society."

This disagreement between activist students and the men who run the universities will continue to provide occasions for demonstrations and disorders. Even so, the university must remain what Rosemary Park calls "the place where discussion between generations is possible." Above all, it must have the courage to remain independent, refusing to seek approval for approval's sake, whether from students, politicians or the public at large.

Such courage ought to be the ultimate product of last week's ugly confrontation at Harvard. The lesson is that force, at best, offers only temporary solutions. What the American university needs above all is a new integrity— moral authority, the unsolicited respect of the young and the old alike. Only thus can the university be immune to extremism and able to follow its calling of truth and reason— the role that Sir Eric Ashby of Cambridge University

defined as providing an "environment for the continuous polishing of one mind by another."

SIGNIFICANCE

The 1969 student protests at Harvard University took many people by surprise as it was assumed that the University's reputation for rational debate and traditional beliefs would outweigh the unrest that was growing among student populations nationwide. Instead, a small group of Harvard students took a stand against University policies they deemed to be supportive of the war in Vietnam. Acknowledging that there was little they could do to affect the president or federal decisions directly, the students turned their attentions to their immediate surroundings and policies they might be able to control.

The University's continued contracts with the Reserve Officers' Training Corps (ROTC) was just one example of Harvard's failure to distance itself from the conflict in Vietnam. Rather than protest national foreign policy on a broad scale, the students made demands of the University governors. They staged a lock-in, taking over the administrative offices, and informed the University that they were not open to negotiations. When the situation escalated and the students were forcibly removed, they went on to boycott classes for several days. Ultimately, the University's decision to use force against the protestors resulted in even more students participating in the strike, because its administration underestimated their students' dedication to their stand.

Political activism did not spring up overnight on the campus of Harvard University. Two years earlier, Harvard students protested against U.S. conscription policy when seventy-one students promised to refuse the draft. When Defense Secretary Robert S. McNamara was a guest speaker at the University, a student attempted to engage him in a debate regarding the war. When McNamara refused to discuss the issue, a group of eight hundred students proceeded to surround his car and McNamara was forced to use the University's underground tunnel system to leave. In the fall of that year, a recruiter from Dow Chemical Company was restrained for several hours by three hundred students who protested the fact that the company manufactured the napalm that was being used in Vietnam. In 1968, one hundred students held a sit-in when they were refused admittance to a faculty meeting where the status of the University ROTC program was scheduled to be discussed. These protests resulted in a number of students being placed on probation, as well as receiving official warnings.

A Harvard University student (l) takes vote of fellow students on whether to continue strike against the school during a gathering of 6,000 students at Harvard Stadium, April 14, 1969. The students voted to continue their strike for another three days. © BETTMANN/CORBIS.

The lesser protests also served as a precursor to the more radical protest held in April 1969. Until that point, the Harvard protests were scattered, with only a small percentage of the student population participating. Often, the Students for a Democratic Society (SDS) instigated the demonstrations, with few non-member students joining them. Despite this, the students who failed to protest still observed the results of these demonstrations, particularly regarding the University's consistent refusal to bend to student demands. When the University reacted to the 1969 protest by using outside force, the general population united in reaction to what they deemed an inappropriately violent means of ending the lock-in.

Student protests in the United States a peaked year later, when National Guard troops attempted to disperse a four-day protest on May 4, 1970 at Kent State University in Kent, Ohio, and fired into the crowd, killing four students and injuring nine. The killings at Kent State resulted in massive protests at universities across the United States and temporary closings of many universities and high schools.

FURTHER RESOURCES
Books

Farrell, James. *The Spirit of the Sixties: The Making of Postwar Radicalism*. Routledge, 1997.

Rosenblatt, Roger. *Coming Apart: A Memoir of the Harvard Wars of 1969*. Little Brown and Company, 1997.

Web sites

The Harvard Crimson. "Reflecting On the 1969 Student Strike." April 9, 1984. <http://www.thecrimson.com/article.aspx?ref=269548> (accessed May 21, 2006).

New York Penal Laws 125.00–125.6

New York State Abortion Laws, 1970

Legislation

By: New York state legislature

Date: July 1, 1970

Source: New York Penal Code

About the Author: In New York state, the power to both introduce and to pass legislation is centered in the state legislature. The legislature has a bicameral structure, as it is composed of a senate and an assembly, each of which is elected. All proposed New York state legislation must pass both branches of the legislature before becoming law. The governor of the state has certain powers of veto available with respect to laws passed by the legislature.

INTRODUCTION

Prior to 1970, there were no American states that permitted pregnant women to freely obtain a legal abortion. Abortion procedures were only available in the limited circumstances of a demonstrated threat to a woman's health should the pregnancy extend to its full term, or where the pregnancy arose due to an act of rape or incest. Illegal abortions were performed with considerable regularity; it was estimated in 1970 that there were between 200,000 and 1.2 million illegal abortions performed annually in the United States.

A number of different groups coalesced around the movement to liberalize American abortion laws in the 1960s, and organizations that were just as fervent in their opposition to legalized abortion were also founded at this time. The most prominent of the pro-abortion groups, the National Association for the Repeal of Abortion Laws (NARAL), was founded in New York in 1969.

A number of distinct issues were advanced by the pro-abortion forces in support of their demand for legislative change. As the public debate intensified, the most important of these issues to be articulated was the ability of women to have access to a safe abortion, performed by a licensed and properly trained doctor, coupled with the claim that a woman had the ultimate right to decide whether a pregnancy proceeded.

In 1967, the state of Colorado enacted a law that provided limited rights to abortion, the same year Great Britain passed the world's first abortion law that legalized the ability of a woman to elect to have an abortion without requiring judicial consent, a concept that became known as "abortion on demand."

The proposed abortion amendments to the New York State Penal Code were the subject of an intense public dialogue both in New York and throughout the United States. The abortion law was ultimately passed in the New York legislature by a single vote on April 9, 1970. The states of Alaska, Hawaii, and Washington each passed similar statues later that year. Within the first year of the passage of the New York abortion legislation, seventeen American states had either permitted abortion on demand, or had otherwise liberalized the ability of women to secure the services of a physician to perform an abortion.

The first crucial feature of the New York state abortion law was the legalization of elective abortions within the first twenty-four weeks of the pregnancy. Abortions performed after the second trimester, or twenty-four weeks, were criminalized as an act of homicide in the abortion law on the part of both the woman undergoing the procedure and the physician performing the abortion. Any abortion performed in any fashion other than that expressly sanctioned in the legislation would render the participants liable to prosecution, including women who attempted to abort a pregnancy themselves. Such abortions were classed as felony offences in the statute.

The second important aspect of the New York law was the absence of a residency requirement. Any woman who was able to travel to New York state could, in theory, secure the services of a physician to perform an abortion so long as her request otherwise complied with the statutory provisions.

PRIMARY SOURCE

NEW YORK LEGISLATURE LEGALIZES ABORTION ON DEMAND
§ 125.00 Homicide defined

Homicide means conduct which causes the death of a person or an unborn child with which a female has been pregnant for more than twenty-four weeks under circumstances constituting murder, manslaughter in the first degree, manslaughter in the second degree, criminally negligent homicide, abortion in the first degree or self-abortion in the first degree.

§ 125.05 Homicide, abortion and related offenses; definitions of terms

The following definitions are applicable to this article:

1. "Person," when referring to the victim of a homicide, means a human being who has been born and is alive.
2. "Abortional act" means an act committed upon or with respect to a female, whether by another person or by the female herself, whether she is pregnant or not, whether directly upon her body or by the administering, taking or prescription of drugs or in any other manner, with intent to cause a miscarriage of such female.
3. "Justifiable abortional act." An abortional act is justifiable when committed upon a female with her consent by a duly licensed physician acting (a) under a reasonable belief that such is necessary to preserve her life, or, (b) within twenty-four weeks from the commencement of her pregnancy. A pregnant female's commission of an abortional act upon herself is justifiable when she acts upon the advice of a duly licensed physician (1) that such act is necessary to preserve her life, or, (2) within twenty-four weeks from the commencement of her pregnancy. The submission by a female to an abortional act is justifiable when she believes that it is being committed by a duly licensed physician, acting under a reasonable belief that such act is necessary to preserve her life, or, within twenty-four weeks from the commencement of her pregnancy.

Sec. 125.40 Abortion in the second degree.

A person is guilty of abortion in the second degree when he commits an abortional act upon a female, unless such abortional act is justifiable pursuant to subdivision three of section 125.05.

Abortion in the second degree is a class E felony.

Sec. 125.45 Abortion in the first degree.

A person is guilty of abortion in the first degree when he commits upon a female pregnant for more than twenty-four weeks an abortional act which causes the miscarriage of such female, unless such abortional act is justifiable pursuant to subdivision three of section 125.05.

Abortion in the first degree is a class D felony.

§ 125.50 Self-abortion in the second degree.

A female is guilty of self-abortion in the second degree when, being pregnant, she commits or submits to an abortional act upon herself, unless such abortional act is justifiable pursuant to subdivision three of section 125.05.

Self-abortion in the second degree is a class B misdemeanor.

§ 125.55 Self-abortion in the first degree.

A female is guilty of self-abortion in the first degree when, being pregnant for more than twenty-four weeks, she commits or submits to an abortional act upon herself which causes her miscarriage, unless such abortional act is justifiable pursuant to subdivision three of section 125.05.

Self-abortion in the first degree is a class A misdemeanor.

Sec. 125.60 Issuing abortional articles.

A person is guilty of issuing abortional articles when he manufactures, sells or delivers any instrument, article, medicine, drug or substance with intent that the same be used in unlawfully procuring the miscarriage of a female.

Issuing abortional articles is a class B misdemeanor.

SIGNIFICANCE

The passage of New York state abortion law in 1970 was the first of several battles waged by the pro-abortion forces in the United States, culminating in the decision of the United States Supreme Court in *Roe v. Wade* in January 1973. The legal and public relations contests between pro and anti-abortion forces during this period reflected the most momentous social policy confrontation since those concerning desegregation in the late 1940s and early 1950s.

The New York state abortion laws were significant not because they represented a conclusion to the abortion issue, but for the fact that the New York legislation was a point of commencement to a fresh round of a national debate whose origins could be traced to the early 1800s. Under the British common law, doctrines that governed the availability of abortion in early years of the United States, abortions were legal so long as they were performed prior to the first discernible movement of the fetus. It was only in the 1850s that American states began to enact statutes to prohibit the performing of abortions.

The legalization of abortion in New York and elsewhere after 1970 had the secondary effect of contributing to the reduction in the death toll attributable to illegal abortions. As recently as the mid 1960s, illegal abortions caused or contributed to approximately seventeen percent of all deaths that resulted from pregnancy or childbirth.

The New York legislation permitted any woman to come to New York and obtain an abortion, and in the first two years of the statute, it is estimated that over sixty percent of those women undergoing an abortion were not residents of New York. Over three hundred and fifty thousand abortions were performed in New York between the passage of the abortion statute and the Supreme Court decision in *Roe v. Wade*.

The American abortion debate has continued long afer *Roe v. Wade*. The subsequent action of the New York legislature with respect to the 1970 abortion law is one example of the continuing struggle on both sides of the abortion debate. The statute passed the New York state legislature by a single vote, and the same legislature voted to repeal the 1970 law in 1972. The repeal legislation was vetoed by Governor Nelson Rockefeller. The subsequent ruling of the Supreme Court in *Roe* confirmed the constitutionality of the New York abortion law.

In the years since the abortion law was passed in 1970, the national debate regarding abortion has shifted its focus. In 1992, the Supreme Court retrenched certain aspects of the concept of abortion on demand in its decision in *Planned Parenthood v. Casey*. The Court ruled that individual states were permitted (but not obligated) to regulate how abortions were performed. States were permitted to prohibit women from proceeding with an abortion if the pregnancy would then result in a viable birth. The Court also rules that states could require parental consent for minors seeking an abortion, a waiting period after the decision to proceed was made by the woman, and the state could mandate counseling as to other options that abortion.

Since the Casey decision, the anti-abortion forces in America, a variety of groups generally described as pro-life, have lobbied the federal government to enact legislation that would have the effect of repealing *Roe v. Wade*. Conversely, the New York abortion legislation has become further entrenched in the political and legal culture in the state. In 2000, New York had the highest abortion rate of any state in the United States. in that year, thirty-nine women in every one thousand in the state ended a pregnancy through abortion. New

York state also provides public funds, through its Medicaid program, to provide for abortions for women who lack the means to pay for the procedure.

A feature of the New York abortion legislation that has manifested itself in other aspects of the national abortion debate is the issue of when human life is said to begin. The legislation does not define life, except through the indirect means of imposing a criminal sanction upon those involved in an abortion in the post-twenty-four week period. The traditional definition of homicide is the killing of a human being. By inference, the New York state law establishes a fetus twenty-four weeks or older as human life. Conversely, the New York statute may be interpreted to mean that human life does not begin to exist until after the fetus has gestated for twenty-four weeks. Disputes concerning such interpretations are at the crux of modern anti-abortion sentiments that hold that life begins with conception.

FURTHER RESOURCES
Books
Risen, James and Judy L. Thomas. *Wrath of Angels: The American Abortion War.* New York: Basic Books, 1998.

Solinger, Rickie, ed. *Abortion Wars: A Half Century of Struggle 1950–2000.* Berkley: University of California Press, 2000.

Web sites
New York Magazine. "The Abortion Capital of America." December 12, 2005. <http://www.newyorkmetro.com/nymetro/features/15248/index.html> (accessed May 20, 2006).

Coat Hangers Used in Abortion Protest

Newspaper article

By: Anonymous

Date: September 8, 1977

Source: "Coat Hangers Used in Abortion Protest." *New York Times* (September 8, 1977).

About the Author: The New York Times Company produces the national newspapers the *New York Times*, the *Boston Globe*, the *International Herald Tribune*, and other local newspapers. Writers, photographers, and cartoonists published in the *New York Times*, founded

in 1851 as the *New-York Daily Times*, have earned a combined total of 116 Pulitzer Prizes.

INTRODUCTION
The 1973 U.S. Supreme Court decision *Roe v. Wade* found state laws banning and restricting abortion unconstitutional. In 1973, the first year that abortion was legal, the Centers for Disease Control reported 615,000 legal abortions; in 1990, the number peaked at 1.4 million, and fell by 2002 to approximately 854,000. Women seeking illegal abortions in states that outlawed the procedure before the *Roe v. Wade* decision faced difficulty finding qualified providers, experienced increased infection rates, avoided seeking medical attention for complications from fear of criminal charges, and an estimated 800–1,000 women died each year from complications resulting from illegal abortions.

After *Roe v. Wade*, state and federal funding for abortions became a critical question in the abortion rights debate. Legalization of abortion helped to lower the price of abortions; black market rates ran as high as $1,000 before legalization. While prices dropped and safety increased, lower income women still were unable to afford abortions, and activists looked to federal and state programs for abortion funds. From 1973 to 1976, Medicaid covered abortions.

In 1976, Congress passed the Hyde Amendment, named for Representative Henry Hyde, a Republican from Illinois. The Hyde Amendment prohibits the use of federal funds for abortions, except in cases of rape, incest, or danger to the life of the mother. Approximately 11.5 percent of all women of reproductive age in the United States are covered by Medicaid; for those women, federal funding is prohibited by law for abortion on demand.

In this article from the *New York Times*, written the year after the Hyde Amendment's passage, abortion rights activists used coat hangers, a symbol of one method women used to perform abortions on themselves before abortion was legal, to drive home their point that using federal funds for abortion would help lower-income women to access safer abortions.

PRIMARY SOURCE

Advocates of Federal funding of abortions delivered about 200 metal coat hangers to a key congressman today as a reminder of the way some abortions used to be performed.

Karen Mulhauser, executive director of the National Abortion Rights Action League, and about a dozen other league members, delivered the hangers in person to

Pro-choice demonstrators rally in Washington D.C. PHOTO BY ROBERT SHERBOW//TIME LIFE PICTURES/GETTY IMAGES.

Representative Daniel J. Flood, Democrat of Pennsylvania, chairman of a Labor and Health, Education and Welfare subcommittee that has jurisdiction over Medicaid funding.

The women conceded that their tactic was emotional but said that some women could resort to the hanger method of ending an unwanted pregnancy if Congress deprived them of the right to a Medicaid-funded abortion.

They said they wanted Mr. Flood to alter his position and help broaden the conditions under which the Government would pay for abortions for poor women.

Mr. Flood heads the House conferees who, with counterparts from the Senate, must recommend a set of conditions to Congress for inclusion in a H.E.W.-Labor funding bill for the fiscal year 1978.

The House has agreed to a position proposed by Mr. Flood that Federal funds should be denied for any abortion unless the life of the woman is jeopardized by a full-term pregnancy. The Senate is maintaining that abortion funding should be restricted to cases of rape, incest or "where medically necessary."

SIGNIFICANCE

After the 1976 Hyde Amendment was enacted, Congress continued to pass restrictions on federal funding for abortion. Hawaii, Maryland, Washington, and New York provided state funds for abortion voluntarily, while thirteen states, including Alaska, Arizona, California, Connecticut, Illinois, Massachusetts, Minnesota, Montana, New Jersey, New Mexico, Oregon, Vermont, and West Virginia all experienced court cases in which state courts determined that state funding of abortions was in line with their state constitutions. Thirty-two states comply with the Hyde Amendment and provide funding for abortion in accordance with the rape, incest, and danger to the life of the mother restrictions. South Dakota is the only state in the nation that refuses to provide funding for any abortions.

The specific parameters of the Hyde Amendment have changed over time. In 1979, the life of the mother exception was excluded, and, in 1981, the exceptions for rape and incest were excluded as well. A 1993 policy change reinstated the Hyde Amendment in its original 1976 format.

The 1977 protests and future protests by abortion rights activists have had some effect on the state level, but the federal government continued to restrict abortion funding. The 1997 Balanced Budget Act permitted Health Maintenance Organizations and other health insurance providers to decline coverage for abortion-related services, if the organization objected on moral or religious grounds. This permitted private providers, such as Catholic Health Maintenance Organizations (HMOs), to restrict funding for abortion-related services.

Supporters of federal funding for abortions point to studies that show that twenty to thirty-five percent of all women on Medicaid who carry pregnancies to term would choose abortion if the procedure were covered. Opponents point to the same statistics to bolster their claims that abortion is a moral issue and a medically elective procedure that should not be performed at the taxpayers' expense. As of 2006, the Hyde Amendment remained in effect in full, with the restriction on federal funding for abortions intact for thirty years.

FURTHER RESOURCES
Books

Hull, N. E. H., and Peter Charles Hoffer. *Roe V. Wade: The Abortion Rights Controversy in American History.* Lawrence: University Press of Kansas, 2001.

Solinger, Rickie. *Abortion Wars: A Half Century of Struggle, 1950–2000.* Berkeley: University of California Press, 1998.

Weddington, Sarah. *A Question of Choice.* New York: Penguin, 1993.

Web sites

Justicia: U.S. Supreme Court Center. "Roe v. Wade. 410 U.S. 113 (1973)." <http://supreme.justia.com/us/410/113/case.html> (accessed May 17, 2006).

NARAL Pro-Choice America. <http://www.naral.org/> (accessed May 17, 2006).

Gallaudet Protesters Claim Victory

Newspaper article

By: The Associated Press

Date: March 11, 1988

Source: The Associated Press

About the Author: The Associated Press is a worldwide news agency based in New York.

INTRODUCTION

In a milestone action for the deaf civil rights movement, Gallaudet University bowed to pressure in 1988 to appoint the first deaf president in the school's history. Gallaudet, founded in 1864, is the world's only university for the deaf. By picking a deaf president, the trustees sought to demonstrate that the deaf are as capable as the hearing in hopes of increasing job opportunities for the deaf.

When President Jerry C. Lee announced his resignation as president of the University in 1987, leaders in the national deaf community joined with Gallaudet alumni, students, faculty, staff and friends in urging the Board of Trustees to select a deaf person as the University's next president. The Board narrowed the field of candidates to three: Dr. Elisabeth Zinser, a hearing woman; Dr. Harvey Corson, a deaf man; and Dr. I. King Jordan, a deaf man. On March 6, 1988, the Board announced the appointment of Zinser as Gallaudet's next president. Students and their supporters reacted swiftly. They refused to accept the board's decision and instead launched the Deaf President Now! (DPN) protest.

The DPN issued four demands: Zinser's resignation, the appointment of a deaf president, the resignation of the board chairman, and the reorganization of the board to include fifty-one percent deaf memberships. Faculty, staff, alumni and members of deaf communities across the country and abroad backed the DPN in support of the notion that it was time that Gallaudet was led by a deaf person. The six day protest ended when Zinser resigned. The board then selected Gallaudet's eighth—and first deaf—president, I. King Jordan, a Gallaudet graduate. Philip Bravin, another Gallaudet alumnus, subsequently became the first deaf chair of the Board of Trustees.

PRIMARY SOURCE

About 2,500 Gallaudet University students and supporters claimed victory in a Capitol Hill rally Friday after Elisabeth Ann Zinser resigned as president of their school for the deaf, but they vowed to continue their protests until their other demands are met.

Zinser, who is not deaf and does not know sign language, was named to the post last Sunday but announced her resignation early Friday morning after protesters virtually halted all classes this week. Zinser said she had stepped down in response "to this extraordinary social movement of deaf people."

Students and activists marched across the Capitol lawn Friday bearing signs and banners and chanting "Deaf President Now," "No Hearing President," and "Deaf Power." "We're still winning. We're still winning," said student leader Jerry Covell. He said he was pleased that Zinser had resigned, but he urged the students to continue their battle to force out the chairwoman of the university's board of trustees and to gain a majority of deaf members on the board. Currently, only four of the twenty board members are deaf.

Gary Olsen, executive director of the National Association of the Deaf, told the students their protests had helped the cause of deaf people nationwide. "Deaf people want to control their destiny," he said. "We will win. I promise you."

Truman Stelle, a Gallaudet faculty member, said, "It is long past time that Gallaudet had a deaf president, as testimony that deaf people are capable of leading themselves." Stelle said the ouster of board chairwoman Jane Bassett Spilman was important because "she clearly sees herself as owner of the Gallaudet plantation, answerable to no one."

Gallaudet, the nation's only liberal arts school for the deaf, has never had a deaf president in its 124-year history. Zinser was the only hearing candidate among the three finalists for the presidency. Despite student demonstrations prior to the selection, Zinser was chosen, setting off a week of protests that have closed down the school. The protesters also have attracted supporters around the country, including members of Congress and some presidential candidates.

At a press conference preceding the rally, Spilman and Zinser acknowledged that the deaf students had made their point but Zinser insisted that the siege itself was not the reason she resigned. "What is happening across the country is a civil rights time of the deaf community," Zinser said. "We have responded to that." The protest, she said, was "a very special moment in time for the deaf community. (That) we could not anticipate." She added that the week's events "should provide no lesson to any other college or university that an action like a campus siege will be tolerated. " I have responded to this extraordinary social movement of deaf people, not to the demands of the students and protesters. "I concluded that the best way to restore order and return this university to its business of education was to pave the way for the board of trustees to consider the selection of a president who is hearing impaired," she said.

Spilman criticized the "external interests of people who perhaps are not as interested or involved in the day-to-day operations of the Gallaudet and not as well informed as the board and the administration," but did not elaborate. Zinser, who was vice chancellor of the University of North Carolina at Greensboro, had never formally submitted her resignation there, and University of North Carolina system President C.D. Spangler told the school's board of governors Friday that Zinser would be welcome back.

In a speech to students at the Capitol Hill rally, Rep. Steve Gunderson, R-Wis., a member of the Gallaudet board of trustees, said, "You have sensitized our nation to the hopes and dreams of not only the hearing impaired but all handicapped."

During the week of protests, he and fellow board member Rep. David Bonior, D-Mich., pressed Zinser and Spilman to find a resolution to the issue. Bonior did not attend the rally, but issued a statement that said Zinser had made a difficult choice. "Her decision is a reflection of her sensitivity to the deaf community and of her true desire to continue moving Gallaudet forward as an outstanding institution for education of the deaf. " The specific challenge to the Gallaudet board of trustees is to select a deaf president as soon as possible. We need further to devise a plan to insure appropriate representation of hearing-impaired and deaf members on the board."

The House Education and Labor Committee's subcommittee on select education, which has jurisdiction over funding for Gallaudet, has scheduled hearings for Tuesday to review the makeup of the board and the controversy over the presidential selection. Three-quarters of the school's $76 million operating budget comes from the federal government. And John Banzhaff, George Washington University law professor and founder of the National Center for Law and the Deaf, has filed a complaint with the District of Columbia Office of Human Rights charging the board with unlawful discrimination for never hiring a deaf president.

SIGNIFICANCE

The deaf rights movement, symbolized by Jordan's ascent and tenure is still establishing itself at the start of the millennium. However, the movement has made enormous advances since 1988. Visual learning is understood and respected as never before while deaf and hard-of-hearing people are earning degrees in unprecedented numbers. Increasingly, many deaf people reject any notion of disability, preferring to view themselves as visually-oriented people. However, the job market for the deaf continues to remain weaker than the market for the hearing.

I. King Jordan retired in 2006, setting off protests across the Gallaudet campus. The trustees selected provost Jane K. Fernandes to replace Jordan, angering many students and faculty. While Fernandes is deaf and would be the first woman president in Gallaudet's history, she grew up speaking and reading lips. As a result, she lacks native fluency in American Sign Language. Many in the Gallaudet community also object to her selection because Fernandes attended mainstream public schools and universities instead of resident schools for the deaf and Gallaudet. Critics view Fernandes as being insufficiently committed to fighting "audism" or discrimination against the deaf both on and off campus. As of May 2006, Fernandes expected to take office. The debate over her selection illustrates the changing definition of what it means to be a deaf person in the twenty-first century.

FURTHER RESOURCES

Books

Christiansen, John B. and Sharon H. Barnartt. *Deaf President Now!: The 1988 Revolution at Gallaudet University*. Washington, D.C.: Gallaudet University Press, 2003.

Gannon, Jack. *The Week the World Heard Gallaudet*. Washington, D.C.: Gallaudet University Press, 1989.

Lane, Harlan. *When the Mind Hears: A History of the Deaf*. New York: Vintage Press, 1989.

Web sites

Gallaudet University. "Gallaudet History." <http:// www.gallaudet.edu/x228.xml> (accessed May 31, 2006).

Freedom of Access to Clinic Entrances Act of 1994

Legislation

By: Edward M. Kennedy

Date: May 26, 1994

Source: Freedom of Access to Clinic Entrances Act. Public Law 103–259, 18 U.S.C. 248.

About the Author: Senator Edward M. Kennedy, a Democrat from Massachusetts, has served in the U.S. Senate since 1962. Known as a progressive, liberal Democrat, Kennedy has championed minimum wage increases, the No Child Left Behind Act, abortion rights, and immigration rights.

INTRODUCTION

Abortion rights legislation, a state matter until the U.S. Supreme Court, in the 1973 case *Roe v. Wade*, stated that women have a constitutional right to privacy and a right to choose abortion, created a flashpoint in American society between pro-choice and anti-choice sectors. Before *Roe v. Wade* abortion laws in the United States were a patchwork of varying laws, with abortion on demand in some states, prohibition of abortion in all cases except the health of the mother in others, and a variety of laws between the two extremes.

Abortion rights activists and women's rights groups, such as the National Abortion Rights Action League (NARAL) and the National Organization for Women (NOW), declared the U.S. Supreme Court decision a victory for women. At the same time, abortion opponents, who consider the act of abortion to be murder, argued vehemently that *Roe v. Wade* sanctioned murder and created a privacy right were none existed.

Justice Harry Blackmun issued the majority decision in *Roe v. Wade* and noted that "We need not resolve the difficult question of when life begins. When those trained in the respective disciplines of medicine, philosophy, and theology are unable to arrive at any consensus, the judiciary, at this point in the development of man's knowledge, is not in a position to speculate as to the answer." According to the doctrine of many Christian denominations such as Catholicism, life begins at conception; Blackmun's statement refers to the Texas state law overturned in the *Roe v. Wade* case, which defined life as such. According to the court, it is not the job of the judicial branch to determine such a complex question.

With *Roe v. Wade* altering the abortion rights landscape, anti-abortion activists began to use coordinated protest and legislative maneuvers to reduce the impact of *Roe*, and later to overturn it. Organizations such as the National Right to Life Council formed in 1973 in response to *Roe*; organizers used legislative appeals, letter writing campaigns, and public protests in their efforts to repeal abortion rights.

By the early 1980s, anti-abortion groups began to target women's reproductive health clinics, such as those operated by Planned Parenthood, a non-profit women's health organization. Operation Rescue, founded by Randall Terry in 1986 and now known as Operation Save America, gained media attention for members' use of graphic images of aborted fetuses on posters during protests in front of women's health centers where abortions were performed. Tens of thousands of Operation Rescue members were arrested at abortion protests in the late 1980s and early 1990s. Members approached women entering health clinics where abortions were performed, pleading with women to look at pictures of aborted fetuses,

Members of the pro-life organization Operation Resuce block the door to a San Diego abortion clinic, during the August 1996 Republican National Convention in that city. © MARK PETERSON/CORBIS.

telling women not to get abortions, threatening violence against abortion providers, and vandalizing health clinic property.

In response, women's rights groups, such as the NOW and NARAL, organized volunteers to provide "clinic defense" for women attempting access to the buildings. Protesters from both sides of the abortion debate thus faced off against each other in person, often resulting in violence. In addition, women's rights groups provided escorts for clinic access.

Violence against abortion providers and clinics escalated. Between 1991 and 1994, more than sixteen murders and attempted murders of abortion providers and clinic staff, as well as eight-seven bombings, arsons, or attempted bombings of abortion clinics, led lawmakers to consider new legislation that would tighten penalties against anti-abortion protesters who used violence as a means to an end. The Freedom of Access to Clinic Entrance Act of 1994 (FACE) was the final result of legislators' efforts.

◼ PRIMARY SOURCE

SECTION 1. SHORT TITLE
This Act may be cited as the 'Freedom of Access to Clinic Entrances Act of 1994.'

SEC. 2. PURPOSE
Pursuant to the affirmative power of Congress to enact this legislation under section 8 of article I of the Constitution, as well as under section 5 of the fourteenth amendment to the Constitution, it is the purpose of this Act to protect and promote the public safety and health and activities affecting interstate commerce by establishing Federal criminal penalties and civil remedies for certain violent, threatening, obstructive and destructive conduct that is intended to injure, intimidate or interfere with persons seeking to obtain or provide reproductive health services.

SEC. 3. FREEDOM OF ACCESS TO CLINIC ENTRANCES
Chapter 13 of title 18, United States Code, is amended by adding at the end thereof the following new section:

ec. 248 Freedom of Access to Clinic Entrances. (a) PROHIBITED ACTIVITIES- Whoever—

1. by force or threat of force or by physical obstruction, intentionally injures, intimidates or interferes with or attempts to injure, intimidate or interfere with any person because that person is or has been, or in order to intimidate such person or any other person or any class of persons from, obtaining or providing reproductive health services;

2. by force or threat of force or by physical obstruction, intentionally injures, intimidates or interferes with or attempts to injure, intimidate or interfere with any person lawfully exercising or seeking to exercise the First Amendment right of religious freedom at a place of religious worship; or

3. intentionally damages or destroys the property of a facility, or attempts to do so, because such facility provides reproductive health services, or intentionally damages or destroys the property of a place of religious worship, shall be subject to the penalties provided in subsection (b) and the civil remedies provided in subsection (c), except that a parent or legal guardian of a minor shall not be subject to any penalties or civil remedies under this section for such activities insofar as they are directed exclusively at that minor.

(b) PENALTIES- Whoever violates this section shall—

1. in the case of a first offense, be fined in accordance with this title, or imprisoned not more than one year, or both; and

2. in the case of a second or subsequent offense after a prior conviction under this section, be fined in accordance with this title, or imprisoned not more than 3 years, or both; except that for an offense involving exclusively a nonviolent physical obstruction, the fine shall be not more than $10,000 and the length of imprisonment shall be not more than six months, or both, for the first offense; and the fine shall be not more than $25,000 and the length of imprisonment shall be not more than 18 months, or both, for a subsequent offense; and except that if bodily injury results, the length of imprisonment shall be not more than 10 years, and if death results, it shall be for any term of years or for life.

SIGNIFICANCE

The Freedom of Access to Clinic Entrances Act (FACE) of 1994 prohibits the use of any form of violence, harassment, or intimidation against any woman entering a reproductive health services clinic. During many anti-abortion protests women seeking non-abortion services, such as prenatal care, birth control access, or routine gynecological care, found themselves interrogated by anti-abortion protesters, subjected to shouts and pleas, and at times became the victims of violent acts. The Freedom of Access to Clinic Entrances Act was written to protect access to all forms of reproductive services; violations that are non-violent result in a $10,000 fine and up to six months in prison, and other actions in violation of FACE can lead to fines exceeding $250,000 and up to ten years in jail, with life imprisonment for murder.

Coming on the heels of the murder of Dr. David Gunn, who performed abortions in a reproductive women's health clinic in Pensacola, Florida, the act also sought to make the murder of workers in abortion clinics a federal crime. The act did not impinge upon protesters' First Amendment rights; protesters could continue to chant, pray, carry posters of aborted fetuses, and call out to women in accordance with local noise regulations, but could not approach women, threaten them verbally, or block access to the clinics. The 1994 U.S. Supreme Court case *Madsen v. Women's Health Center* established a thirty-six foot "buffer zone" around clinic entrances, prohibiting protesters from approaching the clinic or any person within the proscribed zone.

In response to FACE and *Madsen v. Women's Health Center*, anti-abortion organizers began to target clinic workers, tracking down home addresses and telephone numbers and protesting at their homes. In 1997, anti-abortion groups used the Internet to publicize personal information and photographs of known clinic doctors, with the implied message that the murders of such doctors would help the cause of making abortion illegal. The American Coalition of Life Advocates created "The Nuremberg Files," with pictures of abortion providers in the style of wanted posters, including providers' names, phone numbers, and home addresses. If an abortion provider had been killed, his or her face was struck through with a black line; those injured had their names faded to a light shade of gray. The Web site was shut down by court order in 2002.

FACE continues to be used in court cases involving direct intimidation or violent action towards women entering clinics; between 1994 and 2004 the U.S. Department of Justice used FACE in forty-four court cases, resulting in sixty-six convictions.

FURTHER RESOURCES
Books

Blanchard, Dallas A., and Terry J. Prewitt. *Religious Violence and Abortion: The Gideon Project*. Gainesville: University Press of Florida, 1993.

Hull, N. E. H., and Peter Charles Hoffer. *Roe V. Wade: The Abortion Rights Controversy in American History.* Lawrence: University Press of Kansas, 2001.

Solinger, Rickie. *Abortion Wars: A Half Century of Struggle, 1950–2000.* Berkeley: University of California Press, 1998.

Weddington, Sarah. *A Question of Choice.* New York: Penguin, 1993.

Websites

NARAL Pro-Choice America. <http://www.naral.org/> (accessed May 17, 2006).

Operation Rescue/Operation Save America. <http://www.operationsaveamerica.org/> (accessed May 17, 2006).

The Sit-In Begins

Interview

By: Kitty Cone

Date: 2000

Source: Regional Oral History Office of the Bancroft Library at the University of California at Berkeley

About the Author: Kitty Cone, a disability rights activist, helped lead demonstrations to force the implementation of Section 504 of the Rehabilitation Act of 1973. In 2000, she was interviewed by David Landes of the Regional Oral History Office of the Bancroft Library at the University of California at Berkeley.

INTRODUCTION

Section 504 of the Rehabilitation Act of 1973 is the most significant disability rights legislation prior to passage of the Americans with Disabilities Act (ADA) of 1990. The regulations opened up unprecedented opportunities for the disabled and introduced the concept of disability rights to American society.

Section 504 states that no handicapped individual who is otherwise qualified shall be excluded from participating in any program that receives federal funds. At the time of its passage, several states had already passed legislation intended to prohibit discrimination against people with disabilities. The models for Section 504, however, were Title VI of the Civil Rights Act of 1964 and Title IX of the Education Amendments of 1972 that respectively outlawed discrimination against racial minorities and women. Legislators were concerned that disabled individuals who had completed vocational rehabilitation were unable to find work because of discrimination by employers.

Disability activists rejoiced at Section 504, but the legislation could not make an impact until the provisions of the bill were spelled out. In 1977, disabled activists, including Kitty Cone and Judith (Judy) Heumann, began demonstrations in San Francisco to force Department of Health, Education, and Welfare Secretary Joseph Califano to sign regulations implementing Section 504. On April 28, 1977, Califano signed. The regulations required that all new facilities built with federal money be accessible to people with disabilities and that all existing facilities had to be made accessible within two months, although the extension of three years could be granted where major alterations, such as the addition of ramps or elevators, were necessary. All public schools receiving federal funds were required to admit and educate children with disabilities and to make the necessary accommodations to do so.

■ PRIMARY SOURCE

The Sit-in Begins, April 5, 1977

Landes: Let's go to April 5. What do you remember about getting up that morning? [chuckles] Were you nervous? How did you feel as you were leaving home to go to San Francisco?

Cone: I have dead memory. I remember being nervous about what was going to happen. How were we really going to get in the building? Were they going to close the doors on us as we were going in? And having a sort of unclear feeling about—I had no idea what it looked like inside the building; I'm sure we had sent people over there to look at it, but I just didn't have any idea what it was like. I remember being up on the stage and looking out and thinking that it was a very good size crowd and that it was very broad in terms of disability and race and that it was a broad group of people. And then I remember that we all raced for the door. I think we all went in one door, but that can't be right. All the wheelchairs went up this ramp on the side of the building.

Landes: Did somebody say, "Let's go inside!?" How did—

Cone: Yes, Judy—

Landes: Tell me something about Judy's speech.

Cone: I don't remember a thing about it except that it was decided that she was going to say, "Let's go up there and ask them what's happening with the 504

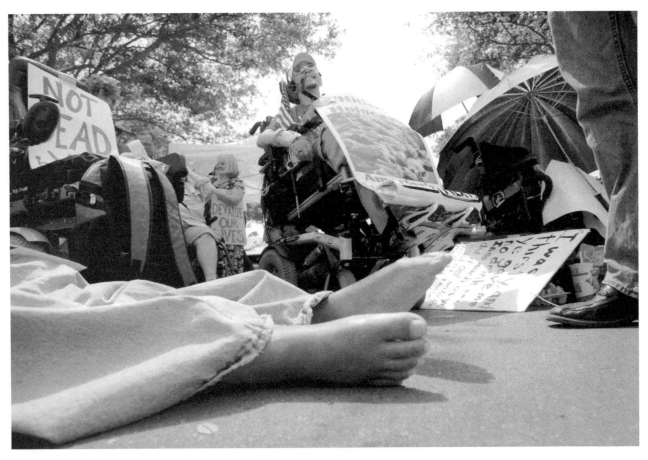

During the Terri Schiavo controversy, demonstrators with disabilities, members of the group "Not Dead Yet," block the driveway of the Woodside Hospice House on March 27, 2005. Schiavo resides inside the hospice. The demonstrators do not believe her feeding tube should have been removed. © TOM FOX/CORBIS.

regulations! Let's go up there and demand to know why they haven't issued them! Everybody, let's go!" Something like that.

Landes: That was the signal.

Cone: That was the signal, and we all just went in [laughs]. We went up to the director's office—his name was Joseph Maldonado, poor man. Judy was acting as the spokesperson, and she said—and the press, of course, was there taking pictures of every bit of it—"We want to know what's happening with the regulations." And this man knew *nothing*; he didn't even have a clue. He didn't even know what 504 was, as I recall [laughs]. He was just made mincemeat out of. He couldn't answer a single question about why they were watering down the regulations or when the regulations were coming out. We wanted assurances, and Judy said, "We're not leaving until we get assurances." So as many as we could, we got into his office and just took it over.

Landes: What were your feeling at that point, when you were inside his office?

Cone: See, this is the difference between me and Judy. This really is the difference. I totally admired Judy's ability to take this man who knew nothing and cream him. But I was feeling slightly sorry for him, actually, [laughs] because he didn't have a clue. But for public relations purposes, it was perfect. It was absolutely perfect. What do you mean you don't know? That kind of thing. It was great.

Landes: You're saying Judy was relentless.

Cone: Oh, always. Yes, fearless.

Landes: Were you relieved to be inside? Earlier you said you were worried that morning as to whether or not they would shut the doors. Once you arrived inside the building and you had a large number of disabled people inside, did you feel that you had taken the next giant step?

Cone: Well, we were in there. There were people inside the building who had no idea that there was going to be a sit-in [laughs]. So it was a process of educating and convincing them that they should stay.

Landes: Some people did not have sleeping bags and had made no preparations to stay more than a few hours.

Cone: Right. But a lot of people had come with a sleeping bag. I remember I brought a couple of pillows out of my van. My attendant stayed for a few days and then left. Some attendants stayed for the entire time; they were absolutely incredible—like Avril Harris, who ended up doing attendant work for the entire—she was just fabulous. Avril had a schedule: every morning she came and brought me two cups of coffee, and she would say, "Here, drink your coffee. I'll go get Judy up and then I'll be back for you." Then she'd go get Judy up—didn't take too long because there was nowhere to take a bath or anything [laughs]. Then she'd come get me up, and then she'd get up a few more people. Nancy Di Angelo was the person that she had come in with.

One thing that amazes me is the physical stamina—I think we were all operating on adrenalin overload for a month. We were going to bed—we would have these mass meetings of everybody in the building, every evening, to discuss how we should respond strategically, and sometimes they didn't end until one or two in the morning, and we'd go to bed and then we'd get up at five thirty in the morning so we could clean up and be prepared for when the workers came into the office the next day.

SIGNIFICANCE

Within ten years of the signing of the Section 504 regulations, people with disabilities constituted seven percent of all first-year college students. New buildings by institutions or agencies funded, even partially, by the federal government were built with ramps, elevators, Braille signage, and curbcuts. Older buildings, when renovated, were required to aim for accessibility. People with disabilities also found it somewhat easier to be hired, although unemployment rates remained substantially higher than in any other group of people.

Section 504 was limited in that it did nothing about groups or organizations that did not receive federal money. Enforcement of 504 was also spotty at best, and federal court decisions about its requirements were often confused and contradictory, tending to

limit its effectiveness. As a result, entire aspects of American public life, such as mass transit and housing, continued to be inaccessible to people with disabilities. By 1983, the National Council for Disability had begun to push for a national law that would become the Americans with Disabilites Act (ADA).

FURTHER RESOURCES

Books

Scotch, Richard. *From Good Will to Civil Rights: Transforming Federal Disability Policy*. Philadelphia: Temple University Press, 2001.

Yell, Mitchell L. *The Law and Special Education*. Upper Saddle River, N.J.: Merrill, 1998.

Zirkel, Perry A. *Section 504: Student Issues, Legal Requirements, and Practical Recommendations*. Bloomington, Ind.: Phi Delta Kappa Educational Foundation, 2005.

USA PATRIOT Act, Section 215

Legislation

By: U.S. Congress

Date: October 24, 2001

Source: *Electronic Privacy Information Center*. "U.S.A. Patriot Act." October 24, 2001 <http://www.epic.org/privacy/terrorism/hr3162.html> (accessed May 16, 2006).

About the Author: The U.S. Senate and House of Representatives, the two houses of the U.S. Congress that enacted this legislation, form the legislative branch of the U.S. government.

INTRODUCTION

The USA PATRIOT Act was passed by both houses of Congress and signed into law by President George W. Bush on October 24, 2001. The acronym stands for Uniting and Strengthening America by Providing Appropriate Tools Required to Intercept and Obstruct Terrorism. Written and enacted in the immediate aftermath of the terrorist attacks of September 11, 2001, it was passed with a little opposition: Only one senator (Russ Feingold, D-WI) and a handful of representatives voted against it.

The act's title declares it is intended "to deter and punish terrorist acts in the United States and around the world, to enhance law enforcement investigatory

A pedestrian studies a sign in the window of Arundel Books in Seattle, February 26, 2004. The store's owner is protesting against aspects of the Patriot Act that give the government access to bookstore and library records. AP IMAGES.

tools, and for other purposes." One of its most controversial provisions is Section 215, which allows Federal Bureau of Investigation (FBI) agents to request "certain business records" after obtaining a warrant from the Foreign Intelligence Surveillance (FISA) court. The FISA court proceedings are secret and its decisions are not subject to appeal. Although libraries and bookstores are not specifically mentioned by the USA PATRIOT Act, many legal experts agree that the section's language allows the FBI to request records from public and university libraries and bookstores. While the language of Section 215 is vague, many privacy and civil liberties advocates claim that authorities may obtain records about who has been borrowing or buying which books or using which Internet resources. Further, the act prevents librarians and booksellers from revealing that they have had to supply records to the FBI—what has been called the "gag

provision" of the bill. The FBI does not need to show the library that there is probable cause for suspecting the person whose records are requested.

Another section of the bill, Section 505, allows the FBI to request records without a court order by issuing a document called a National Security Letter. As with Section 215, recipients of National Security Letters are barred from revealing that they have received such requests. The American Civil Liberties Union (ACLU) has challenged the constitutionality of this controversial section.

PRIMARY SOURCE

H.R. 3162
107TH CONGRESS.

107 1ST SESSION.

IN THE SENATE OF THE UNITED STATES.

OCTOBER 24, 2001.

Received.

AN ACT

To deter and punish terrorist acts in the United States and around the world, to enhance law enforcement investigatory tools, and for other purposes.

Be it enacted by the Senate and House of Representatives of the United States of America in Congress assembled.

SECTION 1. SHORT TITLE AND TABLE OF CONTENTS.

(a) SHORT TITLE.—This Act may be cited as the Uniting and Strengthening America by Providing Appropriate Tools Required to Intercept and Obstruct Terrorism (USA PATRIOT ACT) Act of 2001....

SEC. 215. ACCESS TO RECORDS AND OTHER ITEMS UNDER THE FOREIGN INTELLIGENCE SURVEILLANCE ACT.

Title V of the Foreign Intelligence Surveillance Act of 1978 (50 U.S.C. 1861 et seq.) is amended by striking sections 501 through 503 and inserting the following:

"SEC. 501. ACCESS TO CERTAIN BUSINESS RECORDS FOR FOREIGN INTELLIGENCE AND INTERNATIONAL TERRORISM INVESTIGATIONS.

"(a)(1) The Director of the Federal Bureau of Investigation or a designee of the Director (whose rank shall be no lower than Assistant Special Agent in Charge) may make an application for an order requiring the production of any tangible things (including books, records, papers, documents, and other items) for an investigation to protect against international terrorism or clandestine intelligence activities, provided that such investigation of a United States person is not conducted solely upon the basis of activities protected by the first amendment to the Constitution.

"(2) An investigation conducted under this section shall—

"(A) be conducted under guidelines approved by the Attorney General under Executive Order 12333 (or a successor order); and

"(B) not be conducted on a United States person solely upon the basis of activities protected by the first amendment to the Constitution of the United States.

"(b) Each application under this section—

"(1) shall be made to—

"(A) a judge of the court established by section 103(a); or.

"(B) a United States Magistrate Judge under chapter 43 of title 28, United States Code, who is publicly designated by the Chief Justice of the United States to have the power to hear applications and grant orders for the production of tangible things under this section on behalf of a judge of that court; and

"(2) shall specify that the records concerned are sought for an authorized investigation conducted in accordance with subsection (a)(2) to protect against international terrorism or clandestine intelligence activities.

"(c)(1) Upon an application made pursuant to this section, the judge shall enter an ex parte order as requested, or as modified, approving the release of records if the judge finds that the application meets the requirements of this section.

"(2) An order under this subsection shall not disclose that it is issued for purposes of an investigation described in subsection (a).

"(d) No person shall disclose to any other person (other than those persons necessary to produce the tangible things under this section) that the Federal Bureau of Investigation has sought or obtained tangible things under this section.

"(e) A person who, in good faith, produces tangible things under an order pursuant to this section shall not be liable to any other person for such production. Such production shall not be deemed to constitute a waiver of any privilege in any other proceeding or context.

"SEC. 502. CONGRESSIONAL OVERSIGHT.

"(a) On a semiannual basis, the Attorney General shall fully inform the Permanent Select Committee on Intelligence of the House of Representatives and the Select Committee on Intelligence of the Senate concerning all requests for the production of tangible things under section 402.

"(b) On a semiannual basis, the Attorney General shall provide to the Committees on the Judiciary of the House of Representatives and the Senate a report setting forth with respect to the preceding 6-month period—

"(1) the total number of applications made for orders approving requests for the production of tangible things under section 402; and

"(2) the total number of such orders either granted, modified, or denied."

SIGNIFICANCE

Sections 215 and 505 of the USA PATRIOT Act have been controversial since 2002. The government's authority to obtain personal and business information about persons not accused of any crime struck some Americans as an unconstitutional invasion of privacy; others have defended the Act's provisions as a necessary tool in the struggle against terrorism.

The National Library Association (ALA) became a major opponent of the USA PATRIOT Act, organizing letter-writing and other campaigns to express its views to senators and representatives. In 2003, the organization's executive director said to a reporter for the *Washington Post*, "This law is dangerous. I read murder mysteries—does that make me a murderer? I read spy stories—does that make me a spy? There's no clear link between a person's intellectual pursuits and their actions."

The USA PATRIOT act can require records to be handed over secretly, but it does not require that they be kept to begin with; therefore, some booksellers and librarians began destroying records that could identify who had borrowed or bought books, so that they would have no information to hand over if asked. In 2003, ten libraries in Santa Cruz, California, destroyed borrowing records on a daily basis and posted signs warning patrons that the government can secretly review whatever borrowers read. Several towns in Maine started a campaign to get entire communities to read George Orwell's novel *1984*, a cautionary tale in which the government watches citizens incessantly, justifying its actions as necessary defensive measures in a never-ending war against dangerous enemies. Librarians in Bath, Maine, obliterated all traces of borrowing and Internet records each day. In Monterey Park, California, librarians taped signs to every computer terminal saying, "Beware: Anything you read is now subject to secret scrutiny by federal agents." Similar actions were carried out at many libraries across the country.

Federal officials objected that the new law targeted only those connected to terrorism. "We're not going after the average American," said a Justice Department spokesman. "We're only going after the bad guys." Critics fear that a law that empowers federal agencies to spy on citizens will inevitably be abused for political purposes. Such concerns were apparently bolstered in March 2006 when the American Civil Liberties Union obtained government documents showing that the FBI had spied on a number of nonviolent antiwar groups under the rubric of antiterror investigation, including the Thomas Merton Center of Philadelphia, a pacifist religious organization named in honor of the Catholic monk Thomas Merton (1915–1968).

The USA PATRIOT Act was due to sunset (expire) four years from the bill's original passage. In early 2006, a modified version was passed by the House and Senate and signed into law by President Bush. Many of the new act's provisions were made permanent, with no sunset date, but the new, slightly modified version of Section 215 must be renewed in 2008. The ALA expressed disappointment, stating that the new legislation "offers little improvements to Section 215 regarding individualized suspicion ... [T]he recipient of a Section 215 court order does not have the ability to meaningfully challenge the order or the attached gag order in a court of law." President Bush, welcoming Senate passage of the bill in March 2006, said that "[t]he Patriot Act is vital to the war on terror and defending our citizens against a ruthless enemy."

FURTHER RESOURCES
Books

Baker, Stewart A., and John Kavanagh, eds. *Patriot Debates: Experts Debate the USA Patriot Act*. Chicago: American Bar Association, 2005.

Periodicals

O'Connor, Anahad. "Librarians Win as U.S. Relents on Secrecy Law." *The New York Times*. April 13, 2006.

Sanchez, Rene. "Librarians Make Some Noise Over Patriot Act: Concerns about Privacy Prompt Some to Warn Patrons, Destroy Records of Book and Computer Use." *The Washington Post*. April 10, 2003.

Web sites

American Civil Liberties Union. "With Patriot Act Debate Over, Government Drops Fight to Gag Librarians from Discussing Objections to Controversial Law." April 12, 2006. <http://www.aclu.org/natsec/gen/24995prs20060412.html>.

American Library Association. "USA PATRIOT Act of 2001." April 17, 2006. <http://www.ala.org/ala/washoff/WOissues/civilliberties/theusapatriotact/usapatriotact.htm> (accessed May 16, 2006).

USA PATRIOT Act sec. 213

Legislation

By: U.S. Congress

Date: October 26, 2001

Source: "USA PATRIOT Act sec. 213." U.S. Department of Justice, October 26, 2001.

About the Author: The U.S. Senate and House of Representatives, the two houses of the U.S. Congress that enacted this legislation, form the legislative branch of the U.S. government.

INTRODUCTION

On September 11, 2001, The United States was struck by a series of coordinated terrorist attacks that resulted in the deaths of over three thousand people. The suddenness and the ferocity of the actions created the most calamitous event to have ever taken place on American soil in peacetime. The resulting damage, including the destruction of the World Trade Center in New York, the hijacking and destruction of commercial aircraft, and the significant damage to the Pentagon, was a profoundly disturbing occurrence that called into question the security of American borders. Shortly after the attacks had been carried out, a Middle Eastern Muslim extremist organization, al-Qaeda, headed by Osama bin-Laden, claimed responsibility for the attacks.

In the immediate aftermath of the terrorist attacks, the primary attention of the federal government was directed both to the victims of 9/11 and the determination of whether a further attack might be staged in the aftermath. The Bush administration, supported by the leadership of both the Republican and the Democratic parties in the Senate and the House of Representatives, quickly cast the American response to 9/11 as the commencement of a war on terror. A key issue identified by the American law enforcement community, and one subsequently adopted by American legislators as a basis for the provisions of the Patriot Act, was the quality of domestic intelligence available concerning the actions of potential terrorists operating within the borders of the United States prior to 9/11.

This assertion on the part of law enforcement and national security specialists crystallized into the essential foundation for section 213 of the Patriot Act—that there had been an intelligence gathering failure prior to the 9/11 attacks. Upon this foundation were built the companion notions that the United States must have better intelligence capabilities to ward off any subsequent terrorist attacks and that existing methods by which search warrants are obtained require a streamlining to ensure that in what was now a de facto war, law enforcement agencies are not unduly hindered in their efforts to protect the country.

Protestors rally outside Federal Hall in New York City to protest against the USA Patriot Act, September 9, 2003. AP IMAGES.

Section 213 provided a mechanism by which information could be obtained through searches of premises and seizures of property and electronic data without requiring notice of the search to be given to the investigative target until a later time. This power to "sneak a peek" is contrary to the general—but not absolute—principle of American law that the person who is named as the subject of a search warrant be informed of the search in advance of its execution.

The Patriot Act was drafted and tendered for debate by legislators with remarkable speed. The Act was signed into law by President George W. Bush on October 26, 2001, only forty-five days after the 9/11 attacks had been carried out. The Congressional hearings regarding the Act occurred against a backdrop of intense media commentary concerning the extent and the capabilities of groups such as al-Qaeda, one where fact and speculation were often indistinguishable. It is noteworthy that only one senator voted against the passage of the Patriot Act.

■ PRIMARY SOURCE

USA PATRIOT ACT

Sec. 213. Authority For Delaying Notice Of The Execution Of A Warrant. Section 3103a of title 18, United States Code, is amended—

(1) by inserting '(a) IN GENERAL' before 'In addition'; and

(2) by adding at the end the following:

(b) DELAY—With respect to the issuance of any warrant or court order under this section, or any other rule of law, to search for and seize any property or material that constitutes evidence of a criminal offense in violation of the laws of the United States, any notice required, or that may be required, to be given may be delayed if—

(1) the court finds reasonable cause to believe that providing immediate notification of the execution of the warrant may have an adverse result (as defined in section 2705);

(2) the warrant prohibits the seizure of any tangible property, any wire or electronic communication (as defined in section 2510), or, except as expressly provided in chapter 121, any stored wire or electronic information, except where the court finds reasonable necessity for the seizure; and

(3) the warrant provides for the giving of such notice within a reasonable period of its execution, which period may thereafter be extended by the court for good cause shown.'

SIGNIFICANCE

Section 213 of the Patriot Act has proven to be the most contentious and the most discussed of the provisions designed to combat the threat to American security manifested by 9/11. It is an aspect of the American legal system that is as important for its symbolism as it may be for the actual impact that the section may have had on the abilities of American law enforcement to better counter terrorism. Numerous opponents of the Patriot Act have advocated that no matter how horrific the results of 9/11, American values regarding the sanctity of the person and their property remain paramount.

On one side of the debate, the figures compiled by the United States Department of Justice in 2005 suggest that the impact upon the day-to-day enjoyment of civil liberties in America since the enactment of section 213 is miniscule. Between October 26, 2001 and January 31, 2005, the Department of Justice made 155 applications to execute a delayed notice (sneak a peek) search warrant. These applications represented less than 0.2 percent of all federal warrant requests.

As with other exigent circumstance cases that existed prior to 9/11, a court's power to withhold notification would turn upon whether evidence might be destroyed prior to the search, whether a witness's life might be at risk, or whether the investigation might be jeopardized. The Justice Department adopted a position that based upon its statistics, the provisions of section 213 have functioned as a codification of existing warrant practices as set out in the Federal Rules of Criminal Procedure, where federal courts have held the power to delay the provision of notice of a search warrant to the target.

The counter argument advanced against the Justice Department position by civil libertarians is multi-pronged. The first centers on the language employed in Section 213. The test for whether the target should be notified as to the existence of the

warrant is stated to be that of reasonable cause. The traditional American test for the issuance of a search warrant is that of probable cause; a probability is a significantly higher legal standard than that of the reasonable possibility contemplated by section 213. The critics of section 213 argue that in reducing the legal standard the state has secured an undesirable foothold in the personal liberties of American citizens.

It is also apparent that section 213 was cast more broadly than the other terrorism-specific provisions of the Patriot Act. Section 213 on its face is not restricted to terrorism or national security investigations; it could apply to any federal search warrant application. Unlike most of the other Patriot Act provisions, section 213 was not subject to a sunset clause when signed into law in 2001; sunset clauses are an expiry date built into certain types of legislation that are intended to be short-term in effect.

Congress commenced hearings into the requested reauthorization of the Patriot Act in 2005. The hearings regarding domestic terrorism were significantly colored by the developments of the war in Iraq, which served to reinforce the possibility of terrorist threats from a wide assortment of extremist groups in addition to the impetus behind the Patriot legislation, the al-Qaeda network. The Bush administration advocated that the Patriot Act must be re-authorized to provide domestic security forces the tools to secure America.

The Congressional hearings were not concluded within the expected time frame in December 2005, when information surfaced regarding a covert wiretap program conducted against American citizens by the National Security Agency (NSA); the NSA had not obtained judicial authority for its wiretaps. This conduct raised collateral questions regarding the integrity of other intelligence-gathering programs, including those permitted pursuant to the Patriot Act. The Act was re-authorized on March 10, 2006.

As a result of the re-authorization process, section 213 was amended to expressly provide that notification concerning a search warrant must be provided within thirty days of the date of execution, unless the court specifically approves a longer period.

Throughout the entirety of the post 9/11 period, an intellectual standoff has developed between those favoring broadened government powers to combat terrorism and those who seek what they characterize as a balance between domestic security and the preservation of personal liberty. The battle is primarily an ideological one, because neither side can point to compelling concrete examples to buttress their position. There have been neither demonstrated affronts to personal liberty through the use of section 213, nor have there been prominent investigative successes that would tend to justify its existence. As of the March 10, 2006 re-authorization, section 213 is a permanent part of the American legal structure, pending some later effort to rescind or amend the Patriot Act.

FURTHER RESOURCES

Books

Bouvard, James. *Terrorism and Tyranny: Trampling Freedom, Justice and Peace to Rid the World of Evil*. New York: Palgrave Macmillan, 2003.

National Commission on Terrorist Attacks. *The 9/11 Commission Report: Final Report of the National Commission on Terrorist Attacks Upon the United States*. New York: W.W. Norton, 2003.

Web sites

City Journal. "The Patriot Act is No Slippery Slope." April 8, 2005. <http://www.city_journal.org/html/eon_04_08_05hm.html> (accessed May 21, 2006).

Resolution to Protest the Eroding of Civil Liberties under the USA PATRIOT Act (Public Law 107-56) and Related Federal Orders Since 9/11/01

Resolution

By: City of Ann Arbor

Date: July 7, 2003

Source: City of Ann Arbor, Michigan. "Resolution to Protest the Eroding of Civil Liberties Under the USA PATRIOT ACT (Public Law 107-56) and Related Federal Orders Since 9/11/01." R-281-7-03. July 7, 2003.

About the Author: Ann Arbor is a city in the U.S. state of Michigan with a population of approximately 120,000.

INTRODUCTION

On October 2001, in response to the terrorist attacks of September 11, 2001, a piece of legislation called the USA PATRIOT Act—the Uniting and Strengthening America by Providing Appropriate Tools Required to Intercept and Obstruct Terrorism Act, in full—was passed by Congress and signed by President George W. Bush. Only one Senator (Russ Feingold, D-WI) and a handful of Representatives

voted against the measure. The Act's ostensible purpose was to expand government powers of surveillance and information-gathering for the purpose of preventing terrorism.

However, despite the near-unanimity of the U.S. Congress, the Act was controversial at the popular level. Leftists, libertarians, and even many conservatives had concerns based on historical incidents, such as the FBI's COINTELPRO (Counterintelligence Program, 1956–71), when the government used its policing and surveillance powers to punish and disrupt political organizations and behaviors that some persons found threatening or offensive, even though those activities were nonviolent and were protected by the First Amendment to the U.S. Constitution. Whether or not the PATRIOT Act actually infringes on Constitutional rights has been and continues to be vigorously debated by legal experts, but a number of states and municipalities have passed resolutions defying the PATRIOT Act as unconstitutional, imploring Congress to repeal it, or demanding that it be enforced only in ways that do not infringe on personal liberties guaranteed by the Constitution.

The city council resolution R-281-7-03 of the city of Ann Arbor, Michigan, was the first such act to be passed. In its original form, "Resolution in Support of Due Process for All Members of the Ann Arbor Community," was passed by a 9–2 vote on January 7, 2002, a little over two months after the passage of the PATRIOT Act; the updated version of the resolution, passed July 7, 2003, is given here. One City Council member, Bob Johnson (D-1st Ward), expressed outrage that the Federal government was keeping secret the names of detainees. "People are being held and we can't even find out what their names are. This is so outrageous. It is an outrage to the Constitution."

PRIMARY SOURCE

RESOLUTION TO PROTEST THE ERODING OF CIVIL LIBERTIES UNDER THE USA PATRIOT ACT (PUBLIC LAW 107-56) AND RELATED FEDERAL ORDERS SINCE 9/11/01: R-281-7-03

WHEREAS, The City of Ann Arbor is proud of its long and distinguished tradition of protecting the civil rights and liberties of its residents and knows that these rights and liberties are essential to the well-being of a democratic society;

WHEREAS, The City of Ann Arbor has a diverse population, including recent immigrants and students from other nations, whose contributions to the community are vital to its economy, culture and civic character;

An anarchist, her mouth sealed shut with duct tape reading "Patriot Act," takes part in a demonstration outside the Democratic National Convention in Boston, July 29, 2004. © SHAUL SCHWARZ/CORBIS.

WHEREAS, The Ann Arbor City Council adopted Resolution R-18-1-02, publicly affirming Ann Arbor's support of the due process rights of all who reside in the City;

WHEREAS, The Board of Trustees of the Ann Arbor District Library unanimously adopted the American Library Association Resolution on the USA Patriot Act and Related Measures That Infringe on the Rights of Library Users on June 16, 2003 and stated that the situation created by the USA Patriot Act "presents a clear and present problem to the Library and the public" ;

WHEREAS, Federal, state and local governments should protect the public from terrorist attacks such as those that occurred on September 11, 2001, but should do so in a rational and deliberate fashion to ensure that any new security measure enhances public safety without impairing constitutional rights or infringing on civil liberties;

WHEREAS, The US Attorney General has stated that the federal government may ask local police departments to enforce federal immigration law;

WHEREAS, The City Council is concerned that the adoption of the USA PATRIOT Act (Public Law 107-56) and related executive orders, federal policies, regulations and actions adopted since September 11, 2001 threaten fundamental rights and liberties in the following ways:

Under the provisions of Section 412 of the Act, non-citizens may be incarcerated for 7 days without charge and continue to be incarcerated for six month periods indefinitely, without access to counsel, under the order of the United States Attorney General if he determines release would endanger the security of the country or of a specific person, which decision is subject to limited judicial review.

The provisions of Section 216 of the Act eliminate judicial latitude in issuance of electronic surveillance orders when the state has met its procedural burden.

The provisions of Section 213 of the Act allow federal searches to be conducted and delayed notice to be given to the subject of the search when it has been judicially determined there would be an adverse effect if concurrent notice was given, involving searches for information not protected by the First Amendment. The subject of the search may never be given notice that a search was conducted if criminal proceedings are not initiated after the search.

The provisions of Sections 203 and 215 of the Act, expand federal data collection procedures to now include personal medical, financial, library, and education records and to allow surveillance of religious services, political demonstrations and other public meetings. Also grants ability for federal law enforcement and intelligence agencies to share and maintain the data regardless of whether the individual has committed, is alleged to have committed or is suspected of possible future acts of terrorism.

The provisions of Sections 411 and 802 broadly define acts of domestic or international terrorism, potentially chilling constitutionally protected speech.

WHEREAS, These new powers pose a threat to the civil rights and liberties of all who reside in our City but particularly those who are Muslim and/or those of Arab or South Asian descent and other immigrant populations;

WHEREAS, The Ann Arbor Police Department has undertaken numerous efforts to build police and community trust in its enforcement actions and the USA PATRIOT Act and its related executive orders and regulations as adopted and implemented have the potential to drive a wedge between immigrant communities and the police who protect them; and

WHEREAS, Further federal legislation may be proposed and the Ann Arbor City Council is concerned about any further undermining of civil liberties and freedoms across the United States;

RESOLVED, That the Ann Arbor City Council reaffirms its strong support for fundamental constitutional rights and its opposition to federal measures that infringe on civil liberties;

RESOLVED, That the Ann Arbor City Council affirms current Ann Arbor Police Department commitment to non-discriminatory policing in criminal investigation and supports the Ann Arbor Police Department in conducting its work so that race, religion, ethnicity or national origin is used as a factor only when investigating or seeking to apprehend a specific suspect whose aforementioned characteristics(s) is part of the description of the suspect, but otherwise refrains from relying on such criteria in all policing functions.

RESOLVED, That the Ann Arbor City Council strongly supports the rights of immigrants and opposes measures that single out individuals for legal scrutiny or enforcement activity based solely on their country of origin and/or religion.

RESOLVED, That the Ann Arbor City Council, as a matter of public policy, directs the Ann Arbor Chief of Police, to the extent permitted by law, to:

1. Continue to limit local enforcement actions with respect to immigration matters to penal violations of federal immigration law (as opposed to administrative violations) except in cases where the Chief of Police determines there is a legitimate public safety concern and in such public safety instances, to report the situation to the City Council no later than 60 days after the incident.

2. Continue to refrain from covert surveillance of and/or collection and maintenance of information on individuals or groups based on their participation in activities protected by the First Amendment, such as political advocacy or the practice of a religion, without a particularized suspicion of unlawful activity.

3. Affirm the existing practice, as required by Michigan state law, of providing simultaneous notice of the execution of a state court search warrant to any resident of the City of Ann Arbor whose property is the subject of such a warrant, except in cases of anticipatory search warrants.

4. Report to the City Council any request made by federal authorities for the Ann Arbor Police Department to participate in any activity under the USA Patriot Act, to the extent the Chief of Police has knowledge of such request.

5. Refrain from participating in informational interviews conducted by federal authorities similar to those conducted by the Federal Bureau of Investigation (FBI) in early 2002 in Ann Arbor of individuals not suspected of criminal activity, unless the interviewee has specifically requested the presence of an AAPD official;

RESOLVED, That the City Administrator is directed to seek semi-annually, by form letter, from federal authorities the following information on behalf of the residents of the City of Ann Arbor:

1. The names of all residents of the City of Ann Arbor who have been arrested or otherwise detained by federal authorities as a result of terrorism investigations since September 11, 2001; the location of each detainee; the circumstances that led to each detention; the charges, if any, lodged against each detainee; the name of counsel, if any, representing each detainee;

2. The number of search warrants that have been executed in the City of Ann Arbor without notice to the subject of the warrant pursuant to Section 213 of the USA PATRIOT Act;

3. The extent of electronic surveillance carried out in the City of Ann Arbor under powers granted in the USA PATRIOT Act;

4. The extent to which federal authorities are monitoring political meetings, religious gatherings or other activities protected by the First Amendment within the City of Ann Arbor;

5. The number of times education records have been obtained from public schools and institutions of higher learning in the City of Ann Arbor under Section 507 of the USA PATRIOT Act;

6. The number of times library records have been obtained from libraries in the City of Ann Arbor under Section 215 of the USA PATRIOT Act;

7. The number of times that records of the books purchased by store patrons have been obtained from bookstores in the City of Ann Arbor under Section 215 of the USA PATRIOT Act;

RESOLVED, That the City Administrator transmit to the City Council as an information item at a City Council regular session no less than once every six months a summary of the information obtained pursuant to the preceding paragraph;

RESOLVED, That the City Clerk is directed to transmit a copy of this resolution to President Bush, U.S. Attorney General Ashcroft, U.S. Senator Levin, U.S. Senator Stabenow and U.S. Congressman Dingell, Governor Granholm and State Senator Brater and State Representative Kolb accompanied by a letter urging them to monitor federal anti-terrorism tactics and to work to repeal provisions of the USA PATRIOT Act and other laws and regulations that infringe on civil rights and liberties;

RESOLVED, That upon the passage of additional anti-terrorism legislation that the Ann Arbor City Council believes undermines civil liberties, this resolution may be amended; and

RESOLVED, That the provisions of this resolution shall be severable, and if any phrase, clause, sentence or provision of this resolution is declared by a court of competent jurisdiction to be contrary to the Constitution of the United States or of the State of Michigan or the applicability thereof to any agency, person, or circumstances is held invalid, the validity of the remainder of this resolution and the applicability thereof to any other agency, person or circumstances shall not be affected thereby.

SIGNIFICANCE

Ann Arbor was the first city or state to pass an anti-PATRIOT Act resolution, but by May 2006, some 399 cities and towns—including Chicago, Denver, Las Vegas, Los Angeles, San Francisco, and New York—had passed similar resolutions. Eight states—some with strong Republican majorities—had also passed anti-PATRIOT Act resolutions (Alaska, California, Colorado, Hawaii, Idaho, Maine, Montana, and Vermont). Over eighty-five million Americans now live in localities where either the city or state level of government has expressed its disapproval of the PATRIOT Act and its refusal to cooperate with it. A historical parallel is the Personal Liberty Laws passed by eight states—Connecticut, Kansas, Maine, Massachusetts, Michigan, Rhode Island, Wisconsin, and Vermont—in the 1850s in response to Federal Fugitive Slave Law of 1850, which forbade state agents to assist in the enforcement of the Fugitive Slave Law.

Many of the anti-PATRIOT resolutions have been promoted by local organizations called Bill of Rights Defense Committees, the first of which was formed in November 2001 to respond to legislation its members saw as repressive or potentially repressive effects of new laws or rules, including the PATRIOT Act, the Homeland Security Act, and some Presidential executive orders.

The resolutions are, so far, symbolic. Ann Arbor's resolution was technically not legally binding, being merely a resolution, not an ordinance; many of the other anti-PATRIOT measures are similarly advisory. Further, the PATRIOT Act's powers are given not to state and local police but to Federal agencies; even a binding ordinance would affect the course of events only if state and local agencies were called upon to participate. However, the anti-PATRIOT resolutions and ordinances gain significance as an undeniable record of political will, and as part of a multifaceted resistance to warrantless wiretapping, detention without charge, and other post-9/11 measures. Critics see the measures as pointless posturing, and—if ever effective—as hindering the Federal government in its necessary actions against dire terrorist threats.

FURTHER RESOURCES
Books
Patriot Debates: Experts Debate the USA Patriot Act, edited by Stewart A. Baker and John Kavanagh. Chicago: American Bar Association, 2005.

Periodicals
Howlett, Debbie. "Patriot Act Battle Is Fought Locally." *USA Today.* July 13, 2003.

Weigel, David. "When Patriots Dissent: Surprise: Standing up to the PATRIOT Act Can be Good Politics." *Reason* (November 2005).

Web sites

Bill of Rights Defense Committee. <http://www.bordc.org> (accessed May 31, 2006).

Schabner, Dean. *ABC News*. "Eight Cities in Patriot Act Revolt." July 1, 2002. <http://abcnews.go.com/US/> (accessed May 31, 2006).

Presbyterian Founder of Gray Panthers Documented in "Maggie Growls"

Film review

By: Jerry L. Van Marter

Date: February 4, 2003

Source: Van Marter, Jerry L. "Presbyterian Founder of Gray Panthers Documented in 'Maggie Growls.'" Presbyterian News Service, 2003.

About the Author: Jerry L. Van Marter is the coordinator for the Presbyterian News Service (PNS), a position he has held since 1994. Van Marter has been on the staff of the PNS since 1988. He has served as a Presbyterian minister for over thirty years, and a parish pastor for more than seventeen years. Van Marter is a member of the San Francisco Presbytery (California). The PNS is the authorized news agency for the Presbyterian Church in the United States of America. It is responsible for independently collecting and distributing news and information about the Presbyterian Church.

INTRODUCTION

American social activist Margaret "Maggie" Eliza Kuhn (1905–1995) was born on August 31, 1905, in Buffalo, New York. In 1921, Kuhn graduated from West High School and, in 1926, graduated with a major in English literature and minors in French and sociology from Western Reserve University in Cleveland, Ohio. In 1930, Kuhn became the head of the Professional Department of Business Girls at the Young Women's Christian Association (YWCA) in the Germantown area of Philadelphia, Pennsylvania. Eleven years later, Kuhn transferred to the position of program coordinator and editor for the YWCA's United Service Organizations (USO) division. In 1948, she became the program coordinator for the General Alliance for Unitarian and Other Liberal Christian Women in Boston, Massachusetts. Two years later, in order to take care of her sick parents, Kuhn became the assistant secretary of the Social Education and Action Department at the national headquarters of the Presbyterian Church in Philadelphia.

By this time in her career, Kuhn was already outspoken in her social beliefs, taking strong positions on such issues as the Cold War, desegregation, McCarthyism, nuclear arms, and urban housing. In her capacity with the church, Kuhn urged members to express their opinions so that action would be taken to solve problems. In 1964, the Presbyterian Church gave her a leave of absence in order to teach a course on poverty and ethics at the San Francisco Seminary in California. In 1969, she became program executive for the Council on Church and Race for the Presbyterian Church. At this time, Kuhn became involved with a committee involved with problems facing the elderly.

When Kuhn turned sixty-five years of age (in 1970), retirement was forced upon her by the Presbyterian Church. Kuhn did not want—and was not ready—to stop working. That year, Kuhn met with a group of five friends who had recently retired to discuss problems of the elderly. They formed a group called the Consultation of Older and Younger Adults for Social Change. Within one year, the group possessed one hundred members. In 1972, the members changed the group's name to the Gray Panthers after a New York City television producer suggested the name, which was modeled after the Black Panthers, a militant black political organization founded in the 1960s. The controversial name was appropriate for the action-oriented group that had a sense of exigency with its cause. By 1973, there were eleven chapters of the Gray Panthers regionally within the United States. In 1975, the first national convention of the Gray Panthers was held in Chicago, Illinois. In 1981, the Gray Panthers became an official non-governmental organization (NGO) at the United Nations. In 1990, the group opened its public policy office in Washington, D.C. to better lobby for its priorities.

The Gray Panthers was formed to identify and solve age-related problems of people such as segregating, stereotyping, and stigmatizing—what the organization calls ageism. Since its founding, the organization has advocated for such issues as nursing home reform, world peace, full employment, fair and decent housing, anti-discrimination (ageism, sexism, and racism), pension rights, family security, expanded health care programs, rights for disabled persons, healthy environment, campaign reform, and issues

Maggie Kuhn gestures and yells at the crowd from the podium while giving an address to the Poletown Neighborhood Council. © DAVID TURNLEY/CORBIS.

associated with the United Nations. In 2006, the Gray Panthers have over 20,000 members in local networks within California, Florida, Michigan, Minnesota, New Jersey, New Mexico, New York, Oregon, Rhode Island, Texas, and Washington D.C.

PRIMARY SOURCE

LOUISVILLE—Maggie Kuhn, a Presbyterian who founded the Gray Panthers in 1970 after being forced to retire at age 65 by the former United Presbyterian Church in the United States of America, will be featured in a PBS documentary tonight (Feb. 4) entitled "Maggie Growls."

Check local listings for the exact time in your area. "Maggie Growls" is part of the PBS series *Independent Lens*, which features the work of independent documentary filmmakers.

Kuhn, who died in 1995 at the age of 90, turned her outrage at having to leave the job she loved in the

UPCUSA's Social Education and Action Office in New York into one of the most potent social movements of the 20th century. As a result of the Gray Panthers' efforts, most mandatory retirement laws have been repealed in this country and older Americans have a host of rights they never would have gained otherwise.

"Well-aimed slingshots can topple giants," she said in an understatement of literally biblical proportions. With a disarming mixture of humor, shock value and common sense, Kuhn used her high visibility and the clout of the Gray Panthers to combat media stereotypes that denigrated the elderly and went on to champion universal health care, nursing home reform, shared housing and consumer protections for the most vulnerable in society.

"Maggie Growls" is produced and directed by the award-winning team of Barbara Attie and Janet Goldwater.

SIGNIFICANCE

As of the 2000s, local networks of the Gray Panthers across the United States comprise a national organization of members who call themselves "intergenerational activists dedicated to social change" at the local, state, and federal levels. The group deals with more than just issues of the elderly, believing that they must work to make the United States "a better place to live for the young, the old, and everyone in between."

Many of its members are high school and college students. Believing that neither the young nor the old should be ignored, disregarded, or discarded by the rest of society, the Gray Panthers believe that teenagers and the elderly should be given more responsibilities so as not to waste vast talents and experiences at both ends of the age spectrum. The Gray Panthers refute the notion that retirement is the only alternative for the elderly. Kuhn personally believed that society has treated older persons as problems of society instead of persons experiencing problems caused by society. She has fought to reverse that impression of older persons. Four issues that Kuhn and the Gray Panthers have promoted are the abolishment of forced retirement, exposure of nursing home abuses, reform in the hearing aid industry, and bringing to light the stereotyping of older people in the media.

In 1978, the Gray Panthers helped to enact legislation called the Age Discrimination in Employment Act, which increased the mandatory retirement age in the United States from sixty-five to seventy years in most sectors of the economy. Then, in 1987, the Act abolished mandatory retirement altogether for most people in the United States. (Some people still must abide by mandatory retirement policies, such as pilots, bus drivers, and other such occupations where age has been shown to be a valid occupational requirement.)

Beginning in 1977, the Gray Panthers founded the National Citizens Coalition for Nursing Home Reform and, in 1977, produced the handbook "Nursing Homes: A Citizen's Action Guide," which exposed and documented nursing home abuse.

In 1973, the Gray Panthers joined Ralph Nader's Retired Professional Action Group to produce a documentary called "Paying Through the Ear," a report on health care issues for hearing. In 1982, the Gray Panthers worked with Nader's Public Citizen to persuade the U.S. Food and Drug Administration (FDA) to monitor and regulate the hearing aid industry with respect to deceitful practices.

In 1975, the Gray Panthers began one of its most important programs: the National Media Watch Task Force. Members of the task force monitored how seniors were portrayed on television. When they found inaccurate or offensive portrayals of older people, members relayed that information to the television broadcasters in order to eliminate such portrayals of older people on television. They eventually succeeded in convincing the National Association of Broadcasters to modify the Television Code of Ethics so that seniors were treated with the same respect on the major networks as were being accorded to minorities and women.

At the age of sixty-five years, when she was supposed to retire, the hard-working and committed Maggie Kuhn founded the Gray Panthers. Maggie Kuhn died on April 22, 1995—twenty-five years after her (supposed) retirement. During her lifetime, Kuhn championed the fight for human rights, economic and social justice, international peace, integration, and mental health. She helped to change how society treated and regarded the elderly. The Gray Panthers lives on after her death, helping to deal with policies related to the elderly.

FURTHER RESOURCES
Books

Kuhn, Maggie. *No Stone Unturned: The Life and Times of Maggie Kuhn.* New York: Ballantine Books, 1991.

Web sites

The Gray Panthers. <http://graypanthers.org> (accessed May 31, 2006).

Public Broadcasting Service. "Maggie Growls: Filmmaker Q&A." <http://www.pbs.org/independentlens/maggiegrowls/qanda.html> (accessed May 31, 2006).

Public Broadcasting Service. "The Gray Panthers: Panthers on the Prowl." <http://www.pbs.org/independentlens/maggiegrowls/panthers.html> (accessed May 31, 2006).

Protesting U.S.-Mexico Border Policy

Photograph

By: Denis Poroy

Date: October 1, 2004

Source: Poroy, Denis. "Protesting U.S.-Mexico Border Policy." AP Images, October 1, 2004.

About the Photographer: Denis Poroy is a contributor to The Associated Press, a worldwide news agency based in New York.

Migrant activists lean against the border fence protesting nightly patrols by citizen volunteers who search for people crossing the US-Mexico border. PHOTO BY DAVID MCNEW/GETTY IMAGES.

INTRODUCTION

The long history of Mexican migration to the United States is driven by poverty and a lack of jobs in Mexico, along with a consistently high level of demand for cheap labor from employers in the United States. Mexicans have entered the United States in massive numbers, some legally and some as undocumented immigrants, and they are believed to account for around half of all undocumented immigrants living in the United States.

Over time, there have been variations in the pattern of Mexican migration to the United States and in the policy initiatives that have attempted to control and legitimize the flow of immigrants. Up until the late 1970s, the majority of Mexican migrants exhibited circular migration patterns between the United States and their own country, entering the United States to work on a temporary basis in farming and other seasonal industries. At this time, a temporary laborer policy program was initiated to meet the needs of employers and migrants alike. From the 1980s onward, however, there have been a large number of Mexican migrants wishing to settle permanently in the United States, and unprecedented numbers have entered as undocumented immigrants.

Two major Immigration Acts have been passed in response to the increase in undocumented migration, especially from Mexico: the 1986 Immigration Reform and Control Act (IRCA) and the 1996 Illegal Immigration Reform and Immigrant Responsibility Act (IIRIRA). Both Acts have focused primarily on strengthening the operations of the U.S. Border Control, the enforcement arm of the Immigration and Naturalization Service (INS). In addition, the IRCA introduced penalties for employers found to have knowingly employed undocumented migrants, created a guest worker program for agricultural laborers and provided an amnesty for undocumented migrants who were already long-term U.S. residents. IIRIRA further strengthened the provisions of the IRCA by increasing penalties on undocumented migrants and human smugglers, while at the same time changes were made in welfare legislation, which had the effect of excluding many immigrants, both legal and undocumented, from the public benefits system.

PRIMARY SOURCE

Protesting U.S.-Mexico Border Policy Marchers carry a casket along a section of the US-Mexico border in Tijuana to mark the 10th anniversary of Operation Gatekeeper, October 1, 2004. AP IMAGES.

Although undocumented migrants from Mexico enter the U.S. in a variety of ways, many simply cross the border by foot. Therefore, recent immigration policies have included increasing the budget and employee numbers of the U.S. Border Control, providing it with advanced military equipment and constructing more fences and ditches along the border. The strategy has been to implement specific operations in selected areas known to be main crossing points for migrants. One of these is Operation Gatekeeper, launched in the San Diego border region in 1994. Other intensive border control operations have been conducted in Texas and in central Arizona. The intended purpose of the operations was not only to apprehend undocumented migrants found crossing the border but to act as a deterrent to other potential migrants. It was thought that the terrain along other

parts of the border was too harsh and the climate too extreme for migrants to use as a crossing point. In fact, many migrants have been prepared to risk their lives crossing this inhospitable environment.

Although the border control operations appear to have had some success in reducing border crossings, the overall number of undocumented migrants entering the United States from Mexico remains high. Moreover, the border control activity has had the unintended consequences of redistributing border crossings to the more inhospitable areas of the border and increasing the number of deaths among migrants who succumb to the extremes of climate and environment. They have also apparently led to an increase in the use by migrants of agents or "coyotes" to help them find a route into the United States, as well as the development in Mexico of large-scale criminal activity in illegal trafficking of people.

PRIMARY SOURCE

PROTESTING U.S.-MEXICO BORDER POLICY

See primary source image.

SIGNIFICANCE

Undocumented immigration, particularly from neighboring Mexico, has long been one of the main items on the U.S. political agenda, and one that rouses considerable public interest and attention. Despite various policy initiatives designed to deter potential undocumented migrants, the overall numbers continue to rise. A conservative estimate based on the 2002 census put the total number of undocumented migrants in the United States at 9.3 million; since this is based on official population statistics, the true number is likely to be much higher and also may have risen considerably since 2002.

A key factor underlying the continuing high levels of undocumented migration is that employers continue to have a demand for low-cost labor, which migrants are prepared to provide, whether or not they can enter the United States legally. Policies designed to make entry to and settlement in the United States more difficult—such as increased border control and exclusion of migrants from welfare benefits—may have some deterrent effect but ultimately many migrants will consider that it is worth taking the risk to escape even worse conditions at home.

In 2004, President George W. Bush announced proposals for a guest-worker program under which migrants would be allowed to enter and work in the United States on a three-year, once renewable permit, and would be allowed to apply for green cards to enable them to stay in the country. At the same time, the number of green cards issued to low-skilled workers would be increased to accommodate the higher demand. The advantage of these proposals over previous guest-worker programs is that they take account of changing patterns of migration in which seasonal border crossings for temporary work have been replaced by an increased demand for permanent settlement in the United States. If implemented, along with increased border security measures proposed in 2006, their impact on actual levels of undocumented migration and the number of border crossing deaths remains to be seen.

FURTHER RESOURCES

Books

Delaet, Debra L,. *U.S. Immigration Policy in an Age of Rights.* Westport, Conn.: Praeger Publishers, 2000.

Morto, Alexander. *The Roots of Mexican Labor Migration.* Westport, Conn.: Praeger Publishers, 1994.

Periodicals

Canales, Alejandro I. "Mexican Labour Migration to the United States in the Age of Globalisation." *Journal of Ethnic and Migration Studies* 29 (2003).

Cornelius, Wayne A. "Controlling 'Unwanted' Immigration: Lessons from the United States, 1993–2004." *Journal of Ethnic and Migration Studies* (July 7, 2005).

Griswold, Daniel T. "Confronting the Problem of Illegal Mexican Migration to the U.S." *USA Today* 131 (March 2003).

Orreniou, Pia M. "Illegal Immigration and Enforcement Along the U.S.-Mexico Border: An Overview." *Economic & Financial Review* (January 1, 2001).

Pentagon Will Review Database on U.S. Citizens

Protests Among Acts Labeled "Suspicious"

Newspaper article

By: Walter Pincus

Date: December 15, 2005

Source: Pincus, Walter. "Pentagon Will Review Database on U.S. Citizens: Protests Among Acts Labeled "Suspicious." *The Washington Post.* December 15, 2005.

About the Author: Walter Pincus is the national security reporter for the *Washington Post*, a daily newspaper based in Washington, DC with a circulation of over five million copies weekly.

INTRODUCTION

In December 2005, the television network NBC reported that it had obtained a secret 400 page database from the U.S. Department of Defense (DoD) listing what the military called "suspicious incidents" across the United States. The list, known as the Cornerstone database, was maintained by the Federal agency CIFA (Counterintelligence Field Activity). According to a 2003 report of the DoD to Congress, CIFA is charged with "identification and tracking of terrorists and production of CI [counterintelligence] assessments and advisories and risk assessment in support of DoD force protection and critical infra-structure protection efforts."

One of CIFA's sources of information is the TALON program (Threat and Local Observation Notice). TALON was established by order of Deputy Secretary of Defense Paul Wolfowitz in 2003, when the DoD ordered CIFA to produce and "maintain a domestic law enforcement database that includes information related to potential terrorist threats directed against the Department of Defense." CIFA used TALON information to create the Cornerstone database.

The contents of the database are controversial because among the 1,500 reports in it were almost four dozen describing nonviolent antiwar activities. For example, the database recorded that a small group of activists had met in a Quaker Meeting House (Quakers are a pacifist Christian sect) to plan protests against military recruiting in high schools in Florida. Such records appeared to show that the Pentagon was treating Constitutionally protected, nonviolent, political criticism as a possible source of terrorism.

PRIMARY SOURCE

Pentagon officials said yesterday they had ordered a review of a program aimed at countering terrorist attacks that had compiled information about U.S. citizens, after reports that the database included information on peace protesters and others whose activities posed no threat and should not have been kept on file.

The move followed an NBC News report Tuesday disclosing that a sample of about 1,500 "suspicious incidents" listed in the database included four dozen anti-war meetings or protests, some aimed at military recruiting.

Although officials defended the Pentagon's interest in gathering information about possible threats to military bases and troops, one senior official acknowledged that a preliminary review of the database indicated that it had not been correctly maintained.

"On the surface, it looks like things in the database that were determined not to be viable threats were never deleted but should have been," the official said. "You can also make the argument that these things should never have been put in the database in the first place until they were confirmed as threats."

The program, known as Talon, compiles unconfirmed reports of suspected threats to defense facilities. It is part of a broader effort by the Pentagon to gather counter-terrorism intelligence within the United States, which has

prompted concern from civil liberties activists and members of Congress in recent weeks.

To some, the Pentagon's current efforts recall the Vietnam War era, when defense officials spied on anti-war groups and peace activists. Congressional hearings in the 1970s subsequently led to strict limits on the kinds of information that the military can collect about activities and people inside the United States.

The review of the program, ordered by Undersecretary of Defense for Intelligence Stephen A. Cambone, will focus on whether officials broke those rules, a Pentagon statement said. The regulations require that any information that is "not validated as threatening must be removed from the TALON system in less than ninety days," it said.

The Pentagon stopped short of officially acknowledging fault but strongly implied some information had been mishandled. "There is nothing more important to the U.S. military than the trust and goodwill of the American people," said the statement. "The Department of Defense ... views with the greatest concern any potential violation of the strict DoD policy governing authorized counter-intelligence efforts."

The Talon database—and several affiliated programs—has been described by officials as a sort of neighborhood watch for the military, an important tool in trying to detect and prevent terrorist attacks against the military.

Under the programs, civilians and military personnel at defense installations are encouraged to file reports if they believe they have come across people or information that could be part of a terrorist plot or threat, either at home or abroad. The Talon reports are fed into a database managed by the Counterintelligence Field Activity, or CIFA, a three-year-old Pentagon agency whose budget and size are classified.

The Talon reports—the number is classified, officials said—can consist of "raw information" that "may or may not be related to an actual threat, and its very nature may be fragmented and incomplete," according to a 2003 memo signed by then-Deputy Defense Secretary Paul D. Wolfowitz.

Cambone's review came one day after a sample of the CIFA database, containing reports of 1,519 "suspicious incidents" between July 2004 and May 2005, was disclosed first by NBC News, and by William M. Arkin, a former military intelligence officer and author, on his washingtonpost.com blog Early Warning.

Arkin said he obtained the information, which included a list of entries in the CIFA database, from a military source. The database document included references to incidents in several categories that were deemed suspicious.

Dozens of them involved anti-war and anti-recruiting protests by civilians dating to 2004. A Feb. 5, 2005, Talon report described as a "threat" the planned protest against recruiting at New York University by Army Judge Advocate General personnel. Another entry, concerning Feb. 14, 2005, involved a demonstration planned outside the gates of the base at Fort Collins, Colo.

One refers to a July 3, 2004, "surveillance" report of "suspicious activity by U.S. persons...affiliated with radical Moslems" in Big Bend National Park in Texas.

Another category of reports involved missing identification cards and uniforms of military personnel, which pose threats because they can be used to gain illegal access to Pentagon facilities. Other reports dealt with "test of security," such as when someone drives up to the gate of a military facility or takes photographs or shoots videotape.

There have been no congressional hearings on the Defense Department's growing involvement in domestic intelligence collection, but Rep. Jane Harman (Calif.), the ranking Democrat on the intelligence committee, began raising questions about CIFA's programs after recent articles in The Washington Post.

"CIFA needs to be a tightly controlled program," Harman said yesterday, after she and intelligence committee Chairman Peter Hoekstra (R-Mich.) met privately with Cambone on Capitol Hill. She would not discuss the meeting.

SIGNIFICANCE

Release of the TALON/Cornerstone database was particularly important because it followed a series of revelations that the U.S. government had been spying on U.S. citizens.

Only a month before the database was released, the *Washington Post*" had reported the DoD was "considering expanding the power" of CIFA to collect information about U.S. citizens. Also, documents obtained by the American Civil Liberties Union (ACLU) in 2005 had shown that activities of the type that CIFA was using to gather information had recently come under surveillance by the Federal Bureau of Investigation (FBI) using counterterrorism resources. For example, the FBI had begun a classified investigation into the Thomas Merton Center in Philadelphia, a pacifist Christian group. In May 2006, the ACLU released further government documents showing that the FBI had been using counterterrorism resources to investigate School of the Americas Watch, a church-based organization that protests the training of foreign military personnel on U.S. soil by the U.S. military. "From Quakers to monks to priests," said an ACLU representative, "the

FBI is targeting innocent Americans for counterterrorism surveillance."

Links between the FBI and CIFA increase critics' concern over the possible misuse of information gathered by CIFA. In its 2003 report to Congress, the DoD stated that "CIFA is now furnishing a counterintelligence support team to assist the Federal Bureau of Investigation (FBI)-led Foreign Terrorist Tracking Task Force." In 2005, the *Washington Post*" reported that "the Pentagon has pushed legislation on Capitol Hill that would create an intelligence exception to the Privacy Act, allowing the FBI and others to share information gathered about U.S. citizens with the Pentagon, CIA and other intelligence agencies."

Civil rights advocates, libertarians, and some conservatives fear that government is beginning to use its powers to repress political ideas with which it disagrees. Their fears are at least partly grounded in history: A series of hearings held by Senator Frank Church in the 1970s revealed details of the Counter Intelligence Program (COINTELPRO) run by the FBI from 1956 through 1971. COINTELPRO not only spied upon but actively disrupted (through planted evidence, agents provocateurs, and other illegal tactics) noncriminal activities of the Communist and Socialist Workers parties, Black Power groups, the civil rights movement, anti-Vietnam War groups, and others. The Church Committee's final report characterized COINTELPRO as "a sophisticated vigilante operation aimed squarely at preventing the exercise of First Amendment rights of speech and association" (1976).

In March 2006, Acting Deputy Undersecretary of Defense Roger W. Rogalski wrote a letter to Senator Patrick Leahy (D-VT) stating that "The recent [Pentagon] review of the TALON reporting system identified a small number of reports...that dealt with domestic anti-military protests or demonstrations potentially impacting DoD facilities or personnel. While the information was of value to military commanders, it should not have been retained in the Cornerstone database." The report also stated that "all reports concerning protest activities have been purged" from the database.

However, one DoD briefing document obtained by the National Broadcasting Company (NBC), not related to the TALON program, noted that "we [DoD intelligence officers] have noted increased communication and encouragement between protest groups using the Internet," though no "reoccurring instigators at protests [or] vehicle descriptions." Such statements imply that the DoD is monitoring political internet activity, tracking protestors' identities, and taking the license numbers of cars at protests—all actions which violate the DoD's own guidelines, dating to 1982, for collecting information about U.S. citizens.

Defenders of increased surveillance argue that it is needed to prevent terrorist acts. They argue that surveillance of U.S. citizens is accidental or incidental to such surveillance.

FURTHER RESOURCES

Books

Churchill, Ward and Jim Vander Wall. *The Cointelpro Papers: Documents from the FBI's Secret Wars Against Domestic Dissent.* Boston, MA: South End Press, 1990.

Periodicals

Gellman, Barton and Dafna Linzer. "Bush's Disclosures on Domestic Spying Raise Legal Questions." *The Washington Post.* December 18, 2005.

Pincus, Walter. "Pentagon Expanding Its Domestic Surveillance Activity." *The Washington Post.* November 27, 2005.

Web sites

MSNBC.com. "Pentagon Admits Errors in Spying on Protestors." March 10, 2006. <http://www.msnbc.msn.com/id/10965509/site/newsweek/> (accessed May 26, 2006).

Newsweek. "The Other Big Brother: The Pentagon has its own domestic spying program." January 30, 2006. <http://www.msnbc.msn.com/id/10965509/site/newsweek/> (accessed May 26, 2006).

Activists, Opponents Clash at Immigration Rally

Magazine article

By: Anonymous

Date: May 2, 2005

Source: Boston Globe

About the Author: This news article was written by an unidentified staff writer for the Boston Globe, a daily newspaper with a wide circulation in the Boston, Massachusetts and the greater New England region. Founded in 1872 as a private company, in 1973 it became a public company, which in 1993 merged with the New York Times Company.

INTRODUCTION

The immigrants' rights rally held in Boston in May 2005 reflected the increasing prominence in the mid 2000s of the issue of undocumented migration in the attention of both politicians and the general public. A conservative estimate of the number of undocumented migrants living in the United States, based on 2002 census data, is 9.3 million, but given the clandestine nature of undocumented immigration, the true figure may be much higher than this.

There has been undocumented migration to the United States ever since the Johnson-Reed Immigration Act was passed in 1924, which imposed legislation restrictions on immigration to the United States for the first time by setting quotas on numbers of immigrants of different nationalities and races. The Act also authorized the deportation of anyone found to be entering the United States without valid immigration documents and made undocumented migration a criminal offence. With the passing of this Act, the category of undocumented migrants was first created, and the status of many existing immigrants became illegal.

Although the United States has always attracted significant numbers of undocumented migrants, particularly from Mexico, it is only since the late twentieth century that the problem has risen so high on the political agenda. The factors contributing to this have been a worldwide increase in undocumented migration, with a resulting media focus on the topic, as well as publicity about increasing numbers of deaths among Mexican immigrants who perish in the harsh environment of the border region while trying to avoid the U.S. Border Control.

PRIMARY SOURCE

Clashing with opponents in a few heated exchanges at a Copley Square rally, activists called yesterday for comprehensive immigration overhauls that include fair wages, respect in the workplace, and in-state college tuition and driver's licenses for undocumented immigrants.

"There are so many cases of immigrant workers not being paid wages or being paid under minimum wage," said Elena Letona, executive director of Centro Presente, an immigrants' rights organization based in Cambridge that works with the Latino community. "They've been the most exploited workforce."

The rally included appearances by Councilor Felix Arroyo and Mayor Thomas M. Menino, who said that one in four city residents was born outside the United States.

African immigrants sing and dance in Rome, Italy on December 3, 2005 as part of a protest against an Italian law that cracks down on illegal immigration. AP IMAGES.

Gerthy Lahens, fifty-three, who is studying urban planning on a fellowship at MIT, said coming to America has provided her children with greater opportunities than they would have had in Haiti. Her daughter recently graduated from MIT, and her son is at Boston College.

"We will make America the best country it can be," she said. " I came here to give myself and my children another chance in life, and that's the dream of all immigrants. This is our home, and we will stay."

The event also drew about a dozen protesters.

Mark Sookop, forty, a financial planner from Lincoln, held a sign that read, "Illegals steal jobs." Beside him stood his five-year-old son with a sign that read, " I don't want my college spot given away because I'm American," referring to a bill on Beacon Hill that would allow undocumented immigrants to pay in-state tuition at state colleges instead of out-of-state tuition.

"They have a lot of nerve to say they want the same rights as Americans when they are illegals," Sookop said.

The two sides occasionally exchanged views.

Ralph Filicchia, sixty-nine, a Watertown resident who was shopping in the city yesterday, criticized the expansion of immigrant rights as he made his way through the crowd.

Spotting a sign written in Spanish, he asked the woman why she did not write it in English. Later, he engaged in a heated debate with a small group of Asian-Americans about undocumented immigrants gaining access to healthcare benefits.

" They are costing us millions of dollars," Filicchia said after the exchange. "It's a drain on the country."

Michael Liu, fifty-six, an Asian-American researcher who debated Filicchia, said that immigrants contribute more to the economy than they receive in government benefits. "My parents were immigrants," he said. "I feel immigrants have a right to earn a decent living and be free of harassment."

SIGNIFICANCE

On December 16, 2005, the House of Representatives passed the H.R. 4437 Immigration Rights Bill, which proposed introducing stiff penalties for undocumented migrants and anyone assisting them to enter the United States and making undocumented migration a felony. The proposed reforms in this bill also included fencing some 700 miles of the U.S.-Mexican border to try to reduce the number of illegal border crossings.

On May 25, 2006, the Senate passed an alternative bill, S. 2611, entitled the "Comprehensive Immigration Reform Act," based on the reforms proposed by President George W. Bush in January 2004. A major underlying theme of the Bush proposals was the need to respect family values by preventing families being separated by immigration law and by introducing policies that would help prevent the problem of migrants risking their lives to enter the United States. They also acknowledged the need for immigrants to fill jobs that Americans were not prepared to do. Bush proposed a guest worker program under which migrant applicants would be matched with U.S. employers that had unfilled vacancies. If successful in securing a job, the migrant would receive a three-year temporary residence permit, renewable once, after which they could apply for permanent residence through normal procedures. The scheme would be open to undocumented migrants already in the United States as well as those applying from overseas.

These bills sparked a wave of further demonstrations on the part of immigrant support groups across the nation, highlighting the important role that immigrants have played in the American economy, and the poor wages and conditions of employment that many endure. Pro-immigrant groups were fiercely opposed to the House of Representatives bill, which would treat undocumented migrants as felons, and argued that the Senate bill did not go far enough, as it offered no security or long-term hope to immigrants who might be subject to removal when their temporary permits expired.

Anti-immigration groups also came out in protest, arguing that undocumented immigrants steal the jobs of Americans and represent a financial burden on the economy in terms of health provision, education and other services. These groups were strongly opposed to the Senate bill which they viewed as an amnesty under which millions of undocumented immigrants and their children could receive permanent residence in the United States.

Mixed views were also put forward regarding the likely impact of the Senate proposals on actual levels of undocumented immigration to the United States, with some arguing that they would have little or no effect, unless the borders were also secured more effectively. Others put forward the view that the reforms would be effective in reducing undocumented immigration, citing the example of the "bracero" seasonal worker program of the 1940s–1960s which had reportedly reduced the numbers of undocumented migrants from Mexico during its years of operation.

A demonstration and economic shutdown occurred by immigrant support groups nationwide on May 1, 2006, with undocumented immigrants being asked not to go to work or school on that day, in order to highlight to the public the effects of their absence. Although the overall number of demonstrators was smaller than predicted, there were rallies in most major cities of the United States in which immigrants and their supporters protested against the H.R. 4437 reforms. Some immigrant groups, however, came out in opposition to the event, arguing that it would damage the image of immigrants and that it would be more effective to try to fight the legislation through established political mechanisms.

By June 2006, there had been little progress in achieving agreement on U.S. immigration reform. Any immigration bill must receive the support of both houses of Congress to become law, and this is not expected to be achieved in the near future. In the meantime, the issue of undocumented immigration continues to threaten social stability in many cities of the United States, particularly those with large and visible immigrant populations.

FURTHER RESOURCES

Books

Ngai, Mai. *Impossible Subjects: Illegal Aliens and the Making of Modern America*. Princeton University Press, 2004.

Powers, Mary G and Macisco, John J. Jr. and Center for Migration Studies. *The Immigration Experience in the United States: Policy Implications*. Center for Migration Studies, 1994.

Periodicals

Espenshade, Thomas, J. "Unauthorized Immigration to the United States." *Annual Review of Sociology*. 21, 1995.

Web sites

Migration Policy Institute. "US in Focus.". <http://www.migrationinformation.org/USfocus/> (accessed June 1, 2006).

Santa Cruz Journal: A Protest, a Spy Program, and a Campus in an Uproar

Newspaper article

By: Sarah Kershaw

Date: January 14, 2006

Source: The *New York Times*, January 14, 2006.

About the Author: The *The New York Times* is an American daily newspaper that was first published in 1851, with a circulation of over one million copies. Sarah Kershaw is a staff writer for the newspaper.

INTRODUCTION

Military recruiters were long welcomed onto campuses across the United States. During the Vietnam War, military recruiters came under attack for the first time in American history from students and faculty members who objected to American participation in the conflict. In subsequent years, protests against military recruiters have become common although violence has been extremely rare. Many of these protests focus on the Pentagon's insistence on banning openly gay service members.

In 1990, some law schools that belonged to the Association of American Law Schools began prohibiting the military from recruiting on campus. The schools objected to the military's ban on gays. In response, Congress enacted the Solomon Amendment in 1996. Named after U.S. Representative Gerald Solomon, R-NY, it denied federal funds and assistance to schools and students who attended schools that banned on-campus military recruiting. Many of the schools relented and allowed recruiters back on campus.

The Solomon Amendment did not quiet students or professors. While the military has lessened its presence on campus since the anti-military riots of the Vietnam War era, a number of students and faculty want the military removed entirely from campus. Not all of these protesters are anti-military: Some have stated that they are simply anti-discrimination and that they would not oppose a military that welcomed all sexual orientations into its ranks.

PRIMARY SOURCE

SANTA CRUZ, Calif.— The protest was carefully orchestrated, planned for weeks by Students Against War during Friday evening meetings in a small classroom on the University of California campus here.

So when the military recruiters arrived for the job fair, held in an old dining hall last April 5—a now fateful day for a scandalized university—the students had their two-way radios in position, their cyclists checking the traffic as hundreds of demonstrators marched up the hilly roads of this campus on the Central Coast and a dozen moles stationed inside the building, reporting by cellphone to the growing crowd outside.

"Racist, sexist, antigay," the demonstrators recalled shouting. "Hey, recruiters, go away!"

Things got messy. As the building filled, students storming in were blocked from entering. The recruiters left, some finding that the tires of their vehicles had been slashed. The protesters then occupied the recruiters' table and, in what witnesses described as a minor melee, an intern from the campus career center was injured.

Fast forward: The students had left campus for their winter vacation in mid-December when a report by MSNBC said the April protest had appeared on what the network said was a database from a Pentagon surveillance program. The protest was listed as a "credible threat"—to what is not clear to people around here—and was the only campus action among scores of other antimilitary demonstrations to receive the designation.

Over the winter break, Josh Sonnenfeld, 20, a member of Students Against War, or SAW, put out the alert. "Urgent: Pentagon's been spying on SAW, and thousands of other groups," said his e-mail message to the 50 or so students in the group.

Several members spent the rest of their break in a swirl of strategy sessions by telephone and e-mail, and in interviews with the news media. Since classes began on Jan. 5, they have stepped up their effort to figure out whether they are being spied on and if so, why.

Students in the group said they were not entirely surprised to learn that the federal government might be spying on them.

"On the one hand, I was surprised that we made the list because generally we don't get the recognition we deserve," Mr. Sonnenfeld said. "On the other hand, it doesn't surprise me because our own university has been spying on us since our group was founded. This nation has a history of spying on political dissenters."

The April protest, at the sunny campus long known for surfing, mountain biking and leftist political activity, drew about 300 of the university's 13,000 students, organizers said. (Students surmise that, these days, they are out-agitating their famed anti-establishment peers at the University of California, Berkeley, campus, 65 miles northwest of here.)

"This is the war at home," said Jennifer Low, 20, a member of the antiwar group. "So many of us were so discouraged and demoralized by the war, a lot of us said this is the way we can stop it."

A Department of Defense spokesman said that while the Pentagon maintained a database of potential threats to military installations, military personnel and national security, he could not confirm that the information released by MSNBC was from the database. The spokesman, who said he was not authorized to be quoted by name, said he could not answer questions about whether the government was or had been spying on Santa Cruz students.

California lawmakers have demanded an explanation from the government. Representative Sam Farr, a Democrat whose district includes Santa Cruz, was one of several who sent letters to the Bush administration. "This is a joke," Mr. Farr said in an interview. "There is a protest du jour at Santa Cruz."

"Santa Cruz is not a terrorist town," he added. "It's an activist town. It's essentially Berkeley on the coast."

The university's chancellor, Denise D. Denton, said, "We would like to know how this information was gathered and understand better what's going on here."

"Is this something that happens under the guise of the new Patriot Act?" Ms. Denton asked.

As to the students' insistence that the university is monitoring their activities, Ms. Denton said that she had checked with campus police and other university offices and that "there is absolutely no spying going on."

The antiwar group is working closely with the California chapter of the American Civil Liberties Union, which plans to file a public records request with the federal government on the students' behalf, A.C.L.U. officials said.

Meanwhile, members of the campus's College Republicans, strongly critical of the protesters' tactics last April, are rolling their eyes at all the hubbub.

"I think it's worth looking into, but right now I think they are overblowing it," said Chris Rauer, internal vice president of the College Republicans. "I think people are taking their anger over the war out on this."

The Defense Department has issued a statement saying that in October the Pentagon began a review of its database to ensure that the reporting system complied with federal laws and to identify information that might have been improperly entered. All department personnel involved in gathering intelligence were receiving "refresher" training on the laws and policies, the statement said.

With this happening in academia, there has been a good deal of philosophical contemplation and debate over the socioeconomic and political dynamics underlying the uproar.

"I had multiple reactions," said Faye J. Crosby, a professor of social psychology and chairwoman of the Academic Senate. "One reaction was, 'Gosh, I wonder if we're doing something right?'" Professor Crosby said. "Another reaction was it's a waste of taxpayer money. What are we a threat to?"

"The real sadness," she added, "is the breakdown in discourse of the marketplace of ideas."

Correction: January 18, 2006

An article on Saturday about a protest against military recruitment at the University of California, Santa Cruz, that may have resulted in Pentagon surveillance misspelled the given name of the school's chancellor and because of an editing error misstated the enrollment. She is Denice D. Denton, not Denise. Enrollment is 15,000, not 13,000.

SIGNIFICANCE

A March 6, 2006, Supreme Court opinion required schools to allow military recruiters on campus. In *Rumsfeld, Secretary of Defense v. Forum for Academic and Institutional Rights*, the Supreme Court unanimously found that because Congress could require law schools to provide equal access to military recruiters without violating the schools' freedom of speech, it could also require other schools to provide access. The defendant, FAIR, is an association of law schools and faculty whose members oppose discrimination based on sexual orientation. FAIR hoped to restrict military recruiting because they object to the military's "Don't Ask, Don't Tell" policy on gays and lesbians. Most of the member schools do not permit any recruiters who discriminate to come to their campuses. The organization argued that forced inclusion of military recruiters violated its members' freedoms of speech as well as freedom of association by forcing them to break their own nondiscrimination policies.

Although the Court required schools to provide access for military recruiters, it did not restrict what schools could say about recruiters. While the case worked its way through the legal system, many of the FAIR members permitted recruiters to come to campus. However, announcements of military recruiters on campus were accompanied by statements of the schools' policies against discrimination and an explanation of why the military is exempted from that policy. FAIR members expected to continue the notification policies. A number of non-FAIR schools, such as Notre Dame Law School in Indiana, also notify students that the military's recruiting practices are inconsistent with school principles of equal opportunity.

These statements are also expected to remain as long as the military refuses to recruit gays and lesbians.

FURTHER RESOURCES
Books

Dowell, LeiLani, et al. *We Won't Go: The Truth on Military Recruiters and the Draft*. New York: International Action Center, 2006.

Ostrow, Scott A. *Guide to Judging the Military: Air Force, Army, Coast Guard, Marine Corps, Navy*. Lawrenceville, N.J.: ARCO, 2003.

Finding a Place for 9/11 in American History

Newspaper article

By: Joseph J. Ellis

Date: January 28, 2006

Source: Ellis, Joseph J. "Finding a Place for 9/11 in American History." *New York Times* (January 28, 2006): A17.

About the Author: Joseph J. Ellis, a professor of history at Mount Holyoke College in Massachusetts, is an expert on United States history and democracy. He has written numerous books on the subject, including a biography of Thomas Jefferson for which he was awarded the National Book Award, and *Founding Brothers*, which won the Pulitzer Prize.

INTRODUCTION

On September 11, 2001, four commercial airplanes were hijacked and forced into suicide missions. Targeted at major American landmarks, two of them crashed into the towers of the World Trade Center in New York City, one into the Pentagon in Washington, DC, and one went down in rural Pennsylvania when passengers overthrew the hijackers and thwarted their plan to reach the White House. The suddenness and violence of these terrorist attacks left Americans in shock and searching for both answers and justice. In the days that followed the attacks, Americans wanted to know who was behind the hijackings. Public concern about safety and security also was dramatically heightened. Numerous bomb threats were received in major U.S. cities, and there were rumors that the terrorists had other targets beyond New York and Washington, DC. Traces of anthrax began turning up in the mail, raising the specter of biological warfare,

in addition to the danger of more outright attacks. Americans found it difficult to cope with such a major threat on their own soil, something they had not faced as a nation since the attack on Pearl Harbor sixty years earlier. As a result, they were willing to accept and even embrace the drastic measures set into motion by President George W. Bush and the U.S. Department of Defense, actions they might have considered extreme in other circumstances.

PRIMARY SOURCE

AMHERST, Mass. — IN recent weeks, President Bush and his administration have mounted a spirited defense of his Iraq policy, the Patriot Act and, especially, a program to wiretap civilians, often reaching back into American history for precedents to justify these actions. It is clear that the president believes that he is acting to protect the security of the American people. It is equally clear that both his belief and the executive authority he claims to justify its use derive from the terrorist attacks of Sept. 11, 2001.

A myriad of contested questions are obviously at issue here—foreign policy questions about the danger posed by Iraq, constitutional questions about the proper limits on executive authority, even political questions about the president's motives in attacking Iraq. But all of those debates are playing out under the shadow of Sept. 11 and the tremendous changes that it prompted in both foreign and domestic policy.

Whether or not we can regard Sept. 11 as history, I would like to raise two historical questions about the terrorist attacks of that horrific day. My goal is not to offer definitive answers but rather to invite a serious debate about whether Sept. 11 deserves the historical significance it has achieved.

My first question: where does Sept. 11 rank in the grand sweep of American history as a threat to national security? By my calculations it does not make the top tier of the list, which requires the threat to pose a serious challenge to the survival of the American republic.

Here is my version of the top tier: the War for Independence, where defeat meant no United States of America; the War of 1812, when the national capital was burned to the ground; the Civil War, which threatened the survival of the Union; World War II, which represented a totalitarian threat to democracy and capitalism; the cold war, most specifically the Cuban missile crisis of 1962, which made nuclear annihilation a distinct possibility.

Sept. 11 does not rise to that level of threat because, while it places lives and lifestyles at risk, it does not threaten the survival of the American republic, even though the terrorists would like us to believe so.

My second question is this: What does history tell us about our earlier responses to traumatic events?

My list of precedents for the Patriot Act and government wiretapping of American citizens would include the Alien and Sedition Acts in 1798, which allowed the federal government to close newspapers and deport foreigners during the "quasi-war" with France; the denial of habeas corpus during the Civil War, which permitted the pre-emptive arrest of suspected Southern sympathizers; the Red Scare of 1919, which emboldened the attorney general to round up leftist critics in the wake of the Russian Revolution; the internment of Japanese-Americans during World War II, which was justified on the grounds that their ancestry made them potential threats to national security; the McCarthy scare of the early 1950's, which used cold war anxieties to pursue a witch hunt against putative Communists in government, universities and the film industry.

In retrospect, none of these domestic responses to perceived national security threats looks justifiable. Every history textbook I know describes them as lamentable, excessive, even embarrassing. Some very distinguished American presidents, including John Adams, Abraham Lincoln and Franklin Roosevelt, succumbed to quite genuine and widespread popular fears. No historian or biographer has argued that these were their finest hours.

What Patrick Henry once called "the lamp of experience" needs to be brought into the shadowy space in which we have all been living since Sept. 11. My tentative conclusion is that the light it sheds exposes the ghosts and goblins of our traumatized imaginations. It is completely understandable that those who lost loved ones on that date will carry emotional scars for the remainder of their lives. But it defies reason and experience to make Sept. 11 the defining influence on our foreign and domestic policy. History suggests that we have faced greater challenges and triumphed, and that overreaction is a greater danger than complacency.

SIGNIFICANCE

There is no doubt that the events of September 11 were serious and tragic. They also illustrated the nation's vulnerability in a way that no previous terrorist threat had before by showing that America is not immune to devastation on her own soil. But Ellis argues that the September 11 attacks have assumed a greater role in shaping national policy than seems warranted by the facts of the events. The new government policies enacted to increase the safety of U.S. citizens, both at home and in foreign countries, have been broad and all encompassing, out of proportion to the attacks that took place on a single day in a circumscribed section of the country. While the events were devastating and showed an utter disregard for human life, they did not, in and of themselves, threaten the overall security of the United States. Responses to those events have even, in some cases, created new threats to the well being of the nation.

In an effort to protect the country from the perceived terrorist threat, the Bush administration took measures to increase security by changing the ways in which the U.S. interacts with other countries and their citizens. Such areas as transportation, mail and freight systems, and the ability of foreign students to work and learn in the United States were impacted. Subjects previously studied in cooperation by both American and foreign scientists and students were declared classified, ostensibly to prevent the use of this information by terrorists, but, in effect, limiting the participation of foreign experts and slowing research progress in those fields. Visa delays prevented students from many foreign countries from starting academic programs in the U.S. in a timely manner, and more than three-quarters of those delayed students were in biology, physical science, or engineering programs, all subjects the government flagged as of high interest to potential terrorists. In 2003, enrollment of foreign students in U.S. academic programs was down for the first time since the 1970s. By limiting the participation of foreign students and scientists in U.S. science and engineering endeavors, the United States risks losing their superiority in technical fields.

Some personal sacrifices Americans have made following the events of September 11, primarily as a result of actions taken by the Bush administration, involve a gradual relinquishing of many of the civil liberties upon which the nation was founded. Travelers are strictly limited as to what they are allowed to take onto an airplane, and airport security requires a far earlier arrival so that baggage can be searched and X-rayed. The Patriot Act opened Americans' private lives to scrutiny, giving the government the power to access an individual's medical and tax records, to get lists of books purchased or borrowed without giving any reason, and to enter a person's home and search it in secret without notification. Because the Patriot Act was enacted by Congress only weeks after the events of September 11, the nation was still in a state of emergency and was willing to take unprecedented measures in order to safeguard the country and thwart terrorists. In subsequent years, both Congress and the American people have questioned the scope of the act, and whether the actions taken immediately following September 11, 2001,

Terrorist hijackers fly United Airlines Flight 175 into the south tower of the World Trade Center on September 11, 2001. PHOTOGRAPH BY CARMEN TAYLOR. AP/WIDE WORLD PHOTOS.

were appropriate and proportional to the day's overall place in history.

In 2002, the American Civil Liberties Union launched a campaign against the PATRIOT Act called "Keep America Safe and Free" and began filing lawsuits on behalf of persons who felt victimized by the act. Federal judges, in two separate rulings, also declared sections of the act were unconstitutionally vague and imposed unconstitutional prior restraint on free speech.

In March 2006, Congress approved the extension of an ammended version of the PATRIOT Act.

FURTHER RESOURCES

Books

Chomsky, Noam. *9–11*. New York: Open Media, 2001.

Thompson, Paul. *The Terror Timeline: Year by Year, Day by Day, Minute by Minute: A Comprehensive Chronicle of the Road to 9/11—and America's Response*. New York: Regan Books, 2004.

Periodicals

Chaddock, Gail Russell. "House, Senate Diverge on 9/11 Response." *Christian Science Monitor* (September 27, 2004).

Weiss, Rick. "9/11 Response Hurting Science, ACLU Says." *Washington Post*. (June 22, 2005): A19.

Web sites

National Archives and Records Administration. "National Commission on Terrorist Attacks Upon the United States." September 20, 2004. <http://www.9–11commission.gov/> (accessed May 24, 2006).

Nepal Blocks Protest Rally with Arrests and Curfew

Newspaper article

By: Somani Sengupta

Date: January 21, 2006

Source: The *New York Times*, January 21, 2006.

About the Author: *The New York Times* is an American daily newspaper that was first published in 1851, with a circulation of over one million copies. Somani Sengupta is a staff writer for the newspaper.

INTRODUCTION

Nepal is a small, poor country located between China and India. It is known both for the world's highest mountains, including Mount Everest, and for its troubled political history. In 2006, pro-democracy protests ended the absolute reign of Nepal's king.

Nepal gained independence from Great Britain in 1923, but independence did not bring democracy. In 1948, the country produced its first constitution. However, members of the Rana family continued to hold complete control of the government. In 1959, the first free elections were held and a new constitution approved. In 1960, King Mahendra banned all political parties and suspended the Constitution until 1962. In May 1980, an election resulted in the return of one-party rule. A February 1990 protest by 10,000 people turned violent and resulted in a constitution that permitted multiparty rule. Meanwhile, the Maoists, a strongly republican and nationalistic group, aimed to abolish the monarchy and expel all Indian interests from the country. By drawing on ethnic and socio-economic grievances, they gained supporters in every part of Nepal. The war with the Maoists claimed 10,000 Nepali lives by 2001.

On June 1, 2001, Crown Prince Dipendra gunned down the king, queen, and most of the royal family before committing suicide. The new king, Gyanendra,

Nepalese political activists protest the rule of King Gyanendra in Kathmandu, February 19, 2006. DEVENDRA M SINGH/AFP/GETTY IMAGES.

found himself thrust into a role that he had not been trained to perform and he had little support among the people. Many Nepalese suspected him of engineering the royal massacre. At the time of the murders, the parliamentary opposition had been refusing to cooperate with the government for several months and the country was shut down for three days by opposition groups calling for the resignation of the prime minister. Nepal was on the brink of being a failed state. Observers expected that either the new king or the army would take control and crush the young democracy. The 1990 constitution granted the monarch emergency powers that could be exercised in the event of continued internal strife. Accordingly, King Gyanendra unleashed the Royal Nepalese Army against the Maoists. In February 2005, he appointed himself head of the government and suspended parliament.

PRIMARY SOURCE

NEW DELHI, Jan. 20—Flouting international condemnation, Nepal quashed a pro-democracy protest scheduled

for Friday in the capital, Katmandu, with an all-day curfew enforced by soldiers and the police and mass arrests of organizers.

The police said 200 people had been detained for curfew violations, and armored personnel carriers mounted with machine guns were posted on the streets of the capital, Reuters reported from Katmandu. The leaders of the country's major political parties, which had called for the rally, were placed under house arrest, Reuters said.

The government of King Gyanendra announced a ban on public demonstrations earlier this week, on the grounds that Maoist insurgents waging a decade-long war against the state would use it to foment violence. On Thursday, the police rounded up about 100 people, mostly political party workers involved in the preparations, and blocked telephone communications.

A coalition of seven political parties, once stridently opposed to the rebels and now increasingly vocal against the palace, had planned the rally to call for a full restoration of political rights.

The arrests on Thursday prompted critical statements from the United Nations secretary general, Kofi Annan, as well as from the United States, the European Union and India, a powerful neighbor of Nepal. On a visit to New Delhi on Friday, R. Nicholas Burns, under secretary of state for political affairs, criticized the king and the rebels.

"The United States is very concerned by the actions of His Majesty the King and arresting and detaining of members of the political establishment in the last couple of days," Mr. Burns said.

The fresh crackdown comes nearly a year after King Gyanendra took absolute power, suspended civil liberties and arrested hundreds of political leaders, journalists and others opposed to the royal takeover in an effort to crush the insurgency. The king lifted a state of emergency three months later but kept in place many restrictions on press and political freedoms.

The United States, once an important backer, India and Britain suspended military aid after the takeover by Gyanendra on Feb. 1, 2005.

A unilateral cease-fire declared by the Maoists in September expired this month, raising fears of a resumption of guerrilla attacks.

The Associated Press reported that gunmen suspected of being Maoist rebels killed six police officers late Friday in western Nepal.

King Gyanendra has called for municipal elections to be held next month. But the country's main political parties have vowed to boycott them, and the Maoists have threatened to disrupt them.

The home minister, Kamal Thapa, this week invited the political parties to resume talks with the palace and warned them against supporting the rebels.

SIGNIFICANCE

The weeks of street protests that produced bloody clashes with security forces led to international condemnation of the monarch as well as increased internal demands that he relinquish control. King Gyanendra surrendered to pro-democracy protesters by giving up power at the end of April 2006. By June 2006, the king had become a powerless ceremonial monarch. While he lost support, the notion of a monarchy remains popular. Gyanendra is not well-liked but the monarch is regarded as being semi-divine. A February 2006 article by the respected *Nepali Times* found that among 5,000 people polled, seventy-seven percent supported a ceremonial role for the monarch while only ten percent wanted a republic.

Elections to the new Nepali Congress are scheduled for mid-April 2007. The new assembly will draw up a new constitution and review the monarchy's

future. The Maoists have been invited to join the new government. It is not clear if these steps will bring peace to the small Himalayan nation.

FURTHER RESOURCES
Books

Hutt, Michael ed. *Himalyan People's War: Nepal's Maoist Rebellion.* Bloomington: Indiana University Press, 2004.

Thapa, Deepak, and Bandita Sijaputi. *A Kingdom Under Siege: Nepal's Maoist Insurgency, 1996 to 2004.* London: Zed Books, 2004.

Whelpton, John. *A History of Nepal.* London: Cambridge University Press, 2004.

Moslems Protest Danish Cartoons

Photograph

By: Akhtar Soomro

Date: February 3, 2006

Source: © Akhtar Soomro/epa/Corbis.

About the Photographer: Akhtar Soomro is a freelance photographer based in Karachi, Pakistan, who has contributed photographs to the Associated Press, *The New York Times*, and the European Pressphoto Agency.

INTRODUCTION

On September 30, 2005, a newspaper in Denmark, the *Jyllands-Posten*, published a dozen editorial cartoons depicting Muhammad (570–632), the founder of Islam. The editor of the paper said that he did so after having a conversation with a Danish comedian who did not dare to make jokes about the *Qur'an* (the sacred book of Islam) and with an author of children's books who said that prospective illustrators for his book on Muhammad were afraid to work on the subject except anonymously because of the possibility of fundamentalist Moslem retaliation. To establish that the principle of free speech applied even to this sensitive subject, the editor of *Jyllands-Posten* invited several cartoonists to submit editorial cartoons depicting Muhammad. The results ranged from a mild depiction of the prophet leading a donkey to a caricature showing him with a fizzing bomb for a turban. Another image showed him with a black bar across his eyes, flanked by two veiled women. The Moslem religion forbids the visual depiction of Muhammad.

At first there was little reaction. Then, in October, three of the twelve artists received death threats. This was reported in the Danish press, spreading awareness of the controversy. Islamic diplomats complained to the Danish government about the publication of the cartoons. The Danish prime minister, Anders Fogh Rasmussen, stated that the issue was one of freedom of the press and that it would be inappropriate for the government to comment.

A delegation of conservative Danish imams (Moslem religious leaders) traveled to Egypt and Saudi Arabia with copies of the cartoons from *Jyllands-Posten* as well as several more drastic cartoons that had not been printed in the paper. They showed the cartoons to government officials and other religious leaders. A Norwegian magazine published several of the cartoons on January 10, 2006. Libya and Saudi Arabia withdrew their ambassadors from

Denmark. A boycott of Danish goods was begun in some Moslem countries. The Danish Prime Minister and the editor of *Jyllands-Posten* issued apologies for offending Moslem sensibilities.

Other European publications, angered by these apologies and convinced that they represented a failure to defend free speech, printed the cartoons to demonstrate their freedom to do so. The German magazine *Die Welt* (The World) put the image of Muhammad with a bomb for a turban on its cover. Demonstrations occurred in Indonesia, Lebanon, and Syria. On February 4, demonstrators in Syria stormed the Norwegian and Danish embassies in Damascus, the capital of Syria, and set them on fire. No embassy workers were in the buildings at the time.

On February 6, at least four anti-cartoon protestors were killed in Afghanistan. A teenager was killed

PRIMARY SOURCE

Moslems Protest Danish Cartoons: Cartoons in European newspapers depicting the Prophet Mohammad sparked protests by Muslims worldwide. These men rallied in Karachi, Pakistan, on February 3, 2006, voicing their anger with the cartoons and Pakistan's president, despite a government ban on protests. © AKHTAR SOOMRO/EPA/CORBIS.

Pakistani students run away from tear gas fired by police to disperse a demonstration against European cartoons of the Prophet Mohammad, in Islamabad, Pakistan, February 14, 2006. AP IMAGES.

in a demonstration in Somalia, and a crowd attempted to set fire to the Austrian embassy in Teheran, the capital of Iran. Protestors in Kabul, capital of Afghanistan, burned a Danish flag in front of the Danish embassy and chanted "Death to Denmark" and "Death to America." Over the next several weeks, protests continued, often leading to deaths by trampling or other accidents. The cartoonist who had drawn the most offensive images, Kurt Westergaard, went into hiding after a reward was announced for his death. Rioting in Nigeria killed sixteen protestors on February 18.

PRIMARY SOURCE

MOSLEMS PROTEST DANISH CARTOONS
See primary source image.

SIGNIFICANCE

Slowly, the furor faded. By May 2006, protests had become infrequent. However, the anti-cartoon rioting had claimed approximately 140 lives.

The rioting and diplomatic arguments caused by the Danish editorial cartoons of Muhammad arose from deep-seated beliefs held by liberal Europeans, European Moslems, and Moslems living in majority-Moslem countries such as Syria, Afghanistan, and Pakistan. Europeans often saw their freedom of speech as at stake: Moslems saw blasphemy against the most holy figure of their religion. In Western democracies, blasphemy is usually considered protected speech, at least since the mid-twentieth century; although there are occasional protests against art that is perceived as being irreverent, such as Andres Sorrano's controversial photograph *Piss Christ* (1989), which showed a crucifix submerged in urine, there is little doubt about the legality of such expressions. An exception is Denmark, where the Muhammad cartoon crisis began; on March 30,

2006, a group of Danish Muslims began legal proceedings against *Jyllands-Posten* under a Danish law forbidding blasphemy.

Not all critics of the Muhammad cartoons were devout Muslims. Some Westerners who defended the right of *Jyllands-Posten* to publish the cartoons also argued that the general Western response to Muslim rage was inadequate because it ignored the deeper sources of that rage, namely, centuries of colonization by Western imperial powers. Others argued that Western newspapers that were willing to print the Muhammad cartoons consistently refused to print the most graphic images of civilian injuries arising from the Iraq war. Some defenders of the publication of the cartoons argued that Moslem anger at the appearance of the cartoons reflects an inherent intolerance within the Moslem religion.

FURTHER RESOURCES

Books

Mamdani, Mahmood. *Good Muslim, Bad Muslim: America, the Cold War, and the Roots of Terror*. New York: Pantheon, 2004.

Periodicals

Gall, Carlotta. "Protests Over Cartoons of Muhammad Turn Deadly." *The New York Times*. February 6, 2006.

Web sites

NewspaperIndex.com. "UN to Investigate Jyllands-Posten 'Racism.'" December 10, 2005. <http://blog.newspaper index.com/2005/12/10/un-to-investigate-jyllands-posten-racism/> (accessed May 18, 2006).

National Commission on Terrorism. "Countering the Changing Threat of International Terrorism." January 1, 2004.<http://encyclopedia.laborlawtalk.com/Peter_Kropotkin (verified link)> (accessed April 15, 2006).

5 Politics, Policy, and Political Dissent

Introduction to Politics, Policy, and Political Dissent 245

Politics, Policy, and Political Dissent

That a political action ignites a protest reaction is by no means a new phenomenon. Protest reactions to policy, as demonstrated throughout this volume, are an inextricable part of free and modern politics. This chapter begins with the Sugar Act, one of the policies that brewed colonial displeasure with British rule, eventually fueling the American Revolution. What began as political protest led to demands for sovereignty and eventually revolution. While not all political protest takes this extreme trajectory, political protest has been both catalyst and symptom of political transformation.

Political protest is both individual and social; personal and public. Whether a mass movement, a collective political consciousness trying to reform or reshape government and society, or an individual fight for basic political rights, political protest leaves an indelible mark on modern history. New political theories forged in the nineteenth and twentieth centuries fed protest movements. In consistent tension with fading absolutism and grand empires, political dissidents, revolutionaries, radicals and insurgents embraced democracy, anarchy, socialism, and communism.

"A Chartist Appeal to Lay Down Arms" begins this chapter's discussion of political reform through popular protest. The political saga of twentieth century Russia receives considerable attention here, from the protests that crumbled its monarchy to the decades of Soviet rule that in turn quelled political dissent. From the early years of Bolshivism, when communism itself was a radical protest of Western economics, to

the fall of the Berlin Wall, to the protests that swept the region in the last months before the fall of the Soviet Union, it is a story of the inseparability of policy and protest even when political conscience is most restricted. Also featured is Iran, both at the dawn of the Islamic republic to expatriates abstaining from the 2005 elections in protest of Islamist rule.

Two examples of contentious policy that sparked protest both in the halls of government and in the public square are included here to illustrate the inevitable protest reaction to ever-shifting government policies. "Greenpeace Activists Protest the GOP Policy Agenda 'Contract With America'" discusses public opposition to a new wave of conservative policies in the United States in the mid-1990s, while "Britain's Labour Party Debate The Abandonment of Clause IV" presents the debate within parliament over whether to continue pro-nationalization policies or opt for increased privatization of certain industries in Britain.

The symbols of political protest should not escape the reader's notice. Some images of political oppression and protest included here have defined political protest for generations. The shocking reemergence of Nazi symbols—outlawed across much of Europe—in the protests of racist extremist political groups sharply contrasts images of reunited Berliners tearing down the Berlin Wall. During the Tiananmen Square Protests of June 1989, one man symbolized an entire movement. The anonymous protester halted a line of tanks and captured the attention of the world.

For every piece of foreign linen cloth, called Cambrick, imported from Great Britain, three shillings.

For every piece of French lawn imported from Great Britain, three shillings.

And after those rates for any greater or lesser quantity of such goods respectively.

II. And it is hereby further enacted by the authority aforesaid, That from and after the said twenty ninth day of September, one thousand seven hundred and sixty four, there shall also be raised, levied, collected, and paid, unto his Majesty, his heirs and successors, for and upon all coffee and pimento of the growth and produce of any British colony or plantation in America, which shall be there laden on board any British ship or vessel, to be carried out from thence to any other place whatsoever, except Great Britain, the several rates and duties following; that is to say,

III. For every hundred weight avoirdupois of such British coffee, seven shillings.

For every pound weight avoirdupois of such British pimento, one halfpenny.

And after those rates for any greater or lesser quantity of such goods respectively.

IV. And whereas an act was made in the sixth year of the reign of his late majesty King George the Second, intituled, An act for the better securing and encouraging the trade of his Majesty's sugar colonies in America, which was to continue in force for five years, to be computed from the twenty fourth day of June, one thousand seven hundred and thirty three, and to the end of the then next session of parliament, and which, by several subsequent acts made in the eleventh, the nineteenth, the twenty sixth, and twenty ninth, and the thirty first years of the reign of his said late Majesty, was, from time to time, continued; and, by an act made in the first year of the reign of his present Majesty, was further continued until the end of this present session of parliament; and although the said act hath been found in some degree useful, yet it is highly expedient that the same should be altered, enforced, and made more effectual; but, in consideration of the great distance of several of the said colonies and plantations from this kingdom, it will be proper further to continue the said act for a short space, before any alterations and amendments shall take effect, in order that all persons concerned may have due and proper notice thereof; be it therefore enacted by the authority aforesaid, That the said act made in the sixth year of the reign of his late majesty King George the Second, intituled, An act for the better securing and encouraging the trade of his Majesty's sugar colonies in America, shall be, and the same is hereby further continued, until the thirtieth day of September, one thousand seven hundred and sixty four.

V. And it be further enacted by the authority aforesaid, That from the twenty ninth day of September, one thousand seven hundred and sixty four, the said act, subject to such alterations and amendments as are herein after contained, shall be, and the same is hereby made perpetual.

VI. And it be further enacted by the authority aforesaid, That in lieu and instead of the rate and duty imposed by the said act upon molasses and syrups, there shall, from and after the said twenty ninth day of September, one thousand seven hundred and sixty four, be raised, levied, collected, and paid, unto his Majesty, his heirs and successors, for and upon every gallon of molasses or syrups, being the growth, product, or manufacture, of any colony or plantation in America, not under the dominion of his Majesty, his heir or successors, which shall be imported or brought into any colony or plantation in America, which now is, or hereafter may be, under the dominion of his Majesty, his heirs or successors, the sum of three pence.

. . .

XIV. And it is hereby further enacted by the authority aforesaid, That from and after the tenth day of September, one thousand seven hundred and sixty four, upon the exportation of any sort of white callicoes or muslins, except as herein after is mentioned, from this kingdom to any British colony or plantation in America, besides the one half of the rate or duty commonly called The old subsidy, which now remains, and is not drawn back for the same, there also shall not be repaid or drawn back the further sum of four pounds fifteen shillings for every hundred pounds of the true and real value of such goods, according to the gross price at which they were sold at the sale of the united company of merchants trading to the East Indies, being the third part of the net duties granted thereon respectively by two several acts of parliament, the one made in the eleventh and twelfth year of the reign of King William the Third, intituled, An act for the laying further duties upon wrought silks, muslins, and some other commodities of the East Indies, and for enlarging the time for purchasing certain reversionary annuities therein mentioned; and the other made in the third and fourth year of the reign of Queen Anne, intituled, An act for continuing duties upon low wines, and upon coffee, tea, chocolate, spice, and pictures, and upon hawkers, pedlars, and petty chapmen, and upon muslins; and for granting new duties upon several of the said commodities, and also upon callicoes, China-ware, and drugs; any law, custom, or usage to the contrary notwithstanding.

. . .

SIGNIFICANCE

The Sugar Act marked the first time that the British Parliament adopted duties that were frankly designed to raise revenues in the colonies and were not merely intended to regulate trade. The American colonists strongly objected to this legislation. They resented that the Sugar Act regulated the export of lumber and iron from the colonies. The law thereby restricted the ability of the colonies to produce anything but raw materials. They were angry the new duties on wines meant that wines now had to be brought to America by a roundabout and expensive route. Mostly, they objected to the new molasses duties.

In response to the Sugar Act, lawyer James Otis wrote a pamphlet in which he argued that taxation without representation made slaves of the Americans. Americans responded to the Sugar Act by evading it. By 1765, Grenville had made almost no dent in the British national debt. In response, he escalated his revenue program with the Stamp Act, a tax on all paper used for colonial documents. This act affected nearly everyone in the colonies and had nothing to do with trade. It was obviously a revenue act. The colonists reacted with riots and boycotts. Grenville ultimately received little money from the Stamp Act. In 1767, Charles Townsend, the chief British financial minister, proposed the Townshend Acts to raise money. Colonists again responded with boycotts and demonstrations. The stage had been set for the brewing revolution.

FURTHER RESOURCES

Books

Doerflinger, Thomas. *A Vigorous Spirit of Enterprise: Merchants and Economic Development in Revolutionary Philadelphia*. Chapel Hill: University of North Carolina Press, 1986.

Johnson, Allen S. *A Prologue to Revolution: The Political Career of George Grenville*. Lanham, Md.: University Press of America, 1997.

Schlesinger, Arthur. *The Colonial Merchants and the American Revolution*. New York: Atheneum, 1968.

A Chartist Appeal to Lay Down Arms

Letter

By: Peter Bussey

Date: 1838

Source: Bussey, Peter. "A Chartist Appeal to Lay Down Arms" in Dorothy Thompson, ed. *An Address to the Working Man of England*. New York: Garland, 1986.

About the Author: Peter Bussey (d.1869), one of fifty-three delegates to the first Chartist convention in 1839, owned a pub in Bradford, England. He fled political persecution by emigrating to the United States in 1839, but returned home to die near Leeds.

INTRODUCTION

In the early nineteenth century British citizens enjoyed more freedom than any other people in Europe. However, Britain was far from democratic. A constitutional monarchy with many limits on the powers of king and state, the country was nevertheless dominated by the aristocracy, who controlled the House of Lords as members and the House of Commons as the financiers or sponsors of the elected representatives. The vast majority of people could not vote. New industrial towns were not allowed to elect representatives to Parliament and, often lacking a town organization, could not govern themselves effectively.

Parliament enacted some reforms, repealing the law that banned Catholics and non-Anglican Protestants from government positions and universities. Increasingly, however, reform centered on extending suffrage and enfranchising the new industrial towns. In 1832 Commons passed the Reform Bill, which extended the ballot to 200,000 men—almost doubling the voting rolls. When the House of Lords refused to pass the bill, however, riots and strikes erupted in many cites. King William IV, fearing revolution, pressured the Lords into passing the legislation that gave the middle class the vote and made the House of Commons more representative.

But the people wanted more. The Chartist movement, named after the People's Charter drafted by William Lovett in 1838, sought votes for all men; equal electoral districts; abolition of the requirement that Members of Parliament be property owners; payment for service in Parliament; annual general elections; and the secret ballot. Ironically, these eventually became law after the movement had collapsed.

▮ PRIMARY SOURCE

An Address Fellow Countrymen, Innumerable pages have teemed from the press of this kingdom, against the brutalizing punishment of flogging in the British army, but I have not hitherto seen any production endeavouring to dissuade you from enlisting yourselves as soldiers into such army. This I hold to be a sufficient reason for my addressing you

An illustration of the Chartist riot at Newport, Isle of Wight, Britain, in 1832. © BETTMANN/CORBIS.

on this most important subject, especially the young men of this country, to whom I shall more particularly address myself in these few pages. You, young men, are the strength of the nation, morally and physically the whole of the wealth, power, and happiness of the people are in your hands, and it entirely depends on the manner in which that power is used, whether the people of this country live in the enjoyment of happiness or misery, of freedom or slavery. You are the producers of the nation's wealth, and have, by your skill and industry, raised her pre-eminently above that of any other kingdom in the world—you are also expected to defend her against the aggressions of any other power. Ought not you in return to be invested with the right of citizenship, which has hitherto been denied you? Nothing, in my opinion, could be more fair or reasonable; and let me tell you that the expectations of your fathers rest on you. It is in consequence of your exertions that those necessary alterations in the management of the national affairs of this country may be placed on just and equitable grounds, on which those great and immutable

principles of Truth and Justice may serve as the polar star of all our actions; and the establishment of peace and goodwill amongst mankind, supersede that of war and discord; that universal harmony may prevail through every portion of the earth, and mankind meet as friends and has brothers, those of every clime and colour; then will the fell monster, Selfishness, receive its death blow, and sink into that oblivion it so justly merits, and mankind be free and happy. This can never be the case so long as you continue the wretched dupes of wealth and power, rushing on devastation, misery, and death, to decide their quarrels.

In the first place, I would have you to consider, previous to your enlistment into a standing army, that a soldier is a man hired to kill a fighting man; a butcher, an hired assassin, a legalized murderer, a destroyer of the peace, property, and lives of his fellow-man; not in the dark and gloomy hour of midnight, when nature hath drawn her sable curtain over the dreadful scene of carnage and blood, but in the broad glare of day, when the bright luminary which invigorates the earth is shining in all its enlivening splendour, reflecting its million rays from the upraised instruments of death, manufactured for the express purpose of the better facilitating of human destruction. If we examine into the causes of these inhuman massacres, we shall find they have their origin in the pride, arrogance, and selfishness of a few individuals, who cover their infernal designs, by the following words:—National faith, national honour, and national safety, crowned with glorious war—with which their minions amuse and delude the people; when, at the same time, we have no more business with such war, then those flying men who are said to inhabit the moon. In order to prove this, we will examine into the origin of a few of those wars, wherein we have been particularly active. First, then, we will take the American war, previous to which we find one quarter of the known world subjected to the British Government. Was this because the native Americans found themselves insufficient to the task of governing, and in consequence of which had sent an invitation to this country for governors? No such thing. The ruling few in England, always ready to take that which they have no right to possess, slipping their fingers into everybody's pocket who comes within their reach, in this, as in many other cases, seized upon the land, in the name of (that aristocratic plaything) the King, and christened it part of the British colonies. To this the people were obliged to submit, and things went on pretty smoothly for some time, until the people of America began to imagine that they ought to have a word in the making of those laws by which they had to be governed. This could not be allowed. The poor Americans (in the eyes of aristocrats) were not born to govern the same as we breed them in this country; and to convince them of our superiority, we sent them a quantity of tea, with a tax upon it. This treatment justly aroused the indignation of the Yankees; a riot took place; the taxed tea was thrown overboard; the military interfered and endeavoured to put down the discontents, the ultimate result of which was, the people of America set up governors on their own account, and they have proved themselves worthy of the task. This is raised the spleen of hereditary wisdom, that they determined to chastise them for their insolence. This chastisement, leaving the shedding of the blood of tens of thousands of human beings out of the question, ended in the Independence of thirteen of the United States of America, and entailed a debt on the people of this country, amounting to one hundred and thirty-nine million pounds and upwards. And will any man, not a courtier, have the brazen audacity to assert that this war was necessary for the peace of welfare of England? I maintain that it was not only necessary, but in the highest degree mischievous, dreadful, and horrible, and will stand recorded as an eternal and infamous disgrace on the names of the men at that day in power. . . .

Every person who enlists into a standing army, becomes a part and parcel of that system by which the land that gave him birth is enslaved. A soldier not only engages to shoot at and destroy the inhabitants of other countries, but also those of his own, if commanded to do so by his drivers. He is, as I before stated, a machine which they can direct at pleasure; in proof of which I would ask— would it have been possible for the corruptions of Government to have been carried on in this kingdom to the extent they have, had not a standing army existed? Would Ireland, where thousands of poor creatures have died of starvation, and where thousands more have died by the bullet and the bayonet, have suffered, in such degree, if a standing army had never existed? Would the starvation Corn Laws have been disgracing the English Statute Book, if a standing army had never existed? Would that thing, called the Debt, in consequence of which the labour of millions of unborn ages are mortgaged, have been hung like a millstone round our necks, if a standing army had never existed? Would that poverty-punishing, humanity-disgracing, age-murdering Poor-law Amendment Act ever have been enforced, if a standing army had never existed? In a word, would any of the multifarious acts which disgrace the Statute Book of the British Legislature and oppress the people, ever have been enacted, if a standing army had never existed? I answer—No. The parties well know that the existence and continuance of their system of misrule, depend on the strength and debasement of those who compose the army; but to come more particularly to the ground of objection:—Suppose that their fathers thought proper to change the constitution of the country, which they have a just right to do, when injured by the then existing state of things. The interested few immediately take the alarm,

and assemble the army to keep down the people, whom they designate Rebels, which term, however, is decidedly wrong, as applied in this instance. The majority of a nation never can be rebels; their will ought always to be the acknowledged law of the country: the law based on any other principle can never be just; such being the case, it is only the few who are rebels. However, this few have the command of the army. Then see them assembled, and hear the drivers command the sons to slay their fathers, which, if they refuse to do, according to the existing laws, they must themselves suffer as traitors. Yes, the people must be kept down by force of arms, in that state of abject servitude the few may think proper, or the sons of Britain must kill their sires, mothers, brothers, sisters, or friends, who may be struggling for freedom; perhaps many would refuse thus to murder their most endearing friends. Others have become so far brutalized by the system, that they would rush upon the destruction of the inhabitants of their own country, as they would upon strangers. I have heard a soldier declare, that if ordered by his commanding officer to shoot his own father or mother, he would immediately do it, considering it to be his duty. And have we not known several instances which have occurred in this kingdom, where the military, when called upon, have deliberately fired upon the people? Witness the memorable 16th of August, at Manchester, where a murderous attack was made upon the multitude, peaceably assembled to petition the Parliament for a redress of their grievances. Thus the people are in continual fear of being cut, and hacked, and hewed, by these maddened and infuriated creatures. . . .

Thus you see, to a certain extent, the destruction of life and property, caused by the paltry differences of Kings and Aristocrats. Sometimes the difference was over a small tract of land, to which neither party had any right; at other times, as to what form of Government should exist in a nation, or who should be the Governor, neither of which cases concerned the people of England, any farther than the thirst for conquest and dominion, on the part of the Aristocracy, to enable them to pauperize their progeny on the people, by which they might wallow in the luxuriant productions of the earth, and look down with haughty scorn on the pale, emaciated, and ragged child of want, whose every sinew has been strained to produce the enjoyments in which he revels, and but for whose exertions he must have perished out of want.

Then, my friends, let not the tinseled gew-gaws of a corrupt and profligate government induce you to become the oppressors of your country, by enlisting into a standing army. You may depend upon it that many who have already swallowed the gilded bait, would give every thing they possess, could they throw off the gaudy trappings of the soldier, and exchange them for the clothing of the civilian. Yes, numbers know the value of liberty when it is too late.

They have become thinking men, without the least shadow of an opportunity to change their situation, and are thus rendered the most miserable of human beings. It is all very well to see the recruiting parties strut, and swell, and swagger, through your streets, like some petty despot; but if you saw him on duty, under the daily inspection of his officers you would find the jackdaw stript of his borrowed plume, and trembling under the eagle-eyed glance of an officer....

It might be asked—Would I disband the standing army, and leave the kingdom in a weak, unprotected, and defenseless state?

I answer—NO. Under a rational system of political equality, and internal power of defence would be organized, which would prove a thousand times more formidable to any power, who might be led to commit aggressions upon us, and less objectionable to the community. But more on this subject in a subsequent letter, which I intend to submit for your consideration. In the mean time, I desire of you to give this a fair and candid perusal, trusting that by so doing you will be convinced of the folly and madness of enlisting yourselves into the standing army of the Aristocracy of your country, so that in future should they, by their courtly intrigues, engender and foment quarrels with the aristocrats of other nations, let them decide their own differences in person, and at their own expense.

I remain,

My Friends,

Yours in the Cause of Democracy,

Peter Bussey

SIGNIFICANCE

By 1839 the Chartists had obtained over a million signatures in support of the People's Charter, and the document was presented to the House of Commons that year. When it was rejected by a vote of 235 to 46, many of the movement's leaders, who threatened to call a general strike, were arrested and jailed. When supporters marched on the prison at Newport, Monmouthshire, demanding their release, troops opened fire, killing twenty-four and wounding forty others. A second petition with three million signatures was rejected by Parliament in 1842, and a third in 1848, bringing an end to the movement. The working-class Chartist leadership turned instead to trade unionism, which held the power to bring immediate benefits to workers.

The People's Charter remained the democratic reform program for the rest of the nineteenth century. All of the Chartists' demands, except annual elections

for members of Parliament, were eventually realized. When much of the rest of Europe burst into revolution in 1848, Britain remained quiet in part because British politicians had made timely enough reforms—although not enough to satisfy the working class completely. Despite the Chartists' defeat, their demands laid the foundation for British parliamentary practices, which came to be the model of liberal, progressive, and stable politics.

FURTHER RESOURCES
Books

Jones, David J.V. *Chartism and the Chartists*. London: Allen Lane, 1975.

Saville, John. *1848: The British State and the Chartist Movement*. New York: Cambridge University Press, 1987.

Thompson, Dorothy. *The Chartists: Popular Politics in the Industrial Revolution*. London: Temple Smith, 1984.

Haymarket Riots

Advertisement

By: Anonymous

Date: May 4, 1886

Source: © Bettmann/Corbis.

About the Photographer: This photograph is part of the collection of the Corbis Corporation, headquartered in Seattle, with a worldwide archive of over seventy million images.

INTRODUCTION

In the late nineteenth century, increasing numbers of confrontations between large employers and labor occurred. They were sparked by the growing power of large corporations and monopolies, the loosening of government regulation on corporations by a number of U.S. Supreme Court decisions, and a large influx of immigrant laborers from Europe, some having Socialist political ideas. Various militant unions agitated for improvements in working conditions, including the eight-hour day. Up to this time, working days of ten or twelve hours or even more were common. The eight-hour day was considered by many intellectuals, economists, and capitalists to be a Utopian, absurd demand that would ruin industry. Nevertheless, by 1886, the movement for an eight-hour day had become powerful.

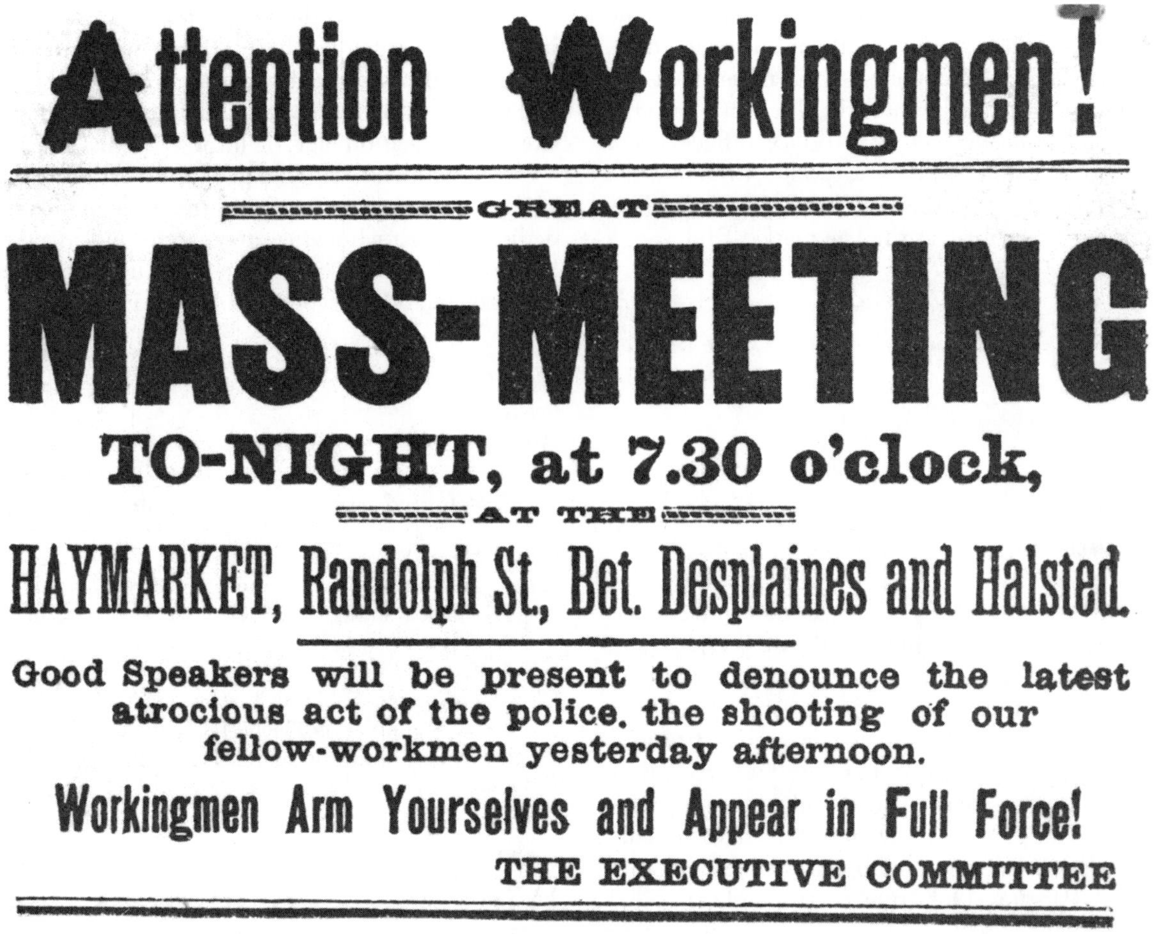

Attention Workingmen!

GREAT
MASS-MEETING
TO-NIGHT, at 7.30 o'clock,
AT THE
HAYMARKET, Randolph St., Bet. Desplaines and Halsted.

Good Speakers will be present to denounce the latest atrocious act of the police, the shooting of our fellow-workmen yesterday afternoon.

Workingmen Arm Yourselves and Appear in Full Force!
THE EXECUTIVE COMMITTEE

PRIMARY SOURCE

Haymarket Riots: A poster calling for striking workers to attend a rally at Haymarket Square in Chicago, on May 4, 1886. The meeting ended in a violent clash between strikers and police that left a dozen dead and over 200 injured. © BETTMANN/CORBIS.

The American Federation of Labor, a collaboration of labor unions, called for a nationwide strike on May 1, 1886, to be observed wherever the eight-hour day was denied by employers. Three hundred and fifty thousand workers took part in the strike, including 40,000 in Chicago. One of the leading labor organizations in the city was the Central Labor Union, a collaboration of twenty-two Chicago unions; two of the leaders of the Central Labor Union were August Spies (1855–1887) and Albert Parsons (1848–1887). Historian Howard Zinn has noted that the *Chicago Mail* newspaper said of these two men on May 1, 1886, "Keep them in view. Hold them personally responsible for any trouble that occurs. Make an example of them if trouble occurs."

On May 3, fighting between strikers and temporary workers (non-union replacement workers or strikebreakers, known derogatively as scabs) took place in front of the McCormick Harvesting Machine Co. Police protected the strikebreakers attempting to enter the factory. When fighting erupted between strikers and strikebreakers, the police beat strikers and fired into the crowd, injuring several strikers and killing one. The flier shown here was part of the outraged response to this killing. It called for a mass meeting at Haymarket Square on the next day, the evening of May 4.

The gathering was smaller than expected, due to rain and cold; only about 1,500–2,000 people attended. Speakers addressed the crowd from the back of a wagon. A contingent of 180 police arrived when the meeting was almost over and only a few hundred protestors were left. Against the mayor's orders, the police approached the wagon platform and ordered the meeting to disperse. Someone—it has never been discovered who—threw a homemade pipe bomb into the midst of the police. Over sixty police officers were wounded and eight died. The police fired on the crowd, killing four workers and injuring 200. This incident became known as the Haymarket Riot.

PRIMARY SOURCE

HAYMARKET RIOTS

See primary source image.

SIGNIFICANCE

The police, who had no suspects for the actual bomb-thrower, essentially attacked the entire labor movement in Chicago, shutting down Socialist and labor-oriented presses, seizing records, and arresting eight leaders of the anarchist movement. (Anarchists are persons who advocate a society lacking institutions that use force, such as armies and police forces; they have often been associated in popular imagery with bomb-throwing, but very few anarchists have actually advocated terrorism.) Among the arrested leaders were Spies and Parsons. Only one of the eight arrested leaders, a man named Fielden, had been present in Haymarket Square when the bombing occurred, and Fielden had been speaking from the wagon at the time the bomb exploded. Nevertheless, all eight were tried for murder on the grounds that their "inflammatory speeches and publications" (in the words of the state court that tried the case) had incited the bomb-throwing.

The *Chicago Mail*'s pre-Haymarket call to "Make an example of them if trouble occurs" was fully heeded: all eight leaders were found guilty of the crime. Seven were sentenced to death and one to fifteen years in prison. The sentence was upheld by the Illinois Supreme Court, and the U.S. Supreme Court declined to hear the case, saying it did not have jurisdiction. In November 1888, four men—including Spies and Parsons—were hanged; one committed suicide in prison by lighting a dynamite stick in his mouth.

Radical and labor movements were ignited by sympathy for the cause of the Haymarket martyrs, as they came to be known. Sixty thousand people signed a petition asking the new governor of Illinois, John Altgeld, to pardon the three surviving Haymarket prisoners. Altgeld re-examined the evidence and pardoned the three men.

A monument to the Haymarket Riot was erected in 2004. It was paid for by $300,000 in state funds and was greeted with mixed reviews. Although city police and organized labor leaders shook hands at the statue site on dedication day, a local anarchist protested, "Those men who were hanged are being presented as social democrats or liberal reformers, when in fact they dedicated their whole lives to anarchy and social revolution. If they were here today, they'd be denouncing this project and everyone involved in it."

FURTHER RESOURCES
Books
Green, James R. *Death in the Haymarket: A Story of Chicago, the First Labor Movement, and the Bombing that Divided Gilded Age America*. New York: Pantheon, 2006.

Periodicals
Kinzer, Stephen. "In Chicago, An Ambiguous Memorial to the Haymarket Attack." *New York Times* (September 15, 2004).

Web sites
Chicago Public Library. "1886: The Haymarket Riot." <http://www.chipublib.org/004chicago/timeline/haymarket.html> (accessed May 22, 2006).

Winston Churchill on Liberalism and Socialism

Speech

By: Winston Churchill

Date: May 4, 1908

Source: Churchill, Winston. "Liberalism and Socialism." May 4, 1908.

About the Author: Winston Churchill (1874–1965) was a member of Parliament in Britain for more than fifty years and, following his time as prime minister during World War II, came to be widely recognized as among the greatest Britons of all time. The son of a former chancellor of the exchequer, Churchill first found fame as a journalist and would later win the Nobel Prize for Literature for his writings.

INTRODUCTION

Winston Churchill was born at Blenheim Palace, Oxfordshire, in November 1874. The son of a Conservative member of Parliament (MP) and later chancellor of the exchequer, Sir Randolph Churchill, and an American socialite, Lady Jennie

Churchill, he was a failure at school and joined the armed forces without attending university. He eventually found success in his early twenties as a war reporter for the *Daily Graphic*, *Daily Telegraph*, and *Morning Star*. Among his early assignments, he covered the Cuban revolt and the British campaign in the Sudan, but found fame for his dispatches during the Anglo-Boer War (1899–1902) in which he was captured and held in a prisoner of war camp, from which he eventually escaped. His escapades and family heritage helped make him among the most famous journalists of his day.

Churchill had tried to follow in his father's political footsteps as early as 1899, when he stood unsuccessfully as a Conservative parliamentary candidate in a by-election [the term given to a mid-term election caused by the death or resignation of a sitting MP] at Oldham, near Manchester. On his return from South Africa in the fall of 1900 he again stood as Conservative candidate in the general election, this time winning a parliamentary seat.

The young Churchill was a charismatic and maverick MP. His fame and huge popularity brought him a prominence not normally associated with a backbench MP, although many of his colleagues in the Conservative Party regarded him a troublemaker. Churchill's opposition to his own party's plans for military spending and trade tariffs brought him into direct opposition with the Conservative leadership and by 1904 he had effectively been cast out of the party. That summer he crossed the floor [the phrase given to MPs switching political allegiance] and became a Liberal MP.

When the Liberals took office in February 1906, Churchill held a variety of ministerial roles within the government. In 1908, he was elevated to the cabinet as president of the Board of Trade. In this role Churchill was closely allied to the maverick chancellor of the exchequer, David Lloyd George (1863–1945), who was in the process of designing the broadest social policy reforms in British history. These reform measures became the basis of British social policy and exist to this day. They included old age pensions, as well as unemployment and sickness benefits. They were to be paid for by increased taxation, particularly of the landed aristocracy who were to be subject to land and inheritance taxes.

The Liberal social reforms attracted a mixture of delight and derision. Liberals saw it as an election winner and a way of checking the progress of the Labour Party, a socialist political party which had begun contesting elections only a few years earlier. Those who benefited from the implementation of the

Former prime minister and leader of the Conservative party, Winston Churchill, speaking at Woodstock, England, on August 4, 1947. He is offering to support Britain's Labour government in securing new loans provided that Britons "labor long and hard." AP IMAGES.

plans were invariably delighted: old people, sometimes lifted out of poverty by the provision of a pension, even referred to their new allowance as the "Lloyd George."

However, in taxing the rich, the Liberals were portrayed as attacking the very fabric of British society. Worse still, they were tainted by accusations of socialism, which at the time was viewed by some as a near-revolutionary political creed, which threatened not just the old order of the monarchy and aristocracy, but the existence of the British Empire. The main plank of the Liberal reforms, the 1908 budget, was blocked by Parliament's unelected upper house, the House of Lords. This house consisted primarily of politically conservative aristocrats who foresaw the threat to their fortunes posed by the Liberal reforms. The legislation passed between the House of Lords and the House of Commons, and the impasse precipitated a constitutional crisis.

At the same time, prominent Liberal MPs such as Lloyd George, Prime Minister Herbert Asquith, and Churchill assiduously waged a press and public speaking campaign to allay voter's concerns and sell the benefits of their reform program.

■ PRIMARY SOURCE

Liberalism is not Socialism, and never will be. There is a great gulf fixed. It is not only a gulf of method, it is a gulf of principle. There are many steps we shall take which our Socialist opponents or friends, whichever they like to call themselves, will have to take with us; but there are immense differences of principle and of political philosophy between the views we put forward and the views they put forward.

LIBERALISM AND SOCIALISM—A CONTRAST.

Liberalism has its own history and its own tradition. Socialism has its formulas and its own aims. Socialism seeks to pull down wealth; Liberalism seeks to raise up poverty. Socialism would destroy private property; Liberalism would preserve private interests in the only way in which they can be safely and justly preserved, namely, by reconciling them with public right. Socialism would kill enterprise; Liberalism would rescue enterprise from the trammels of privilege and preference. Socialism assails the pre-eminence of the individual; Liberalism seeks, and shall seek more in the future, to build up a minimum standard for the mass. Socialism exalts the rule; Liberalism exalts the man. Socialism attacks capital; Liberalism attacks monopoly.

These are the great distinctions which I draw, and which, I think you will agree, I am right in drawing at this election between our respective philosophies and our ideas. Don't think that Liberalism is a faith that is played out, that it is a philosophy to which there is no expanding future. As long as the world rolls round, Liberalism will have its part to play—grand, beneficent, and ameliorating—in the relation of men and States.

SOCIALIST PREACHING AND SOCIALIST PRACTICE.

Ah gentlemen, I don't want to embark on bitter or harsh controversy, but I think the exalted ideal of the Socialists—a universal brotherhood, owning all things in common–is not always supported by the evidence of their practice. They put before us a creed of universal self-sacrifice. They preach it in the language of spite and envy, of hatred and all uncharitableness. They tell us that we should dwell together in unity and comradeship. They are themselves split into twenty obscure factions, who hate and abuse each other even more than they hate and abuse us.

LEAVING OUT HUMAN NATURE.

They wish to reconstruct the world. They begin by leaving out human nature. 'Equality of reward, irrespective of service rendered'—is not this their maxim? It is expressed in other ways. You know the phrase, 'From each according to his ability, to each according to his need.' How nice that sounds. Let me put it another way. 'You shall work according to your fancy; you shall be paid according to your appetite.' Although I have tried my very best to understand these propositions, I have never been able to imagine the mechanical heart in the Socialist world which is to replace the ordinary human heart that palpitates in our breasts. What motive is to induce men, not for a day, or an hour, or a year, but for all their lives, to make a supreme sacrifice of their individuality? What motive is to induce Scotsmen, who spread all over the world and win their way by various paths to eminence and power in every land and climate, to make the great and supreme sacrifice of their individuality? I have heard of loyalty to a Sovereign. We have heard of love of country. Ah, but it is to be a great cosmopolitan republic. We have heard of love of family and wives and children. These are the mere weaknesses of the bad era in which we live. We have heard of faith in a world beyond this when all its transitory pleasures and perils shall have passed away, a hope that carries serene consolation to the heart of men. Ah, but they deny its existence.

NEVER SO GRIM A JOKE.

And what then are we to make this sacrifice for? It is for the sake of society. And what is society? I will tell you what society is. Translated into concrete terms, Socialistic 'society' is a set of disagreeable individuals who obtained a majority for the caucus at some recent election, and whose officials in consequence would look on humanity through innumerable grills and pigeon-holes and across innumerable counters, and say to them 'Tickets, please.' Truly this grey old world has never seen so grim a joke.

COLLECTIVISM AND INDIVIDUALISM.

Now, ladies and gentlemen, no man can be either a collectivist or an individualist. He must be both; everybody must be both a collectivist and an individualist. For certain of our affairs we must have our arrangements in common. Others we must have sacredly individual and to ourselves. We have many good things in common. You have the army, the navy, the police, the fire brigade, the civil service in common. But we don't eat in common; we eat individually. And we don't ask the ladies to marry us in common. And you will still find the truth lies in these matters, as it always lies in difficult matters, midway between extreme formulas. It is in the nice adjustment of the respective ideas of collectivism and individualism that the problem of the world and the solution of that problem lie in the years to come.

ROOM FOR MORE COLLECTIVISM.

But I have no hesitation in saying that I am on the side of those who think that a greater collective element should be introduced into the State and municipalities. I should like to see the State undertaking new functions, particularly stepping forward into those spheres of activity which are governed by an element of monopoly. Your tramways and so on; your great public works, which are of a monopolistic and privileged character—there I see a wide field for State enterprise to enter upon. But when we are told to exalt and admire a philosophy which destroys individualism and seeks to replace it by collectivism, I say that is a monstrous and imbecile conception which can find no real acceptance in the minds and hearts—and the hearts are as trustworthy as the minds—in the hearts of sensible people....

THE DESTINY OF LIBERALISM.

Liberalism will not die. Liberalism is a quickening spirit—it is immortal. It will live on through all the days, be they good days or be they evil days. No, I believe it will even burn stronger and brighter and more helpful in evil days than in good—just like your harbour lights which shine out across the waters, and which on a calm night gleam with soft refulgence, but through the storm flash a message of life to those who toil on the rough waters.

SIGNIFICANCE

The constitutional crisis caused by the Liberal reform budget would bubble on until 1911 at which point King George V agreed to create as many Liberal peers as were needed to overcome the Conservative opposition in the House of Lords. Faced with this prospect, the Lords backed down and the Liberal social reform program was able to continue. Limited reform of the House of Lords would also take away some of its earlier powers.

By this time, however, the Liberal majority in the House of Commons had been substantially weakened. Although this only slightly impeded their social reformism, it marked the onset of a brief period when Irish political parties held the balance in the House of Commons. This would have a profound effect on the politics of Ireland. Reliant on Irish Nationalist support to form a government after the December 1910 General Election, the Liberals promised home rule. After the Easter Rising of 1916 and the War of

Independence (1919–21) this manifested as outright independence, although shorn of the six northern counties that remained under British rule.

Churchill became home secretary in 1910 and First Lord of the Admiralty a year later. He held this position until World War I, but was forced to resign after overseeing the disastrous Gallipoli Campaign in the Dardanelles. This proved so catastrophic that it almost wrecked Churchill's career and the specter of it still hung over him even when he later achieved far greater glories. A spell fighting in the trenches helped restore some of his reputation, and Churchill returned to government in July 1917 as Minister of Munitions, later serving as secretary of state for the Colonies.

The Liberals, however, were a declining political force, gripped by infighting and splits. Churchill lost his parliamentary seat at the 1922 general election and failed to win back a seat at the following year's general election. Slowly, however, he was edging back towards the Conservative Party. He was elected Constitutionalist MP for Epping in 1924, though with Conservative backing, and was formally welcomed back into the party ranks a year later. "Anyone can rat," he would muse, "But it takes a certain ingenuity to re-rat." [One of the meanings of to "rat" is to switch allegiance.]

Churchill served as Chancellor of the Exchequer in Stanley Baldwin's Conservative government (1924–1929), but his earlier "ratting", high profile political failures (Gallipoli; Britain's fateful return to the Gold Standard; his largely inglorious reign as chancellor), and differences over fundamental issues of policy, such as free trade, left him marginalized within his party and widely discredited in the public's eyes. He spent much of the 1930s consumed with depression and fighting a lonely battle speaking out against Nazi Germany and appeasement. Although he would go on to achieve political immortality with his extraordinary conduct as prime minister during World War II, had that war never happened Churchill would probably have faded from the political scene, forgotten and discredited.

Churchill's political infidelities, his changing of parties, and his greatness as a wartime leader (when party politics were rendered largely irrelevant) have tended to blur his political viewpoints. In essence he was a traditional Conservative—a backer of imperialism, *l'aissez faire* economics, and limited social reform—but was an MP at a time when the Conservative Party was taking a different course.

If anything, what consistently marked Churchill's politics over time was a vehement anti-Socialist stance that occasionally bordered on hysteria. At various times in his career he used force to break up strikes; said that the miners of the 1926 General Strike should be shot with machine guns; sought to deploy the British army to defeat the Bolsheviks after the Russian Revolution; praised Benito Mussolini for defeating Italian Communists; and was contemptuous of Labour Party MPs, even those, such as Clement Atlee, who would participate in his wartime government.

FURTHER RESOURCES
Books

Cook, Christopher. *A Short History of the Liberal Party 1900–2001*. Basingstoke: Palgrave Macmillan, 2002.

Dangerfield, George. *The Strange Death of Liberal England*. London: Paladin, 1983.

Jenkins, Roy. *Churchill*. London: Macmillan, 2001.

Lloyd-George, Robert. *David and Winston*. London: John Murray, 2005.

One Aspect of Bolshevist Liberty

Magazine article

By: Ludovic Naudeau

Date: 1917

Source: Naudeau, Ludovic. "One Aspect of Bolshevist Liberty." *Current History*. New York: New York Times, 1918.

About the Author: Ludovic Naudeau was a correspondent for the *Paris Temps* based in Petrograd (St. Petersburg), Russia, when he wrote this article in 1917.

INTRODUCTION

At the beginning of the twentieth century Russia's feudal agricultural economy struggled to provide food for its rapidly increasing population and to support a growing number of industrial cities. The country's involvement in the First World War (1914–1918) only exacerbated these problems. Her industrial infrastructure could not equip the army for modern warfare, and she suffered major defeats and heavy losses as a result. At home, the economy collapsed from the pressure, and severe food shortages and riots became commonplace.

From 1916 onward, public demonstrations and strikes protesting the Tsar's refusal to withdraw from the war increased steadily, culminating in a series of violent demonstrations in February 1917. On

A Russian special police officer stands by the portrait of Bolshevik leader Vladimir Lenin in the town of Gudemes in Chechnya, January 19, 2000. © REUTERS/CORBIS.

returning from visiting the troops at the front, Nicholas II heeded his ministers's advice to abdicate.

Russia's legislative body, the Duma, then established a provisional government to replace the tsar and restore public order. Headed by Alexander Kerensky, a socialist member of the Duma, the new government consisted of both liberals and socialists. The new administration, however, continued to fight the war instead of tackling Russia's domestic problems; this undercut its authority, and chaos erupted. Resistance to all forms of government became common over the following months, in both the countryside and the cities.

Between February and October there was no clear political leadership in Russia, although several groups vied for power. When the First All Russian Congress of Soviets was held in June, the Socialist Revolutionaries, the largest single bloc, outnumbered the Bolsheviks—then a radical Marxist splinter group. Although small, the Bolsheviks gained support over the following months as people became increasingly dissatisfied with the provisional government. Bolshevik efforts to incite military and civilian rebellion against the government and the continuation of the war met with little success, however, and Vladimir Lenin, the Bolshevik party leader, began to execute his plan to take control of the government by force.

On October 24, 1917, Lenin's Red Army stormed the Winter Palace, and the Bolsheviks established a totalitarian state, which they called a "dictatorship of the proletariat." Civil war broke out between the "Reds" (communists) and "Whites" (those who opposed their rule and wanted to establish a democratic government). After the Bolshevik victory in 1919, Lenin established a police state, making communist rule because even more oppressive.

■ PRIMARY SOURCE

One Aspect of Bolshevist Liberty *Ludovic Naudeau, a Petrograd correspondent of the Paris Temps, writing in October, 1917, drew this amusing sketch of one phase of life in the Russian capital:.*

One morning recently I was awakened by the cries of my neighbor in the next room. His boots had been stolen. The same day the manager of a newspaper office told me that he had been robbed of six pairs of pantaloons. What use could any one have for six nether garments? The star reporter came in with eyes bulging. "Four hundred thefts every night!" he cried; "that is the average for the last two weeks. The Petrograd militia are vainly seeking for the 18,000 criminals who are living in liberty among us. It is frightful!"

Under the old regime we were guarded by 5,750 police agents—large, strong men—who cost $2,500,000 a year. Those Pharaohs have been replaced by 7,000 small, mean-looking militiamen, who cost, in present taxes, $8,500,000 annually. Formerly we enjoyed sweet security. Today things fly out of one's pockets of themselves; watches escape from their fobs; apartments empty themselves automatically of their objects of value. Every night one-half of the population is busy robbing the other half. Sometimes the thieves are civilians dressed as soldiers, and sometimes they are solders dressed as civilians. It is robbery made free-for-all—a socialistic budge-all-catch-all.

Besides, the persons whom one meets in prison do not stay there. One no longer stays in prison; it is not good form. Sometimes a new outburst of popular wrath opens the doors; sometimes the guards and sentinels give the

prisoner to understand that the best thing he can do is to go away. There is talk of organizing a mass patrol of the streets, in which all the honest men of the city would have to go on guard by turns "in squads."

All this is true, confirmed by a thousand witnesses. During the weeks immediately following the fall of the empire, the capital, in a sort of solemn and anguished waiting, enjoyed absolute peace, a truce of the underworld, a sort of petrification of crime. But today robbery has risen to the rank of a social institution. And yet, as Russia has not ceased to be a land of contrasts, there are no Apaches in the streets, no highwaymen, no hold-up men, none of those bloodthirsty thugs who menace life at night in other capitals. Many petty thieves and relatively few assassins! I wrote this note in a street car, and when I put my notebook in my pocket I discovered that I had been relieved of my purse; a fact that is not without its good side, since I had forgotten to mention the pickpockets, who are as numerous as the pockets of honest men.

The Russian people lived for centuries under an autocracy, and yet they are by nature the most parliamentary of all the nations, doubtless because they are the most placid, the least irritable. We observed this once more at the All-Russian Congress, where a few momentary tumults did not destroy our general impression of a dignified and rather sad calmness. In that old and pompous Alexandra Theatre, under the blaze of the candelabra, amid the dull radiance of gilding almost a century old, we saw 1,5000 [sic] delegates. Their controversies were long, grave, sometimes noisy, but the spectator who recalled the Boulanger episode and the Dreyfus affair noticed how much less irascible and excitable the Russians were by comparison. If the Russian people did not have, deep in their nature, a vast fund of cheerful and accommodating plasticity, a great tendency to prevent or rather to postpone conflicts by means of discussion and pacific "readjustment," of provisional agreement, civil war would have broken out fifty times since last March. . . .

■

SIGNIFICANCE

The social and economic changes that occurred in early twentieth-century Russia made its monarchy unsustainable. Although the Tsar recognized the need to modernize the country and industrialization proceeded rapidly, the new cities and factories provided opportunities for organized political opponents to develop, while rapid industrialization resulted in overcrowding and poor living conditions that increased frustration among the working classes.

Under these conditions, political change was inevitable. While some scholars argue that a coup staged by a minority party does not qualify as a true "revolution," there is no doubt that the changes in Russian politics and in the lives of ordinary people were revolutionary, indeed. The revolution ended Russia's longstanding feudal autocratic rule by the tsars, only to replace it with a totalitarian communist state that finally disintegrated in 1991.

FURTHER RESOURCES

Books

Chamberlin, William Henry. *The Russian Revolution, 1917–1921*. Princeton, NJ: Princeton University Press, 1987.

Figes, O. *A People's Tragedy: the Russian Revolution, 1891–1924*. London: J. Cape, 1996.

Miller, M., ed. *The Russian Revolution: The Essential Readings*. Oxford University Press, 2001.

Periodicals

Darby, Graham. "The October Revolution (Russia's Bolshevik Revolution of 1917)." *History Review* (Issue 28) September 1997.

Lenine: The Man and His Beliefs

Magazine article

By: "A Russian Social Worker"

Date: January 1918

Source: A Russian Social Worker. "Lenine: The Man and His Beliefs." *Current History* 7 (January 1918): 14–18.

About the Author: *Current History* claims to be the oldest U.S. publication devoted exclusively to world affairs. It was founded by the *New York Times* in 1914 to provide detailed coverage of World War I. "A Russian Social Worker" is a pseudonym taken by the writer to preserve anonymity in the dangerous political climate in Russia in 1918.

INTRODUCTION

Vladimir Illyich Ulyanov (Lenin) was the leader of the Bolshevik movement and would lead this small Marxist party to power in the Russian Revolution of October 1917. In doing so he established his brand of Marxist rule in Russia and laid the basis for seven decades of Soviet Communism.

Born into a middle class family in Simbirsk in 1870, Lenin trained and briefly practiced as a lawyer, although he spent most of his life as a professional revolutionary. Indeed, Lenin had revolutionary antecedents. His older brother, Alexander, was executed when Lenin was a teenager for his part in a plot to murder Tsar Alexander III in 1887. Lenin later claimed that this event instilled in him a deep hatred of the Russian royal family and committed him to the revolutionary cause.

Lenin did not become involved in revolutionary politics until the early 1890s when he was a young lawyer and began studying the works of Karl Marx (1818–1883). As was the case with many political texts at the time in Russia, Marx's work was illegal and Lenin was arrested in 1895 and sentenced to exile in Siberia. It was during his Siberian exile that Lenin decided to devote his life to furthering the cause of Marxism. Living in spartan conditions, he spent much of his time studying Marxist texts and working on his own interpretations, many of which were published secretly in Russia and other countries in the late 1890s. He left Russia with his wife Nadezhda Krupskaya and for nearly two decades lived in a variety of European cities.

Freed from the censorship and persecution of the Tsarist regime, Lenin became a prolific and, within his own circles, high-profile writer and speaker, promoting his own interpretation of Marxism. He co-founded a Russian-language newspaper, *Iskra* (the Spark), which was sold in émigré communities across Europe. In these émigré communities, Lenin found a small, but dedicated, following of intellectuals and fellow revolutionaries, such as Leon Trotsky (1879–1940). Ironically, most of them—like Lenin himself—were from the sort of "petit-bourgeoisie" backgrounds that he fulminated against.

In 1902, Lenin wrote *What Is To Be Done?* Although it wasn't recognized as such at the time, this became his seminal text. In it, he wrote that the ultimate goal of Marxism was complete freedom, but this could only be attained through a rigidly disciplined party. He criticized the lack of discipline among his fellow revolutionaries, saying that no fundamental changes to society could be attained while dissent and controversy raged within their ranks. Marx's dream was a society governed by a dictatorship of the proletariat, with the workers ruling over the old order. When Lenin's revolution took place in 1917, an opposite social order was, in fact, established, with a dictatorship ruling over the proletariat. Lenin claimed that this was a temporary measure, but it became the defining characteristic of Marxism-Leninism.

When revolution erupted in Russia in February and October 1917, it was seen as the test case of European socialism and Marxism. Lenin's comrades

Vladimir Ilyich Ulianov, the communist revolutionary better known as Lenin, in Moscow, Russia, 1918. P. OTCHUPA/AFP/GETTY IMAGES.

across Europe leapt to congratulate the hero of what seemed like the first successful socialist revolution and the beginning of a new world order. Left-leaning newspapers, magazines, and journals published hagiographic and eulogizing profiles of the new Russian leader.

■ PRIMARY SOURCE

More than one clue to the meaning of the Bolshevist upheaval in Russia is to be found in the life of Lenine, its leading spirit. Until a few weeks ago it did not matter very much who Lenine was, or what his ideas were, but when soldiers, workmen, and peasants have suddenly translated him to the highest office in the land, it becomes important that the facts of his career should be known.

The question whether or not Lenine is a tool of the German Government may be left unanswered for the present. He undoubtedly received facilities from the German Government to return to Russia from Switzerland immediately after the revolution in March, but what motive prompted the German authorities to pick an archenemy of all autocracies for such a privilege is something of a mystery. Certainly, Lenine's previous career does not suggest him as very pliable material for German intrigue.

Nikolai Lenine was born at Simbirsk, in Central Russia, in the year 1870, and he is thus now 47 years of age. His real name is Vladimir Ilitch Ulyanov, and Lenine is only one of the several aliases which he, like other revolutionists, has found it necessary to adopt at various times. A son of a Government official employed in the Department of Public Instruction, Lenine received his preliminary education in his home town. In his early twenties he went to Petrograd to continue his studies in the political science department of the Petrograd University. Here he at once became affiliated with a group of radical students who took an active interest in the political and social problems of the day.

His brother, A. Ulyanov, also a student of the same university, was already a member of the Populist Party (Narodniki) which secretly advocated violence against the existing authorities as one of the means of bringing about the abolitions of autocracy. In 1887 this brother was arrested, and charged with participation in a "terrorist" plot to wreck the imperial train carrying Alexander III. After a secret trial and without many preliminaries he was condemned to death and was hanged shortly thereafter. Lenine was also arrested at the time, but was released, as there was no evidence found against him. This arrest, however, caused his expulsion from the university.

WORK AS A PROPAGANDIST

At this time the Russian Social-Democratic movement was still in its infancy. Underground propaganda and organizing were carried on among factory employees by the enlightened and idealistic intelligentsia pledged to the "cause." It was then that Lenine spent his Sundays in a circle of uneducated workmen, explaining to them the elements of Socialist economies and the fundaments of the teachings of Karl Marx....

Because of his socialist activities Lenine was compelled to leave Russia on several occasions. Switzerland, France, and Austria were the countries of his temporary domicile. From these foreign posts he directed the work of one of the factions of the Social-Democratic Party, developing a leadership of great power and initiative....

A direct actionist, Lenine believed in the seizure of political power by means of a violent revolution and in establishing a proletarian government. Then only, he held, could there be accomplished an economic readjustment of the country, bringing with it a more equitable social order. Also, as a thorough Marxian, he had utmost faith in the ultimate triumph of the proletariat.

After the revolution of 1905 and the reaction that followed, the Lenine faction dwindled down to but a few émigrés and it seemed as if Bolshevism was destined to die out. But in 1911–12, when the spell of the reaction began to break up, and when, with the awakening, a new spirit began to permeate the political and social life of Russia, a sudden impetus to renewed activities was given to the Bolsheviki. This may also be explained by the fact that the leaders of this faction were the first to understand the momentous significance of this national resurrection. They immediately set to work, and the first Socialist daily paper, Pravda, (the Truth,) was one of the results of their efforts. Undoubtedly this daily has exercised considerable influence upon the working masses who rallied to it and gave it their whole-hearted support. Since then there has been a gradual growth of Bolshevism in the industrial centres of Russia under the intellectual guidance and leadership of Lenine. The movement gained in strength from year to year. As early as in 1913 the Bolsheviki sent six representatives to the Duma.

At the outbreak of the war in 1914 Lenine was in Cracow, at that time the headquarters of the organizations which directed the revolutionary movement in Russia. It should be remembered that Lenine, like other revolutionary leaders, was compelled to live in exile. The Austrian authorities immediately arrested him on suspicion of being a Russian spy, but as he was easily able to prove that he had no connection with the Czar's Government, he was released and permitted to go to Switzerland, where he remained until March, 1917. The news of the successful revolution caused him to endeavor to return to Russia and the German Government gave him the necessary permission to pass through Germany.

CHIEF RUSSIAN PARTIES

On his arrival in Petrograd, Lenine gathered together his followers and began the agitation in favor of the Bolshevist program. This program was outlined by Lenine in a remarkable statement which in the light of recent events has become an important document for the understanding of the situation. According to this statement, the chief groupings of political parties in Russia are:

1. The representatives of the feudal landholders and the more conservative sections of the bourgeoisie.
2. The Constitutional Democrats (Cadets) and other liberal groups representing the majority of the bourgeoisie, that is, the captains of industry and those landholders who have industrial interests.
3. The Socialist groups which represent the small entrepreneurs, small middle-class proprietors, more or less well-to-do peasants, petite bourgeoisie, as well as those workers who have submitted to a bourgeois point of view.
4. The Bolsheviki, who ought properly to be called the Communist Party, which is at present termed the Russian Social Democratic Workers' Party, and which represents class-conscious workers, day laborers, and the poorer strata of peasantry, which are grouped with them as the semi-proletariat.

THE BOLSHEVIST PLATFORM

The Bolshevist platform, as outlined by Lenine, reads as follows:

The councils of Workers', Soldiers' and Peasants' Delegates must at once take every practicable and feasible step for the realization of the Socialist program.

The Bolsheviki demand a republic of the Councils or Workers', Soldiers' and Peasants' Delegates: abolition of the standing army and the police, substituting for them an armed people; officials to be not only elected but also subject to recall and their pay not to exceed that of a good worker.

Sole authority must be in the hands of the Councils of Workers', Soldiers' and Peasants' Delegates. There must be no dual authority.

No support should be given to the Provisional Government. The whole of the people must be prepared for the complete and sole authority of the Councils of the Workers', Soldiers' and Peasants' Delegates.

A constituent assembly should be called as soon as possible, but it is necessary to increase the members and strengthen the power of the Councils of Workers', Soldiers' and Peasants' Delegates by organizing and arming the masses.

A police force of the conventional type and a standing army are absolutely unnecessary. Immediately and unconditionally a universal army of the people should be introduced, so that they and the militia and the army shall be an integral whole. Capitalists must pay the workers for their days of service in the militia.

OFFICERS SUBJECT TO THEIR MAN

Officers must not only be elected, but every step of every officer and General must be subject to control by special soldiers' committees.

The arbitrary removal by the soldiers of their superior officers is in every respect indispensable. The soldiers will obey only the powers of their own choice; they can respect no others.

The Bolsheviki are absolutely opposed to all imperialist wars and to all bourgeois Governments which make them, among them our own Provisional

Government. The Bolsheviki are absolutely opposed to "revolutionary defense" in Russia.

The Bolsheviki are against the predatory international treaties concluded between the Czar and England, France, etc., for the strangling of Persia, the division of China, Turkey, Austria, etc.

The Bolsheviki are against annexations. Any promise of a capitalist Government to renounce annexations is a huge fraud. To expose it is very simple, by demanding that each nation be freed from the yoke of its own capitalists.

The Bolsheviki are opposed to the (Russian) Liberty Loan, because the war remains imperialistic, being waged by capitalists in alliance with capitalists, and in the interests of capitalists.

The Bolsheviki refuse to leave to capitalist Governments the task of expressing the desire of the nations for peace.

All monarchies must be abolished. Revolutions do not proceed in fixed order. Only genuine revolutionaries may be trusted.

THE PEASANTS TO SEIZE ALL LAND

The peasants must at once take all the land from the landholders. Order must be strictly maintained by the Councils of Peasants' Delegates. The production of bread and meat must be increased and the soldiers better fed. Destruction of cattle, of tools, etc., is not permissible.

It will be impossible to rely upon the general Councils of Peasants' Delegates, for the wealthy peasants are of the same capitalist class that is always inclined to injure or deceive the farmhands, day laborers, and the poorer peasants. We must at once form special organizations of these latter classes of the village population both within the Councils of Peasants' Delegates and in the form of special Councils of Delegates of the Farmers' Workers.

We must at once prepare the Councils of Workers' Delegates, the Councils of Delegates of Banking Employees, and others for the taking of all such steps as are feasible and completely realizable toward the union of all banks in one single national bank, and then toward a control of the Councils of Workers' Delegates over the banks and syndicates, and then toward their nationalization, that is, their passing over into the possession of the whole group.

The only Socialist International, establishing and realizing a brotherly union of all the workers in all countries, which is now desirable for the nations,

is one which consists of the really revolutionary workers, who are capable of putting an end to the awful and criminal slaughter of nations, capable of delivering humanity from the yoke of capitalism. Only such people (groups, parties, etc.) as the German Socialist, Karl Liebknecht, now in a German jail, only people who will tirelessly struggle with their own Government and their own bourgeoisie, and their own social-patriots, and their own "centrists," can and must immediately establish that International which is necessary to the nations.

The fraternization between soldiers of the warring countries, at the front, must be encouraged; it is good and indispensable.

It will be noticed that the Bolsheviki have actually attempted to carry out the greater part of this program, and in some cases have apparently succeeded, at least temporarily.

SIGNIFICANCE

The program outlined by Lenin in 1917 echoed directly his then largely forgotten 1902 tract *What Is To Be Done?* Indeed, it was his call for unity and discipline that allowed the Bolsheviks to prevail over larger and more populist political organizations in the chaos of war-torn and hunger-ravaged Russia.

After seizing power by a coup d'état in October 1917, the Bolsheviks began persecuting their opponents and denying any form of free political expression in the interests of a disciplined revolution. The necessity of discipline within party ranks spoken of in his Bolshevik platform and in *What Is To Be Done?* was quickly implemented across not just the Bolshevik party but in Russia as a whole. There was no allowance for dissent, no matter how nuanced. Even Leon Trotsky, once one of Lenin's closest allies and the architect of the Bolshevik revolution, was forced into exile after stepping out of line and was later murdered by Soviet agents.

Lenin came to power on a slogan of "Peace, Land and Bread." One of his first acts as Russian leader was to withdraw Russian troops from World War I and to make peace with Germany. However, Lenin soon found himself fighting a civil war against the so-called White Army, a loose coalition of anti-Bolshevik forces, which was to continue from 1918 until 1922. His call for global revolution and anti-imperialist rhetoric marked him as an enemy of most nations and some, such as Great Britain, sent expeditionary forces to assist the White Army.

Another of Lenin's early acts as Russian leader was to establish the Council of People's Commissars (the Cheka and later the NKVD), a secret police force whose pervasiveness soon surpassed that of the old tsarist police force. Initially, its role was limited to rounding up Bolshevik opponents, but its mandate quickly expanded to include overseeing agrarian reforms and forcing the collectivization of farms. These reforms were widely and often violently opposed by peasants, who refused to produce crops, plunging Russia into famine and contributing to its ongoing civil war. This increased the zeal of the Cheka and their assault on the peasantry became known as "the Terror." During this chaotic time, as many as nine million people died. Agrarian collectivization was the USSR's foremost problem in its early years. As a result, a second famine occurred in the early 1930s in which at least another four million people died.

In August 1918, Lenin survived an assassination attempt by Fanya Kaplin, a factory worker, despite being shot three times. Although he recovered, a bullet remained lodged in his shoulder near his neck, and this severely impaired his health within a few years. He suffered three strokes between May 1922 and March 1923, which first left him paralyzed down one side and eventually unable to speak or move. He died in January 1924.

Although Lenin never lived to see the most profound effects and worst excesses of Soviet Communism, his ideas were fundamental to its initiation and to the course it took. He instigated a totalitarian system, where any limited form of democracy or debate was not just suppressed, but actively persecuted. He saw the "making" of a true proletarian state coming after an organized campaign of violence against capitalists. In the event, "capitalist" became a catch-all term for virtually every social class in Russia and almost every person in the country suffered, either under the terror instigated by Lenin, as a result of the famine caused by his policies, or under the horrific policies of his successor, Joseph Stalin (1879–1953).

Even in the years following the Russian revolution when it became clear that Lenin had forsaken the utopian ideals of his comrades, both in Russia and elsewhere, his socialist allies continued to defend him. They dismissed the reports of brutality, famine, and hardships emerging from Russia as capitalistic propaganda. This state of denial persisted for most of the USSR's history, with famous writers such as George Bernard Shaw and Kingsley Amis defending the excesses of Lenin and Stalin. Even historians

traditionally portrayed Lenin as the "least worst" face of Soviet Communism, particularly when compared to Stalin. Not until the collapse of the USSR in the late 1980s and the opening up of previously secret archives was the extent of Lenin's crimes realized and the historical record revised.

FURTHER RESOURCES

Books

Figes, Orlando. *A People's Tragedy: The Russian Revolution 1891–1924*. London: Jonathan Cape, 1996.

Hill, Christopher. *Lenin and the Russian Revolution*. London: Penguin, 1971.

Pipes, Richard. *Russia Under the Old Regime*. London: Penguin, 1995.

Web sites

Marxist Internet Archive. "What Is To Be Done?" <http://www.marxists.org/archive/lenin/works/1901/witbd/> (accessed May 22, 2006).

Hitler's Propaganda Machine

Newspaper article

By: Roger B. Nelson

Date: June 1933

Source: Nelson, Roger B. "Hitler's Propaganda Machine." *New York Times* (June 1933).

About the Author: The *New York Times* is a daily U.S. newspaper, which was founded in 1851. It is published daily in New York City and is distributed to many other countries. The newspaper printed this additional information at the top of the article, revealing the author's insight into his topic: "The writer of this article has had unusual opportunities of studying the Nazi movement in Germany at first hand and of obtaining the views of the outstanding leaders in private and informal conversations with them, rather than by questioning them in set interviews."

INTRODUCTION

The article reveals the ways in which the National Socialists (Nazis) under Adolf Hitler (1889–1945) were so effective in using propaganda to build support for their party and its preparations for war. In the early 1930s, Germany was suffering from the devastating effects of a worldwide depression, a humiliating defeat

A Nazi war propaganda item, 1943. PHOTO BY WALTER SANDERS//TIME LIFE PICTURES/GETTY IMAGES.

in World War I, and the equally degrading impact of the Versailles Treaty, which had required Germany to return huge areas of territory gained during the war to their former owners. It had faced steeply rising inflation and high levels of unemployment. Social and economic policies were failing, and the morale of the people was low. Adolf Hitler, the leader of the Nationalist Socialist party, swept into power in 1933. He became Chancellor of Germany as a result of a bargain made with President Hindenberg by a group of influential landowners and industrialists, who were fearful of the growth of support for the political left.

Within weeks of taking power, the Nazis established the Ministry for Popular Enlightenment and Propaganda, with Joseph Goebbels (1897–1945) as its head. This Ministry developed a program of propaganda that infiltrated every area of German life and that was cleverly tailored to appeal to the weaknesses and aspirations of various groups in the population. All forms of media, education, industry, and scientific

activity were used to propagate National Socialist ideals, while Hitler himself frequently appeared in circus-like mass rallies to arouse nationalist fervor by delivering the propaganda in person.

The key themes of National Socialist propaganda were the supremacy and racial purity of the German people and their betrayal by both foreign aggressors and enemies who had infiltrated their country. All Germany's recent troubles could be blamed on these groups. The German people had been stabbed in the back following World War I, it was claimed, and their domestic fortunes had been ruined by the actions of groups such as the Communists and, above all, the Jewish people. The Jews were singled out as the scapegoat for many of Germany's problems and for any of the Nazi party's failures. Anti-Semitism became the key tool in the party's efforts to unite the German people.

At the same time, the Nazis embarked on a massive rearmament program that created many jobs, thereby addressing the unemployment problem and securing the support of the working classes. In addition, the Nazis were able to appeal to the lower middle classes, whose businesses had suffered under the difficult economic conditions, by blaming the Jews for their problems, and to the middle classes by promoting the idea of a racially pure, powerful nation. In doing so, they cleverly manipulated the fears and weaknesses of each group with targeted propaganda tools.

The rebuilding of Germany's military strength appealed to all Germans who wanted their nation to regain its former power and glory. Military themes permeated the Nazi party, and their uniforms, ranks, and hierarchy formed an important part of the propaganda program. The military style of organization appealed to the people's need for order and authority, which had been lacking in recent years, and the uniforms and ranks gave a much-needed sense of identity, pride, and self-importance to party members.

War itself was glorified as the way of avenging Germany against its enemies, and once Hitler took power he focused on preparing the nation for another conflict. He was able to secure the support of the German people by promoting the idea of a "Thirty Years War"—a war that had started in August 1914 and would only be over when Germany was restored to its former glory—and by encouraging the belief that foreign aggressors were planning to attack Germany. When Hitler attacked Poland in 1939 and World War II started, he could, therefore, justify his actions to the German people in the name of self-defense.

■ PRIMARY SOURCE

Most observers have been amazed by the speed and thoroughness with which the National Socialist German Labor (Nazi) party has reorganized the government apparatus of Germany, in eliminating opposition and in transforming the entire social and political landscape of the Reich—and all this after the Nazis' fortunes had been buried deep last December by most of the foreign correspondents and the overwhelming majority of their opponents at home—Democratic, Catholic, Socialist and official Communist.

Why did German fascism grow and triumph? Was it a result of the Versailles Treaty? Was the victory a by-product of the weakness, blundering, confusion and division of its enemies? Is it the outcome of the economic crisis? All these are fundamental factors and have received their merited consideration.

But the mechanics of popularizing fascism among the German people has been completely overlooked. A special, carefully planned technique of propaganda and agitation has enabled the National Socialists to sell their comprehensive and ambitious program with an ease which might well make America's most brilliant publicity agent envious. This propaganda involved the skillful exploiting of German psychology.

Specific, peculiar German conditions were systematically capitalized. The strategy was always to find the weakest link in the bourgeois democratic and working-class revolutionary chain of opponents and there to apply the greatest pressure. This is what Leopold Pleichinger, chief asset in Hitler's unadvertised "brains trust," meant when he said "We National Socialists have learned much from the Russian Bolsheviki." In view of this, it is interesting to speculate why Hitler did not proscribe Lenin's books, *The Infantile Sickness of Communism* and *The Proletarian Revolution of 1917*, when he ordained a nation-wide burning of Marxist literature.

In the color, spirit and drama of the Nazi propaganda technique, or Fascist "salesmanship-*kultur,*" is to be found the soul and vision of German fascism.

The German Fascists have learned to dramatize their talk, their deeds, their very existence. It is the drama of Fascist propaganda and the smooth functioning of the Nazi propaganda machine, under the direction of Joseph Goebbels, that have generated the phenomenal rise of Hitler's party.

Above all, the Nazi promotion machine emphasizes good acting. Millions of Germans, of all classes, like to play at soldiers and office-holding. As Herr Scheller of the *Angriff* staff told me, "The masses want it. We can and must give it to them. It can only help our movement. We must see through the eyes of the masses." Hitler and his aides-de-camp well understand how much the soldier spirit, the military spirit, has been bred into the German people for many generations.

That is why military pomp pervades the Nazi organization and its propaganda. Hence the handing out of offices and "titles" to large numbers in the party. Even the office of doorkeeper in a party building becomes coveted once it is conferred by the Nazi party leadership. A doorkeeper, let us say in the Berlin district office, no longer considers his services menial. Has he not been given a party uniform and charged with the guardianship of party headquarters! He has "military" orders. He has been made to feel that he is a soldier in the cause, with power to give as well as to execute orders.

The form of Nazi party organization is built around this idea of "playing soldier." The regular army, the Reichswehr, has its uniform. The party Storm Troops (*Sturm Abteilung*) and Safety, or Security Squad (*Schutzstaffel*) have theirs. At one Nazi mass meeting I asked a leader of the Security Squad: "Why do you all salute each other so much? And why do you throw your shoulders back and click your heels so often?" He automatically threw back his shoulders, clicked his heels, stood erect and said: "Our party salute, the raised, forward-stretched hand, and our 'Heil' (hail) infuse us with solidarity, impress upon us all our feeling of 'soldiership,' our fighting comradeship in our great cause, the rebuilding of a strong and beautiful Germany."

This very profitable game of soldiers goes on zestfully in every Nazi party headquarters. In the Berlin party building one sees uniforms continuously rushing and strutting from room to room. The Nazi clerk in the book shop, collecting small change from a customer, acts as if he were working in the commissary of any army division. Every wall is plastered with the *Hakenkreuz* (swastika), the party emblem. Post cards, pins, uniforms, neckties, flags, pennants, standards, banners, charms, posters, watch-chains and boots, all bear the sign of the *Hakenkreuz* and are for sale in the book store. Here one can also buy paintings, book-ends, silhouettes, plaques, and post-card pictures of Hitler, Goebbels, Rosenberg, von Epp, Goering and other Nazi chiefs. Pictures of German national heroes of the past are very cleverly confused with Nazi heroes of today. On one wall there is Hitler posing as Bismarck. Beside him is Goebbels masquerading as Frederick the Great, and Captain Goering aping von Moltke.

Certainly, these leaders, these firstline performers in the Nazi show, know how to drape themselves. They are past-masters in exploiting "the callings-up of the dead upon the stage of universal history."

The Nazi concept of leadership, discipline and organization and the attitude toward party propaganda work are military to the core. Party discipline is based solely on formal orders from above. The leader, *der Fuehrer*, is all-powerful in himself. Today in Germany the leader is Adolf Hitler. He is above all, but not of all. Let Joseph Goebbels explain this concept of leadership: "It is an old lesson of history that when a young party sure of its aim wrecks the rule of a corrupt and inwardly foul system, when it takes into its own hands the power of the State, it gives the responsibility to a dictator, who must conquer the State with new ideas and put them through. That is what we are going to do." When Wilhelm Frick, the first Nazi to take over a ministerial post, assumed office in Thuringia, Hitler grasped the occasion to show who is who in the party and whose party it was. He declared himself: "I have selected Party comrade Frick to take over the post of Ministry of Interior and Education *** only to represent the ideas of our *Weltanschauung* (world philosophy)."

. . .

These Nazi propagandists are superb salesmen. They do not overlook anything. When they push the sales of

their own cigarettes they pack in Nazi publicity. Here is a package of ten, called "Kommando," with a lusty *Hakenkreuz*-breasted eagle on its face. On one end is printed the fighting slogan, "Struggle Against Trust Rule"; on the opposite end the name *Kameradschaft Zigaretten* (Comradeship Cigarettes). Inside is a premium-coupon bearing more Hitler propaganda. This time it is in verse and closes with an appeal and a lesson in Nazi economics: "And do not forget—*Kameradschaft Zigaretten* are hand-packed to help overcome German unemployment. *** Smoke K.Z. everywhere, all the time." Here is another package called *Sturm* (Storm), with more Nazi insignia on its face and another call to action on its sides; "Against the Trust and Corporations." And inside, a beautifully colored picture, one of a series portraying types of soldiers and uniforms in the days of Frederick the Great. Then there are cigarettes called "New Front," "Alarm" and "Drummer." All these cigarettes proudly emphasize in their pleas to be smoked that "a virile nation can never go down, because at the right time there comes to it the right leader, who, fearless of whatever fate may befall him, raises new armies (*neue Fronten*) to deliver and save it."

The same all-inclusive propaganda is used with candy, gramophone records, stationery and other articles of consumption. On all sides the Nazi cause is being promoted and streamers proclaim: "All power to Hitler, the Leader, the Deliverer!"

From platform and street corner, in movie and pulpit, from broadcasting station and airplane the Nazi propagandists have pounded away at the misery, the confusion and corruption of German parliamentary democracy. Every Nazi orator has time and again proclaimed that "it is the Versailles Treaty and the 'system' it forced upon Germany that has brought all the trouble." And the Nazi editors have emphasized and re-emphasized that "it is the 'November Men,' the Marxists, the Red-Black (Social Democratic-Catholic Centre) coalition who stabbed us in the back during the war, signed the degrading peace, disgracefully agreed to the tribute payment of the Dawes and Young Plans and let in the Jews, bolshevism and international high finance." To such propaganda the jobless students, bankrupt storekeepers, poverty-stricken professional workers, hungry housewives and slum proletarians not only lent a ready ear but soon added a powerful fist. The Nazis never missed the slightest chance to coin this misery, growing out of a lost war and a world-wide economic crisis, into political capital for themselves. To a defeated Germany they glorified nationalism and raised the banner of a new Germany. Hitler's aim was to impound these nationalist tides so that they might generate a current which would energize his followers and paralyze his opponents.

"The People," as a sort of mythical, all-stirring and all-vanquishing concept, was dinned into every Nazi propagandist, great and small, into every Nazi political stagehand and star. Every election manifesto proclaimed: "You, the people, in your hands lies the future. You have to decide whether Germany should continue as a paradise of money speculators and swindlers or should again become a land of honor, well-regulated life, and conscientious responsibility. ***You, the people, look up and act. Drive the bureaucrats out of their easy chairs. Give Hitler the power and responsibility!"

. . .

The mistakes and difficulties of other parties became grist for the Nazi mills. The arrogant bureaucracy of the German republican government was generally abhorred. No one exploited this in the workers' ranks with greater cunning and with more deadly effect than Hitler. Here was an excellent entering wedge for the Nazi propagandist into even the class-conscious proletariat. The bureaucrats must go! This became the battle cry of the Nazi agitators in the industrial sections of the country. Recruits were thus gained in new strata of German society—in the proletarian camp. Nor were they ordinary recruits. They soon proved to be most militant, especially in the Storm Troops.

Again let Goebbels show us how the Nazi propaganda machine works. Addressing himself to the pick of the Storm Troops and Security Squad, massed in the Lustgarten of Berlin, he waxed eloquent in masterly demagogy: "We do not want to think any more in terms of classes; we are no proletarians and are no bourgeoisie. We do not ask whether you are manual laborer, worker or prince. A great common cause welds us together. The day of freedom and bread is drawing near. *** Now they [the Social Democrats] are out on the streets calling for freedom. For fourteen long years they had the opportunity to achieve freedom, but, instead, they took away the bread from the people; instead of providing work they slugged the German workers with hard rubber clubs (Gummiknueppel)."

The Nazi propaganda machine has been quick throughout to steal whatever it could use from the camp of the working-class revolutionists. The Nazis were taught to fight bolshevism with some of the weapons of communism itself. Thus, the Fascist storm banners bear this symbol and song: "We are the army of the Hakenkreuz. Wave the red banners high. We shall bring the German workers to the road of a new liberty!"

The appeal of martyrdom rings throughout all Nazi propaganda. At all meetings before Hitler took power members of the party went around with collection boxes urging you to give, to "help the Nazi prisoners and their dependent families"—prisoners as a result of street brawls, fights at meetings with communists and Socialists, attempts on political opponents' lives, and so on. These collection boxes were labeled in big red letters: "Think of Nazi Prisoner-Relief. *** Not a single Nazi prisoner must feel neglected. Loyalty to the loyal." A sketch of a Nazi in his prison cell tops the message. Throughout the period of the struggle for power, every Nazi paper made the most of announcements of party comrades being slain, often with a picture of the dead. Gruesome murder evidence or impressive funeral scenes of their fallen party heroes were constantly featured.

. . .

Nazi agitators were provided with pamphlets to teach them how to fire the imagination of their listeners in the manner of Hitler and Goebbels. The pamphlets contained specially inserted loose leaves Hilfszettel (helping notes), each leaf containing an argument with facts and figures either explaining some Nazi plank or setting forth the Social Democrats' voting record in the Reichstag for fifty years or unmasking them as "traitors to the working class," as "lackeys of high finance," and as "vassals of the Stock Exchange."

The middle classes were by no means neglected. The Nazis saw despair turning many of them to astrology, fortune-telling and all sorts of quackery for hope and relief. Poorer middle-class housewives, particularly, were attracted to astrology. From July 31 to Aug. 3, 1932, the German astrologers held a national convention at Stettin. Here such subjects as "Astrology and Education," "Astrology, the Press and Criticism" and even "Politics in the Light of Astrology" were discussed. Among the popularizers of astrology, Jan Janussen, recently mysteriously murdered and since discovered to have had Jewish blood in his veins, was the most successful. His weekly paper, Hanussen's Berliner Wochenschau, led the field in circulation.

In stepped the Nazis. A middle class in misery is the most fertile field for fascism. Astrology and clairvoyance soon became the best Nazi fertilizers in the ranks of these disillusioned and despairing people. No time was lost to make Hanussen a Nazi prophet, so as to create the impression that the future lay with the Nazis. In Hanussen's weekly the wildest of Nazi dreams, hopes and plans were established as coming and foreseen in the horoscope of von Hindenburg, von Papen, von Schleicher, Hitler and others. In this fashion the lower strata, culturally speaking, were stirred. "Here, at last, is a chance for success," said the middle-class housewife to herself. For the first time she had the stars and planets on her side.

. . .

Time and again Hitler had told the world: "I am convinced nothing will happen to me, because I believe destiny has assigned a task to me." Conveniently the Nazi propagandists mobilized their supernatural department and had Hanussen turn to his crystal with the question:

"Will Hitler become Chancellor of the Reich?" On this point Hitler's horoscope was clear: "The sun is big and is in the division consisting of the three signs of Jupiter (Trigon)—the majestic Trigon! With this also comes the three-sign division of Sun-Moon, Moon-Venus and Jupiter-Venus which only strengthens the royal Trigon. All these would be strong signs for Hitler's assuming the post of Chancellor—and later even higher posts."

The keystone of the whole Nazi theoretical arch is the race question. And the race question means anti-Semitism. The Nazis have a special index of individuals in public life whom they suspect of having even the slightest trace of Jewish blood. No effort was spared to make anti-Semitic propaganda effective. Cartoons, caricatures, high-sounding slogans were at a premium. Here is a typical advertisement in *Der Angriff* of Aug. 6, 1932: "Artist Wanted—For anti-Semitic caricatures, talented, current contributions. Also similar literary contributions are wanted. Applicants should forward their replies to B.V. 449 *Angriff* Hedemannstrasse." Anti-Semitism, as a philosophy, was well rooted in Germany, and the Nazis feverishly exploited the prejudice for their own ends. In their propaganda manual they characterized the Jew as the personification of all evil in Germany, the cause of all misery and destitution, the power behind the forces which brought about Germany's defeat in the last war, the mainspring of Marxism and internationalism. Just as astrology drew the backward housewife and the bewildered, hopeless rural middle classes to the Nazi heaven, so did anti-Semitism inflame and capture urban middle-class people, the small storekeepers, standing bankrupt before the growing department stores owned by Jewish merchants.

When we see how the Nazis succeeded with their propaganda, it is interesting to listen to G. Stark, the Hitlerite theorist: "Political propaganda is quite different from advertising, though it utilizes in part the same methods. Propaganda on the political or spiritual field is not commercial advertising which seeks only monetary success, but rather it seeks systematic education to win followers for a world philosophy *(Weltanschauung)*. We always remember the great number of comrades who sacrificed their life for the movement. They were propagandists of the deed until their last breath." Indeed, even the American advertising experts can learn much from the Nazi publicity technique. And the kings of the underworld can take lessons from the Nazis in the field of "the propaganda of the deed" in which they have been especially effective. The Beuthen incident and the sweeping "achievements" of the Storm Troops against their political opponents and the Jews are notorious. In the Nazi propaganda arsenal, terrorism, demonstrations, parades and raids are the accepted weapons. Often, undoubtedly, terrorism has been the chief and most forceful. The Nazis

have elaborated a complicated technique in their preparation of terrorist campaigns to "educate" whole communities, to strike fear into whole towns, to make them swallow their creed, if necessary with castor oil and time bombs.

The Nazis boast of the realism in their propaganda machine. "To be able to see with the eyes of the masses, this is the whole secret of the key to successful political propaganda," asserts Herr Stark. It must be admitted that Nazi propaganda has equaled its highest hopes in weaving generalizations, illusions, promises and prejudices around the everyday interests and activities of the people.

The *Kampfschatzmarken* (fighting fund stamps), often beautifully printed in the Soviet colors of red and gold and bearing such slogans as "Freedom and Bread" and "The Future Belongs to the People," have circulated by the millions with telling effect. Nazi placards with striking and colorful pictures of farmers, housewives and workers, make a direct appeal. Quite often the posters are copied outright from those of the Russian or German Communists. Nazi leaflets have been rich in simple fighting slogans, with rousing calls to action in picturesquely vague language. In recent months special efforts have been directed to harnessing the movie and the theatre to the Nazi vehicle of propaganda. The Hitler-*Schallplatte* (phonograph record), taking eight and one-half minutes of playing time, is a big attraction at all meetings in small towns and rural areas which Hitler does not reach in person. Many are glad to pay to listen to the master's voice.

In the big cities where addresses are delivered by such eloquent speakers as Hitler or Goebbels, the admission prices often run as high as $1.75 a seat. The meeting is held in a huge stadium. An aviator in a Nazi plane thrills the audience with dare-devil stunt flying. The Storm Troops march onto the field to the tune of the Frederick Rex March and assemble in a huge swastika formation. The air is charged with a martial spirit—drums, trumpets, bells, cymbals and plenty of brass on every side. While waiting for the speakers to arrive the audience puffs Nazi cigarettes or chews Nazi swastika-stamped candy. Hundreds of Roman-candle fireworks flare through the dark at night meetings. The main speaker advances to be greeted by a torchlight parade. His aim is to arouse a spirit of revivalism which sweeps the vast mass off its feet. At the end of the meeting as many as 150,000 may arise in unison to sing "Deutschland Ueber Alles." They march out in disciplined fashion and find on the streets battalions of Storm Troops who unfurl their crimson banners with the tiny black swastika on them, and sing Nazi songs, now in the melody of a Polish revolutionary peasant song, now in the tune of the "Red Guard March," and finally in the melody of the "Volga Boat Song."

The three maxims of Nazi propaganda success are:

1. Dramatize your propaganda. All the world is a stage. Act well.
2. Always maintain the initiative. Always spring something new. Always let something loose; let there be something happening, something going on. And always be on the offensive—in your propaganda of the word as well as in your propaganda of deed.
3. See with the eyes of the masses, with the eyes of all who should be Nazis. Speak in their language. Give them what they want—in your propaganda. Know your people, the Germans. Be of the Germans. And, above all, learn to draw your followers en masse into your propaganda work. Make every one feel he is an actor on the stage of history building a new Germany.

SIGNIFICANCE

After Hitler became chancellor of Germany in 1933, another world war was inevitable. The whole program to rebuild Germany was based on the idea that Germany had been betrayed and that the only way for Germany to avenge itself upon its enemies and put an end to the conflict that had begun in 1914 was through military action. In this context, Germany's invasion of Poland was almost incidental—just the excuse that Hitler needed to go to war against his enemies.

The effectiveness of the Nazi propaganda program can only be understood in the context of the utter demoralization of the German people that resulted from their defeat in World War I, the humiliating peace terms, and the effects of the Depression. In fact, the Depression was already lifting in many nations, and it is likely that Germany's fortunes would have improved in the 1930s even if the Nazis had not been in power. Instead, the Nazis were able to incite in the German people the belief that it was right to punish the groups who they believed were to blame for their troubles. This led directly to World War II and the horrors of the Holocaust and cost the lives of many millions of people worldwide.

FURTHER RESOURCES

Books

Berghahn, V. R., John A. Broadwin, and Hilmar Hoffmann. *The Triumph of Propaganda: Film and National Socialism, 1933–1945*. New York: Berghahn Books, 1997.

Fraser, Lindley. *Germany Between Two Wars: A Study of Propaganda and War-Guilt*. New York: Oxford University Press, 1945.

First Inaugural Address of President Franklin D. Roosevelt

Speech

By: Franklin D. Roosevelt

Date: March 4, 1933

Source: *U.S. National Archives and Records Administration.* "Teaching with Documents: FDR's First Inaugural Address." <http://www.archives.gov/education/lessons/fdr-inaugural/> (accessed June 2, 2006).

About the Author: Franklin D. Roosevelt (1882–1945) was the thirty-second president of the United States. Elected to a historic four terms, Roosevelt took office in 1933 in the midst of the Great Depression. His presidency ended with his death in April 1945, just prior to the conclusion of World War II.

INTRODUCTION

During the 1920s, the United States experienced a period of great prosperity. By the end of the decade, however, the economy had begun to slow down and had become increasingly unstable. After a volatile few weeks of record-high losses, the stock market crashed on October 29, 1929. The crash marked the beginning of the decade-long Great Depression, a devastating financial crisis that affected the entire industrialized world. A number of American stock-market investors suffered massive losses, and consumer confidence plummeted. Even those who still had money purchased only necessities, a reflection of the post-crash sense of insecurity and vulnerability. Following the sudden decline in consumer spending, many stores and factories closed their doors. The economy quickly spiraled downward: tens of thousands of businesses failed, thousands of banks closed, millions of workers became unemployed, farmers lost their land, and families all over the country lost their life savings.

President Herbert Hoover (1874–1964), who had taken office in early 1929, responded slowly and inadequately to the crisis. He did enact some measures to

President Franklin Roosevelt delivers his first inaugural address at the U.S. Capitol on March 4, 1933. © UNDERWOOD & UNDERWOOD/CORBIS.

stimulate the economy, but he was reluctant to take drastic measures and he did little to provide immediate relief for the millions who had been plunged into poverty. Resentment toward Hoover spread among the populace. When Franklin D. Roosevelt received the Democratic Party's nomination for president in 1932, he pledged dramatic policy changes—a "New Deal" for the American people. In the presidential election that November, Roosevelt beat Hoover by a substantial margin amid promises of relief for an ailing nation. In the months leading up to Roosevelt's inauguration, the financial crisis worsened. Dozens of state governors declared extended bank holidays in an attempt to prevent the total collapse of the nation's banking system. The national unemployment rate reached twenty-five percent. By the time of the inauguration on March 4, 1933, the American economy was in dire straits and the people were desperate for signs of improvement.

PRIMARY SOURCE

I am certain that my fellow Americans expect that on my induction into the Presidency I will address them with a candor and a decision which the present situation of our Nation impels. This is preeminently the time to speak the truth, the whole truth, frankly and boldly. Nor need we shrink from honestly facing conditions in our country today. This great Nation will endure as it has endured, will revive and will prosper. So, first of all, let me assert my firm belief that the only thing we have to fear is fear itself—nameless, unreasoning, unjustified terror which paralyzes needed efforts to convert retreat into advance. In every dark hour of our national life a leadership of frankness and vigor has met with that understanding and support of the people themselves which is essential to victory. I am convinced that you will again give that support to leadership in these critical days.

In such a spirit on my part and on yours we face our common difficulties. They concern, thank God, only material things. Values have shrunken to fantastic levels; taxes have risen; our ability to pay has fallen; government of all kinds is faced by serious curtailment of income; the means of exchange are frozen in the currents of trade; the withered leaves of industrial enterprise lie on every side; farmers find no markets for their produce; the savings of many years in thousands of families are gone.

More important, a host of unemployed citizens face the grim problem of existence, and an equally great number toil with little return. Only a foolish optimist can deny the dark realities of the moment.

Yet our distress comes from no failure of substance. We are stricken by no plague of locusts. Compared with the perils which our forefathers conquered because they believed and were not afraid, we have still much to be thankful for. Nature still offers her bounty and human efforts have multiplied it. Plenty is at our doorstep, but a generous use of it languishes in the very sight of the supply. Primarily this is because rulers of the exchange of mankind's goods have failed, through their own stubbornness and their own incompetence, have admitted their failure, and abdicated. Practices of the unscrupulous money changers stand indicted in the court of public opinion, rejected by the hearts and minds of men.

True, they have tried, but their efforts have been cast in the pattern of an outworn tradition. Faced by failure of credit they have proposed only the lending of more money. Stripped of the lure of profit by which to induce our people to follow their false leadership, they have resorted to exhortations, pleading tearfully for restored confidence. They know only the rules of a generation of self-seekers. They have no vision, and when there is no vision the people perish.

The money changers have fled from their high seats in the temple of our civilization. We may now restore that temple to the ancient truths. The measure of the restoration lies in the extent to which we apply social values more noble than mere monetary profit.

Happiness lies not in the mere possession of money; it lies in the joy of achievement, in the thrill of creative effort. The joy and moral stimulation of work no longer must be forgotten in the mad chase of evanescent profits. These dark days will be worth all they cost us if they teach us that our true destiny is not to be ministered unto but to minister to ourselves and to our fellow men.

. . .

Restoration calls, however, not for changes in ethics alone. This nation asks for action, and action now.

Our greatest primary task is to put people to work. This is no unsolvable problem if we face it wisely and courageously. It can be accomplished in part by direct recruiting by the Government itself, treating the task as we would treat the emergency of a war, but at the same time, through this employment, accomplishing greatly needed projects to stimulate and reorganize the use of our natural resources.

Hand in hand with this we must frankly recognize the overbalance of population in our industrial centers and, by engaging on a national scale in a redistribution, endeavor to provide a better use of the land for those best fitted for the land. The task can be helped by definite efforts to raise the values of agricultural products and with this the power to purchase the output of our cities. It can be helped by preventing realistically the tragedy of the growing loss through foreclosure of our small homes and our farms. It can be helped by insistence that the Federal, State, and local governments act forthwith on the demand that their cost be drastically reduced. It can be helped by the unifying of relief activities which today are often scattered, uneconomical, and unequal. It can be helped by national planning for and supervision of all forms of transportation and of communications and other utilities which have definitely public character. There are many ways in which it can be helped, but it can never be helped merely by talking about it. We must act and act quickly.

Finally, in our progress toward a resumption of work we require two safeguards against a return of the evils of the old order; there must be a strict supervision of all banking and credits and investments; there must be an end to speculation with other people's money, and there must be provision for an adequate but sound currency.

. . .

In the field of world policy I would dedicate this Nation to the policy of the good neighbor—the neighbor who resolutely respects himself and, because he does so, respects the rights of others—the neighbor who respects his obligations and respects the sanctity of his agreements in and with a world of neighbors.

If I read the temper of our people correctly, we now realize as we have never realized before our interdependence on each other; that we cannot merely take but we must give as well; that if we are to go forward, we must move as a trained and loyal army willing to sacrifice for the good of a common discipline, because without such discipline no progress is made, no leadership becomes effective. We are, I know, ready and willing to submit our lives and property to such discipline, because it makes possible a leadership which aims at a larger good. This I propose to offer, pledging that the larger purpose will bind upon us all as a sacred obligation with a unity of duty hitherto evoked only in time of armed strife.

With this pledge taken, I assume unhesitatingly the leadership of this great array of our people dedicated to a disciplined attack upon our common problems.

Action in this image and to this end is feasible under the form of government which we have inherited from our ancestors. Our Constitution is so simple and practical that it is possible always to meet extraordinary needs by changes in emphasis and arrangement without loss of essential form. That is why our constitutional system has proved itself the most superbly enduring political mechanism the modern world has produced. It has met every stress of vast expansion of territory, of foreign wars, of bitter internal strife, of world relations.

It is to be hoped that the normal balance of executive and legislative authority may be wholly adequate to meet the unprecedented task before us. But it may be that an unprecedented demand and need for undelayed action may call for temporary departure from that normal balance of public procedure.

I am prepared under my constitutional duty to recommend the measures that a stricken nation in the midst of a stricken world may require. These measures or such other measures as the Congress may build out of its experience and wisdom, I shall seek, within my constitutional authority, to bring to speedy adoption.

But in the event that the Congress shall fail to take one of those two courses, and in the event that the national emergency is still critical, I shall not evade the clear course of duty that will then confront me. I shall ask the Congress for the one remaining instrument to meet the crisis—broad Executive power to wage a war against the emergency, as great as the power that would be given to me if we were in fact invaded by a foreign force.

For the trust reposed in me I will return the courage and the devotion that befit the time. I can do no less.

We face the arduous days that lie before us in the warm courage of national unity; with the clear consciousness of seeking old and precious moral values; with the clean satisfaction that comes from the stern performance of duty by old and young alike. We aim at the assurance of a rounded and permanent national life.

We do not distrust the future of essential democracy. The people of the United States have not failed. In their need they have registered a mandate that they want direct, vigorous action. They have asked for discipline and direction under leadership. They have made me the present instrument of their wishes. In the spirit of the gift I take it.

SIGNIFICANCE

Roosevelt's inaugural address touched on a number of the elements that would form the foundation of the New Deal. He spoke of the immediate need to reverse the banking crisis and of the critical tasks of creating jobs for the unemployed and providing assistance to farmers. He explained the strong role the government must play—particularly the executive branch—in reviving the national economy, and he urged the American people to be ready to sacrifice for the good of the country. In this speech and many others after it, Roosevelt projected confidence and strength, offering a measure of calm to a worried public.

Upon taking office, President Roosevelt acted quickly. He declared a federal banking holiday and called for a special session of the U.S. Congress to pass legislation that would avert a collapse of the banking system. Congress convened on March 9, 1933, and by that evening, Roosevelt had signed into law the Emergency Banking Act. This law began the New Deal and brought on a gradual renewal of the public's faith. Over the next few months, a period known as the Hundred Days, Roosevelt and the U.S. Congress passed a number of significant New Deal laws.

The watchwords of the New Deal were "relief, recovery, and reform." Relief measures provided immediate assistance to people suffering from dire poverty or to businesses on the brink of collapse. Laws aimed at recovery focused on fixing the damage wrought during the first few years of the Depression, and reforms attempted to strengthen the economy to prevent future depressions. While the New Deal did not reverse the course of the Depression overnight, it did result in a slow but sure economic recovery. One of the most significant changes initiated by the Roosevelt administration, exemplified by the passage of the Social Security Act of 1935, was the notion that the federal government had an obligation to provide for its neediest citizens.

FURTHER RESOURCES
Books

Burg, David E. *The Great Depression*. New York: Facts on File, 1996.

Davis, Kenneth Sydney. *FDR: The New Deal Years, 1933–1937*. New York: Random House, 1986.

Depression America. 6 vols. Danbury, Conn.: Grolier Educational, 2001.

Kyvig, David E. *Daily Life in the United States, 1920–1940*. Chicago: Ivan R. Dee, 2004.

Nardo, Don, ed. *The Great Depression*. San Diego, Calif.: Greenhaven Press, 2000.

Web sites

Franklin D. Roosevelt Presidential Library and Museum. "Franklin D. Roosevelt." <http://www.fdrlibrary.marist.edu/fdrbio.html> (accessed June 2, 2006).

New Deal Network. <http://newdeal.feri.org/> (accessed June 3, 2006).

A Statement by Frank E. Gannett, Publisher, Gannett Newspapers

Letter

By: Frank E. Gannett

Date: February 23, 1937

Source: *The National Archives.* "Teaching With Documents: Constitutional Issues: Separation of Powers." <http://www.archives.gov/education/lessons/separation-powers/#documents> (accessed May 19, 2006).

About the Author: Frank E. Gannett (1876–1957) founded the newspaper organization that bears his name in 1906. By 1937, Gannett had constructed a media empire that today remains one of the most influential in the United States. Gannett was a vociferous opponent of the New Deal policies of President Franklin Roosevelt. He expressed his opposition to Roosevelt both through his newspapers and through his leadership of the National Committee to Uphold Constitutional Government, an organization founded in response to the Roosevelt plan to increase the size of the Supreme Court in 1937.

INTRODUCTION

Franklin Roosevelt's election as president of the United States in 1932 precipitated a series of legislative initiatives designed to counter the toll that had been exacted by the Great Depression upon both the American economy and large segments of the American population. Between 1933 and 1935, Roosevelt and his Democratic administration passed into law the National Recovery Administration, the Agricultural Adjustment Act, and a host of other measures designed to provide relief to the disadvantaged and a stimulus to the American economy. These programs are best known by the collective term used by Roosevelt, the New Deal.

The New Deal was roundly attacked by both the Republican Party leadership and elements of Roosevelt's own Democratic Party. Conservative elements equated the New Deal with socialism, and many Americans were concerned about the potential centralization of power in the office of the President. A number of challenges to the constitutionality of the various components of the New Deal were initiated. As these challenges worked their way for determination to the U.S. Supreme Court, it became apparent that the New Deal initiatives were not viewed favorably by the court. In May 1935, the Supreme Court ruled three of Roosevelt's initiatives to be unconstitutional, precipitating a series of statements by Roosevelt regarding the hostile attitude of the court towards progress.

Roosevelt's resounding victory in the November 1936 presidential election set the stage for his plan to redefine the composition of the Supreme Court in a fashion that was favorable to the New Deal legislation yet to come before the Court. On February 5, 1937, Roosevelt announced his intention to introduce the Judicial Reorganization Bill of 1937. The Bill would provide the President with the power to appoint an additional Supreme Court justice for every current sitting justice who was 70.5 years of age or older. Roosevelt's stated rationale for the bill was a desire to have a sufficient number of justices to carry out the work of the Court; critics of the plan labeled the proposal "court packing," setting the stage for one of the most bitter constitutional battles in American history.

In a less-publicized aspect of Roosevelt's plan, Supreme Court justices could be transferred to lower courts to rule on cases; in such a structure, pro–New-Deal judges could be assigned to rule on New Deal legislation.

At the heart of the controversy was the structure of American government as mandated by the U.S. Constitution. The Constitution created a three-part system of government, where the powers of the executive branch, headed by the president, the legislative branch, comprised of the Senate and the House of Representatives, and the judiciary are evenly balanced. Influential conservatives such as Frank Gannett saw the Judicial Reorganization Act as an attempt by the president to take control of the judiciary and thus take control of government itself.

Defenders of the existing Supreme Court structure pointed to the fundamental importance of judicial impartiality that the Constitution sought to protect. Supreme Court justices are appointed for life to make them less vulnerable to either political influence or swings in public opinion.

Frank Gannett during his 1940 campaign for president of the United States. PHOTO BY HANS KNOPF/PIX INC./TIME LIFE PICTURES/GETTY IMAGES.

Roosevelt introduced the judicial reorganization bill in the Senate in February 1937. Public sentiment was not favorable to its passage, even though large segments of the American public felt the Supreme Court was essentially defeating the will of the people in ruling New Deal legislation as unconstitutional. Other events overtook the proposed legislation. A New York State minimum wage law—a crucial piece of New Deal legislation—was unexpectedly approved by the Court when Justice Owen J. Roberts aligned himself with the pro–New-Deal wing of the Court. This event prompted the expression, "A switch in time saved nine." The proposed judicial reorganization legislation was never passed, resulting in an apparent victory for Roosevelt's opponents, such as Frank Gannett.

PRIMARY SOURCE

President Roosevelt had cleverly camouflaged a most amazing and startling proposal for packing the Supreme Court. It is true that the lower courts are slow and overburdened, we probably do need more judges to expedite litigation but this condition should not be used as a subtle excuse for changing the complexion and undermining the independence of our highest court. Increasing the number of judges from nine to fifteen would not make this high tribunal act any more promptly than it does now, but it would give the President control of the Judiciary Department.

A year ago I predicted that this is exactly what would happen if Roosevelt was reelected. The Supreme Court having declared invalid many of the administration measures the President now resorts to a plan of creating a Supreme Court that will be entirely sympathetic with his ideas. Provision has been made for amending the Constitution. If it is necessary to change the Constitution it should be done in the regular way. The President is mistaken, if he thinks he can conceal his real purpose of packing, influencing and controlling the Supreme Court by confusing that objective with a long dissertation on the slow action of our various courts.

The Supreme Court has been the anchor that has held America safe through many storms. Its absolute independence and integrity must never be in doubt.

Our Government is composed of three departments, Legislative, Executive and Judiciary. These are the foundations of our Democracy. As a result of the election and the transfer of powers by so-called emergency measures, the Executive now dominates the Legislative Department. The President now proposes also to dominate the Judiciary. Do we want to give to this man or any one man complete control of these three departments of our Government which have from the beginning of the Republic been kept entirely separate and independent?

This proposal should give every American grave concern for it is a step towards absolutism and complete dictatorial power.

Frank E. Gannett.

SIGNIFICANCE

The constitutional issues detailed by Frank Gannett in his open letter of February 1937 represent one of the most concerted challenges to the function of American government in the history of the nation. The ability of a president to appoint Supreme Court justices to fill a vacancy is inherent in the power of the American executive branch, but to create a court that was as large as the President needed it to be to pass his legislative programs was a remarkable attempt to extend his executive authority.

Roosevelt's desire to impose his will upon the Supreme Court composition was all the more remarkable when it is assessed against the entire history of the

Court. Created in 1789, the historical attitude adopted by the Court towards the constitutionality of legislation was remarkably conservative—only two government bills were held to be unconstitutional between 1789 and the end of the American Civil War in 1865. Six bills were ruled to be unconstitutional between 1865 and 1930. The Supreme Court's apparent lack of regard for the constitutionality of the components of the Roosevelt New Deal is an isolated approach when considered against the sweep of history.

Roosevelt's judicial reorganization scheme had some curious features. Roosevelt had made the age of the Supreme Court justices a significant issue in his public comments about the reorganization; six of the nine justices were then over seventy years of age, yet Roosevelt made no mention of whether the election of a president or a member of Congress should be similarly limited by age considerations. It is noteworthy that Roosevelt's concerns regarding the age of a sitting justice have never prompted the imposition of an age limit. A U.S. Supreme Court appointment remains one made for life, or until the justice retires or dies. By contrast, Canada, a country that shares a common legal heritage with the United States, mandates the retirement of its Supreme Court members at age seventy-five.

The attempt by Roosevelt to control the Supreme Court remains a classic example of losing a battle but winning the war. Whether in response to the attempts by Roosevelt to change the Court composition, or as a result of a genuine change in the judicial outlook towards the New Deal initiatives that remained to be considered by the Court, the Supreme Court took a more favorable view of the New Deal program from 1937 forward. Roosevelt gained the further advantage of the passage of time between 1937 and 1941; as justices retired or died, Roosevelt exercised his prerogative to appoint justices whom he believed would be favorable to his administration. By 1941, seven of the Supreme Court justices were Roosevelt appointees.

A further significance of the efforts of Roosevelt to control the Supreme Court rests with the contrast between Roosevelt's reorganization initiative and the entirety of his political career. His desire to pack the Supreme Court must be seen as Roosevelt's most ill-conceived decision in a long and successful political career. As president, he artfully maneuvered the nation to accept the New Deal as necessary to the survival of America's economic structure; his policies provided some measure of relief to those devastated by the Depression, and the related environmental impacts of the Midwest droughts. Roosevelt, through careful statesmanship, brought the United States into the

European war indirectly, through his support of Great Britain from 1939 through 1941. The transparency of his characterization of the judicial reforms he desired in 1937 as necessary to assist with the workload of the Supreme Court are remarkable, given Roosevelt's obvious political talents.

The Supreme Court issues of 1937 are also significant for the fact that in the intervening period, there have been relatively few public issues concerning the structure and the composition of the court. Modern American judicial history includes some heated nomination hearings (Robert Bork in 1987 and Justice Clarence Thomas in 1991 are notable examples), but there have been no serious efforts to fundamentally alter how the Court conducts its business.

FURTHER RESOURCES

Books

Brandt, J. Donald. *A History of Gannett 1906–1993.* Arlington, Va.: Gannett Company, 1993.

Leuchtenburg, William E. *The Supreme Court Reborn: The Court Revolution in the Age of Roosevelt.* New York: Oxford University Press, 1995.

Web sites

Notable American Unitarians. "Frank Gannett: Newspaper Publisher, 1876–1957." <www.harvardsquarelibrary.org/unitarians/gannett.html> (accessed May 19, 2006).

PBS. "American Experience: Franklin Delano Roosevelt." <www.pbs.org/wgbh/amex/presidents/32_f_roosevelt/index.html> (accessed May 19, 2006).

American Indian Movement Siege of Wounded Knee

Photograph

By: Anonymous

Date: March 19, 1973

Source: © Bettmann/Corbis.

About the Photographer: Photograph residing in the Bettmann Archives of Corbis Corporation, an image group headquartered in Seattle, with a worldwide archive of over seventy million images.

INTRODUCTION

The American Indian Movement (AIM) is part of the Red Power civil rights movement of the late 1960s

PRIMARY SOURCE

American Indian Movement Siege of Wounded Knee: A roadblock on the road to Wounded Knee, South Dakota, is manned by armed members and supporters of the American Indian Movement (AIM), March 19, 1973. © BETTMANN/CORBIS.

and 1970s. Founded in Minneapolis by a group of Anishinabe Indians, it modeled the confrontational style of the Black Panther Party. In 1973, AIM members undertook a major civil rights campaign in South Dakota that led to the seventy-one day siege at Wounded Knee.

On the Pine Ridge reservation in South Dakota, the recently-installed Oglala Sioux tribal president Dick Wilson sought to establish himself as a dictator. He signed away a large and mineral-rich tract of reservation land in exchange for being allowed by the federal government to set up his feudal barony. Wilson had been provided with federal funds to create a paramilitary organization that called itself the Guardians of the Oglala Nation (GOONs). Heavily armed, the GOONs were employed in an effort to terrorize Wilson's opponents, mostly AIM supporters, into submission. As one example, AIM member and Oglala tribe member Russell Means, who owned land on Pine Ridge, was barred from the reservation by GOONs.

Wilson's opponents obtained enough signatures to call for his removal from office. However, the Bureau of Indian Affairs placed Wilson in charge of his own impeachment. A sixty-man Special Operations Group of U.S. marshals was posted on the reservation to support Wilson. Stymied in their efforts to resolve their grievance by conventional due process methods, the elders (comprising the traditional Oglala leadership) next called upon AIM to intervene. On February 27, 1973, AIM planned to hold a press conference at a site heavy with symbolism. It picked the mass grave containing the remains of 350 Lakotas massacred by the U.S. Army at Wounded Knee in 1890 to expose the situation on Pine Ridge. However, on the night before the press conference, Wilson's GOONs had set up roadblocks on every road by which the press could enter the settlement, simultaneously sealing the AIM people inside. The siege of Wounded Knee had begun.

PRIMARY SOURCE

AMERICAN INDIAN MOVEMENT SIEGE OF WOUNDED KNEE
See primary source image.

SIGNIFICANCE

The siege ended on May 7, 1973 when federal officials agreed to conduct a full-scale investigation of the Wilson regime and to meet with traditional Oglala leaders concerning violations of the 1868 Fort Laramie Treaty that had legally defined U.S./Lakota relations. AIM had achieved its purpose. The situation on Pine Ridge and the oppressive conditions in Indian country more generally had riveted international attention. Within a year, AIM translated this media attention into the establishment of its diplomatic arm, the International Indian Treaty Council (ITC). The council became the world's first indigenous organization to attain formal consultative status with the United Nations.

During the siege, Wilson publicly announced that AIM would die at Wounded Knee. In the three years between March 1973 and March 1976, at least sixty-nine AIM members and their supporters were murdered on or near Pine Ridge. Another 350 AIM members and supporters suffered serious physical assaults and/or attempts on their lives. The FBI declined to investigate the murders and assaults because it was short of manpower. AIM members and supporters, disputing this claim, charged the FBI with continuing the long American pattern of abusing and suppressing Native Americans.

AIM held its last general membership meeting in 1975. Its last national officer, John Trudell, resigned in 1979 shortly after his entire family was mysteriously murdered on the Duck Valley Reservation in Nevada. There were occasional bursts of AIM activity in subsequent years, but AIM was effectively finished by 1980.

FURTHER RESOURCES
Books

Burnett, Robert and John Koster. *The Road to Wounded Knee.* New York: Bantam, 1974.

Churchill, Ward and Jim Vander Wall. *Agents of Repression: The FBI's Secret Wars Against the Black Panther Party and the American Indian Movement.* Cambridge, MA: South End, 2002.

Sayer, John William. *Ghost Dancing the Law: The Wounded Knee Trials.* Cambridge, MA: Harvard University Press, 1997.

Smith, Paul Chaat and Robert Allen Warrior. *Like a Hurricane: The American Indian Movement from Alcatraz to Wounded Knee.* New York: New Press, 1996.

Iranian People Vote for an Islamic Republic

Magazine article

By: Anonymous

Date: April 7, 1979

Source: "Iranian People Vote for an Islamic Republic." The *Economist.* April 7, 1979.

About the Author: The *Economist* is a British-based magazine covering business and global issues.

INTRODUCTION

On February 1, 1979, the Ayatollah Ruhollah Khomeini returned to Iran after fourteen years in exile. By the end of March, Khomeini had successfully led the movement to replace the constitutional monarchy with an Islamic state. The modern monarchy had been in place since 1925, when the parliament of Persia voted to vest the crown of Iran in Reza Shah Pahlavi. In 1935, Persia adopted the new name of Iran. During World War II (1938–1945), the shah allied with the Axis powers leading to post-war occupation by Britain and Russia, as the two nations divided Iran into spheres of influence. In 1951, a power struggle between the shah and the prime minister followed the parliament voting to nationalize the oil industry which, at the time, had been dominated by the British-owned Anglo-Iranian Oil Company. With the assistance of the United States and Britain, a coup in Iran installed a new prime minister into power and the shah, who had fled during the power struggle, returned. By 1963, the shah began the "White Revolution," a campaign to modernize the country by implementing land reform and policies of social and economic reform. The shah utilized the state secret police to control opposition to his reform.

The shah's movement to modernize Iran was funded by the vast oil revenues; however, inflation, official corruption, and a growing income gap began to lead to unrest by 1976. In addition, the modernization policies began to alienate the Muslim clergy in the

Iranian women in burqas show their identity cards to a solider as they line up to vote in a 1979 election. © CHRISTINE SPENGLER/SYGMA/CORBIS.

country. By 1978, approximately 60,000 foreigners resided in Iran. Their influence in the form of dress, culture, and entertainment along with the shah's modernization policies created the perception that Iran was sacrificing its Islamic values and cultural identity. Externally, the creation of a one-party state in 1975 and the heavy-handed tactics used to implement the shah's reforms created international concern that basic freedoms were being suppressed under the shah's rule. Secular leadership from the middle class led by intellectuals, lawyers, and secular politicians began a campaign of protest against the shah in the form of letters, declarations, and resolutions calling for the restoration of constitutional rule.

In 1978, religious protests signaled the beginning of the end of the shah's rule in Iran. The religiously based protests began after an article appearing in the newspaper, *Ettelaat*, questioned the piety of Khomeini and suggested that he was working as a British agent. Khomeini, although in exile, was considered the spiritual leader to many Shiite Muslims in Iran. This accusation was not received well and resulted in

orchestrated demonstrations and strikes. From exile, Khomeini issued proclamations calling for the overthrow of the shah and continued protests. His supporters declared their goal of creating an Islamic state with Khomeini as its leader. One such protest came on September 4, 1978, at the public prayers to commemorate the end to Ramadan, the Muslim month of fasting. The assembly of approximately 100,000 quickly turned into an anti-shah protest. The protests continued for several days until martial law was declared in Tehran and eleven other cities. September 9th became known as "Black Friday" to those protesters when troops fired into the crowds at Tehran's Jaleh Square and killed at least eighty-seven people, by Iranian government accounts. This move escalated the violence of the protests as the opposition became radicalized and began to target symbols of the shah's modernization program. Nightclubs and movie theaters, viewed as symbols of moral corruption, were bombed. Banks, signs of economic corruption, were also hit by the opposition. In addition, police stations, representing political repression, were also targeted.

Khomeini, by October 1978, had been expelled from Iraq and reestablished his headquarters in France outside of Paris. This new location afforded Khomeini better exposure in the world press, as well as better communication with his followers in Iran. In November, leaders of the National Front, an opposition political party, met with Khomeini and issued a statement which called for the removal of the shah and the creation of a new government in Iran. At this same time, the shah began to negotiate with moderate oppositions, some of whom were also members of the National Front. After meeting with the shah, National Front leader, Shapour Bakhtair arranged to form a government as long as the shah left Iran.

On January 16, 1979, the shah departed Iran. Bakhtair began to initiate polices that would appease the opposition. However, Bakhtair could not gain the support of Khomeini who was committed to the creation of a new political structure in Iran and an end to the monarchy. The National Front expelled Bakhtair as a traitor and on February 1, 1979 Khomeini returned to Iran from exile. Shortly thereafter, Khomeini would declare a new state, the Islamic Republic of Iran, as determined through a referendum throughout Iran.

PRIMARY SOURCE

Under the gaze of their spiritual advisers, Iranians voted overwhelmingly if not exactly secretly in favour of an Islamic republic on March 30th and 31st. Ayatollah Khomeini has got the rubber-stamp he wanted for the new regime he intends to put in place of the Shah's.

It could hardly have been otherwise. The ballot papers had a green section (the colour of Islam) for Yes, and a red section—guess whose colour that is—for those intrepid enough to vote No. The choice had to be made in full view of the mullahs and other guardians of the revolution who manned the polling stations. Few voters exercised the "right" of dissent.

Away from the polling stations, there was muffled opposition. The new political party of the middle class, the National Democratic Front, called for a boycott. Ayatollah Shariatmadari, who used to be Iran's foremost religious leader, expressed reservations about the absence of a real choice. And several of the country's minorities are manifestly uneasy. The Turkomans, in particular, are putting up a tough fight for autonomy. For the minorities, non-Persians and in many cases Sunni Moslems, not Shiates like most Persians, the way the referendum was run hints at the emergence of a new tyranny.

SIGNIFICANCE

Khomeini and his followers asserted that the 1979 referendum represented the popular will to create a new Islamic state, in which the economy and society would be managed by the tenets of Islam. The ultimate authority in the new structure was to be held by the supreme leader. The supreme leader is a member of the *ulama*, or Muslim scholars whose role is the interpretation of Islamic law. The new government also provided for a president, and assembly of experts, from which the supreme leader is chosen. The guardian council serves as a constitutional court and the *Majlis* serves as the parliament of Iran.

FURTHER RESOURCES

Periodicals

Bakhash, Shaul. "Iran: The Coming of the Revolution." *Countries of the World.* January 1, 1991.

Gheissari, Ali; Nasr, Vali. "Iran's Democracy Debate." *Middle East Policy.* July 1, 2004.

Web sites

BBC. "Timeline: Iran." <http://news.bbc.co.uk/2/hi/middle_east/country_profiles/806268.stm> (accessed May 10, 2006).

Nation Building and Singapore's People's Association

Magazine excerpt

By: Lee Kuan Yew

Date: 1980

Source: Yew, Lee Kuan. "Nation Building and Singapore's People's Association." *The First Twenty Years of the People's Association.* 12 (1980): 7–17.

About the Author: Lee Kuan Yew was the first Prime Minister of Singapore, taking office in 1959. He guided the nation's economic and political growth and was repeatedly re-elected, holding office until 1990.

INTRODUCTION

Singapore, an Asian city whose history extends back many centuries, first became involved with the western powers in 1819. In that year, the British established a trading post in Singapore to refit and resupply their far-ranging merchant fleet and to serve as a military buffer against possible expansion by the Dutch.

Parade goers and policemen look at a display of one of Singapore's founders during Singapore's 40th anniversary of independence on August 9, 2004. AP IMAGES.

The settlement proved to be almost immediately profitable for the British and two treaties soon formalized the relationship between the Crown and its new possession.

By the middle 1800's, Singapore had become a major trading port, with a population of over 80,000, and had also became the world's leading processor and exporter of natural rubber. The city's prosperity was interrupted when the Japanese bombed and invaded it in 1941, occupying the area for more than three years. After British forces retook it in 1945, the British military governed until the following year, when Singapore was designated a Crown Colony of Great Britain. Singapore was then led by regimes incorporating both British and local elements until 1959, when the colony elected its first Parliament and Prime Minister and became a sovereign nation.

Lee Kwan Yew, Singapore's first elected prime minister, faced numerous challenges. While Singapore was technically independent, Great Britain retained control of the nation's foreign policy, creating resentment among some of Singapore's citizens. In the years following his election, Lee worked diligently to secure his nation's complete independence from its former colonial master.

While Singapore jostled with Great Britain over its independence, a larger conflict was engulfing Asia as communists battled for control of numerous countries. In Singapore itself, communist sympathizers held important political positions, and Lee's own political party, the People's Action Party (PAP), consisted of a moderate wing, which Lee headed, and a strongly pro-communist wing. Following the PAP's election victory, numerous other nations expressed concern that the win might empower communists in Singapore, and some businesses relocated their operations to other Asian locales.

While the two wings of the PAP had joined forces to win control of the nation, their ultimate objectives were incompatible. Lee and the moderates foresaw an inevitable union between Singapore and Malaya, resulting in complete autonomy from Britain for the newly joined countries; the communist wing of the party hoped to achieve a takeover of Singapore and closer ties to other communist nations. With the two sides hopelessly at odds over the future of the nation and the party, the communists eventually chose to leave PAP and form their own party in 1961.

Beyond political concerns, Lee also faced economic problems. Though relatively prosperous, Singapore remained a tiny nation with little land and few natural resources. One of Lee's early initiatives proposed merging Singapore with its larger neighbor Malaya and two other colonies to form the new nation of Malaysia; the agreement created central control for matters such as defense and trade but allowed local autonomy for regional issues. In addition to vastly expanding Singapore's resource base, Lee believed the merger would allow Malaysia to finally and completely throw off all vestiges of British control. With overwhelming public support, the merger was approved in 1963.

Lee's achievement proved to be short-lived. The marriage between Singapore and its Malaysian partners proved difficult to consummate, as political and racial tensions led to conflict and violence. The distribution of power within the new nation was also a point of contention, and food shortages resulting from the riots exacerbated an already tense situation. In 1965, Lee appeared on television to announce Singapore's exodus from Malaysia. The smaller nation would now be forced to survive on its own, without the benefit of a much larger marketplace and resources.

■ PRIMARY SOURCE

Few people know how crucial a role the People's Association has played in Singapore in the last twenty years, and what a key institution it still is. When we took office in 1959, we knew that the average person in Singapore did not want to be openly identified with any political party, whatever his personal feelings or loyalties may be. He was more fearful than apathetic. The communists were all-powerful and intimidating and most people, especially the Chinese, believed with good reason that if they were seen opposing the communists, then if the communists won, retribution would be inevitable.

Hence the Government decided to set up the People's Association with forty-five founder institution members. It inherited some twenty-nine community centers and five youth clubs. People need not be openly identified with a political party like the PAP, or a government department like the Social Welfare Department, but with a semi-independent, semi-government statutory board. The PA's objective was to get the discrete, almost self-contained, social and communal groups to meet across racial, language, religious, and cultural barriers. The PA had to bring these diverse groups together in joint recreational, social, and educational activities, all of a non-political nature.

The PA recruited some fifty highly politicized Chinese-educated young men as community centre organizers. They were the activists to form the nucleus as ground workers in these community centers. They had run PAP literacy and recreational activities in PAP branches. They were therefore familiar with the habits and preferences of the young boys and girls from poor working-class homes. Many of these youths were early school leavers and worse, they were unemployed. The community centers began to spring to life with literacy classes, cooking lessons, chess games, basketball, ping-pong, and other simple pleasures.

In June 1961, the pro-communists in the PAP broke off. Most of these fifty organizers in the PA also broke off to support Barisan Sosialis. They believed Barisan would win and topple the PAP. They deliberately disrupted the activities and programs in the community centers. Nevertheless, these new activities carried on, although at a reduced pace. The Ministers and Assemblymen were too busy rallying the ground against the communists to do much about repairing the damage in the PA. This phase, a daily ding-dong propaganda, life and death struggle between the PAP and the communists, fought in desperate earnestness, ended with a decisive seventy-one percent vote for merger in a referendum in favor of Malaysia in September 1962. Once this battle was over, we set out to rebuild the ground organization for the next round against the communists. . . .

At first, it was a slow and tentative regrouping of the ground. Our strategy was simple. Once we showed that the communists were not invincible, we were able to get some local leaders to come forward and identify themselves openly with the PAP government. The first three constituency tours got off the ground with warm and even enthusiastic responses, despite silent communist intimidation in rural constituencies where their influence had always been strong. Then more and more influential leaders volunteered to "welcome" my visits, arranging more welcoming committees in more stops in a constituency to attend receptions and functions. During those stops, speeches of support and requests for government action were made. Invariably, I had to reply impromptu. Often I made as many as twenty speeches in one day, some nearly one hour long. . . .

The constituency tours gathered momentum. People watched on TV the spontaneous response of the crowds to the speeches made. The visits gathered steam. The ground swell surged in the government's favor. I could feel the tide turn against the communists. People were no longer so afraid of Barisan Sosialis. Communist intimidation lost its chilling fear since they were unable or unwilling to risk violence and assassinations. Masses of people openly supported the government and welcomed me on those tours. More and more leaders came forward, prepared to stand up against the communists and be counted.

The communists set out to disrupt the tours. The first attempt was on 12 January 1963 at Kampong Kembangan. Along Jalan Eunos, the members of the communist-controlled Rural Residents' Association held up banners and posters criticizing the government and shouting protests as we passed by their premises. On 19 January 1963 in Jalan Kayu, three women affected by resettlement, were instigated by the Country People's Association to create a scene. They vociferously confronted me and demanded increased compensation.

On 2 February 1963, a revolt took place in Brunei. Barisan Sosialis leaders were involved in the conspiracy with Azahari. A sweep was made of the pro-communist leaders. Operation Cold Store was ordered by the Internal Security Council. It was supported by the Singapore Government.

A month later, on 10 March 1963, I toured Nee Soon, another rural constituency with many blank votes. Barisan wrote up "blackboard news" viciously attacking the government and condemning me for the detentions. They placed the "blackboard news" where I had to see it on my way to a reception at the Lim Clan Association. But after Operation Cold Store, they were careful not to use force....

There were many such incidents of protests and disruptions. On 8 September 1963 at Towner Road (now renamed Whampoa Drive), when I passed the premises of the Singapore School Canteen Vendors' Union, the Hawkers' Union, and the Singapore business Houses Employees' Union, (adjacent to one another), they booed and jeered at me. They started to jostle me as I passed by. They pressed on me and tried to push me into the drain. Fortunately, my alert and attentive security officer, Ng Choon Soon (retired recently), strenuously interposed himself between them and me. He absorbed he jostle and enabled me to jump across, instead of falling into, the one-meter deep monsoon drain....

Ten months after my first tour in Jurong, I toured Mountbatten, completing the last of the fifty-one constituencies. I remember that I finished my last tour in the dawn hours of the morning of nomination day, 12 September 1963. The newspapers recorded that I finished my tour of Telok Blangah at 2:15 A.M. of 12 September, then went on to Mountbatten and finished my visit at 6:15 A.M. I wanted to finish all visits before the general election campaign began. I went home to Oxley Road to doze for a few hours. Then I changed, and presented myself at the nomination centre at the Polytechnic that same morning at about 11 A.M.

Polling day was on Saturday, 21 September 1963. The PAP won the elections with 46.5 percent of the votes, winning thirty-seven seats. Thirteen seats went to Barisan. The last seat went to Ong Eng Guan in Hong Lim. But his majority was much reduced compared to what he had in the by-election in May 1961.

In October 1964, we formalized the functioning of management committees for sixteen community centers, including Duxxton Plain in Tanjong Pagar. These men who formed the earliest management committees had carried on working actively after my constituency tours. We drew upon this reservoir of active community leaders. These men had formed the various Welcoming Committees in each constituency.

In June 1964, there were communal riots in Singapore. We formed Goodwill Committees in many areas, especially in Geylang Serai, Geylang, Nee Soon, Sembawang and Jalan Kayu. They helped to dampen inter-communal fears and panic. They provided ground leadership.

By 26 January 1965, the PA formed another twenty-one management committees; and by 3 August 1965, another forty-four management committees.

Those who did not want to have daily involvement in the work of the community centers were brought into the Citizens' Consultative Committees. The first four Citizens' Consultative Committees were formed on 24 March 1965 for Nee Soon, Punggol, Sembawang and Serangoon Gardens.

These men were already established leaders of the communities they lived in. Through them, we explained our policies to the people. Through them, we received accurate feedback on how people were affected, and what needed to be modified. Without this network of local community leaders throughout every constituency, the government would not have had so sensitive a feel of the ground. Without our fingers on the pulse, we could not have made swift modifications to policies to minimize upsetting our people's lives. We did not abandon our policies for economic development and urban renewal, but we mitigated the upsets caused to people's lives.

I cannot adequately express my abiding gratitude to all those officers who sacrificed so many weekends to accompany me on all the tours through the fifty-one constituencies....

They were dedicated men. They understood what was at stake. They slogged with me to help the government win over the ground. Had the PAP lost in September 1963, the history of Singapore would have been different.

Singaporeans are indebted to these public officers and to these community leaders. They were the interface between the administration and the people whose lives were affected by the rapid changes set in motion by the government's economic and social policies. These officers and community leaders became something like a clutching system that enabled the government to change gears without wrenching the gear box. They were not great public figures known to the press. They were known only in their own villages, known to people only in their own streets, known to members of their own clans. They had lived amongst their followers for decades. Only trustworthy men became leaders in such close and intimate situations. Without such men in the Management Committees and the Citizens' Consultative Committees, the PA would have been just another paper organization, running the headquarters in the old Kallang Airport building, with 186 community centers it had at its maximum in 1969, as so many symbols marked on a chain-of-command chart. Now, there are only 158 community centers as some small under-utilized rural centers have been closed.

The future types of community leaders will be different. Whole communal groups have moved out and are spread throughout the different new towns and housing estates. All dialect, religious, and ethnic groups are now mixed in the new towns. Nevertheless, new leaders will emerge. The PA must facilitate the identification, selection and training of trustworthy men who will become the accepted leaders of these new communities. If we do not actively create social situations for such leaders to emerge, they will nevertheless emerge, but more gradually over a longer time frame. They will be the modern day counterparts of the old kepala kampung, or the penghulu, or the ketua, or the zhu xi of the huay kuan, in the Residents' Committees. As they prove their worth, we must absorb the most reliable and active of them into the Management committees and the Citizens' Consultative Committees. In this way, we can ensure that the government remains sensitive to the changing needs of the people.

This is the key task of the PA. It is not the lavishness of the modern amenities in impressive "new generation" community centers that guarantees success. Success depends on the quality and dedication of the men on the ground; men who command respect; men who are trusted by their fellow citizens; men who will give the government honest feedback so that modifications and amendments to government policies are made in time to minimize the adverse impact of these policies. Those who are naturally active and socially committed are bound to be noticed and selected for the Residents' Committees. The most effective members of the Resident's Committees will go on to serve on the Management Committees and Citizens'

Consultative Committees. Then people will always have clear channels up to the government.

SIGNIFICANCE

Singapore today is among the most impressive economic success stories in Asia, a democracy that enjoys low levels of corruption and a booming economy based primarily on electronics manufacturing and export. The nation's Gross Domestic Product per person is roughly equal to that of the largest nations in Europe, making it a highly competitive producer in international markets. In 2005, Singapore's economy experienced an inflation rate of just one percent, while its industrial production grew by more than eight percent.

After choosing not to run for Prime Minister in 1990, Lee remained active in the PAP and in national politics. Today, he is a respected elder statesman and is widely viewed as one of the primary forces behind Singapore's rise to prosperity. By 1999, the ruling PAP had developed such a stranglehold on national politics in Singapore that its leaders seriously considered dividing it into two parties in order to create a more credible opposition. In 2004, Lee's oldest son, Lee Hsien Loong was chosen as Singapore's third Prime Minister.

FURTHER RESOURCES
Books
Farrell, Brian P. et al. *Between Two Oceans: A Military History Of Singapore From First Settlement To Final British Withdrawal.* New York: Avon Books, 1977.

Vasil, Raj. *Governing Singapore: A History of National Development and Democracy.* Eastern University Press, 2004.

Yew, Lee Kuan. *From Third World to First : The Singapore Story: 1965–2000.* New York: HarperCollins, 2000.

Periodicals
Anonymous. "China's Dispora Turns Homeward." *The Economist.* 329(1993):33-34.

Straczek, J. H. "Sixty Years On: The Fall of Singapore Revisited." *International History Review.* 24(2004):893-895.

Wong, Ting-Hong and Michael Apple. "Rethinking the Education/State Formation Connection: Pedagogic Reform in Singapore, 1945–1965." *Comparative Education Review.* 46(2002):182–200.

Web sites
Central Intelligence Agency. "World Factbook: Singapore." <http://www.cia.gov/cia/publications/factbook/geos/sn.html> (accessed June 29, 2006).

University of Texas International Information Systems. "Singapore: History." 1994 <http://inic.utexas.edu/asnic/countries/singapore/Singapore-History.html> (accessed June 29, 2006).

The Party That Isn't

North Korea's "Unification Revolution Party"

Book excerpt

By: Research Center for Peace and Unification

Date: May 1980

Source: *The Party That Isn't: North Korea's Unification Revolution Party*. Seoul, South Korea: Research Center for Peace and Unification, 1980.

About the Author: The Research Center for Peace and Unification is located in Seoul, the capital of South Korea. The Center has published numerous books and articles on issues related to economic development, security, and other unification topics pertinent to North and South Korea.

INTRODUCTION

The development of the Unification-Revolution party (URP) was a move by North Korea's longtime leader Kim Il-Sung (1912–1994) to unify the Korean peninsula under common Communist rule in the 1960s and 1970s. There had been earlier unsuccessful attempts to take over democratic South Korea by Kim Il-Sung and his Workers' Party, including the three-year multinational Korean War (1950–1953), which involved the United States, the Soviet Union, and Chinese forces. With restrictions on media, education, and travel in and out of the country, North Korea's largely peasant population has been isolated from much of the outside world since the country was formed in 1948. For the nearly fifty years he was in power, Kim Il-Sung was determined to gain control of Koreans in the south of the peninsula as well. Kim Il-Sung died in 1994 without having achieved that goal.

Prior to surrendering power to the Allied Forces at the end of World War II, Japan ruled the Korean peninsula as a single country for thirty-five years. In 1945, control of Korea was handed to the United States, the Soviet Union, Britain, and China. Differences between American and Soviet political ideology made it difficult to develop an agreed upon plan to give Korea the independence its citizens were demanding. American fears that the Soviets would take over Korea led to the division of the peninsula into North and South at the 38th parallel, the line of latitude 38 degrees north of the equator. The United States supported the development of the democratic Republic of Korea in the South, while the Soviet Union fostered the development of the Communist Democratic People's Republic of Korea (DPRK) in the North.

The Workers' Party, which started as an anti-imperialist group throughout the Korean peninsula during the Japanese rule, gained support of North Korean peasants by speaking about the ideals of achieving self-reliance. The charismatic Kim Il-Sung implemented popular economic and political reforms, which included the redistribution of land to the people and the seizing of property previously controlled by the Japanese. However, many of the wealthier educated and skilled workers in North Korea disagreed with the Communist ideals and quickly fled to South Korea. North Korea struggled to maintain its self-reliance, requiring assistance from both the Soviet Union and China.

South Korea's early years were not free from political turmoil. Tensions between the government and the people climaxed in April 1960, since unemployment was high and many people believed the recent presidential elections had been rigged. Protests ensued, with the Korean police killing 125 students and injuring 1,000 others, during a week of demonstrations. The riots forced the president to step down, and a reorganization of the government followed.

PRIMARY SOURCE

FABRICATION OF THE "UNIFICATION-REVOLUTION PARTY"

When the Ap[ril] 19 Student Uprising created a politically and socially chaotic situation in the Republic of Korea in 1960, the North Koreans were overjoyed—as if a Communist revolution had broken out in the South—and spared no effort for agitation through its radio broadcasts to South Korea, hoping to inspire a Communist revolution.

But at the fourth Party Congress held in September of the following year, Kim Il-sung regretted that the Student Uprising could not be developed into a "popular revolution." Emphasizing that "for the success of the South Korean revolution there must be a revolutionary party which takes Marxism-Leninism as its guiding principle," he had support for the South Korean revolution adopted as a party policy.

The North Korean Communists judged that, due to the absence of a revolutionary party, they not only missed a

The North Korean government holds a reporting convention in Pyongyang, its capital, on September 8, 2005 to mark the 57th anniversary of the founding of the nation. AP IMAGES.

favorable revolutionary opportunity in the April 19 Student Uprising, but also failed to prevent the May 16 Military Revolution in 1961, thereby allowing the birth of the strongest-ever anti-Communist government in Seoul and causing enormous damage to the South Korean revolutionary force....

As part of the policy to secure a revolutionary base in preparation for the decisive moment, Kim Il-sung began to hasten the organization of a violent underground party in the South by infiltrating professional espionage agents.

At the eighth fourth-term meeting of the Party Central Committee on February 27, 1964, Kim declared, "The North will support the revolution in the south, but can never wage it in lieu of the south. We should organize the party's leading echelon with excellent persons from both the North and the South. For this purpose, the Communists who come originally from the south must be trained and dispatched to the South in large numbers."

In accordance with Kim's instructions, Ho Bong-hak, director of the party's external liaison department, dispatched a professionally trained espionage agent, Kim Song-ku, to the South on March 15, 1964, to win over former pro-communist collaborators Kim Chong-tae and Lee Mun-kyu, among others. Kim Chong-tae was summoned to Pyongyang on four occasions, in March 1964,

April 1965, July 1966 and April 1968, received intensive espionage training and was sent back South to perform special missions.

Beside Lee Hyo-sun, party secretary in charge of anti-South operations, and Ho, the director of the general bureau of anti-South operations, Kim Il-sung personally met with Kim Chong-tae to instruct him on the South Korean revolution. Ho furnished him a total of US $70,000, 5,000,000 Japanese yen and 23.5 million Korean won in operational funds, in addition to weapons, poisons and other espionage equipment.

The North Korean instructions were: 1) to form a basic underground party organization with former members of the defunct South Korean Workers' Party as the nucleus; 2) to stage a campaign to propagate communist ideology among the masses by use of publications; 3) to cultivate party cadres with Seoul National University as the center; 4) to develop intellectual, student and youth circles into party teams and vanguards under the disguise of progressive movements; 5) to facilitate the revolutionary period through ideological indoctrination of the masses by use of booklets on Communism; 6) to study special warfare tactics for armed struggle and prepare for guerrilla warfare; 7) to organize a United Front for Korean National Liberation for a Vietcong-style united front struggle; and 8) to take over the metropolitan areas by violent means when the time is ripe and destroy major public installations and assassinate key figures in the ROK Government....

PURPORTED ACTIVITIES OF THE URP

Although North Korea has been spreading false propaganda about the nonexistent Unification-Revolution Party, it is all too clear that the whole affair is a fraud.

In an attempt to make the world believe that such an organization does exist in the South, North Korea has been staging various dramas. For instance, on such public occasions as a Workers' Party Congress or Kim Il-sung's birthday celebrations in Pyongyang, alleged representatives of the Unification-Revolution Party deliver speeches denouncing the Republic of Korea while praising the North.

SIGNIFICANCE

Efforts by North Korea to infiltrate South Korea with the URP were largely unsuccessful. In 1970, spies and armed forces affiliated with the URP from North Korea were sentenced to death and sent to prison in South Korea. A high level politician from North Korea's Central News Agency was also put to death, after his claim of having defected to South Korea from the North proved false. Opponents of South Korea's government made claims that politicians were using the threat of Communist infiltration from North Korea as a way to scare the population and stay in power. However, with strong ties to the West, there was never a serious move towards communism in South Korea.

North Korea has found few allies since the country became a major arms supplier to Iran, Syria, and Libya. Threats of nuclear attack on South Korea and Japan by North Korea have brought further tensions to the region. The United States and other western countries have maintained economic sanctions against North Korea, only easing the sanctions to convince North Korea to freeze its nuclear weapons program, and to persuade North Korea to hold talks about ending the country's isolation. The people of North Korea suffer high levels of poverty and famine. In contrast, South Korea has seen high rates of economic growth, and the country maintains vigorous trading relationships throughout the Western world.

Although differences between the North and South remain, there continues to be a desire among the Korean people for reunification. Through the efforts of the Ministry of Unification, established by South Korea primarily as a research and publicity organization in 1968, there have been some efforts to forge economic and social ties between North and South Korea. Talks concerning economic cooperation between the North and South have taken place, and trials of a train link between the North and South are scheduled in 2006. Although in reduced numbers, U.S. troops continue to stand guard in South Korea at the 38th parallel.

FURTHER RESOURCES
Books

Grinker, Roy R. *Korea and Its Futures: Unification and the Unfinished War*. New York: St. Martin's Press, 1998.

Martin, Bradley K. *Under the Loving Care of the Fatherly Leader: North Korea and the Kim Dynasty*. New York: St. Martin's Press, 2004.

Suh, Dae-Sook. *Kim Il Sung*. New York: Columbia University Press, 1995.

Periodicals

Kim, Joungwon Alexander. "Divided Korea 1969: Consolidating for Transition." *Asian Survey, A Survey of Asia, Part I* 10 (January 1970): 30–42.

Web sites

PBS, NewsHour. "North Korea: Nuclear Standoff." October 24, 2005. <http://www.pbs.org/newshour/bb/asia/northkorea/index.html> (accessed May 21, 2006).

Republic of Korea. Ministry of Unification. <http://unikorea.go.kr/index.jsp> (accessed May 21, 2006).

Fall of the Berlin Wall

Photograph

By: John Gaps III

Date: November 12, 1989

Source: AP Images.

About the Photographer: John Gaps III is a photographer with the Associated Press (AP), the largest and oldest news organization in the world. It serves thousands of daily newspapers, radio and television channels, and online customers by providing comprehensive news coverage. AP is a nonprofit organization with 3,700 employees working in more than 240 offices in 121 countries.

INTRODUCTION

On July 25, 1945, two months after victory in Europe, the Allies met in the German city of Potsdam to discuss Germany's fate. Intended to give Germans "the opportunity to prepare for the eventual reconstruction of their life on a democratic and peaceful basis," the country was divided into four occupied zones, one for each of the Allies—Britain, France, United States, and Soviet Union. The first three zones were capitalist and democratic; the Soviet zone, under the control of Joseph Stalin (1879–1953), became communist.

On May 23, 1949, the British, French, and American zones became the Federal Republic of Germany or West Germany, a capitalist state that advanced rapidly toward social and economic reform. In October of that year, the Soviet quadrant became East Germany, the socialist German Democratic Republic (GDR).

The situation in East Germany was dismal. Food and resources were scarce; there was little political freedom and even less economic development. Millions of East Germans left their homes to move to the West, a drain of labor that threatened East Germany with economic collapse. On April 1, 1948, the Soviet Union blockaded routes in and out of East Germany, causing food and fuel shortages. After the blockade was lifted in 1949, the number of East Germans migrating west increased. As many as 2.5 million people fled the country between 1949 and 1961.

Starting in 1952, East Germany tried to stop the exodus with fences, walls, barbed wires, and mine fields around its borders. By the end of May, the only way to get out of East Germany and escape to freedom was through Berlin.

Berlin was a problem, as it was the seat of the Allied Control Council, yet it was situated in the Soviet-occupied zone. Its western sector, a capitalist oasis in a communist country, became a magnet for those hoping to escape to freedom. As the final push in its effort to seal its borders, the GDR began to build a wall around the three western sectors of Berlin on August 13, 1961, using barbed wire and cinder blocks; these were later replaced with concrete, guard towers, electrified fences, and mines.

The wall divided not only the city, but segregated whole families and communities. And it slowed—but did not stop—escape attempts. As many as 10,000 people tried to get over the wall—as many as 5,000 made it. 260 people died while trying to cross the wall between 1961 and 1989.

By the mid 1980s, however, the Soviet Union was imploding, the Cold War was waning, and the Warsaw Pact was disintegrating. Mass protests against the East German government began in the fall of 1989, and Erich Honeker, the country's prime minister, resigned. On November 9, 1989, his replacement, Egon Krenz, decreed at a press conference that East Germans would be allowed to apply for visas to travel to the West. Ecstatic crowds swarmed the city's checkpoints, demanding entry into West Berlin.

The overwhelmed guards, faced with the option of opening the border or opening fire, chose the former. Gates along the Wall were opened, and Berliners united amidst joyous celebrations on both sides. Jubilant crowds climbed on top of the wall and began to attack it with sledgehammers. In less than a year, the two countries were reunited.

PRIMARY SOURCE

FALL OF THE BERLIN WALL
See primary source image.

SIGNIFICANCE

The Berlin Wall was a potent symbol of communist tyranny and the Cold War. Although by the 1960s and 1970s, East Germany was not officially governed by the Soviet Union, the country was strongly influenced by its policies and allied to it by the Warsaw Pact.

When Mikhail Gorbachev became head of the Soviet Union in 1985, he instigated democratic reforms in an effort to improve his economically ailing country. While commending Gorbachev for the improvements, President Ronald Reagan (1911–2004) delivered a challenge in 1987 at the Brandenburg Gate in West Berlin: "General Secretary Gorbachev, if you seek peace, if you seek prosperity for the Soviet Union and Eastern Europe, if you seek liberalization: Come here to this gate! Mr. Gorbachev, open this gate! Mr. Gorbachev, tear down this wall!"

Two years later, the Berlin Wall had been destroyed and the Cold War effectively ended. The first free parliamentary elections were held in East Germany on March 18, 1990; the Treaty of Union united the two regions into one Germany on October 3, 1990.

The new country, however, was confronted with several challenges, the most significant of

PRIMARY SOURCE

Fall of the Berlin Wall: A man hammers away at the Berlin Wall on November 12, 1989, as the border barrier between East and West Germany was torn down after 28 years, symbolically ending the Cold War. AP IMAGES.

which was incorporating the communist East German economy into capitalist West Germany. Another was the high rate of unemployment among East Germans, thousands of whom lost their jobs to more progressive West German workers and companies.

More than fifteen years after the wall's demise, marked cultural and economic differences remain between east and west. The cost of reunification appeared to be a sore spot for westerners, while east Germans resented their lower wages and standard of living. A 2004 survey conducted by the Forsa Institute found thirty-seven percent of West Germans said that the government is focused only on development projects in the east, whereas almost a third of former East Germans indicated dissatisfaction towards development in the eastern part of Germany.

FURTHER RESOURCES

Books

Buckley, William F. *The Fall of the Berlin Wall*. Hoboken, NJ: Wiley & Sons, 2004.

Powaski, Ronald E. *The Cold War: The United States and the Soviet Union, 1917–1991*. New York: Oxford University Press, 1998.

Web sites

BBC News. On This Day. " November 9, 1989: Berliners Celebrate the Fall of the Wall." <http://news.bbc.co.uk/onthisday/hi/dates/stories/november/9/newsid_2515000/2515869.stm> (accessed May 24, 2006).

CNN: Cold War. "The Wall: 1958–1963." <http://edition.cnn.com/SPECIALS/cold.war/episodes/09/> (accessed May 24, 2006).

MSNBC. "One in 5 Germans Wants Berlin Wall Rebuilt." <http://www.msnbc.msn.com/id/5942091> (accessed May 24, 2006).

East Germans climb onto the Berlin Wall at the Brandenburg Gate shortly after the opening of borders between East and West Germany, November 10, 1989. © REUTERS/CORBIS.

Reagan Foundation. "Tear Down This Wall." June 12, 1987. <http://www.reaganfoundation.org/reagan/speeches/wall.asp> (accessed May 24, 2006).

Time—The Berlin Wall: Ten Years After. "The Wall That Defined Us." <http://www.time.com/time/daily/special/berlin/opener.html> (accessed May 24, 2006).

Library of Congress. Country Studies. "Germany." <http://lcweb2.loc.gov/frd/cs/detoc.html> (accessed May 24, 2006).

Tiananmen Square Protests of June 1989

Photograph

By: Jeff Widener

Date: June 5, 1989

Source: AP Images.

About the Photographer: Jeff Widener is an Associated Press photographer and has been nominated for a Pulitzer Prize. As of 2006, he is also photographer for the *Honolulu Advertiser*.

INTRODUCTION

In June 1989, an unprecedented protest in Tiananmen Square in Beijing which had begun two months before was brought to a violent end. As the world watched, China's People's Liberation Army (PLA) forcibly removed thousands of demonstrators from Tiananmen Square. An estimated 1,000-2,600 people were killed by the military in the events that unfolded beginning in April of that year. In 1991, the Chinese government confirmed that 2,578 demonstrators from the events in Tiananmen Square in 1989 had been arrested. The events which led to the unparalleled suppression of the protests in June of 1989 actually began in 1985. At this time, students and workers began to rally in support of extensive democratic reforms throughout China. These demonstrations began on university campuses as students opposed the presence of the PLA in the schools. In addition, protesters demonstrated against nuclear testing that had recently taken place in the Xinjiang province. This movement adopted slogans of "Law, not authoritarianism" and "Long Live Democracy" in its quest for democratic reform in China. As these protests escalated into nationwide demonstrations, members of the Chinese Communist Party (CCP) supported a swift military response on the part of the government. However, party chairman Hu Yaobang was sympathetic to the reformers and refused to respond with military force. As a result, in 1987 he lost his position as party chairman.

After Hu Yaobang's death on April 15, 1989, students began to gather in Tiananmen Square to express their grief for his passing. These demonstrations developed into demonstrations in support for his political stand against military response to the pro-democracy demonstrations that occurred in 1985. On April 26, an editorial appeared in the *People's Daily Newspaper* discrediting the gathering of Hu Yaobang's supporters. In response, the mood changed from an outpouring of grief to a political stand for democratic reforms. These demonstrations which began in Tiananmen Square began to spread to twenty-nine provinces and eighty-four cities, according to Chinese government figures. Students began a hunger strike on May 13, and by May 17, approximately one million demonstrators had converged on Tiananmen Square. Many of these protesters were students. However, unlike demonstrations in the past, this became a cross-class protest which included students, urban workers, party and

PRIMARY SOURCE

Tiananmen Square protests of June 1989: An anonymous protestor stands alone in the middle of Beijing's Cangan Boulevard in Tiananmen Square, blocking the advance of a line of tanks, on June 5, 1989. AP IMAGES.

government employees, and over seven hundred organizations participated.

The CCP leadership, under the control of Deng Xiaoping, declared martial law on May 20. During this period, the PLA attempted to dispel the protestors, but failed. On May 30, the protesters constructed the "Goddess of Democracy," a ten-meter-high plaster statue, inspired partly by the Statue of Liberty. The statue was raised to face the portrait of Mao Tse Tung hanging in Tiananmen Square. Shortly thereafter, the Chinese government approved a policy of forceful removal and disbursement of the protesters. The implementation of this policy began on June 1 by cutting off access of foreign journalists. On June 2, convoys of tanks and soldiers moved into central Beijing. By the next day, the military began to use tear gas and rubber bullets to force the demonstrators to leave the square. The PLA's tanks entered

Tiananmen Square by midnight of June 3, at which time many demonstrators agreed to leave the square peacefully. However, in the early morning of June 4, the army began to open fire on the protesters.

The American Embassy in Beijing reported that approximately ten thousand troops surrounded the three thousand remaining protesters. This confrontation resulted in violent clashes along Changan Boulevard, the main thoroughfare in Tiananmen Square. As a result, the military used automatic weapons, tanks and armored personnel carriers to end the protests, which until this point had been peaceful. According to these reports, the military opened fire on unarmed civilians, to include members of the press. The U.S. Embassy reported that journalists for CBS had been beaten by the PLA and their equipment, to include cameras, had been smashed.

PRIMARY SOURCE

TIANANMEN SQUARE PROTESTS OF JUNE 1989

See primary source image.

SIGNIFICANCE

On June 5, 1989, the PLA had obtained control of Tiananmen Square and the demonstrators had been quieted. As a column of tanks moved along Changan Boulevard toward Tiananmen Square, a lone man emerged to confront the column. The lead tank attempted to go around the man, but the man continued to stand in the path of the tank. At one point, the man jumped onto the tank and addressed the driver. Shortly thereafter, the man was apprehended by a group of people and taken away. Although many have speculated the name and fate of the lone protester, no one has accurately identified the man or what has become of him.

The U.S. Embassy in Beijing reported that relative calm had been restored to the region by June 8. Human rights organizations assert that approximately 1,000–2,600 people were killed during the events. By 1991, the Chinese government had confirmed 2,578 arrests of those involved in participating and organizing the protests. Unlike the gentle handling of the 1985–1986 pro-democracy protests, the CCP leadership enacted sweeping responses to prevent future demonstrations from occurring. In addition to jailing protesters, many of the demonstration's leadership were exiled. Policy changes also occurred. The CCP intensified the political education of students through programs such as an eight week university program that teaches party principles. Many schools adopted a state-written curriculum which focuses on China's achievements and the excesses of the West.

FURTHER RESOURCES

Periodicals

Clements, Jonathan. "Tiananmen Square 13 Years After: The Prospects for Civil Unrest in China." *Asian Affairs: An American Review.* 29 (2002): 159.

Web sites

PBS. "Frontline: The Memory of Tiananmen Square, 1989." <http://www.pbs.org/wgbh/pages/frontline/tankman/cron/> (accessed May 10, 2006).

National Security Archive Electronic Briefing Book No.16. "Tiananmen Square, 1989." <http://www.gwu.edu/~nsarchiv/NSAEBB/NSAEBB16/> (accessed April 30, 2006).

The Guardian Unlimited. "Tiananmen: Ten Years On." 1999. <http://www.guardian.co.uk/Tiananmen/0,2759,193066,00.html> (accessed April 30, 2006).

An Urgent Appeal From Our Anguished Hearts

Tibetan Protest Against Chinese Rule, 1989

Letter

By: Friends in the Struggle of the Lhasa Tiger-Leopard Group

Date: September 27, 1989

Source: Schwartz, Ronald David. *Circle of Protest: Political Ritual in the Tibetan Uprising.* New York; Columbia University Press, 1994.

About the Author: The Lhasa Tiger-Leopard Group was one of the groups of political activists who opposed the Chinese occupation of Tibet. A prominent member of this group was Lhakpa Tsering, whose death while in Chinese custody in 1989 focused international attention on the treatment of the Tibetan people under Chinese rule.

INTRODUCTION

Until 1950, Tibet was a sovereign nation, a remote and rugged land situated in the Himalayan Mountains. Tibet had been a sanctuary for the Buddhist faith since A.D 700. For many centuries, Tibetan political leadership and religious direction were linked to the authority of the Buddhist spiritual leader, the Dalai Lama. The current Dalai Lama is the fourteenth to hold this title. In 1950, Buddhist monks comprised approximately one sixth of the population of the capital city of Lhasa.

In 1950, China invaded Tibet and took control of all government institutions. Chinese rulers claimed Tibet as a part of their empire at various times in the previous five hundred years, and the newly founded People's Republic of China relied upon this historical connection as a basis to occupy the country. Years of unrest first boiled into an armed uprising against the Chinese occupiers in 1959. The Tibetan opposition to the Chinese occupation was brutally suppressed, as numerous Tibetan leaders were summarily executed by the Chinese. The Dalai Lama and other prominent religious leaders fled to India, where they established a government-in-exile.

Free Tibet graffiti stands on a wall in a street in Darjeeling, India, 1989. Protests against Chinese rule in Tibet have been commonplace in India since the Dalai Lama fled to India in 1959. © ALISON WRIGHT/CORBIS.

In the years that followed the 1959 uprising, there were repeated allegations of atrocities committed by the Chinese against the local population. Numerous Buddhist monasteries in Lhasa and throughout Tibet were destroyed and their contents sold. The Chinese government placed significant restrictions on the observance of the Buddhist faith in Tibet. Tibetan nationals were the subject of discrimination by the Chinese. The Dalai Lama petitioned numerous world leaders to come to the aid of the Tibetan people against the Chinese occupation, with little success. Tibet was now ruled by China as the Tibetan Autonomous Region, a component part of the greater People's Republic of China.

Another popular uprising occurred in various parts of Tibet in 1987. This revolt was spearheaded by young political dissidents, and it attracted a vigorous armed response from the Chinese military. Demonstrations continued in Lhasa into 1988, as the Dalai Lama and the Tibetan government-in-exile renewed their efforts to secure international support for the Tibetan nationalist cause. Martial law was imposed by China in March 1989, and a series of prison terms in excess of fifteen years were imposed upon the various leaders of the insurgency.

In 1989, one of the Tibetan dissident leaders, twenty year old Lhakpa Tsering, died in Chinese custody at the notorious Drapchi Prison in Lhasa. Tsering was a member of the Tiger-Leopard Group whose members and supporters authored the letter of September 27, 1989.

PRIMARY SOURCE

The great Protector Deities long ago commanded by Padmasambhava have not lost their power.

Though we have brought this fate upon ourselves, it is not time for the end of the aeon.

Are we not under the domination of misfortune and demonic hindrances?

Look with your eye of wisdom and see if it is time now for the forces of power to rise up.

One deity of this land of snow mountains incarnates the compassion of all the Buddhas and Bodhisattvas.

A pure unmistaken line of incarnations has come to Tibet.

Now, when the melodious sound of the wheel of Dharma is spoken, everywhere in foreign lands,

Look with your eye of wisdom on those who have stayed behind, like the corpse of a dead lion.

In the midst of the ruins of the great monasteries, magnificent places of pilgrimage, blades of grass sing a sad song.

The disputations of the monks arguing the five bundles of Sutras are not heard; a foreign song is sung.

Wild animals dwell in the hermitages and caves of practitioners of Tantra and Mantra.

Look with your eye of wisdom, you gods, how have we erred to make this happen?

Although the Buddha's wisdom is always as close to the faithful as a body and its smell,

Because of the two obstructions, I and those like me are deprived of the Buddha's words, and commentaries.

Like the agony of a baby bird whose training is not yet complete,

Look soon with your eye of wisdom upon the suffering of those sentient beings so we may see his face.

Because Tibetans are a people with great compassion and faith in Dharma,

The precious life and warm blood of our heroes and heroines is flowing in the streets of Lhasa.

Look soon with your eye of wisdom upon the torment of our friends in the struggle,

Held in the court of the Lord of Death, brought by inhuman foreign enemies to the land of men.

Unexcelled, most powerful Protectors of Tibet,

Were we not like mother and child, we could not ask this of you.

This is the anguished appeal of a child separated from its mother.

Though unbidden, we are powerless not to speak out, please be patient.

Though the ripening of our sins is relentless, there must be and end.

The Dalai Lama has said the great star of the dawn has already risen.

If we hold fast to the words of truth of the Tibetans,

There is no doubt we will soon be victorious.

From all the friends in the struggle of the Lhasa Tiger-Leopard Group

27 September 1989

SIGNIFICANCE

Contemporaneous to the mobilization of Tibetan opposition against the Chinese, the national government of China was engaged in the suppression of the dissident movement that instigated the public demonstrations held at Tiananmen Square in Beijing between April 1 and June 4, 1989. Hundreds of protestors were killed or injured when the Chinese troops ended the demonstrations, events that touched off world-wide condemnation of Chinese tactics and attitudes toward apparently peaceful forms of protest.

The letter (in the form of a poem) written by the Friends of the Lhasa Tiger-Leopard Group does not mention China or the occupation of Tibet by name. However, the authors employ a mix of traditional Tibetan images, such as the mountains and the lion, against the context of death, blood, and foreign intervention. It is apparent that the passion for Tibetan nationalism had not faded in the almost forty years between the writing of the poem and the occupation of Tibet by China. The reference in the poem to blood flowing in the streets is with respect to the imposition of martial law by the Chinese in March 1989 and the further repressive steps taken to quell political protests in Lhasa.

At the time of the publication of the letter by the Lhasa Group, the Dalai Lama had advanced his work to engage Western governments to support Tibetan nationalism. The Dalai Lama was awarded the Nobel Peace Prize on December 10, 1989, in recognition of his efforts to promote a peaceful resolution to the Chinese occupation of Tibet.

The award of the Peace Prize to the Dalai Lama is significant on a number of levels, as it appeared to stimulate a greater international interest in the Tibetan conflict. Between 1990 and 1993, there was a massive exodus of Buddhist monks from Tibet to India. At the same time, a number of nations passed resolutions that condemned the actions of the Chinese government as taken against the Tibetan population to limit their religious practices and cultural traditions. In 1991, the United States Senate passed a resolution declaring that Tibet was an occupied country, and that the Dalai Lama headed a government in exile. A similar resolution was passed by the Australian Senate in the same year.

The weight of international political opinion continued to favor the Tibetan nationalist cause in August of 1991, when the United Nations passed a resolution in support of Tibet as a national entity, as did the European Parliament in 1992. In the United States, President Bill Clinton signed legislation that supported the efforts of the Dalai Lama and Tibetan nationalists to preserve their identity.

It is clear that the various political pronouncements made on behalf of the Tibetan nationalists had a limited impact upon the conduct of the Chinese in Tibet. It is also clear that little or no effort was made by any nations to compel change in Tibet through the direction of economic pressure upon China. Shortly after signing the Tibetan legislation in 1994, the United States re-affirmed China's 'Most Favored Nation' trading status; this designation confirmed China's desirability as an American economic partner. The apparently contradictory signals of the United States in 1994 regarding China, in contrast to the 1991 Senate resolution can only be interpreted as a belief on the part of the United States that the fostering of Chinese trade was of greater national importance than the use of trade sanctions to pursue a resolution in Tibet.

The Chinese actions against Tibetan national symbols continued in 1996 when the public display of photographs of the Dalai Lama was banned.

In recent years, there has been a status quo maintained with respect to the Chinese governance of Tibet and the resolution of the human rights concerns raised by Tibetans. The Dalai Lama has persisted in his world wide efforts to pursue a solution to the dispute with China. It is significant that while the government-in-exile continues to work from its base in northern India, the Dalai Lama has now advanced a desire to negotiate a resolution with China where Tibet would not be an independent nation, but an autonomous area within China where Tibetan religious and cultural practices can be preserved. Current American policy with respect to Tibet mirrors this attitude; In September 2002, the Foreign Relations Authorizations' Act as signed by President George W. Bush affirmed American support for the preservation of Tibetan language and culture.

FURTHER RESOURCES
Books

Dreyer, June Teufel and Barry Sautman, ed. *Contemporary Tibet; Politics, Development, and Society in a Disputed Region*. Armonk, New York; M.E.Sharpe, 2005.

Goldstein, Melvyn C. *The Snow Lion and the Dragon: China, Tibet, and the Dalai Lama*. Berkley; University of California Press, 1997.

Web sites

Nobel Prize Committee. "Nobel Peace Prize, 1989." April 1, 2005. <http://www.nobelprize.org/peace/laureates/1989/index.html> (accessed May 26, 2006).

Anti-Soviet President Gorbachev Caricatured Protest Sign During Soviet Armed Crackdown on Independence-bent Baltic SSR

Photograph

By: Igor Gavrilov

Date: 1991

Source: Photo by Igor Gavrilov/Time Life Pictures/Getty Images.

About the Photographer: Igor Gavrilov is a Russian photographer and one of the most noted and prolific chroniclers of the breakup of the USSR. This photograph is part of the collection at Getty Images, a worldwide provider of visual content materials to such communications groups as advertisers, broadcasters, designers, magazines, new media organizations, newspapers, and producers.

INTRODUCTION

Following the death of Soviet President Konstantin Chernenko in February 1985, Mikhail Gorbachev was elevated to General Secretary of the Communist Party and leader of the USSR. Following years of economic stagnation, Gorbachev immediately set about revitalizing the USSR with a series of reforms. Its central tenets were *glasnost* ("Change" or "openness), *perestroika* ("reconstruction") and *uskoreniye* ("acceleration") which were launched at the Communist Party's 27th Congress in February 1986.

The most profound impact for those living within the USSR would be the introduction of *glasnost*. This gave new and comparatively wide-ranging freedoms, particularly greater freedom of speech, which had long been suppressed by the Soviet government. The press became far less controlled and there was an amnesty for thousands of political prisoners and dissidents. Gorbachev also called for democracy within the parameters of the Soviet state and established a limited parliament—the Congress of People's Deputies—with elections in March and April 1989.

The new atmosphere created by the Soviet President encouraged the non-Russians of Estonia, Latvia and Lithuania to exert their own long-suppressed national identities. Initially this was done in small and ostensibly trifling ways: for instance, in December 1987 the Estonian Heritage Society was founded, and the following year its banned pre-war flag started appearing once more. Emboldened by such moves, nationalism quickly re-emerged in these three states.

It was Lithuania that led the initially tentative moves to break from Moscow. In November 1988, a law making Lithuania the official language of the Soviet republic and restoring its pre-war flag and national anthem was passed. This gave impetus to a nationalist people's front, called *Sajudis*, which began to articulate an increasingly vocal political voice for its long-suppressed people.

On May 18, 1989, the Supreme Soviet in Vilnius declared economic and political sovereignty for Lithuania. On August 23, 1989, around two million people formed a chain about 370 miles (600 kilometers) long across the three Baltic states to mark the fiftieth anniversary of the Molotov-Ribbentrop pact, which had effectively doomed the three countries to an era of Soviet domination. This was followed in December by the abolition of the Soviet Communist Party (CSPU) authority in Lithuania and permission for non-communist political parties to be established. Even set against the backdrop of revolution across eastern Europe, this was a staggering development and it made Lithuania the first Soviet republic to establish a multi-party democracy and discard years of adherence to Marxist-Leninism.

Moscow, caught unaware as its Eastern European client states collapsed like dominoes, was unsure how to proceed. It had countenanced economic independence in the summer of 1989 but seemed unprepared to concede political power. At the same time the three Baltic states continued to test the limits of their newfound national confidence. On March 11, 1989, the Lithuanian Supreme Soviet renamed itself the Supreme Council and declared independence as the Republic of Lithuania. It was followed by Estonia on March 30 and Latvia on July 28. (This would nevertheless not be widely recognized by other countries for a further eighteen months).

For Moscow this was a step too far. That summer it placed a fuel embargo on Lithuania, forcing it to "suspend" its independence. This merely exacerbated

tensions between the republic and Moscow and failed to silence its people, who spoke even louder for freedom from Soviet rule.

PRIMARY SOURCE

ANTI-SOVIET PRESIDENT GORBACHEV CARICATURED PROTEST SIGN DURING SOVIET ARMED CRACKDOWN ON INDEPENDENCE-BENT BALTIC SSR

See primary source image.

SIGNIFICANCE

In January 1991, the world watched as the USSR sent troops into Vilnius in an apparent attempt to end the move toward secession. The show of strength, though less violently articulated, had echoes of Soviet intervention in Czechoslovakia in 1968 and Hungary in 1956. President Mikhail Gorbachev claimed to be the recipient of "thousands" of telegrams demanding presidential rule be reapplied in Lithuania; an exact echo of Leonid Brezhnev's response to the Prague Spring twenty-three years earlier. The main flashpoint came on the night of January 13, when Soviet troops fired upon a television center in Vilnius, killing thirteen unarmed protesters.

However, the USSR was not in a similar position in 1991 and was beset by internal differences. Press censorship had largely been lifted in the USSR and widely denounced the attack on the Lithuanian protesters. Rival politicians to Gorbachev, such as Boris Yeltsin, used the events to attack the Soviet President and gain political leverage. *Glasnost* had seemingly spun out of the Kremlin's control.

The Lithuanians responded by organizing a referendum in which nine out of ten backed secession. Iceland became the first country to recognize Lithuanian independence in February 1991, and Sweden opened an embassy there shortly thereafter.

Gorbachev, for his part, drew up a new response to the growing secession agitation not just in the Baltics, but throughout the USSR. He drew up a new union treaty, designed to create a voluntary federation within the parameters of the USSR. This move would have effectively dissolved the USSR and was strongly opposed by many Communist Party hardliners in Moscow. In August 1991 they tried to oust Gorbachev in a coup d'etat. Although this collapsed within days and Gorbachev returned to power, it crushed the Soviet leader's hopes that the union could be held together. The following month Moscow recognized the Baltic states' independence

PRIMARY SOURCE

Anti-Soviet President Gorbachev Caricatured Protest Sign During Soviet Armed Crackdown on Independence-bent Baltic SSR: A protest poster from Vilnius, Lithuania, caricaturing and demonizing Soviet leader Mikhail Gorbachev during a 1991 Soviet military crackdown on independence-minded Lithuanians. PHOTO BY IGOR GAVRILOV//TIME LIFE PICTURES/GETTY IMAGES.

and on September 17, 1991, they joined the United Nations. On December 25, Gorbachev resigned as Soviet President and the USSR was dissolved.

Full independence was nevertheless replete with numerous complexities attributable to the interwoven nature of Soviet economics and the presence of Red Army troops and ethnic Russians on Baltic soil. However, Lithuania's path to independence was replete with less antagonism than in its Baltic neighbors, Latvia and Estonia. Lithuania, where Russians and Byelorussians formed just twelve percent of the population, was not as threatened by the minority problem as were Estonia and Latvia. As such, the citizenship laws of post-independence Lithuania were relatively generous to its minorities and allowed for a relatively smooth transition from Soviet rule. By contrast, Estonia's minority was a third of its population and Latvia's two-fifths. The post-independence

citizenship laws in these two countries were based around race and language, were severely prejudiced against those associated with the old regime and socially and politically disenfranchised non-ethnic Latvians and Estonians. Invariably they provoked outrage in Russia (and also the European Union, which held back aid until they were revised) and were a severe impediment to successfully negotiating full secession, particularly over the withdrawal of Red Army troops and border crossings. A complete divorce with the old regime was agreed later and less amicably than had been the case in Lithuania.

FURTHER RESOURCES
Books

Crampton, R J. *Return to Diversity: A Political History of East Central Europe Since World War II.* London: Routledge, 1997.

A Soviet soldier sticks his head up out of his armored personnel carrier in Vilnius, Lithuania, during a 1991 crackdown by the USSR.
PHOTO BY IGOR GAVRILOV//TIME LIFE PICTURES/GETTY IMAGES.

Kotkin, Steven. *Armagadden Averted: The Soviet Collapse 1970–2000*. Oxford, U.K.: Oxford University Press, 2000.

Marples, David R,. *The Collapse of the Soviet Union 1985–1991*. Harlow, U.K.: Longman, 2004.

Britain's Labour Party Debate

The Abandonment of Clause IV

Report

By: Anonymous

Date: 1994

Source: "Labour Party Conference Report 1994." *Labour Party* (1994): 191–199.

About the Author: The Labour Party is the United Kingdom's principal left-wing political party. It describes itself as a "democratic socialist party."

INTRODUCTION

In February 1900, the Trades Union Congress hosted a conference in London's Memorial Hall called the Conference on Labour Representation. Over seventy organizations convened at the meeting with the goal of creating a political party that would represent trade unions and socialists. As such, the Labour Representation Committee was created. The party consisted only of organizations and did not have individual members. From 1906 through 1914, this newly created Labour Party worked closely with the Liberal governments. In 1918, Labour adopted clause 4 to the party's constitution calling for a nationalization of the economy through the "common ownership of the means of production, distribution and exchange" of wealth. In 1924, despite winning sixty-seven fewer seats than the reigning Conservative party, Labour was asked to form a government. This newly found power was lost in the next election due to the Zinoviev letter, a forged letter suggesting a link between Labour and Communists. By 1929, Labour was once again in power and began to implement changes, such as the reorganization of the coal and iron industries. Under the economic guidance of Cambridge economist John Maynard Keynes (1887–1946), the Labour government sought to implement economic changes to combat widespread unemployment following the 1929 stock market crash. By 1931, Labour had lost its majority once more.

Following the end of World War II, Labour won a landslide victory in the 1945 election by gaining 393 seats. Much of the success of Labour during the 1945 election was attributed to its newest manifesto, "Let Us Face the Future," which consists of the party's pledge to destroy the five evil giants of want, squalor, disease, ignorance, and unemployment. The party was led by Clement Attlee (1883–1967), who initiated substantial reforms. Attlee and Labour sought to promote the sense of community and cooperation that had been prevalent during the war. As a result, the party received cross-class support from trade unions and working classes. Attlee successfully created the National Health Service, established a universal welfare state, worked toward accomplishing full employment through the implementation of Keynesian economic theories and limited state planning, and nationalized twenty percent of British industry. During this period privately owned coal and rail industries were inefficient, prone to industry conflicts, and had a record of poor treatment of workers. As a result, Labour asserted that the state must intervene to ensure economic stability, rather than wait for the market to correct itself. This was the first successful implementation of the goals and objectives outlined in clause 4 of the party's constitution. Despite leading widespread reform, the Labour party lost its momentum and failed to win majorities in subsequent elections.

After losing a series of elections, the party began to modernize in 1980 led by Neil Kinnock (1942–). Kinnock pushed the party to accept market mechanisms for economic change rather than the Keynesian demand-side policies. While Kinnock's attempt to reform the party was failing, Margaret Thatcher (1925–) was dismantling much of the nationalization of industry that had occurred under previous Labour governments. Successes of privately owned companies such as British Airways and British Telecommunications led to continued Labour election losses. Kinnock's successor, John Smith, was more successful at modernizing the Labour party. Although Kinnock had abandoned policies of high taxation and nationalization, the party was still in conflict. Smith first addressed the power of unions to vote as a block. In 1993, Smith succeeded at the party

London's Waterloo Station, April 2, 1993. AP IMAGES.

conference in passing the One Man One Vote measure, thereby dismantling the union block power in the party. Smith died in 1994 as the Labour party was gaining support for the reforms that he had implemented.

PRIMARY SOURCE

Jim Mearns (Glasgow Maryhill CLP) moved Composite 57.

He said: Comrade Chair, comrade delegates and friends, I am proud to be a socialist, proud to be in the Labour Party and proud of Clause IV of our Constitution. (Applause)

This composite calls for clear, radical socialist policies. It calls for the party to commit itself to working towards a fundamental and irreversible shift in power in favour of working people. It calls for a measure of public ownership, and everyone here knows that public ownership for railways, the Post Office, water and other utilities makes sense. It is concerned with emphasising the party's socialist principles as set out in clause IV (4), that is "to secure for the workers by hand or by brain the full fruits of their industry and the most equitable distribution thereof that may be possible upon the basis of the common ownership of the means of production, distribution and exchange, and the best obtainable system of popular administration and control of each industry or service" —not the words of left wing revolutionaries, but of the Fabian Society.

These words are a symbol of our commitment to the working class and a succinct statement of our core philosophy. They did not stop us winning elections in the past and they will not stop us winning elections in the future. (Cheers and applause)...

Jane Carroll (South Debyshire CLP) seconded composite 57.

She said: this composite reaffirms our commitment to democratic socialism. These principles founded our great victories in the past and should be the basis of our new strategies. These principles are not new; they coincide with the principles of the Cooperative movement, from which we have just heard, and of course the trade union movement. Indeed, some trade union rule books include the selfsame principles about the redistribution of wealth and the improvement of conditions in the workplace and in the home....

During the past decade we were persuaded that we had to move to the right if we were to gain office, but it now appears that the electorate have more radical visions than some of us realize. A MORI poll, commissioned by The Economist, not well known for its left wing views, was published this week. It gives credence to the essence of this composite, and if opinion polls are important, as we are told they are, we should certainly take notice of this one. The Economist poll indicates that the return of privatized industries, such as water and electricity, to public ownership is backed by 68 per cent, and even by many of those still intending to vote Conservative. A wealth tax on fortunes above 150,000 is supported by an overwhelming majority—perhaps people would favour a maximum wage as well as a minimum wage. There is more. A 46 per cent majority is in favour of increasing income tax to pay for spending on education; a majority is in favour of more state intervention in the economy. Finally, a staggering 84 per cent supported the reduction of VAT on domestic fuel bills to 5 per cent....

Alan Johnson (Union of Communication Workers): Supporting Composite 56 on behalf of 180,000 public sector workers in the Post Office and opposing Composite 57.

To my members public ownership is not some vague concept, but is crucial to the future of the Post Office and to their working lives. We have been publicly owned for 300 years and are still waiting for our members who work by hand or brain to get the full fruits of their labour....

It is 20 years since we last won a general election. In those 20 years, the command economy has been discredit—forget about it: it is never going to be restored. If those people who are worried about an open review within the party of every dot and comma of our constitution are so worried that they cannot defend Clause IV in open debate, then Clause IV is not worth defending. We need objectives and principles that are relevant to the 21st century and to the working class, not principles written by two middle class Fabians in 1918. We want to fight the election on policies, not on shibboleths. I oppose Composite 57. (Applause)

David Winnick (Ex-Officio, MP for Walsall, North):

I have come here this morning to make a plea that we should not waste the next 12 months on an internal debate about Clause IV. There is no reason why we should be engaging in such a debate: Clause IV should stand.

I remember that in 1959/1960 we were told by the ten arch-modernisers that unless we deleted Clause IV we would never win another election. Some of you will remember it. Well, we did: we won in 1964, in 1966 and twice in 1974, with Clause IV intact. We win when we have confidence in ourselves, our socialism and what we stand for. We stand now examining our navel. Next week the Tories will not be doing that. When they gather, they will not be saying that they need to start apologizing for their wholehearted belief in capitalism and privatization. They have that self-confidence, and we should do the same.

Tony Blair said that we should not apoligise for our socialism. You are absolutely right, Tony. Some of us have never tried to start apologising. Neither is there any need to start apologizing for Clause IV. It is a long term objective. We have always recognized it and always recognized that it needs the consent and enthusiasm of the large majority of British people. But, Alan Johnson, it is nonsense to believe that we have been in the wilderness for the past 15 years because of Clause IV. When you go on the doorstep, do people ask about Clause IV? I will tell you what they talk about, poverty and unemployment and the disasters that they bring; they talk about the breakdown of law and order.

In his excellent speech—except for the last part— Tony Blair concentrated on what we should be doing in the two to two-and-a-half years that are left. We are now on the offensive; we have got the Tories on the run; in the House of Commons and in the country we are winning elections—Euro-elections, local elections, by-elections. Why should we spend the next 12 months going through the nightmare and agony of Clause IV? What sense is there in that? *(Applause)*

With the greatest respect to our leader, sometimes ideas that come during a holiday season on the beach are not necessarily the best ideas in practice. I say to Tony and to the National Executive Committee, let us drop this nonsense. The most decisive way to profit is by passing Composite 57 today. You may not agree with every dot and comma—after all, you pass NEC statements where you might not agree with every dot and comma—but passing Composite 57 would have this virtue above all else: it would stop the nonsense of ensuring that we go through the agony of having a debate on Clause IV. They would be bound to drop it; therefore I plead with Conference that if we want to concentrate on the real enemy—and we know who that is—let us make sure that we pass Composite 57. That is the way forward. *(Applause)*

George Sands (Graphical, Paper and Media Union) . . .

Clause IV is central to the philosophy of the Labour Party. It is this, and our clear, unambiguous policies, that differentiate our programme from our opponents' and gives the means of providing purpose and vision to every member of this society. Support composite 57. *(Applause)* . . .

Chair: . . . What we have before us here today are two composites. The NEC support Composite 56 and ask you to remit Composite 57, so that it can be part of that wide-ranging debate.

There are parts of Composite 57 with which we can all agree, but we cannot accept the motion as it stands. It both attacks the present position of the party, which you have all voted on and applauded earlier in the week, and distorts the historic role of Clause IV in our history and constitution. Labour remains totally committed to the public ownership of public services. . . .

Co-operation, both with a large and small 'c', was very much part of the thinking around Clause IV, as it is today. Common ownership was not seen, as it has subsequently all too often become, as a matter of nationalized corporations and state monopolies. We all know that the cost of the mistakes of capitalism are all around us, but we also have to admit that socialism has made a few mistakes too: too great a concentration on state ownership and public corporations and too little on real control and real popular administration. We do not want a narrow definition of socialism. Massive extensions of "public ownership", as understood in that sense, are not on the agenda of the next Labour government. That is only partially because of the restraints on resources. Let us not forget that, enormous though those constraints will be, the next Labour government will require massive money and resources to reverse

the inequalities of 17 years of Tory rule and to get the economy going. We will not have that much money for extension of ownership.

But also we have learnt the lesson from here and from Eastern Europe that "top-down" socialism very rarely works. What is needed is something that was in the minds of the drafters of Clause IV, the subtler, more varied, multi-layered approach in Europe and elsewhere, to which Denis referred, that is subject to popular administration and very much part of the socialism of the 21st century, whichever way we update the words and whether or not we update Clause IV. The aims and values and the constitution of the party may need updating, but I ask you today to understand the reality of your history and the commitment that the front bench and the party leadership are making to the future of socialism. We ask you to support Composite 56 and to remit Composite 57 and get on with this debate so that we can redefine the socialism of the 21st century. *(Applause)*

Chair: Conference, there are two composites in front of us.

(A vote was taken and Composite 56 was carried.)

Composite 57, the NEC recommendation is to remit. *(Interruption)* Does the mover refuse to remit? No. Then the recommendation of the NEC must be to oppose. The mover has served notice that he wanted to call for a card vote.

(Card vote 3 was taken on Composite 57: Votes for, 50.9 per cent; votes against, 49.1 per cent. The composite is carried.)

SIGNIFICANCE

Tony Blair (1953–) succeeded Smith as leader of the Labour Party. Before his election to the party leadership, Blair called state collectivism inappropriate during the time of globalization and stated that social and economic change and individual prosperity made Clause IV outdated. As a result, he led the push to modernize the amendment. Blair asserted that the clause didn't relate to present day issues, such as gender equality, race relations, employment, and education. The new clause expresses the goals of a dynamic economy, a just society, an open democracy, and a healthy environment. Under the new clause, Labour began to officially move away from the welfare state that was created by Attlee in 1945. The new Labour Party, under the guidance of Blair, supports private enterprise and stresses the rights and responsibilities of citizens. The newly adopted policies removed government from everyday monetary policies and stripped away the socialist rhetoric of the Labour party of the past. As a result, the new Labour Party has attracted a wide spectrum of middle class voters and retained a majority since the 1994 election.

FURTHER RESOURCES

Periodicals

Fielding, Steven, Peter Thompson, and Nick Tiratsoo. "New Labour and 1945? (Britain's Party Since Its Majority Election to Power in 1945)." *History Today* (July 1, 1995).

Trimdon, Barry Hillenbrand. "Britain on the Attack and on Track: Tony Blair Has Won the Battle to Reform the Labour Party." *Time International* (March 27, 1995).

Turner, Royce. "'New Labour' and Whatever Happened to the British Left?" *Contemporary Review* 256 (August 1995).

Web sites

Assinder, Nick. "How Blair Created a New Party." *BBC*, July 20, 2004. <http://news.bbc.co.uk/1/hi/uk_politics/3724233.stm> (accessed May 10, 2006).

The Labour Party. "History of the Labour Party." <http://www.labour.org.uk/428> (accessed May 10, 2006).

Greenpeace Activists Protest GOP Policy Agenda

Photograph

By: Terry Ashe

Date: February 9, 1995

Source: Photo by Terry Ashe/ Time Life Pictures/Getty Images.

About the Photographer: Terry Ashe is a photographer for Time-Life. This photograph is in the collection at Getty Images, a worldwide provider of visual content materials to advertisers, broadcasters, designers, magazines, new media organizations, newspapers, and producers.

INTRODUCTION

In 1994, with Congressional elections looming in the middle of the first term of President Bill Clinton (1946–), the Republican congressional leadership announced a dramatic national campaign strategy—virtually all Republicans running for seats in the U.S. House of Representatives, whether incumbents or challengers, would sign a document called the Contract with America. The contract spoke of reforming government practices and promised to bring ten specific bills to a vote during the first 100 days of the 104th Congress. The language of the contract was pre-tested by pollster Frank Luntz using focus groups (groups of people randomly selected from the general population); only provisions that scored an approval rating of sixty percent or higher were retained. The ten bills were given attractive names like the Taking Back Our Streets Act and the Personal Responsibility Act.

This photograph shows activists from the environmental group Greenpeace staging a die-in in Washington, DC, to dramatize what they believed would be the deadly effects of the contract. Greenpeace is a global environmental group established in 1971 that specializes in nonviolent direct action, civil disobedience, and media-targeted street theatre to oppose whaling, genetic engineering, pollution, rainforest destruction, greenhouse gas emissions, and the like.

Greenpeace and other critics of the Contract with America claimed that not only were some of the promised policy changes unwise or cruel on their face—such as the contract's call for "prohibiting welfare to minor mothers [mothers under 18 years of age] and denying increased [Aid to Families with Dependent Children] for additional children while on welfare "—but that the descriptions were a misleading characterization of the actual changes that were proposed. For example, although ten acts were specifically listed, some of the promised acts were voted on as a series of smaller acts. Environmentalists, in particular, criticized the contract as a stalking horse that, while speaking attractively of reform, liberty, and responsibility, would actually constitute a "war on the environment" (in the words of the University of Buffalo's energy officer, 1995). The Sierra Club stated that "buried within the bills—which sport advertising-slogan names such as the 'American Dream Restoration Act'—lie a number of provisions that would indirectly undermine the foundation of environmental, health, and safety protections."

PRIMARY SOURCE

GREENPEACE ACTIVISTS PROTEST GOP POLICY AGENDA
See primary source image.

SIGNIFICANCE

Environmentalists pointed to the following provisions of the Contract with America, explicitly listed or

PRIMARY SOURCE

Greenpeace Activists Protest GOP Policy Agenda: Greenpeace activists in gas masks protest the Republican policy agenda "Contract With America" outside the U.S. Capitol on February 9, 1995. PHOTO BY TERRY ASHE//TIME LIFE PICTURES/GETTY IMAGES.

"buried within the bills" (Sierra Club, 1994), as harmful to the environment:

1. The Private Property Rights Protection and Compensation Act. This bill was intended to fulfill the contract's proposal that the federal government be required to pay compensation "when federal government actions reduce the value of [private property]." The Sierra Club claimed that this bill would allow compensation for "businesses, polluters, and others who claim environmental protections reduce their property values by 10 percent or more," making it too costly to "enforce and enact environmental, health and safety protections."

2. The Federal Regulatory Budget Control Act. This act would have set a numerical upper limit for the number of federal regulations. Needful regulations might, environmentalists said, be blocked simply because a quota had already been filled.

3. The Risk Communication Act. This act would require panels of scientists to review and possibly reject proposed environmental regulations. Scientists working for the industries to be regulated could serve on the panels, creating a conflict of interest.

The Republican Party gained majority control of the U.S. House of Representatives in the mid-term elections of 1994, although whether this victory was due to the appeal of the contract (which was announced fairly late in the election cycle) is debated by electoral experts. Many of the changes proposed by the contract were, in any case, implemented. Nine out of the ten items specifically listed were passed by the U.S. House of Representatives, although not all were passed by the U.S. Senate and became law. Some of the measures passed by the Republican-controlled House and Senate were made with the cooperation

House Minority Whip Newt Gingrich of Georgia announces the "Contract with America" plan for government reform before a crowd of Republican congressional candidates and supporters, September 27, 1994. AP/WIDE WORLD PHOTOS. REPRODUCED BY PERMISSION.

of President Clinton, such as the contract's proposed changes to the welfare system. However, Clinton resisted some of the changes to environmental laws attempted by Republicans. In July 1995, when the House passed an appropriations bill that would have cut the Environmental Protection Agency's budget by a third and changed the Clean Water Act of 1972 to allow development of wetlands and loosen pollution controls on cities and industries, Clinton called its actions "a stealth attack on our environment in the guise of a budget bill" and "a polluter's protection act."

In general, political conservatives have continued to favor the elimination or relaxation of government regulations on all forms of industrial activity, including those that pollute. They argue that market mechanisms will assure that greater good (including acceptable levels of pollution) are more likely to be produced by such a system than by one in which government seeks to regulate specific behaviors. Opponents of such claims, such as

Greenpeace, argue that they are misleading, and that conservative-controlled governments actually funnel resources to large corporations. More fundamentally, they argue that businesses and corporations, motivated by the short-term need to generate profits, cannot be trusted to interact with the Earth in a sustainable way that promotes long-term global health.

FURTHER RESOURCES
Periodicals

Garrett, Major. "Beyond the Contract." *Mother Jones* (March/April 1995).

Roff, Peter. "Analysis: The Contract With America at 10." *Washington Times* (September 29, 2004).

Web sites

The Sierra Club. "Year in Review: Contract On America's Environment." <http://www.sierraclub.org/planet/199412/yir-contract.asp> (accessed May 26, 2006).

U.S. House of Representatives. "Contract With America." <http://www.house.gov/house/Contract/CONTRACT.html> (accessed May 26, 2006).

Berlin Police Use Tear Gas to Quell Anti-Nazi Protest

News article

By: Tony Paterson

Date: December 2, 2001

Source: Paterson, Tony. *The Telegraph Group.* "Berlin Police Use Tear Gas to Quell Anti-Nazi Protest." December 2, 2001. <http://www.telegraph.co.uk/news/> (accessed June 3, 2006).

About the Author: Tony Paterson is a contributor to the *Daily Telegraph*, a British daily broadsheet newspaper, which has been published since 1855. It was the first national British newspaper to introduce an electronic version online, in 1994.

INTRODUCTION

The primary source presented here highlights the threat in current-day Germany of the growth of neo-Nazism and its damaging effect on social stability.

There was very little neo-Nazi activity in Germany during the period between 1945 and the 1960s. This was largely due to the success of the process of "denazification," under which the new German governments and the allied occupation forces removed all Nazi sympathizers from positions of influence or authority and banned extreme right-wing political groups and activities. However, Nazi beliefs and sympathies have been passed down through the generations and have emerged over the last few decades, especially since German reunification in the 1990s, in the form of the neo-Nazi movement and the extreme right-wing National Democratic Party. This trend has been fueled by increasing levels of immigration to Germany, particularly of asylum seekers and refugees.

The neo-Nazis glorify Germany's National Socialist past and revere Adolf Hitler. They are fiercely anti-Semitic and racist, and believe that all of Germany's problems can be attributed to the presence of foreigners in the country, particularly Jews. Many neo-Nazis deny the existence of the Holocaust and claim that the mass murder of millions of Jews during Nazi Germany was exaggerated or was a story

fabricated by Germany's enemies. Neo-Nazi sympathizers often adopt insignia from the Nazi regime, such as the swastika and the red-and-black clothing scheme. Although it is now illegal in Germany to produce or own anything representing Nazism, it is relatively easy to import such products from other countries that have neo-Nazi movements.

Since there are now extremely small numbers of people of Jewish ancestry living in Germany, most neo-Nazi attacks are against other non-German groups such as the large community of Turkish guest-workers, and non-white asylum seekers and refugees. The anti-Semitic activities of the movement tend to be directed at symbolic targets such as Jewish cemeteries and museums. For example, in September 2002, the Museum of the Death March in Germany's Belower Forest was burned down by neo-Nazis.

Violent racial attacks against foreigners perpetrated by extreme right-wing political groups have been a common occurrence in Germany, particularly since the reunification in 1990. There have also been a high number of racially motivated arson attacks on the homes of people seeking asylum in Germany.

Germany has a large population of disaffected young people, especially from the east, many of whom are attracted by neo-Nazi ideology and the options it offers to blame their problems on Jews and recent immigrants. The incorporation of the German Democratic Republic into the Federal Republic of Germany brought about severe economic and social pressures due to the weakness of the East German economy, and the policy of de-industrializing much of the former East Germany has resulted in a very high unemployment rate in that part of the country. At the same time, levels of immigration to Germany have increased sharply, particularly from the former Soviet Union and among foreign nationals seeking refugee status or asylum in the country.

The violent attacks against foreign nationals in Germany have provoked many demonstrations across the country in which thousands of people have protested against the extreme right-wing violence. These in their turn have encouraged the neo-Nazis to demonstrate publicly, increasing their visibility in the public arena. There have been a number of violent clashes in German cities between the National Socialists and their extreme left-wing counterparts, which have necessitated intervention by anti-riot police.

Left-wing demonstrators celebrate in front of a police water cannon in Berlin, after a day of mostly peaceful anti-Nazi demonstrations turned into fierce streetfights, May 1, 2004. © ARND WIEGMANN/REUTERS/CORBIS.

PRIMARY SOURCE

Riot police used tear gas and water cannon to quell violent Left-wing protests against the largest neo-Nazi demonstration in Berlin since the Second World War yesterday when 3,500 members of the extreme-Right National Democratic Party tried to march through a Jewish quarter of Berlin.

Witnesses said that dozens of protesters and several police officers were injured as about 1,200 anti-Nazi demonstrators hurling cobblestones and bottles tried to break through a security cordon near the capital's main synagogue to get to a group of neo-Nazis on the other side.

Riot police equipped with helmets and shields responded by driving back the demonstrators with water cannon, truncheons and tear-gas grenades. Police said that at least 20 protesters were arrested. Earlier, Jewish community leaders and the German government had described the decision by the 6,000-member NPD to hold a march near the Jewish quarter of Berlin as "an unbearable provocation."

The NPD had called its rally and demonstration to protest against the reopening on Wednesday of a controversial exhibition entitled Crimes of the Wehrmacht which graphically documents the war crimes perpetrated by the German army in Nazi-occupied eastern Europe and the Soviet Union during the Second World War.

The exhibition, which shows how ordinary German soldiers took part in the massacre of Jews and other civilians, was withdrawn from public view two years ago after historians discovered that some of its photographs showed murdered victims of the Soviet secret police and not those killed by the German army.

All 180 members of Berlin's Social Democrat-led government yesterday attended the exhibition, located in the Jewish quarter of the city, as a gesture of protest against the neo-Nazi march. "We are here to show our solidarity," said

Berlin's governing mayor Klaus Wowereit. "Unfortunately we have no legal power to stop this march," he added.

Despite attempts by the Berlin authorities to prevent the NPD demonstration, the city's courts ruled on Friday that the march should be allowed to go ahead, citing the German constitutional right to freedom of political expression.

NPD members wearing skinhead haircuts and "bovver boots" were, however, prevented from passing directly through the city's central Scheunenviertel district which was largely Jewish before the war and has since enjoyed a modest increase in Jewish inhabitants from Russia.

The NPD protesters, bused to Berlin from throughout Germany, were shielded from Left-wing protesters by 4,000 riot police. NPD demonstrators chanted slogans and brandished placards claiming that the Wehrmacht exhibition was an "insult to courageous German fighters and the German Fatherland."

Paul Spiegel, the leader of Germany's 81,000-strong Jewish community, said: "It is unbearable to think that these people should be allowed to pass through an area of Berlin in which Jews were once rounded up and sent to the concentration camps."

SIGNIFICANCE

Neo-Nazism is a growing movement in the western world, but mainly operates underground. It is reported to have organized groups in every western country and sophisticated international links between them. In some countries it is moving into mainstream society and politics as Euro-nationalism, in which the anti-Semitic beliefs of the movement are suppressed in the interest of capitalizing on public concerns about the influxes of non-western immigrants, including Muslims and non-white asylum seekers.

In response to the growing wave of racism in Germany, the government has introduced integration programs and language instruction in order to help immigrants to assimilate into German society. However, some immigrants have resisted participation in these, preferring to retain their own language and characteristics and to build their own communities of fellow nationals. This has exacerbated the problems of racial tension and helped to strengthen support among some elements of the German population for the ideals of the National Democratic Party and the neo-Nazi movement.

The German government has also taken legal action against neo-Nazi groups, banning around twenty organizations since the early 1990s. Its attempts to ban the National Democratic Party itself, however, have so far been unsuccessful. In the meantime, the party is

gaining support in mainstream politics, winning parliamentary seats in two states in the former East Germany in 2004 and declaring its intention to win representation in future federal elections.

FURTHER RESOURCES

Books

Niven, Bill. *Facing the Nazi Past: United Germany and the Legacy of the Third Reich*. New York: Routledge, 2002.

Periodicals

Rosenthal, John. "Anti-Semitism and Ethnicity in Europe." *Policy Review* 121 (2003).

Web sites

DW-World.de. "Report: Number of Neo-Nazis Rises in Germany." May 21, 2006. <http://www.dw-world.de/dw/article/0,2144,2027557,00.html> (accessed June 3, 2006).

Spiegel Online. "Why Germans Can Never Escape Hitler's Shadow." March 10, 2005. <http://service.spiegel.de/cache/international/0,1518,345720,00.html> (accessed June 3, 2006).

Expatriates Urge Fellow Iranians to Boycott Presidential Election

News article

By: Laura Wides

Date: June 17, 2005

Source: Wides, Laura. "Expatriates Urge Fellow Iranians to Boycott Presidential Election." *Associated Press*. June 17, 2005.

About the Author: Laura Wides has written many articles on a wide range of topics for the Associated Press, a worldwide news agency based in New York.

INTRODUCTION

The Iranian expatriate reform movement called for a boycott of the 2005 presidential elections to protest the country's political structure, which critics say gives too little power to the country's citizens. Iran is an Islamic theocratic republic led by religious leaders, or mullahs, and (nominally) elected officials. Much of the protest against the country's political structure is generated by Iranians in the United States and other Western countries, who fled during the 1979 Islamic Revolution. Political views of the exiled reformers

A police officer directs a protester during a demonstration outside Loews Santa Monica Beach Hotel in Santa Monica, California, June 8, 2001. The hotel is one of the sites where Iranians living abroad could vote in Iran's elections. AP IMAGES.

reach through television and radio programs broadcast into Iran via satellite, and through messages posted on websites.

The Supreme Leader and twelve-member Guardian Council hold most political power. Six council members are clerics appointed by the Supreme Leader, and six are lawyers recommended by the head of the judicial branch (who is appointed by the Supreme Leader) and approved by the legislature. The council reviews laws passed by the parliament to ensure their adherence to the constitution and Islamic Law.

The Assembly of Experts, a body of 86 members who are *mujtahids*, or experts in *fiqh*, or Islamic Law, selects the Supreme Leader, who serves for life (although in theory he could be replaced by the assembly at any time). There are public elections for president, parliament and the Assembly of Experts. However, the Guardian Council approves all candidates, rejecting any who have a reform agenda.

The 1979 Islamic Revolution overthrew Iran's last king, Shah Mohammed Reza Pahlavi. Although he improved living standards for many Iranians and gave women the right to vote, he abolished all political parties but his own, jailed opponents and activists, and enforced strict censorship. Iranian religious leaders, or *mullahs*, denounced many of the shah's rulings as un-Islamic, and many ordinary Iranians distrusted his economic policies and believed his decisions were controlled by the United States. Violent pro-democracy protests ousted the shah, allowing the exiled cleric Ayatollah Ruhollah-Khomeini to return. When he took control of Iran as the Supreme Leader, hundreds of thousands opposed to the new theocracy fled the country.

The mullahs claim that the country supports their rule, citing high turnouts for prayers and elections. In the 2001 presidential election, for example, 68 percent of the 42 million eligible voters went to the polls. President Mohammad Khatami, whose term ended in 2005, had been elected by young Iranians and women who believed his campaign promises to bring about industrialization, democracy, and the rule of law. He was frequently defeated in his efforts to bring about social change, however, and lost most of his battles with the Guardian Council. His support waned, and expatriates encouraged their fellow Iraqis to boycott the 2005 election to show that this dissatisfaction was widespread. Politicians and researchers predicted that the 2005 elections would have a 30 to 60% voter turnout.

PRIMARY SOURCE

Expatriates Urge Fellow Iranians to Boycott Presidential Election
Iranian exiles are campaigning against presidential elections in their homeland, urging would-be voters in the Islamic republic and around the globe to boycott what they call a sham.

In Los Angeles, half a dozen television and radio stations that for years have criticized the Iranian government are beaming their message into Iran by satellite and Internet ahead of Friday's voting.

Reformists say that whether a hardliner or more moderate wins, the election only legitimizes the current regime, where supreme leader Ayatollah Ali Khamenei has the final word on every important national issue.

"We are encouraging people to stay home," said Los Angeles-based TV journalist Homa Sarshar. "We want to show the world empty streets."

Sarshar and other expatriates see little difference between the leading candidates.

"One may be a little bit more liberal, one may be a little more conservative, but all are in the same camp. They accept the constitution, and the constitution is about a supreme leader who has the final word," she said.

Nacsrin Mohammadi—whose brothers have been tortured in prison since their 1999 arrest for leading the student movement in Iran—gave more than two-dozen interviews this week in Los Angeles, her voice hoarse from repeating her plea to other Iranis to boycott the election.

"I want people to stay home, not only for me, because my family has been destroyed, but so nobody else will

have to go what we have gone through," she said through an interpreter.

Earlier, Mohammadi, 28, went on a three-day hunger strike to bring attention to students like her brothers, Manouchehr and Akbar, whom she says were starved and forced to watch each other being beaten until the bottoms of Akbar's feet split open and his toenails fell off. "We want the people of the world to know that Iranians, especially the youth, do not want this regime," she said.

Hossein Hedjazi, program director and host at KIRN AM 670 radio station, said he took an informal poll of listeners and all planned to boycott the election.

Those expatriates who do plan to vote may find it difficult. People born in Iran or to Iranian parents can cast their ballot, even if they become citizens of another country, but first they have to find a polling center. About 35 centers were announced nationwide. Yet in Southern California, where a third of the nation's roughly 1 million Iranians live, few organizations knew where the poll sites were as of Thursday. No Los Angeles sites were made public.

Despite the media storm, Hedjazi said he worried that some youth, who make up the majority of Iran's 70 million people, may be swayed by the heavy western-style campaigns.

Iranian rock and American rap has blared at political rallies. Candidates have given out free Internet access cards, and girls on roller skates have campaigned in knee-length tunics.

Hedjazi said some students may believe that even a conservative like front-runner Hashemi Rafsanjani, a former Iranian president and successful businessman, is better than hardliner Mohammad Bagher Qalibaf, a former police chief backed by Khamenei's allies.

Reformist candidate Mostofa Moin, who was initially barred from running, has warned that a boycott could pave the way for a totalitarian state, but many expatriates say his win won't change things as long as Khamenei remains in power.

"Even if 50 percent turnout, they think that this will be a big victory," Hedjazi said of the current regime. "It doesn't matter if they vote for or against them, that will demonstrate their legitimacy."

But Mohammadi said she believes people will not be swayed by the slick campaigns or political pressure to vote.

"All these changes will go away after the election," she said. "After 26 years, the people are very well informed and familiar with the tricks of the regime."

SIGNIFICANCE

The boycott failed to dissuade voters, more than 70% of whom turned out to elect conservative Mahmoud Ahmadinejad, the former mayor of Tehran, to the presidency. While mayor, Ahmadinejad had overturned decisions made by previous moderate leaders. Ahmadinejad's presidency began by taking a hard-line stance on international issues, particularly the development of nuclear energy. The United States, Europe, and Israel fear that Iran's uranium enrichment program is being used to develop nuclear weapons, despite reassurances that it is intended only for domestic electricity production. Ahmdinejad's government has not cooperated with UN and IAEA inspection requests, resulting in a referral to the Security Council and possible economic or even military sanctions.

Many of those who supported the election boycott are against tough action against Iran, saying sanctions would only hurt the people, not change the government. Many Iranians also support the United States, something reformists think would change with a rigid approach. Stanford University's Iran Democracy project recommends focusing U.S. foreign policy on support for the struggling reform movement and involving the many young unemployed Iranians who are dissatisfied with the government. Increasing the broadcast of radio and television news and talk programs into Iran, and establishing diplomatic ties to Iran could also help bring change to Iran.

FURTHER RESOURCES

Books

Alavi, Nasrin. *We Are Iran: The Persian Blogs*. Brooklyn, N.Y.: Soft Skull Press, 2005.

Milani, Mohsen M. *The Making of Iran's Islamic Revolution: From Monarchy to Islamic Republic*. Boulder, CO: Westview Press, 1994.

Periodicals

MacFarquhar, Neil. "Iran Reformists Split on Election Boycott." *New York Times*. June 10, 2005.

MacFarquhar, Neil. "Most Iranian Exiles in U.S. Oppose Military Attack." *New York Times*. May 9, 2006.

Shahidian, Hammed. "To Be Recorded in History: Researching Iranian Underground Political Activists in Exile." *Qualitative Sociology*. 24, no. 1 (2001): 55–81.

Web sites

BBC News. "Country Profile: Iran." April 20, 2006. <http://news.bbc.co.uk/1/hi/world/middle_east/country_profiles/790877.stm> (accessed May 22, 2006).

6 Labor, Trade, and Globalization

Labor, Trade, and Globalization

The Industrial Revolution changed the physical landscape with railroads, large factories, automated farming, and booming cities. It also altered society, creating a new working class whose lives centered on the factory, mine, or construction project. During the nineteenth century, this work was arduous and often dangerous. There were few assurances of safety and no guarantees of a living wage. Children worked alongside adults. Labor organizations and unions arose to address these issues. While skilled laborers had long organized into gilds, mass organization of the working class was often met with repression—at the hand of both the company boss and the government. Denounced as insurgents, agitators, and radicals, labor protesters fought for worker's rights, fair pay, limitations on the working week, and safer working conditions—from the depths of coal mines to the top floor of the factory sweatshop.

While labor protest takes many forms, this chapter emphasizes the strike—a protest weapon unique to the labor movement. The sources here present accounts of strikes in various forms, from speeches to song. "Which Side Are You On?" is an oft-adapted anthem of striking workers and union organizers. With lyrics frequently changed to suit the particular action, the Depression-era song has found repeated use for generations of protesters. Included here is President Ronald Reagan's controversial response to the 1981 air traffic controllers' strike in the United States. Finally, to demonstrate the power of a labor union turned mass political protest movement, "Solidarity's Message to the Working People of Eastern Europe"

discusses the role of Solidarity in Poland's independence movement and break with communism.

Just as the methods of production revolutionized in the modern era, so to did trade. International trade is not the invention of the modern world, but it is fully entrenched as the fixture of an increasingly global economy. Whereas protesters in the nineteenth century pressed for freer markets ("Great Free Trade Demonstration At Liverpool"), some now lobby for more restricted markets to protect local workers or farmers. Some oppose the trend of outsourcing work to lower paid, less protected workers in developing nations; other protesters argue that globalization and free-trade agreements weaken developing nations.

The current anti-globalization movement, or global justice movement, opposes many aspects of increased globalization including the perceived control of trade associations and international monetary policy by a small handful of the wealthiest nations and most powerful corporations. Though a majority of anti-globalization protests are peaceful, many have employed tactics of vandalism. Frequent targets are overseas locations of American owned companies. Pictures of damaged McDonald's, similar to the one included in this chapter, have become the U.S. media's iconic image of anti-globalization protests abroad. The diversity of aims and tactics of the global justice movement is discussed in "What Charles and Evan Did for Spring Break," a first-hand account of two youth protesters at one of the past decade's largest anti-globalization demonstrations.

Great Free Trade Demonstration At Liverpool

Magazine article

By: The Economist

Date: September 2, 1843

Source: "Great Free Trade Demonstration At Liverpool." *The Economist* (September 2, 1843).

About the Author: *The Economist* is a news magazine, owned by The Economist Group, which has been published weekly since 1843. It is produced in London, but has a worldwide readership. It mainly covers international affairs, politics, business, and finance issues, and maintains an editorial stance in support of free trade and fiscal conservatism.

INTRODUCTION

The public meeting in support of free trade reported on in this 1843 article was organized in Liverpool, England, by the Anti-Corn Law League. It was addressed by one of the movement's leading figures, John Bright. The Anti-Corn Law League, formed in the northeast of England in 1839, was a political pressure group. Its main objective was to bring about the repeal of the English Corn Laws and the establishment of free trade between England and other countries.

The Conservative (Tory) government had passed a series of new Corn Laws in 1815 in response to pressure from landowners who were concerned about falling profits. These laws restricted the import of grain from other countries to protect the price of locally produced grain in the interest of English farmers and landowners. The import of wheat was banned completely if the average price of domestically produced grain fell below a certain level, and a sliding scale of duties was imposed on all wheat imports.

Enactment of the Corn Laws coincided with a time of rapid population growth, as England made the transition from an agricultural to an industrial country, and they put severe pressure on the ability of the country to produce enough food to feed its population. The effect was to substantially increase the price of bread, the staple food of the poor agricultural and industrial workers.

The Anti-Corn Law League's active membership consisted mainly of industrialists, manufacturers, merchants, and Liberal politicians, led by John Bright and Richard Cobden. Bright was the son of a Lancashire cotton manufacturer. A Quaker by religious background, he held strong laissez-faire capitalist views, and his powerful oratory skills were instrumental in gaining support for the League among many different groups, including industrial workers, agricultural laborers, and tenant farmers. Demonstrations and public meetings were held throughout the country, and the League published many books and pamphlets promoting its views. These had strong religious undertones, which may have helped to increase their appeal to the population.

The Anti-Corn Law movement came to represent the focus of a general campaign against the Conservative government and the landowner classes, who were regarded by League members and Liberal politicians as having a monopoly on power that was harmful to England's industrial progress. It was part of a Liberal political movement that placed a high value on individual freedom from state control. At this time, there were still many medieval restrictions on trade and manufacturing, and the ruling landowner classes held many aristocratic privileges. Freedom of trade and economic activity, and a reduction in the privilege and power of the ruling classes, were seen as necessary for advancement and the economic well-being of the nation. Free trade was needed, it was argued, so that other countries could obtain the capital they needed to buy British manufactured goods. In the absence of free trade, other countries would develop their own products and the British manufacturing industry would be threatened.

Although the main focus of the League's campaign was free trade and the repeal of the Corn Laws, monopoly in any form was opposed. The League spoke out against not only the landowners and the politicians, but against the established church, the military, and the universities, all of which were seen as having vested interests in preserving the status quo and hampering economic progress.

The League also focused its efforts on highlighting the poor conditions of both agricultural and industrial workers under the prevailing social structure, conditions that were blamed on the effect of the Corn Laws. It campaigned for improved conditions for workers, including changes in the land tenure system, abolition of the game laws, and fair housing rents.

In response to these arguments, Tory politicians countered that the League members were campaigning for their own interests. If the price of bread was lower, the profits of industrialists and manufacturers would increase, since they could pay their workers lower wages, and people would have more money to spend on their products.

Liverpool, England, 1945. © HULTON-DEUTSCH COLLECTION/CORBIS.

Eventually, however, the Conservative Prime Minister Robert Peel was convinced by the arguments of the League, and repealed the Corn Laws in 1846. In doing so, he acted against the wishes of many members of his own party, who soon dismissed him from power. The Conservative Party itself lost a great deal of support as a result of the Anti-Corn Law Campaign and the growing popularity of free trade principles. They were ousted from control of the government by the Whigs and did not win another election until 1866.

PRIMARY SOURCE

One of the greatest, if not the greatest public demonstration ever made in Liverpool in favour of free-trade principles, was made on the evening of Wednesday last, on the occasion of the regular monthly meeting of the Liverpool Anti-Monopoly Association.... Long before the hour at which the doors of the theatre were announced to be opened, the street opposite the house was densely crowded by persons eager to obtain admittance, and soon after the doors were thrown open the pit and gallery, to which the admission was free, were completely packed in every corner with individuals. The boxes, which were principally reserved for ladies, and to which there was a charge of sixpence for admission, were quite filled, but not inconveniently crowded. The stage was crammed, although there was also a charge of sixpence for admission to that part of the house. Never has it been our lot to see a more numerous or more enthusiastic meeting. Thousands were obliged to go away without obtaining admission, although every available corner of the capacious building was filled up. Even from the ventilating aperture in the centre of the ceiling there were numbers of individuals to be seen peering upon the animated and densely crowded assembly below. The theatre was appropriately fitted up with banners, bannerets, and free-trade devices.

About half-past seven o'clock William Rathbone, Esq., entered the house, and was received with the most enthusiastic cheering. He was followed shortly afterwards by

John Bright, Esq., M.P., who was welcomed with deafening applause. As soon as the cheering had subsided, James Mellor, Esq., proposed that William Rathbone, Esq., take the chair, which was seconded by Lawrence Heyworth, Esq., and carried by acclamation.

The Chairman, who was warmly received, addressed the meeting, after which Mr. John Smith, in an effective speech, proposed the first resolution, which was as follows:—

"That, as the distress which all classes of the community have long been suffering, and the exemplary patience with which it has been endured, have been fully acknowledged by her Majesty's Ministers, this meeting desires to record their extreme dissatisfaction that another session of Parliament has been permitted to close without a single attempt to apply a remedy; and this dissatisfaction is aggravated by the knowledge of the fact that such guilty neglect of all just legislation has neither the excuse of ignorance on the one hand, nor the want of power on the other; but that, while constantly acknowledging the truth of the principles of free trade, and possessed of a large majority in both Houses of Parliament, her Majesty's Ministers still continue to sacrifice the national prosperity to a selfish, but shortsighted, system of monopoly."

Mr. James Mulleneux supported the resolution, which was then put by the chairman, and literally a forest of hands were held up in its favour. Not one was extended in opposition, and it was declared as passed unanimously.

Richard Sheil, Esq., considered himself particularly fortunate in having to propose a resolution which needed no recommendation from him, and which only required to be read to ensure its adoption. It was:—

"That the Anti-Corn-law League, by their energetic and unwearied exertions in proving to the community generally, and especially to the agriculturalists, the evils of the so-called protective system, have well earned the gratitude of their countrymen; and this meeting testify their high gratification in being honoured by the presence of John Bright, Esq., a distinguished member of that body, and, thanking him most earnestly for his past exertions, rejoice that his sphere of usefulness is enlarged by his triumphant election of the city of Durham."

That was the resolution he had to propose, and all he begged was, that they would reflect a little upon it. Just let them consider what effect the election of John Bright for the city of Durham must necessarily have upon the community at large, on the great change which had taken place in that city, a change which was rapidly spreading throughout the country, a change which would soon place the representatives of the people in the House of Commons in the position from which they ought never to have been removed. (Loud cheers.)

...John Bright, Esq., M.P., then rose, and his reception was most enthusiastic. When the repeated rounds of cheering had subsided, he addressed the audience in his able and eloquent style, dwelling with great point on topics similar to those urged in the Preliminary Number of THE ECONOMIST, touching on sugar, coffee, wool, etc., and then addressed himself to the question of the opinions of the Liverpool constituency. He knew that the 10l. householders of Liverpool were in favour of free trade. (Hear, hear.) He would not make a speech on party politicshe would not say a word of any man as the representative of any constituency whatever, on any ground whatever, except as being for or against free trade. The 10/. householders of Liverpool would declare in favour of free trade if an election took place tomorrow morning. (Great cheering.) But their borough had been handed over, bound hand and foot, to the monopolists, by that portion of the electors who were themselves the greatest sufferers by this system—men who were the first crushed by it, and who would be plunged into the intensest suffering unless this system were abolished. (Hear, hear.) He had a right to speak to freemen. He was almost going to say that he had no claim to sit in Parliament, except as the representative of the freemen and working classes of the city of Durham. (Great cheering.) He had canvassed them over and over, and over again. They had always been asked to vote for either red or for blue, he believed that was the other colour, they had always voted for either Whig or Tory without thinking that it was of any sort of consequence to them what sort of opinions were held by the one or the other. But he had sat with them in their cottages; he saw them taking their breakfast and their tea; he showed them how monopoly robbed them of their coffee and sugar, and of bread and butter for their children; he showed them how stonemasons, shoemakers, carpenters, and every kind of artisan suffered if the trade of the country were restricted; he showed them that if their families increased, if the population increased, and trade did not increase, those who had no property but their labour, who must have work or must starve, suffered most; he showed them how the fierce competition for labour thus created reduced the rate of wages; he showed them that the foul fiend of monopoly stood upon, and had been called into existence by the law of England, that law which they by their conduct at former elections had assisted to make, and he proved to them that that fiend deprived them of one-third or one-half of the miserable pittance of wages that they earned. They never made a single party speech at that election; the words Whig and Tory were never used; they talked of free trade—of the rights of industry, of the trampling of the poor under the hoof of monopoly; there was no sinister interest there, no West India monopolists there—they had their labour only to depend upon; they were honest men and had intelligence, and when their intelligence and their sympathies were thus appealed to, it was not possible for all the intimidation, all the influence of the rich and the powerful, to prevent them from voting for a man of whom they knew nothing excepting as connected with the Anti-Corn-law League, and as an advocate for the abolition of all monopolies. (Great cheering.) He wished that all the freemen of Liverpool were then present at that meeting; he would stay till twelve o'clock at night—nay, he would stay till twelve o'clock to-morrow night to discuss with them all points connected with this great question; he wished he could have one shake of the hand with the whole body of the freemen of Liverpool. There was no class of people for whom he had so sincere a sympathy as for those who lived by their labour, well knowing that the effects of bad laws must come into every cottage, and that good laws would send some sunshine and some comfort to every cottage and to every heart in the land. (Much cheering.) There was no remedy for the existing distress amongst the working classes but the abolition of those laws which restricted their trade and which bound down an increasing population to restricted employment and an insufficient supply of food. At another election, he called upon them to think no more of party, which was but a miserable bone of contention thrown amongst them to distract their attention, whilst somebody else was running away with all that was worth contending for. He was glad to see that last session had destroyed the adherence to party objects in Parliament. The ministry had found out that by strict adherence to their party they could do nothing for the people: on the one hand they found that if they attempted to do much for the people, their party would forsake them, on the other, that if they adhered strictly to party objects they could not withstand the opposition of the people. The Whig party dared not march with their principles; they had been the most powerless opposition that ever confronted a government; they knew what the people wanted; but somehow or other there was a clinging to aristocratic prejudices; and he (Mr. Bright) told the people that they had nobody to rely upon but themselves. (Hear, hear.) Tell him that Whig or Tory, or any other aristocracy could save England! It was a foolish and a hopeless tale; their salvation must come from themselves, and it must come from them at the polling booth. (Enthusiastic cheering.) There were two methods only, one by the sword, the other by the vote. He had nothing to do with the sword. Take away the sword; the state might be saved without it; but let them think of their votes; the vote of the working man was as good as the man who owned a county.

(Hear, hear.) Let not the working man think himself merely an atom in the political machine; his vote might turn the election for Liverpool, and the one vote for Liverpool might destroy for ever this odious corn law. (Great cheering.) When he thought what Liverpool was, what it would be if this law were abolished, he was anxious that that night should not pass away without producing some effect. When he thought of their noble, their exulting river, he saw in it a source of great and increasing prosperity. A friend of his left this river on the 4th of this month, and in twenty-five days he had a letter from him from Halifax, Nova Scotia; in six hours they could travel from London to Boulogne; and was it to be tolerated, that a people who could effect such wonders as these should submit any longer to such an imbecile system as that of monopoly? (Loud cheers.) Talk not of the continuance of such a childish and wicked system, a system to which there was no parallel in any age or nation. (Continue cheering.) The people of Egypt, who built pyramids to last till the end of time, were a people so ignorant and imbecile as to worship monkeys: why the people of Liverpool bore some resemblance to the people of Egypt in that. (Much laughter and cheering.) If he were an inhabitant of Liverpool he should be ashamed to acknowledge in foreign countries that he belonged to it, for the people of Liverpool did something as absurd as the worshipping of monkeys. They did things to endure for ages, they had led the world in many a grand career, and yet they bowed down to this miserable creature monopoly, compared with which the monkey of the Egyptians was indeed a god. (Great cheering.) He asked them on behalf of the people of Rochdale, who sent their produce through the port of Liverpool, who imported their cotton and their wool through the port of Liverpool, he asked them, on behalf of that industrious population, amongst whom he lived, to vote for the abolition of the corn laws; and on behalf of that constituency who had entrusted him with the representation of their city, because he came fearlessly amongst them to advocate the abolition of all monopolies, on their behalf, and on behalf of the suffering people of this country, and on behalf of the great principles of justice and humanity all the world over, and on behalf of that Christianity for which they professed to be willing to make some sacrifices, he called upon them to think on this question, and having thought upon it to decide, and give their voices and their votes in favour of the abrogation of the worst law that any human legislature ever passed to the misery and misfortune of any people. The Hon. Gentleman resumed his seat amidst enthusiastic and prolonged acclamations, having spoken exactly an hour and twenty minutes.

The Chairman said, that after what they had heard, and they had heard a great deal, the next thing was to go and remember what they had heard, and act upon it. The meeting was now dissolved, and he felt proud in seeing such an assembly as the one before him that evening; one so well conducted, and free from any of that clap-trap by which they had been so often allured. He trusted they would remember what they had heard and act upon it.

A vote of thanks to the Chairman was then moved by Mr. Charles Edward Rawlins, jun., which was put to the meeting and carried.

The Chairman briefly returned thanks for the honour conferred upon him, and hoped that the people of Liverpool would show, not only in word, but in deed, that which would tell on the next generation and on children yet unborn.

Three cheers having been given for Mr. Cobden, and the same for Mr. Bright, the meeting separated at a quarter to ten o'clock.

SIGNIFICANCE

The Anti-Corn Law movement was a manifestation of the massive social and economic changes that were taking place in Great Britain at the time. The country was undergoing rapid industrialization and the break up of traditional rural society. As a result, long-established customs and beliefs were being weakened. New groups, such as the industrialists, were emerging whose interests were in direct conflict with those of the landowning ruling classes, but who needed the support of the masses to challenge the political system and advance these interests. At the same time, many of the Anti-Corn League campaigners were genuinely in favor of better living and working conditions for the poor, and believed that this could best be achieved if the economy were allowed to regulate itself, free from state interference.

The repeal of the Corn Laws was a major milestone in British history in two important respects. First, it represented a watershed, at which point the legacy of Britain's feudal past was finally broken, with the landowners no longer able to assert the same power as they had in the past. Second, it was the first example of mass public opinion being successfully mobilized against the government, and it remains one of the most striking examples of democratic governance.

FURTHER RESOURCES
Books

Pickering, Paul A., and Alex Tyrell. *The People's Bread; A History of the Anti-Corn Law League.* Leicester: Leicester University Press, 2000.

Periodicals

Spall, Richard F. "Landlordism and Liberty: Aristocratic Misrule and the Anti-Corn-Law League." *Journal of Libertarian Studies* 8 (1987).

Ward, Tony. "The Corn Laws and English w\Wheat Prices, 1815–1846." *Atlantic Economic Journal* (September 1, 2004).

Decrees of the Provisional Government Relating to the Workingmen

Declaration

By: Provisional Government of France

Date: 1848

Source: J. H. Robinson, ed., *Readings in European History.* Boston: Ginn, 1906.

About the Author: The Provisional Government of France took control of the country in 1848 after the abdication of Louis Philippe. It was out of power by the end of the year.

INTRODUCTION

In 1848, revolutionary political and social theories combined with a severe economic crisis to produce a massive upheaval across Europe. Only Great Britain and Russia escaped untouched. Governments were toppled while monarchs and politicians fled. National independence, social reform, and liberal democratic constitutions suddenly seemed within reach. Yet, the revolutions of 1848 ultimately led to little change.

There were troubles throughout Europe in the 1840s. A civil war broke out in Switzerland, while the Poles attempted a revolution and the people of Naples, Italy, took up arms. In this climate, revolution was expected. It happened in France. Louis Philippe's monarchy had been categorized by inaction. Despite a clear need, the government produced no social reforms and preferred to cater to wealthy special interests. The government's refusal to consider electoral reforms heightened a sense of class injustice among middle class shopkeepers, skilled artisans, and unskilled working people. On the night of February 22, 1848, the revolt began in Paris when barricades went up. Two days later, Louis Philippe abdicated in favor of his grandson.

The common people no longer wanted a monarchy. They proclaimed a provisional republic, headed

An illustration showing the French revolution of 1848. Armed men stand on an improvised barricade in a city street. Officials stand on the ground before them. © BETTMANN/CORBIS.

by a ten-man executive committee and certified by shouts of approval from the revolutionary crowd. The committee immediately set about drafting a constitution for France's Second Republic.

■ PRIMARY SOURCE

The provisional government of the French republic decrees that the Tuileries shall serve hereafter as a home for the veterans of labor.

The provisional government of the French republic pledges itself to guarantee the means of subsistence of the workingman by labor.

It pledges itself to guarantee labor to all citizens.

It recognizes that workingmen ought to enter into associations among themselves in order to enjoy the advantage of their labor.

The provisional government returns to the workingmen, to whom it rightfully belongs, the million which was about to fall due upon the civil list.

The provisional government of the French republic decrees that all articles pledged at the pawn shops since the first of February, consisting of linen, garments, or clothes, etc., upon which the loan does not exceed ten francs, shall be given back to those who pledged them. The minister of finance is ordered to meet the payments incidental to the execution of the present edict.

The provisional government of the republic decrees the immediate establishment of national workshops. The minister of public works is charged with the execution of the present decree.

■

SIGNIFICANCE

The 1848 upheaval held the promise of making France into the world's model for social advance. The Provisional Government reduced the working day in Parisian factories to ten hours and formed a commission to study labor problems. Slavery in the colonies was abolished while every adult male gained the right to vote. Political leaders spoke of guaranteeing the right to work and of adding a minister of labor to the cabinet. By the end of 1848, the proposals had been abandoned and most of the reforms repealed. French voters had favored moderate republicans over the radicals and a republican army had crushed the rebellious Parisian working class. The workers were left more bitter and frustrated than ever. In response, they supported the rise of Napoleon III, who was supposed to be a friend of the common man. Napoleon did enact a few reforms, but they came late in his reign and were relatively minor efforts. Major improvements for workers in France did not occur until the twentieth century.

The rest of Europe fared about as well as France. In March 1848, the Hungarians demanded autonomy from the Austrian Empire. In August 1849, Austrian and Russian forces defeated the Hungarian independence movement. In March 1848, Frederick William IV of Prussia was forced to agree to a liberal constitution. In December, the king disbanded the Prussian Assembly and granted the country a conservative constitution. In March 1849, he reasserted his royal authority. Overall, the moderate, nationalistic middle classes were unable to expand on their initial victories. Instead, they drew back when radical workers presented much more revolutionary demands. Radical change would not come for generations.

FURTHER RESOURCES

Books

Dowe, Dieter, ed., et al. *Europe in 1848: Revolution and Reform.* New York: Berghahn Books, 2001.

Smith, W.H.C. *Second Empire and Commune: France, 1848–1871.* New York: Longman, 1996.

Tacke, Charlotte, ed. *1848: Memory and Oblivion in Europe.* New York: Lang, 2000.

Which Side Are You On?

Song lyrics

By: Florence Reece

Date: 1931

Source: Reece, Florence. "Which Side Are You On?" Stormking Music, 1933.

About the Author: Florence Reece (1900–1986), the wife of a coal miner and organizer for the National Miner's Union in Harlan County, Kentucky, wrote "Which Side Are You On?" in 1931 during an especially violent strike. She penned the song after Harlan County deputies ransacked her home in search of her husband.

INTRODUCTION

Of the many songs born out of labor strife in America's coal mines, Florence Reece's classic 1931 union song, "Which Side Are You On?" is one of the best known. Written in response to a violent strike in Harlan County, Kentucky, the song roused people across the nation in support of the right to organize. It ultimately helped the Wagner Act pass into law.

In the spring of 1931, during the Great Depression, coal miners suffered dangerous conditions and low pay in Harlan County. The pay of the miners had been slashed repeatedly by the mine owners, who also fired thousands of workers. In desperation, the miners contacted the small United Mine Workers (UMW) and began to organize. They were opposed by the local Coal Operators' Association and local law enforcement. The strike soon became one of the most violent labor episodes of the 1930s. The coal companies responded harshly by immediately evicting thousands of miners from their company-owned homes. On May 5, 1931, one hundred armed miners engaged in open warfare with company guards in a skirmish that left one miner and three company men dead. Hundreds of state troopers then arrived to halt

the conflict and the UMW declared that the Harlan County miners were on their own. Still seeking to organize, the miners turned to the National Miners' Union (NMU), a group that was supported by the Communist Party.

Florence Reece, the wife of a rank-and-file organizer for the NMU in Harlan County, was at home one day in 1931 when Sheriff J. H. Blair and several of his deputies broke into her cabin to search for her husband. (Known to the workers as "thugs," most of the deputies were mine guards who were still being paid by mine owners, as Blair later admitted.) As her young daughters cried, the police poked their rifles into closets, under beds, and into piles of dirty clothes before finally leaving. A furious Reece then tore a calendar off the wall and wrote "Which Side Are You On?" She set the lyrics to the tune of an old Baptist hymn. "Lay the Lily Low."

■ PRIMARY SOURCE

"Which Side are You On?"

Come all of you good workers,
Good news to you I'll tell,
Of how that good old union
Has come in here to dwell.

Which side are you on?
Which side are you on?
Which side are you on?
Which side are you on?

My daddy was a miner,
And I'm a miner's son,
And I'll stick with the union,
Till every battle's won.

They say in Harlan County,
There are no neutrals there.
You'll either be a union man,
Or a thug for J.H. Blair.

Oh, workers can you stand it?
Oh, tell me how you can.
Will you be a lousy scab,
Or will you be a man?

Don't scab for the bosses,
Don't listen to their lies.
Us poor folks haven't got a chance,
Unless we organize.

SIGNIFICANCE

"Which Side Are You On?" became an anthem of the labor movement. Various labor activists, such as Pete Seeger, picked up the song and changed its lyrics to fit their situation. The song eventually passed over from the union movement to the civil rights movement. In 1961, Congress of Racial Equality (CORE) leader James Farmer revised the lyrics to suit the circumstances in the South during the Freedom Rides. Whenever CORE members perceived that other African Americans were betraying the cause, they sang Reece's song. In 1965, the song inspired marchers for voting rights at Selma, Alabama. It has outlived Reece, who died in 1986 at her home in Knoxville, Tennessee.

Unionism finally came to Harlan County in May 1933 when the National Industrial Recovery Act recognized the legal right of workers to organize unions. The UMW organized the coal mines in a matter of months. By autumn of 1933, the workers had signed their first collective bargaining agreement with the coal operators.

For people around the country, Harlan County came to demonstrate the limits of company paternalism. In times of trouble, the coal companies abandoned the miners. The episode in Kentucky, publicized so well by Reece's song, helped pave the way for the Wagner Act of 1935. This legislation, among the most significant for labor in American history, guaranteed workers the right to organize and created a legal process for obtaining recognition of the union as the representative of workers.

FURTHER RESOURCES

Books

Hevenor, John W. *Which Side Are You on?: The Harlan County Coal Miners, 1931–39*. Urbana. Ill.: University of Illinois Press, 1978.

Taylor, Paul F. *Bloody Harlan: The United Mine Workers of America in Harlan County, Kentucky, 1931–1941*. Lanham, Md.: University Press of America, 1990.

Wooley, Bryan. *When the Morning Comes*. Lexington, Ky.: University Press of Kentucky, 1975.

Single Women of Boston Picket Relief Headquarters

Photograph

By: Anonymous

Date: June 24, 1935

Source: © Corbis/Bettmann.

About the Photographer: The photographer is unknown. Otto Bettmann, a librarian and curator in Berlin in the 1930s, began collecting photographs to preserve as a historical archive. Fleeing Germany with several trunks of photographs in his possession, he settled in the United States. By 1995, his collection included over 11 million items, including this picture of single women picketing in Boston.

INTRODUCTION

The Roaring Twenties, a time of great economic gains in the stock market and of a widening in the gap between rich and poor in the United States, came to an abrupt end on Black Tuesday, October 29, 1929, when the stock market lost twelve percent of its value in one day. The stock market continued to decline for the next thirty-two months, finally bottoming out in June 1932, losing 89.2% of its value from October 28, 1929 levels. The country sank into the Great Depression as Republican President Herbert Hoover struggled to prevent economic freefall.

Unemployment went from 3.3 percent to 8.9 percent in one year; by 1933 unemployment hit 24.3 percent, the worst rate on record. Unemployment rates in the U.S. would not dip below 10 percent again until 1941, at the start of U.S. involvement in World War II (1941–1945). The 1930s saw farm prices drop forty to sixty percent, and the depression affected countries worldwide.

Franklin D. Roosevelt campaigned as a Democrat for the presidency in 1932; Americans viewed Hoover as uncaring and unwilling to take needed measures to pull the country out of the Great Depression, in spite of his efforts to establish protective tariffs and to encourage business leaders to keep wages high for those who were still employed. Roosevelt was elected in November 1932 and by March 1933, when he took office, he initiated a series of programs that fell under the umbrella title "The New Deal."

Job creation was one of Roosevelt's primary goals; Hoover had created the Federal Emergency Relief Administration, sometimes known as the ERA or FERA, and Roosevelt expanded it. Between May 1933 and December 1935, when it was replaced by the Works Progress Administration, the FERA provided jobs for more than 20 million Americans, at a government cost of more than $3.1 billion.

In this photograph, single women in the Boston area—single, widowed, and divorced—picketed the local headquarters of the FERA in protest of their belief that married women were receiving a higher percentage of FERA jobs and the higher paying positions.

PRIMARY SOURCE

Single Women of Boston Picket Relief Headquarters: Single women rally in front of Boston's emergency relief agency on June 24, 1935. They are demanding that needy single women be given preference for jobs over married women. © CORBIS/BETTMANN.

PRIMARY SOURCE

SINGLE WOMEN OF BOSTON PICKET RELIEF HEADQUARTERS

See primary source image.

SIGNIFICANCE

Women poured into the workforce during the Great Depression of the 1930s in an attempt to secure any form of employment; many employers would hire women over men because women's wages were set at lower rates. As the Depression continued, men began to accept the lower wages, and women at times found themselves jobless as well. During the 1930s married and single women increased their numbers in the workforce; when the FERA was established men and women flocked to the local headquarters in search of aid or jobs.

With no husband or partner to help shoulder the burden of support during the Depression, and for those women with no sons or other male relatives to help, the lack of a job could literally mean the difference between life and death. As the signs in this photograph show, single women viewed themselves as subjects of discrimination in the assignment of FERA jobs. Some local FERA agencies assigned single women and married men supporting families priority over married women; the Boston picketing is in

Demonstrators march to protest the layoff of Works Progress Administration workers in San Francisco, California, 1936. © HORACE BRISTOL/CORBIS.

response to the perception that such prioritization was not applied at that location.

In the mid 1930s—with the Great Depression at its peak in terms of unemployment—public sentiment turned sharply against married women "taking jobs" from married men or single women and men. A 1936 survey of Americans showed that eighty-two percent believed that married women should not work if their husbands held jobs. By the late 1930s, twenty-six states considered laws that would restrict a married woman's right to work. Nevertheless, by 1940 more than twenty-five percent of all married women would be in the workforce.

The single women's protest at the FERA headquarters helped to shape federal job allocation as the FERA closed and its responsibilities fell under a new agency, the Works Progress Administration, in late 1935. The WPA restricted both spouses in a marriage from working, believing that this took a job away from another person in need. The WPA hired women,

minorities, and immigrants according to need, and single women found the need-based policy in line with their protest. After the United States entered into World War II in 1941, millions of men were drafted into the military and demand for industrial products for military use soared. This created a situation in which men and women, married or otherwise, had little trouble finding work; and the WPA and similar job creation programs soon came to an end.

FURTHER RESOURCES
Books

Breyer, Stephen. *Active Liberty: Interpreting Our Democratic Constitution*. New York: Knopf, 2005.

Nelson, Samuel P. *Beyond the First Amendment: The Politics of Free Speech and Pluralism*. Johns Hopkins University Press, 2005.

Stone, Geoffrey R. *Perilous Times: Free Speech in Wartime: From the Sedition Act of 1798 to the War on Terrorism*. New York: W.W. Norton, Inc., 2005.

Web sites

United States Department of Labor. "Compensation from before World War I through the Great Depression." 2001. <http://www.bls.gov/opub/cwc/cm20030124ar03p1.htm> (accessed June 3, 2006).

Deportee

Song lyrics

By: Woody Guthrie

Date: 1948

Source: Guthrie, Woody. "Plane Wreck at Los Gatos (Deportee)." The Woody Guthrie Foundation and Archives, 1948.

About the Author: American guitarist, singer/songwriter, and political activist and social protestor, Woodrow Wilson "Woody" Guthrie (1912–1967) is considered one of the most influential folk singers of the twentieth century, with nearly three thousand songs to his credit. He is best remembered for "This Land is Your Land" and "So Long, Its Been Good to Know You." Guthrie was born in Okemah, Oklahoma, but in 1931 moved into the Texas panhandle after local economic conditions and his mother's lingering illness left his family destitute. Guthrie barely survived in Texas as the Great Depression dominated the country. When the Dust Bowl came to the Great Plains in 1935, Guthrie headed to California in search of work. As Guthrie walked, hitchhiked, and rode hobo trains over the next two years, he experienced the life of the poor and often homeless people of the Depression era. He performed odd jobs but, more often than not, sang and played guitar for food and sundries. Many of his songs used themes of social justice, the American Dream, everyday living of everyday people, pro-labor, and anti-fascist communism. He soon became a popular personality and opinionated spokesperson among the people who inspired his songs. While working for the Los Angeles newspaper *The Light*, Guthrie investigated the plight of migrant workers. The research prompted Guthrie to support organized labor and to speak out about migrant rights. He wrote about migrant workers in such songs as "Plane Wreck at Los Gatos (Deportee)."

INTRODUCTION

The governments of Mexico and the United States agreed to establish an amnesty through deportation program in 1947. Under its terms, undocumented Mexican workers who had been apprehended in the United States would be sent back to Mexico—only to return as temporary contract laborers if they signed employer contracts. This arrangement of cheap seasonal labor for U.S. growers and assurances of not being deported for migrant workers became known as Drying Out Wetbacks or Storm and Drag Immigration.

On January 29, 1948, the *New York Times* reported an airplane crash 20 miles (32 kilometers) west of Coalinga, California, over the Los Gatos canyon. The airplane contained twenty-eight Mexican farm workers who were being flown from Oakland, California, to the El Centro, California deportation center.

Woody Guthrie read a news report about the wreck that supposedly did not give the names of the victims, only referred to them as deportees (illegal immigrants in the process of deportation). One news spokesperson stated that the deaths were dismissed as unimportant because all were deportees except for the pilot. Perceiving the incident as racial injustice, Guthrie wrote a poem he called "Plane Wreck at Los Gatos (Deportee)," in which he assigned symbolic names to the nameless Mexicans. The poem was not set to music, but Guthrie merely chanted the words when he performed it as a protest song. Guthrie's poem was made into a song in the 1950s by schoolteacher Marty Hoffman. Thereafter, folk singer Pete Seeger popularized the song by singing it at concerts. Since then, the song has been sung by such performers as Bob Dylan, The Byrds, Dolly Parton, Judy Collins, Arlo Guthrie (Woody Guthrie's son), and Bruce Springsteen.

PRIMARY SOURCE

The crops are all in and the peaches are rott'ning,
The oranges piled in their creosote dumps;
They're flying 'em back to the Mexican border
To pay all their money to wade back again.

Goodbye to my Juan, goodbye, Rosalita,
Adios mis amigos, Jesus y Maria;
You won't have your names when you ride the big airplane,
All they will call you will be "deportees"

My father's own father, he waded that river,
They took all the money he made in his life;
My brothers and sisters come working the fruit trees,
And they rode the truck till they took down and died.

Some of us are illegal, and some are not wanted,
Our work contract's out and we have to move on;
Six hundred miles to that Mexican border,

They chase us like outlaws, like rustlers, like thieves.

We died in your hills, we died in your deserts,
We died in your valleys and died on your plains.
We died 'neath your trees and we died in your bushes,
Both sides of the river, we died just the same.

The sky plane caught fire over Los Gatos Canyon,
A fireball of lightning, and shook all our hills,
Who are all these friends, all scattered like dry leaves?
The radio says, "They are just deportees"

Is this the best way we can grow our big orchards?
Is this the best way we can grow our good fruit?
To fall like dry leaves to rot on my topsoil
And be called by no name except "deportees" ?

SIGNIFICANCE

Governmental labor statistics throughout the twentieth century showed that migrant workers had been paid lower-than-normal wages while working and living in poverty-like conditions with little access to the protections supplied to most U.S. workers.

In 1917, migrant workers were first organized in the United States under guest-worker programs. The Farm Security Administration (FSA) was established during the Great Depression (1929–early-1940s) to improve the condition of the country's rural poor. The FSA also placed migrant workers into areas that had labor shortages. However, migrant workers were excluded from labor protection policies that were enacted through President Roosevelt's New Deal programs. In 1942, United States and Mexico agreed to permit temporary Mexican agricultural workers into the United States under a series of minimum wage, maximum hour, and elementary labor protection rules. When the agreement did not succeed, the U.S. government created the Bracero program, which supplied temporary, undocumented Mexican agricultural workers to U.S. growers. The Bracero program was officially ended by Congress in 1948, but continued into 1951 through a series of informal binational agreements.

Beginning in 1952, a temporary agricultural worker (H-2A) program became part of the Immigration and Nationality Act (INA). This action, in essence, consolidated various immigration provisions into the INA. The Act allowed H-2A visas for foreign visitors to work in the United States when American workers are unwilling, unable, or unqualified to perform specific work at specific locations.

In 1986, Congress reformed its immigration laws when it passed the Immigration Reform and Control Act (IRCA). It provided for legalization of undocumented persons in the United States who had met specific admissions criteria, sanctions against anyone who employed undocumented workers, and border restrictions to stop further undocumented migrations. Although the IRCA legalized about 1.1 million individuals, over the next twenty years the Act did not succeed in its goals. In 1988, the number of undocumented workers into the United States was estimated to be between 1.5 and 3 million, while in 2002, it was estimated to have reached 9.3 million. Analysis from the PEW Hispanic Center shows that 11.1 million unauthorized migrants were in the United States as of March 2005.

In 2005, legislation was introduced in Congress called The Border Protection, Antiterrorism, and Illegal Immigration Control Act. The bill targets enforcement of illegal immigration but does not provide any means for the legalization and citizenship of undocumented workers. As a result, protests concerning immigration reform were held in 2006 at various locations across the country. The legislation was criticized by various civil rights, business, and religious groups. Many legislators countered with compromise measures such as The Agricultural Job Opportunities, Benefits, and Security Act, commonly known as AgJobs.

As of May 2006, immigration reform legislation has yet to pass in Congress. Tensions continue in the agricultural labor sector as disagreements occur concerning the requirements for foreign guest workers and legalization status of undocumented farm workers. Undocumented workers continue to cross U.S. borders to work at jobs that American workers refuse to do. In 2005, it was reported by the federal government that between fifty-two and eighty-five percent of all farm workers are undocumented, with most of them originating from Mexico. Over a half-century after Woody Guthrie wrote about the plight of migrant workers, most migrant farm workers remain among the poorest U.S. workers, with annual earnings of between $5,000 and $10,000. Without such migrant workers, the abundant crops grown in the United States could not be fully harvested, which would undoubtedly cause fruits and vegetables to be sought increasingly from foreign markets.

A group of deportees are processed prior to departure for Europe from Hoboken, New Jersey, May 1, 1952. AP IMAGES.

FURTHER RESOURCES

Books

Cray, Ed. *Ramblin' Man: The Life and Times of Woody Guthrie*. New York: W.W. Norton, 2004.

Partridge, Elizabeth. *This Land Was Made for You and Me: The Life and Songs of Woody Guthrie*. New York: Viking, 2002.

Hard Travelin': The Life and Legacy of Woody Guthrie, edited by Robert Santelli and Emily Davidson. Hanover, N.H.: University Press of New England for Wesleyan University Press, 1999.

Periodicals

Gilbert, Lauren. "Fields of Hope, Fields of Despair: Legisprudential and Historic Perspectives on the AgJobs Bill of 2003." *Harvard Journal on Legislation* 42 (Summer 2005): 417.

Web sites

The American Immigration Law Foundation. "The Value of Undocumented Workers: The Numbers Behind the U.S.–Mexico Immigration Debate." <http://www.ailf.org/ipc/policy_reports_2002_value.asp> (accessed May 25, 2006).

The Library of Congress. "Woody Guthrie and the Archive of American Folk Song: Correspondence 1940–1950." <http://memory.loc.gov/ammem/wwghtml/wwghome.html> (accessed May 25, 2006).

The PEW Hispanic Center. "Size and Characteristics of the Unauthorized Migrant Population in the U.S." <http://pewhispanic.org/reports/report.php?ReportID=61> (accessed May 25, 2006).

The Woody Guthrie Foundation and Archives. "Wood Guthrie: Biography." <http://www.woodyguthrie.org/biography.htm> (accessed May 25, 2006).

Rip in the Silk Industry

America's Great Silk Worker's Strike

Book excerpt

By: William D. Haywood

Date: March 1913

Source: Kornbluh, Joyce, L., ed. *Rebel Voices: An IWW Anthology.* Ann Arbor: University of Michigan Press, 1968.

About the Author: William D. Haywood (1869–1928) was one of the founders of the International Workers of the World (IWW), America's first socialist trade union organization. The IWW, through Haywood and a group of activists that included Elizabeth Gurley Flynn (1890–1964), took control of the union organizing in support of the Paterson, New Jersey, silk worker's strike that began on January 27, 1913.

INTRODUCTION

In 1913, Paterson, New Jersey, was the center of the American silk manufacturing industry. Known variously as "Silk City" and the "Lyons of America," in reference to the French silk making capital, one-third of Paterson's work force of approximately 75,000 people was engaged in one of three enterprises broadly aligned as the silk trade—the ribbon weavers, the broad silk weavers, and the dye makers. Many of the silk workers were recent immigrants to the United States.

At the heart of the manufacture of silk was the loom, the machine that wove silk thread into fabric. Until about 1890, much of the Paterson silk manufacturing was done on small looms that were often privately owned machines that weavers operated in their own homes. The introduction of large looms was critical to the centralization of silk weaving into factories in Paterson.

By 1912, the wages paid to a typical silk worker had not been increased in twenty years. In both Paterson and the nearby Pennsylvania towns where silk mills were located, poverty was the norm among the families of silk trade workers. Working conditions in the silk mills were difficult, with ten- to twelve-hour days the standard work day.

Further mechanization was on the horizon. In the Paterson factories, each weaver operated two separate looms, but many factories planned to introduce either three-loom or four-loom systems. In January 1913, a four-loom system was first imposed in the silk mill owned by Henry Doherty. His workers attempted to negotiate a solution with Doherty, fearing that the new system would result in widespread unemployment and that wages would further decline. Doherty refused to negotiate with the workers, who then turned to the local office of the International Workers of the World (IWW) for assistance. Eight hundred silk workers from Doherty's mill went on strike on January 27, 1913, setting in motion one of the most contentious and far reaching labor disputes in American history.

Prior to 1912, the prevailing belief among American capitalists was that those businesses with a largely immigrant workforce could never be successfully unionized, since the constituent groups in such workforces were often fractious and divided by old national rivalries. The Lawrence, Massachusetts, textile industry strike of 1912 altered that perception forever, as the IWW organized a union from a workforce comprised of over twenty different worker nationalities. The Lawrence strike had ended favorably for the IWW and the local workers.

In the first days of the Paterson strike, it appeared that the dispute would be confined to the Doherty factory. However, within days, the industry-wide discontent concerning the four-loom system spread throughout the 300 mills in the Paterson silk industry. At the peak of the dispute, as many as 50,000 silk workers were on strike in the region. The IWW advanced a formal platform that sought the abolition of the four-loom system, an eight-hour work day, and increased wages.

By modern standards, the dispute was remarkable for the degree to which public authorities were directed against the striking workers. Accounts vary as to the precise number of silk workers and IWW sympathizers taken into custody during the strike. The most conservative estimates exceed 1,900 persons. Many of those arrested for their part in the demonstrations served ten-day jail sentences. Two strikers were killed during of an altercation with private detectives hired by the mill owners.

For both sides, the strike became a simple war of attrition. By June, 1913, the IWW was staging weekly rallies that attracted thousands of spectators to nearby Haledon, New York, to rouse public sentiment for the strikers and their cause. A pageant was organized in June, 1913, by a group of New York intellectuals who sympathized with the silk worker's cause. The proceeds of the pageant, held at Madison Square Garden, were directed to the relief of the silk workers, most of whom had no other source of income. Given the importance of the silk trade to the city, by June, 1913, the Paterson economy had collapsed.

Striking silk workers at Turn Hall, Paterson, New Jersey, February 25, 1913. © BETTMANN/CORBIS.

In July, 1913, a group of ribbon weavers returned to work, and the Paterson strike was soon over. Perceiving that they had an advantage, various mill owners offered to permit their workers to return at their previous wages, on condition that the workers resigned from the IWW.

PRIMARY SOURCE

When the broad silk weavers in Henry Doherty's mill in Paterson, N. J., left their machines last February they inaugurated what has proved to be the closest approach to a general strike that has yet taken place in an American industry.

They revolted against the 3 and 4 loom system which until recently has been confined to the state of Pennsylvania. This system is restricted to the lower grades of silk, messaline and taffeta.

There are almost 300 silk mills in Paterson. Doherty was the first manufacturer to introduce this system there and later it was carried into 26 other mills. The silk workers soon realized that unless this scheme for exploiting them still further was checked, it would in time pervade the entire industry in the Jersey city.

The silk workers of Paterson are the most skilled in the United States and the employers thought that if there was anywhere in the country where this system could be successfully adopted it was in Paterson. They thought that their workers would stand for it. The workers themselves were not consulted, as the manufacturers afterward realized to their sorrow, when a general strike was called embracing the industry in all its branches and extending to all states where silk is manufactured.

At present no less than 50,000 silk workers are on strike in New Jersey, Pennsylvania, New York and Connecticut, including those in the preparatory processes, the "throwster" mills, dye houses, broad silk making in all grades, as well as in nearly all the ribbon mills.

In many respects this strike is hardly less significant than that at Lawrence. It involves nearly as many workers and the conditions are just as bad. But the Paterson revolt has attracted less public attention than did the woolen fight. This is due to several reasons.

In the first place, the manufacturers, through their control of outside newspapers, were able to bring about a general conspiracy of silence. The New York papers, for example, after the first few days in which they gave prominence to the strike, were warned through subtle sources that unless there was less publicity they would be made to suffer through loss of support and advertising. Then the Paterson strikers were fortunate in having among them several trained veterans in the labor movement, such as Adolph Lessig, Ewald Koettgen, and Louis Magnet, who had been members of the I.W.W. since 1906, and knew what to do towards putting the strike on an organized basis. For a time they were able to take care of themselves without relying much on outside help. Besides, the authorities kept their hands off for a time, after their first fright in which they threw Elizabeth Gurley Flynn, Carlo Tresca and later Patrick Quinlan and Alex Scott, the Socialist editor, into jail. These organizers got on the job instantly and have done excellent work.

THE LYONS OF AMERICA

Paterson is the Lyons of America. It practically has a monopoly in the making of the finer grades of silk in this country. It has 25,400 people engaged in the silk industry and in the manufacture of silk machinery and supplies. Therefore, when practically all these workers came out, the industry was tied up tight.

Fifty-six per cent of the Paterson silk workers are women and children and they have been among the most devoted and enthusiastic strikers.

As this is written, the strike has entered upon its seventh week and the demands of the workers have crystallized around a determination to have the eight-hour day. This will apply to all the workers involved, except the broad silk weavers whose principal demand, as stated, is the abolition of the grinding 3 and 4 loom system.

So greatly have wages been reduced in recent years that the weavers are now demanding the restoration of the 1894 price list which was imposed on them at the time. With the improvements in machinery that have been made, this would be a great advantage to the ribbon weavers. The dye house workers are holding out for a minimum wager of $12 a week. In other branches there is a general demand for a 25 per cent increase in wages.

Present wages, according to the manufacturers' figures, average $9.60 a week. A general call at one of the mass meetings for pay envelopes brought out hundreds which showed the average wage is much lower than this and as all wages are determined by working periods, the actual yearly wage would bring average "earnings" down to $6 or $7 a week.

Paterson manufacturers have an absolute monopoly on the finer grades of silk, like brocades, that are made on the Jacquard loom, and it would be easy for them to raise prices to meet wage increases, but because of the cutthroat competition among them, silk is cheaper, on the whole, than it was 15 years ago. This reduction in price, needless to say, has been taken out of the flesh and blood of the workers.

UNTRUSTIFIED INDUSTRY

The big capitalists have never tried to enter the silk trade, because it deals with a luxury. They are too busy securing their grip on the necessities of life, like food, clothing, steel, transportation, etc.

The Paterson workers, then, have not had to fight a concentrated trust, such as existed at Lawrence, but a gang of scattered employers, all jealous and fearful of each other. The strike undoubtedly would have ended much sooner had it not been for the desire of the richer manufacturers to see the smaller makers starved out and driven into bankruptcy, which already has occurred to a number of them.

The manufacturers as a whole have used as any excuse for not raising wages the plea that they cannot afford it on account of Pennsylvania's competition. But this is untrue, because the Pennsylvania mills are controlled largely by the same interests that center in Paterson.

The Pennsylvania silk mills are situated generally in mining camps and industrial centers where the wages of the men have been so reduced that women and children have been compelled to seek employment in the mills. Ninety-one percent of the workers in the Pennsylvania silk mills are women and children.

Wages in the Pennsylvania silk mills average much less than in New Jersey and it is a peculiar fact that the men get less than the women. The men get $6.06 a week while the women are making $7.01.

There are six prominent processes in the making of silk and they are usually done in different establishments. "Throwing" is largely done in Pennsylvania—reeling the raw silk as it comes from cocoon, etc. The dyeing is done in separate factories. . . .

THE RED BADGE OF TOIL

In this connection it is worth while to relate an incident—one of the most dramatic of the strike. The Paterson bosses lost no time in injecting the "patriotic" issue, after the fashion of Lawrence, Little Falls and Akron. The red flag, they howled, stood for blood, murder and anarchy—the Star Spangled Banner must be upheld, etc., etc. Elizabeth Gurley Flynn was on the platform at a big strike meeting one day explaining the significance of the red flag when a striking dyer sprang up from the middle of the audience crying: "I know! Here is the red flag!"

And aloft he held his right hand—stained a permanent bloody crimson, gnarled from years of toil, and corroded by the scarlet dye which it was his business to put into the fabrics worn by the dainty lady of the capitalist class as well as by the fawning prostitute.

For an instant there was silence and then the hall was rent by cries from the husky throats as all realized this humble dyer indeed knew the meaning of the red badge of his class.

Ribbon weaving is largely done by men and women. In this department the bosses have developed a speeding up system with reductions in pay, overlooking no opportunity to introduce improved machinery. Thus they increase production, at the same time they lowered the pay, until the workers are now demanding a scale which 19 years ago was imposed upon them! That is, the weavers now ask a wage that prevailed two decades ago.

The significance of this demand makes it plain that in the evolution of industry and the introduction of new machinery the workers have obtained no benefit, while the bosses have reaped ever increasing profits.

Many children are employees in the silk industry, most of them being between the ages of 14 and 16. However, there are few violations of the child labor law, not because the manufacturers care anything about either the law or the children, but because the making of high grade silk requires the careful and efficient work that only adults can give. However, the Paterson capitalists have begun to set up plants in the southern states as well as in the mining regions of Pennsylvania, installing there new style looms which can be operated by girls and children.

MEETING FOR CHILDREN

One of the best and most enthusiastic meetings held during the strike was that for the benefit of the children of the mills. They packed Turner Hall and listened eagerly and with appreciation as speakers outlined to them the development in the manufacture of silk from the cocoon to the completed fabric lying on the shelves of the rich department store.

The strike has been viciously fought from the very beginning. The usual combination of press, pulpit and police has labored both openly and secretly to weaken it and break it, but without avail. For seven weeks the Paterson newspapers have delivered screams of rage and fury day after day. They have not hesitated to urge any measure that might break the strike, from tar-and-feathers to murder. Day after day in big, black headlines in their front pages they have demanded that the "I.W.W. blatherskites" be driven out of town. They have constantly incited the police to violence and urged the authorities to take "drastic measures." All in vain. On the day this is written the leading organ of the manufacturers admits that the police, the administration and the courts have been helpless and it now begs the workers themselves to "drive the I.W.W. out of town," promising that if they will organize into "a decent, dignified, American union," the whole city will demand that the bosses give them the conditions for which they ask.

LITTLE VIOLENCE

Despite this, another paper admits in its editorial columns that Paterson after all ought to be thankful. "Though 25,000 people have been on strike here for seven weeks," it says, "there has been remarkably little violence."

As was the case in Lawrence, nearly every nationality on earth is represented in the strike. The Italians and Germans are the most numerous, with thousands of Russians, Poles, Hungarians and Armenians besides. Shoulder to shoulder they have stood, with a spirit and loyalty that nothing could break or weaken. For seven long weeks they have held out and in place of food many of them have simply taken up another link in their belts and drunk a glass of water. Some relief money has come in but not enough to help any except the most needy cases.

Incidents without number could be given to show the spirit of self sacrifice and devotion among the Paterson workers. The jail has had no terrors for them, since accommodations there are hardly worse than in the "homes" they are compelled to live in. On occasions when the police have started wholesale arrests they have vied with each other in placing themselves in the hands of the "bulls." One day when the police gathered in more than 200 of them, they refused to walk to jail but demanded the patrol wagon. When the police pleaded that the patrol wagon would hold only a few at a time, they said they would wait! And the patrol wagon the police were compelled to get, making trip after trip to the jail while the arrested strikers stood in a group and laughed and sang.

The meetings we have held have been wonders. Day after day strikers have crowded into Turner and Helvetia Halls with enthusiasm just as rampant as on the first day of the strike and on the Sundays when the Socialist city of

Haledon is visited, at the invitation of Socialist Mayor William Brueckmann, for open air meetings, it has seemed as if the whole population of the northern part of New Jersey was present. To speak at such meetings is worth a whole lifetime of agitation.

SIGNIFICANCE

When William Haywood wrote "The Rip in the Silk Industry" in 1913, he was arguably the most experienced and battle-hardened union organizer in American history. "Big Bill" Haywood spent fifteen years organizing Idaho and Colorado miners in an atmosphere that was one of open warfare between owners and workers. In 1907, Haywood was charged with the murder of the former governor of Idaho, who had acted aggressively against the miners while in office. Haywood was subsequently acquitted in one of the most famous trials in American legal history, with Clarence Darrow leading his defense.

Given Haywood's experiences, his article is remarkable on a number of levels. Haywood adopts the measured and persuasive tone of an advocate, not the call to arms of a stereotypical union firebrand. He presents the Paterson strikers case with a mixture of local economic statistics and concrete examples of owner- and state-sponsored wrongdoing. Haywood states that the Paterson strike is a virtual general strike of 50,000 workers, a claim that was reasonably square to the facts. The strike is only seven weeks old at the time of Haywood's writing; Haywood clearly believes that the strikers, and his International Workers of the World, are not only determined to win the strike, they are taking the first steps towards a better life for the Paterson silkworkers.

The non-violent approach of the Paterson strikers is noteworthy in what would become a desperate struggle by June, 1913. The concept of strike funds or other relief payments to striking workers was unknown at the time, and since over 1,900 strikers or other protestors were ultimately arrested and jailed for illegal picketing or related demonstrations, heightened emotions and overt violence might otherwise have been expected.

The Paterson strike followed the Lawrence, Massachusetts, textiles strike in 1912, a dispute in which the workers were led by the IWW. The IWW had achieved a measure of victory in Lawrence and sought to apply the same tactics of non-violence and persistent, sometimes strident advocacy of their cause to secure public support. Much of the IWW success in Lawrence had turned on its ability to successfully organize immigrant workers from a number of different backgrounds and cultures. Those organizing tactics were refined in Paterson, whose silkworkers were of similarly diverse backgrounds.

The Paterson strike was also significant in establishing Elizabeth Gurley Flynn as a force within both organized labor and other types of social activism. Flynn was twenty-two years old when the strike began, and she was one of the most passionate of its leaders. Flynn made many speeches at the IWW-sponsored rallies held in support of the strikers in nearby Haledon, New York, in the spring of 1913. These events served to both attract thousands of spectators, as well as to publicize the strike and its issues to the broader public.

The workers' demand for a shorter work day was expressed by the phrase, eight hours of work, eight hours of rest, and eight hours of pleasure. The Paterson workers would ultimately receive their eight-hour work day in 1919. However, the mill owners in Paterson would work over the next two decades to relocate their factories away from Paterson and its perceived militant labor force.

The Paterson strike represented a convergence of disparate forces into the union cause that was unique in American history to that time. The Paterson silk workers, whose concerns were primarily economic, gained the support of both the socialist IWW, as well as that of a group broadly described as the Greenwich Village intellectual class. Margaret Sanger, a registered nurse who would later advocate birth control and public sexual education, was a member of that intellectual class. When Flynn organized temporary housing in New York and Boston for hundreds of the strikers' children, to help the strikers cope with their diminished financial resources during the strike, Sanger was a prime mover in securing accommodation for the children.

The Paterson strike ended badly for the IWW. The strikers returned to work after almost five months of unemployment and they received very little in the way of concessions from the mill owners. The mill owners, fearful of another crippling strike, did not implement the four-loom system for another ten years. The failure of the IWW in Paterson foreshadowed the general decline of the union. By 1920, the IWW was a spent force. Flynn went on to become one of the founders of the American Civil Liberties Union. Haywood was charged with sabotaging the American war effort in 1918, and he fled to Russia while on bail in 1921. He died in Moscow in 1928.

FURTHER RESOURCES

Books

Flynn, Elizabeth Gurley. *The Rebel Girl: An Autobiography.* New York: New York University Press, 1955.

Golin, Steve. *The Fragile Bridge: Paterson Silk Strike, 1913.* Philadelphia: Temple University Press, 1988.

Web sites

PBS. "The American Experience: The Paterson Silk Strike of 1913." <http://www.pbs.org/wgbh/amex/goldman/peopleevents/e_strike.html> (accessed May 19, 2006).

Address by César Chávez, President United Farm Workers of America, AFL–CIO

The Grape Boycott

Speech

By: César E. Chávez

Date: March 1989

Source: Chávez, César. "Address by César Chávez, President United Farm Workers of America, AFL–CIO." *The César E. Chávez Foundation.*

About the Author: César Estrada Chávez (1927–1993) was a Mexican-American labor leader and activist for civil and social rights. He gained international recognition for improving the working and living conditions of migrant farm workers, especially the elimination of harmful pesticides. With fellow activist Dolores Huerta, Chávez founded the National Farm Workers Association (NFWA)—now the United Farm Workers of America (UFW)—in 1962; they led a five-year grape boycott that eventually brought growers to the bargaining table. Chávez was posthumously awarded the Presidential Medal of Freedom in August 1994. His birthday, March 31, became an official California state holiday in 2000.

INTRODUCTION

In September 1965 César Chávez and 2,000 members of the National Farm Workers Association (NFWA) declared its first boycott of grapes. Putting the plight of farm workers in the national spotlight, and with support from political, religious, and student groups around the country, Chávez pressured growers to provide better wages and working conditions for their field workers. One year later, NFWA merged with an AFL–CIO union to become the United Farm Workers Organizing Committee (UFWOC). The strike, considered one of the most successful in American history, ended in 1970, when most California grape growers signed labor contracts.

In 1973 the UFWOC—now the United Farm Workers of America (UFW)—called a second grape boycott when the United Farm Workers of America (UFW) lost most of its labor agreements to the Teamsters. Gaining national attention, in part due to concurrent boycotts of nonunion lettuce and Gallo wine, the boycott ended four years later with the landmark California Agricultural Labor Relations Act.

In 1984 Chávez announced a third boycott called the "Wrath of Grapes" to protest the continuing use of toxic pesticides. At the same time, Chávez himself went on a thirty-six day hunger strike he dubbed the "fast for life." Chávez continued this third boycott until his death in 1993. Arturo Rodriquez succeeded him as president of the UFW.

■ PRIMARY SOURCE

Address by César Chávez, President United Farm Workers of America, AFL–CIO

Pacific Lutheran University

March 1989

Tacoma, Washington

What is the worth of a man or a woman? What is the worth of a farm worker? How do you measure the value of a life?

Ask the parents of Johnnie Rodriguez.

Johnnie Rodriguez was not even a man; Johnnie was a five year old boy when he died after a painful two-year battle against cancer.

His parents, Juan and Elia, are farm workers. Like all grape workers, they are exposed to pesticides and other agricultural chemicals. Elia worked in the table grapes around Delano, California until she was eight months pregnant with Johnnie.

Juan and Elia cannot say for certain if pesticides caused their son's cancer. But neuroblastoma is one of the cancers found in McFarland, a small farm town only a few miles from Delano, where the Rodriguezes live.

"Pesticides are always in the fields and around the towns," Johnnie's father told us. "The children get the chemicals when they play outside, drink the water, or when they hug you after you come home from working in fields that are sprayed.

"Once your son has cancer, it's pretty hard to take," Juan Rodriguez says. "You hope it's a mistake, you pray.

César Chávez announces the end of a seven and one-half years boycott against the California lettuce and grape industries in January 1978. AP IMAGES.

He was a real nice boy. He took it strong and lived as long as he could."

I keep a picture of Johnnie Rodriguez. He is sitting on his bed, hugging his [t]eddy bears. His sad eyes and cherubic face stare out at you. The photo was taken four days before he died.

Johnnie Rodriguez was one of 13 McFarland children diagnosed with cancer in recent years; and one of six who have died from the disease. With only 6,000 residents, the rate of cancer in McFarland is 400 percent above normal.

In McFarland and in Fowler childhood cancer cases are being reported in excess of expected rates. In Delano and other farming towns, questions are also being raised.

The chief source of carcinogens in these communities are pesticides from the vineyards and fields that encircle them. Health experts believe the high rate of cancer in McFarland is from pesticides and nitrate-containing fertilizers leaching into the water system from surrounding fields.

Last year California's Republican [g]overnor, George Deukmejian, killed a modest study to find out why so many children are dying of cancer in McFarland. "Fiscal integrity" was the reason he gave for his veto of the $125,000 program, which could have helped 84 other rural communities with drinking water problems.

Last year, as support for our cause grew, Governor Deukmejian used a statewide radio broadcast to attack the grape boycott.

There is no evidence to prove that pesticides on grapes and other produce endanger farm workers or consumers, Deukmejian claimed.

Ask the family of Felipe Franco.

Felipe is a bright seven year old who is learning to read and write.

Like other children, Felipe will some day need to be independent. But Felipe is not like other children: [H]e was born without arms and legs.

Felipe's mother, Ramona, worked in the grapes near Delano until she was in her eighth month of pregnancy. She was exposed to Captan, known to cause birth defects and one of the pesticides our grape boycott seeks to ban.

"Every morning when I began working I could smell and see pesticides on the grape leaves," Ramona said.

Like many farm workers, she was assured by growers and their foremen how the pesticides that surrounded her were safe, that they were harmless "medicine" for the plants.

Only after Ramona took her son to specialists in Los Angeles was she told that the pesticides she was exposed to in the vineyards caused Felipe's deformity. The deep sadness she feels has subsided, but not the anger.

Felipe feels neither anger nor sadness. He is lavished with the care and love he will always need. And he dreams of what only a child can hope for: Felipe wants to grow arms and legs. "He believes he will have his limbs someday," his mother says. "His great dream is to be able to move around, to walk, to take care of himself."

Our critics sometimes ask, 'why should the United Farm Workers worry about pesticides when farm workers have so many other more obvious problems?' The wealth and plenty of California agribusiness are built atop the suffering of generations of California farm workers. Farm labor history across America is one shameful tale after another of hardship and exploitation.

Malnutrition among migrant children. Tuberculosis, pneumonia, and respiratory infections. Average life expectancy more than twenty years below the U.S. norm.

Savage living conditions. Miserable wages and working conditions. Sexual harassment of women workers. Widespread child labor. Inferior schools or no school at all.

When farm workers organize against these injustices they are met with brutality and coercion—and death.

There is nothing we care more about than the lives and safety of our families.

There is nothing we share more deeply in common with the consumers of North America than the safety of the food all of us rely upon.

We are proud to be a part of the House of Labor.

Collective bargaining is the traditional way American workers have escaped poverty and improved their standard of living. It is the way farm workers will also empower themselves.

But the UFW has always had to be something more than a union.

Because our people are so poor. Because the color of our skin is dark. Because we often don't speak the language. Because the discrimination, the racism, and the social dilemmas we confront transcend mere economic need.

What good does it do to achieve the blessings of collective bargaining and make economic progress for people when their health is destroyed in the process?

If we ignored pesticide poisoning—if we looked on as farm workers and their children are stricken—then all the other injustices our people face would be compounded by an even more deadly tyranny.

But ignore that final injustice is what our opponents would have us do.

"Don't worry," the growers say.

"The UFW misleads the public about dangers pesticides pose to farm workers," the Table Grape Commission says. "Governor Deukmejian's pesticide safety system protects workers," the Farm Bureau proclaims.

Grapes is [sic] the largest fruit crop in California. It receives more restricted use pesticides than any fresh food crop.

About one-third of grape pesticides are known carcinogens—like the chemicals that may have afflicted Johnnie Rodriguez; others are teratogens—birth defect–producing pesticides—that doctors think deformed Felipe Franco.

More than half of all acute pesticide-related illnesses reported in California involve grape production.

In 1987 and '88, entire crews of grape workers—hundreds of people—were poisoned after entering vineyards containing toxic residues.

In all those episodes, the grapes had been sprayed weeks before. All the legal requirements were followed. The vineyards were thought to be "safe."

But farm workers were still poisoned.

Farm workers and their families are exposed to pesticides from the crops they work. The soil the crops are grown in. Drift from sprays applied to adjoining fields—and often to the very field where they are working.

The fields that surround their homes are heavily and repeatedly sprayed. Pesticides pollute irrigation water and groundwater.

Children are still a big part of the labor force. Or they are taken to the fields by their parents because there is no child care.

Pregnant women labor in the fields to help support their families. Toxic exposure begins at a very young age—often in the womb.

What does acute pesticide poisoning produce?

Eye and respiratory irritations. Skin rashes. Systemic poisoning.

Death.

What are the chronic effects of pesticide poisoning on people, including farm workers and their children, according to scientific studies?

Birth defects. Sterility. Still births. Miscarriages. Neurological and neuropsychological effects. Effects on child growth and development.

Cancer.

Use of pesticides are governed by strict laws, agribusiness says. Growers argue reported poisonings involved only one (1) percent of California farm workers in 1986.

True.

But experts estimate that only one (1) percent of California pesticide illness or injury is reported. The underreporting of pesticide poisoning is flagrant and it is epidemic.

A World Resources Institute study says 300,000 farm workers are poisoned each year by pesticides in the United States.

Even the state Department of Food and Agriculture reported total pesticide poisoning of farm workers rose by 41 percent in 1987.

Yet the Farm Workers aren't sincere when we raise the pesticide issue, grape growers complain.

They won't admit that the first ban on DDT, Aldrin, and Dieldrin in the United States was not by the Environmental Protection Agency in 1972, but in a United Farm Workers contract with a grape grower in 1967.

Forty-four (44) percent of the pesticides used on grapes that pose potential health hazards to humans can't be detected by tests used to check for toxic residues.

A recent report by the National Academy of Sciences concludes that pesticides in 15 commonly eaten foods, including grapes, pose the greatest pesticide-caused dietary cancer risk to people.

Many pesticides used on food—that have government tolerance levels—can cause cancer in human beings.

Almost all tolerance levels of pesticides in food were set by the federal government without adequate testing for potential harmful health effects on consumers.

Some safety studies on these pesticides were conducted by an Illinois laboratory that was closed after it was found to be reporting fraudulent data to the EPA. Two of its toxicologists are in jail.

The U.S. General Accounting Office estimates that it will take EPA until well into the 21st century to ensure all pesticides now on the market meet current health and safety standards.

The U.S. Food and Drug Administration takes an average of 18 days to test food for pesticide residues. Before test results are available, the food has been marketed and consumed.

Most pesticides were approved by the U.S. Department of Agriculture in the 1940s and '50s. Little or no testing for chronic health effects was required.

Not long ago the Delaney Amendment, passed by Congress, banned any food additive known to cause cancer in animals or humans. That ban applies to everything—except farm pesticides.

In 1978, EPA allowed new chemicals to be registered conditionally without complete testing for chronic health effects. Testing on half of all new pesticides registered between 1978 and 1984 did not meet current health and safety testing standards.

All this means that we do not know if pesticide residues on the food you buy in supermarkets cause cancer, birth defects, and other tragedies.

You can't fool Mother Nature. Insects can outfox anything we throw at them. In time, they will overcome.

People thought pesticides were the cure-all—the key to an abundance of food. They thought pesticides were the solution; but they were the problem.

The problem is this mammoth agribusiness system. The problem are [sic] the huge farms. The problem is the pressure on the land from developers. The problem is not allowing the land to lay fallow and recover. The problem is the abandonment of cultural practices that have stood the test of centuries: crop rotation, diversification of crops.

The problem is monoculture—growing acres and acres of the same crop; disrupting the natural order of things; letting insects feast on acres and acres of a harem of delight ... and using pesticides that kill off their natural predators.

Oscar Wilde once said, "A cynic is someone who knows the price of everything and the value of nothing."

We look at the price, but we don't look at the value. Economics and profit drive everything.

People forget that the soil is our sustenance. It is a sacred trust. It is what has worked for us for centuries.

It is what we pass on to future generations.

If we continue in this thoughtless submission to pesticides—if we ruin the top soil—then there will not be an abundance of food to bequeath our children.

I studied this wanton abuse of nature. I read the literature, heard from the experts about what pesticides do to our land and our food.

I talked with farm workers, listened to their families, and shared their anguish and their fears. I spoke out against the cycle of death.

But sometimes words come too cheaply. And their meaning is lost in the clutter that so often fills our lives.

That is why, in July and August of last year, I embarked on a 36-day unconditional, water-only fast.

The fast was first and foremost directed at myself. It was something I felt compelled to do to purify my own body, mind and soul.

The fast was an act of penance for our own members who, out of ignorance or need, cooperate with those who grow and sell food treated with toxics.

The fast was also for those who know what is right and just. It pains me that we continue to shop without protest at stores that offer grapes; that we eat in restaurants that display them; that we are too patient and understanding with those who serve them to us.

The fast, then, was for those who know that they could or should do more—for those who, by not acting, become bystanders in the poisoning of our food and the people who produce it.

The fast was, finally, a declaration of non-cooperation with supermarkets that promote, sell, and profit from California table grapes. They are as culpable as those who manufacture the poisons and those who use them.

It is my hope that our friends everywhere will resist in many nonviolent ways the presence of grapes in the stores where they shop.

The misery that pesticides bring farm workers—and the dangers they pose to all consumers—will not be ended with more hearings or studies. The solution is not to be had from those in power because it is they who have allowed this deadly crisis to grow.

The times we face truly call for all of us to do more to stop this evil in our midst.

The answer lies with you and me. It is with all men and women who share the suffering and yearn with us for a better world.

Thank you. And boycott grapes.

SIGNIFICANCE

In November 2000, the UFW ended its sixteen-year boycott of California table grapes. UFW president Arturo Rodriquez noted that many of the union's goals—some originated by Chávez himself—had been fulfilled. One of the union's major goals had been to eliminate pesticides harmful to farm workers, especially Phosdrin, dinoseb, methyl parathion, methyl bromide, and Captan.

Dinoseb, a highly toxic herbicide, fungicide, and insecticide, was banned in 1986 due to the risk of potential adverse health effects such as sterility and birth defects. The insecticide methyl parathion (or Parathion) was severely restricted for most food crops and banned for indoor use in 1978 after the EPA determined that it had caused over 600 poisonings and about 100 farm worker deaths since 1966. Phosdrin, a pesticide, was banned in 1994 after farm workers Ricardo Guzman, Martin Martinez, and Miguel Farias, along with twenty-three other workers in Washington state, were poisoned. Methyl bromide, an agricultural soil fumigant, was finally phased out on January 1, 2005, (except for certain permissible exemptions). In 1989, the fungicide Captan was severely restricted in the United States for use on many food crops because it was shown to produce tumors in rats and mice.

In 1994, the UFW began to focus more on union organizing and contract negotiations than on boycotts. By 2000, it had won eighteen union elections and gained twenty-four new contracts with growers. Rodriquez also hoped to increase membership, which had dropped to 20,000 in 1994 after a peak of 80,000 in 1970–1971. In 2000, UFW membership stood at 27,000.

The cause that César Chávez spearheaded in the 1960s has strengthened the rights and protections of farm workers across the United States. Many local, state, and federal laws, regulations, and bans have been implemented due to the UFW. One of the most important of these is the California Agricultural Labor Relation Act, passed in June 1975. The act guarantees farm workers the right to join unions, organize, and bargain with their employers. It also protects them from unjust labor practices. Even with such laws, however, problems still occur: UFW spokespersons maintain that farm workers are still exposed to pesticides used by agribusinesses.

Chávez originally hoped to establish a labor union for farm workers that would represent them in their fight for better working and living conditions. He used nonviolent means to convince powerful grape growers and influential political groups that farm workers had the right to organize, and went on hunger strikes to bring national attention to the plight of his constituents. The UFW continues to organize and bargain for grape, lettuce, mushroom, rose, strawberry, and other vegetable and fruit workers in California, Florida, and Washington.

FURTHER RESOURCES

Books

Bruns, Roger. *César Chávez: A Biography*. Westport, CT: Greenwood Press, 2005.

La Botz, Dan. *César Chávez and la Causa*. New York: Pearson Longman, 2006.

Web sites

César E. Chávez Foundation. "An American Hero." <http://Chávezfoundation.org/CésareChávez.html> (accessed May 9, 2006).

Public Broadcasting Service. "The Fight in the Fields: César Chávez and the Farmworkers' Struggle." <http://www.pbs.org/itvs/fightfields/> (accessed May 9, 2006).

United Farm Workers. "History." <http://www.ufw.org/> (accessed May 9, 2006).

Casey Jones—The Union Scab

Song lyrics

By: Joe Hill

Date: 1912

Source: Kornbluh, Joyce L., ed. *Rebel Voices: An IWW Anthology*. Ann Arbor: University of Michigan Press, 1968.

About the Author: Joe Hill was a Swedish-born labor organizer with the Industrial Workers of the World, or IWW, and an influential writer of protest songs that rallied working people throughout the United States and beyond.

INTRODUCTION

At the turn of the twentieth century, clashes between workers and business owners reached epic proportions. As industries accumulated wealth and power during the latter decades of the 1800s, millions of American workers struggled in poverty, working long hours in unsafe conditions for low pay. Rapid growth of the labor force, fed in part by the massive influx of immigrants to the United States, resulted in increased union membership. The two sides of the labor movement—restive workers demanding better wages and wealthy owners protecting their profits—reached an impasse many times, and the period was marked by a number of major strikes, many of which ended in violent repression by owners and law enforcers.

The success of any strike relies upon widespread participation among workers; strikes that are unable to significantly inhibit a company's operation fail to command the attention of management. The inspiration for Joe Hill's song "Casey Jones—The Union Scab" was a strike by thousands of shop workers at the Harriman and Illinois Central Railroad System, which included the Southern Pacific—the "S.P. line" referred to in the song. While shop workers had walked off the job, the engineers and others continued to work, enabling the trains to run and undermining the shop workers' ability to negotiate with management.

Hill's song parodies legendary railroad engineer Casey Jones, depicting Jones as a scab, a traitor to the union cause. Born in 1864, John Luther "Casey" Jones became a renowned railway engineer working on the Illinois Central line. In April 1900, Jones was killed when his passenger train collided with a freight train in the town of Vaughan, Mississippi. According to the oft-retold story, Jones told his fireman, Sim Webb, to save his own life and jump from the train, while Jones himself stayed in the cab and died with the brake cord still in his hands. His determination to stay on the train and slow it down reportedly saved many lives among the train's passengers. Jones became a legend after his death, a romantic symbol of the early American railroading tradition. A railroad worker named Wallace Saunders memorialized the beloved engineer in the song "Casey Jones," which became a folk-music classic. By depicting him as a "union scab" rather than a railway hero in "Casey Jones—The Union Scab," Joe Hill turned the Casey Jones legend on its head, converting a heroic figure into an enemy of the working man.

■ PRIMARY SOURCE

(Tune: "Casey Jones")
The Workers on the S.P. line to strike sent out a call;
But Casey Jones, the engineer, he wouldn't strike at all;
His boiler it was leaking, and its drivers on the bum,
And his engine and its bearings, they were all out of plumb.

Chorus:

Casey Jones kept his junk pile running;
Casey Jones was working double time;

The Department Store Workers Union called a strike at the West 14th Street, New York City, Woolworth's in March 1937. Half the store's employees stayed on the job, including these salespeople. © BETTMANN/CORBIS.

Casey Jones got a wooden medal,
For being good and faithful on the S.P. Line.

The Workers said to Casey: "Won't you help us win this strike?"
But Casey said: "Let me alone, you'd better take a hike."
Then some one put a bunch of railroad ties across the track,
And Casey hit the bottom with an awful crack.

Chorus:

Casey Jones hit the river bottom;
Casey Jones broke his blessed spine,
Casey Jones was an Angeleno,
He took a trip to heaven on the S.P. line.

When Casey Jones got up to heaven to the Pearly Gate,
He said, "I'm Casey Jones, the guy that pulled the S.P. freight."
"You're just the man," said Peter; "our musicians went on strike;

"You can get a job a-scabbing any time you like."

Chorus:

Casey Jones got up to heaven;
Casey Jones was doing mighty fine;
Casey Jones went scabbing on the angels,
Just like he did to workers on the S.P. line.

The angels got together, and they said it wasn't fair,
For Casey Jones to go around a-scabbing everywhere.
The Angels Union No. 23, they sure were there,
And they promptly fired Casey down the Golden Stair.

Chorus:

Casey Jones went to Hell a-flying.
"Casey Jones," the Devil said, "Oh, fine;
Casey Jones, get busy shoveling sulpher-
That's what you get for scabbing on the S.P. line."

SIGNIFICANCE

Joe Hill, a rank-and-file member of the Industrial Workers of the World, may not have been known personally by many workers, but his songs were adopted as anthems by laborers throughout the United States. Songs such as "Casey Jones—The Union Scab," "The Preacher and the Slave," and "The Rebel Girl" made Hill famous among laborers hailing from all over the world and working in a variety of industries. Many of Hill's songs were published in the IWW's *Little Red Song Book*, a collection of songs designed to unite and inspire the Wobblies, as IWW members were known.

Decrying the exploitation of working people and emphasizing the importance of laborers uniting for social and economic justice, Hill became an influential protest songwriter and an effective communicator of the IWW's agenda. Begun in 1905 by labor pioneers William "Big Bill" Haywood (1869–1928), Mary "Mother" Jones (1830–1930), and Eugene Debs (1855–1926), the IWW embraced all members of the working class from all types of industries. This philosophy, represented by the slogan "one big union for all," set the IWW apart from other major unions of the period, many of which were intended only for skilled workers, or only for workers in a particular industry. The IWW promoted a socialist agenda, asserting that tensions between workers and employers would persist until society was restructured and workers took over the means of production. In part because of the radical politics the union espoused, the IWW developed a reputation as a violence-prone organization that encouraged workers to commit acts of sabotage.

In January 1914, during an attempted robbery of a grocery store in Salt Lake City, Utah, a grocer named John Morrison and his son were shot to death. The two masked assailants, one of whom had been shot by the grocer's son, fled the scene. The same day, Joe Hill, living in Salt Lake City at the time, sought medical attention for a gunshot wound that he claimed was the result of an argument about a woman. The doctor reported Hill's injury to the police, and Hill was arrested on suspicion of involvement in the deaths of the Morrisons. In the months leading up to his trial, Hill's case became an important cause for the IWW. The union protested that Hill was being prosecuted not because he was truly suspected of killing the Morrisons but because of his past actions as a Wobbly agitator and organizer. Local newspapers repeatedly emphasized Hill's association with the IWW and portrayed the union in dark and dangerous terms. With minimal evidence and questionable tactics, the prosecution obtained a guilty verdict, and in July 1914 Joe Hill was sentenced to death.

Upon Hill's conviction, a widespread protest arose. Hill's impending death brought him far more fame than he had achieved previously, and he became an idealized symbol of the honorable, brave, and determined working man. Supporters from all over the United States and other nations as well sent letters to the governor of Utah seeking a pardon for Hill. The Swedish ambassador to the United States intervened on his behalf, sending telegrams to President Woodrow Wilson (1856–1924). Wilson wrote to the Utah governor asking that the execution be delayed and a full investigation conducted. The efforts on Hill's behalf failed, however, and on November 19, 1915, Hill was executed by a firing squad. The night before his execution, Hill sent a telegram to IWW leader Bill Haywood, concluding with a phrase that became part of his legend: "Don't waste any time in mourning. Organize."

Hill's death transformed him into a martyr for the union cause, and he became a symbol of the sacrifice necessary to achieve a new social order. Many years later, his death inspired Alfred Hayes and Earl Robinson to write a song, "Joe Hill," proclaiming Hill as a man who "never died." Like the famed railroad engineer Casey Jones, Hill became a mythic character and a working-man's icon, memorialized in literature and song, in the wake of his death.

FURTHER RESOURCES

Books

Dubofsky, Melvyn. *We Shall Be All*. Chicago: Quadrangle Books, 1969.

Fowke, Edith and Joe Glazer. *Songs of Work and Protest*. New York: Dover Publications, 1973.

Le Blanc, Paul. *A Short History of the U.S. Working Class*. New York: Humanity Books, 1999.

Murolo, Priscilla and A. B. Chitty. *From the Folks Who Brought You the Weekend: A Short, Illustrated History of Labor in the United States*. New York: New Press, 2001.

Reef, Catherine. *Working in America*. New York: Facts on File, 2000.

Web sites

KUED. University of Utah. "'I Never Died...': The Words, Music, and Influence of Joe Hill." <http://www.kued.org/joehill/voices/article.html> (accessed May 30, 2006).

Grand Jury Indictment of the Chicago Seven

Indictment

By: United States District Court

Date: September 1968

Source: Indictment. *United States.v. David T. Dellinger, Rennard C. Davis, Thomas E. Hayden, Abbott H. Hoffman, Jerry C. Rubin, Lee Weiner, John R. Froines, and Bobby G. Seale.* United States District Court, Northern District of Illinois, Eastern Division, 1968.

About the Author: United States District Courts are part of the federal judicial system. They oversee both civil and criminal trials, as determined by Congress and the Constitution. The system is divided into ninety-four districts, with a minimum of one district per state and one each for the District of Columbia and Puerto Rico. Illinois has both a Northern and Southern district, each of which is further subdivided.

INTRODUCTION

In August 1968 the Democratic National Convention was held in Chicago, Illinois, amid a series of protests against the Vietnam War. The protests began in an organized, almost entertaining manner, but escalated as the convention progressed, causing police to become concerned about the number of people involved. When an 11:00 P.M. curfew was announced, some members of the crowd began to throw rocks. The protest then morphed into a riot, with police using tear gas and batons to drive protestors back. While numerous participants were arrested, the "Chicago Eight" were indicted for conspiracy to riot. During the trial the following year, Black Panther Party activist Bobby Seale was separated from the group and tried alone due to his uncontrollable behavior in court, turning the Chicago Eight into the Chicago Seven.

◼ PRIMARY SOURCE

UNITED STATES DISTRICT COURT NORTHERN DISTRICT OF ILLINOIS EASTERN DIVISION

UNITED STATES OF AMERICA

–vs–

DAVID T. DELLINGER, RENNARD C. DAVIS, THOMAS E. HAYDEN, ABBOTT H. HOFFMAN, JERRY C. RUBIN, LEE WEINER, JOHN R. FROINES, and BOBBY G. SEALE

No. 69CRI80 Violation: Title 18, United States Code, Section 371, 231 (a) (1) and 2 101

INDICTMENT

The SEPTEMBER 1968 GRAND JURY charges:

1. Beginning on or about April 12, 1968, and continuing through on or about August 30, 1968, in the Northern District of Illinois, Eastern Division, and elsewhere,

DAVID T. DELLINGER,
RENNARD C. DAVIS,
THOMAS E. HAYDEN,
ABBOTT H. HOFFMAN,
JERRY C. RUBIN,
LEE WEINER,
JOHN R. FROINES and
BOBBY SEALE,

defendants herein, unlawfully, wilfully and knowingly did combine, conspire, confederate and agree together and with

WOLFE B. LOWENTHAL
STEWART E. ALBERT,
SIDNEY M. PECK,
KATHIE BOUDIN,
SARA C. BROWN,
CORINA F. FALES,
BENJAMIN RADFORD,
BRADFORD FOX,
THOMAS W. NEUMANN,
CRAIG SHIMABUKURO,
BO TAYLOR,
DAVID A. BAKER,
RICHARD BOSCIANO,
TERRY GROSS,
DONNA GRIPE,
BENJAMIN ORITZ,
JOSEPH TORNABENE
and
RICHARD PALMER

being co-conspirators not named as defendants herein, and with diverse other persons, some known and others unknown to the Grand Jury, to commit offenses against the United States, that is:

a. to travel in interstate commerce and use the facilities of interstate commerce with the intent to incite, organize, promote, encourage, participate in, and carry on a riot and to commit acts of violence in furtherance of a riot, and to aid and abet persons in inciting, participating in, and carrying on a riot and committing acts of violence in furtherance of a riot, and during the course of such travel, and use, and thereafter, to perform overt acts for the purpose of inciting, organizing, promoting, encouraging, participating in, and carrying on a riot, and committing acts of violence in furtherance of a riot, and aiding and abetting persons in inciting, participating in, and carrying out a riot, and committing acts of violence in furtherance of a riot, in violation of Section 2101 of Title 18, United States Code; and

b. to teach and demonstrate to other persons the use, application, and making of incendiary devices, knowing, having reason to know, and intending that said incendiary devices would be unlawfully employed for use in and in furtherance of civil disorders which may obstruct, delay and adversely affect commerce and the movement of articles and commodities in commerce and the conduct and performance of federally protected functions, in violation of Section 231 (a) (l) of Title 18, United States Code; and,

c. to commit acts to obstruct, impede, and interfere with firemen and law enforcement officers lawfully engaged in the lawful performance of their official duties incident to and during the commission of civil disorders which obstruct, delay, and adversely affect commerce and the movement of articles and commodities in commerce and the conduct and performance of federally projected functions in violation of Section 231 (a) (3) of Title 18, United States Code.

2. It was a part of said conspiracy that from on or about April 12, 1968, through on or about August 24, 1968, the defendants DAVID T. DELLINGER, RENNARD C. DAVIS, THOMAS E. HAYDEN, ABBOTT H. HOFFMAN and JERRY C. RUBIN, and other co-conspirators not named as defendants herein, would organize and attend various meetings, would publish and cause to be published articles, and would make and cause to be made long distance telephone calls for the purpose of encouraging persons to come to Chicago, Illinois, to participate in massive demonstrations during the period of on or about August 25, 1968, through on or about August 29, 1968.

3. It was a further part of said conspiracy that the defendants DAVID T. DELLINGER, RENNARD C. DAVIS and THOMAS E. HAYDEN, and other co-conspirators not named as defendants herein, would maintain and cause to be maintained an office of the National Mobilization Committee to End the War in Vietnam at 407 South Dearborn Street, Chicago, Illinois, and other "movement centers," to be used for the planning and organizing of activities to take place in Chicago during the period of on or about August 25, 1968, through on or about August 29, 1968.

4. It was a further part of said conspiracy that from on or about August 13, 1968, through on or about August 24, 1968, the defendants DAVID T. DELLINGER, RENNARD C. DAVIS, THOMAS E. HAYDEN, ABBOTT H. HOFFMAN, JERRY C. RUBIN, LEE WEINER and JOHN R. FROINES and other co-conspirators not named as defendants herein, would select and cause to be selected persons

designated as "marshals" and would conduct and cause to be conducted training sessions for such "marshals" at which instructions would be given in techniques of resisting and obstructing police action, including karate, Japanese snake dancing, methods of freeing persons being arrested, and counter kicks to knee and groin.

5. It was further part of said conspiracy that from on or about August 1, 1968, through on or about August 29, 1968, the defendants DAVID T. DELLINGER, RENNARD C. DAVIS, THOMAS E. HAYDEN, ABBOTT H. HOFFMAN, JERRY C. RUBIN, LEE WEINER, JOHN R. FROINES and BOBBY G. SEALE, and other coconspirators not named as defendants herein, would plan, carry into effect, and cause to be carried into effect actions and tactics to be employed by groups of persons in Chicago, Illinois, during the period of on or about August 25, 1 968, through on or about August 29, 1968, which actions and tactics would include but would not be limited to the following:

a. large numbers of persons would march to the International Amphitheatre, Chicago, Illinois, even if permits authorizing such marches were denied;

b. large numbers of persons would remain in Lincoln Park, Chicago, Illinois, after 11:00 p.m., even if permits authorizing such persons to remain were denied, and would set up defenses and would attempt to hold the Park against police efforts to clear it, were permits denied;

c. large numbers of persons would break windows, set off false fire alarms, set small fires, disable automobiles, create disturbances at various hotels in the Chicago Loop area, and throughout the city of Chicago, for the purpose of disrupting the city and causing the deployment of military forces;

d. on or about August 28, 1968, large numbers of persons would block, obstruct and impede pedestrian and vehicular traffic in the Chicago Loop area, and would occupy and forcibly hold all or part of the Conrad Hilton Hotel in Chicago.

6. It was a further part of said conspiracy that from on or about August 25, 1968, through on or about August 29, 1968, the defendants DAVID T. DELLINGER, RENNARD C. DAVIS, THOMAS E. HAYDEN, ABBOTT H. HOFFMAN, JERRY C. RUBIN, LEE WEINER, JOHN R. FROINES and BOBBY G. SEALE, and other coconspirators not named as defendants herein, would make statements and speeches to assemblages of persons encouraging them to remain in and hold Lincoln Park against police efforts to clear it after permits to remain therein had been denied; to march to the International Amphitheatre after permits authorizing such march had been denied; to make weapons to be used against the police; to shout obscenities at, throw objects, threaten and physically assault policemen and National

Guard troops; and to obstruct traffic and damage and seize property in the city of Chicago.

7. It was a further part of said conspiracy that on or about August 27, 1968, BOBBY G. SEALE would travel to Chicago, Illinois, where he would speak to assemblages of persons for the purpose of inciting, organizing, promoting and encouraging a riot.

8. It was a further part of said conspiracy that JOHN R. FROINES and LEE WEINER would teach and demonstrate to other persons the use, application and making of an incendiary device, intending that said incendiary device would be employed to damage the underground garage at Grant Park, Chicago, Illinois, on the evening of August 29, 1968.

9. It was a further part of said conspiracy that the defendants and co-conspirators would misrepresent, conceal, and hide and cause to be misrepresented, concealed and hidden, the purpose of and the acts done in furtherance of said conspiracy.

Overt Acts

At the times hereinafter mentioned the defendants committed, among others, the following overt acts in furtherance of the conspiracy and to effect the objects thereof:

1. The Grand Jury realleges and incorporates by reference the allegations contained in Counts 11 through VIII of this indictment, each of which count is alleged as a separate and distinct overt act.

2. On or about July 23, 1968, JERRY C. RUBIN spoke to an assemblage of persons at 48th Street and Park Avenue, New York, New York.

3. On or about July 25, 1968, THOMAS E. HAYDEN spoke to an assemblage of persons at the Diplomat Hotel, New York, New York.

4. On or about August 1, 1968, RENNARD C. DAVIS spoke to an assemblage of persons at 30 West Chicago Avenue, Chicago, Illinois.

5. On or about August 15, 1968, RENNARD C. DAVIS, THOMAS E. HAYDEN and JOHN R. FROINES participated in a meeting at Lincoln Park, Chicago, Illinois.

6. On or about August 18, 1968, RENNARD C. DAVIS, LEE WEINER and JOHN R. FROINES participated in a meeting at 1012 North Noble Street, Chicago, Illinois.

7. On or about August 20, 1968, RENNARD C. DAVIS, ABBOT H. HOFFMAN, LEE WEINER and JOHN R. FROINES participated in a meeting at the National Mobilization Committee office at 407 South Dearborn Street, Chicago, Illinois.

8. On or about August 24, 1968, DAVID T. DELLINGER, RENNARD C. DAVIS, THOMAS E. HAYDEN, ABBOTT H. HOFFMAN, LEE WEINER and JOHN R. FROINES attended a "marshal" training session at Lincoln Park, Chicago, Illinois.

9. On or about August 25, 1968, DAVID T. DELLINGER, RENNARD C. DAVIS, THOMAS E. HAYDEN and ABBOTT H. HOFFMAN met at the National Mobilization Committee office at 407 South Dearborn Street, Chicago, Illinois.

10. On or about August 26, 1968, RENNARD C. DAVIS, JERRY C. RUBIN, LEE WEINER, and JOHN R. FROINES met at Lincoln Park, Chicago, Illinois.

11. On or about August 27, 1968, JERRY C. RUBIN, BOBBY G. SEALE and others spoke to an assemblage of persons at Lincoln Park, Chicago, Illinois.

12. On or about August 28, 1968, DAVID T. DELLINGER, THOMAS E. HAYDEN, JERRY C. RUBIN and others spoke to an assemblage of persons at Grant Park, Chicago, Illinois.

13. On or about August 29, 1968, LEE WEINER and JOHN R. FROINES engaged in a conversation at Grant Park, Chicago, Illinois.

All in violation of Section 371 of Title 18, United States Code.

Count II

The SEPTEMBER 1968 GRAND JURY further charges: That during the period beginning on or about July 20, 1968, through on or about August 22, 1968,

DAVID T. DELLINGER,

defendant herein, did travel in interstate commerce from outside the State of Illinois to Chicago, Illinois, Northern District of Illinois, Eastern Division, with intent to incite, organize, promote and encourage a riot and, thereafter, on or about August 28, 1968, at Grant Park, Chicago, Illinois, he did speak to an assemblage of persons for the purpose of inciting, organizing, promoting and encouraging a riot, in violation of Title 18, United States Code, Section 2101.

Count III

The SEPTEMBER 1968 GRAND JURY further charges: That during the period beginning on or about July 20, 1968, through on or about August 1, 1968,

RENNARD C. DAVIS,

defendant herein, did travel in interstate commerce from outside the State of Illinois to Chicago, Illinois, Northern District of Illinois, Eastern Division, with intent to incite, organize, promote and encourage a riot, and thereafter, on or about August 1, 1968, at 30 West Chicago Avenue, Chicago, Illinois, and on or about August 9, 1968, at 407 South Dearborn Street, Chicago, Illinois, and on or about August 18, 1968, at 1012 North Noble Street, Chicago, Illinois, and on or about August 26, 1968, at Grant Park, Chicago, Illinois, he did speak to assemblages of persons for the purpose of inciting, organizing, promoting and encouraging a riot; in violation of Title 18, United States Code, Section 2 101.

Count IV

The SEPTEMBER 1968 GRAND JURY further charges: That during the period beginning on or about July 20, 1968, through on or about August 22, 1968,

THOMAS E. HAYDEN,

defendant herein, did travel in interstate commerce from outside the State of Illinois to Chicago, Illinois, Northern District of Illinois. Eastern Division, with intent to incite, organize, promote and encourage a riot and, thereafter, on or about August 26, 1968, at Grant Park, Chicago, Illinois, he did speak to assemblages of persons for the purposes of inciting, organizing, promoting and encouraging a riot; in violation of Title 18, United States Code, Section 2101.

Count V

The SEPTEMBER 1968 GRAND JURY further charges: That during the period beginning on or about August 1, 1968, through on or about August 7, 1968,

ABBOTT H. HOFFMAN,

defendant herein, did travel in interstate commerce from outside the State of Illinois to Chicago, Illinois, Northern District of Illinois, Eastern Division, with intent to incite, organize, promote and encourage a riot and, thereafter, on or about August 26, 1968, at Lincoln Park, Chicago, Illinois, and on or about August 27, 1968, at Lincoln Park, Chicago, Illinois, and on or about August 29, 1968, at Grant Park, Chicago, Illinois, he did speak to assemblages of persons for the purpose of inciting, organizing, promoting, and encouraging a riot; in violation of Title 18, United States Code, Section 2101.

Count VI

The SEPTEMBER 1968 GRAND JURY further charges: That during the period beginning on or about July 23, 1968, through on or about August 21, 1968,

JERRY C. RUBIN,

defendant herein, did travel in interstate commerce from outside the State of Illinois to Chicago, Illinois, Northern District of Illinois, Eastern Division, with intent to incite, organize, promote and encourage a riot and, thereafter, on or about August 25, 1968, at Lincoln Park, Chicago, Illinois, and on or about August 26, 1968, at Lincoln Park, Chicago, Illinois, he did speak to assemblages of persons for the purposes of inciting, organizing, promoting and encouraging a riot; in violation of Title 18, United States Code, Section 2101.

Count VII

The SEPTEMBER 1968 GRAND JURY further charges: That on or about August 29, 1968, at Chicago, Illinois, in the Northern District of Illinois, Eastern Division,

JOHN R. FROINES and LEE WEINER,

defendants herein, did teach and demonstrate to other persons the use, application and making of an incendiary device knowing, having reason to know and intending that said incendiary device would be unlawfully employed for use in and in furtherance of a civil disorder which may obstruct, delay and adversely affect commerce and the movement of articles and commodities in commerce; in violation of Title 18, United States Code, Section 231 (a) (1).

Count VIII

The SEPTEMBER 1968 GRAND JURY further charges: That on or about August 27, 1968,

BOBBY G. SEALE,

defendant herein, did travel in interstate commerce from outside the State of Illinois to Chicago, Illinois, Northern District of Illinois, Eastern Division, with intent to incite, organize, promote and encourage a riot and, thereafter, on or about August 27, 1968, at Lincoln Park, Chicago, Illinois, and on or about August 28, 1968, at Grant Park, Chicago, Illinois, he did speak to assemblages of persons for the purposes of inciting, organizing, promoting and encouraging a riot; in violation of Title 18, United States Code, Section 2101.

SIGNIFICANCE

Before the 1968 Democratic convention, several radical groups met to discuss how the event could be used as an opportunity to demonstrate their opposition to the Vietnam War and other government policies. The National Mobilization to End the Vietnam War (MOBE) had a political agenda, while Yippies, members of the Youth International Party (YIP), were mostly counterculture media hounds concerned with attention-getting publicity stunts. In addition, the Black Panther Party and the Southern Christian Leadership Conference wanted to protest the racist nature of many American policies. Several potential protest strategies were discussed among the groups, including a boycott, uniting behind an antiwar candidate such as Eugene McCarthy, staging an event that would completely disrupt the conference itself, or a series of peaceful protests and teach-ins involving as many antiwar protestors as they could convince to join them.

Ultimately, they settled on a nonviolent protest. The Yippies also planned a festival to coincide with the protests, promoting music, theater, dance, and poetry. They billed the event as an alternative to the staid convention and support of Lyndon Johnson, and a way to advocate the freeing of America.

However, Mayor Richard Daley and other Chicago officials were concerned that the demonstrations

Harvard professor and LSD guru Timothy Leary sits with Yippie leader Abbie Hoffman and Jerry Rubin at a news conference announcing plans to disrupt the 1968 Democratic convention, August 1968. AP IMAGES.

would reflect badly on the city during the convention, which they considered a prime opportunity to promote Chicago as a business and tourist destination. When demonstrators applied for permits to sleep in the parks, for example, their requests were denied; other permit requests were turned down, too, in an attempt to control crowd numbers. The 11:00 P.M. curfew was posted, and the city arranged for extra police, army, and national guardsmen to serve during the convention as a precautionary measure. Although protest leaders sued to have the curfew overturned and to gain access to the parks, the federal district court denied their request.

Ultimately, the protestors chose to ignore the city's mandates: they set up camps in the parks and refused to leave at curfew. The police charged the parks at 11:00 to force the protestors to vacate, while the protestors were determined to hold fast, encouraged by leaders such as Abbie Hoffman and Rennie Davis, the latter of whom communicated via a bullhorn.

After their arrests, the Chicago Eight (later Seven), continued to protest on any stage available. During their trials, they refused to stand at the judge's entrance, blew kisses to the jury, and on occasion wore judicial robes and hurled insults at members of the court. The judge found both the defendants and their attorneys in contempt, ultimately issuing more that 150 citations. (These were later overturned by a court of appeals because contempt sentences of that length required jury trials.)

Before 1968, such protests would have been dealt with by local police, but the Civil Rights Act had made it illegal to cross state lines with the intention of inciting a riot, and so many of the organizers arrested during the protest were held and later indicted on this charge. Ultimately, five members of the Chicago Seven were convicted of intent to incite a riot across state lines, but were acquitted on all conspiracy charges. The five convictions were overturned on appeal.

FURTHER RESOURCES
Books
Farber, David. *Chicago '68*. Chicago: University of Chicago Press, 1988.

Wiener, Jon, ed. *Conspiracy in the Streets: The Extraordinary Trial of the Chicago Eight*. New York: New Press, 2006.

Schultz, John. *Chicago Conspiracy Trial*. New York: Da Capo, 1993.

Web sites
University of Missouri-Kansas City Law School. "Famous American Trials: 'The Chicago Seven' Trial—1969–1970" <http://www.law.umkc.edu/faculty/projects/ftrials/Chicago7/Account.html> (accessed May 25, 2006).

President of the E.U. Commission Jaques Santer shakes hands with Microsoft chairman Bill Gates in Belgium on February 4, 1998. AP IMAGES.

PRIMARY SOURCE

Bill Gates Hit with Pie: Bill Gates, chairman of Microsoft, shortly after being hit in the face with a cream pie. Gates was arriving at a meeting with business and government leaders in Brussels, Belgium, when he was surprised by pranksters. AP IMAGES.

Bill Gates Hit with Pie

Photograph

By: The Associated Press

Date: February 4, 1998

Source: AP Images.

About the Photographer: The Associated Press is a worldwide news agency based in New York that works with thousands of journalists, photographers, and videographers around the world.

INTRODUCTION

Bill Gates is the world's wealthiest man and the founder and director of Microsoft, one of the world's largest companies. With Microsoft operating systems used in a majority of computers around the world, Gates has amassed a fortune of over $40 billion. He donates hundreds of millions of dollars each year to thousands of charities, which helped him (along with his wife Melinda and pop star Bono) earn *Time* magazine's People of the Year award in 2005. Gate's wealth has made him a highly publicized figure and the target of anti-globalization and anti-capitalist attacks.

Microsoft's influence is felt all over the globe, but this dominance has made it vulnerable to lawsuits charging that the company has attempted to monopolize the world of personal computing. In addition, many of the company's harshest critics are dedicated computer users and programmers who accuse Microsoft of placing profits over quality and releasing products before errors are fully corrected.

One of the factors that drive protests against Bill Gates and Microsoft is the fear of globalization, which opponents claim allows large international companies to drive smaller competitors out of business. Protestors believe that globalization has the potential to destroy local economies and concentrate profits in the hands of a few international corporations.

PRIMARY SOURCE

BILL GATES HIT WITH PIE
See primary source image.

SIGNIFICANCE

Neil Godin, arrested in the pie incident, is a self-described "comical terrorist" and anarchist who has been involved with similar attacks for more than thirty years. While making an effort to avoid actually injuring his targets, Gordon seeks out high-profile personalities at public occasions to humiliate them, preferably generating headlines and images that ricochet around the world, gaining publicity for his anarchist cause.

Godin selected Gates because he held that Gates was a person of power and that exposing him would help spread the message of the anarchists, who oppose most forms of power or rule. Although Gates is a businessman and not an elected political figure, many view him as an influential world leader because of his company's economic power. Critics of globalization feel that international corporations dictate policies in the same manner as sovereign governments.

FURTHER RESOURCES
Books
Boyd, Aaron. *Smart Money; The Story of Bill Gates*. Greensboro, NC: Morgan Reynolds, Inc., 2004.

Web sites
Microsoft. "Bill Gates." <http://www.microsoft.com/billgates/default.asp> (accessed May 25, 2006).

Institute for Anarchist Studies. <http://www.anarchist-studies.org> (accessed May 25, 2006).

Anti-WTO Protests Escalate

Newspaper article

By: Anonymous

Date: December 3, 1999

Source: "WTO Protests Escalate." *Seattle Post-Intelligencer* (December 3, 1999).

About the Author: This article was contributed by a staff writer for the *Seattle Post-Intelligencer*, a newspaper based in Seattle, Washington.

INTRODUCTION

The World Trade Organization (WTO) is an organization of over 140 states that have signed a series of agreements about the details of global trade. The WTO was formed in 1995 and meets annually to set global trade policy.

Since its beginning, the WTO has been a political target of anti-globalization activists who view the organization as manipulating international trade in order to steal from the poor and give to the rich on a global scale. Such activists see the WTO as systematically undermining environmental, consumer, labor, and other protections in order to protect the profits of multinational corporations. Defenders of the WTO and the neoliberal economic policies it promotes argue that unrestricted international corporate activity—often referred to as free trade—actually produces greater prosperity, on average, for poorer as well as for wealthier countries.

The WTO's annual meeting occurs in a different city each year. In 1999, the city was Seattle, Washington. Organized labor, environmentalist, and anti-globalization activists planned protests against the organization's meeting on a large scale. Groups organizing included the AFL-CIO (American Federation of Labor and Congress of Industrial Organizations), Public Citizen, Friends of the Earth, church groups, the Sierra Club, Peoples' Global Action, the War Resisters League, and more. Before the event, these preparations caused some apprehension—a Republican member of the King County Council who was consulting with protestors in hopes of organizing a peaceful outcome said that the upcoming event was a "security nightmare."

The outcome was not peaceful. There were 587 arrests and some property damage, including smashed storefronts and looting. The struggle was widely reported as "the battle in Seattle" in national and world media. All mainstream media sources agree that only a small minority of the protestors were violent. The WTO meeting itself failed to produce an agreement.

PRIMARY SOURCE

Anti-WTO protesters took to the streets in downtown Seattle again Friday night, with one contingent calling on city officials to release fellow demonstrators from jail and another calling on WTO delegates to go home.

What began Monday as a fight against the WTO ended yesterday with a candlelight vigil and a battle for civil rights.

"I think it started out about workers' rights and human rights around the world," said Ryan Hinkel, a plumber who took part in a labor march yesterday. "And then it developed more into being about the right to protest as the week went on."

As night fell, hundreds of people gathered peacefully at the King County Jail, the Westin Hotel and Denny Park. Amid the smell of burning incense at the jail, people broke into small groups to discuss what to do next.

Earlier in the day, protesters twice staged brief demonstrations inside the Washington State Convention and Trade Center, where the conference is being held. Around noon, eight people unfurled a banner in the center's press room that read: "Defend Forests. Clearcut the WTO."

"President Clinton is a clear and present danger to the world's forests!" shouted Randy Hayes of the Rainforest Action Network.

Seattle Police hauled off the protesters, and reporters questioned the WTO for limiting the activists' right to free speech.

But WTO spokesman Keith Rockwell said people who shout and unfurl banners are not welcome.

The WTO conference ended Friday night after talks to set a trade agenda collapsed.

Community and city leaders, meanwhile, announced some incentives to get residents to return to downtown, which earlier this week was the scene of frequent large demonstrations, occasional violent outbursts, vandalism and looting by a small group of activists.

But first Seattle had to get through its fourth night of street-clogging demonstrations.

Just like they did Thursday night, a large crowd assembled at the King County Jail, with protesters calling for release of several hundred jailed demonstrators inside. City officials agreed the night before to let the group's lawyers in to talk to the jailed protesters if the crowd would disperse, which it did.

Another group of protesters reportedly chained themselves to doors at the Westin hotel and called on delegates, many of whom are staying at the hotel, to go home.

The Westin is not far from the convention center where WTO delgates are meeting and were two minor protests occurred earlier today.

Just before noon, seven environmental activists unfurled a large banner that said: "Defend Forests. Clearcut the WTO," referring to a U.S. initiative to slash border taxes on timber and paper products.

Environmentalists oppose the move because it would boost the rate of deforestation overseas and could eventually hobble domestic forest-protection laws.

"President Clinton is a clear and present danger to the world's forests," shouted Randy Hayes of the Rainforest Action Network. "We have got to stop this madness."

Another sign held by a protester with duct tape on her mouth said, "WTO is a global no-protest zone."

After about three minutes, reporters began to lose interest and return to their desks, then Seattle police rushed in and escorted the protesters out of the building at the request of WTO officials.

The protesters gained access to the press room using media credentials, which activists can obtain if they are writing for specialized publications, such as environmental newsletters.

Police said the seven were admonished and barred from the building, but they were not arrested on what is expected to be the final day of the WTO conference.

After the brief protest, reporters asked why the WTO was limiting the activists' right to free speech, considering many officials have held press briefings this week.

WTO spokesman Keith Rockwell said the difference was that in those briefings, officials did not unfurl banners and did not shout.

"Everyone is welcome to come in," he said. "Everyone is allowed to distribute information, but disturbing the work of people who are reporters and who are trying to get their jobs done will not be permitted."

A second wave of demonstrations hit the convention center several hours later.

Protesters shouting "sea turtles are not trade barriers" unfurled a banner on the sixth floor so delegates hanging out in the fourth-floor smoking area could see it high in the atrium.

It showed a sea turtle snared in a fishing net and gave the Web address of the Sea Turtle Restoration Project, a San Francisco Bay-area group.

"Clinton say No to the WTO," the banner read. It hung for about 45 seconds before the activist holding it was grabbed by police. Like the earlier protesters, this activist was admonished and barred from the building.

The protests inside the convention center marked the only exceptions to a week that saw delegates, reporters and assorted hangers-on going easily about their business inside the convention center, insulated from assorted outbursts of anarchy on the streets.

Those inside the convention center wanted for little, having at their disposal Kinko's, Starbucks, Subway and several other fast-food outlets, a full-service restaurant and bar, a post office and several retail shops. The gym was closed.

Access to the convention center has been limited to people with proper credentials. The convention center also is in a "police perimeter" zone or "no-protest" zone that further restricts access.

Across town at about the same time as the press room demonstration, hundreds of demonstrators gathered for a rally and march through downtown on behalf of fair trade, free speech, worker rights and the environment. It was that rally that eventually wound up back at the county jail and at the Westin.

Many people in this afternoon's march said they saw the week shift from an indictment of the WTO and its powers, procedures and policies to concern over excessive police force and trampled constitutional rights.

"I think it started out about workers' rights and human rights around the world," said Ryan Hinkel, a plumber. "And then it developed more into being about the right to protest as the week went on."

Wearing a hard hat, harness and tool belt, Vulka Staab of Seattle extended his lunch break from his job as a carpenter erecting a 25-story building downtown to join the union procession.

He too was disappointed in police handling of demonstrations this week.

"I don't think a few vandalized doors is enough to declare a state of emergency," he said. "I always thought our Seattle cops were better than that. I definitely think less of them now."

Others praised police efforts to keep order.

Still others regretted that the WTO had chosen Seattle for its conference.

"It was a mistake to have invited them here," said Bill Bankhead of Seattle. "I wondered why they were invited here when they caused so much trouble in Geneva."

Earlier this week, police frequently used tear gas, pepper spray, rubber bullets and other measures to control what they said were defiant or law-breaking WTO protesters.

Tensions were particularly high Tuesday, when violence broke out and a small group of protesters smashed downtown windows, set Dumpsters on fire and looted stores.

A state of emergency was declared, curfews were imposed and hundreds of extra law officers—including two National Guard units—were called in to keep the peace during the final days of the WTO conference. By Wednesday night, more than 500 protesters had been arrested.

Protests continued Thursday, but police did not need to resort to force to control crowds and only two people were arrested.

Seattle's mayor called for calm, lifted a general curfew, shrunk the no-protest zone around the convention center and agreed to let lawyers into the county jail to talk to demonstrators who had been arrested.

SIGNIFICANCE

The Seattle protests and riots have often been cited as the coming-of-age of the anti-globalization movement in the United States and the most significant revival of student protest since the Vietnam War era. Never before had such a wide array of activists—labor, peace, human rights, environmental, anti-corporate, feminist, and others—converged on a single target. California Senator Tom Hayden wrote shortly after the unrest that "the Seattle protestors represent the breakthrough of the vast hip-hop generation into a public effort to challenge the system." Conservative critics, on the other hand, cited the protests as evidence of the irrationality and potential for violence of the movements involved.

Media coverage of the event was itself controversial. Mainstream outlets such as the *Washington Post* frequently referred to the protestors as "anti-trade activists" or characterized the protests as being against world trade, but protestors insisted that they were advocating for "fair trade" rather than no trade or the system generally referred to as "free trade." An editorialist in the *New York Times* wrote, "When protestors shout about the evils of globalization, most are not calling for a return to narrow nationalism, but for the borders of globalization to be expanded, for trade to be linked to democratic reform, higher wages, labor rights and environmental protections."

Much media coverage of the Seattle protests emphasized the violence of protestors, especially property damage caused by a relatively small number of self-identified anarchists. Some media critics argued that police assaults on nonviolent demonstrators preceded the looting incidents and that police sometimes

South Korean protesters in Seoul brandish bamboo sticks at riot police during a rally held for a South Korean farmer who committed suicide the week before during the World Trade Organization (WTO) talks in Cancun, Mexico. © RHEE DONG-MIN/REUTERS/CORBIS.

ignored vandals in order to attack demonstrators non-violently blockading the entrance to the WTO meeting. The Seattle Chief of Police at the time of the protests, Norm Stamper, later wrote of seeing criminal assaults by police: "I saw a cop kicking a retreating demonstrator in the groin before shooting him in the chest with a rubber pellet... Then there was the cop who, spotting two women in a car videotaping the action, ordered one of them to roll down her window. When she complied, he shouted, 'Film *this*!' and filled their car with mace." Left-leaning journalists Alexander Cockburn and Jeffrey St. Clair argue that "the evidence of a civilian riot was nonexistent. With tens of thousands of demonstrators on the streets for a week, under near constant assault by cops, there were no firearms confiscated, no Molotov cocktails discovered, and no police officers seriously injured ... minor acts of [property damage] served as a kind of Gulf of Tonkin incident, used to justify the violent onslaughts by police and the National Guard." Moreover, there were allegations of beatings and deprivation of food, water, and medical care for protestors in detention. Direct Action Network spokesperson told Agence France-Presse on December 4, 1999 that "Our legal team has gone in [to jails where arrested protestors were being held] and found out that beatings in detention were severe, and there has been repeated use of pepper spray in detention." The accuracy of accounts of abuse in detention was disputed by Seattle police.

Protests at WTO meetings and the meetings of other organizations instrumental in the globalized free-trade regime (e.g., the meetings of the World Bank and International Monetary Fund in Washington, D.C. in 2001) have continued. Media coverage of such events tends to focus on clashes between protestors and police rather than on the substantive agendas of either the protestors or the organizations being protested.

FURTHER RESOURCES
Books

Cockburn, Alexander and Jeffrey St. Clair. *Five Days that Shook the World: Seattle and Beyond.* New York: Verso, 2000.

Periodicals

Hayden, Tom. "The Battle in Seattle: What Was That All About?" The *Washington Post* (December 5, 1999).

Klein, Naomi. "Rebels in Search of Rules." The *New York Times* (December 10, 1999).

May Day in the Soviet Union

Photograph

By: Anonymous

Date: c. 1970

Source: Photo by Keystone/Getty Images.

About the Photographer: This photograph is part of the collection at Getty Images, a worldwide provider of visual content materials to such communications groups as advertisers, broadcasters, designers, magazines, new media organizations, newspapers, and producers. The identity of the photographer is not known.

INTRODUCTION

May Day's origins lie in northern Europe as a pagan festival commemorating a cross quarter day (a day falling halfway between two of the four main solar events—the two solstices and two equinoxes) and the official end of the winter months. More recently it has continued to be celebrated as an early summer festival—particularly in Britain, Germany, the Netherlands, and among some immigrant communities in the United States. It is traditionally marked with dancing around a Maypole, bonfires, and heavy drinking. Across most of Europe, the day is usually marked by a public holiday.

For the last 125 years, May Day has been appropriated by trade union and Socialist movements as a day commemorating the accomplishments of workers. It was adopted at the First Congress of the Second International (a coalition of international Socialist and workers movements) in 1889 to mark Chicago's Haymarket protests of May 1886. During the Haymarket protests, workers successfully demonstrated in favor of an eight-hour day, but during the skirmishes that broke out between police and protesters, eleven people were killed. After the Second International's Congress, May Day became a worldwide celebration of the international labor movement and was celebrated as much by workers marching in the colors of their trade unions as it was by neo-Pagan rituals.

Nowhere, however, was May Day celebrated with more fervor than in the USSR and its client states. As elsewhere, it was a public holiday with demonstrations of worker solidarity, but with the onset of the Cold War it increasingly became a propaganda show for Soviet technological achievements and military might. In Red Square, troops paraded their latest military hardware in front of huge, stage-managed crowds.

Presidents of friendly regimes were invited to inspect the parades and, under effigies of Socialist heroes such as Vladimir Lenin and Karl Marx, synchronized demonstrations of dance, music, and flag waving took place. These May Day parades and demonstrations were one of the few occasions when the West was allowed a peek behind the Iron Curtain and the displays were designed to inspire either admiration or fear.

The Soviet leadership also choreographed their May Day parades as statements on contemporary global politics. In 1946, Red Army troops, recently returned from defeating Fascism in Europe, took center-stage. In 1963, shortly after the Cuban missile crisis, May Day was a defiant show of military and technological might, in which the latest weaponry was paraded through Red Square. By the late 1960s, with mounting criticism across the world of America's role in the Vietnam War, the May Day parades increasingly became a demonstration of solidarity with the Viet-Cong (whom the USSR were also covertly funding) and an attack on the perceived imperialism and brutality of America's actions in Vietnam.

PRIMARY SOURCE

MAY DAY IN THE SOVIET UNION
See primary source image.

SIGNIFICANCE

Although the origins of May Day as an international workers day lay in the United States, it was never an officially sanctioned U.S. holiday because of its associations with the deeply divisive Haymarket protests and later because of its Socialist connotations. Instead, American workers are recognized and celebrated on Labor Day, a September holiday that also informally marks the end of summer. However, as elsewhere in the world, May Day became a focal point for popular demonstrations of solidarity and discontent in the United States as well. This was especially true in the days surrounding May Day in 1970 and 1971.

Mirroring events in Red Square, protesters in Washington, DC turned May Day into a massive anti-Vietnam war protest in 1970. About 100,000 people turned out in a relatively spontaneous, but highly visible, demonstration against recent U.S. incursions into Cambodia. The following year the demonstrations were more organized and were met by huge police and National Guard resistance. Following a

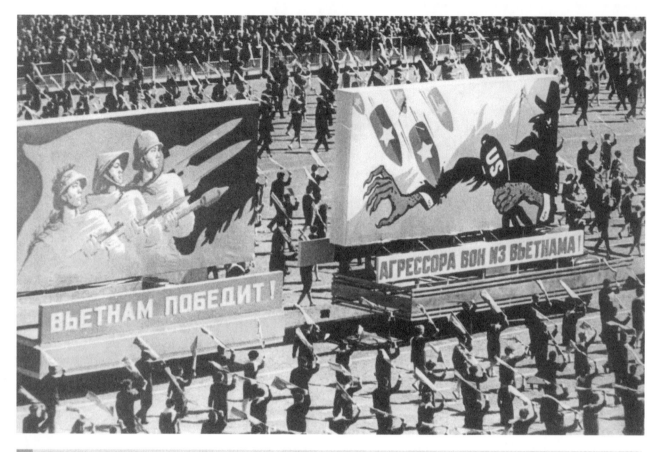

PRIMARY SOURCE

May Day in the Soviet Union: A May Day parade in Moscow, circa 1970, expressing support for North Vietnam and opposition to the United States. PHOTO BY KEYSTONE/GETTY IMAGES.

month of veteran protests, 500,000 people converged on Washington, DC, aiming to shut down the federal government by non-violent action. Over several days, they listened to speakers and music, manned barricades and dominated global news reports. Some 12,000 protesters were arrested.

Since the fall of Communism in Europe, May Day has tended to be marked in these countries by demonstrations of adherents to the old regime, or by those disaffected by the inequalities of the post-Communist era. May Day celebrations continue to be important events in the remaining Communist countries, such as China and Cuba, and the day is still widely observed as a public holiday across the West.

In recent years, May Day has been taken over by anti-capitalist and anti-globalization protesters. In London on May Day 2000, anti-capitalist demonstrations in and around Parliament developed into a large scale riot. Branches of McDonalds and Starbucks were

vandalized, as was the cenotaph—a monument commemorating the victims of World War I and World War II—and a statue of Winston Churchill was defaced. Following these disturbances, the British government enacted legislation forbidding demonstrations within the vicinity of Parliament. The following year, police contained about 1,000 demonstrators at Oxford Circus, the busiest junction on London's main shopping street, for several hours lest there be a repeat of the previous year's violence. The police actions prompted widespread criticism, with critics complaining that the police were over-reaching themselves and barring the right to legitimate protest.

May Day protests elsewhere in the early twenty-first century have tended to reflect the concerns of individual peoples at that particular time. Thus, in 2002, the May Day demonstrations in France were directed against Fascism, since that country was experiencing a resurgence of far right political groups.

Thousands line the street, in front of the Kremlin, to watch the May Day Parade in Moscow's Red Square on May 1, 1928. AP IMAGES.

In 2006, relatively small, but significantly defiant, demonstrations were held in Belarus and Zimbabwe, where opposition politicians had been incarcerated. Arguably the most significant protest of that year came in the United States, when millions of Latino immigrants staged nationwide protests against proposed immigration reform.

FURTHER RESOURCES
Books

McCauley, Martin. *Russia, America and the Cold War, 1949–1991.* 2nd ed. New York: Longman, 2004.

Thompson, Bill. *The Soviet Union Under Brezhnev: 1964–82.* New York: Longman, 2003.

Web sites

Guardian Unlimited. "May Day Protests: Special Report." <http://www.guardian.co.uk/mayday/story/0,7369,481318,00.html> (accessed May 22, 2006).

Life. "May Day Classic Photographs." <http://www.life.com/Life/classicpictures/mayday/9.html> (accessed May 22, 2006).

Solidarity's Message

Declaration

By: Anonymous

Date: September 9, 1981

Source: Warsaw Radio, September 9, 1981

About the Author: Solidarity had its origins as a labor and protest organization among the shipworkers of Gdansk, Poland, in 1980. It quickly came to play a central role in opposition to the communist government of Poland, which outlawed it in 1981. Solidarity continued its efforts, however, eventually leading to the establishment of a democratic government in Poland.

INTRODUCTION

The Solidarity movement is generally recognized as one of the most significant and successful of the various movements that opposed communism in Eastern Europe. As a result of its successes in Poland, Solidarity has been credited with playing a major role in initiating the wave of reforms which led to the fall of communism throughout Europe in the late 1980s and 1990s.

While fighting Nazi Germany during World War II (1939–1945), the Soviet Union occupied most of Eastern Europe, including Poland. After the war, the Soviet Union established communist governments to rule the countries under its control in a manner consistent with Soviet goals. Poland was no exception. Not all Poles were happy with this situation. Many claimed that while communist rule caused industrial production to increase, the domestic economy and the population suffered as a result. Protests against the government took place in 1956, 1968, 1970, and 1976, but none were successful in bringing about major changes.

In 1980, economic conditions in Poland were poor. After meat prices in Poland reached an all-time high, a collection of shipyard workers in Gdansk came together under the umbrella of an independent trade union that would soon come to be known as Solidarity. Led by labor activist Lech Walesa, Solidarity demanded reforms in the Polish economy and civil society. It was met with widespread popular support, and Poland's government felt it had no choice but to concede many of its demands. Solidarity continued to grow in size and strength, and came to be seen as a threat to the communist government itself. In response, the government cracked down. In December, 1981, martial law was imposed and many of Solidarity's leaders, including Walesa, were imprisoned. The Solidarity movement was outlawed.

This proved to be only a temporary setback for Solidarity. Martial law was lifted in 1983, and Walesa and other Solidarity members were freed from prison. Also in 1983, Walesa received the Nobel Peace Prize, a sign of international support for Solidarity's aims. While Solidarity itself remained outlawed, the spirit of reform that it embodied remained a powerful force in Poland. Combined with a continued poor economy, it led to unrest throughout the 1980s.

By 1989, times were changing throughout Soviet-dominated Eastern Europe. Led by Mikhail Gorbachev, the Soviet Union was undergoing reforms of its own. Inspired in part by Solidarity's example, pressures for reform were mounting in other communist countries as well. Gorbachev made it clear to Polish leaders that Soviet troops would not intervene to maintain the status quo; the Poles would have to deal with the continued unrest in their country on their own.

The communist Polish government decided that the only way to restore order was to re-legalize Solidarity, and try to reach some form of compromise with it. Accordingly, Solidarity was legalized again in April, 1989. Negotiations on reforms began immediately. At first, the government and Solidarity agreed to a new parliament where non-communists could have significant representation, although communists would still control key aspects. The resulting election was a resounding success for Solidarity; the party won all but one of the seats not reserved for the Communist Party and its allies. Faced with these results, the remaining support for the communists quickly collapsed. By August of 1989, Solidarity was in control of the government. In 1990, Walesa was elected president, and in 1991 Poland had its first completely free parliamentary elections since the 1930s. Gorbachev, a reformer, was now president of the Soviet Union, and had made it clear that the Soviet Union would not intervene militarily in Poland.

In 1989, the government agreed to talks with Solidarity leading to elections, which resulted in an overwhelming victory for the Solidarity candidates and the fall of the communist government. After Solidarity was able to bring down communism in Poland, reform movements began to be seen in other European countries, including Hungary as well as East Germany, which ultimately resulted in the fall of the Berlin Wall. Lech Walesa received the Nobel Peace Prize in 1983 and went on to become the president of Poland.

PRIMARY SOURCE

MESSAGE TO THE WORKING PEOPLE OF EASTERN EUROPE

Delegates assembled in Gdansk at the first . . . Solidarity congress send workers of Albania, Bulgaria, Czechoslovakia, GDR, Romania, Hungary and all nations of the Soviet Union greetings and expressions of support. As the first independent trade union in our postwar history, we are profoundly aware of the fact that we share the same fate. We assure you that despite lies disseminated in your countries, we are an authentic representative organ

Poles march in the streets with "Solidarity" banners during Pope John-Paul II's 1987 visit to Poland. © BERNARD BISSON/CORBIS SYGMA.

of workers with 10 million members, an organ that was created as a result of workers' strikes.

Our goal is to struggle to improve the lives of all working people. We support those of you who have decided to embark on the difficult path of struggle for a free union movement. We believe that it will not be long now before our representatives will be able to meet your representatives in order to exchange their experiences as unionists.

SIGNIFICANCE

Solidarity's success was the beginning of a wave of reform and revolution that resulted in the end of communist rule in Europe. Within months of Solidarity coming to power in Poland, communist governments in East Germany and Hungary were topled. Others followed soon after. All were inspired by Solidarity's example. In 1991, communism collapsed in the Soviet Union itself, and the USSR split into fifteen independant nations.

Solidarity, while it did eventually rise to power in the national government, was not built as a political party, and was established with the principle goal of finding a way to better the lives of average Poles. The achievements of Solidarity have often been pointed to as an example of how with the proper organization and commitment, ordinary citizen groups are able to impact national politics and even bring down reigning governments. The major uniqueness of Solidarity was their accomplishments largely through democratic means without resorting to expressions of violence that is often associated with labor unrest.

For Poland, as a country that throughout much of modern history has been occupied by foreign powers, the rise of Solidarity to bring independence from the Soviets has been viewed as a very important step in the national development. Just months prior to the creation of Solidarity, Pope John Paul II, a Polish priest, assumed the highest position in the Catholic Church. Many Polish citizens rallied behind this event to exhibit feelings of nationalism, a feeling they could embrace by supporting Solidarity, which allowed

Poland to emerge from communism. Pope John Paul II has long been credited with supporting efforts to bring independence from communism to Poland and other countries in Eastern Europe.

Today, Poland is a developing democracy with a capitalist economy. The country is closely allied with Western superpowers and bears little institutional or economic resemblance to the communist period. Solidarity has been largely credited with allowing the formation of the new Polish government and economy, and is recognized as being among the most significant social movements of the latter half of the twentieth century.

FURTHER RESOURCES

Books

Ash, Timothy Garten. *The Polish Revolution: Solidarity*. New Haven, Conn.: Yale University Press, 2003.

Web sites

National Commission of Independent Self-Governing Trade Union. "Solidarity Web Site." <http://www.solidarnosc.org.pl/eng1.htm> (accessed May 24, 2006).

Globalization and the Maquiladoras

Magazine article

By: Jen Soriano

Date: November 24, 1999

Source: Soriano, Jen. "Globalization and the Maquiladoras." *Mother Jones* (November 24, 1999).

About the Author: Jen Soriano is a staff writer for *Mother Jones*, an independent, nonprofit magazine known for its commitment to social justice and its investigative reporting.

INTRODUCTION

The Maquiladora Program is an attempt to provide economic development for Mexico and cheap labor for Mexico's trading partners as well as low prices for consumer goods. It is a set of international trade policies and regulations that permit a business in the U.S. or another originating nation to temporarily transfer goods to Mexico, where the products receive added value with minimal or no tariffs being applied to the goods as long as they are shipped back to the originating nation.

Protestors rallying against the North American Free Trade Agreement (NAFTA) in San Francisco, California, September 20, 1993. © REUTERS/CORBIS.

The Maquiladora Program has its roots in the Border Industrialization Program (BIP) enacted by the Mexican government in 1965. This program allowed foreign-owned firms to build assembly plants in Mexico. These plants were known as maquiladoras, after *maquilar* meaning "to assemble." The government expected to promote economic development by attracting foreign investment and to provide employment opportunities for Mexicans. Although the BIP provided the opportunity for maquiladoras to be established and to operate, several modifications since 1965 have resulted in a more formalized, more highly regulated and controlled program.

In order to provide for more standardization, the Mexican government issued the Maquila Decree on December 22, 1989 that established the Maquiladora Program. The decree named the Mexican Secretariat of Commerce and Development as the agency responsible for the regulation of maquiladoras and specified that while the maquiladora is a registered Mexican corporation, 100% of the capital investment, ownership, and management of the firm may be foreign.

PRIMARY SOURCE

Increased competition across borders means business needs to keep costs and prices down. One tried-and-true way to do that is to move factories out of developed nations and into poorer ones, where worker safety regulations are rare and wages are often exploitatively low. Maquiladora workers are converging on Seattle to be heard.

Martha Ojeda has a message for the thousands of government officials meeting at the Seattle WTO summit to discuss how best to promote global free trade. "We want fair jobs, not free trade," says Ojeda, executive director of the San Antonio-based Coalition for Justice in the Maquiladoras.

Ojeda is leading a squadron of Mexican factory workers to the streets of Seattle for the summit to denounce the ways free trade impacts the lives of working people in developing countries.

"We will be there to ask what happened to the promises of free trade," says Ojeda. "Where are the improved living conditions? Where are the better jobs?"

In Mexico, nearly six years after the passage of the North American Free Trade Agreement, which was supposed to create more jobs and higher wages throughout North America, one of the consequences of free trade has been the proliferation of maquiladora factories, which critics call little better than sweatshops. Relaxed rules on foreign investment and export duties have made it far easier for foreign companies to open these low-wage assembly plants where workers make everything from leather gloves to televisions for multinational companies including BMW, Chrysler, Fisher Price, Sony, and Xerox, mostly for export to the US.

There are by now some 4,000 maquiladoras concentrated along the U.S.-Mexico border. According to the Mexican business journal El Financiero, employment in the maquiladoras nearly doubled between 1993 and 1998, and now stands at over one million people.

According to a Workers University of Mexico study, maquiladora workers earn between $3.50 and $5 a day—enough to do little more than survive in the border towns, where the cost of living is thirty percent higher than in the rest of the country.

Life inside the factories is often grim. "Workers labor from sunrise to sunset. They never see day light," says Ojeda, who was a maquiladora worker for twenty years. "They are sometimes exposed to toxic chemicals, and in one case workers were given "vitamins" which turned out to be amphetamines. They rarely see their families; often wives will work for one shift, then switch with their husbands who take the next shift." Sexual harassment of women employees, who are the majority of maquiladora workers, is common—and not prohibited by Mexican law. Some have even been murdered.

While NAFTA promoted free trade among Mexico, Canada, and the U.S., the WTO promotes free trade among 135 member nations. More free trade, say critics, means more maquiladora-style manufacturing.

"The maquiladoras are one manifestation of the global sweatshop," says Larry Weiss, labor and globalization program director at the Resource Center of the Americas. "These same export processing zones can be found in Jakarta, Manila, Zimbabwe, Costa Rica—all over the Third World and in the former Soviet Bloc. This is what globalization is all about."

At workshops and rallies throughout the Seattle meetings, the maquiladora delegation will join farm workers, union members, and activists from all over the world in trying to get their concerns heard. "We are not expecting to make $500 a week," says Ojeda. "In Mexico, as everywhere, we simply want fair wages, good working conditions, and the ability to live with dignity." In short, she says, "We want our rights to be included in the WTO's commercial agenda."

SIGNIFICANCE

The Mexican government made attempts to protect maquiladora workers, but these workplace regulations have not been effectively enforced. Workers are officially limited to a maximum work week of six eight-hour shifts with paid pregnancy leave, profit-sharing, national holidays, vacations, and severance benefits. In reality, pregnant workers are often fired to avoid the payment of pregnancy leave and rampant corruption has allowed businesses to ignore the other rules. The result is a continued brutalization of workers that has fueled anti-globalization activism.

The implementation of the North American Free Trade Agreement (NAFTA) in 1994 raised concerns among reformers. Many anti-globalization and anti-maquiladora activists feared that it would negatively affect Mexican workers. NAFTA did result in a rapid expansion of trade between Mexico and the United States. However, the direct impact of NAFTA on the operation of maquiladoras and the overall maquiladora output has been minor. U.S. industrial production combined with international currency and wage variability had the greatest influence on maquiladora employment in the first decade of NAFTA. The future of the maquiladoras in the face of social, political, and economic upheavals in Mexico at the start of the twenty-first century is not clear.

FURTHER RESOURCES
Books

Bacon, David. *The Children of NAFTA: Labor Wars on the U.S./Mexico Border*. Berkeley: University of California Press, 2004.

Cravey, Altha J. *Women and Work in Mexico's Maquiladoras*. Lanham, MD: Rowman and Littlefield, 1998.

Kopinak, Kathryn. *Desert Capitalism: Maquiladoras in North America's Western Industrial Corridor*. Tucson: University of Arizona Press, 1996.

What Charles and Evan Did for Spring Break

News article

By: MacNeil-Lehrer Productions/PBS

Date: April 19, 2000

Source: MacNeil/Lehrer Productions/PBS

About the Author: MacNeil/Lehrer Productions—founded by Jim Lehrer and Robert MacNeil, along with Liberty Media—was the organization behind the *MacNeil/Lehrer NewsHour*. Initially, Lehrer and MacNeil teamed up to co-anchor the 1975 Senate Watergate hearings for PBS (Public Broadcasting Service). Eventually, the partnership turned into The *MacNeil/Lehrer Report* beginning in October 1975, and The *MacNeil/Lehrer NewsHour*, starting in 1983. The MacNeil/Lehrer NewsHour was hosted by Jim Lehrer, who was also its executive editor and co-producer, and Robert MacNeil, who was also its reporter and writer. The show won two Emmy Awards, along with numerous other awards, during its thirty years of news reporting for PBS. When MacNeil retired in 1995, the program was renamed The *NewsHour* with Jim Lehrer. Public Broadcasting Service (PBS) is a network of U.S. public television stations that is owned and directed by about 350-member public television stations across the country, which themselves are operated by such groups as community organizations, local and state agencies, and educational facilities.

INTRODUCTION

On April 16, 2000, Charles Olbert and Evan Scott, who were members of the group SURGE (Students United for a Responsible Global Environment), joined other activists to protest at the spring meetings of the International Monetary Fund (IMF) and The World Bank (WB). SURGE is an activist organization dedicated to promoting economic, environmental, political, and social justice throughout the world through action and education.

Established by the United Nations (UN), the IMF is an international economic organization that examines the world's economy, promotes international monetary cooperation, and provides short-term economic aid (often times, emergency loans) to developing countries (usually in exchange for free-market reforms) to expedite the growth of international trade. Also established by the UN, the World Bank (formally called the International Bank for Reconstruction and Development) is an international economic organization that provides long-term loans and grants, along with developmental and technical assistance, to help developing countries around the world implement social programs. World Bank financing is often used for social projects such as modernizing educational and health systems, and for environmental and infrastructure projects such as improving or creating roads and highways, national parks, and dams.

Olbert and Scott, as participants of the SURGE protest against the IMF/WB, were protesting the two organizations' actions with respect to globalization. The concept of globalization is generally defined as activities that promote countries to trade goods and services with other countries around the world. Recent trends seen as a direct result of globalization include an increased movement/expansion of commodities, information, infrastructures (such as communications), legal systems, money, organizations (such as multinational companies), people, and technologies around the world.

Proponents of globalization, such as the IMF, define globalization as "the process through which an increasingly free flow of ideas, people, goods, services, and capital leads to the integration of economies and societies." Critics of globalization, such as the International Forum on Globalization, define globalization as "the present worldwide drive toward a globalized economic system dominated by supranational corporate trade and banking institutions that are not accountable to democratic processes or national governments."

PRIMARY SOURCE

Charles Olbert and Evan Scott ran an unusual errand in early April: the two high school juniors made a special trip

Smoke billows from a burning billboard during riots on the opening day of the meeting of the IMF and World Bank in Prague, on September 26, 2000. AP IMAGES.

to the Army Navy Surplus store in their home town of Durham, North Carolina to buy gas masks.

The masks, along with other basic supplies, were part of their preparations for a trip to Washington D.C. This was not a typical school field trip.

Charles and Evan are part of a North Carolina student group called SURGE (Students United for a Responsible Global Environment).

SURGE joined other activists who plan peaceful protests coinciding with the April 16 spring meetings of the International Monetary Fund (IMF) and The World Bank.

COPS SHOP

The Washington DC Police Department also did a little shopping.

They bought a million dollars worth of extra supplies, including tear gas, riot gear, plastic bullets and gas masks.

Police officials say the supplies are just a precaution, in case the protests get too chaotic.

When a similar protest took place in Seattle last December, violence erupted. Downtown store windows were smashed and several hundred protesters were arrested, hundreds of others were sprayed with tear gas.

A BANK WITH NO TELLERS

So what exactly is everyone getting so excited about?

The IMF and The World Bank are international organizations that lend huge chunks of money (billions) to poor countries.

Both rich and poor countries are members of both organizations.

The IMF generally lends money to countries going through an economic crisis. Each of its 182 member countries contributes to the pool of funds. For example, when the Brazilian economy crashed in 1998, the IMF organized a "bail out" to help stabilize Brazil's currency.

When the World Bank was started in 1946 it collected contributions from its wealthier member countries. It reinvested a portion of this money in the world's capital markets to grow the fund from which loans are made. The World Bank, which has 181 members, loans close to $30 billion annually to many of its poorer member countries.

The World Bank invests in countries to help them modernize. In general, loans are given to build roads, develop industry and start education programs.

The World Bank's slogan is "Our Dream is A World Free of Poverty."

THEY DON'T BUY IT

But Charles doesn't buy the slogan and he's heading to Washington DC to make it known.

"On the surface, the IMF and World Bank seem good," he says. "They appear like they're helping the economy of poor nations get going. But if you dig deeper, you realize all they do is hurt working people, damage the environment and help big corporations get richer."

Charles has spent a lot of time reading about the IMF and The World Bank on the net. He hangs out everywhere from new sites like CNN.com to radical anarchy sites.

Specifically, Charles objects to the terms of the IMF's economic recovery loans.

When the IMF lends money to a struggling country, they also specify what the country must do to shore up their economy and pay back the loan. These are called Structural Adjustment Programs or Economic Stabilization Programs.

Charles believes countries end up having to cut spending on things like education, health care and environmental protection and he feels the programs give rich nations too much control over the economies of poorer nations.

"These institutions just want their money paid pack," says Charles, referring to the IMF and World Bank. "For example, the IMF might pressure a nation to start producing cotton because it's a cash crop and it brings a high price when you export it. But if you use land for cotton in a country where people are starving, it just means you're producing less food locally and then you have to import food for even higher prices."

ON THE OTHER SIDE OF THE DEBATE

The IMF says its programs are aimed at getting countries to adopt strategies that will help them succeed in a new global market place and build long term economic stability.

According to the IMF, there is no question of forcing a member to adopt any policy. The IMF says that what authority they do have is to require member countries to disclose information on certain economic policies and to avoid, as far as possible, putting restrictions on the flow of money in and out of their country.

The World Bank counters that it's a development institution whose goal is to reduce poverty by promoting sustainable economic growth in its client countries.

Development is about putting all the component parts in place—balanced economic and social programs, according to the World Bank.

"I think that people are worried about the future. I think they don't understand a lot of the big international institutions. We are ready to talk, and we have been ready to talk, we're very anxious to do it, and some of the mystery will go. But we are entering a new age of globalization, and I think there's a lot of fear," says James Wolfensohn, the president of World Bank.

IS FREE TRADE FREE?

The IMF believes that, in general, taxes and regulations on trade between all countries should be kept to a minimum or eliminated. This is referred to as "free trade."

Evan's concerns about the IMF center around free trade.

"There's an underlying conflict between free trade and the preservation of the environment, protection of the human rights and other social issues," says Evan. "Free trade means that countries that produce goods for the least amount of money succeed."

The cost of things like minimum wage laws and environmental regulations have to be met by governments and businesses. Evan says the free trade system will reward countries where factory workers earn very little money or governments fail to enforce environmental protections.

Those who favor free trade say it is the best basis for an international market economy. They say it's the most efficient way to bring together buyers and sellers.

BATTLE OF SEATTLE

None of these issues are simple—that's why they've spurred protests.

Late last year, activists protested in Seattle against the policies of the World Trade Organization, another international group which supports free trade. The protests became a battle between police and demonstrators.

Charles and Evan say watching news footage of the "Battle of Seattle" piqued their interest in these global economic issues.

"It was a real turning point for me," says Evan. "Kids were getting gassed, the cops were in riot gear. Very few people here at school knew what it was about it."

The protesters in Seattle included activists from many backgrounds, including environmentalists, worker's rights groups and human rights advocates.

The media coverage of the chaos made people pay more attention to these global economic issues—including Evan and Scott, who got together and started trying to educate other students.

UNITED WE STAND

Charles and Evan are part of a growing wave of student organizing.

Activism has gathered strength on college campuses over the past few years as groups have pressured school administrations and companies to boycott clothes produced in oppressive factories, sometimes called sweatshops, where workers are not paid a decent hourly wage or are forced to work in unsafe conditions.

Now, the activist spirit is being felt in high schools.

The International Student Activism Alliance, a new high school group which promotes peaceful protest, already has 160 chapters and thousands of members.

STARC (the Student Alliance to Reform Corporations) launched just five months ago already has 2,000 members from both high schools and colleges. They also advocate peaceful means of getting one's point across.

Groups like these have organized at lightning speed with the help of the Internet. Their causes differ—ranging from anti-sweat shop campaigns, to gay rights to environmental concerns—but they're linked by a desire to be a force for positive social change.

STAND AND BE COUNTED

SURGE, the student group Charles and Evan are part of, has chartered three buses to join the East Coast caravan to Washington D.C.

Charles says he's excited about being part of the action—but he's not planning to be in the front lines.

"This is a magnet school so if you get in any trouble at all, they can kick you out," he says.

And Evan says even if he doesn't wind up in a cloud of tear gas this weekend, he's already found a use for his gas mask.

"I used it in a photo project about environmental pollution . . . and the mask is also just pretty entertaining."

SIGNIFICANCE

The proponents of globalization and critics of globalization (anti-globalists) have been in conflict for years over the ways that globalization has developed. The effects of globalization on the poorest people and countries are at the heart of the dispute. The conflict centers around the role that governments, corporations, and individuals play in globalization and free trade while, at the same time, dealing with the social and environmental problems.

On one side are the anti-globalists, including activist groups as SURGE, that demonstrate against globalization, equity differences between rich and poor, and the methods by which the IMF/WB conduct business. Activist groups contend that the IMF/WB, which are termed "global loan sharks" by anti-globalists, often attract desperate countries for low-interest loans and then demand economic policies that actually worsen their countries. They criticize the IMF/WB for pushing globalization onto countries through methods that are imperialistic, unaccountable, and corporate-focused. Within these groups, globalization is seen as another term for Americanization because the United States is viewed as one of only a few countries that will profit from globalization. Rather than calling it free trade, anti-globalists talk of corporate-managed trade because poor countries are strictly managed concerning their trading practices. They contend that more people become poor because their native industries and natural resources, such as coasts, fisheries, forests, lands, and rivers, are degraded or destroyed so loans will not default.

The anti-globalists maintain that these poor countries spend so much money on interest payments that they are unable, or limited in their ability, to continue with social and human rights issues. They also declare that when countries deal with IMF/WB policies, the quality of the environment is often sacrificed. Responsibility to corporations, what is call corporate globalism, is seen as the primary force behind the IMF/WB rather than to the peoples of the debtor nations. Activists say that such policies make the division between the rich and the poor even wider.

On the other side of the debate are the pro-globalists, including organizations such as the IMF and the WB. IMF/WB leaders state that they are making consistent and long-term progress in helping low-income countries become more prepared to live in the global economic market by increasing their financial growth and decreasing poverty levels. Such leaders contend that when loans are made with poor countries, the contract helps to deal with social issues. In the case of worker displacement, for instance, training programs are setup to re-train workers. Generally, pro-globalists declare that globalization efforts are helping advance poor countries that did not participate in the technological revolution of the twentieth century. As part of this practice, private companies are brought in to introduce new technologies, educational opportunities, and financial incentives to help countries become competitive.

In some cases, IMF/WB leaders state that countries have borrowed so much money that it is unlikely they will meet their obligations to repay the debt. In such cases, a certain amount of debt is removed so the country can return to investing in social and economic programs. In addition, pro-globalists contend that it is necessary to use readily available natural resources. In cases where non-renewable resources such as fossil fuels are used to create economic opportunity, environmental protection programs are also initiated.

In summary, pro-globalists contend that some problems, such as workers losing their jobs, inevitably occur in short term globalization, but that they can be solved over time, and healthy economic incentives will eventually bring more jobs and goods to a global market. Anti-globalists, on the other hand, contend that the progress of globalization is being strictly directed by large industry, and if left to develop on its own accord or by institutions with social consciences, different policies would be created that more equitably would address social, human rights, and environmental concerns.

FURTHER RESOURCES
Books

Frieden, Jeffry A. *Global Capitalism: Its Fall and Rise in the Twentieth Century.* New York: W.W. Norton, 2006.

Gerdes, Louise I., ed. *Globalization.* San Diego, CA: Greenhaven Press, 2006.

Kadragic, Alma. *Globalization and Human Rights.* Philadelphia, PA: Chelsea House, 2006.

Lemert, Charles C. *Deadly Worlds: The Emotional Costs of Globalization.* Lanham, MD: Rowman and Littlefield Publishers, 2006.

McDonald, Kevin. *Global Movements: Action and Culture.* Malden, MA: Blackwell Publishing, 2006.

Web sites

International Forum on Globalization (IFG). "Globalization." <http://www.ifg.org/analysis.htm> (accessed June 1, 2006).

International Monetary Fund (IMF). "Globalization: A Framework for IMF Involvement." March 2002 <http://www.imf.org/external/np/exr/ib/2002/031502.htm> (accessed June 1, 2006).

Students United for a Responsible Global Environment (SURGE) <http://surgenetwork.org/> (accessed June 1, 2006).

The World Bank (WB). <http://www.worldbank.org/> (accessed June 1, 2006).

On the Air Traffic Controllers Strike

Press release

By: Ronald Reagan

Date: August 3, 1981

Source: White House Press Release. "On the Air Traffic Controllers Strike." August 3, 1981.

About the Author: Ronald Reagan (1911–2004) served as the fortieth president of the United States from 1981 to 1989. Noted for his conservative politics, the popular Republican focused on economic reforms that reversed some of the gains made by labor during previous presidential administrations.

INTRODUCTION

Ronald Reagan's high-profile battle with the Professional Air Traffic Controllers' Organization (PATCO) served as a pivotal moment in the labor movement. Besides showing Reagan to be tough and confident, the struggle gave notice to business executives that the federal government approved of breaking the power of labor unions. Reagan reversed fifty years of federal support for unionization.

PATCO members ran the sophisticated technology that controlled air traffic in the U.S. They regarded themselves as highly trained professionals in stressful jobs, made worse by long hours and outmoded equipment. During the 1980 presidential campaign, Reagan had met with the president of PATCO to promise that he would take every necessary step to provide the best air traffic equipment available and to

Two PATCO air traffic controller union members picket at La Guardia Airport in New York, August 6, 1981. AP IMAGES.

improve working conditions by hiring more controllers. PATCO then became one of the few labor unions to endorse Reagan over incumbent Jimmy Carter. After the election, Reagan changed his course. The PATCO contract expired in March 1981 and Reagan's advisers warned him that the administration's position in those negotiations would send signals to several other unions. Particularly worrying, the contract of the massive postal workers' union was set to expire shortly after the PATCO contract. Reagan was also warned that a strike would possibly cost the nation $150 million per day in lost domestic commerce alone.

PATCO sought a $10,000 per year raise, a thirty-two-hour work week, and a better early retirement package. Reagan offered $2,300 in additional benefits and pay. The controllers were banned from legally striking or staging a slowdown because they were federal employees. However, in years past, controllers had effectively slowed plane traffic at various airports to win improvements in every area from staffing to pay. On August 2, 1981, the controllers went on strike. The

action was inconveniencing and potentially dangerous as well as illegal. In a press conference on August 3, Reagan joined Secretary of Transportation Drew Lewis and Attorney General William French Smith to announce that the 15,000 striking PATCO members would be fired if they did not return to work. Lewis added that there would be no negotiations during the strike and that supervisory personnel, joined by 150 military controllers, had the system running at fifty percent capacity.

PRIMARY SOURCE

This morning at 7 A.M. the union representing those who man America's air traffic control facilities called a strike. This was the culmination of seven months of negotiations between the Federal Aviation Administration and the union. At one point in these negotiations agreement was reached and signed by both sides, granting a $40 million increase in salaries and benefits. This is twice what other government employees can expect. It was granted in recognition of the difficulties inherent in the work these people perform. Now, however, the union demands are seventeen times what had been agreed to—$681 million. This would impose a tax burden on their fellow citizens which is unacceptable.

I would like to thank the supervisors and controllers who are on the job today, helping to get the nation's air system operating safely. In the New York area, for example, four supervisors were scheduled to report for work, and seventeen additionally volunteered. At National Airport a traffic controller told a newsperson he had resigned from the union and reported to work because, "How can I ask my kids to obey the law if I don't?" This is a great tribute to America.

Let me make one thing plain. I respect the right of workers in the private sector to strike. Indeed, as president of my own union, I led the first strike ever called by that union. I guess I'm maybe the first one to ever hold this office who is a lifetime member of an AFL-CIO union. But we cannot compare labor-management relations in the private sector with government. Government cannot close down the assembly line. It has to provide without interruption the protective services which are government's reason for being.

It was in recognition of this that the Congress passed a law forbidding strikes by government employees against the public safety. Let me read the solemn oath taken by each of these employees, a sworn affidavit, when they accepted their jobs: "I am not participating in any strike against the Government of the United States or any agency thereof, and I will not so participate while an employee of the Government of the United States or any agency thereof."

It is for this reason that I must tell those who fail to report for duty this morning they are in violation of the law, and if they do not report for work within forty-eight hours, they have forfeited their jobs and will be terminated.

SIGNIFICANCE

In the wake of the firing of the PATCO members, it still remained more difficult to fire a union member than a non-union worker. Union membership had started to decline before the PATCO strike, despite claims that the episode led to a weakening of unions. In 1945, thirty percent of Americans belonged to a union. As industries deregulated, new business formed around high-technology products, and less-educated workers failed to join unions, union membership dropped to twenty-three percent by the start of Reagan's presidency.

The PATCO union, however, was destroyed. On August 5, Reagan announced that thirty-eight percent of PATCO members had returned to work. On August 13, the government announced that 10,438 controllers had been fired and flight schedules had returned to eighty percent normal. On December 9, Reagan confirmed his position that fired controllers would not be rehired, although they could apply for other government positions. Polls showed that sixty-seven percent of Americans approved of Reagan's handling of the strike, including sixty-one percent of blue-collar workers who would normally back labor unions. In 1987, controllers approved the National Air Traffic Controllers Association as their bargaining agent. The new union gained support because of disputes among the controllers and Federal Aviation Administration (FAA) that reprised many of the issues that had angered PATCO members: poor labor-management communications, inadequate staffing levels, high traffic volume, and outdated equipment. In 1987, the U.S. air traffic control system handled three million more flights than it had in 1981 with 3,000 fewer controllers than in 1981. By 2006, 4,000 of the 16,000 controllers hired after the 1981 strike were ready for retirement. Union leaders predict an upcoming shortage of controllers.

FURTHER RESOURCES
Books

Northrup, Herbert R. and Amie D. Thornton. *The Federal Government as Employer: The Federal Labor Relations Authority and the PATCO Challenge*. Philadelphia: Wharton School, University of Pennsylvania, 1986.

Pemberton, William E. *Exit with Honor: The Life and Presidency of Ronald Reagan*. Armonk, NY: M.E. Sharpe, 1998.

Reeves, Richard. *President Reagan: The Triumph of Imagination*. New York: Simon and Schuster, 2005.

Shostak, Arthur B. and David Skocik. *The Air Controllers' Controversy: Lessons from the PATCO Strike*. New York: Human Science Press, 1986.

Protesters Smash the Window of a McDonald's

Photograph

By: Pontus Lundahl

Date: June 15, 2001

Source: © Pontus Lundahl/epa/Corbis.

About the Photographer: This photograph was taken by Swedish photographer Pontus Lundahl. This photograph is part of the collection of the Corbis Corporation, headquartered in Seattle, Washington, with a worldwide archive of over 70 million images.

INTRODUCTION

The world began to experience an unparalleled movement of currency, capital, trade, and human resources between nations beginning in the 1950s, a phenomenon referred to as globalization. Globalization implies an international economy where goods and services move across borders without difficulty. Due to its impact on workers and the environment in developing nations, this transfer of resources across borders has fueled debates regarding development and economic theory. Advocates of globalization, led by multi-national corporations (MNCs) and Trans-national corporations (TNCs), argue that the free flow of trade and currency has created an expansion of democracy as well as economic growth and opportunities globally. Those who oppose globalization assert that the globalization trend has allowed multi-national corporations and transnational corporations to engage in unfair labor practices and environmentally detrimental policies in low-income countries, as well as an increase in the income gap between high-income and low-income nation-states. Dissenters in the globalization debate suggest that these corporations are the cause of a decline in standards in developing countries. They assert that the integration of global markets has allowed MNCs and TNCs to pressure low-income countries to relax environmental regulations and labor standards or risk losing jobs and international investment.

◼ PRIMARY SOURCE

Protesters smash the window of a McDonald's: Demonstrators smash windows of a McDonalds restaurant in downtown Gothenburg, Sweden. They are protesting globalization and the European Union during the June 2001 European Union summit that took place nearby. © PONTUS LUNDAHL/EPA/CORBIS.

◼ PRIMARY SOURCE

PROTESTERS SMASH THE WINDOW OF A MCDONALD'S

See primary source image.

SIGNIFICANCE

In 1999, in Seattle, Washington, the World Trade Organization met to discuss international trade rules. At this World Trade Organization conference, anti-globalization activists began to protest the disparity of income distribution between developed and developing countries, as well as the environmental impact of globalization. The demonstration, which began as a group of 150–250 demonstrators, swelled to thousands. Members of the group began to block traffic, smash storefront windows and spray graffiti. Continued clashes with police brought a response by the National Guard and police that included tear gas and arrests. The next large scale anti-globalization protests occurred in Prague in September 2000 at the World Trade Organization and International Monetary Fund summit. Prague police estimated that approximately 15,000 protesters were involved in the demonstration, many of which were neutralized by tear gas after trying to enter the summit. At subsequent meetings of international organizations, such as the European Union, activists targeted symbols of globalization in the form of American TNCs like McDonald's restaurants.

In June 2001, members of the European Union (EU) planned to meet in Gothenburg, Sweden. Several issues to be discussed at the summit included the expansion of the EU from fifteen to twenty-seven members. In addition, as U.S. President George W. Bush was to attend the summit, several issues regarding EU—U.S. relations were also on the agenda. The summit was set to establish a joint EU—U.S. declaration on the Middle East, as well as present the EU's displeasure with George Bush's decision to abandon the Kyoto Protocol which deals with environmental issues. As a result, the summit became a target for protesters. As the members of the EU and U.S. met in Gothenburg, Sweden, approximately 25,000 protesters began to congregate near the summit. Demonstrators began to vandalize shop windows, including a McDonald's restaurant, and create makeshift barricades from the tables and chairs taken from outside cafes. Some of the protesters threw stones and firecrackers at the police, leading to the shooting of three protesters and the injuring of police.

However, these protesters are not a cohesive group of likeminded activists. In fact, the protesters are a disparate group each with its own defining cause. Many of the protesters that engaged in violence in Prague and Gothenburg considered themselves anarchists. In addition to anarchists, those loosely incorporated protesters include environmentalists, opponents to free trade, and worker's rights advocates. The groups banded together to create massive displays against globalization, while promoting their own agendas. The groups share information regarding summits and organize to promote their own policies. By creating massive protests that consists of thousands of demonstrators, the groups gain media attention and the attention of those meeting at the various summits.

These protests gained more than publicity for the anti-globalization cause. In 2000, the coffee mogul Starbucks agreed to begin buying a limited amount of coffee determined by the activists to be the product of fair trade.

FURTHER RESOURCES
Periodicals

Ross, Robert J. S., and Anita Chan. "From North-South to South-South." *Foreign Affairs* (September 1, 2002).

Taylor, Timothy. "The Truth About Globalization." *Public Interest* (April 1, 2002).

Vayrynen, Raimo. "Anti-Globalization Movements at the Crossroads." *Kroc Institute Policy Briefs* (November 2000).

Web sites

CNN. "Three Protesters Shot at EU Summit." June 18, 2001. <http://transcripts.cnn.com/2001/WORLD/europe/06/16/eu.protests/> (accessed May 26, 2006).

Global Exhange. "Global Exchange and USFT Respond to Starbucks' Fair Trade Announcement." April 29, 2004. <http://www.globalexchange.org/campaigns/fairtrade/coffee/1795.html> (accessed May 26, 2006).

Anti-FTAA Protestors Clash with Police

Photograph

By: Spencer Platt

Date: November 20, 2003

Source: Photo by Spencer Platt/Getty Images.

About the Photographer: Spencer Platt is a staff photographer for Getty Images. Getty Images is a worldwide provider of visual content materials to advertisers, broadcasters, designers, magazines, new media organizations, newspapers, and producers.

INTRODUCTION

The Free Trade Area of the Americas (FTAA) is a proposed trade agreement originally intended to encompass all countries in North and South America other than Cuba. However, as of mid-2006, Brazil, Bolivia, Paraguay, Uruguay, and Venezuela had all dropped out of FTAA negotiations.

The FTAA is intended as an extension of the North American Free Trade Agreement between Canada, Mexico, and the United States. Its stated goal is to lower trade barriers between participating nations. Critics of NAFTA, who have also opposed the FTAA, have claimed that it encourages the migration of industrial production from the U.S. and Canada to Mexico and bankrupts Mexican farmers by forcing them to compete directly with heavily-subsidized U.S. agriculture. Defenders of NAFTA and the FTAA argue that such trade agreements, by allowing market principles to work on an international level, produce net gains in prosperity for all nations involved.

Opponents of FTAA, which include North American labor unions and middle-class activists as well as farmers and indigenous peasants across much of Latin America, have sought to block it through political lobbying, electoral processes (e.g., in Venezuela and Bolivia), and nonviolent public protest and civil disobedience at the sites of FTAA summit meetings. These summits are gatherings at which representatives of prospective member states negotiate the terms of a possible FTAA agreement.

PRIMARY SOURCE

Anti-FTAA Protestors Clash with Police: Police arrest an anti-globalization protester during the fourth day of the summit to create a Free Trade Area of the Americas, on November 20, 2003. PHOTO BY SPENCER PLATT/GETTY IMAGES.

The 2003 FTAA summit was held in Miami, Florida. (The city of Miami hoped that the FTAA headquarters would be built there and it offered to pay half of the estimated $12–16 million cost of building the facility.) The response of the city police to the protests that occurred during the summit was controversial. Miami spent almost $24 million on security for the FTAA summit ($10.6 million for the Miami-Dade County Police, $13 million for the Miami Police Department), not counting payments on lawsuits brought against city police. Lawsuits were brought for various violations of protestor's civil rights, including mass arrests and improper arrests; criminal violence by police; and illegal mass strip searches of female prisoners. Miami received $8.5 million in federal money from the $87-billion 2003 Iraq

spending bill to cover some of the costs of defending the FTAA meeting.

PRIMARY SOURCE

ANTI-FTAA PROTESTORS CLASH WITH POLICE
  See primary source image.

SIGNIFICANCE

Miami police forces were determined to avoid a repeat of the chaotic situation that surrounded the World Trade Organization meeting in Seattle in 1999. To this end, the actions of over three dozen law-enforcement agencies were coordinated by the

A protester wears a gas mask during a demonstration outside the site of the Organization of American States foreign ministers meeting in Windsor, Ontario, on June 4, 2000. AP IMAGES.

Miami Police Department. Police were equipped with concussion grenades, tear gas, body armor, tazers, and other gear. After being shown video footage of Seattle by the city police, the city commissioners passed a law forbidding protestors to carry sticks, water balloons, and other objects (the law was repealed by the commissioners a few months after the FTAA meeting, in March 2004).

Accusations of criminal behavior by the police were numerous. Alleged police crimes included shooting rubber-coated steel bullets at retreating (therefore non-threatening) protestors; spraying the eyes of non-resisting protestors at point-blank range with pepper spray, which causes extreme pain and sometimes permanent damage; arresting persons for not dispersing without giving them an opportunity to disperse; tazering and beating nonviolent protestors; arresting people for merely looking like protestors; targeting of medics

and journalists; and more. The human rights advocacy group Amnesty International stated in a December 16, 2005, letter to Governor Jeb Bush that police actions had violated the United Nations Basic Principles on the Use of Force and Firearms by Law Enforcement Officials: "Concerns include reports of the indiscriminate and inappropriate use of nonlethal weapons on nonviolent protestors resulting in scores of injuries, the obstruction of those providing medical treatment, multiple and random arrests ...and the denial of the right to freedom of expression and association." A Florida circuit court judge, Richard Margolius, stated in open court in December 2003 that he saw "no less than 20 felonies committed by police officers" during the protests. When told that no police officers had been charged in the protest crackdown he said, "None? Pretty sad commentary. At least from what I saw."

In April, 2005, several thousand women who were illegally strip-searched after being arrested on misdemeanor charges during the FTAA protests were awarded $6.25 million in a class-action lawsuit brought against Dade County, Florida. Only women were strip-searched, not men, apparently as a humiliation tactic. Under Florida law, it is only legal to strip-search a person charged with a felony.

The actual FTAA-protests operations plan of the Miami Police Department has remained secret, its exclusion from public records laws being affirmed by a Florida appeals court in April 2005. In 2005, other cities expecting to host controversial international economic organizations sent police representatives to Miami to study the operations plan and to model their own police responses to it. By May 2006, five lawsuits based on police actions during the protests had been brought against the Miami police and other law-enforcement agencies by the American Civil Liberties Union. As of this writing, all five cases were still being litigated.

An internal review of the response to the protests by the Miami Police Department admitted minor mistakes, but said that the response was "an overall success." It also stated that "The people and businesses of Miami faced a minimum of inconvenience with resiliency and good humor. Those who came to commit violence faced an intelligent, measured police plan determined to minimize the effect of their criminal tactics."

The FTAA summit at Mar Del Plata, Argentina, in November 2005 failed to produce an agreement. As of mid-2006, prospects for the formation of a Free Trade Area of the Americas appear dim.

FURTHER RESOURCES

Books

Vizentini, Paulo, and Marianne Wiesebron. *Free Trade for the Americas?: The United States' Push for the FTAA Agreement.* New York: Zed Books, 2004.

Periodicals

Driscoll, Amy. "Judge: I Saw Police Commit Felonies." *Miami Herald* (December 20, 2003).

Driscoll, Amy. "Ordinary People Join Protests." *Miami Herald* (November 19, 2003).

Marrero, Diana. "Security at Miami's Free Trade Meeting Cost Taxpayers $23.9 Million." *Miami Herald* (February 24, 2004).

Rodriguez, Ihosvani. "Appeals Court Protects Secrecy Involving Police Strategy for Miami Trade Talks." *South Florida Sun-Sentinel* (April 19, 2005).

Salazar, Caroly, and Susannah A. Neshmith. "Summit was 'Success,' Miami Police Conclude." *Miami Herald* (February 5, 2004).

Schwartz, Noaki, and Trenton Daniel. "Lawsuit on Strip Searches Settled." *Miami Herald.* April 19, 2005.

Web sites

American Civil Liberties Union. "Police Trampled Civil Rights During 2003 Free Trade Protests in Florida, ACLU Charges." November 17, 2005. <http://www.aclu.org/freespeech/gen/21621prs20051117.html> (accessed May 24, 2006).

National Lawyers' Guild. "The Assault on Free Speech, Public Assembly, and Dissent." <http://www.nlg.org/resources/DissentBookWeb.pdf> (accessed May 24, 2006).

Globalization: Environmental and Health Practices of American Companies Abroad

Photograph

By: Indranil Mukerjee

Date: August 14, 2003

Source: INDRANIL MUKHERJEE/AFP/Getty Images.

About the Photographer: Indranil Mukherjee is a professional photographer and journalist. This photograph is part of the collection at Getty Images, a worldwide provider of visual content materials to such communications groups as advertisers, broadcasters, designers, magazines, new media organizations, newspapers, and producers.

INTRODUCTION

Since the end of World War II, the world has engaged in an unparalleled transfer of currency, capital, trade, and human resources between countries, called globalization. This flow across borders has created debates about development, economic theory, and fair trade practices, due largely to its effect on workers and the environment in developing countries. Supporters of globalization assert that this transparent flow of trade and currency facilitates the expansion of economic growth and opportunities globally. Opponents to globalization maintain that it has promoted unfair labor and trade practices and environmentally harmful policies in developing countries. In addition, globalization has increased the income gap between high-income or developed countries, referred to as countries of the North, and low-income or developing nations, referred to as countries of the South (due to their relative geographic locations).

Globalization implies a global economy where goods and services move across borders without difficulty. This movement across borders includes investments, capital, labor, and technology. The phenomenon of globalization involves an increased integration of global economies in the form of advanced world trade and fast-moving international financial markets. Supporters of globalization maintain that globalization has also allowed the spreading of knowledge and democracy, which facilitates a robust, more widely employed workforce and, therefore, a future without conflict. Leading the globalization movement are multi-national corporations (MNCs) and trans-national corporations (TNCs). Opponents of globalization assert that these corporations are responsible for a continued decline in standards in developing countries. They suggest that the integration of global markets has allowed MNCs and TNCs to force developing countries in the South to relax regulations governing environmental and labor standards or risk losing international investment and jobs.

PRIMARY SOURCE

GLOBALIZATION: ENVIRONMENTAL AND HEALTH PRACTICES OF AMERICAN COMPANIES ABROAD
    See primary source image.

PRIMARY SOURCE

Globalization: Environmental and Health Practices of American Companies Abroad: An Indian schoolgirl stands behind signs asking if people will choose between "poison drinks" such as Pepsi and Coca-Cola or "healthy drinks" like lemon juice in Bangalore on August 14, 2003. This protest is part of a nationwide movement against Pepsi and Coca-Cola after reports found that these soft drinks sold in India have dangereous amounts of pesticides in them. INDRANIL MUKHERJEE/AFP/GETTY IMAGES.

SIGNIFICANCE

One of the leading TNCs expanding its global reach is the American based Coca-Cola Company. Coca-Cola operates in over 200 countries and possesses an iconic status due to its historical longevity and global reach. In 1999, the Coca-Cola company opened up a bottling facility in Plachimada, Palghat district, Kerala in India. The company located the factory amidst an agricultural region with access to common ground water. When the company began to access the groundwater, also accessed by local farmers, the corporation drew 1.5 million liters a day from the water resource. After six months of drawing from the local groundwater, the community began to feel the affects of the plant's activities. Villagers began to see a decrease in their water tables. The water shortage also affected Coke, as the company was only able to extract

800,000 liters per day. Local villagers affected by the decreased water supply claim that Coke's mining of groundwater has dried up and contaminated local wells. As a result, the Coke facility has been the site of continued protests.

The Coca-Cola Company addressed the water scarcity issue as a part of its 2005 annual report. The company provides two villages most affected by the water shortage with daily truckloads of water. However, many consider this a short-term cure to a larger issue. Protesters at the Coca-Cola plant accuse local leaders of corruption and collusion with the company. Protesters cite the lack of laws regulating private industries from extracting groundwater. However, officials have acted by closing the bottling facility, pending a courts decision on the fate of the plant. The Coca-Cola company has also begun to work

Global Business Coalition President and CEO Richard Holbrooke, Secretary of State Condoleeza Rice and Senator Hillary Clinton speak during the Global Business Coalition Gala Awards in Washington, September 28, 2005. AP IMAGES.

with environmentally minded non-governmental groups, such as the World Wildlife Fund and CARE, implement new water resource policies that will capture enough water without affecting the local environment.

In addition to the water shortage issue, the Coca-Cola Company was also cited for the presence of pesticides in its products. The Centre for Science and Environment, located in New Delhi, conducted research on the top soda brands marketed in India by Coca-Cola and PepsiCo. The study showed elevated levels of insecticides and pesticides in the sodas. The insecticides DDT, malathion, lindane, and chloropyrifos were present in 81 percent of samples tested. A Delhi High Court mandated retest resulted in a confirmation of the original tests results. The initial publication of these results resulted in an initial decrease in the sales of sodas in India. However, subsequent tests revealed that the insecticides and pesticides were

present in the groundwater extracted locally, not added by the companies.

The increased movement of goods and services created by globalization has created an unprecedented openness among countries. It has also led to increasing competition between different countries and regions for factories, jobs, and tax revenue. Given these competitive pressures, many countries have resisted efforts to improve environmental and labor standards for fear that they will drive up costs and hurt their ability to compete in the global marketplace. Those who support the implementation of international fair labor standards and environmental regulations argue that the lack of such standards and regulations propels the developing countries toward lower wages and declining environments.

Those who oppose globalization suggest that the concern regarding environmental exploitation is not merely a production issue. These groups cite that the control of a nation's natural resources, such as oil, diamonds, water and timber frequently lead to civil wars and unrest. As natural resources become scarcer and the global population increases, the threat of continued conflict remains due to the struggle to possess control over these resources.

FURTHER RESOURCES
Periodicals

Ross, Robert J S; Chan, Anita. "From North-South to South-South." *Foreign Affairs*. September 1, 2002.

Taylor, Timothy. "The Truth about Globalization." *Public Interest*. April 1, 2002.

Indonesian Village Chiefs Protest Pulp Mill

Anti-World Bank Protests

Photograph

By: Bay Ismoyo

Date: June 13, 2003

Source: BAY ISMOYO/AFP/Getty Images.

About the Photographer: Bay Ismoyo is a photographer for Getty Images, a worldwide provider of visual content materials to such communications groups as advertisers, broadcasters, designers, magazines, new media organizations, newspapers, and producers.

INTRODUCTION

The World Bank is an international organization that loans money to the governments of poorer nations. Although technically a United Nations project (formed 1944), it is in practice run by its member states, whose voting power is proportional to the amount of money they invest in the bank. Thus, the United States holds over sixteen percent of voting power at the World Bank, more than twice as much as its next most powerful member, Japan (with 8% of voting power). This gives the U.S. an automatic veto of World Bank decisions; moreover, the World Bank president has always been an American nominated by the American president.

The stated purpose of the Bank is to lend money for development projects such as dams, utilities, factories, agriculture, and so forth, with the ostensible goal of reducing poverty worldwide. Virtually all the loans made by the Bank are to poor countries in Asia, Africa, and South America. However, the Bank is a controversial institution. Critics argue that it imposes a free-

trade ideology on debtor nations that does not relieve poverty but instead deepens poverty while allowing transnational corporations to make greater profits, often at the expense of local human rights. Critics charge that the Bank causes a net reverse flow of money to the rich nations in the form of interest payments on unpayable debts.

The Bank itself has admitted several mistakes. One was its backing of the Indonesian transmigration program in the 1970 and 1980s, which sought to resettle 65 million people from the most densely populated islands of the archipelago to more rural islands. The result is widely acknowledged as disastrous, with poorly-planned agricultural settlements failing and indigenous peoples displaced by waves of government-backed newcomers. Another Indonesian case of controversial World Bank funding is the pulp operation run by PT Inti Indorayon Utama starting in the 1980s in the remote Toba-Samosir regency in North Sumatra. The purpose of the operation was to produce approximately 90,000 to 100,000 tons of wood pulp per year, seventy percent for export to China, South Korea, and Taiwan. The operation also produced rayon, a synthetic fiber derived from wood cellulose and used to make clothing. Operations commenced in the early 1980s, but by 1986 conflicts between the company and the rural villagers around the operation began to intensify. Villagers accused the company of clearing community lands for planting eucalyptus trees for pulp and dumping toxic waste into local rivers and Lake Toba, one of the world's largest lakes. Tens of thousands of people joined in the protests and some were imprisoned, beaten, or shot by security forces.

Protests and road blockades shut down the PT Indorayon plant in 1999. In 2002, the government announced its intention to reopen the plant (then renamed PT Toba Pulp Lestari, PTL). Protests and blockades resumed, along with arrests and beatings of villagers. In June 2003, the heads of fifty-two villages in the area of the plant traveled to Jakarta, the capital of Indonesia, to protest the plant reopening. One was quoted in the Indonesian press as saying, "There is no point in us continuing to go about our everyday affairs if the government does not listen to the views of our people, who have consistently demanded a permanent closure of the pulp mill."

PRIMARY SOURCE

INDONESIAN VILLAGE CHIEFS PROTEST PULP MILL
See primary source image.

SIGNIFICANCE

The World Bank has long operated on the Washington Consensus, a set of policies based on capitalist theories of economics which shape the conditions that the bank imposes on borrowing nations. Through lists of demands called Structural Adjustment Programs, the Bank requires borrowing governments to lift trade barriers, deregulate markets, sell off state-owned assets such as utilities and water supplies, and cut aid to the poor. The ostensible goal of structural adjustment is to alleviate poverty by promoting growth through industrial developments such as the pulp and rayon operations in northern Sumatra. However, these policies have been cited by movements resisting free-market globalization. Such discontent contributed to the election in the early 2000s of a number of leftist, anti-globalization presidents in Latin America (e.g., Evo Morales in Guatemala, who nationalized the natural-gas industry in early 2006). The anti-globalization movement has charged that the rich countries have run the World Bank to enrich themselves at the expense of poorer nations.

In February, 2006, the World Bank released a report admitting that two decades of the Washington Consensus had not cut poverty in one of the world's poorest regions, Latin America, but worsened it. The report, apparently questioning free-market doctrines promoted by the Bank for decades, stated that private-sector growth does not necessarily relieve poverty and that policies must directly target inequity (rather than trusting to the invisible hand of the market to distribute benefits). Moreover, it argued that governments must do more, not less, to control economies: "Converting the state into an agent that promotes equality of opportunities and practices efficient redistribution is, perhaps, the most critical challenge Latin America faces in implementing better policies that simultaneously promote growth and reduce inequality and poverty" (quoted in "Breaking Ranks at the World Bank," the *Washington Post*, Feb. 17, 2006).

Nevertheless, opposition to the TPL pulp plant in Indonesia remains stalled. The Indonesian government, which has been repeatedly penalized in recent years by the World Bank and International Monetary Fund for official corruption, has been historically unwilling to enforce environmental laws or to side with rural peoples against corporations, which can afford to pay cash bribes to military and political figures.

■ PRIMARY SOURCE

Indonesian Village Chiefs Protest Pulp Mill: Indonesian local village chiefs from Toba Samosir, North Sumatra, protest against the Indonesian government reopening of pulp company PT Inti Indorayon Utama, outside the presidential palace in Jakarta, June 13, 2003. BAY ISMOYO/AFP/GETTY IMAGES.

FURTHER RESOURCES
Books
Woods, Ngaire. *The Globalizers: The IMF, the World Bank, and Their Borrowers*. Ithaca, NY: Cornell University Press, 2006.

Periodicals
Sanchez, Marcela. "Breaking Ranks at the World Bank." *The Washington Post*. February 17, 2006.

Web sites
Trudeau Centre for Peace and Conflict Studies, U. of Toronto. "Environmental Scarcities, State Capacity and Civil Violence: The Case of Indonesia." May, 1997. <http://www.library.utoronto.ca/pcs/state/indon/indon3.htm> (accessed May 26, 2006).

A boy searches for food in a garbage pile while a rally against the Haitian government's internationally-supported privatization plan passes by on May 1, 1996. AP IMAGES.

Communities Oppose Wal-Mart

Photograph

By: Scott Olsen

Date: May 26, 2004

Source: Photo by Scott Olson/Getty Images.

About the Photographer: This photograph is part of the collection maintained at Getty Images, a worldwide provider of visual content materials to such communications groups as advertisers, broadcasters, designers, magazines, new media organizations, newspapers, and producers. The photographer, Scott Olsen, is a freelance photojournalist based in Chicago, Illinois.

INTRODUCTION

Wal-Mart is the best known retail company in North America. It is the largest private employer in the United States, operating almost 4,000 stores and warehouse outlets. Wal-Mart has expanded at a rate that has approached sixty stores per month at various times since the year 2000.

The core philosophy of Wal-Mart is to provide a wide range of consumer goods to the public at the lowest possible price, with a corresponding emphasis on customer service. Wal-Mart has an unsurpassed purchasing power in the manufacturing sector. Having goods offered for sale in Wal-Mart stores is an important factor in the success of many producers of consumer goods. An example of Wal-Mart's market dominance is illustrated by the agreement signed by American country music singer Garth Brooks with Wal-Mart in 2005, making the retailer the exclusive vendor of his music.

The rise of Wal-Mart from a single retail outlet located in Rogers, Arkansas, in 1962 to its position as one of the world's most powerful companies occurred in a span of less than forty years. In many North American cities, Wal-Mart expansion plans invariably attract both supporters and detractors. The debates about the location of a Wal-Mart store in an urban area are often particularly volatile, since a wide range of issues are raised, including the nature of the jobs created in the proposed stores, the non-union work-force policy of Wal-Mart generally, and the impact of the full service Wal-Marts on existing businesses and neighborhoods.

In 2004, Wal-Mart had approximately fifty stores located in the greater Chicago area. The company decided that it wanted to build two new stores within the city limits of Chicago, one on the south side and one on the west side. For most of its history, Wal-Mart's policy was to locate its stores in rural or suburban areas to take advantage of generally lower land acquisition and labor costs. Each of the proposed Chicago Wal-Marts required the approval of a re-zoning application to permit the land to be used for this large-scale, commercial purpose.

Both of the Chicago neighborhoods selected by Wal-Mart were historically disadvantaged. Each area had a largely African American population, a segment of the community that Wal-Mart opponents have charged is under-represented in the Wal-Mart workforce. Prior to the formal hearing of the re-zoning applications, Wal-Mart made a concerted effort to demonstrate a commitment to these communities, through both advertising and contributions to local religious and educational groups.

The battle lines in each re-zoning application were clearly drawn. Wal-Mart, supported by a number of local Chicago politicians, argued that the new stores would have a positive economic impact on each community. Wal-Mart claimed that the employees for the new store would be hired primarily from the local community. The political supporters of Wal-Mart pointed to the construction jobs that would be created by the projects themselves, as well as the likelihood that other retail businesses would establish themselves in close proximity to Wal-Mart.

A coalition of community and labor groups opposed the construction of the two new Chicago Wal-Marts. The community groups saw a negative impact on the existing community, fearing that local businesses would be destroyed by Wal-Mart. Labor unions used the re-zoning applications as an opportunity to criticize Wal-Mart for its aggressive opposition to unionized workers anywhere in its empire, as well as to point out what the labor interests described as the low wages and poor benefits of Wal-Mart employees.

PRIMARY SOURCE

COMMUNITIES OPPOSE WAL-MART

See primary source image.

SIGNIFICANCE

Shortly after this photograph was taken on May 26, 2004, a split decision was rendered in the fight to establish Wal-Mart stores within Chicago's city limits. The west side proposal was approved, while the south side application failed to pass the Chicago assembly.

The events in Chicago represent in microcosm the issues facing Wal-Mart's expansion into large urban centers across North America. In each case, the issues are the same—a large, successful retailer engenders fear that a local commercial landscape will be irrevocably changed by its presence in an area. Community opponents of Wal-Mart developments often argue that "big box" stores destroy the economic viability of an older commercial district in an urban area.

A second question that is inextricably linked to Wal-Mart's commercial power concerns what protection, if any, a local government should provide to other retailers who are not able to offer comparable goods for sale as cheaply as Wal-Mart or its large scale competition, such as Target and Costco. This question, in turn, requires consideration of the reasons why Wal-Mart occupies such a pre-eminent position in the retail market, involving such issues as Wal-Mart's policies concerning its workforce. These debates are often focused on what Wal-Mart stands for, rather than on the merits of a particular local re-zoning application.

Given its buying power, Wal-Mart can in many cases dictate the terms upon which it purchases goods from manufacturers. Wal-Mart asserts that it must seek the lowest possible price because its customers demand these kinds of goods; to do otherwise would be bad business. Since its founding, Wal-Mart has operated under the theory that consumers are more interested in buying cheap and

PRIMARY SOURCE

Communities Oppose Wal-Mart: Signs confiscated from protestors entering a meeting of the Chicago City Council lie on the floor outside the council chambers, May 26, 2004. PHOTO BY SCOTT OLSON/GETTY IMAGES.

reliable goods than in purchasing a particular product brand. It is the volume of sales that makes Wal-Mart profitable—the company earns less than four cents in margin for each dollar of revenue generated.

Much of the Chicago opposition focused on the wages to be paid in the proposed stores. The labor groups that worked to defeat the Wal-Mart applications pointed to the aggressive anti-union history of the company; at the time of the Chicago applications, no Wal-Mart store anywhere in North America had successfully unionized. Wal-Mart maintained that its employees received wages comparable to the rest of the North American retail sector.

Wal-Mart's attitude towards unions was demonstrated in a dispute at the Wal-Mart store in Jonquiere, Quebec, Canada, in 2005. The company

closed its store there after an employee union was certified in accordance with Quebec labor law. Wal-Mart claimed that the unionization of the store and the union demand that thirty more employees be hired rendered the store unprofitable. The battle created a division between the Wal-Mart employees in Jonquiere. Some believed that Wal-Mart closed the store to demonstrate the extreme measures it was prepared to take to combat unionization of its workforce, while others believed that the margins in the retail industry are so slender that the additional costs traditionally associated with unionized workforces cannot be sustained. Even after the store closed, these questions remained open.

Wal-Mart lost its south side Chicago zoning application battle, but it may ultimately have won the regional retail war. Wal-Mart built a large store within four miles of the proposed south side site, outside of the Chicago city limits where it could obtain the necessary municipal approvals more readily.

FURTHER RESOURCES

Books

Dicker, John. *United States of Wal-Mart*. New York: Penguin Books, 2005.

Fishman, Charles. *The Wal-Mart Effect: How the World's Most Successful Company Really Works—and How It's Transforming the American Economy*. New York: Penguin, 2006.

Zukin, Sharon. *Point of Purchase: How Shopping Changed America*. New York: Routledge, 2004.

Periodicals

Struck, Doug. "Wal-Mart Leaves Bitter Chill/Quebec Store Closes after Vote to Unionize." *Washington Post* (April 14, 2005): E1.

Surowiecki, James. "The Customer Is King." *The New Yorker* (February 14, 2005).

Web sites

Swanson, Al. "Analysis: Wal-Mart Keeps Coming." *Washington Times* June 3, 2004. <http://www.washtimes.com/upi-breaking/20040603-024504-8072r.htm> (accessed June 2, 2006).

7 Sovereignty

Sovereignty

The desire of a people for a homeland, self-government, or tribal or national sovereignty is among the leading instigators for protest, conflict, and war throughout recorded history. In the modern age, pleas for autonomy often begin as protests of government policy. When such appeals are repeatedly suppressed, when declarations of independence and self-government are ignored, sovereignty movements often wage war. Religion, ethnicity, history, imperialism, and race often fan the fires of many of these conflicts. Great nations and peoples have begun their quest for independence with protest. The American Revolution gained momentum from colonial protests over the Sugar and Stamp Acts. Two of the seminal events of the era, the Boston Tea Party (featured in this chapter) and the signing of the Declaration of Independence are both examples of protests for sovereignty.

While many such movements have led to bloodshed and war, a few have achieved their goals through non-violent revolution. Included in this chapter is the Dandi March, a peaceful protest of British imperial policies in India that sparked the movement for Indian independence.

Also profiled in this chapter are several sources on the Israeli-Palestinian conflict, from the formation of the nation of Israel to the 2005 removal of Jewish settlements in the Gaza Strip. Settlers resisting removal by members of the Israeli Defense Force invoked haunting images of the Holocaust to peacefully protest Israeli disengagement policies.

Since sovereignty movements often culminate with violent conflict, some individuals who were once dissidents or protesters are likely to later be called separatists, combatants, insurgents, freedom fighters, or terrorists. Though it may be cliché to claim "one man's terrorist is another's freedom fighter," the maxim does hold some truth. Much of how protests—and even warfare—for sovereignty are memorialized in history books depends on the perspective of the author. "The IRA Hunger Strikers" illustrates this grave juxtaposition of protest, terrorism, and the fight for autonomy.

The editors do not condone terrorism; violent acts against innocent civilians intended to induce fear are not legitimate acts of protest. However, it is left to readers to decide when actions move beyond justified protest into acts of riot or terrorism. The reader should understand that with many of these issues there are varying degrees of opposition—from non-violent protest to paramilitary action—and that acts of the most extremist and violent fringes should not dilute the message or actions of peaceful protesters who espouse the same cause.

The Boston Tea Party

Book excerpt

By: George R. T. Hewes

Date: 1834

Source: Hawkes, James A. *Retrospect of the Boston Tea Party, with a Memoir of George R. T. Hewes* ... New York: S. S. Bliss, 1834.

About the Author: George R. T. Hewes was a shoemaker who lived in Boston, Massachusetts, during the mid–1700s. He both witnessed and participated in several of the major revolutionary events of that time period, including the Boston Massacre and the Boston Tea Party. He later provided historian James Hawkes with an account of his experiences.

INTRODUCTION

The Boston Tea Party was one of several events leading up to the start of the American Revolutionary War. In the 1760s, the British passed several laws that regulated taxes on the colonists, including the Sugar Act of 1764, taxing sugar, coffee, and wine; the Stamp Act of 1765, which taxed items such as newspapers and playing cards; and the Townshend Acts of 1767, which levied taxes on glass, lead, paint, paper, and tea. The money raised by the taxes was supposedly to cover the cost of governing the colonies. At the same time, colonists were denied representation in the British parliament.

This lack of representation led to numerous pre-Revolution protests, most notably that led by John Hancock (1737–1793). Hancock organized a boycott of tea provided by the East India Company, which was subject to an import tax, and helped to enforce the boycott by smuggling tea in so that the colonists would not go without their favored beverage. The result was the Tea Act, passed by the British to enable the East India Company to sell directly to the colonies. Most American ports refused to allow the ships bringing in the tea to land, however, the British-appointed governor in Boston, Governor Hutchinson, assisted the tea merchants. The tea would be brought ashore by force, and the British military docked at the wharf would provide backup. The Boston Tea Party resulted from the colonists' refusal to allow the British governor or the East India Company to force them to accept the merchandise.

PRIMARY SOURCE

The tea destroyed was contained in three ships, lying near each other at what was called at that time Griffin's wharf, and were surrounded by armed ships of war, the commanders of which had publicly declared that if the rebels, as they were pleased to style the Bostonians, should not withdraw their opposition to the landing of the tea before a certain day, the 17th day of December, 1773, they should on that day force it on shore, under the cover of their cannon's mouth.

On the day preceding the seventeenth, there was a meeting of the citizens of the county of Suffolk, convened at one of the churches in Boston, for the purpose of consulting on what measures might be considered expedient to prevent the landing of the tea, or secure the people from the collection of the duty. At that meeting a committee was appointed to wait on Governor Hutchinson, and request him to inform them whether he would take any measures to satisfy the people on the object of the meeting.

To the first application of this committee, the Governor told them he would give them a definite answer by five o'clock in the afternoon. At the hour appointed, the committee again repaired to the Governor's house, and on inquiry found he had gone to his country seat at Milton, a distance of about six miles. When the committee returned and informed the meeting of the absence of the Governor, there was a confused murmur among the members, and the meeting was immediately dissolved, many of them crying out, "Let every man do his duty, and be true to his country"; and there was a general huzza for Griffin's wharf.

It was now evening, and I immediately dressed myself in the costume of an Indian, equipped with a small hatchet, which I and my associates denominated the tomahawk, with which, and a club, after having painted my face and hands with coal dust in the shop of a blacksmith, I repaired to Griffin's wharf, where the ships lay that contained the tea. When I first appeared in the street after being thus disguised, I fell in with many who were dressed, equipped and painted as I was, and who fell in with me and marched in order to the place of our destination.

When we arrived at the wharf, there were three of our number who assumed an authority to direct our operations, to which we readily submitted. They divided us into three parties, for the purpose of boarding the three ships which contained the tea at the same time. The name of him who commanded the division to which I was assigned was Leonard Pitt. The names of the other commanders I never knew.

We were immediately ordered by the respective commanders to board all the ships at the same time, which we promptly obeyed. The commander of the

A reproduction of a Currier and Ives lithograph depicting the Boston Tea Party. © BETTMANN/CORBIS.

division to which I belonged, as soon as we were on board the ship appointed me boatswain, and ordered me to go to the captain and demand of him the keys to the hatches and a dozen candles. I made the demand accordingly, and the captain promptly replied, and delivered the articles; but requested me at the same time to do no damage to the ship or rigging.

We then were ordered by our commander to open the hatches and take out all the chests of tea and throw them overboard, and we immediately proceeded to execute his orders, first cutting and splitting the chests with our tomahawks, so as thoroughly to expose them to the effects of the water.

In about three hours from the time we went on board, we had thus broken and thrown overboard every tea chest to be found in the ship, while those in the other ships were disposing of the tea in the same way, at the same time. We were surrounded by British armed ships, but no attempt was made to resist us.

We then quietly retired to our several places of residence, without having any conversation with each other, or taking any measures to discover who were our associates; nor do I recollect of our having had the knowledge of the name of a single individual concerned in that affair,

except that of Leonard Pitt, the commander of my division, whom I have mentioned. There appeared to be an understanding that each individual should volunteer his services, keep his own secret, and risk the consequence for himself. No disorder took place during that transaction, and it was observed at that time that the stillest night ensued that Boston had enjoyed for many months.

During the time we were throwing the tea overboard, there were several attempts made by some of the citizens of Boston and its vicinity to carry off small quantities of it for their family use. To effect that object, they would watch their opportunity to snatch up a handful from the deck, where it became plentifully scattered, and put it into their pockets.

One Captain O'Connor, whom I well knew, came on board for that purpose, and when he supposed he was not noticed, filled his pockets, and also the lining of his coat. But I had detected him and gave information to the captain of what he was doing. We were ordered to take him into custody, and just as he was stepping from the vessel, I seized him by the skirt of his coat, and in attempting to pull him back, I tore it off; but, springing forward, by a rapid effort he made his escape. He had, however, to run a gauntlet through the crowd upon the wharf nine each one, as he passed, giving him a kick or a stroke.

Another attempt was made to save a little tea from the ruins of the cargo by a tall, aged man who wore a large cocked hat and white wig, which was fashionable at that time. He had sleightly slipped a little into his pocket, but being detected, they seized him and, taking his hat and wig from his head, threw them, together with the tea, of which they had emptied his pockets, into the water. In consideration of his advanced age, he was permitted to escape, with now and then a slight kick.

The next morning, after we had cleared the ships of the tea, it was discovered that very considerable quantities of it were floating upon the surface of the water; and to prevent the possibility of any of its being saved for use, a number of small boats were manned by sailors and citizens, who rowed them into those parts of the harbor wherever the tea was visible, and by beating it with oars and paddles so thoroughly drenched it as to render its entire destruction inevitable.

SIGNIFICANCE

Compared to many of the other events leading up to the start of the Revolutionary War, the Boston Tea Party was a peaceful, quiet protest—no one was injured or killed and damage was minimal. In addition, the action was the colonists' last resort, following their attempts to go through proper channels by appealing to Governor Hutchinson to intervene regarding the threatened unloading of the tea. Only after this attempt failed did the colonists finally decide to take matters into their own hands. The colonists gathered at the South Meeting House before heading to the wharf. Although it has not been proved, Samuel Adams (1722–1803) is rumored to have been the organizing force behind the protest. The participants, known as the Sons of Liberty, dressed as Mohawk Indians as a way to disguise their identities rather than attempting to actually impersonate Indians or to appear more frightening. During the event itself, they remained focused on their task, destroying the tea by throwing it off of the ships in the harbor. A total of forty-five tons of tea was dumped off of the three ships. The colonists carefully guarded against theft for personal gain or any other type of illegal activity, their goal being to make a political statement, not to be labeled as criminals.

The Boston Tea Party engendered mixed reactions. Some colonists felt that vandalism of any sort, even the destruction of the tea, was inappropriate behavior. Benjamin Franklin (1706–1790) went so far as to offer to compensate the East India Company for their monetary loss. Prior to the protest, the East India Company had been experiencing financial difficulties due to mismanagement and corruption. This was a part of the reason that the company had been so anxious to maintain a monopoly on tea sales to the colonies. The British labeled the colonists as criminals and accused them of behaving as spoiled children. They retaliated by enacting the Coercive Acts, also known as the Intolerable Acts, by way of punishment. These acts included a bill that banned the port in Boston from loading or unloading any ship in Boston harbor. Any royal official in Massachusetts was offered protection, and any court cases dealing with the suppression of riots or tax collection were remanded to England. As a final blow, the British took over the appointment of Massachusetts' government officials, essentially stripping the colony of its government charter.

Not all of the results were negative, however. Other colonial ports took note of the events of the Boston Tea Party and, sympathizing with the Boston colonists, began taking a stronger stand in their own harbors. Tax collectors working for the British governors found it more difficult than ever to collect revenue, and some were even tarred and feathered. Tension escalated as the colonists resisted the stricter edicts set by the British government. This led to more protests and, eventually, to the formation of the First Continental Congress as a means of organizing the colonies to present a unified front in their rebellion against Britain. After that it was only a matter of months before the colonists went to war against the British.

FURTHER RESOURCES
Books
Young, Alfred F. *The Shoemaker and the Tea Party: Memory and the American Revolution*. Boston, Mass.: Beacon Press, 2000.

Web sites
Boston Tea Party Historical Society. "The Boston Tea Party." <http://www.boston-tea-party.org/> (accessed May 24, 2006).

University of Virginia. Institute for Advanced Technology in the Humanities. "Resistance to Revolution." <http://www.iath.virginia.edu/seminar/unit1/mob.html> (accessed May 24, 2006).

Petition Against the Annexation of Hawaii

Photograph

By: Anonymous

Date: September 11, 1897

Source: "Petition Against the Annexation of Hawaii." *Records of the U.S. Senate: National Archives and Records Administration* (September 11, 1897) Record Group 46. Courtesy of the National Archives and Records Administration.

About the Photographer: The United States National Archives and Records Administration (NARA) is an independent agency of the U.S. federal government. The NARA is responsible for documenting and preserving governmental and historical records such as presidential proclamations and executive orders, Congressional acts, and federal regulations.

INTRODUCTION

In 1891, Queen Lili'uokalani (1838–1917) was the reigning monarch of Hawaii (locally spelled Hawai'i). However, the previous government—led by her brother King David Kalakaua (1836–1891) from 1874 to 1891—had continuing disputes with American and European businesspersons who were doing business in Hawaii, primarily in the agricultural industry as owners of sugar cane plantations. By the end of the 1890s, non-native white farmers and businesspersons had taken control over most of Hawaii's privately held land.

King Kalakaua's primary goal was to preserve Hawaii's culture, which ran against powerful American and European goals. During this time, the Hawaiian economy increasingly relied on trade with the United States. Trade agreements eventually helped sugar plantation owners dominate the local economies and national politics. Perceiving the King as dishonest, unreliable, and anti-American, and wanting large tariffs to be removed from their sugar sales, a group of American and European business leaders gained control of the monarch with assistance of an armed militia. A new constitution was implemented—called the Bayonet Constitution because it was signed by Kalakaua against his wishes—which limited the authority of the King's government, focused power with wealthy white land owners, and eliminated many rights from native Hawaiians.

When Queen Lili'uokalani accepted her country's leadership upon her brother's death, she attempted to return power to the native Hawaiians and resume friendly relations with the American and European business and political leaders. However, on January 16–17, 1893, a group of American sugar farmers and business leaders, along with the help of U.S. Minister to Hawaii John Stevens and Marines from the *U.S.S. Boston*, deposed Lili'uokalani and overthrew her monarchy. They established a new government headed by Sanford Ballard Dole (1844–1926), an attorney, justice, and former advisor to the monarch. Without approval from the U.S. State Department, Stevens recognized the new government and declared Hawaii, as of February 1, 1893, to be a protectorate of the United States.

Immediately, the leaders of the new government negotiated a treaty of annexation with the United States. However, President Grover Cleveland, who had succeeded President Benjamin Harrison in March 1893, did not agree with their imperialistic acts. After deciding that Stevens' actions were inappropriate, Cleveland stopped the treaty and ordered Queen Lili'uokalani to be returned to the throne. Unfortunately, Dole and the Hawaiian revolutionaries ignored his demands, stating that the United States did not have the right to interfere with internal Hawaiian affairs. Instead, they developed plans to make Hawaii an independent republic. On May 30, 1894, a constitutional convention was assembled and, on July 4, 1894, the new constitution took effect with Dole as the country's president. The United States recognized the Republic of Hawaii.

During the next three years, the native Hawaiians protested the overthrow of the Lili'uokalani government and the possible annexation of Hawaii. In particular, on January 5, 1895, native Hawaiian protestors used violence in an attempt to stop annexation plans. However, the violence was quelled by governmental forces, with leaders of the revolt and Queen Lili'uokalani jailed.

In March 1897, William McKinley, who succeeded Cleveland as president, held the opposite view of Cleveland—he wanted to annex Hawaii. On June 16, 1897, McKinley and Hawaiian representatives signed a treaty of annexation. However, native male Hawaiians formed the *Hui Hawaii Aloha Aina* (loosely translated as Hawaiian Patriotic League) and native female Hawaiians formed the *Hui Hawaii Aloha Aina o Na Wahine* in order to block the annexation. The two groups conducted a petition drive from September 11 to October 2, 1897, hoping to show the U.S. government that most Hawaiians were opposed to annexation. They collected over 21,000 signatures from natives on the five main Hawaiian islands—or more than fifty percent of all native Hawaiians. The Petition Against Annexation helped lobbying efforts to convince members of the U.S. Congress not to ratify the annexation treaty. On February 27, 1898, only forty-six senators voted for annexation, less than the two-thirds majority needed for approval.

PRIMARY SOURCE

PETITION AGAINST ANNEXATION OF HAWAII
See primary source image.

PRIMARY SOURCE

Petition Against Annexation of Hawaii: Page 6 of Men's Petition Against Annexation of Hawaii, September 11, 1897. COURTESY OF THE NATIONAL ARCHIVES AND RECORDS ADMINISTRATION.

During Hawaii's annexation ceremony, the Republic of Hawaii's flag is removed from a flag pole at Lolani Palace in Honnolulu on August 12, 1898. AP IMAGES.

SIGNIFICANCE

The struggle to stop annexation by members of the Hawaiian Patriotic League and their female counterparts, along with lobbying efforts by the native Hawaiian representatives, did not last long. On February 15, 1898, the U.S.S. Maine was destroyed in Havana harbor in Cuba, which provoked the Spanish American War. With much of the fighting around the Philippine Islands, the United States needed a fueling station and naval base in the Pacific Ocean. U.S. political and military leaders saw that Hawaii was best positioned strategically for those needs. The U.S. Congress—needing only a simple majority in both houses—approved the annexation of Hawaii. The president signed the resolution on July 7, 1898, and the transfer of power was held on August 12, 1898. On June 14, 1900, Hawaii became a U.S. territory, with its people now considered U.S. citizens and Dole appointed territorial governor. The resolution ceded 1.8 million acres (728,400 hectares) of the Hawaiian lands—nearly fifty percent of the total—to the United States. However, the native Hawaiians and their government never directly relinquished their claims, nor were they ever compensated for their lands and possessions.

From 1900 to 1959, Hawaii remained a U.S. territory. Hawaii was admitted as the fiftieth state of the United States on August 21, 1959. Active opposition to statehood occurred on that day in Hawaii.

The petition against annexation of Hawaii by the United States on September 11, 1897, was an attempt by native Hawaiians to preserve their cultural heritage, to maintain their national identity, and to prevent further power to be gained by white businesspersons. The majority of native Hawaiians were against annexation of their land to the United States. However, the actions of the white businesspeople driven by their monetary goals were stronger than the actions of the native Hawaiian people with their cultural goals.

On November 23, 1993, the U.S. Congress passed a joint resolution that was signed by President William Clinton. The Apology Resolution, named Public Law No. 103–150, acknowledged that the United States acted improperly in its role supporting the overthrow of Hawaii, and acknowledged the ramifications of the illegal overthrow in 1893. The apology was a first step in the reconciliation process of the United States toward Hawaii.

Now, in the early years of the twenty-first century, citizens of Hawaii are divided with respect to their future and their state's relationship with the United States. Three major divisions have arisen with the following desires: (1) a country-within-a-country arrangement, similar to the one granted to the American Indians and Alaska Natives, (2) secession from the United States, with independent nationhood status, and (3) abolishment of any Native Hawaiian entitlement programs. Civil rights and self-determination continue to be difficult questions being asked by Hawaiians. As the petition against the annexation of Hawaii showed in 1897, Hawaiians still struggle to preserve their culture, heritage, and identity. Some believe that native Hawaiians have been able to preserve their culture, while others believe that because of the large number of immigrants and the U.S. domination of their land, native Hawaiians have lost their identities. Some even consider native Hawaiians as outsiders in their own land. Over the years, native Hawaiians have lost economic and political power to more affluent immigrant inhabitants.

FURTHER RESOURCES
Books

Bell, Roger John. *Last Among Equals: Hawaiian Statehood and American Politics*. Honolulu, Hawaii: University of Hawaii Press, 1984.

Liliuokalani, Queen of Hawaii. *Hawaii's Story by Hawaii's Queen*. Rutland, Vt.: C.E. Tuttle Co., 1964.

Tate, Merze. *The United States and the Hawaiian Kingdom: A Political History*. New Haven, Conn.: Yale University Press, 1965.

Web sites

Hawaii Advisory Committee to the U.S. Commission on Civil Rights, National Asian American Pacific Islander Mental Health Association. "Reconciliation at a Crossroads: The Implications of the Apology Resolution and *Rice v. Cayetano* for Federal and State Programs Benefiting Native Hawaiians." June 2001. <http://www.naapimha.org/issues/Reconciliation-Crossroads.pdf> (accessed May 31, 2006).

PBS (Public Broadcasting Service) Online, WGBH Educational Foundation. "Hawaii's Last Queen." <http://www.pbs.org/wgbh/amex/hawaii> (accessed May 31, 2006).

University of Hawaii at Manoa Library. "The Annexation Of Hawaii: A Collection Of Documents." <http://libweb.hawaii.edu/digicoll/annexation/annexation.html> (accessed May 31, 2006).

Dandi March

Photograph

By: Anonymous

Date: April 7, 1930

Source: © Bettmann/Corbis.

About the Photographer: This photograph is part of the collection of the Corbis Corporation, headquartered in Seattle, with a worldwide archive of over 70 million images.

INTRODUCTION

During the eighteenth and nineteenth centuries, India was ruled by the British. Considered to be among the most significant movements in the world, the Indian independence struggle began on May 10, 1857, when a few Indian soldiers in the British Indian Army united to rebel against the rulers. Known as 'India's First War of Independence,' this uprising paved the way for future rebellions against British rule. For many years after the Revolt of 1857, there was a growing political and social awareness in India, and Indian leadership emerged at the national and provincial levels.

In 1885, the Indian National Congress (INC) was established with a fundamental motive of developing an Indian presence in legislative councils, universities, and special commissions. By 1900, led by the INC (or Congress), now a national political organization, the Indian Independence Movement had gained momentum. In 1905, the Governor General of India, Sir George Curzon, ordered a partition of Bengal (an eastern state in India) that led to widespread agitation and a Congress-led boycott of British goods. Called the *Swadeshi* Movement (using only Indian-made goods), the boycott was widespread, and it prompted the British government to introduce several legislative reforms.

In 1915, Mohandas Karamchand Gandhi (1869–1948; later referred to as Mahatma Gandhi), a barrister

PRIMARY SOURCE

Dandi March: Mahatma Gandhi (center, bald with glasses) arrives in Dandi, India, at the end of his famous march to protest the Salt Laws of the British colonial government, on April 7, 1930. He is surrounded by other protest marchers. © BETTMANN/CORBIS.

by profession, returned to India from South Africa. While in South Africa, Gandhi protested against the racial discrimination policies of the government. On witnessing numerous cases of discrimination against Indians in India, Gandhi (as a leader of INC) initiated the historic Non-cooperation Movement in 1918. The movement encouraged Indian citizens to use non-cooperation as a means of passive revolt against the British government. During the Non-cooperation Movement, Gandhi and other leaders vehemently protested the Rowlatt Acts (or the Black Acts of 1919), which prohibited freedom of the press and gave the British government unprecedented authority to arrest anyone. In 1922, however, the movement came to an abrupt end when the non-violent philosophy of Gandhi was violated by an angry mob that set a police station on fire in Chauri Chaura, a town in the northern Indian state of Uttar Pradesh.

In 1930, the Civil Disobedience Movement—another non-violent method of protest—was initiated.

Adopting the underlying principles of the Non-cooperation Movement, the Civil Disobedience Movement targeted the Salt Act implemented by the British. The Salt Act stated the that production or sale of salt by anyone other than the British government was illegal. In addition, heavy taxes were levied on salt. Most Indians (who were agricultural laborers at the time) were not allowed to collect easily accessible salt from coastlines. Instead, they had to pay a substantial price for the salt. Stating that the Salt Act symbolized the discriminatory and unjust attitude of British rule, Gandhi and his followers decided to launch a movement to defy the Salt Act.

On March 12, 1930, Gandhi and his supporters set out, on foot, for the coastal village of Dandi in the western state of Gujarat, some 240 miles from their starting point in Sabarmati Ashram, Ahmedabad, Gujarat. The march is popularly known as the Salt Satyagraha (persuasion of truth) or the Dandi March. The primary source is a photograph taken of Gandhi with other prominent members of India's freedom movement participating in the Dandi March of 1930.

PRIMARY SOURCE

DANDI MARCH

See primary source image.

SIGNIFICANCE

For decades, the British had imposed a tax on salt that adversely affected poor Indians. The tax was levied at one thousand percent the cost and amounted to five percent of the total tax collected by the British in India. International communities and press, including the American press, severely criticized the British rule for taxing a basic and naturally available commodity.

Considered as the turning point in the Indian independence movement, the Dandi March gained huge popularity and nationwide attention. As the march progressed, thousands of activists joined in. At every stop along the way, Gandhi addressed the crowds with the purpose of educating them about the independence movement. Twenty-five days after it started, the non-violent march ended on April 5, 1930, at the small coastal town of Dandi. The following day, Gandhi set out to the seashore, picked up a lump of salt, and declared, "With this, I am shaking the foundations of the British Empire."

Soon after breaking the law, Gandhi encouraged other Indians to produce and distribute salt themselves. Consequently, millions of people nationwide broke the salt law. The British government arrested thousands of people (including Gandhi and other leaders of the INC) for making and selling salt.

Gandhi's non-violent march, widely acknowledged as an event that shook the British Empire, reverberated throughout the nation, becoming a milestone in the Civil Disobedience Movement for Indians independence. Gandhi continued to work towards India's independence which was achieved seventeen years after the Dandi March in August 1947.

The Dandi March and the Civil Disobedience Movement inspired many other individuals working for freedom and independence, including Martin Luther King, Jr. and Nelson Mandela. As of the 2000s, the Dandi March is re-enacted in India and other countries every year.

FURTHER RESOURCES

Books

Weber, Thomas. *On the Salt March: The Historiography of Gandhi's March to Dandi*. New York: HarperCollins Publishers India, 1997.

Web sites

Bombay Sarvodaya Mandal. "Defiance of Salt Tax." <http://www.mkgandhi.org/civil_dis/civil_dis.htm> (accessed May 22, 2006).

Country Studies US. "Mahatma Gandhi." <http://countrystudies.us/india/20.htm> (accessed May 22, 2006).

Economist.com. "Gandhi, Salt and Freedom." December 23, 1999. <http://www.economist.com/diversions/millennium/displayStory.cfm?Story_ID=347107> (accessed May 22, 2006).

Mahatma Gandhi Foundation. "The Salt March." <http://www.saltmarch.org.in> (accessed May 22, 2006).

Ministry of Home Affairs, Government of India. "History: Milestones in Indian History." <http://mha.nic.in/his3.htm> (accessed May 22, 2006).

The Zionist People's Council Proclaim the Establishment of the State of Israel

Government record

By: The Jewish National Council

Date: May 14, 1948

Source: "The Zionist People's Council Proclaim the Establishment of the State of Israel." In *Major Knesset Debates: 1948–1981*, edited by Netaniel Lorch. Lanham, Md.: University Press, 1993.

About the Author: The Jewish National Council, referred to as the *Vaad Leumi* in Hebrew, was the official body of the Zionist movement in Palestine in the years leading up to the declaration of the State of Israel in May of 1948. Also known as the Jewish National Council on Palestine or the Jewish People's Council, the organization was made up of many Jewish parties that worked towards the creation of a Jewish State. After the declaration of statehood, the Council formed the provisional government of the new State of Israel.

INTRODUCTION

The creation of the State of Israel in May of 1948 gave birth to one of the world's most recognized conflicts

Dr. Abba Hillel Silver addresses an estimated crowd of 19,000 people in Madison Square Garden in New York City on May 16, 1948, during a rally organized by The American Zionist Emergency Council, to salute the new state of Israel. AP IMAGES.

between Israel and the Arab states that surround it. Israel's creation was viewed as a success of the modern Zionist movement born in the later nineteenth century. Modern Zionism was developed by the Austrian journalist Theodor Herzl (1860–1904) with the goal of creating a modern state for the Jewish people in the face of rising anti-Semitism and assimilation. In the early twentieth century the movement gained political and social momentum amongst many segments of the European Jewish communities, leading to massive immigration of Jews to Palestine. Located on the Mediterranean Sea, this land that would become Israel had been the center of Jewish activity in ancient times and is recognized as sacred to the world's three major religions, Islam, Christianity, and Judaism.

The declaration of the State of Israel brought an end to the British Mandate over Palestine, which had

been in place since the British took control over the region during the course of World War I. The Jewish immigration, which had intensified during the 1930s and 1940s as a result of the Nazi persecution of European Jews, had caused a great deal of conflict between the Zionists and the Arab inhabitants of Palestine. The issue was turned over to the United Nations, which in November of 1947 voted in favor of a plan that would allow for the partition of Palestine into two states, one for the Arabs and one for the Jews. Given this international support for the Zionist cause and upon the departure of the British government from Palestine in May of 1948, the Jewish National Council immediately declared the creation of the State of Israel as the Jewish homeland.

Within hours of the declaration, the Arab governments surrounding Palestine announced their rejection of the Jewish State and their opposition to the Partition Plan and launched an attack on Jewish forces. The result was the Israeli War of Independence, which was waged over the course of 1948. The war was eventually won by the Israeli army but gave birth to the Arab-Israeli conflict, which has become one of the globe's more costly and recognized conflicts. Since 1948, Israel has attracted millions of Jewish immigrants from Europe as well as Arab countries, and despite the political tensions has a thriving economy.

PRIMARY SOURCE

DRAFT OF THE DECLARATION OF THE ESTABLISHMENT OF THE STATE OF ISRAEL

Sitting 3 of the People's Council 14 May 1948 (5 Iyar 5708) JNF building, Tel Aviv

The Chairman, D. Ben-Gurion: Today is a day of greater opportunities and graver dangers than we have faced for many generations. a) The Mandate has ended and we must establish Jewish rule; b) War has been declared on us. This war may be intensified by an invasion by the regular Arab armies.

Our defense forces are functioning with the utmost dedication on all fronts and will do their duty. Arrangements have been made with regard to the danger of invasion.

We have assembled here today to make preparations and dispositions for independent Jewish rule. You have before you two documents for consideration: the first, a declaration; the second, the first draft of an interim constitution, which is urgently needed so that the Jewish institutions will be able to function during this period.

We will start with the first document: "The Declaration by the People's Council of the Establishment of the State of Israel."

A. In the Land of Israel the Jewish people came into being. In this land their spiritual, religious and national character was shaped. Here they lived in sovereign independence. Here they created a culture of national and universal import, and gave to the world the eternal Book of Books.

B. Exiled by force, still the Jewish people kept faith with their land in all the countries of their dispersion, steadfast in their prayer and hope to return and here revive their political freedom.

C. Fired by this attachment to history and tradition, the Jews in every generation strove to renew their roots in the ancient homeland, and in recent generations they came home in their multitudes. Veteran pioneers and defenders, and newcomers braving blockade, they made the wilderness bloom, revived their Hebrew tongue, and built villages and towns. They founded a thriving society, master of its own economy and culture, pursuing peace but able to defend itself, bringing the blessing of progress to all the inhabitants of the land, and dedicated to the attainment of sovereign independence.

D. In 1897 the First Zionist Congress met at the call of Theo Herzl, seer of the vision of the Jewish state, and gave public voice to right of the Jewish people to national restoration in their land.

E. This right was acknowledged by the Balfour Declaration of November 1917, and confirmed in the Mandate of the League of Nations which accorded international validity to the historical connection between the Jewish people and the Land of Israel, and to their right to reestablish their National Home.

F. The Holocaust that in our time destroyed millions of Jews in Europe again proved beyond doubt the compelling need to solve the problem of Jewish homelessness and independence by the renewal of the Jewish state in the Land of Israel, which would open wide the gates of the homeland to every Jew and endow the Jewish people with the status of a nation with equality of rights within the family of nations.

G. Despite every hardship, hindrances and peril, the remnant towns survived the grim Nazi slaughter in Europe, together with Jews from other countries, pressed on with their exodus to the Land of Israel and continued to assert their right to a life of dignity, freedom and honorable toil in the homeland of their people.

H. In the Second World War the Jewish community in the Land of Israel played its full part in the struggle of the nations championing freedom and peace against the Nazi forces of evil. Its war effort and the lives of its solders won it the right to be numbered among the founding peoples of the United Nations.

I. On 29 November 1947, the General Assembly of the United Nations adopted a resolution calling for the establishment of a Jewish [state] in the Land of Israel, and required the inhabitants themselves to take all measures necessary on their part to carry out the resolution. The recognition by the United Nations of the right of the Jewish people to establish their own state is irrevocable.

J. It is the natural right of the Jewish people, like any other people, to control their own destiny in their sovereign state.

K. Accordingly we, the members of the People's Council, representing the Jewish people in the Land of Israel and the Zionist movement have assembled on the day of the termination of the British Mandate in Palestine, and by virtue of our natural and historic right and of the resolution of the General Assembly of the United Nations, do hereby proclaim the establishment of a Jewish state in the Land of Israel—the State of Israel.

L. We resolve that from the moment the Mandate ends, at midnight on the Sabbath, 6 Iyar 5708, 15 May 1948, until the establishment of the duly elected authorities of the state in accordance with a constitution, be adopted by the elected constituent Assembly not later than 1 October 1948, the People's Council shall act as the Provisional Council of State and its executive arm, the National Administration, shall constitute the Provisional Government of the Jewish state, and the name of that state shall be Israel.

M. The State of Israel will be open to Jewish immigration and the ingathering of the exiles. It will devote itself to developing the land for the good of all its inhabitants. It will rest upon foundations of liberty, justice and peace as envisioned by the prophets of Israel. It will ensure complete equality of social and political rights for all its citizens, irrespective of creed, race or sex. It will guarantee freedom of religion, conscience, education and culture. It will safeguard the holy places of all religions. It will be loyal to the principles of the Charter of the United Nations.

N. The State of Israel will be prepared to cooperate with the organs and representatives of the United Nations in carrying out the General Assembly resolution of 29 November 1947, and will work for the establishment of the economic union of the whole Land of Israel.

O. We appeal to the United Nations to assist the Jewish people in the building of their state, and to admit the State of Israel into the family of nations.

P. Even amidst the violent attacks launched against us for months past, we call upon the sons of the Arab people dwelling in Israel to keep the peace and to play their part in building the state on the basis of full and equal citizenship and due representation in all its institutions, provisional and permanent.

Q. We extend our hand in peace and good-neighborliness to all the States around us and to their peoples, and we call upon them to cooperate in mutual helpfulness with the independent Jewish nation in its land. The State of Israel is prepared to make its contribution in a concerted effort for the advancement of the entire Middle East.

R. We call upon the Jewish people throughout the diaspora to join forces with us in immigration and construction, and to be at our right hand in the great endeavor to fulfill the age-old longing for the redemption of Israel.

S. With trust in the Rock of Israel, we set our hands in witness to this Declaration, at this session of the Provisional Council of State, on the soil of the homeland, in the city of Tel Aviv, on this Sabbath Eve, 5 Iyar 5708, 14 May 1948.

The Vote Those in favor of the entire document: 16

Those abstaining: 8

The Draft of the Proclamation The Chairman, D. Ben-Gurion: We will now discuss the constitutional document, the draft of which you have before you.

P. Rosenblueth (Aliya Hadasha): The purpose of this proclamation is to fill a void, particularly as regards the law. I am sure that it speaks for itself and that no lengthy explanations are necessary; a reading will suffice.

By right of the Declaration of Independence published today, 14 May 1948 (5 Iyar 5708), according to which the Provisional Council of States and the Provisional Government of the State of Israel were established the Provisional Council proclaims:

1. The Provisional Council of State is the legislative authority. The Provisional Council of State is entitled to and hereby does delegate some of its legislative powers to the Provisional Government for the purpose of urgent legislation.

2. Such provision of the law as arise from the White Paper of 1939 are hereby declared null and void. Sections 13–15 of the Immigration Ordinance, 1041 and regulations 102–107c of the Defense (Emergency Regulations, 1945 are hereby repealed. The Land Transfer Regulations, 1940 are herby repealed retroactively as of 18 May 1939 (29 Iyar 5699).

3. Apart from the above clauses, and as long as no laws have been enacted by or on behalf of the Provisional Council of State, and insofar as this is consistent with these laws and with changes arising from the establishment of the state and its authorities, the law which existed in Palestine on 14 May 1948 (5 Iyar 5708) shall continue in force in the State of Israel....

N. Nir-Rafalkes (Mapam): The first clause of the Proclamation is phrased clearly, but "urgent legislation" is very ambiguous.... There will be a sitting on Sunday evening. The Administration has guaranteed that nothing will be done until then. Why should we decide something now to which people object in principle? One of the principles of democracy is the separation of the legislature from the executive. But we are giving our administrators the power to legislate. There is a danger that the council will become a fiction, and my experience in the People's Council and the Administration during recent months indicates that someone wants to do this. According to the resolution, two institutions were established, the People's Council and the National Administration, and until now the People's Council has met only once. Since the matter is not extremely urgent, I suggest that at this point we do not accept the first clause, and discuss it on Sunday evening.

M. Wilner (Communists): I support Council Member Nir's proposal. Since I object to this anti-democratic practice, I object more strongly to its endorsement by a resolution. Simple logic says that we, the council, have decided to abolish the Council. That is the proposal and it has no other meaning. Since there is not time now, I suggest postponing the date on the first clause until the council meets on Sunday, leaving just the beginning of the clause, i.e., that the Provision council of State is the legislative authority. We can discuss the additions when we have time.

G. Myerson (Mapai): It appears to me that the clause can remain provided the words "and does delegate" are removed.

The chairman. D. Ben-Gurion: I notified you of the Administration's decision not to use its authority until Sunday, even if it is delegated to it...As for Council Member Wilner's objections, every parliament, especially during an emergency situation, delegates this type of authority to its executive arm. We are at war. No one knows what will happen tomorrow. There is no guarantee that Tel Aviv will not be bombed or that something even worse will happen. I think that the members of the Administration deserve the confidence of the council Members...but if events take an unforeseen turn, we do not want to be left completely without authority. The Mandatory laws have come to an end, we must legislate and issue instructions immediately, that is why the clause is worded in this way.

N. Nir-Rafalkes (Mapam): We could omit the phrase "The Provisional council of State is entitled to delegate," and pass an internal resolution stating: "Until Sunday evening the Government can do nothing." The Council may not be able to meet on Sunday.

The Chairman, D. Ben-Gurion: I suggest a different internal resolution. By the way, an internal resolution is not a law, and no internal resolution will authorize the government to legislate if we accept your proposal. Unless a situation arises which physically prevents the Council from meeting on Sunday, the Provisional Government is not allowed to act though the authorization has been given.

M. Bentov (Mapam): There is a way out of this. The Council can [meet] regardless of the number of members present. Till now we had no charter, and there is no reason why we should not decide that in emergency any number of members may act on behalf of the Council.

The Chairman, D. Ben-Gurion: In my opinion, from the point of view of democracy that is worse. I suggest an amendment stating that a resolution passed by a quorum is temporary, and when the entire Council meets it may amend the decision of the quorum. This means that Council meets with however many members are present, but when entire council meets it supercedes the quorum.

(Council Member Bentov's proposal is put to a vote and adopted.)

D. Remez (Mapai): I suggest replacing "is entitled to delegate" with "has the right to delegate," and wording paragraph 3 as follows: [as] long as no laws have been enacted by or on behalf of the Provisional Council of State, the law which existed in Palestine on 14 May 1948 (Iyar 5708) shall continue to be in force in the State of Israel, insofar as this is consistent with the contents of this proclamation and with changes arising from the establishment of the state and its authorities.

The Chairman, D. Ben-Gurion: We will vote on the entire Proclamation.

(The Proclamation is adopted. The sitting is closed.)

Declaration of the Establishment of the State of Israel Sitting 4 of the People's Council

14 May 1848 (5 Iyar 5709)

Museum Auditorium, Tel Aviv

Present: members of the People's Council, representatives of the Jewish Agency, the Zionist Organization, the National Committee of the Jews of Palestine, the Jewish National Fund, the Jewish Foundation Fund, representatives of literature, art and journalism, party leaders, the Chief Rabbis, members of the Tel Aviv Municipality, the Chief of the General Staff of the Hagana and his associates, founders of the Yishuv and representatives of the Ishuv's economic bodies.

D. Ben-Gurion: I will now read out to you the Declaration of Independence of the State of Israel as it was approved at its first reading by the People's Council (see above)...

We will now rise to adopt the Declaration of Independence of the Jewish state. (All present stand). Kindly be seated. Those Council Members who wish to make statements regarding the Declaration of Independence will be able to do so at the next sitting of the People's Council which will be held on Sunday evening, we hope... I now give the floor to Rabbi Fishman.

Rabbi Fishman: Blessed art thou, O Lord our God, King of the Universe, who has kept us in life and hast preserved us, and hast enabled us to reach this season.

D. Ben-Gourion: All the Jerusalem members of the People's Council, who were unfortunately unable to be here for obvious reasons, met in the Jewish

Agency offices today and informed us that they join us in adopting this declaration. I will now read out to you the proclamation of the People's Council (see above) . . .

The Council Members are requested to approach the President's podium in alphabetical order. The Secretary of the Provisional Government will call out their names and each one will sign the Declaration of Independence. Places will be kept for the members from Jerusalem, in alphabetical order.

The signatories to the Declaration of Independence of the State of Israel:

David Ben-Gurion
Daniel Auster
Mordecai Bentov
Yitzhak Ben-Zvi
Eliyahu Berligne
Fritz Bernstein
Rabbi Wolf Gold
Meir Grabowski
Yitzhak Gruenbaum
Dr. Abraham Granowsky
Eliyahu Dobkin
Meir Wilner-Kovner
Zerah Warhaftig
Herzl Vardi
Rachel Cohen
Rabbi Kalman Kahana
Saadia Kobashi
Rabbi Yitzhak Meir Levin
Meir David Lowenstein
Zvi Luria
Golda Myerson
Nathum Nir
Zvi Segal
Rabbi Yehuda Leib Hacohen Fishman
David Zvi Pinkas
Aharon Zisling
Moshe Kolodny
Eliezur Kaplan
Abraham Katznelson
Felix Rosenblueth
David Remez
Berl Repetur
Mordecai Shattner
Benzion Sterrnberg
Behor Shitrit
Moshe Shapira
Moshe Shertok

D. Ben-Gurion: The State of Israel has come into being. The sitting is now closed.

SIGNIFICANCE

The Declaration of the State of Israel has been viewed by many members of the international Jewish community and supporters of the state as the realization of an ancient biblical promise that the Jews would return to Israel after their expulsion from the region nearly two thousand years earlier. As this declaration makes clear, the return en masse of the Jewish people in the area was viewed as a religious and cultural desire to once again have a Jewish presence in this place referred to as the Holy Land.

Israel, despite its small geographic size, represents importance both for its inhabitants and for religious people all over the world. This declaration shows how the Zionists saw a religious and historical right to justify the creation of the State of Israel, a right which was ratified by the international community. Specific attention was placed to the plight of the Jews as a result of the Holocaust and the role that Israel should play in offering a refuge to the survivors.

This document, in creating the State of Israel, served to intensify the conflict between the Zionists and the Arab world to a new level. While the dispute over Palestinian territory had been violent prior to 1948, with the creation of a national identity for Israel the violence would spill over into one of the world's most significant international conflicts. The result was five major wars, local and international terrorism, and ethnic and religious strife that continues indefinitely.

The declaration clearly recognized the risk for violence that Israel's establishment would likely create, but it also set the stage for a policy of negotiation and peacemaking that could bring an end to the conflict and allow the two sides to co-exist. As of 2006, Israel is home to about 6.5 million people, almost four million of whom are Jewish. Nineteen percent of Israeli residents are Arab, about the same number as when the country was established in 1948.

FURTHER RESOURCES
Books
Lacquer, Walter. *A History of Zionism*. New York: MJF Books, 1972.

Sachar, Howard M. *A History of Israel: From the Rise of Zionism to Our Time*. New York: Alfred A. Knopf, 1996.

Web sites
American-Israeli Cooperative Enterprise. "Jewish Virtual Library—Israel."<http://www.jewishvirtuallibrary.org/jsource/israel.html> (accessed May 25, 2006).

State Department Telegram to Diplomats and Consulates Regarding the Recognition of Israel

Telegram

Date: May 14, 1948

Source: *The National Archives.* "Teaching With Documents Lesson Plan: The U.S. Recognition of the State of Israel." <http://www.archives.gov/education/lessons/us-israel/> (accessed May 25, 2006).

About the Author: President Harry S. Truman (1884–1972) directed the U.S. Department of State to issue this telegram the same day in 1948 that Israel's Provisional Government proclaimed the new State of Israel.

INTRODUCTION

The term Zionism refers to the movement for the creation of a Jewish state. Following waves of anti-Semitism throughout Europe in the latter decades of the nineteenth century, the move to create a Jewish homeland gained popularity among Jews. Russian political problems after the assassination of the Tsar were blamed on Jews. As such, Jews became the target of violence. In addition, the Dreyfus affair, during which a Jewish army captain was convicted of treason based on forged evidence, highlighted the institutionalized nature of anti-Semitism in France. Writers such as Leon Pinsker (1821–1891) and Theodor Herzl (1860–1904) began to assert that Jews would continue to be the target of discrimination wherever they remained a minority. In 1896, Herzl published *Der Judenstaat (The State of the Jews)*, which suggests that the condition of the Diaspora, or Jews residing throughout the world, would continue to deteriorate. As a result, the first Zionist Congress met in August 1897 and the goal to gain a Jewish home was established. After Herzl's death, Chaim Weizmann (1874–1952) led the Zionist movement and met with British leaders in the hopes of gaining British support for a homeland. By 1907, Weizmann had visited Palestine and concluded that the region should be colonized by the Jews. As a result, a trickle of immigrants began to move into the region.

During this time, Western powers viewed Palestine as a region that lacked national settlement. Approximately 200,000 Arabs, a delineation based on language rather than national identity, resided in the region, but they lacked a formal governmental structure. As World War I began to spread, Britain negotiated policies with both Arabs and the Jews who resided in the Middle East. In 1917, the Balfour declaration identified the British sympathy for Zionist goals and the British intent to sponsor a national home for the Jews. British occupying troops in the Middle East allowed Britain to become the dominant power following the defeat of Germany and Turkey in World War I. At the San Remo Conference in 1922, Western powers divided the Middle East using self-interest to determine their mandates. While the Western powers carved up the region, Jews began to immigrate to Palestine in larger numbers. From 1919–1931, the Jewish population in Palestine increased from 60,000 to 175,000.

In 1933, Adolf Hitler (1889–1945) began his rise to power and also began to implement his policies for the eradication of European Jews. During this period, Arabs became increasingly resistant to the growing numbers of Jewish immigrants to Palestine. After a series of conflicts that resulted in the deaths of Britons, Jews, and Arabs, the White Paper of 1939 established a new policy for Britain. The white paper asserted that Britain sought an independent Palestinian state, governed by Jews and Arabs who shared authority. Perceiving a betrayal on the part of British policy makers, the Zionists began to pursue support from the United States where many of the Jews resided. As World War II came to an end, Zionists gained popular support for a Jewish state as the details of the Holocaust became apparent. On the political front, however, Britain and the U.S. recognized the importance of the Middle East in the ramp up to the Cold War. By 1948, United Nations Resolution 181 terminated the Mandate for Palestine, by which the British had administered the region. As a result, the Jewish inhabitants of the region declared their independence and the statehood of Israel. Arab nations rejected the state of Israel while western powers acknowledged the new country.

PRIMARY SOURCE

NO DISTRIBUTION.

US URGENT.

TO.

CERTAIN AMERICAN DIPLOMATIC AND CONSULAR OFFICERS
NIACT.

For your secret info and for such precautions as you may consider it necessary to take this Govt may within next few

School children from Camden, New Jersey, wave Israeli flags at a rally celebrating the foundation of Israel as a sovereign nation, on May 16, 1948. © BETTMANN/CORBIS.

hours recognize provisional Jewish govt as de facto authority of new Jewish state.

Send to following posts:

MISSIONS
Cairo
Jidda
Baghdad
Beirut
Damascus

CONSULATES
Alexandria
Port Said
Dhahran
Jerusalem
Haifa

Aden
Basra.

SIGNIFICANCE

After the British left the newly formed state, several Arab nations including Egypt, Syria, Iraq, Lebanon, Jordan, and Saudi Arabia declared war on Israel. Invasions by Egyptian, Syrian, and Jordanian forces began the Israeli War of Independence. The armistice for this war, signed in 1949, partitioned more land to Israel than was originally agreed to by the United Nations resolution. By 1967, the Cold War between the U.S. and the Soviet Union was in full swing. Many Arab countries received military and financial support from the Soviet Union, while the U.S., Britain, and France continued to support Israel. The Six-Day War occurred in June 1967 as a response to the actions of Egyptian President Gamal Abdel Nasser who closed the straits of Tiran to Israeli shipping and expelled UN peacekeepers. In response, Israel launched attacks on the Egyptian air force and began an occupation of Sinai and Gaza, as well as the West Bank and Golan Heights. Peace was established through UN Resolution 242. However, many Arabs, including those within the Palestine Liberation Organization (PLO), rejected the terms of the resolution. As a result, on October 6, 1973, Egyptian and Syrian forces launched an attack on Israel on Yom Kippur, the Jewish holy day of atonement. Both the U.S. and the Soviet Union participated indirectly by supplying their respective allies with arms.

Conflict between Israel and its Arab neighbors continued to result in violence and unrest in the region. Then, in 1979, Egypt and Israel signed the Camp David Accords. These agreements, which included a peace treaty between Egypt, one of the most powerful Arab states, and Israel, demonstrated that negotiations with Israel were possible. This summit laid the framework for the 1993 Oslo Agreement between Israel and the Palestine Liberation Organization. By 2000, the peace process set in motion by the Oslo agreement had stalled. Attempts by the U.S. to restart the peace process have met with resistance in the following years. In 2006, Hamas, an Islamic fundamentalist organization, won the Palestinian National Authority's general legislative elections. The future of negotiations is in doubt, since Hamas is viewed by Israel and the Western powers as a terrorist organization due to their violent activities against Israel.

FURTHER RESOURCES
Books
Brenner, Michael. *Zionism: A Brief History*. Princeton, N.J.: Markus Weiner Publishers, 2003.

Sacher, H. M. *A History of Israel*. New York: Alfred Knopf, 1979.

Periodicals
Ovendale, Ritchie. "The Origins of the Arab-Israeli Conflict." *The Historian* (January 2002).

Prague Spring

Photograph

By: Anonymous

Date: August 21, 1968

Source: © Bettmann/Corbis.

About the Photographer: This photo was taken by an anonymous Czech photographer and smuggled out of Czechoslovakia. It now resides in the archive of the Bettmann Archive of the Corbis Corporation.

INTRODUCTION

The arrival of Communism in Czechoslovakia differed from other countries in Soviet Eastern Europe. Whereas Communism elsewhere followed some form of Soviet occupation after World War II, from December 1945 there were no Soviet troops on Czechoslovakian soil and the country was democratic with full parliamentary elections. How it came to adopt Communist rule in 1948 has been dubbed the 'elegant takeover,' but it was hardly a takeover at all. Rule was effectively handed over to the Communist Party, the country's largest political organization, after a string of parliamentary crises brought the collapse of the liberation government of Edvard Benes.

Although Czechoslovakian Communism had popular roots it was soon discredited. The democratic system was dismantled and the country underwent a harsh period of Sovietization in the 1950s, which was marked by purges, summary arrests, and repression. Economic problems also arose, which, by the late 1960s, were crippling the country and further undermining Communist Party rule.

In an attempt to rectify these problems, the Slovak Alexander Dubček was made the Communist Party's First Secretary on January 5, 1968. Aged forty-six, he was seemingly the model Soviet apparatchik, having spent thirteen years of his youth in the USSR and another three as an adult student of Moscow's Soviet Higher Party School. Yet Dubček, for all his apparent immersion in the ways of the Communist Party, was by Soviet standards a progressive leader brought in to mitigate reformist pressure from within Czechoslovakia.

The task facing the new leader was complex, since he had to please Moscow and the Czechoslovakian people simultaneously. Dubček had to revitalize the Czechoslovakian economy, but needed to do so within the rigid parameters imposed by Marxist economics. He needed to earn public confidence by loosening the stifling party control of state and social institutions, but had to accomplish this without provoking a negative Russian response, such as occurred in Hungary twelve years earlier.

Dubček quickly set about reviving the ranks of the Communist Party. A stream of dismissals and resignations (as well as several suicides) purged senior party

PRIMARY SOURCE

Prague Spring: The period of debate and reforms in Communist Czechoslovakia known as the Prague Spring ended with Soviet troops occupying the country to reimpose strict control. Here, a student protestor climbs atop a Soviet tank in the streets of Prague on August 21, 1968. © BETTMANN/CORBIS.

ranks of many of the hardliners so despised by the Czechoslovakian people. Dubček appointed known reformers to key positions within the government, including the Defense and Interior Ministries. He helped restore the credibility of the party by denouncing the terror of the 1950s and rehabilitating its victims, both living and dead.

Although Dubček would profess and maintain his commitment to Marxism-Leninism and the rule of the Communist Party, he authorized a vast public debate in the spring and summer of 1968. Officials met the people and engaged in discussions about the country's future. Interest groups were formed and flourished, and students and intellectuals debated Czechoslovakia's future. This period became known in the West as the Prague Spring (although it lasted long into the summer).

This debate was never seriously directed against Communism or Socialism, and a return to capitalism or the decollectivisation of agriculture were never formally or substantially broached. Nor did it assume an anti-Russian tone, despite the grievances against the USSR nursed by many Czechoslovakians. Rather it was seen by Communist Party bosses in Prague and initially Moscow as an experiment in 'Socialism with a human face' and a way of renewing the Communist system.

PRIMARY SOURCE

PRAGUE SPRING
See primary source image.

SIGNIFICANCE

It was not long before the momentum behind the Prague Spring moved beyond Dubček's control and provoked deep concerns in Moscow. In particular, Dubček's rehabilitation of purge victims gave way to a paroxysm of revulsion against the preceding two decades of Communist rule. Rather than revitalize the Communist Party, it diminished its credibility, even if it added to Dubček's growing stature. On June 27, 1968, a group of Czechoslovakian intellectuals issued a statement entitled "Two Thousand Words." It was an indictment of two decades of Communist dictatorship and mixed ringing endorsements of Dubček and demands for a faster pace of reform with veiled criticisms of Moscow. Dubček distanced himself from the statement, but it gained enormous popularity amongst his countrymen.

Before the publication of the "Two Thousand Words" statement, Moscow had looked at developments in Czechoslovakia with restraint. The USSR did not intervene in Czechoslovakian affairs, despite clamoring from its East German and Polish client states, who viewed the developments just over their borders with concern, fearing that the reform movement could bubble over and compromise their own regimes.

However, the "Two Thousand Words" statement seemed to tip the balance against Dubček. On July 3, the Soviet President, Leonid Brezhnev, warned that "we cannot remain indifferent to the fate of socialism in another country" and *Pravda*, the newspaper and Soviet Communist Party mouthpiece, began comparing the situation in Czechoslovakia with that of Hungary in 1956, when Soviet tanks were sent in to quell reformists. On July 15, the Warsaw Pact members collectively demanded Dubček reimpose censorship; a demand he rebutted three days later.

The final straw for Moscow seemed to come on August 10 with the publication of a draft of new party statutes, which were to be formalized at an Extraordinary Party Congress the following month. Key among these was a statute calling for the election of party officials by secret ballot. This notion was regarded as heretical by adherents to Marxism-Leninism, for whom unity and discipline were their central tenets. This statute would also likely lead to the removal of conservatives from the political offices they still retained, further loosening Moscow's grip on the country.

On the night of August 20, 1968, 7,500 Soviet tanks rolled into Czechoslovakia to suppress what it now deemed a politically and ideologically dangerous renaissance. They were joined by up to 500,000 troops from the USSR and Soviet client states. About eighty

A Czechoslovakian poster shows Vladimir Lenin's crying face over an image of a Soviet tank. It is a criticism of the Soviet Union's crackdown on Czechoslovakia's movement towards greater freedom, 1968. PHOTO BY THREE LIONS/GETTY IMAGES.

Czechoslovaks were killed and hundreds were wounded as the invasion met huge non-violent civil resistance and attracted global criticism. Moscow, for its part, claimed that the invasion had been 'invited' by concerned Czechoslovakian Communist Party members.

Dubček was arrested and sent to Moscow for "negotiations." These so-called negotiations resulted in the Moscow Protocol of August 26, an arrangement forced upon the Czechoslovakian leader, which banned all organizations that violated Socialist principles and restored censorship. A later treaty was signed that allowed for the "temporary" stationing of Soviet troops in Czechoslovakia to oversee the "normalization" of the country. Dubček was replaced as Communist Party Secretary the following year and given the ambassadorship to Turkey, apparently in the hope that he would defect. When he didn't he was recalled and banned from the Communist Party in 1970.

The invasion of Czechoslovakia was justified under the terms of what became known as the "Brezhnev Doctrine." This doctrine held that if Socialism was threatened in any state, then other Socialist governments had an obligation to defend it. For most of the next two decades, it was this doctrine that supported the edifice of Communism in Eastern Europe, even when the region suffered chronic economic crises in the late 1970s and 1980s. Although Soviet tanks were not dispatched in the same way again, the threat of invasion by Russian and Warsaw Pact forces stymied reformism across the region and served as the impetus for the imposition of martial law in Poland after Solidarity's emergence in 1980–1981. Not until the rule of President Mikhail Gorbachev would the Brezhnev Doctrine be abandoned. This was the first step leading to the collapse of Communism in Eastern Europe.

Rather than strengthen the hold of Communism on Czechoslovakia, the Soviet invasion undermined the ideology and dissipated any Russophilia that had lingered after the USSR's liberation of the country from Nazi Germany. The economic difficulties that the reforms of the Prague Spring intended to rectify were never properly addressed, leaving Czechoslovakia teetering towards stagnation. Moreover, as one reformist pointed out, Moscow's intervention "proved something most Czechoslovak reformers... did not even dare to believe at the time, namely, that the established Marxist-Leninist theory is incompatible with a genuine, modern, democratic, economic and political system and, what is more, that it is not even open to reform." [Radoslav Selucky, *Czechoslovakia: The Plan that Failed.*]

On his return from Turkey, Alexander Dubček was sent into internal exile with an appointment as a "forestry official." In reality he lived under severe restrictions and for years was not permitted to associate with anyone beyond his immediate family. In 1989, he re-emerged into public life, this time as a key ally of Vaclav Havel, who led Czechoslovakia's "Velvet Revolution." He was elected speaker of the country's Federal Assembly and, when Czechoslovakia was poised to split into two countries in 1993, he was positioned to become a leading figure in post-independence Slovakia. Just two months before Slovakia became an independent country, Dubček was killed in a road accident at the age of sixty-eight.

FURTHER RESOURCES

Books

Crampton, R. J. *Eastern Europe in the Twentieth Century—and After*. London: Routledge, 1997.

Rothschild, Joseph, and Nancy M. Wingfield. *Return to Diversity: A Political History of East Central Europe Since World War II*. 3rd edition. New York: Oxford University Press, 1999.

Selucky, Radoslav. *Czechoslovakia: The Plan that Failed*. London: Nelson, 1970.

Gordon-Skilling, H., Jaromir Navrotil, Antonin Bencik, Vaclav Kural, Marie Michalkuva, Jitka Vondorova, and Vaclav Havel. *The Prague Spring 1968*. Budapest: Central European University Press, 1998.

IRA Hunger Strikes

Book excerpt

By: Gerry Adams

Date: 2003

Source: Adams, Gerry. *A Farther Shore: Ireland's Road to Peace*. New York, N.Y.: Random House, 2003.

About the Author: Gerry Adams is the president of Sinn Fein, the political arm of the Irish Republican Army. He has been an active player in the Ireland peace process since the 1980's, representing the republican position which advocates the unification of all segments of Ireland under one authority.

INTRODUCTION

As one of the world's most watched territorial disputes, the conflict over the future control in Northern Ireland has been waged for many decades as a battle between the unionists, who support British control over the region and the republicans or nationalists, who call for a unification of Ireland and complete independence from Great Britain. Both within Irish circles, and often internationally, the debate over authority in Ireland is referred to simply as "the Troubles."

The conflict over control over Northern Ireland can be traced back to the twelfth century when the Norman Conquest led to the English king Henry II declaring authority over much of the area that makes up Ireland. In 1916, many movements aimed at unifying Ireland under Irish rule had failed, and the Irish Republican Brotherhood, which would become the Irish Republican Army, the IRA, was born. Led by Michael Collins, the IRA would institute a War for Independence, which by 1920 was quieted enough to allow for negotiations with the British government.

Demonstrators march in Belfast, Northern Ireland, on May 4, 1981. Those marching in front bear portraits of IRA activists on hunger strike at the time. © MICHEL PHILIPPOT/SYGMA/CORBIS.

In December of 1921, the area was officially divided into two countries, the Republic of Ireland and Northern Ireland. The southern portion of the country became an independent nation, whereas Northern Ireland remained a part of the United Kingdom. Despite this resolution, which appeased many and reduced tensions, the efforts of the IRA to unite all of Ireland continued to be carried out throughout the twentieth century. At times the IRA resorted to acts of terrorism including attacks aimed against British interests and carried out on English soil.

In the early 1980's, the IRA's political party Sinn Fein, led by Gerry Adams, began to hold negotiations aimed at developing a peace process to bring an end to the conflict. Talks resulted in a cease-fire declared by the IRA in 1994, which later fell apart but was reinstated in 1997 with the signing of the Belfast Agreement. This agreement created a framework to end the conflict without providing specific details for implementation. Following the agreement, even while tensions remained, there was a dramatic decrease in violence and peace talks that have continued on

occasion aimed at discovering a final resolution to the conflict.

PRIMARY SOURCE

In February '78, I was back in prison again. After a particularly horrific IRA bombing at the La Mon Hotel in which twelve people were killed, there was a roundup of Belfast republicans. I was among them. I wasn't questioned at all about the La Mon bombing. All my interrogation was about Sinn Fein activities. After seven days' detention I was charged with IRA membership. I was held for seven months and then, after a fiasco of a trial, the charges were dismissed. My solicitor P.J. McGrory's submission that I had no case to answer won the day and set an important legal precedent.

I spent part of my imprisonment in the H-Blocks of Long Kesh where I joined the protesters on the remand wing. I also met with some of the men whom I knew from Cage 11. I was shocked by the conditions they were living under and the extent of the brutality by the administration.

I came out of prison determined to change that. We organized the Sinn Fein POW department and formed a small committee to concentrate on the prisoner issue.

We moved to provide a more effective lobbying support for the prisoners. They were persuaded to adopt five demands which expressed in a humanitarian way the substance of their required conditions. Our objective was to try and make it easier for the British government to compromise, while at the same time opening the prison issue up for support from a broader range of people. It was from these initiatives that the prisoner campaign, organized mainly by family members in the Relatives Action Committees, moved into a broad front phase with the establishment of the H-Block/Armagh Committee.

At that time, Cardinal Tomas O Fiaich was the head of the Catholic Church in Ireland. He was a popular Church leader, scholarly but down-to-earth and close to his native South Armagh roots. It was Father Reid who suggested that we meet with Cardinal O Fiaich on the prison issue, and myself, Father Des, Danny Morrison (then editor of the Belfast-based *Republican News*), and Kevin Hannaway traveled regularly to Ara Coeili—the Primate's residence in Armagh—to discuss the situation. The Cardinal informed the British Secretary of State, Humphrey Atkins, of these meetings and tried to mediate a resolution of the prison protest.

In August 1978, Cardinal O Fiaich visited the H-Blocks at our request. After the visit he said: "One could hardly allow an animal to remain in such conditions, let alone a human being. The nearest approach to it that I have ever seen was the spectacle of hundreds of homeless people living in the sewer pipes of the slums of Calcutta. The stench and the filth in some of the cells with the remains of rotten food and human excreta scattered around the walls was almost unbearable. The authorities refused to admit that these prisoners are in a different category from the ordinary, yet everything about their trials and family background indicates that they are different. They were sentenced by special courts without juries. The vast majority were convicted on allegedly voluntary confessions obtained in circumstances which are now placed under grave suspicion by the recent report of Amnesty International. Many are very youthful and come from families which had never been in trouble with the law, though they lived in areas which suffered discrimination in housing and jobs. How can one explain the jump in the prison population of Northern Ireland from 500 to 3,000 unless a new type of prisoner has emerged? The problem of these prisoners is one of the great obstacles to peace in our community. As long as it continues it will be a potent cause of resentment in the prisoners themselves, breeding frustration among their relatives and friends and leading to bitterness

between the prisoners and prison staff. It is only sowing the seeds of future conflict."

The Cardinal's public intervention was the first major breakthrough on the prisoner issue. It occurred against the background of ongoing conflict and at a time in which the British government was pushing ahead with its other counterinsurgency strategies.

Sinn Fein was also being radically overhauled by the leadership at that time, led by Ruairi O Bradaigh. We were reviewing our attitude to a wide range of issues. Debating and discussing ways to make political advances. Speaking at the annual Bodenstown commemoration at the graveside of republican Wolfe Tone, I acknowledged, "Our most glaring weakness to date lies in our failure to develop revolutionary politics and to build a strong political alternative to so-called constitutional politics.

The revamped prisoner campaign intensified its outreach, publicity, and street campaigning. Despite all of the efforts publicly and privately, the British government remained unmoved. The possibility of such a strategy had been canvassed by the prisoners for some time. It was mainly pushed by some of the older or more experienced men, like Bobby Sands and Brendan Hughes. The Sagart was close to both of them and was often visiting them in their cells. Brendan Hughes was the officer commanding (or OC) of the prisoners at that time. He became the leader of the first hunger strike and Bobby Sands replaced him as OC.

Father Reid was devastated by the commencement of the first hunger strike. He had lobbied ferociously for an end to the dispute. He wrote reams of letters, including a number of appeals to the British authorities. Not long after the beginning of the first hunger strike, he took seriously ill. The stress of trying and failing to get a resolution of this issue took its toll and the Sagart was moved by his superiors out of Belfast. I used to visit Father Alex in Drogheda Hospital. On one occasion, Colette and I found him in a very distressed state as the health of the hunger strikers deteriorated. Paradoxically, while the plight of the prisoners and their families and the ongoing conflict continued to wear him down, he took great comfort from the messages of support which the blanket men smuggled out to him.

The Sagart was almost a year out of commission—an awful year for all of us. The first hunger strike ended just before Christmas. By then, three women prisoners in Armagh and the seven men in the H-Blocks had been joined by thirty more H-Block prisoners. The condition of one of the original seven, Sean McKenna, deteriorated quickly.

But with the commencement of the hunger strike, the British government opened up contact with republicans. Through this contact in the British Foreign Office—

code-named "Mountain Climber" —a channel of communication which had been used during the 1974 IRA-British government truce was reactivated. Father Reid's role had been filled by another Redemptorist priest, Father Brendan Meagher. The British said they wanted a settlement of the issues underpinning the protest and committed to setting out the details in a document to be presented to all of the prisoners formally and publicly after they came off their hunger strike.

Mountain Climber brought the document to Father Meagher, who delivered it to Clonard Monastery where I and a few people who were assisting the prisoners were waiting for him. As he was briefing us, Tom Hartley, the head of our POW department, burst into the room where we were meeting to tell us that the hunger strike was over in the Blocks.

Sean McKenna's condition had continued to deteriorate. As the leader of the hunger strike and, knowing that a document was on its way, Brendan Hughes had intervened in order to save Sean's life. The women in Armagh ended their fast later when they got news of the H-Blocks' decision.

In this new situation, without the pressure of a hunger strike to focus them, the British moved away from their commitments and from the document. The channel of communication was once more closed down. The prisoners were furious. Bobby Sands had wanted to recommence the fast almost immediately after there was evidence of British duplicity. We persuaded him to hang on. He manfully tried to work with the prison administration to find a way through the difficulties.

But someone somewhere somehow within the British system had decided that the prisoners were defeated. This was best illustrated by Prime Minister Margaret Thatcher on a visit to Belfast on May 28 when she declared that the hunger strike "may well be their [IRA] last card." A sensible, more strategic administration would have kept to its commitments and defused the prison issue by building a settlement. But the stakes were high. This had never been solely a prison dispute.

Criminalization was but one element in an integrated British strategy. The prison was the battlefield because the British system was intent on making it the breakers yard for the republican struggle. They were intent on defeating that struggle, not on finding a political and peaceful settlement.

So despite all our efforts, despite the Herculean efforts of Bobby Sands and his comrades, the die was cast. In March of 1981, the second hunger strike commenced. It was led by Bobby Sands. When it ended seven months later on October 3, ten hunger strikers were dead. Bobby Sands had been the first to die on May 5. He was followed over the following four summer months up to August by Francis Hughes, Raymond McCreesh, Patsy O'Hara, Joe McDonnell, Martin Hurson, Kevin Lynch, Kieran Doherty, Thomas McElwee, and Micky Devine....

The events of that awful summer of '91 polarized Irish society, north and south.

The prisoners were perceived to be the soft underbelly of the republican struggle. The British thought they could be isolated, beaten, intimidated, and coerced into accepting the label of criminal. But republican prisoners are political prisoners—men and women of conviction, commitment, and determination. The H-Block and Armagh prisoners resisted. They endured horrendous conditions and bore great physical cruelty with fortitude and courage. At the end, when no other course of action was open to them, they went on hunger strike in defense of their integrity as republican political prisoners, in defense of this republican struggle, in defense of their comrades in the prison, and to assert their humanity....

In the course of the hunger strike, Bobby Sands was elected as MP (Member of the British Parliament in London) for Fermanagh and South Tyrone in the north. In the south of Ireland, other hunger strikers were elected. The hunger strike had a particular impact there. It raised a fundamental moral question about the role of the south in Britain's' war in Ireland. It made a political impact that shook the system to its foundations. It was not just the fact that one hunger striker, Kieran Doherty, was elected TD (Teachta Dala, elected Member of the Irish Parliament, the Dail) for Cavan-Monaghan. Or that another prisoner, Paddy Agnew, was elected TD for Louth, and other prisoners, including Joe McDonnell and Mairead Farrell, attracted substantial electoral support. It was the fact that the hunger strike unmasked the unwillingness of the south's political establishment to do anything for the hunger strikers, or indeed do anything to challenge British rule in a part of Ireland.

The stories of the hunger strikes have been told elsewhere. For those of us who were part of that period, it is hard to imagine that it was over twenty years ago. It is as if it was yesterday. It can be understood only if we appreciate the incorruptibility, and unselfishness and generosity of the human spirit when that spirit is motivated by an ideal of an objective greater than itself.

People are not born as heroes. The hunger strikers were ordinary men who in extraordinary circumstances brought the struggle to a moral platform which became a battle between them and the entire might of the British state. In the course of their protest, the hunger strikers smashed British policy. Efforts to criminalize the political prisoners failed. When ten men died in the H-Blocks, Margaret Thatcher and her regime were seen to be the criminals. The hunger strikers were rightly viewed by most fair-minded people as highly idealistic and politically motivated young men. Today, years later, it is clear to me that their legacy is still unfolding. The idealism of the hunger strikers and the other prisoners in the blocks and Armagh remains an example to republicans, even those who were only children during that terrible time.

SIGNIFICANCE

Having killed more than 3,000 people and injured more than 30,000, the conflict over Northern Ireland has become one of the most watched territorial debates, and many international leaders and diplomats have committed themselves towards developing a comprehensive and lasting peace plan. While the number of casualties is low in comparison to other current conflicts, for a nation with a smaller population like Ireland, these numbers are viewed as quite substantial, and the conflict has a dramatic effect on the political and social environments throughout Ireland and many parts of the United Kingdom.

Gerry Adams, as the head of Sinn Fein, the political arm of the Irish Republican Army (IRA), has become the principle figure from the side of the nationalist camp working towards finding a peaceful resolution to the ages-old conflict. While the IRA has been largely portrayed as a violent organization, and often viewed as a terrorist entity, Adams's actions and statements, including this passage, have attempted to legitimize the positions of the IRA, and have the world better appreciate the position of the organization. The hunger strike as a form of protest that has been used on many occasions by protest movements throughout history, is often designed to help increase public support for the positions of the protesters. As Adams describes it, the strike successfully made the general public, particularly those in southern areas of Ireland, relate to the republican arguments.

As a result of the strike, which became, according to Adams, one of the more significant efforts of the IRA to gather public support for their cause, sentiments about the IRA began to change. Adams, in this section, argues that rather than the IRA activists being viewed as criminals, the British were faulted for a situation which allowed ten political prisoners to die. As a result of this new perception and a slow development of empathy with the IRA's stance, some question how long British rule might be able to withstand these types of protests. In achieving these types of successes, the IRA and Sinn Fein became more integrated into the political process allowing for the commencement of

negotiations and the hopes for a final and peaceful resolution to the conflict.

FURTHER RESOURCES
Books
Tonge, Jonathan. *Northern Ireland, Conflict and Change*. New York, N.Y.: Longman, 2002.

Web sites
Community Dialogue. "Community Dialogue: Understanding In the Northern Ireland Conflict." <http://www.communitydialogue.org/> (accessed June 3, 2006).

University of Ulster. "Conflict Archive on the Internet; Northern Ireland Conflict, Politics and Society." <http://cain.ulst.ac.uk/index.html> (accessed June 3, 2006).

Jewish Settlers Protest Israeli Withdrawal from Gaza

Photograph

By: Marco Di Lauro

Date: August 17, 2005

Source: Photo by Marco Di Lauro/Getty Images.

About the Photographer: Marco Di Lauro is a stringer for Getty Images, a worldwide provider of visual content materials to such communications groups as advertisers, broadcasters, designers, magazines, news media organizations, newspapers, and producers.

INTRODUCTION

The Gaza Strip is a roughly rectangular piece of land on the east coast of the Mediterranean, just south of Israel and just north of Egypt. It is about 140 square miles in size (362 square kilometers), with a population of about 1,325,000 Palestinian Arabs and, until late 2005, some 7,500–8,000 Israeli Jews living in twenty-one segregated enclaves. The settlers, about 0.6% of Gaza's population, occupied approximately 18% of the area.

From 1918 to 1948 Gaza was part of the League of Nations mandate of Palestine, administered by Great Britain. When the United Nations divided Palestine into Jewish and Arab states after World War II, seven allied Arab armies attacked the new state of Israel, triggering the 1948 Arab–Israeli war. Heavy fighting and political expulsion drove about 800,000

Palestinian Arabs into Gaza both during and after the war. The strip was occupied by Egypt both during and after the war; its boundaries were drawn up during the armistice agreements of 1949. In 1967, Israel fought a second war with Egypt, Syria, and Jordan, and again prevailed, this time winning control of the Sinai Peninsula, the Golan Heights, the West Bank of the Jordan River, and the Gaza Strip. The Sinai was returned to Egyptian control in 1979–1982. In 2005, Israel removed Jewish settlements from Gaza as part of a broad disengagement program in the region.

Soon after 1967 Israel began to build settlements in the occupied territories, hoping to establish the largest possible Israeli Jewish population there with the ultimate goal of making the territories a de facto part of Israel, facilitating eventual official annexation. Settlers were attracted by a combination of economic, religious, and nationalistic motives. The Israeli government made very low land and housing prices available; in addition, most Israeli domestic law did not apply in the Occupied Territories, so minimum-wage laws, required vacations, and benefits for workers (who are mostly Palestinian—and in Gaza, Thai nationals—and work for low wages) do not apply. Some Orthodox settlers also believe that Gaza and the West Bank are part of *Eretz Israel*, "the land of Israel" —which they believe was given to them by God. Such settlers believe that by living in the Occupied Territories they fulfilled a divine command.

In December 2003 Deputy Prime Minister Ehud Olmert announced that Israel would withdraw from the settlements in Gaza, a policy approved by the Knesset (parliament) in August 2004. Although a majority of Israelis approved the policy, it was opposed by most Orthodox and Jewish nationalist Israelis. President George W. Bush announced American support for the withdrawal in April 2004, and the removals began in August 2005, carried out by some 50,000 unarmed Israeli police and troops. Settlers at Kfar Darom settlement threw acid at the police, but there was little or no outright combat between settlers and Israeli forces during the withdrawal process.

Settlers removed from the Gaza strip were relocated to Israel. Each family received between $150,000 and $400,000 in cash compensation (depending on the size of their house, family size, and length of residence in Gaza) plus moving expenses and two years' rent in new housing. Israel asked the U.S. for an additional $2 billion in aid in 2005 to help pay for the cost of the resettlement program.

PRIMARY SOURCE

Jewish Settlers Protest Israeli Withdrawal from Gaza: Israeli settlers in the Gaza Strip protest being forced to leave their homes as part of the government's withdrawal policy, August 17, 2005. PHOTO BY MARCO DI LAURO/GETTY IMAGES.

PRIMARY SOURCE

JEWISH SETTLERS PROTEST ISRAELI WITHDRAWAL FROM GAZA
  See primary source image.

SIGNIFICANCE

The emotional nature of the Israeli withdrawal from Gaza was emphasized in much reporting on the event: "Duty Exacts Emotional Toll on Troops," read a *Washington Post* subheadline for August 18, 2005. Photographs dramatizing the grief and outrage of Israeli settlers forced to leave their homes, such as this primary source, were widely circulated in the

Jews are rounded up by the Nazis in Warsaw, Poland during the German invasion in World War II, 1943. Jewish settlers protested their removal from the settlements in the Gaza Strip by invoking this photograph, one of the most famous images of the Holocaust. AP IMAGES.

media. Some Israeli Jewish critics of Israel's settlement policy, such as Uri Avnery, argued that media calls for extraordinary compassion were exaggerated. "[A]s far as simple human compassion is concerned," Avnery argued in the liberal Jewish journal *Tikkun*, "the settlers demand it from us, but never seem to feel it for anyone else. There is something disgusting about their inability to see the Other. It's a kind of emotional insanity: The mass expulsion of Arabs is OK. The expulsion of some thousands of Jews within the country is a 'second Holocaust.'"

Critics of Israeli government policy were also skeptical about the motives for the withdrawal. They noted that Israel would continue to exercise complete military control over Gaza's airspace, territorial waters, the Gaza/Egypt border, and the land between Gaza and the West Bank. The most common criticism of the policy was that Israel was withdrawing a relatively tiny number of settlers from Gaza while allegedly accelerating a far more massive settlement program in the West Bank, where there are a total of

187,000 Israeli settlers (plus 177,000 in East Jerusalem). While 7,500–8,000 Israeli settlers were removed from Gaza in 2005, several thousand other Jewish residents moved to settlements in the West Bank. Then-president of the Palestinian National Authority, Mahmoud Abbas, writing in the *Wall Street Journal* on October 20, 2005, complained that "Israel has accelerated its settlement expansion in the Palestinian heartland."

Proponents of the Israeli policy said this indicated that Israel's desire for a peaceful settlement with an independent Palestinian state was sincere. Israel withdrew from four settlements in the northern West Bank in August 2005. In May 2006, the administration of the new Israeli Prime Minister, Ehud Olmert, announced a unilateral plan to withdraw 60,000 settlers from 72 Israeli settlements in the West Bank. Under the plan, up to 28% of settlers in the West Bank would be withdrawn (70,000 out of about 250,000) and a handful of the least populous settlements would be annexed to Israel. (The figure of 250,000 settlers does not include

East Jerusalem.) Under the plan, about 15% of the West Bank's land area would be annexed by Israel. Olmert asserts that the plan would increase security by better defining Israel's borders. Like the withdrawal from Gaza, this plan has been criticized by some. According to the *Washington Post* for May 23, 2006, "many European officials fear Olmert's plan is an attempt by Israel to set permanent borders without negotiating with the Palestinians."

FURTHER RESOURCES

Books

Gelvin, James L. *The Israel-Palestine Conflict: One Hundred Years of War*. New York: Cambridge University Press, 2005.

Periodicals

Fattah, Hassan M. "Some Arabs See Withdrawal as Hollow Victory." *The New York Times*. August 17, 2006.

Kessler, Glenn. "U.S. Uneasy About Israel's Plans for West Bank." *The Washington Post*. May 23, 2006.

Wilson, Scott. "Soldiers Use Force, Persuasion in Gaza Settler Evacuation." *The Washington Post*. August 18, 2005.

Web sites

Congressional Research Service. "Israel's Proposal to Withdraw from Gaza." February 2, 2005. <http://fpc.state.gov/documents/organization/> (accessed May 23, 2006).

Congressional Research Service. "Israeli-United States Relations." April 28, 2005. <http://fpc.state.gov/documents/organization/47089.pdf> (accessed June 12, 2006).

Tikkun. "On Limits of Compassion for Israeli Settlers in Gaza: A Jewish Perspective (by Uri Avnery)." 2005. <http://www.tikkun.org/rabbi_lerner/Uri%20Avnery%20on%20Gush%20Settlers> (accessed May 23, 2006).

8 Health, Environment, and Animal Rights

Health, Environment, and Animal Rights

Many of the subjects of global environmental and health protest movements are basic and fundamental—clean air, pure water, preservation of natural resources, and access to healthcare and health information. Similarly, animal rights protestors assert that all animals deserve a life of dignity, free of captivity and cruelty, whether they inhabit the wild or our domestic surroundings. They are movements that foster a comprehensive well-being of the individual and its social and natural environment. Like other protest movements, the environmental and animal rights movements advocate not only a shift in social policy but also changes in human behavior. For example, many mainstream animal rights protest campaigns protest the conditions in which animals are raised and encourage vegetarianism. Environmental justice protesters may protest deforestation and encourage consumer boycotts of companies that destroy forest resources.

Some factions of the environmental justice and animal rights movements rely on direct-action as a means of protest. From camping in trees to prevent their removal to destroying laboratory equipment, direct actions range from non-violent acts of civil disobedience to the aggressive destruction of property. The articles "Animal Rights Raiders Destroy Years of Work" and "Neighbors of Burned Homes Pained by Suburban Sprawl" feature two direct action campaigns described as acts of protest by movement members and crimes of vandalism and terrorism by law enforcement agencies. When individuals employ violence and vandalism as means of intimidation, their actions may fit within current definitions of terrorism. While the actions of extremists should not dilute the message of less-radical protesters, the editors leave it to the reader to determine when illegal acts are legitimate forms of protest or mere criminal conduct.

In contrast to the sometimes violent campaigns of the Animal Liberation Front and the Earth Liberation Front, the People for the Ethical Treatment of Animals' (PETA) "We'd Rather Go Naked" campaign combined a media blitz of scantily clad celebrity advertisements with naked protests at businesses that sell fur products. Also, the chapter begins by featuring the first Earth Day, created to raise awareness of environmental issues and proactive solutions to environmental crises. Current environmental policy issues such as the Kyoto Treaty and the European Union agreement governing genetically modified organisms (GMOs) are also highlighted here.

Finally, this chapter brings to light policy, protest, and activism surrounding current international health issues. Several of these articles focus on the international AIDS crises because the movement to combat AIDS has captured a large share of media and public attention. Across the globe, the fight against AIDS spurs dramatic activism—from activists in developing nations defying local prohibitions on distributing condoms to the gay rights movements' embrace of AIDS activism and protest in more developed nations.

The First Earth Day

Photograph

By: Anonymous

Date: April 22, 1970

Source: Photo by Hulton Archive/Getty Images.

About the Photographer: This photograph is part of the Getty Images collection, a worldwide provider of visual content materials to advertisers, broadcasters, designers, magazines, news media organizations, newspapers, and producers. The photographer is not known.

INTRODUCTION

Earth Day observes and celebrates the environmental health of the Earth, emphasizing the need for a clean and healthy environment for all living things. It is usually celebrated on April 22 of each year; however, some events are planned for the weekends before or after the date and can last for days or weeks. Wisconsin Senator Gaylord Anton Nelson (1916–2005) established the first Earth Day celebration on April 22, 1970. (Some people celebrate Earth Day on the vernal equinox, the first day of spring in the northern hemisphere, an idea first proposed by John McConnell in 1970.)

According to Nelson, his idea of dedicating a day to celebrate the Earth's environment developed over a seven-year period. In 1962 he realized that while many people in the United States were concerned about the environment, few American politicians were. He persuaded President John Kennedy to tour eleven states in September 1963 to emphasize conservation. Although the trip did not generate national publicity, Nelson felt it provided a foundation for later actions. Over the next six years, he talked to audiences around the country about the need to protect the ecosystem.

Then in the summer of 1969, after observing anti-Vietnam War demonstrations, he decided to organize a grass roots protest to bring attention to environmental damage. In September 1969 he announced his plans to launch a nationwide protest the following spring. The news media carried the story, spurring interest from individuals and groups across the country. On November 30, 1969, environmental journalist Gladwin Hill published a story in *The New York Times* that related growing public concern over the environment.

On April 22, 1970, about 20 million American schoolchildren, college students, and adults participated in Earth Day rallies and demonstrations to honor the Earth and show support for environmental reform. One of the more notable events was held in New York City—Mayor John Lindsay closed Fifth Avenue for an ecology fair in Central Park.

Nelson received many awards in his lifetime, including the Ansel Adams Conservation Award in 1990, an award given to federal officials who have dedicated themselves to conservation and land ethics; the Only One World award from the United Nations Environment Programme in 1992; followed by the Presidential Medal of Freedom, the highest U.S. civilian honor, in 1995. Nelson served ten years (1948–1958) as a state senator in Wisconsin; one term as governor of Wisconsin (1958–1963); and eighteen years (1963–1981) as a U.S. senator from Wisconsin. After leaving the Senate, Nelson became a counselor for the Wilderness Society.

PRIMARY SOURCE

THE FIRST EARTH DAY
See primary source image.

SIGNIFICANCE

By the beginning of the twenty-first century, Earth Day was celebrated annually by more than 500 million people in over 140 countries. Many environmental groups organized events to emphasize local, regional, national, and global environmental problems and suggest ways to solve them. Air, soil, and water pollution are popular subjects for Earth Day events, as are the destruction of habitats and ecosystems, depletion of nonrenewable resources, and reduction in the number of animal and plant species. Environmental exhibitions at Earth Day celebrations often focus on ways that individuals can help, such as recycling, conserving, leading healthier lifestyles, making lands friendlier to wildlife, picking up litter, cleaning up bodies of water, and planting trees.

Coordinating Earth Day activities worldwide is one function of the environmental awareness organization called Earth Day Network (EDN), founded by organizers of the first Earth Day. Its mission is to encourage individuals, organizations, governments, and corporations to take responsibility for a clean and healthy environment. EDN activists promote environmental citizenship by helping about 12,000 groups in 174 countries each year with Earth Day and general

PRIMARY SOURCE

The First Earth Day: The first Earth Day conservation awareness celebration in New York, New York, on April 22, 1970. PHOTO BY HULTON ARCHIVE/GETTY IMAGES.

environmental activities. Its American program helps over 3,000 groups and more than 100,000 educators by coordinating efforts for millions of community development and environmental protection activities.

Nelson credited the first Earth Day celebration with convincing politicians to develop environment-friendly legislation. Since then, Congress has passed many laws that protect, manage, and preserve the environment. In fact, the Environmental Protection Agency (EPA), which began operations on December 2, 1970, was one of the first federal organizations created by environmental legislation. The EPA is responsible for the environmental health of the country as specified through various facets of federal legislation. One such law is the Clean Air Act, enacted in 1970, which directs the EPA to establish and enforce national air-quality standards to protect both the public health and environment. According to the EPA, between 1970 and 2005, the gross domestic product increased 19 percent, motorized vehicle miles traveled by 178 percent, energy consumption by 48 percent, and the U.S. population by forty-two percent. During this same thirty-five year period, however, the total emission of the six major air pollutants—carbon monoxide, lead, nitrogen dioxide, ozone, particulate matter, and sulfur dioxide—dropped by fifty-three percent.

Congress also passed the Occupational Safety and Health Act (1970), Clean Water Act (1970), Endangered Species Act (1973), Safe Drinking Water Act (1974), Toxic Substances Control Act (1976), and the Comprehensive Environmental Response, Compensation, and Liability Act (CERCLA or Superfund, 1980).

Many environmental organizations were also created or revitalized by Earth Day. Greenpeace, for instance, was founded in 1971 to concentrate on diminished whale populations and problematic nuclear power plants. The Nature Conservancy began to expand in the early 1970s by purchasing undeveloped lands for nature preserves. The Sierra Club and the National Audubon Society began to sue companies that it considered harmed the environment with their practices, such as northwestern logging companies that harvested old-growth forests.

Many American citizens were spurred to recycle in the 1970s, and communities began to establish recycling programs in the 1980s. By the 1990s, many recycling programs were converting trash into useful products, reducing the amount of trash dumped into landfills. During that same decade, many corporations began to adopt more efficient industrial operations.

Throughout its history, Earth Day has strengthened the support for environmental programs, and helped build volunteerism in communities around the world. When Earth Day celebrated its thirty-fifth anniversary in 2005, its legacy showed that the environment's health is a major concern for everyone.

FURTHER RESOURCES
Books

Christofferson, Bill. *The Man from Clear Lake: Earth Day Founder Gaylord Nelson*. Madison, WI: University of Wisconsin Press, 2004.

Graham, Mary. *The Morning after Earth Day: Practical Environmental Politics*. Washington, DC: Governance Institute, Brookings Institution Press, 1999.

Nelson, Gaylord, with Susan Campbell, and Paul Wozniak. *Beyond Earth Day: Fulfilling the Promise*. Madison, WI: University of Wisconsin Press, 1992.

Young adults assume a meditative pose as they observe Earth Day, March 21, 1971, in Central Park, New York. © BETTMANN/CORBIS.

Web sites

Earth Day Network. <http://www.earthday.net/default.aspx> (accessed May 11, 2006).

EarthDay.gov. "Environmental Highlights: Federal Government Actions." <http://www.earthday.gov/fedactions.htm> (accessed May 11, 2006).

EnviroLink: The Online Environmental Community. "How the First Earth Day Came About." <http://earthday.envirolink.org/history.html> (accessed May 11, 2006).

Animal Rights Raiders Destroy Years of Work

Newspaper article

By: Anonymous

Date: March 8, 1992

Source: The New York Times

About the Author: *The New York Times* is a major newspaper headquartered in New York City that is published by the New York Times Company, a major newspaper publisher and media company. The New York Times Company owns newspapers such as the *Boston Globe* and the *International Herald Tribune*, television and radio stations, and electronic information services.

INTRODUCTION

According to the U.S. District Court that serves the Western District of Michigan (Southern Division), animal rights activists going by the name of the Animal Liberation Front (ALF) had been participating in terrorist activities within the United States since at least 1984. ALF is a general term used to represent any animal liberation activist/extremist that uses terrorist actions and methods to protest against organizations and individuals that promote animal testing. Such organizations include the dairy, egg, fur, and meat industries and such individuals as breeders, corporate researchers, farmers, fisherpersons, ranchers, and university professors. ALF members use such tactics as

Animal rights demonstrators gather near the unfinished Oxford University medical laboratory science site in Oxford, England, August 25, 2004. AP IMAGES.

firebombing buildings, breaking into laboratories, destroying research documents and information, and other such illegal acts that are intended to end the human exploitation of animals. Although ALF does not exist as a formal organization, its members informally act as small underground cells dedicated to the ALF philosophy.

According to domestic U.S. terrorist investigators, animal research facilities at universities and private businesses have been the most frequent targets of arson and vandalism from ALF members, at least since 1991. Generally, it has been found that after a target has been attacked, a press report is released that claims the action was committed to end animal research and exploitation and that future acts will occur if demands are not met. In 1991, the U.S. Federal Bureau of Investigation (FBI), along with the U.S. Bureau of Alcohol, Tobacco and Firearms (ATF), began to investigate activities of ALF members with respect to a series of crimes against organizations associated with the fur industry.

The FBI stated that the first known target of ALF was Oregon State University (OSU) in Corvallis, Oregon. Its mink farm was firebombed and burglarized on June 10, 1991. Later that day, various news agencies in Oregon were given ALF press releases related to the incident. Then, on June 15, 1991, the Northwest Farm Food Cooperative was firebombed. An ALF press release was issued stating that the cooperative was targeted because it provided animal feed to fur breeders, gave financial support to mink research, and was associated with OSU. Then, on August 12, 1991, the fur animal research facility at Washington State University was vandalized. A press release was issued by ALF, which included threats to other universities and scientists if they did not stop exploiting animals. Two other acts of arson occurred at the Fur Breeders Agriculture Co-op in Sandy, Utah, on August 28, 1991, and the Malecky Mink Ranch in Yambill, Oregon, on December 21, 1991.

The largest attack occurred on February 28, 1992, when arson, burglary, and property damage occurred at Michigan State University (MSU). On that date, the

MSU offices of scientists Richard J. Aulerich (a professor of animal science) and Karen Chou (an assistant professor of animal science) were destroyed and major damage occurred at MSU's mink facilities. Thirty years of Aulerich's work was destroyed. This time, however, the press reports were released by the People for the Ethical Treatment of Animals (PETA), the largest animal rights organization in the United States. PETA is dedicated to animal rights through rescue, celebrity participation, education, legislation, protest campaigns, research, special events, and undercover investigations.

In 1993, a U.S. Department of Justice report documented over 300 cases of acts of vandalism, fire bombings, physical assaults, and other illegal acts committed by animal rights extremists in the United States over the previous fifteen years. According to the Justice report, ALF had accepted credit for most of the crimes.

PRIMARY SOURCE

EAST LANSING, Mich.

Animal rights advocates entered two research areas at Michigan State University on Feb. 28, set fire to one and destroyed thirty-two years' worth of animal science research, the university administration said. The vandals also inadvertently destroyed fertility research that could have helped both humans and endangered species.

The raid was directed against Richard J. Aulerich, an animal science professor, the university said. The raid destroyed equipment and property worth $75,000 to $125,000, said Maynard G. Hogberg, the chairman of the Animal Science Department at M.S.U.

Of the thirty-two years of data lost, two to three years' worth had not been published, he said.

Karen Chou, an associate professor of animal science, said she lost ten years' worth of data on the effects of chemicals in animal reproduction. Her research was aimed at testing the viability of sperm before fertilization and at studying the effects of chemicals on reproduction.

Professor Chou said her fertility research could have helped solve reproductive problems in endangered species. It could also have uncovered the effects chemicals have on human reproduction, she said.

RAIDS AT OTHER CAMPUSES

The Animal Liberation Front, which conducted similar raids at Oregon State University one and one-half years ago and at Washington State University six months ago, claimed responsibility for the acts in a press release. The group says it seeks to end all animal experimentation and in

particular calls experimentation on minks, such as Professor Aulerich was doing, cruel and worthless.

Professor Aulerich had been conducting research on toxins and their effect on animals, Professor Hogberg said. The research involves feeding minks, which are especially susceptible to toxics, food containing toxic chemicals or other contaminants. Professor Hogberg said the minks had recently been fed fish caught in Saginaw Bay in Michigan, which is contaminated by PCB's.

The research was intended to be used to benefit humans and other animals, he said.

Professor Hogberg said that he did not know how many of the 350 minks kept at the lab were euthanized each year, but said that the number was "very low." He said the animals were not maimed during the research.

Gregory Maas, the chairman of the Incurably Ill For Animal Research, based in Bridgeview, Ill., offered a $5,000 reward for information leading to the arrest of the vandals. The group works for the continuation of animal research to aid human medical research, Mr. Maas said.

According to Bill Wardwell, a lieutenant with the Michigan State University Department of Public Safety, members of the Animal Liberation Front broke into Anthony Hall on campus about 5 A.M. and entered Professor Aulerich's office. Files and papers were strewn around the office and a fire was started, he said.

The fire gutted Professor Aulerich's office and smoke extensively damaged two other offices, a conference room and a reception area. Lieutenant Wardwell said similar devices were used in the break-ins at both Washington State and Oregon State.

At the Poultry Research Facility, where Professor Aulerich conducts his research, vandals destroyed research documents and poured sulfuric acid into laboratory equipment, including devices used to feed the minks, Lieutenant Wardwell said. They also opened the minks' cages, but the animals remained inside, he said.

"Aulerich tortures minks" and "Fur is murder" were sprayed on the wall with red paint. The slogans were signed "A.L.F.," for Animal Liberation Front.

A FEDERAL CASE

Lieutenant Wardwell said a nationwide alert was sent to warn police departments of the possibility of similar actions. Increased security is planned for research laboratories on campus, he said, including more patrols.

The United States Bureau of Alcohol, Tobacco and Firearms and the Federal Bureau of Investigation have been brought in to investigate the case. Dennis B. Anderson, the senior resident agent in Lansing, Mich., said the F.B.I was involved because Professor Aulerich used Federal financing for his experiments and because police suspect that the vandals crossed state lines to commit the crime.

The animal-rights group issues its press releases through People for the Ethical Treatment of Animals, a national animal rights group in Washington, D.C. Steven I. Simmons, a spokesman for People for Ethical Treatment of Animals, said his organization was not linked to the Animal Liberation Front. But he said his group was usually alerted by the front before and after a raid.

SIGNIFICANCE

Government investigators began to study the crimes perpetrated allegedly by ALF members (what they called Operation Bite Back) with regards to MSU, along with the other smaller crimes that were similar in attributes. Upon researching the crimes, the investigators discovered that one person was likely behind the crimes. Rodney Adam Coronado (alias, Jim Perez and Martin Rubio), a long-time advocate of animal rights, was found to have personally issued several press releases under the name of Coalition Against Fur Farms. In fact, it was verified that he had earlier helped to damage a whaling station in Iceland and sink two whaling ships.

At this time, an arrest warrant was issued for Coronado after he was interviewed by a local television station in which he stated he participated in past ALF activities and acknowledged performing illegal acts. Identification of Coronado by eyewitnesses at several ALF crime scenes was also verified. Forensic evidence confirmed that Coronado played a major role in planning and executing these illegal acts. In addition, material evidence, including documents from Aulerich's office that were known to have been stolen during the ALF raid, was found in Coronado's possession.

In July 1993, Coronado was indicted on five counts by the grand jury (in the Western District of Michigan) for his role in Operation Bite Back and with the February 28, 1992 break-in at MSU. Coronado was apprehended by law enforcement officials in November 1994 while on the Pasqua Yacqui reservation in Arizona. On March 3, 1995, Coronado pled guilty. When found guilty, Coronado was sentenced to fifty-seven months in prison.

After Coronado was arrested, further fire bombings and property damage to universities and businesses associated with perceived mistreatment of animals by ALF members stopped. However, because other animal rights extremists continue to act against scientists, business owners, and farmers who deal with animals, these people are aware that they may be targeted in the future. Increased security measures have been implemented to counter possible attacks. Since Coronado's sentencing to prison, he has publicly asked other people to take over his leadership role in the animal rights movement.

In 2004, the FBI opened an investigation called Operation Backfire to investigate domestic terrorism by the environmental activist group Earth Liberation Front (ELF) and ALF. Because of its actions, ALF was named by the U.S. Department of Homeland Security, in January 2005, as a domestic terrorist threat to the United States. FBI and ATF officials stated at a Senate hearing, on May 18, 2005, that violent animal rights extremists—specifically stating that ALF was one such group—pose one of the most serious threats to the United States with respect to domestic terrorism. At about the same time, the British newspaper the *Daily Telegraph* called ALF one of its country's most active terrorist groups.

FURTHER RESOURCES

Books

Best, Steven and Anthony J. Nocella, editors. *Terrorists or Freedom Fighters?: Reflections on the Liberation of Animals.* New York: Lantern Books, 2004.

Committee on the Judiciary, Senate, United States Congress. *Animal Rights: Activism vs. Criminality: Hearing Before the Committee on the Judiciary, United States Senate, One Hundred Eighth Congress, Second Session, May 18, 2004.* Washington, DC: U.S. Government Printing Office, 2004.

Libby, Ronald T. *Eco-wars: Political Campaigns and Social Movements.* New York: Columbia University Press, 1998.

National Research Council of the National Academies. *Science, Medicine, and Animals.* Washington, DC: National Academies Press, 2004.

Web sites

Animal Liberation Front (ALF). "Homepage of ALF." <http://www.animalliberationfront.com/> (accessed May 29, 2006).

People for the Ethical Treatment of Animals (PETA). "Homepage of PETA." <http://www.peta.org/> (accessed May 29, 2006).

AIDS Die-in Protest

Photograph

By: Scott Perry

Date: April 19, 1992

Source: AP Images.

About the Photographer: Photographer Scott Perry worked for many years as a freelance photographer, primarily for the Associated Press and the *Maine Times*. His pictures appeared in publications around the world, including the *New York Times, USA Today*, and *National Geographic*. He has since shifted his focus to creating specialized panoramic landscape photographs in Maine and New Hampshire.

INTRODUCTION

Acquired Immune Deficiency Syndrome (AIDS) is a disease characterized by damage to the immune system caused by the human immunodeficiency virus (HIV). It is contracted through an exchange of body fluids, including semen, vaginal secretions, blood, or breast milk. Believed to have originated in sub-Saharan Africa in the 1950s, the disease began to appear in the United States in 1979, with only a few cases. Throughout the 1980s, more people were diagnosed with this mysterious virus, which appeared to be uniformly fatal. People everywhere in the world were infected, but, in the United States, the illness initially spread most quickly through the homosexual community and among intravenous drug users. As a result, the general public was slow to learn of the threat, often considering themselves safe since they did not belong to one of the high-risk populations. However, AIDS continued to spread, until it reached pandemic proportions. As of the beginning of 2006, an estimated forty million people are living with the virus and as many as twenty-five million have died. Although treatments have improved and life expectancy is far greater following an HIV diagnosis than it was in decades past, AIDS remains a fatal illness. It also remains a moral and political battleground, as protestors stand up for the rights of AIDS patients around the globe.

PRIMARY SOURCE

AIDS DIE-IN PROTEST

See primary source image.

SIGNIFICANCE

During the early days of the AIDS epidemic, when less was known about how it spread, fear of the illness led to protests targeting those suffering from the disease. There was concern about how safe it was to allow AIDS patients to continue attending school or going to work with healthy people; some questioned whether AIDS patients were putting other people at risk by exposing them to the illness. Many AIDS patients found

themselves discriminated against: fired from their jobs, forced out of school, and shunned. Protestors who backed the rights of AIDS patients fought for legislation that would prevent this sort of discrimination, often staging sit-ins that they dubbed die-ins, since the stakes when dealing with AIDS were ultimately life and death. The story of Ryan White, a thirteen-year-old hemophiliac who contracted AIDS through a blood transfusion and was hounded out of his school in 1985, became a rallying point for protestors trying to gain sympathy for people suffering from the illness. In 1988, the U.S. first banned discrimination against federal workers who had the AIDS virus. At the time, President Reagan was criticized for limiting the protection; a call for legislation protecting all workers with HIV had been discussed. In 1990, after the death of Ryan White at age eighteen, the U.S. Congress passed the Ryan White CARE Act, a last-resort payment source for treatment for AIDS patients with no other recourse.

Education became the most powerful and most accessible weapon in the war against AIDS. As more information about the disease became available, people were forced to accept that anyone could contract HIV, not just those in high-risk categories. The media joined forces with the federal government and the medical community to educate the public, providing public service announcements and highlighting examples of people living with the disease. By the 1990s, the spread of AIDS had slowed in the United States, but in parts of the world where education is limited and money for treatment nonexistent, people have continued to become infected in epidemic numbers.

Protestors continue to call for education, both in the U.S. and abroad, and also focus on the need for additional funding for AIDS research, which still can only be treated, not cured. Although federal funding has been promised for both research and social service programs, the dollars delivered are often less than the amounts originally discussed. In some cases, much of the funding for educational programs has been funneled into programs that preach abstinence only, rather than providing people with the knowledge necessary to engage in protected sexual relations. Protestors also target drug companies providing AIDS treatment in developing nations, accusing them of putting high profits above people's lives. In the developing world, AIDS medications are often prohibitively expensive and limited in availability, so that few people receive treatment. The United Nations also has been criticized, with protestors going so far as to chain themselves together in the building's lobby to emphasize their displeasure with world leaders who fail to provide adequate health services to AIDS patients.

PRIMARY SOURCE

AIDS Die-in Protest: A group of AIDS activists stage a die-in on the road leading to President Bush's vacation home in Kennebunkport, Maine, April 18, 1992, demonstrating against the Bush administration's AIDS policies. AP IMAGES.

Their demands centered on the need for more funding for vigorous, scientific AIDS research in an effort to find a cure for this deadly disease.

FURTHER RESOURCES

Books

Behrman, Greg. *The Invisible People: How the U.S. Has Slept Through the Global AIDS Pandemic, the Greatest Humanitarian Catastrophe of Our Time.* New York: Free Press, 2004.

Shilts, Randy, and William Greider. *And the Band Played On: Politics, People, and the AIDS Epidemic.* New York: Stonewall Inn Editions, 2000.

Periodicals

Liebert, Larry. "Reagan Assailed for Directive on AIDS." *San Francisco Chronicle* (August 3, 1988): A1.

Schapiro, Rich, and Paul H. B. Shin. "UN Rapped on AIDS." *New York Daily News* (June 1, 2006).

Web sites

Aegis. "So Little Time: An AIDS History." <http://www.aegis.com/topics/timeline/> (accessed June 2, 2006).

AIDSaction.org. <http://www.aidsaction.org/> (accessed June 2, 2006).

United Nations Program on HIV/AIDS. "2006 Report on the Global AIDS Epidemic." <http://www.unaids.org/en/HIV_data/2006GlobalReport/default.asp> (accessed June 2, 2006).

Greenpeace Protests French Nuclear Tests in the Mururoa Atoll

Photograph

By: Philippe Wojazer

Demonstrators protest that President Reagan misused funds to support Nicaraguan contras at the same time his administration refuses to support funding for AIDS prevention, Washington, D.C., June 1, 1987. © JP LAFFONT/SYGMA/CORBIS.

Date: September 1, 1995

Source: Wojazer, Philippe. "Greenpeace Protests French Nuclear Tests in the Mururoa Atoll." AP Images.

About the Photographer: Philippe Wojazer is a contributor to the Associated Press, a worldwide news agency based in New York.

INTRODUCTION

The first nuclear weapon was exploded by the United States in 1945. In 1960, France became the fourth country to explode an atomic bomb. Between 1960 and 1996, when it ceased testing permanently, France conducted 192 nuclear weapons test explosions, forty-one in the atmosphere and 134 underground.

French nuclear testing began in the Sahara Desert, but after Algeria won its independence in 1962, the French established the Centre d'Expérimentation du Pacifique (CEP, Pacific Experimentation Center) at Moruroa Atoll in French Polynesia.

In 1992, France announced a unilateral moratorium on nuclear weapons testing. In 1995, the new President of the French Republic, Jacques Chirac, announced that France would resume bomb testing at the CEP, with seven or eight explosions scheduled for 1995 and 1996. The governments of Japan, Australia, New Zealand, and the Philippines condemned the proposed tests, as did environmental organizations. One objection was that weapons testing undermined negotiations for a Comprehensive Test Ban Treaty, which had begun in 1993. The international environmental group Greenpeace also objected to the environmental damage that, it argued, would be done even by an underground test.

For many years Greenpeace had been drawing attention to French nuclear testing by defying its ban on vessels within a 12-mile (19-kilometer) radius of the CEP. The French government resented Greenpeace's efforts and had even resorted to international terrorism to quash them; in 1985, the first *Rainbow Warrior* was sunk at anchor in Auckland harbor, New Zealand, by a bomb set off by agents of the French equivalent of the Central Intelligence Agency, the Direction Générale de la Sécurité Extérieure (DGSE, General Directorate for External Security). The sinking of the vessel, which had been scheduled to lead a flotilla of small vessels into the CEP exclusion zone to interfere with French nuclear testing plans, killed a Greenpeace photographer. Several agents involved in the operation were convicted in New Zealand courts but served light sentences and were promoted upon returning to France.

After France's 1995 announcement of resumed testing, the *Rainbow Warrior II* (launched in 1989) was sent to the Moruroa area to repeat the mission of the first *Rainbow Warrior*: protest, publicize, and, if possible, disrupt. Two ships, the *Rainbow Warrior II* and the *Greenpeace*, approached the edge of the CEP exclusion zone on September 1, 1995. The French warship *Prairial* asked the vessels to turn back but they did not. French commandos stormed the Greenpeace vessels with grappling hooks and tear gas and arrested all on board, including American Samoa's Delegate to the U.S. Congress, Eni Faleomavaega (1943–). Meanwhile, two Greenpeace divers in high-speed inflatable boats penetrated to the center of the zone and dived under an offshore platform at Moruroa. Greenpeace claimed that the platform was the one where the nuclear test was scheduled to be conducted, while France claimed that it was a different platform.

The *Greenpeace* and the *Rainbow Warrior II*, which had already been seized in a similar confrontation in July, 1995, were towed to Hao, an island 375 miles (604 kilometers) north of the CEP, and held there by the French Navy for five months.

■ **PRIMARY SOURCE**

GREENPEACE PROTESTS FRENCH NUCLEAR TESTS IN THE MURUROA ATOLL

See primary source image.

■ **PRIMARY SOURCE**

Greenpeace Protests French Nuclear Tests in the Mururoa Atoll: A French Navy Commando dingy prepares to storm Greenpeace's ship Rainbow Warrior after it entered the 12-nautical mile (20kms) military restricted zone around the Mururoa atoll nuclear testing site, September 1, 1995. A French naval vessel stands by. AP IMAGES.

SIGNIFICANCE

When France announced in 1995 that it intended to carry out a series of nuclear tests, it also said that when the tests were over it would sign the Comprehensive Test Ban Treaty (CTBT), which had been under negotiation since 1993. The CTBT was conceived as a successor to the Partial Test Ban Treaty of 1963, which forbade nuclear tests in the oceans, atmosphere, and space and was eventually signed by 113 nations, including the United States and the Soviet Union, but not China or France. The CTBT, in contrast, would ban all nuclear explosions, including underground tests.

The last French nuclear test occurred on January 26, 1996. In 1998, France ratified the CTBT. (The United States has refused to ratify the treaty.) France is the only country having nuclear weapons to have dismantled all its nuclear testing facilities. In partial fulfillment of its

Office employees gather outside the French embassy at suburban Makati in Manila, the Philippines on September 11, 1995, to protest nuclear testing conducted by the French at Mururoa atoll in Pacific. AP IMAGES.

obligations under the CTBT, France has set up twenty-seven seismic monitoring stations to help detect possible test explosions. France also, in the late 1990s, began to dismantle its facilities for producing weapons-grade plutonium. France has also reduced the size of its nuclear arsenal, but still maintains a number of nuclear weapons and delivery systems, including a fleet of four nuclear submarines carrying nuclear-armed missiles.

FURTHER RESOURCES
Books

Weyler, Rex. *Greenpeace: How a Group of Journalists, Ecologists, and Visionaries Changed the World.* Emmaus, PA: Rodale, 2004.

Periodicals

Danielsson, Bengt. "Poisoned Pacific: The Legacy of French Nuclear Testing." *The Bulletin of the Atomic Scientists* 46, 2 (1990): 22–31.

Shenon, Philip. "France Seizes 2 Ships Owned by Greenpeace." *The New York Times* (September 2, 1995).

——— "French Navy Seizes a Third Ship At Site of Planned Nuclear Tests." *The New York Times* (September 4, 1995).

Web sites

Comprehensive Test Ban Treaty Organization. May 16, 2006. <http://www.ctbto.org> (accessed May 25, 2006).

GlobalSecurity.org. "Nuclear Weapons: France." April 28, 2005. <http://www.globalsecurity.org/wmd/world/france/nuke.htm> (accessed May 25, 2006).

Kyoto Protocol

United Nations document

By: United Nations

Date: December 11, 1997

Source: *United Nations.* "Kyoto Protocol to the United Nations Framework on Climate Change."

December 11, 1997. <http://unfccc.int/resource/docs/convkp/kpeng.html> (accessed May 16, 2006).

About the Author: The United Nations is an organization comprising almost all the world's recognized nations. It facilitates international cooperation in matters pertaining to law, security, economic development, and human rights.

INTRODUCTION

The Kyoto Protocol is an international agreement, signed by 163 countries, that was appended to the United Nations Framework Convention on Climate Change in 1997. The protocol opened for signature in 1997 and entered into force—that is, became law for those countries that had both signed and ratified it—in 2005. The purpose of the protocol is to control the production of six greenhouse gases, most notably carbon dioxide, that are released by agriculture and industry and that many believe are changing the climate of the Earth.

In 1988, the United Nations created the International Panel on Climate Change to study the question of whether the world's weather was becoming warmer or cooler. The first report of the panel was issued in 1990. It affirmed that the Earth was probably warming as a result of human activity. In 1992, the greatest number of national leaders to attend any gathering up to that time met in Rio de Janeiro, Brazil, for the United Nations Conference on Environment and Development, also known as the Earth Summit. This group created the United Nations Framework Convention on Climate Change, also known as the Rio Convention. The Rio Convention called for the stabilization of greenhouse-gas emissions by 2000. The United States was among the countries that ratified the Rio Convention.

Starting in 1995, the signatories of the Rio Convention held a meeting called the Conference of Parties every year. The third Conference of Parties was held in Kyoto, Japan, in 1997. Here the Kyoto Protocol to the Rio Convention was negotiated. The Kyoto Protocol called for a more aggressive approach to the reduction of greenhouse gases than the 1990 convention. Specifically, it sought a global reduction of greenhouse-gas emission of five percent from 1990 levels by 2008–2012. Individual country targets varied; Germany agreed to a twenty-five percent cut, the United Kingdom to a fifteen percent cut, and the United States to a seven percent cut. The United States signed the Kyoto Protocol but has neither ratified nor officially withdrawn from it.

A crane lifts up a huge solar panel on the Kyosela's new head office building in Kyoto, Japan, December 1,1997. AP IMAGES.

■ PRIMARY SOURCE

The Parties to this Protocol,

Being Parties to the United Nations Framework Convention on Climate Change, hereinafter referred to as "the Convention",
In pursuit of the ultimate objective of the Convention as stated in its Article 2,
Recalling the provisions of the Convention,
Being guided by Article 3 of the Convention,
Pursuant to the Berlin Mandate adopted by decision 1/CP.1 of the Conference of the Parties to the Convention at its first session,
Have agreed as follows:

ARTICLE 2

1. Each Party included in Annex I, in achieving its quantified emission limitation and reduction commitments under Article 3, in order to promote sustainable development, shall:

(a) Implement and/or further elaborate policies and measures in accordance with its national circumstances, such as:

(i) Enhancement of energy efficiency in relevant sectors of the national economy;

(ii) Protection and enhancement of sinks and reservoirs of greenhouse gases not controlled by the Montreal Protocol, taking into account its commitments under relevant international environmental agreements; promotion of sustainable forest management practices, afforestation and reforestation;

(iii) Promotion of sustainable forms of agriculture in light of climate change considerations;

(iv) Research on, and promotion, development and increased use of, new and renewable forms of energy, of carbon dioxide sequestration technologies and of advanced and innovative environmentally sound technologies;

(v) Progressive reduction or phasing out of market imperfections, fiscal incentives, tax and duty exemptions and subsidies in all greenhouse gas emitting sectors that run counter to the objective of the Convention and application of market instruments;

(vi) Encouragement of appropriate reforms in relevant sectors aimed at promoting policies and measures which limit or reduce emissions of greenhouse gases not controlled by the Montreal Protocol;

(vii) Measures to limit and/or reduce emissions of greenhouse gases not controlled by the Montreal Protocol in the transport sector;

(viii) Limitation and/or reduction of methane emissions through recovery and use in waste management, as well as in the production, transport and distribution of energy;

(b) Cooperate with other such Parties to enhance the individual and combined effectiveness of their policies and measures adopted under this Article, pursuant to Article 4, paragraph 2(e)(i), of the Convention. To this end, these Parties shall take steps to share their experience and exchange information on such policies and measures, including developing ways of improving their comparability, transparency and effectiveness. The Conference of the Parties serving as the meeting of the Parties to this Protocol shall, at its first session or as soon as practicable thereafter, consider ways to facilitate such cooperation, taking into account all relevant information.

2. The Parties included in Annex I shall pursue limitation or reduction of emissions of greenhouse gases not controlled by the Montreal Protocol from aviation and marine bunker fuels, working through the International Civil Aviation Organization and the International Maritime Organization, respectively.

3. The Parties included in Annex I shall strive to implement policies and measures under this Article in such a way as to minimize adverse effects, including the adverse effects of climate change, effects on international trade, and social, environmental and economic impacts on other Parties, especially developing country Parties and in particular those identified in Article 4, paragraphs 8 and 9, of the Convention, taking into account Article 3 of the Convention. The Conference of the Parties serving as the meeting of the Parties to this Protocol may take further action, as appropriate, to promote the implementation of the provisions of this paragraph.

4. The Conference of the Parties serving as the meeting of the Parties to this Protocol, if it decides that it would be beneficial to coordinate any of the policies and measures in paragraph 1(a) above, taking into account different national circumstances and potential effects, shall consider ways and means to elaborate the coordination of such policies and measures.

ARTICLE 3

1. The Parties included in Annex I shall, individually or jointly, ensure that their aggregate anthropogenic carbon dioxide equivalent emissions of the greenhouse gases listed in Annex A do not exceed their assigned amounts, calculated pursuant to their quantified emission limitation and reduction commitments inscribed in Annex B and in accordance with the provisions of this Article, with a view to reducing their overall emissions of such gases by at least 5 per cent below 1990 levels in the commitment period 2008 to 2012.

2. Each Party included in Annex I shall, by 2005, have made demonstrable progress in achieving its commitments under this Protocol. . . .

ARTICLE 28

The original of this Protocol, of which the Arabic, Chinese, English, French, Russian and Spanish texts are equally authentic, shall be deposited with the Secretary-General of the United Nations.

DONE at Kyoto this eleventh day of December one thousand nine hundred and ninety-seven.

SIGNIFICANCE

The administration of President Bill Clinton was only moderately friendly to the Kyoto Protocol. Key figures in the Administration admitted the reality of global climate change, but the administration never submitted the protocol to the U.S. Congress for ratification. With the election of George W. Bush in 2000, U.S. policy turned strongly against the Kyoto Protocol. President Bush and his supporters have repeatedly emphasized that they consider global climate change itself to be uncertain or, if real, not necessarily caused by human activity. Both the Clinton and Bush administrations feared that implementation of the Kyoto Protocol would harm the economy of the United States.

Although the reality of global climate change is disputed by a few scientists, the great majority of scientists who study climate agree that the Earth's weather is not only changing, but changing as a result of human activities that release carbon dioxide and other greenhouse gases into the air. Carbon dioxide is released primarily by burning coal and petroleum products, such as gasoline. Statements affirming that human activity is modifying the climate have been issued by many scientific groups, including the American Meteorological Society (2003), the American Geophysical Union (2003), and the American Association for the Advancement of Science (2004). The latter urged that "governments and consumers in the United States and worldwide should take immediate steps to reduce the threat of global warming and to prepare for a future in which coastal flooding, reduced crop yields and elevated rates of climate-related illness are all but certain." Whether or not the Kyoto Protocol's carbon-dioxide reduction goals would be adequate even if implemented by all its signatories—including the United States, the world's largest greenhouse-gas emitter, both per-capita and overall—is scientifically uncertain. Proponents of the protocol argue that given the global stakes, it is better to begin taking even inadequate steps rather than no steps at all. Opponents fall into several camps. Some, including many political conservatives in the U.S., argue that global climate change may not be happening, may not be caused by human activity if it is happening, and may not be avoidable even if it is happening and is caused by human activity. Others argue that the Kyoto Protocol is economically irrational and would cause net harm to human well-being even if it succeeded in mitigating global climate change. U.S. criticism of the protocol argues that it does not ask for sufficient greenhouse-gas reductions from China, the second-largest greenhouse-gas emitter.

As the scientific consensus that greenhouse warming is real, potentially disastrous, and human-caused becomes more complete, U.S. political attitudes toward greenhouse-gas mitigation appear to be changing. In July 2005, the U.S. Senate approved a nonbinding bipartisan resolution affirming that "there is growing scientific consensus that human activity is a substantial cause of greenhouse gas accumulation" and calling for "mandatory market-based limits" on greenhouse-gas emissions. In April 2006, the

California Legislature began consideration of the Global Warming Solutions Act, which would set the first mandatory statewide caps on greenhouse-gas emissions. Since the bill reflects targets for greenhouse-gas reductions set by the Republican governor, Arnold Schwarzenegger, it is likely to pass. "I say, the debate is over," Schwarzenegger said in June 2005. "We know the science. We see the threat, and we know that the time for action is now." In May 2005, 132 mayors of U.S. cities and towns formed a bipartisan coalition to implement the Kyoto Protocol's emissions targets at a community level.

In May 2006, a study by the National Academy of Sciences that had been commissioned by President George W. Bush announced that global warming is "real and particularly strong within the past 20 years" and attributed the warming primarily to carbon dioxide released by burning fossil fuels. The report said that "Global warming could well have serious adverse societal and ecological impacts by the end of this century."

FURTHER RESOURCES
Books
Cameron, Peter D., and Donald Zillman. *Kyoto: From Principles to Practice*. New York: Kluwer Law International, 2001.

Periodicals
Kintisch, Eli. "Climate Change: Along the Road From Kyoto." *Science* 311 (2006): 1702–1703.

Oreskes, Naomi. "The Scientific Consensus on Climate Change." *Science* 306 (2004): 1686.

Web sites
American Association for the Advancement of Science. "Climate Experts Urge Immediate Action to Offset Impact of Global Warming." June 16, 2004. <http://www.aaas.org/news/releases/2004/0616climate.shtml> (accessed May 16, 2006).

A Bitter Pill For the World's Poor

Drug companies Do Care for the Suffering—If They Have Some Cash

Magazine article

By: Isabel Hilton

Date: January 5, 2000

Source: Hilotn, Isabel. "A Bitter Pill For the World's Poor." *The Guardian*. January 5, 2005.

About the Author: Isabel Hilton is a reporter, journalist, writer, and radio broadcaster born in Aberdeen, Scotland. She is a lecturer on international relations and a member of the Royal Institute of International Affairs. She is also a regular contributor to distinguished publications such as the *New Yorker*, *The Guardian*, *The Observer*, and *New York Times Magazine*.

INTRODUCTION

According to the World Health Organization (WHO), more than fourteen million people die in developing countries each year due to curable diseases (such as diarrheal diseases, tuberculosis, and malaria). The HIV/AIDS epidemic is one example of how access to affordable drugs in impoverished nations, a key component in disease intervention, is complicated by trade restrictions, policy, and the interests of the pharmaceutical industry.

Brazil's National AIDS Program (NAP) is regarded as a successful model of combating the HIV/AIDS epidemic. Since its inception, HIV death rates in Brazil have dropped fifty percent. Despite spending $232 million by 2001 to implement this national health initiative, Brazil has estimated a savings of more than $1.1 billion in healthcare costs. Many researchers urge immediate action using this model of intervention in other developing nations in Asia and Sub-Saharan Africa. However, others are more cautious and argue that a methodical approach (slower to enact) is necessary to implement a system that is sustainable and effective for the long term. Often, developing countries lack the resources and infrastructure to assure adequate delivery of the drugs to the population targeted for prevention and treatment. To further cloud the issue, are factors such as intellectual property rights and trade policy. With a market worth more than $65 billion per year, some human rights organizations ask why drug companies aren't investing more research and development dollars where it's needed most, on diseases that primarily affect poor nations.

PRIMARY SOURCE

In a tiny village in Bihar, in northern India, a young man of 17 was sitting outside his house. He was shaking and sweating profusely, the whites of his eyes were yellow, and his spleen was found to be enlarged. He was suffering from leishmaniasis, known once to the British as dum dum fever and today in India as kalaazar. Untreated, the illness attacks the immune system until the victim succumbs to some opportunistic infection—most likely tuberculosis—and dies.

The young man had tried to get treatment, despite his family's poverty. His father was a rickshaw puller, so every penny the family had was laboriously earned. They had spent several months' income on treatment, but the young man had been given a drug that had lost its effectiveness. Now there was no money and no more treatment.

It is a story repeated daily in towns and villages across the developing world. Whatever the recorded cause of death—leishmaniasis, tuberculosis, pneumonia—the real cause is poverty. Poor people in tropical countries are at risk from a range of diseases for which they cannot get treatment—either because medicines are available at prices they cannot afford or, worse still, because no medicines are available.

The most common treatments for leishmaniasis were discovered by British doctors in the closing years of British rule. They applied their minds to leishmaniasis because they needed to keep their soldiers healthy. For the same reason, the U.S. invested in malaria research during the Vietnam war. But when there is no pressing military or colonial imperative, the developed world loses interest in tropical diseases. Multinational pharmaceutical companies neglect the diseases of the tropics, not because the science is impossible but because there is, in the cold economics of the drugs companies, no market.

There is, of course, a market in the sense that there is a need: millions of people die from preventable or curable diseases every week. But there is no market in the sense that, unlike Viagra, medicines for leishmaniasis are needed by poor people in poor countries. Pharmaceutical companies judge that they would not get sufficient return on research investment, so why, they ask, should we bother? Their obligation to shareholders, they say, demands that they put the effort into trying to find cures for the diseases of affluence and longevity—heart disease, cancer, Alzheimer's. Of the thousands of new compounds drug companies have brought to the market in recent years, fewer than 1% are for tropical diseases.

We could just shrug, of course, and say that's what you get for being poor. Or, if we were feeling more charitable at the dawn of the new millennium, we could post off a batch of (probably outdated) medicines and feel better. The companies have their own equivalent of those care packages in donation programmes—short-term gestures that look good in the annual report. They can also be cited to counterbalance charges of neglect or of dumping drugs in developing countries that cannot be marketed where regulation is more stringent. (That is so widespread that there is a grim little joke in the industry: if there are no side effects, they say, it must be Honduras.) The trouble with charitable gestures is that they are only gestures. If we want to have an effect, something more systematic is required.

Why should we? Because, as the economist Jeffrey Sachs points out, it is no good waiting for developing countries to attain the degree of affluence that would allow them to buy themselves an effective health service, equipped with the medicines we take for granted. The fact is that ill health in tropical countries is a huge drag on development, and without intervention in health, other aid is the less effective.

And who should intervene? The pharmaceutical companies have the capacity to do so, as well as a moral debt that they have not begun to pay. But it is unrealistic to suppose that they act without public stimulus. The World Health Organisation has the public authority but not the technical capacity. As a partnership, the industry and international public health bodies could make a significant difference, if they were prepared to set aside, respectively, corporate greed and bureaucratic complacency.

There are signs of a change of approach at the WHO, as the impact of the arrival of the former Norwegian prime minister, Gro Harlem Bruntland, is felt. For the first time in years, the organisation is displaying energy and initiative. How far this will go, though, will depend on how the industry responds.

In the corporate headquarters of major drug companies, the public relations posters display the image they like to present: of caring companies that bring benefit to humanity, relieving the suffering of the sick. What they don't say, is that, so far, their humanity has not extended beyond the limits of the pockets of the sick.

SIGNIFICANCE

On the advent of the 25th anniversary of the beginning of the AIDS epidemic, over forty million people are living with HIV worldwide. Over 4,900,000 new infections occurred in 2005. HIV/AIDS is a pandemic with increasing rates of infection. There is immediate need for intervention on a global scale; however, the scientific community is divided on the issue of how to halt one of the largest public health threats of the twenty-first century.

In 2003, WHO launched the 3 by 5 Initiative to treat three million HIV positive people with anti-retroviral (ARV) therapy in poor countries by the end of 2005. This approach involves a strategic framework for antiretroviral therapy in five categories: global leadership, partnership and advocacy; urgent, sustained country support; standardized tools to implement ARV therapy; effective and dependable medical

and diagnostic supplies; and quickly recognizing and applying advances.

Health disparities are exacerbated as this disease continues to thrive in marginalized populations (i.e. developing countries, drug users, the poor, rural areas, and minorities). HIV infection in American infants has nearly vanished due to prophylactic (preventative) therapy with antiretroviral (ARV) drugs. In North America and Europe, death rates within ten years of diagnosis for those with HIV have dropped almost eighty percent with ARV use. However, in developing countries, of the six million in need of treatment, only 400,000 actually received ARV therapy in 2003. Fifty percent of the population requiring treatment is located in sub-Saharan Africa and India. Moreover, most of the fourteen million HIV/AIDS orphans in the world reside in Africa. Without timely intervention, this figure is estimated to climb as high as twenty-five million by the year 2010. According to the WHO,

> immense advances in human well-being co-exist with extreme deprivation. In global health, we are witnessing the benefits of new medicines and technologies. But there are unprecedented reversals. Life expectancies have collapsed in some of the poorest countries to half the level of the richest—attributable to the ravages of HIV/AIDS in parts of sub-Saharan Africa and to more than a dozen 'failed states.'

Anti-retroviral therapy is a key component to fighting HIV/AIDS worldwide, but access to therapy in developing countries remains problematic. In January 2006, Oxfam (a United Kingdom-based international aid agency) submitted a letter to the WHO asking for a review of global trade agreements. Oxfam argues that these treaties unfairly increase intellectual property rights, which in the end hinders the impoverished access to affordable drugs.

In 2003, UNAIDS established a Global Reference Group on HIV/AIDS and Human Rights. The result is that access to HIV/AIDS therapy is now a human rights issue (as well as a financially sound strategy). In the end, an integrated approach is needed using medical, structural, and cultural interventions, with the cooperation of politicians, governments, private industry, and others.

FURTHER RESOURCES
Books

World Health Organization. *Treating 3 Million by 2005: Making it Happen.* Geneva, Switzerland: World Health Organization, 2003.

World Health Organization. *World Health Report 2006.* Geneva, Switzerland: World Health Organization, 2006.

A four-year-old girl holds her vaccination certificate at a medical clinic in Craquixajay, a small rural village 65 miles west from Guatemala City, November 17, 2004. AP IMAGES.

Periodicals

de Carvalho Mesquita Ayres, J.R., et al. "Vulnerability, Human Rights, and Comprehensive Health Care Needs of Young People Living With HIV/AIDS." *American Journal of Public Health*. 96 (2006): 1001–1006.

Desvarieux, M., et al. "Antiretroviral Therapy in Resource-Poor Countries: Illusions and Realities." *American Journal of Public Health*. 95 (2005): 1117–1122.

McCoy, D., et al. "Expanding Access to Antiretroviral Therapy in Sub-Saharan Africa: Avoiding the Pitfalls and Dangers, Capitalizing on the Opportunities." *American Journal of Public Health*. 95 (2005): 18–22.

Web sites

Oxfam GB. "Drug Companies vs. Brazil: The Threat to Public Health." May 2001. <http://www.oxfam.org.uk/what_we_do/issues/health/papers.htm> (accessed May 14, 2006).

Oxfam GB. "Public Health at Risk." April 2006. <http://www.oxfam.org.uk/what_we_do/issues/health/papers.htm> (accessed May 14, 2006).

PETA's "We'd Rather Go Naked" Campaign

Photograph

By: Mike Theiler

Date: November 29, 2001

Source: Photo by Mike Theiler/Getty Images.

About the Photographer: Mike Theiler is a freelance photographer who is a regular contributor to Reuters, AFP, Getty, and the Associated Press news agencies. Getty Images in a photo agency that covers breaking events from around the world. The agency covers sports, news and entertainment events with hundreds of photographers located in many international locations.

PRIMARY SOURCE

PETA's "We'd Rather Go Naked" Campaign: Demonstrators from the People for the Ethical Treatment of Animals (PETA) rally partially naked as they protest the fur industry November 29, 2001 in front of the White House in Wasington, D.C. PHOTO BY MIKE THEILER/ GETTY IMAGES.

INTRODUCTION

People for the Ethical Treatment of Animals (PETA) is an animal rights advocacy organization that is famous for provocative advertising aimed at promoting vegetarianism and combating any forms of perceived mistreatment of animals. The organization, which is based in the United States with operations in the United Kingdom, Germany, the Asia-Pacific region, and India, was founded in 1980 to protect the rights of animals. The more than one million members of PETA around the world support the organization's mission that eating, wearing, experimenting on animals should not take place. PETA is also opposed to animals being used for entertainment in shows or circuses, which they contend is abusive to the rights of the animals.

PETA focuses its activities in four primary areas—factory farms, laboratories, entertainment venues, and the clothing industry—where the organization says animals are being most abused. To publicize its message, PETA has historically developed controversial advertising campaigns aimed at shocking its audiences into realizing how animals are being mistreated. A past campaign included imagery of victims of the Holocaust placed alongside pictures of animals in captivity. The campaign called "Holocaust on Your Plate," presented the murder of six million Jews by the Nazis as being comparable to the slaughter of animals for human consumption.

The organization has targeted specific campaigns at younger children with the goal of producing future generations more strongly committed to vegetarianism. The organization released a comic book entitled "Your Mommy Kills Animals" with images of a woman taking a knife to a bunny rabbit. As a result of PETA's well established record of public exposure and use of the mass media, the organization has had numerous successes in stopping specific acts of alleged mistreatment of animals. Meat and fur producing companies that have been targeted by PETA's publicity campaigns have occasionally been moved to change their operations or even shut down facilities. The organization is actively involved in promoting the spaying and neutering of family pets with the goal of limiting the numbers of unwanted animals.

PRIMARY SOURCE

PETA'S "WE'D RATHER GO NAKED" CAMPAIGN
See primary source image.

SIGNIFICANCE
Since it was first organized in 1980, shock has been PETA's primary tactic for publicizing its core message that animals are being mistreated by humans. The organization routinely uses controversy and sexual explicitness to gain the attention of their target audience. In certain cases, particularly where PETA has compared animal slaughter to historical incidents of genocide, there has been a general public outcry of disgust. While many people around the world choose vegetarianism as a form of protest against animal slaughter for eating purposes, PETA's tactics have caused it to be viewed by many as a fringe group that uses means usually shunned by more moderate organizations to make its point.

This photo shows that PETA does not shy away from using sexuality and nudity to advertise its message. Naked or nearly naked models have often been used by PETA as a means of turning heads and adding to the shock value of its campaigns. The organization gained considerable notoriety for a campaign entitled "We'd Rather Go Naked than Wear Fur." This ad campaign poses models, often well known and recognized celebrities in the nude, with a text message bearing the name of the campaign. Singer Melissa Ethridge, basketball star Dennis Rodman, and supermodel Christy Turlington are just some of the more famous individuals that have been featured in the campaign. Although the campaign was condemned and shunned by many family value and conservative groups, PETA did succeed in stirring up considerable public sentiment against the fur industry. The result, according to PETA, was that several major clothing lines, including Calvin Klein, agreed to remove real fur from their products.

The decision to pose for this photo in front of the White House demonstrates the extent to which PETA activists appreciate the need for sensationalism to get their messages across. Washington, D.C. and the White House in particular are among the most scrutinized and closely watched places in the world by the mass media. For activists and protesters looking to sensationalize their messages, this location has long been a top choice. With the knowledge that they would be arrested for public indecency, the protesters chose to demonstrate outside the White House because their arrests would draw the attention of photographers, like the one who took this picture.

FURTHER RESOURCES
Books
Workman, Dave P. *Peta Files: The Dark Side of the Animal Rights Movement*. Bellevue, WA: Merril Press, 2003.

Web sites
People for the Ethical Treatment of Animals (PETA). <www.peta.org> (accessed May 25, 2006).

The AIDS-Drug Warrior

Web magazine article

By: Daryl Lindsey

Date: June 1, 2001

Source: Lindsey, Daryl. *Salon*. "The AIDS-drug Warrior." June 1, 2001. <http://archive.salon.com/news/feature/2001/06/18/love/print.html> (accessed May 30, 2006).

About the Author: Daryl Lindsey is the editor of the online English edition of *Speigle*, a German magazine. He has also contributed to the *Guardian* and other

English-language newspapers. Founded in 1995, *Salon* has received several awards including "Best Online Magazine" by Yahoo Internet Life and "Best 50 Websites" by Time Life. *Salon* reaches more than 2.5 million visitors, most of who reside in the U.S.

INTRODUCTION

According to The World Bank, "Sub-Saharan Africa has just over ten percent of the world's population, but is home to more than sixty percent of all people living with HIV—25.8 million." The solution to managing the worldwide HIV/AIDS situation is complex, especially in developing nations. According to Africa Action, a Washington, D.C.-based organization that works for political, social, and economic justice in Africa,

> an effective response to HIV/AIDS requires a more urgent and comprehensive approach from the U.S. and the international community. It requires greater funding, a scale-up of effective prevention, treatment, care and support programs, support for the rights and needs of women and girls, and new investments in Africa's human resources and health care infrastructure.

Large multinational pharmaceutical companies are under more scrutiny of late. Critics charge that drug makers focus more on diseases that affect the affluent rather than tropical diseases and other diseases that affect developing countries.

Historically, medical research of tropical diseases was driven by war and colonialism—the need to keep specific populations of people alive and healthy (i.e. soldiers and settlers). Today, the advancement of medical science has resulted in cures for many diseases, but affluent people in developed nations have the most access to lifesaving drugs and technology, while millions in the least developed countries continue to die. Lack of health care infrastructure, lack of affordable drugs, and lack of political stability deter access to treatment and worsen the HIV/AIDS crisis.

There are two sides to this debate. While critics argue drug makers can do more to help, pharmaceutical companies claim that reducing drug prices will significantly decrease profits that are funneled to research and development of new drugs. Critics say drug makers hinder progress by offering over-priced drugs and trying to block efforts to produce generic drugs. Frustrated by high pricing and corporate influence, countries like Brazil and South Africa sought to develop their own drugs or import cheaper versions from other countries. In response, the U.S. government petitioned the World Health Organization (WHO) to sanction both countries.

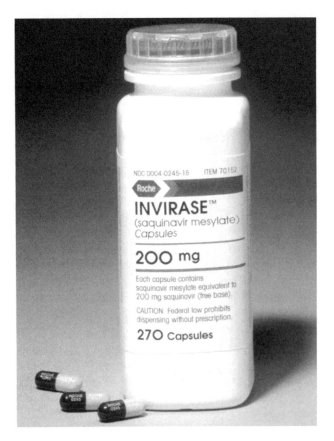

The new AIDS treatment drug "Saquinavir" was approved by the Food and Drug Administration on December 7, 1995, to be sold under the brand name "Invirase". AP IMAGES.

Critics point out that the U.S. government, backed by the pharmaceutical industry, has challenged international treaties aimed at providing poor countries access to affordable medicine and generic drugs. Many researchers, activists, and citizens assert that the right to health (including affordable medicines) is a human rights issue.

PRIMARY SOURCE

WASHINGTON—Every day a new headline emerges touting a victory in the global fight against the AIDS epidemic. One day, a pharmaceutical company announces it will deeply discount its drugs for the African market. The next, Yale University and Bristol-Myers Squibb announce they will no longer enforce their patent on an AIDS drug used in HIV-ravaged South Africa. Then 39 companies abruptly withdraw their lawsuit against the South African government over a 1997 law that would make it easier for the country to produce generic versions of patented drugs or import brand-name drugs from other countries to sell at cheaper prices.

All good news, right?

Wrong, says Jamie Love. It's just slick humanitarian-flavored spin.

For Love, one of the leading—and most outspoken—activists on the front lines of the AIDS-drug pricing wars, the real issue is that the major pharmaceutical companies still maintain control over who can manufacture their patented drugs and how much they cost. As the head of the Ralph Nader-founded Consumer Project on Technology, Love has been trying for years to persuade governments in developing nations to wrest control of AIDS-drug policy and pricing from the pharmaceuticals. Love argues that by issuing so-called compulsory licenses that would allow generic drug manufacturers to create cheap and ubiquitous versions of AIDS drugs, developing nations would drive down the cost of raw materials, increase competition and make the drugs more widely available.

Love is a blue-eyed firebrand whose silver-streaked locks of brown hair are the only thing that hint at his 51 years of age. The day I visited Love's modest digs at the Carnegie Foundation offices in Washington—Love's operation runs on a fraction of the budget of most NGOs involved in AIDS policy—he had just returned from yet another trip to Europe, where he attended an international meeting on AIDS and intellectual property. He took me on a quick tour, through a fortress of bookshelves and metal filing cabinets, where he gave terse orders to colleagues and tried to make the world of intellectual property policy more thrilling for a reporter.

Love explained that he is pursuing a three-part strategy in his push for compulsory licensing, with South Africa as the centerpiece. First, he's working with CIPLA, the generic drug manufacturer, to demonstrate what it actually costs to manufacture AIDS drugs: Love and CIPLA claim that it costs less than $1 a day to manufacture a three-drug cocktail for one patient. Second, he's turning to the private sector, lining up the international mining company Anglo American and healthcare providers to demand compulsory licenses from the South African and other governments. Finally, if those licenses are issued, he will work with CIPLA to get drugs to the corporations and healthcare providers that want to provide them to their employees and patients.

The foundations of Love's compulsory licensing push were laid in 1997, when the South African government passed a law that would make compulsory licensing and parallel importing easier. (Parallel importing is the practice of purchasing drugs from a third party in another country instead of directly from the manufacturer. It's cheaper because pharmaceutical companies usually charge lower prices in poorer countries.) The United States, under the stewardship of then-Vice President Al Gore, pressured South Africa to abandon or revise the legislation, and the pharmaceutical companies sued. In 1998, the South African government backed off, saying it would not issue compulsory licenses. Then, in March, a month before the trial was slated to begin, it also said it would not seek to do parallel imports. A month later, the pharmaceutical companies dropped their case against South Africa.

It's been over a month since the case was dismissed. Unwilling to take on a difficult legal battle against the South African government, few companies have stepped forward to demand licenses to produce generic versions of AIDS cocktail drugs: Only CIPLA and Aspen Pharmacare, South Africa's largest generic drug manufacturer, have attempted to do so. Meanwhile, drug companies have been slashing their prices—in order to discourage South Africa from succumbing to the temptation of compulsory licensing. But he says they haven't dropped them to rock-bottom production cost, and working with CIPLA, he has numbers to prove it.

The pharmaceutical GlaxoSmithKline, for example, announced on June 11 that it would discount Combivir—a two-drug combination—to $2 a day for governments, charity organizations and NGOs in Africa. CIPLA, however, has offered the same drug combination of Lamivudine and zidovine plus a third drug, nevirapine, for between 96 cents a day for nonprofits or $1.64 for governments—at a low-end cost of $350 a year, as much as 50 percent less than Glaxo's lowest bid, according to the World Health Organization.

Given these numbers, in a situation where even pennies more in cost mean lives lost, Love keeps hammering away on the generic-licensing theme. And he's lined up some heavy hitters in the private sector to back him: The international mining company Anglo American, the largest mining company in South Africa, has proposed supplying as many as 50,000 of its HIV-positive employees with generic drugs made by CIPLA. In March, CIPLA registered a request with the South African government for a compulsory license for the key drugs it needs to produce the cocktail. The company expects a prolonged legal battle with the government.

Love turned to the private sector in part because of his frustration with the South African government's slow response to the AIDS crisis—a frustration born of his experiences during the South African trial, when he served as an advisor to the Health Ministry, a party to the suit. South Africa's hesitations and missteps on the issue are well-chronicled. President Thabo Mbeki has expressed concerns about the safety of cocktail treatments and even questioned publicly, to international dismay, whether HIV is the true cause of AIDS. The South African government has so far refused to declare the AIDS crisis a national emergency—although a staggering 4.7 million South Africans are infected. And it has been reluctant to issue compulsory licenses or support proposals like Love's. In a recent interview with the U.K. Guardian, South African Health Minister Manto Tshabalala-Msimang said: "To be frank...we haven't thought it through." In her Guardian interview, Tshabalala-Msimang asked the reporter whether Anglo American, the company that Love is working with to distribute anti-retrovirals to its workers, would provide the families of its miners with access to the drugs and also what effect the heat in the mines would have on workers taking the drugs. These were not questions that inspired confidence that the minister was fully informed.

To be fair, the South African government also has a more legitimate reason for its ambivalent attitude toward drug treatment: Proper use of retrovirals requires a healthcare infrastructure that the country lacks. Anglo American has a better chance of efficiently delivering and administering the drugs—which is another reason Love is optimistic about private initiatives. Lending credence to his position is the decision made by auto giant DaimlerChrysler earlier this week to provide anti-HIV cocktail treatments to employees and their families, totaling as many as 23,000 patients.

Mention the global AIDS bureaucracy, centered in the U.N. organization UNAIDS and spread through innumerable NGOs, and Love scoffs derisively. "I pitched this private-sector stuff because if you sit around and wait for these assholes at the U.N. agencies to get their acts together, a lot of caskets are going to go into the ground," he says. "They're not men of action. They're followers, not leaders. There's no leadership taking place at the U.N. agencies. There's a lot of great pensions that are coming down. There are some high salaries being paid and sumptuous meals being consumed and business-class tickets being given out. But I have to say: Leadership? No, I'm sorry. I mean, this is Basic 101 stuff. What are we doing? We're figuring out how much it costs to manufacture drugs, we're figuring out how you can solve the intellectual property problems, how you can solve the drug registration problems. We're trying to get people to act," he says.

Love isn't impressed when I point out that UNAIDS has met with CIPLA, and that international organizations monitoring essential drug pricing routinely cite CIPLA's quotes in their comparison charts. "When things are on the front page of the New York Times, they have to acknowledge them," he says, raising his voice. "They haven't been the people pushing compulsory licensing. Instead, they're the ones making the big bucks. And that's wrong because they're the ones with the big megaphone and the big voice."

The United Nations recently announced that it would create a $7 billion superfund to fight AIDS, malaria and tuberculosis. Details of that plan are expected to be announced at a

U.N. General Assembly meeting on the AIDS crisis in New York next week. But Love has little confidence that the money will be used in the most effective way.

Officials from the United Nations and global AIDS organizations, for their part, say that activists like Love, fixated on treatment, ignore the crucial element of prevention. Instead of emphasizing widespread administration of AIDS cocktail treatments, organizations like WHO and UNAIDS have stressed education and prevention programs, which are easier to administer and potentially have the most long-term impact. Pieter Piot, the famous Belgian epidemiologist who helped identify the Ebola virus and is executive director of UNAIDS, recently described his view for how the U.N. plan should work in the New York Times: "We feel strongly that the response to AIDS has to be a balanced one: prevention and treatment. In the current climate, people forget that. I'm really getting tired of the fact that a terribly complex problem of treatment and care for people having H.I.V. is reduced to the price of anti-retroviral drugs."

Those are exactly the kinds of statements that raise Love's ire. "Are we supposed to say that since we can't save all of them, we're going to let them all die? That's an appalling, racist attitude. We're going to do all we can to save them," he says. "We make our little contribution on the intellectual property side and you'd think we'd raped Queen Mary."

Love says that when famous AIDS bureaucrats like Piot criticize his work, they fail to see the forest for the trees. He says that what he and his organization are doing is just one part of the puzzle, though admittedly one that's currently getting a lot of attention. "We're not saying prevention's not important. We don't campaign against those things—everyone knows those are important."

What of the argument, preferred by pharmaceuticals and the South African government, that sloppy distribution and administration of cocktail drugs not only undermine their effectiveness but could lead to more resistant strains of HIV—that it would be more effective to focus on HIV education and prevention, and on use of the drug AZT, which can reduce transmission of the virus from mothers to babies? Such arguments were recently echoed by the Bush administration's highest-ranking foreign aid official, Andrew Natsios, who told the Boston Globe that monies given to the United Nation's new AIDS superfund should be used almost exclusively for prevention.

In his comments to the paper, Natsios cited poor medical infrastructure and a lack of familiarity with Western ways, including the ability to tell time effectively enough to administer cocktail treatments. "You have to take these [AIDS] drugs a certain number of hours each day, or they don't work," Natsios told the Globe. "Many people in Africa have never seen a clock or a watch their entire lives. And if you say, one o'clock in the afternoon, they do not know what you are talking about. They know morning, they know noon, they know evening, they know the darkness at night."

Love joins other AIDS activists (and New York Times columnist Bob Herbert, who accused Natsios of perpetuating stereotypes about African culture) in rejecting the argument that anti-retrovirals are too complex to be effective in Africa. He points out that combinations of different medicines now enable HIV patients who have access to such pills to take as few as four pills each day. This treatment regimen is currently being used on HIV-positive homeless both in San Francisco and in South Africa, where Doctors Without Borders is providing cocktail treatments to one village.

The real issue, Love says, is price. And by teaming with CIPLA, he is attempting to prove that AIDS drugs can be made affordable, even in impoverished nations like South Africa. In CIPLA, Love found a company willing to stick its neck out—and take the heat for doing so. When CIPLA made headlines around the world by quoting $350, the lowest cost ever for a three-drug anti-HIV cocktail, the pricing came as the result of Love's negotiations with CIPLA CEO Yusuf Hamied—the generic drug mogul who has become a huge thorn in the side of the pharmaceutical giants with his rock-bottom pricing. It was a watershed moment for international activists fighting for inexpensive access to AIDS drugs. Even the international organizations Love scoffs at cite the figure as a standard in international drug pricing.

"It shocked everyone and blew up in smoke the idea that the pharmaceutical companies were making donations," says Love. "It was a third of the best prices you could get out of the branded guys in what they thought were donations."

Not surprisingly, the action didn't exactly elicit praise from the pharmaceutical industry. At a recent industry conference GlaxoSmithKlein CEO Jean-Pierre Garnier described CIPLA as price-undercutting "pirates," and said the company "is not doing this to get a Nobel prize." CIPLA's Hamied responds to such criticism by saying, "Indeed, we are a commercial company. But I market 400 products in India. If I don't make money on a half-dozen of them, it's no big deal. I don't make any money on the cancer drugs we sell or drugs for thalassemia, a blood disorder that's common in India. We sell these drugs virtually at cost because I don't want to make money off these diseases which cause the whole fabric of society to crumble. India alone will have 35 million HIV cases by 2005, and it's something we can't afford."

SIGNIFICANCE

Since the inception of this debate, a number of new initiatives to encourage the delivery of drugs

used in the treatment of AIDS to developing countries were begun, each with modest success. For example, the President's Emergency Plan for AIDS Relief (PREFAR) was drafted in 2003 with $15 billion to be distributed in five years. Critics argue that this initiative proposed by President Bush does not mesh well with current programs that have proven success and that it is under-funded. In fact, a recent UNAIDS report shows needed funding of more than $18 billion alone in 2007 to effectively combat the pandemic in developing countries. In addition, PREFAR adds more barriers to access of affordable drugs, as it relies on brand name formulations. The high cost of brand name drugs reduces the number of recipients.

Despite more international programs and more funding, the situation continues to escalate, especially in Africa. Researchers describe more than three million new cases of HIV in 2005 (and a total of twenty-six million people currently living with the disease in Africa alone). The 2006 *World Health Organization Annual Report* describes a coming shortage worldwide in trained health-care workers of "over four million, affecting fifty-seven countries, thirty-six of which are in sub-Saharan Africa." In response to these problems, in early 2006, the WHO Commission on Intellectual Property Rights, Innovation, and Public Health (CIPH) passed a new declaration proposed by Kenya and Brazil, which the U.S. supported. Daryl Lindsey, author of the primary source, who observed these negotiations, also wrote, "This initiative is important. If we can create a global framework that stimulates R&D [research and development] in areas of medical priority and also promotes access, we may be able to replace or de-emphasize global agreements that simply raise drug prices."

FURTHER RESOURCES
Books

Love, James. Remuneration Guidelines for Non-voluntary use of a Patent on Medical Technologies. TCM Series No. 18. World Health Organization, 2005.

UNAIDS. *AIDS Epidemic Update—December, 2005*. Geneva, Switzerland: UNAIDS, 2005.

World Bank and UNAIDS. *Responding to HIV/AIDS Crisis: Lessons from Global Best Practices*. Geneva, Switzerland: The World Bank, 2005.

World Health Organization. *World Health Report 2006*. Geneva, Switzerland: World Health Organization, 2006.

Periodicals

Berkman, A., et al. "A Critical Analysis of the Brazilian Response to HIV/AIDS: Lessons Learned for Controlling and Mitigating the Epidemic in Developing Countries." *American Journal of Public Health*. 95 (2005): 1162–1172.

Centers for Disease Control and Prevention. "HIV/AIDS Surveillance Report, 2004." *U.S. Department of Health and Human Services, Centers for Disease Control and Prevention.* 16 (2004).

de Carvalho Mesquita Ayres, J.R., et al. "Vulnerability, Human Rights, and Comprehensive Health Care Needs of Young People Living With HIV/AIDS." *American Journal of Public Health.* 96 (2006): 1001–1006.

Desvarieux, M., et al. "Antiretroviral Therapy in Resource-Poor Countries: Illusions and Realities." *American Journal of Public Health.* 95 (2005): 1117–1122.

Galvão, J. "Brazil and Access to HIV/AIDS Drugs: A Question of Human Rights and Public Health." *American Journal of Public Health.* 95 (2005): 1110–1116.

McCoy, D., et al. "Expanding Access to Antiretroviral Therapy in Sub-Saharan Africa: Avoiding the Pitfalls and Dangers, Capitalizing on the Opportunities." *American Journal of Public Health.* 95 (2005): 18–22.

Web sites

Africa Action. "Betraying Africa's Priorities: A Short Analysis of U.S. Policies on HIV/AIDS in Africa." May 22, 2006. <http://www.africaaction.org/newsroom/index/> (accessed May 30, 2006).

Consumer Project on Technology. "Drug Development Incentives to Improve Access to Essential Medicines." May 2006. <http://www.cptech.org/ip/health/rnd/love-who052006.pdf> (accessed May 31, 2006).

Oxfam GB. "Public Health at Risk." April 2006. <http://www.oxfam.org.uk/what_we_do/issues/health/papers.htm> (accessed May 14, 2006).

The World Bank. "HIV/AIDS in Africa—Regional Brief." <http://web.worldbank.org/WBSITE/EXTERNAL/COUNTRIES/AFRICAEXT/EXTAFRHEANUTPOP/EXTAFRREGTOPHIVAIDS/0,contentMDK:20411613~menu PK:717155~pagePK:34004173~piPK:34003707~theSitePK:717148,00.html> (accessed May 31, 2006).

Commission Recommendations on Coexistence of Genetically Modified Crops with Conventional and Organic Farming

Report

By: Commission of the European Communities

Date: July 23, 2003

Source: *Commission of the European Communities.* "Commission Recommendation 23 July 2003 on Guidelines for the Development of National Strategies and Best Practices to Ensure the Co-existence of Genetically Modified Crops with Conventional and Organic Farming." <http://ec.europa.eu/comm/agriculture/publi/reports/coexistence2/guide_en.pdf> (accessed May 29, 2006).

About the Author: The Commission of the European Communities, also known as the European Commission, is the representative lawmaking body for the European Union. It is located in Brussels, Belgium.

INTRODUCTION

Genetically modified (GM) crops are plants, such as cotton, corn, or soybeans, whose genetic makeup (DNA) has been directly modified using genetic engineering techniques. GM animals are also being produced, but GM plants have been of special concern to critics of genetic engineering because plants broadcast their DNA on the wind in the form of pollen, whereas animals can only transfer their DNA by mating. GM plants and animals are often lumped together under the term genetically modified organisms (GMOs).

The use of GM plants and animals in agriculture has been controversial, with many citizens' groups and a minority of scientists maintaining that genetic modification presents unknown risks for both the environment (since engineered genes, unlike other pollutants, can potentially reproduce themselves without limit) and for the health of humans who eat genetically modified food. The majority of scientists in industry and government have maintained that such concerns are unfounded. Public opinion in Europe has been more negative about the introduction of GM crops into the food supply than in the United States, leading the European Union to take several restrictive steps regarding the production and importation of GM foods in Europe.

In 2003, the European Commmission—the executive branch of the European Union, consisting of one commissioner from each of the Union's twenty-five member states—released its recommendations for the farming of GM plant crops in Europe. This document described some of the concerns that arise when mixing GM crops and organic or conventional crops in the landscape, and offered suggestions for coexistence of GM crops with other crops. The suggestions were generalized, not specific. For example, a typical recommendation is, "For self-pollinating crops and plants where the harvested product is not a seed, such as beets and potatoes, shorter distances are possible. Isolation

Protesters march to the Statehouse in Montpelier, Vermont to call for a time out on genetically engineered crops, February 26, 2004. AP IMAGES.

distances should minimize but not necessarily eliminate gene flow by transfer. The objective is to ensure a level of adventitious [accidental] presence below the tolerance threshold."

PRIMARY SOURCE

THE COMMISSION OF THE EUROPEAN COMMUNITIES,
Having regard to the Treaty establishing the European Community, and in particular Article 211 thereof,

Having regard to the Communication from the Commission to the European Parliament, the Council, the Economic and Social Committee and the Committee of the Regions on "Life sciences and biotechnology—A strategy for Europe" . . . and in particular Action 17 thereof,

Whereas:

1. No form of agriculture, be it conventional, organic or agriculture using genetically modified organisms (GMOs), should be excluded in the European Union.

2. The ability to maintain different agricultural production systems is a prerequisite for providing a high degree of consumer choice.

3. Coexistence refers to the ability of farmers to make a practical choice between conventional, organic and GM-crop production, in compliance with the legal obligations for labelling and/or purity standards.

4. Specific coexistence measures to protect the environment and the human health, if needed, are included in the final consent of the authorisation procedure in accordance with Directive 2001/18/EC of the European Parliament and of the Council, with a legal obligation for their implementation.

5. The issue of coexistence addressed in this Recommendation concerns the potential economic loss and impact of the admixture of GM and non-GM crops, and the most appropriate management measures that can be taken to minimise admixture.

6. Farm structures and farming systems, and the economic and natural conditions under which farmers in the European Union operate, are extremely diverse, and efficient and cost-effective measures for coexistence vary greatly between the different parts of the European Union.

7. The European Commission considers that measures for coexistence should be developed and implemented by the Member States.

8. The European Commission should support and advise Member States in this process by issuing guidelines for addressing coexistence.

9. Such guidelines should provide a list of general principles and elements for the development of national strategies and best practices for coexistence.

10. Two years after the publication of the present Recommendation in the Official Journal of the European Union, and based on information from Member States, the Commission will report to the Council and the European Parliament on the experience gained in the Member States concerning the implementation of measures to address coexistence, including, if appropriate, an evaluation and assessment of all possible and necessary steps to take.

HEREBY RECOMMENDS:

1. In developing national strategies and best practices for coexistence Member States should follow the guidelines provided in the Annex to this Recommendation.

2. This Recommendation is addressed to the Member States.

Done at Brussels, 23 July 2003.
For the Commission
Franz Fischler
Member of the Commission

1. INTRODUCTION

1.1. The concept of coexistence The cultivation of genetically modified organisms (GMOs) in the EU is likely to have implications for the organisation of agricultural production. On the one hand, the possibility of the adventitious (unintended) presence of genetically modified (GM) crops in non-GM crops, and vice versa, raises the question as to how producer choice for the different production types can be ensured. In principle, farmers should be able to cultivate the types of agricultural crops they choose, be it GM crops, conventional or organic crops. None of these forms of agriculture should be excluded in the EU.

On the other hand, the issue is also linked to consumer choice. To provide European consumers with a real choice between GM food and non-GM food, there should not only be a traceability and labelling system that functions properly, but also an agricultural sector that can

provide the different types of goods. The ability of the food industry to deliver a high degree of consumer choice goes hand in hand with the ability of the agricultural sector to maintain different production systems.

Coexistence refers to the ability of farmers to make a practical choice between conventional, organic and GM-crop production, in compliance with the legal obligations for labelling and/or purity standards.

The adventitious presence of GMOs above the tolerance threshold set out in Community legislation triggers the need for a crop that was intended to be a non-GMO crop, to be labelled as containing GMOs. This could cause a loss of income, due to a lower market price of the crop or difficulties in selling it. Moreover, additional costs might incur to farmers if they have to adopt monitoring systems and measures to minimise the admixture of GM and non-GM crops. Coexistence is, therefore, concerned with the potential economic impact of the admixture of GM and non-GM crops, the identification of workable management measures to minimise admixture and the cost of these measures.

The coexistence of different production types is not a new issue in agriculture. Seed producers, for example, have a great deal of experience of implementing farm management practices to ensure seed purity standards. Other examples of segregated agricultural production lines include yellow dent field maize for animal feed, which successfully coexists in European agriculture with several types of "speciality maize" grown for human consumption, and waxy maize grown for the starch industry.

1.2. Economic aspects of coexistence versus environmental and health aspects It is important to make a clear distinction between the economic aspects of coexistence and the environmental and health aspects dealt with under Directive 2001/18/EC on the deliberate release of GMOs into the environment.

According to the procedure laid down in Directive 2001/18/EC, the authorisation to release GMOs into the environment is subject to a comprehensive health and environmental risk assessment. The outcome of the risk assessment can be one of the following:

- a risk of an adverse effect to the environment or health that cannot be managed is identified, in which case authorisation is refused,
- no risk of adverse effects on the environment or health is identified, in which case authorisation is granted without requiring any additional management measures other than those specifically prescribed in the legislation,
- risks are identified, but they can be managed with appropriate measures (e.g. physical separation and/ or monitoring); in this case the authorisation will carry

the obligation to implement environmental risk management measures.

If a risk to the environment or health is identified after the authorisation has been granted, a procedure for the withdrawal of the authorisation or for modifying the conditions of consent can be initiated under the safeguard clause set out in Article 23 of the Directive.

Since only authorised GMOs can be cultivated in the EU, and the environmental and health aspects are already covered by Directive 2001/18/EC, the pending issues still to be addressed in the context of coexistence concern the economic aspects associated with the admixture of GM and non-GM crops. . . .

1.5. Purpose and scope of the guidelines The present guidelines, which take the form of non-binding recommendations addressed to the Member States, should be seen in this context. Their scope extends from agricultural crop production on the farm up to the first point of sale, i.e. "from the seed to the silo."

The document is intended to help Member States develop national strategies and approaches to address coexistence. Focusing mainly on technical and procedural aspects, the guidelines provide a list of general principles and elements to aid Member States in establishing best practices for coexistence.

SIGNIFICANCE

The Commission's recommendations imply that farming with GM organisms must be allowed in Europe and that only the detailed arrangements are in question. The very title of the report—which declares the Commission's intention "to ensure the coexistence of genetically modified crops with conventional and organic farming"—rules out the possibility of banning GM foods altogether. This is politically significant because of widespread popular opposition to GM foods in Europe and elsewhere in the world. In July 2005, a Europe-wide survey conducted by the Commission found that fifty-four percent of Europeans agreed with the statement that "food made from genetically modified organisms is dangerous." (Note that the poll question refers to dietary hazard only, not to the possibility of ecological danger from engineered genes mixing with wild populations.) Similar majorities in Russia, China, and Canada disapprove of GM foods, with widespread opposition in Africa as well (where polling figures are not available). In some European countries, especially Germany and France, the percentage of persons disapproving of GM foods is near ninety percent.

This situation—where GM foods are supported by most experts and opposed by many citizen groups and a minority of experts—has created political tensions. Since 1990, European consumers have repeatedly been told that certain food products are safe only to find later that they were not. Beef contaminated by bovine spongiform encephalopathy (mad cow disease) is, perhaps, the most notorious example. Such occurrences have eroded the public trust in experts' reassurances.

When the European Commission held a conference entitled "Co-existence of Genetically Modified, Conventional and Organic Crops" in Vienna, Austria, in April 2006, representatives from citizen groups gave presentations in which they strongly objected to the idea of coexistence with GM crops. The International Federation of Organic Agriculture Movements stated that "we have zero acceptance of GM contamination [of organic crops]" and that the "Commission proposal to simply allow contamination in organic food [up to a fixed threshold] is totally inadequate and inappropriate." The group called for "prohibition of GMOs in agriculture" and "strict liability and compensation to protect non-GM farmers" from contamination of their crops with modified genes spread through pollen or seed. The Friends of the Earth, a global coalition of environmental organizations, argued that "genetic contamination . . . is a new type of pollution created by industry" and called for a European "ban of GMOs currently authorized for cultivation and a moratorium on all GMO cultivation until an EU law preventing contamination and establishing strict liability and allowing EU Regions to be GMO-free is in place."

About two-thirds of the world's GM crops are grown in the United States, mostly corn, soybeans, and cotton, and canola (called "rape" in Europe—the plant name derives from the Latin for turnip and has nothing to do with sexual assault). In 2004, eighty-five percent of all soybeans, forty-five percent of all corn, and seventy-six percent of all cotton planted in the U.S. were GM varieties and over seventy percent of processed foods in American supermarkets contain at least traces of GM crops.

In 1998, the European Union placed a six-year moratorium on the importation of new GM crop varieties. In 2003, the United States, at the urging of pro-biotechnology groups, led the second and third largest GM-producing countries (Argentina and Canada) in complaining to the World Trade Organization (WTO) that Europe's refusal to import GM crops was an unfair trade practice. In February 2006, the WTO ruled in favor of the GM crop producers (but, the European Commissions guidelines of 2004 had already, in effect, lifted the moratorium). Yet European consumers remain mostly hostile to GM foods, and European law requires labeling of foods that contain GM crops. Therefore, many European food-store chains refuse to stock GM foods. It may remain economically difficult to market GM foods in Europe even if the European Union complies with the WTO's order to accept GM imports.

Some Europeans have complained of U.S. bullying in the GMO affair. A European Union briefing document said in 2006 that "the U.S. appears to believe that GMOs that are considered to be safe in the U.S. should be de facto deemed to be safe for the rest of the world." A representative of Friends of the Earth said in response to the 2006 WTO ruling that "The WTO undermines democracy and puts business interests before the welfare of the public. It should not be allowed to rule on what we eat or what our farmers grow."

FURTHER RESOURCES

Books

Ruse, Michael, and David Castle, eds. *Genetically Modified Foods: Debating Biotechnology*. Amherst, NY: Prometheus Books, 2002.

Periodicals

Gillis, Justin, and Paul Blustein. "WTO Ruling Backs Biotech Crops." *Washington Post* (February 8, 2006).

Web sites

European Commission. "Conference, 4–6 April 2006, Vienna: Co-existence of Genetically Modified, Conventional, and Organic Crops." <http://ec.europa.eu/comm/agriculture/events/vienna2006/index_en.htm> (accessed May 29, 2006).

Pew Initiative on Food and Biotechnology. "Fact Sheet: Genetically Modified Crops in the United States." 2004. <http://pewagbiotech.org/resources/factsheets/display.php3?FactsheetID=2> (accessed May 29, 2006).

Robbing the Poor to Pay the Rich?

Briefing paper

By: Anonymous

Date: November 2003

Source: "Robbing the Poor to Pay the Rich?" *Oxfam G.B.* December 2003. <http://www.oxfam.org.uk/what_we_do/issues/health/bp56_medicines.htm> (accessed May 31, 2006).

About the Author: This briefing was written by staff members of Oxfam G.B., a British charitable organization affiliated with Oxfam International. Oxfam is a worldwide strategic partnership that works with other organizations to find solutions to poverty and suffering. Some of Oxfam's allies are the European Commission, ECHO, Department of International Development, and The United Nations.

INTRODUCTION

According to the Biotechnology Industry Organization (BIO), as of 2006 there are more than three hundred drugs and vaccines in clinical trials for more than two hundred diseases (including AIDS, arthritis, and Alzheimer's Disease). In 2003 there were 1,473 biotechnology companies in the United States (314 were public companies). Revenues from this industry have grown from $8 billion in 1992 to $39 billion in 2003. In 2003 nearly $17.9 billion was spent on research and development. The Biotechnology industry is regulated by the Food and Drug Administration (FDA), the Environmental Protection Agency (EPA), and Department of Agriculture (USDA).

BIO is clear with regard to ethical issues: "Biotechnology has extraordinary potential to improve the health and well-being of people in the developing world, but significant impediments exist to the development and dissemination of diagnostics, therapeutics, and vaccines for the infectious diseases prevalent in developing countries...BIO and the biotechnology industry respect the power of the technology we are developing, and we accept the need for appropriate regulation. We work with state, federal and international regulatory bodies to shape the development of regulatory policies that foster safe, effective and beneficial products."

Pharmaceutical Research and Manufacturers of America (PhRMA) is one of the largest and most influential lobbying organizations in Washington. PhRMA represents forty-eight pharmaceutical companies and employs over 1,200 lobbyists to advocate policies that advance its interests. PhRMA's mission is "winning advocacy for public policies that encourage the discovery of life-saving and life-enhancing new medicines for patients by pharmaceuticals/biotechnology research companies." Despite these lofty proclamations, the pharmaceuticals/biotech industry has come under intense scrutiny. The numbers reveal some startling truths: despite claims of putting the interests of public health and well-being before profit, big PhRMA has

Government doctors and nurses stage a picket outside a suburban Quezon City hospital in the Philippines, December 6, 2005. They are protesting the World Trade Organization Ministerial Conference in Hong Kong. The protesters opposed the government hospitals, high prices of medicines, and exodus of health professionals which they claimed were caused by the globalization policy. AP IMAGES.

used its clout and connections to reap bigger profits in the U.S. and abroad.

Consumer advocacy groups and human rights organizations alike (Public Citizen, the Center for Responsive Politics, and Oxfam International) describe some alarming trends. In 2001 the government inflation rate was only 1.6 percent while prescription drug prices increased by ten percent. In the same year, the pharmaceutical industry led all of *Fortune* magazine's measures of profitability. In addition, while profits of Fortune 500 companies dropped fifty-three percent, profits of top U.S. drug companies jumped from $28 billion to $37 billion (a thirty-three percent increase). These companies also spent 12.5 percent of revenues on research and development while keeping 18.5 percent for profit. In the past decades, the industry has

experienced increased profitability—two times more than the median for all industries in the Fortune 500 in the 1970s, four times more in the 1990s, and, in 2001, eight times more than all industries in the Fortune 500.

Increasing profits are only part of the picture. Drug companies and their representatives contributed at least $29 million to federal candidates in 2002. The pharmaceutical industry ranked tenth in total campaign contributions compared to more than eighty other industries. During the election-year campaigns of 2002, pharmaceutical companies donated $21 million to Republican candidates and causes, $7 million to Democrats, and $19 million in soft money contributions.

Drug companies also invest millions in lobbying. It has been so successful that it won coverage for prescription drugs through Medicare and blocked imports of cheaper drugs from foreign counterparts, including Canada. More importantly, U.S. drug companies have learned to circumvent international policies that were designed to give developing countries access to affordable drugs. These companies have alliances and partnerships that lend the industry the power to influence national and international policy.

PRIMARY SOURCE

ROBBING THE POOR TO PAY THE RICH?

Impressive advances in medicine and technology have boosted health and extended life expectancy—but not for everyone. Vital new medicines for diseases such as HIV/AIDS are priced out of reach of the millions of sick people in the developing world, in part due to global patent rules which restrict the availability of affordable generic versions of patented medicines. In 2001, all members of the World Trade Organization adopted the 'Doha Declaration', promising to prioritize public health over private patent rights and to promote 'access to medicines for all.' This paper examines how the government of the United States is contravening this commitment by using technical assistance, bilateral and regional trade agreements, and the threat of trade sanctions to ratchet up patent protection in developing countries. This policy benefits the influential U.S. pharmaceutical industry while pushing medicines further out of the reach of poor people.

EXECUTIVE SUMMARY

In 2001, WTO members unanimously adopted the 'Doha Declaration', which affirmed the primacy of public health over international patent rules. Trade ministers recognized that WTO patent rules—known as TRIPS—lead to higher drug prices, placing medicines out of reach of patients in poor countries and undermining public health. They made a commitment to interpret patent rules in a way that prioritized health standards, and to ensure that countries too poor to buy branded drugs and unable to make cheap generic substitutes could obtain medicines more easily.

The United States signed the Doha Declaration, promising to promote 'access to medicines for all.' But in the two years since Doha, it has not only failed to uphold this commitment but has actively undermined the letter and spirit of the Declaration. The U.S. Trade Representative is pursuing standards of patent protection which go far beyond WTO patent rules, and it is doing so regardless of the devastating impact that this could have on the capacity of developing countries to treat health problems such as Acquired Immune Deficiency Syndrome (AIDS).

Oxfam believes the U.S. government is pursuing this pro-patent agenda on behalf of its powerful pharmaceutical lobby, PhRMA. The industry has an interest in strong patent protections, which limit generic competition and therefore protect its market share and profits. In 2000, the industry contributed approximately $20,142,583 in campaign contributions, 76 per cent of which went to the Republican Party. In 2003, the industry gave $29,371,406, with $21,719,527 of that money going to Republicans. In addition, it spends approximately $120 million each year on lobbying. This is a drop in the ocean compared with its yearly sales: an estimated $400 billion in 2002. The ten largest U.S. drug companies made $35.9 billion in profit in 2002, with a rate of return for shareholders of 27.6 per cent, more than two and a half times the Fortune 500 average of 10.2 per cent.

Fourteen million people die each year from infectious diseases, and more than 42 million people are living with HIV/AIDS, including 3.2 million children under the age of 15, the majority in developing countries. And patients in developing countries now account for 59 per cent of the 56.5 million annual global deaths from non-communicable diseases such as cardiovascular disease, cancers, diabetes, respiratory disease, obesity, and others.

Much of this suffering and death could be prevented if people had regular access to medicines, yet one-third of the world's population does not. Many factors are responsible, including poverty, lack of finance, and poor health-service infrastructure—but the high cost of new patented medicines is also a key factor. The absence of cheap generic versions of these medicines means that poor people must simply go without the drugs that could save or prolong their lives. The most notorious example is medicines to treat HIV/AIDS, but the problem will extend to all new medicines whether for drug-resistant strains of existing killers such as TB, malaria, and pneumonia, new improved treatments for hepatitis, cancers, diabetes, or treatments for new emerging diseases, such as Severe Acute Respiratory Syndrome (SARS) or anthrax.

Poor countries with fewer resources to dedicate to healthcare and medicines need access to the cheapest drugs available to fight such problems of public health. But the cheapest generic versions of new patented drugs are being blocked from developing-country markets by U.S. trade policies on intellectual property, at the urging of the drug companies that benefit from the monopoly position that patents confer.

During the two years since Doha, the U.S. has contravened the goal of the Declaration—'access to medicines for all'—by pressuring developing countries to implement 'TRIPS-plus measures': patent laws which go beyond TRIPS obligations and do not take advantage of its public-health safeguards. The USA does this in a number of ways. It provides biased technical assistance in countries such as Uganda and Nigeria, which benefits its own industry by increasing drug prices and limiting the availability of generics, but reducing access. It uses bilateral and regional free trade agreements to ratchet up patent protection in developing countries. It has recently concluded free trade agreements with Chile and Singapore and is using the high intellectual property standards in the latter as a model for negotiations on the FTAA (Free Trade Area of the Americas) (see OI briefing paper 'From Cancun to Miami: the FTAA threat to development in the hemisphere', November 2003) and with Central American, Southern African, and other countries. And lastly, the U.S. bullies countries into increasing patent protection by threatening them with trade sanctions under section 301 of the Trade Act of 1974; nearly all those targeted are developing countries, including countries in compliance with their WTO obligations. The Costa Rican Pharmaceutical Industry estimates that the implementation of such TRIPS-plus patent rules would mean an increase in the cost of medicines of up to 800 per cent, because these rules would seriously restrict competition from generics.

At the WTO, the U.S. pressured developing countries to accept an unnecessarily restricted and complex deal which was intended to safeguard access to generic drugs for countries that are too poor to buy patented drugs and which lack domestic drug-production capacity. Action on this issue was promised as part of the Doha Declaration, but regrettably the U.S. and other rich countries rejected a simple solution initially proposed by developing countries, the World Health Organization (WHO) and NGOs. The U.S. has also pressured Cambodia (the first of the least-developed countries [LDCs] to join the WTO since its foundation) to agree to introduce patenting now, even though the Doha Declaration permitted the LDCs to defer the introduction of pharmaceutical patenting until at least 2016.

The pro-health interpretation of international patent rules was a key promise made by rich countries in launching the current 'Doha Round' of trade talks. This Round has been dubbed the 'Doha Development Round', since it was meant to address the needs and interests of poorer countries. But developing countries are now rightly skeptical, doubting that their rich-country trading partners—especially the U.S.—ever intended to focus on development. In the two years since Doha, the U.S. has been excessively responsive to industry interests, while failing to consider the importance of generic medicines for fighting public-health problems in developing countries that lack health-care resources. Unless the U.S. adjusts its trade policies to reflect its commitment at Doha, medicines will be priced further out of reach of poor patients. Millions of people will suffer or die needlessly because the U.S. government refuses to look beyond the short-term commercial interests of its drug lobby.

Oxfam recommends the following measures:

- WTO members should ensure the simplification of the final TRIPS amendment aimed at lifting restrictions on the export of affordable generic versions of new drugs to countries without drug-production capacity. Unnecessary red tape should be removed, and there should be no mandatory limits on country eligibility, or on the diseases for which such medicines can be procured, in keeping with the Doha Declaration. WTO member states should amend their legislation accordingly.
- The U.S. should stop using the threat of trade sanctions to bully countries into adopting 'TRIPS plus' intellectual property protections. TRIPS-plus rules further limit the availability of affordable generics in countries where they are urgently needed, and they contravene the Doha Declaration. The U.S. should also stop using its bilateral trade agreements such as CAFTA, regional agreements such as the FTAA, or negotiations over to WTO accession to pressure developing and least-developed countries to adopt TRIPS-plus patent rules.
- The U.S. should provide technical assistance to developing countries that will benefit public health and access to affordable medicines, rather than the interests of the pharmaceutical industry.
- Developing countries should resist pressures to implement TRIPS-plus measures, and should make full use of the TRIPS flexibilities, including but not limited to the recent WTO deal, in order to gain access to medicines, in line with the Doha Declaration

The international community must continue to monitor the health impacts of the TRIPS Agreement, and should consider further future reforms to the Agreement in order to give developing countries greater freedom to decide the appropriate length and scope of patents protection for medicines based on the needs of public health. More broadly, evidence from authoritative sources indicates the need for a substantive review of the entire TRIPS Agreement in the light of its detrimental impact on innovation, access to knowledge-based goods, and development.

SIGNIFICANCE

The pharmaceutical/biotech industry asserts that it wants to take part in the global fight against disease but must also protect small businesses and start-ups that need to recoup investments years in development. They argue that the only asset these small fragile companies have is their intellectual property (IP), and that IP needs safeguards from piracy and imitation to ensure industry survival.

"Access for All" was the unifying theme for the XV International IDS Conference in Thailand in 2004. Brazil's National AIDS Program (NAP) was held up as the standard of a successful national HIV/AIDS program. Central to Brazil's success was lobbying by human rights advocates—voicing that access to affordable medicine and healthcare is a human right. Studies of the NAP demonstrate how "free universal access to antiretroviral treatment has had a dramatic impact on morbidity and mortality from AIDS in Brazil and has gained considerable international recognition for its efforts." Also, the World Health Organization 3 by 5 initiative, to treat three million people with HIV/AIDS by the end of 2005, is part of the global campaign to provide better access to drug therapy in developing countries.

As of May 2006 there are more than two million children less than fifteen years of age infected with HIV (most in sub-Saharan Africa). Of these, less than five percent have access to pediatric AIDS treatment. In addition, fourteen million people die every year in developing nations of preventable diseases such as TB and malaria. These people and their countries need affordable drugs—often generic derivatives—to combat disease along with strengthened healthcare systems. The U.S. pharmaceutical industry is in a position to help in the global fight against one of the worst public health threats in recent decades.

FURTHER RESOURCES
Books
UNAIDS. *AIDS Epidemic Update—December, 2005.* Geneva, Switzerland: UNAIDS, 2005.

World Health Organization. *Treating 3 Million by 2005: Making it Happen*. Geneva, Switzerland: World Health Organization, 2003.

Periodicals

de Carvalho Mesquita Ayres, J.R., et al. "Vulnerability, Human Rights, and Comprehensive Health Care Needs of Young People Living With HIV/AIDS." *American Journal of Public Health* 96 (2006): 1001–1006.

Desvarieux, M., et al. "Antiretroviral Therapy in Resource-Poor Countries: Illusions and Realities." *American Journal of Public Health* 95 (2005): 1117–1122.

Galvão, J. "Brazil and Access to HIV/AIDS Drugs: A Question of Human Rights and Public Health." *American Journal of Public Health* 95 (2005): 1110–1116.

McCoy, D., et al. "Expanding Access to Antiretroviral Therapy in Sub-Saharan Africa: Avoiding the Pitfalls and Dangers, Capitalizing on the Opportunities." *American Journal of Public Health* 95 (2005): 18–22.

Web sites

Biotechnology Industry Organization. "Biotechnology Industry Facts." <http://www.bio.org/speeches/pubs/er/statistics.asp?p=yes> (accessed May 31, 2006).

Center for Responsive Politics. "Background: Pharmaceuticals/Health Products." April 2006. <http://www.opensecrets.org/industries/background.asp?Ind=H04> (accessed May 31, 2006).

Neighbors of Burned Homes Pained by Suburban Sprawl

Newspaper article

By: Felicity James

Date: December 11, 2004

Source: James, Felicity. "Neighbors of Burned Homes Pained by Suburban Sprawl." *New York Times.* December 12, 2004.

About the Author: Felicity James is a staff writer for the *New York Times* a daily newspaper based in New York with a daily circulation of over one million copies.

INTRODUCTION

The Earth Liberation Front (ELF) is an eco-terrorist group that has been active in the U.S. since 1997. ELF attacks individuals, corporations, and governments that, in the organization's view, place monetary gain ahead of the natural environment. It uses economic sabotage to inflict financial suffering on those deemed objectionable.

ELF, modeled after the Animal Liberation Front, formed in England in the early 1990s after the splintering of Earth First! The organization spread to the U.S. in 1997. It is a loosely-knit collection of individual cells without any centralized leadership. Anyone can join the group as long as the individual follows the ELF philosophy of protecting the environment by targeting corporate budgets. Since there is no formal membership, anyone can claim an action on behalf of ELF. Many but not all cells send a communiqué to the ELF press office for distribution to law enforcement and media, thereby claiming responsibility for a violent action.

ELF began by spiking trees and sabotaging logging equipment. It moved out from the forests and into more densely populated areas in 2004. The shift reflected anger at suburban sprawl into previously undeveloped areas and a clash between long-time rural residents and refugees from suburbs. ELF began targeting building developers who logged land or filled in wetlands to make way for new homes. Fire became the ELF weapon of choice. Arsons and attempted arsons around the nation, but mostly in the West, were linked to ELF by the federal government.

PRIMARY SOURCE

WASHINGTON, Dec. 11—Blue plastic ribbons dangle from some saplings that line the mouth of Araby Bog, delineating the wetland boundary, as recognized by the State of Maryland and the development companies that are building 500 homes in the area. About one hundred feet away, the tree branches hold a few pale pink ribbons, marking the edge of the future housing lots.

Up the small hill from the mouth of the bog, clearly visible through the naked trees of December, are the large houses of Hunters Brooke, where thirty fires were set before dawn on Monday and ten houses were consumed by the flames.

W. Faron Taylor, the deputy state fire marshal, said on Saturday that investigators had not narrowed their search for a suspect, but after the blaze it was widely noted that a group of eco-terrorists had set fires at other new buildings or developments from San Diego to Long Island, NY. In those cases, however, a loosely knit group, the Earth Liberation Front, explicitly took credit—and that has not happened here.

Whatever the motive, the fires have highlighted a long and contentious battle over whether this instant dose of suburban density belonged here. The flames seem unlikely to alter the outcome: the developer of Hunters Brooke said this week that the houses would be rebuilt.

Deputy Fire Marshall Bruce Pulver examines the remains of a newly built home that was destroyed by arson near Snohomish, Washington, on April 20, 2004. Supporters of the Earth Liberation Front are believed to have burned the homes to protest urban sprawl and the destruction of the natural environment. AP/WIDE WORLD PHOTOS.

For years, local citizens fought their way from the Charles County Planning Commission to the federal courts to preserve the bog. It was not just the wetland, one of the few remaining magnolia bogs in the mid-Atlantic region they sought to preserve. They cherish their isolation from Washington's inexorably spreading suburbs. They do not want to lose their chance to see the full panoply of stars in the deeper dark of a rural night.

For Patricia Stamper, a sixty-six-year-old government statistician who has lived up a dirt road in the Mason Springs area with her horses for thirty years, it is impossible to untangle her concern for the environment from her anger that "a high density housing complex is being dumped on us all at once."

She lives less than a mile from Hunters Brooke and a few hundred yards from the companion planned development called Falcon Ridge, which will also border the bog. Asked which was more important, keeping the bog pristine or preserving the quiet life she sought when she moved here, Ms. Stamper said, "You're asking me to make an artificial choice."

David Boswell is also feeling crowded. His great-great-grandmother, in 1902, bought the old slave quarters he owns one mile down another dirt road near the rear of Hunters Brooke. Mr. Boswell, who is thirty-seven, said: "there was a woman in the paper who said she wanted to move out here in the country and see a hawk in the trees. What about me? I'm already here. I've been working on my house for years. Now I'll have their street lights across the way."

The clash of cultures that has been an inevitable consequence of suburban sprawl for fifty years has slowly changed its context. Rising environmental awareness has coincided with the ability of ever-more-distant national homebuilding conglomerates to plant dense modern developments far into the countryside.

Of the 1.7 million dwellings constructed in 2003, fifteen percent were in rural areas, according to Gopal Ahluwalia, a statistician with the National Association of Home Builders.

Now, however, many rural areas are home to sophisticated transplants like Ms. Stamper, or her friend Ellie Cline, a former real estate agent who lives in Araby House, a colonial-era home. They can find their way around a county government. They know or are quick studies on environmental rules. They can reach out to experts and environmental groups with money and muscle when a fragile environmental area, like Araby Bog, is jeopardized by loss of water, polluted runoff or any other incidental consequence of development.

They can form organizations like Save Araby, Mattawoman and Mason Springs, or Samms. With aid from pro bono lawyers, they can sue.

The 6.5-acre magnolia bog, soon to be flanked by developments, is one of the last of its kind in the mid-Atlantic region. Roderick Simmons, a botanist with Maryland Native Plants Society, said that the 100,000 gallons of water flowing daily from the bog into

Mattawoman Creek, and eventually into the Chesapeake Bay, is" ultra-pure spring water."

It is ringed by sweet bay magnolias and carpeted with sphagnum moss, and is home to several rare or threatened plants. Robert DeGroot, president of the Maryland Alliance for Greenway Improvement and Conservation, said, "this is a very small pristine area just full of plants that you don't see anywhere else."

A Charles County spokeswoman said the one hundred-foot buffer zones would protect the bog, but a geologist's report prepared for Samms this summer said this had failed to protect from "dense residential development" in the surrounding acreage whose groundwater refreshes the bog.

"This is akin to saving Niagara Falls while allowing the St. Lawrence River to be diverted," the geologist, Tony Fleming, wrote. If development must proceed, he said, lots should cover several acres. Hunters Brooke has quarter-acre lots.

The bog was not on many people's radar when Hunters Brooke LLC first applied for county government approval in 1993. Preliminary approval of their plans was granted in 1994. Beginning in 1998, there followed a minuet of appeals and lawsuits by the opponents, coupled with county commission decisions that favored the developers.

After final approval, appeals and state and federal lawsuits helped delay construction until this year. One county commissioners' meeting after another, according to the files of The Maryland Independent, a local weekly, ended with the developers—subsidiaries of the Lennar Corporation, one of the largest developers in the nation—getting the needed waivers and postponements.

The average time from application to construction is two to four years, Mr. Ahluwalia said. This took more than a decade, if the end point is marked at the dismissal of the environmentalists' suit against the Army Corps of Engineers last month.

Then, Monday, came the fires. Environmental groups and their local allies were quick to condemn the arson. Investigators pointedly refused to rule out any possible motive, from financial interest to eco-terrorism to thrill-seeking.

Gale Bailey, a Charles County native who lives close to the bog, said that the fires were upsetting, but that she had no fear for her own home. David Boswell, asked if anyone local could be responsible, said quickly, "I didn't do it," then smiled and blushed. Rod Coronado, who sometimes acts as a spokesman for the Earth Liberation Front, took no credit when reached by telephone in Arizona this week but said he supported the idea of the arson.

Some say such fights over development, whether waged with matches or lawsuits, are usually futile, because the growth of areas like Washington will continue.

Jacque Hightower, a federal government executive whose new Hunters Brooke home suffered moderate damage in the fire, said, "my wife and I, we've worked hard to be able to buy a home such as this." He added: "Times are changing. Everything's changing around us. It's going to change, regardless."

Correction: December 16, 2004, Thursday An article on Sunday about a proposed real estate development near an environmentally endangered bog in Maryland referred incorrectly to the neighbors' lawsuit against the Army Corps of Engineers over its decision to allow construction. A partial summary judgment in favor of the neighbors was issued in July, and last month the corps withdrew an appeal of that decision. The suit itself was not dismissed.

SIGNIFICANCE

In February 2002, the Federal Bureau of Investigation (FBI) listed the ELF as the largest and most active U.S.-based terrorist group. Between 1997 and 2003, ELF claimed to have inflicted more than $100 million in damages from "ecotage." Although no one has died as of mid–2006 in any of these operations, ELF's campaign against loggers, SUV dealerships, and others it considers threats to the planet have galvanized and polarized the environmental movement. While some environmentalists argue that success can only be achieved by combining legal and illegal tactics, others regard the ELF attacks as dangerous stunts that make environmentalists seem irrational and dangerous. Those opposed to the environmental movement have already lumped bombing in with nonviolent tree-sits, boycotts, lawsuits, and picket lines. In doing so, they have found support for new laws against environmental activism in the West.

As of May 2006, several federal court cases against ELF members were currently pending. The eco-terrorists were charged with plotting to blow up a U.S. Forest Service genetics lab in Placerville, California; the Nimbus Dam and a nearby fish hatchery in Rancho Cordova, California, and cellular telephone towers and electric power stations in unspecified locations. The attacks do not always stop the development. The arson of a $12 million Vail, Colorado ski resort building in lynx habitat led to the collapse of the established grass-roots opposition, and the construction of an even larger resort with even more habitat destruction.

FURTHER RESOURCES
Books

Foreman, Dave. *Confessions of an Eco-Warrior*. New York: Three Rivers Press, 1993.

Rosebraugh, Craig. *Burning Rage of a Dying Planet: Speaking for the Earth Liberation Front*. New York: Lantern Books, 2004.

Zakin, Susan. *Coyotes and Town Dogs: Earth First! and the Environmental Movement*. Tucson: University of Arizona Press, 2002.

World AIDS Day: Human Rights Watch Calls for Increased Support

Protections for Global AIDS Activists

Website

By: Anonymous

Date: December 1, 2005

Source: *Human Rights Watch*. "World AIDS Day: Human Rights Watch Calls for Increased Support, Protections for Global AIDS Activists." December 1, 2005. <http://hrw.org/english/docs/2005/12/01/global 12114_txt.htm> (accessed May 30, 2006).

About the Author: Founded in 1978, the Human Rights Watch (HRW) is the largest human rights organization in the U.S. HRW is composed of 150 professionals including lawyers, journalists, and academics and a cadre of volunteers. Based in New York, its motto is "Defending Human Rights World Wide."

INTRODUCTION

World AIDS Day takes place each year on the first day of December. Millions of people worldwide wear red ribbons on this day as a symbol of support for those living with HIV/AIDS and the hope for a cure in the future. Activists mark the day with demonstrations and gatherings to highlight current issues in the fight against AIDS.

One of the key issues in the global war on HIV/AIDS is protecting those with the illness and activists from discrimination, intimidation, and violence. The stigmatization of those with AIDS has hindered the progress of education, prevention, and treatment campaigns especially in countries such as India, China, and those of Africa. According to Jane Galvao, a researcher who studied the history of the HIV/AIDS crisis in Brazil, "people affected by HIV/AIDS who are living in areas where discrimination, stigmatization, and threats against individuals with HIV/AIDS are high are less inclined to seek testing, thereby postponing treatment if available, which means that opportunities to decrease HIV transmission are lost."

The AIDS epidemic is among the largest public health threats of the twenty-first century. In response to the growing trend of human rights violations, the Carr Center issued a report in 2001 stating:

> But the pandemic represents more than a health catastrophe. It is both a product of, and exacerbated by, pervasive violations of human rights. HIV/AIDS is a preventable and manageable disease that has been turned into a pandemic by ignorance, neglect, and violations of human rights. The disease most deeply affects those least able to enjoy their rights: the poorest, the weakest, the least educated, the most stigmatized.

In June 2001, the United Nations (UN) General Assembly acknowledged the role of Human Rights in

Filipinos light candles to memorialize AIDS victims and mark World AIDS Day, December 1, 2003. © ERIK DE CASTRO/REUTERS/ CORBIS

HIV/AIDS with their "Declaration of Commitment on HIV/AIDS." In addition, in 2003, UNAIDS formed the Global Reference Group on HIV/AIDS and Human Rights-validating the connection between human rights and HIV/AIDS.

In 2002, UNAIDS released the HIV/AIDS and Human Rights International Guidelines. Then, in 2004 UNAIDS and UNESCO proposed the initiative "An AIDS-free Generation in Less than a Generation."

PRIMARY SOURCE

AIDS activists around the world face frequent government repression and abuse and need substantially increased support and protections, said Human Rights Watch on World AIDS Day.

"The few success stories we have in the global fight against AIDS are the result of the heroic efforts of courageous individuals mobilizing impoverished, marginalized, and stigmatized populations to action," said Joe Amon, director of the HIV/AIDS Program at Human Rights Watch. "But AIDS activists and outreach workers are often harassed or even jailed by their governments for simply standing up and speaking out about AIDS, and the international donor community is doing too little to protect them."

Human Rights Watch has documented numerous cases of AIDS activists and non-governmental organizations being harassed, intimidated, or jailed for their work. In China, government officials have jailed activists seeking to expose government complicity in a tainted blood scandal that has infected hundreds of thousands of rural villages with HIV in the country's Henan province. In India and Bangladesh, outreach workers delivering services to sex workers, to men who have sex with men, and to other hidden populations, have faced widespread police harassment and violence.

In Uganda, activists protesting the government's recent turn toward moralistic "abstinence-until-marriage" programs face intimidation from officials and accusations of immorality. In the Philippines, police routinely arrest women and accuse them of prostitution for simply carrying condoms. In Russia, the parliament is considering legislation that would tighten government control over Russian and foreign non-governmental organizations, threatening vital outreach and education programs for injecting drug users and sex workers.

Activists have encountered government violence for doing nothing but demonstrating peacefully for access to health care. This year in Queenstown, South Africa, police fired rubber bullets and teargas at members of the Treatment Action Campaign (TAC) who were protesting the slow progress of the government's antiretroviral treatment program. Human Rights Watch has called for a full investigation into this incident.

"Bitter experience has shown that repressing civil society only fuels AIDS epidemics," said Amon. "Where repression rules the day, AIDS wins."

Since 2002, Human Rights Watch has honored six individuals or organizations for their courageous work defending the rights of people living with or affected by AIDS. They are:

Meena Seshu (2002) is founder and general secretary of SANGRAM, an organization based in Sangli, Maharashtra State, India, that has helped women in prostitution become AIDS educators among themselves and in the wider community.

Dr. Wan Yanhai (2002) is coordinator of the AIZHI (AIDS) Action Project, a nongovernmental organization he founded in 1994 that provides some of the only basic information on HIV/AIDS available to people in China through a widely used web site (www.aizhi.org).

AIDS Law Project (2003) is a pioneering organization that helps combat HIV/AIDS by protecting the rights of the millions affected by the disease in South Africa and that co-founded the Treatment Action Campaign.

The Thai Drug Users' Network (2004) has worked with few resources to help protect the human rights of drug users in Thailand since 2002, even during a brutal anti-drug crackdown that resulted in as many as 3,000 killings.

Humanitarian Action (2005) is a ground-breaking HIV/AIDS organization which has shown that providing outreach and care to Russia's most marginalized populations—such as syringe exchange for drug users, outreach to street-based sex workers, and medical services for street children—is the best way to stem the tide of HIV/AIDS.

Beatrice Were (2005), is one of Uganda's most courageous and compelling AIDS activists. She founded an organization that supports women living with HIV/AIDS and engages in advocacy on behalf of AIDS-affected families and was one of the first Ugandan women to openly declare her HIV status.

SIGNIFICANCE

In her analysis of the HIV/AIDS crisis in Brazil, Galvao argues "the participation of civil society had a key role in bringing about and sustaining the Brazilian government's ARV (anti-retroviral drug) distribution policy" Cooperation among communities has a significant impact on better health outcomes; however, it is only a beginning in the fight against factors that exacerbate the war on HIV/AIDS including discrimination and poverty.

Research on HIV/AIDS prevention shows that human rights issues associated with AIDS prevention are in need of greater attention. Sexual violence, prostitution, poverty, illiteracy, inadequate health services and condoms, lack of information about safe sex practices, and drug use fuel the spread of AIDS in the developing world. Effective human rights based campaigns against AIDS combat not only discrimination and social stigmas, but also address warfare, rape, prostitution, women's rights and access to healthcare. Many human rights activists and medical professionals also assert that both developed and developing nations must work to improve the availability of effective and reasonably priced medication for HIV/AIDS patients

Since 1980, nearly twenty-three million people across the globe have died of HIV/AIDS and AIDS-related illnesses. As many as ninety-five percent of individuals with HIV/AIDS live in developing nations. World AIDS Day, observed annually on December 1st, was created in 1998 to draw international attention to HIV/AIDS prevention, treatment, and human rights issues. Some past annual themes for World AIDS Day include "Stigma & Discrimination," "Children Living in a World with AIDS," and "Women & AIDS."

FURTHER RESOURCES
Books

UNAIDS. *2006 Report on the Global AIDS Epidemic*. Geneva, Switzerland: UNAIDS, 2006.

World Health Organization. *World Health Report 2006*. Geneva, Switzerland: World Health Organization, 2006.

Periodicals

Berkman A., et al. "A Critical Analysis of the Brazilian Response to HIV/AIDS: Lessons Learned for Controlling and Mitigating the Epidemic in Developing Countries." *American Journal of Public Health*. 95 (2005): 1162–1172.

de Carvalho Mesquita Ayres, J.R., et al. "Vulnerability, Human Rights, and Comprehensive Health Care Needs of Young People Living With HIV/AIDS." *American Journal of Public Health*. 96 (2006): 1001–1006.

Galvão, J. "Brazil and Access to HIV/AIDS Drugs: A Question of Human Rights and Public Health." *American Journal of Public Health*. 95 (2005): 1110–1116.

Web sites

United Nations. "HIV/AIDS and Human Rights: from Awareness to Action." 2004 <http://www.un.org/cyberschoolbus/student/2004/theme.asp> (accessed May 31, 2006).

Sources Consulted

BOOKS AND WEBSITES

A Century of Lawmaking. "Library of Congress." <http://rs6. loc.gov/ammem/amlaw/lawhome.html> (accessed on July 19, 2006).

Abrams, Floyd. *Speaking Freely: Trials of the First Amendment.* New York: Viking Adult, 2005.

Adams, Gerry. *A Farther Shore: Ireland's Road to Peace.* New York, N.Y.: Random House, 2003.

Aegis. "So Little Time: An AIDS History." <http://www. aegis.com/topics/timeline/> (accessed June 2, 2006).

Africa Action. "Betraying Africa's Priorities: A Short Analysis of U.S. Policies on HIV/AIDS in Africa." May 22, 2006. <http://www.africaaction.org/newsroom/index/> (accessed May 30, 2006).

Agency for Healthcare Research and Quality. "Agency for Healthcare Research and Quality." <http://www. ahrq.gov> (accessed on July 19, 2006).

Agnew, Spiro T. *Go Quietly ... Or Else.* New York: Morrow, 1980.

Agosin, Marjorie. *Tapestries of Hope, Threads of Love: The Arpillera Movement in Chile, 1974–1994.* Albuquerque: University of New Mexico Press, 1996.

AIDS Research Institute (ARI). "AIDS Research Institute (ARI)." <http://ari.ucsf.edu> (accessed on July 19, 2006).

Alabama Department of Archives and History. "Statement and Proclamation of Governor George C. Wallace, University of Alabama, June 11, 1963." <http://www. archives.state.al.us/govs_list/schooldoor.html> (accessed May 31, 2006).

Alavi, Nasrin. *We Are Iran: The Persian Blogs.* Brooklyn, N.Y.: Soft Skull Press, 2005.

Albert, Peter, and Ronald Hoffman. *We Shall Overcome: Martin Luther King, Jr., and the Black Freedom Struggle.* Philadelphia, Penn.: Da Capo, 1990.

Alistair Cooke. *Letters From America: 1946–2004.* New York: Penguin, 2004.

Allison Carter, The University of Alabama. "James Hood: Still Working for Equality." <http://www.ccom.ua.edu/od/ article_hood.shtml> (accessed May 31, 2006).

Alonso, Harriet Hyman. *Peace as a Women's Issue: A History of the U.S. Movement for World Peace and Women's Rights.* Syracuse, N.Y.: Syracuse University Press, 1993.

Alterman, Eric. *When Presidents Lie: A History of Official Deception and its Consequences.* New York: Viking, 2004.

Ambrose, Stephen. *Nixon.* New York: Simon and Schuster, 1987.

American Association for the Advancement of Science. "Climate Experts Urge Immediate Action to Offset Impact of Global Warming." June 16, 2004. <http://www. aaas.org/ news/releases/2004/0616climate.shtml> (accessed May 16, 2006).

American Civil Liberties Union. "Free Speech Under Fire: The ACLU Challenge to 'Protest Zones.'" September 23, 2003. <http://www.aclu.org/freespeech/protest/ 11419res20030923.html> (accessed May 23, 2006).

American Immigration Law Foundation. "The Value of Undocumented Workers: The Numbers Behind the U.S.–Mexico Immigration Debate." <http://www. ailf.org/ipc/policy_reports_2002_value.asp> (accessed May 25, 2006).

American Library Association. "USA PATRIOT Act of 2001." April 17, 2006. <http://www.ala.org/ala/washoff/ WOissues/civilliberties/theusapatriotact/usapatriotact. htm> (accessed May 16, 2006).

American Memory. "Library of Congress." <http://memory.loc.gov/ammem/index.html> (accessed on July 19, 2006).

American Rhetoric. "American Rhetoric." <http://www.americanrhetoric.com/> (accessed on July 19, 2006).

American Rhetoric. "Dr. Martin Luther King, Jr.: 'I Have a Dream.'" <http://www.americanrhetoric.com/speeches/Ihaveadream.htm> (accessed June 2, 2006).

Amnesty International. "Amnesty International." <http://www.amnesty.org/> (accessed on July 19, 2006).

Amnesty International. "Chile—Torture: An International Crime." <http://web.amnesty.org/library/index/engamr220101999> (accessed May 8, 2006).

Animal Liberation Front (ALF). "Homepage of ALF." <http://www.animalliberationfront.com/> (accessed May 29, 2006).

Appleton Public Library. "Biography, Joseph McCarthy (1908–1957)." <http://www.apl.org/history/mccarthy/biography.html> (accessed May 25, 2006).

Asbury, Herbert. *The Great Illusion.* New York: Doubleday, 1950.

Ash, Timothy Garten. *The Polish Revolution: Solidarity.* New Haven, Conn.: Yale University Press, 2003.

Avrich, Paul. *An American Anarchist: The Life of Voltairine de Cleyre.* Princeton, N.J.: Princeton University Press, 1978.

Bacon, David. *The Children of NAFTA: Labor Wars on the U.S./Mexico Border.* Berkeley: University of California Press, 2004.

Bailey, Beth, William H. Chafe and Howard Sitkoff, ed. *A History of Our Time: Readings on Post-War America.* New York: Oxford University Press, 2002.

Baker, Stewart A., and John Kavanagh, eds. *Patriot Debates: Experts Debate the USA Patriot Act.* Chicago: American Bar Association, 2005.

Baskir, Lawrence M., and William A. Strauss. *Chance and Circumstance: The Draft, the War, and the Vietnam Generation.* New York: Vintage, 1978.

Bass, S. Jonathan. *Blessed Are the Peacemakers: Martin Luther King, Jr., Eight White Religious Leaders, and the Letter from Birmingham Jail.* Baton Rouge: Louisiana State University Press, 2001.

Bates, Daisy. *The Long Shadow of Little Rock: A Memoir.* Fayetteville: University of Arkansas Press, 1986.

Behrman, Greg. *The Invisible People: How the U.S. Has Slept Through the Global AIDS Pandemic, the Greatest Humanitarian Catastrophe of Our Time.* New York: Free Press, 2004.

Bell, Roger John. *Last Among Equals: Hawaiian Statehood and American Politics.* Honolulu, Hawaii: University of Hawaii Press, 1984.

Bennett, Andy, ed. *Remembering Woodstock.* Burlington, Vt.: Ashgate, 2004.

Berghahn, V. R., John A. Broadwin, and Hilmar Hoffmann. *The Triumph of Propaganda: Film and National Socialism, 1933–1945.* New York: Berghahn Books, 1997.

Bernstein, Irving. *Guns or Butter: The Presidency of Lyndon Johnson.* New York: Oxford University Press, 1996.

Best, Steven and Anthony J. Nocella, editors. *Terrorists or Freedom Fighters?: Reflections on the Liberation of Animals.* New York: Lantern Books, 2004.

Biographical Directory of the United States Congress. "McCarthy, Joseph Raymond (1908–1957)." <http://bioguide.congress.gov/scripts/biodisplay.pl?index=M000315> (accessed May 25, 2006).

Blanchard, Dallas A., and Terry J. Prewitt. *Religious Violence and Abortion: The Gideon Project.* Gainesville: University Press of Florida, 1993.

Bombay Sarvodaya Mandal. "Defiance of Salt Tax." '<http://www.mkgandhi.org/civil_dis/civil_dis.htm> (accessed May 22, 2006).

Boston Tea Party Historical Society. "The Boston Tea Party." <http://www.boston-tea-party.org/> (accessed May 24, 2006).

Bosworth, Patricia. *Marlon Brando.* New York: Viking, 2001.

Bouvard, James. *Terrorism and Tyranny: Trampling Freedom, Justice and Peace to Rid the World of Evil.* New York: Palgrave Macmillan, 2003.

Boyd, Aaron. *Smart Money; The Story of Bill Gates.* Greensboro, NC: Morgan Reynolds, Inc., 2004.

Branch, Taylor. *Parting the Waters: America in the King Years, 1954–63.* New York: Simon & Schuster, 1988.

Brando, Marlon, with Robert Lindsey. *Brando: Songs My Mother Taught Me.* New York: Random House, 1994.

Brandt, J. Donald. *A History of Gannett 1906–1993.* Arlington, Va.: Gannett Company, 1993.

Brecher, Jeremy. *Strike!* Revised and updated edition. Cambridge, Mass.: South End Press, 1997.

Brenner, Michael. *Zionism: A Brief History.* Princeton, N.J.: Markus Weiner Publishers, 2003.

Breyer, Stephen. *Active Liberty: Interpreting Our Democratic Constitution.* New York: Knopf, 2005.

Brinkley, Douglas. *Rosa Parks.* New York: Viking Penguin, 2000.

British Library. "British Library Images Online." <http://www.imagesonline.bl.uk/britishlibrary/> (accessed on July 19, 2006).

Bruns, Roger. *César Chávez: A Biography.* Westport, CT: Greenwood Press, 2005.

BUBL LINK Social Sciences. "Centre for Digital Library Research." <http://bubl.ac.uk/link/linkbrowse.cfm?menuid=2822> (accessed on July 19, 2006).

Buckley, William F. *The Fall of the Berlin Wall*. Hoboken, NJ: Wiley & Sons, 2004.

Buele, Mary Jo and Paul Buehle. *The Concise History of Woman Suffrage: Selections from History of Woman Suffrage*. University of Illinois Press, 2005.

Burg, David E. *The Great Depression*. New York: Facts on File, 1996.

Burnett, Robert and John Koster. *The Road to Wounded Knee*. New York: Bantam, 1974.

César E. Chávez Foundation. "An American Hero." <http://Chávezfoundation.org/CésareChávez.html> (accessed May 9, 2006).

Cameron, Peter D., and Donald Zillman. *Kyoto: From Principles to Practice*. New York: Kluwer Law International, 2001.

Caputo, Philip. *13 Seconds: A Look Back at the Kent State Shootings*. New York: Chamberlain Brothers, 2005.

Carey, Gary. *Marlon Brando: The Only Contender*. New York: St. Martin's Press, 1985.

Carter, Dan T. *The Politics of Rage: George Wallace, the Origin of the New Conservatism, and the Transformation of American Politics*. New York: Simon and Schuster, 1995.

Census Bureau. "United States Census Bureau." <http://www.census.gov/> (accessed on July 19, 2006).

Center for Responsive Politics. "Background: Pharmaceuticals/Health Products." April 2006. <http://www.opensecrets.org/industries/background.asp?Ind=H04> (accessed May 31, 2006).

Central Intelligence Agency. "World Factbook: Singapore." <http://www.cia.gov/cia/publications/factbook/geos/sn.html> (accessed June 29, 2006).

Chaffee, Lyman G. *Political Protest and Street Art: Popular Tools for Democratization in Hispanic Countries*. Greenwood Press, 1993.

Chamberlin, William Henry. *The Russian Revolution, 1917–1921*. Princeton, NJ: Princeton University Press, 1987.

Chicago Public Library. "1886: The Haymarket Riot." <http://www.chipublib.org/004chicago/timeline/haymarket.html> (accessed May 22, 2006).

Chomsky, Noam. *9–11*. New York: Open Media, 2001.

Christiansen, John B. and Sharon H. Barnartt. *Deaf President Now!: The 1988 Revolution at Gallaudet University*. Washington, D.C.: Gallaudet University Press, 2003.

Christofferson, Bill. *The Man from Clear Lake: Earth Day Founder Gaylord Nelson*. Madison, WI: University of Wisconsin Press, 2004.

Churchill, Ward and Jim Vander Wall. *Agents of Repression: The FBI's Secret Wars Against the Black Panther Party and the American Indian Movement*. Cambridge, MA: South End, 2002.

Churchill, Ward and Jim Vander Wall. *The Cointelpro Papers: Documents from the FBI's Secret Wars Against Domestic Dissent*. Boston, MA: South End Press, 1990.

Clark, E. Culpepper. *The Schoolhouse Door: Segregation's Last Stand at the University of Alabama*. New York: Oxford University Press, 1993.

Cockburn, Alexander and Jeffrey St. Clair. *Five Days that Shook the World: Seattle and Beyond*. New York: Verso, 2000.

Commission of the European Communities. "Commission Recommendation 23 July 2003 on Guidelines for the Development of National Strategies and Best Practices to Ensure the Co-existence of Genetically Modified Crops with Conventional and Organic Farming." <http://ec.europa.eu/comm/agriculture/publi/reports/coexistence2/guide_en.pdf> (accessed May 29, 2006).

Committee on the Judiciary, Senate, United States Congress. *Animal Rights: Activism vs. Criminality: Hearing Before the Committee on the Judiciary, United States Senate, One Hundred Eighth Congress, Second Session, May 18, 2004*. Washington, D.C.: U.S. Government Printing Office, 2004.

Community Dialogue. "Community Dialogue: Understanding In the Northern Irelaxsnd Conflict." <http://www.communitydialogue.org/> (accessed June 3, 2006).

Comprehensive Test Ban Treaty Organization. May 16, 2006. <http://www.ctbto.org> (accessed May 25, 2006).

Congressional Research Service. "Israeli-United States Relations." April 28, 2005. <http://fpc.state.gov/documents/organization/47089.pdf> (accessed June 12, 2006).

Consumer Project on Technology. "Drug Development Incentives to Improve Access to Essential Medicines." May 2006. <http://www.cptech.org/ip/health/rnd/love-who052006.pdf> (accessed May 31, 2006).

Conway, Jean. *Housing Policy*. Gildredge, 2000.

Cook, Christopher. *A Short History of the Liberal Party 1900–2001*. Basingstoke: Palgrave Macmillan, 2002.

Country Studies US. "Mahatma Gandhi." <http://countrystudies.us/india/20.htm> (accessed May 22, 2006).

Coyne, John R, Jr. *The Impudent Snobs: Agnew vs. the Intellectual Establishment*. New York: Arlington House, 1972.

Crampton, R J. *Return to Diversity: A Political History of East Central Europe Since World War II*. London: Routledge, 1997.

Crampton, R. J. *Eastern Europe in the Twentieth Century—and After*. London: Routledge, 1997.

Cravey, Altha J. *Women and Work in Mexico's Maquiladoras*. Lanham, MD: Rowman and Littlefield, 1998.

Cray, Ed. *Ramblin' Man: The Life and Times of Woody Guthrie*. New York: W.W. Norton, 2004.

Cross, Charles. *Room Full of Mirrors: A Biography of Jimi Hendrix*. New York: Hyperion, 2005.

Dallek, Robert. *Flawed Giant: Lyndon Johnson and His Times, 1961–1973*. New York: Oxford University Press, 1998.

Dangerfield, George *The Strange Death of Liberal England*. London: Paladin, 1983.

Daniels, Roger. *The Bonus March: An Episode of the Great Depression*. Westport, CT: Greenwood, 1971.

Davis, Kenneth Sydney. *FDR: The New Deal Years, 1933–1937*. New York: Random House, 1986.

DeBenedetti, Charles. *An American Ordeal: The Antiwar Movement of the Vietnam Era*. Syracuse, NY: Syracuse University Press, 1997.

Degen, Marie Louise. *The History of the Women's Peace Party*. The John Hopkins Press, 1939.

Delaet, Debra L. *U.S. Immigration Policy in an Age of Rights*. Westport, Conn.: Praeger Publishers, 2000.

DeLamott, Eugenia C. *Gates of Freedom: Voltairine de Cleyre and the Revolution of the Mind*. Ann Arbor, Mich.: University of Michigan Press, 2004.

Dicker, John. *United States of Wal-Mart*. New York: Penguin Books, 2005.

Dickson, Paul and Thomas B. Allen. *The Bonus Army: An American Epic*. New York: Walker, 2005.

Doctors Without Borders. "Doctors Without Borders." <http://www.doctorswithoutborders.org/> (accessed on July 19, 2006).

Doerflinger, Thomas. *A Vigorous Spirit of Enterprise: Merchants and Economic Development in Revolutionary Philadelphia*. Chapel Hill: University of North Carolina Press, 1986.

Dowe, Dieter, ed., et al. *Europe in 1848: Revolution and Reform*. New York: Berghahn Books, 2001.

Dowell, LeiLani, et al. *We Won't Go: The Truth on Military Recruiters and the Draft*. New York: International Action Center, 2006.

Dreyer, June Teufel and Barry Sautman, ed. *Contemporary Tibet: Politics, Development, and Society in a Disputed Region*. Armonk, New York: M.E. Sharpe, 2005.

Dubofsky, Melvyn. *We Shall Be All*. Chicago: Quadrangle Books, 1969.

Duram, James C. *A Moderate among Extremists: Dwight D. Eisenhower and the School Desegregation Crisis*. Chicago; Nelson-Hall, 1981.

Dwight D. Eisenhower Presidential Library and Museum. "Little Rock School Integration Crisis." <http://www.eisenhower.archives.gov/dl/LittleRock/littlerockdocuments.html> (accessed May 23, 2006).

Earth Day Network. <http://www.earthday.net/default.aspx> (accessed May 11, 2006).

Electronic Privacy Information Center. "U.S.A. Patriot Act." October 24, 2001 <http://www.epic.org/privacy/terrorism/hr3162.html> (accessed May 16, 2006).

Elmer, Jerry. *Felon for Peace: The Memoir of a Viet Nam-era Draft Resister*. Nashville, Tennessee; Vanderbilt University Press, 2005.

Epstein, Barbara. *Political Protest and Cultural Revolution: Nonviolent Direct Action in the 1970s and 1980s*. University of California Press, 1991.

Estes, Steve S. *I Am a Man!: Race, Manhood, and the Civil Rights Movement*. Chapel Hill: University of North Carolina Press, 2006.

European Commission. "Conference, 4–6 April 2006, Vienna: Co-existence of Genetically Modified, Conventional, and Organic Crops." <http://ec.europa.eu/comm/agriculture/events/vienna2006/index_en.htm> (accessed May 29, 2006).

Fager, Charles. *Selma, 1965*. New York: Scribner, 1974.

Fairclough, Adam. *To Redeem the Soul of America: The Southern Christian Leadership Conference and Martin Luther King, Jr*. Athens: University of Georgia Press, 1987.

Falkner, David. *Great Time Coming: The Life of Jackie Robinson, from Baseball to Birmingham*. New York: Simon and Schuster, 1995.

Farber, David. *Chicago '68*. Chicago: University of Chicago Press, 1988.

Farrell, Brian P. et al. *Between Two Oceans: A Military History Of Singapore From First Settlement To Final British Withdrawal*. New York: Avon Books, 1977.

Farrell, James. *The Spirit of the Sixties: The Making of Postwar Radicalism*. Routledge, 1997.

Federal Government Agencies Directory. "Louisiana State University." <http://www.lib.lsu.edu/gov/fedgov.html> (accessed on July 19, 2006).

Federation of American Scientists. "Federation of American Scientists, ProMED Initiative." <http://www.fas.org/promed> (accessed on July 19, 2006).

FedStats. "FedStats." <http://www.fedstats.gov> (accessed on July 19, 2006).

Felder, Deborah G. *A Century of Women: The Most Influential Events in Twentieth-Century Women's History*. Kensington Publishing Corp., 1999.

Figes, O. *A People's Tragedy: the Russian Revolution, 1891–1924*. London: J. Cape, 1996.

Figes, Orlando. *A People's Tragedy: The Russian Revolution 1891–1924*. London: Jonathan Cape, 1996.

Findlaw. "Findlaw/West." <http://public.findlaw.com/library/> (accessed on July 19, 2006).

Fishman, Charles. *The Wal-Mart Effect: How the World's Most Successful Company Really Works—and How It's*

Transforming the American Economy. New York: Penguin, 2006.

Fletcher, Ian Christopher and Laura E. Nym Mayhall et al. *Women's Suffrage in the British Empire; Citizenship, Nation and Race*. Routledge, 2000.

Flynn, Elizabeth Gurley. *The Rebel Girl: An Autobiography*. New York: New York University Press, 1955.

Foley, Michael S. *Confronting the War Machine: Draft Resistance During the Vietnam War*. Chapel Hill: University of North Carolina Press, 2006.

Foreman, Dave. *Confessions of an Eco-Warrior*. New York: Three Rivers Press, 1993.

Fowke, Edith and Joe Glazer. *Songs of Work and Protest*. New York: Dover Publications, 1973.

Frady, Marshall. *Wallace*. New York: Random House, 1996.

Frank, Anne. *Anne Frank; Diary of a Young Girl*. New York: Doubelday, 1995.

Franklin D. Roosevelt Presidential Library and Museum. "Franklin D. Roosevelt." <http://www.fdrlibrary. marist.edu/fdrbio.html> (accessed June 2, 2006).

Fraser, Lindley. *Germany Between Two Wars: A Study of Propaganda and War-Guilt*. New York: Oxford University Press, 1945.

Fried, Albert. *McCarthyism, The Great American Red Scare: A Documentary History*. New York: Oxford University Press, 1996.

Frieden, Jeffry A. *Global Capitalism: Its Fall and Rise in the Twentieth Century*. New York: W.W. Norton, 2006.

Gaillard, Frye. *The Cradle of Freedom: Alabama and the Movement that Changed America*. Tuscaloosa, Ala.: University of Alabama Press, 2004.

Gallaudet University. "Gallaudet History." <http://www. gallaudet.edu/x228.xml> (accessed May 31, 2006).

Gannon, Jack. *The Week the World Heard Galludet*. Washington, D.C.: Gallaudet University Press, 1989.

GAO (Government Account Office). "Site Map." <http://www. gao.gov/sitemap.html> (accessed on July 19, 2006).

Garrow, David J. *Protest at Selma: Martin Luther King, Jr. and the Voting Rights Act of 1965*. New Haven, Conn.: Yale University Press, 1978.

Gelvin, James L. *The Israel-Palestine Conflict: One Hundred Years of War*. New York: Cambridge University Press, 2005.

Gerdes, Louise I., ed. *Globalization*. San Diego, CA: Greenhaven Press, 2006.

Glen, John. *Highlander: No Ordinary School*. Knoxville: University of Tennessee Press, 1996.

Goldstein, Melvyn C. *The Snow Lion and the Dragon: China, Tibet, and the Dalai Lama*. Berkley: University of California Press, 1997.

Goldstein, Robert Justin. *Flag Burning and Free Speech: The Case of Texas v. Johnson*. Lawrence: University Press of Kansas, 2000.

Golin, Steve. *The Fragile Bridge: Paterson Silk Strike, 1913*. Philadelphia: Temple University Press, 1988.

Gordon-Skilling, H., Jaromir Navrotil, Antonin Bencik, Vaclav Kural, Marie Michalkuva, Jitka Vondorova, and Vaclav Havel. *The Prague Spring 1968*. Budapest: Central European University Press, 1998.

Graham, Mary. *The Morning after Earth Day: Practical Environmental Politics*. Washington, DC: Governance Institute, Brookings Institution Press, 1999.

Gray Panthers. <http://graypanthers.org> (accessed May 31, 2006).

Green, James R. *Death in the Haymarket: A Story of Chicago, the First Labor Movement, and the Bombing that Divided Gilded Age America*. New York: Pantheon, 2006.

Grinker, Roy R. *Korea and Its Futures: Unification and the Unfinished War*. New York: St. Martin's Press, 1998.

Grobel, Lawrence. *Conversations with Brando*. New York: Cooper Square Press, 1999.

Halberstam, David. *The Best and the Brightest*. Ballantine Books, 1993.

Hansen, Drew. *The Dream: Martin Luther King, Jr., and the Speech that Inspired a Nation*. New York: HarperCollins, 2003.

Harding, Walter. *The Days of Henry Thoreau: A Biography*. New York: Dover, 1962.

Harries, Meiron and Susie Harries. *The Last Days of Innocence: America at War, 1917–1918*. New York: Vintage, 1997.

Harriet Beecher Stowe Center. <http://www. harrietbeecherstowe center.org/index_home.shtml> (accessed June 4, 2006).

Hawaii Advisory Committee to the U.S. Commission on Civil Rights, National Asian American Pacific Islander Mental Health Association. "Reconciliation at a Crossroads: The Implications of the Apology Resolution and Rice v. Cayetano for Federal and State Programs Benefiting Native Hawaiians." June 2001. <http://www.naapimha.org/ issues/econciliationCrossroads.pdf> (accessed May 31, 2006).

Health Resources and Services Administration (HRSA). "Health Resources and Services Administration (HRSA)." <http://www. hrsa.gov> (accessed on July 19, 2006).

Hedrick, Joan D. *Harriet Beecher Stowe: A Life*. New York and Oxford: Oxford University Press, 1994.

Hensley, Thomas R., with James A. Best. *The Kent State Incident: Impact of Judicial Process on Public Attitudes*. Westport, CT: Greenwood Press, 1981.

Herman, Arthur. *Joseph McCarthy: Reexamining the Life and Legacy of America's Most Hated Senator*. New York: Free Press, 2000.

Herman, Didi. *Rites of Passage: Struggles for Lesbian and Gay Legal Equality*. Toronto: University of Toronto Press, 1994.

Herring, George C. *America's Longest War: The United States and Vietnam, 1950–1975*. New York: Alfred A. Knopf, 1986.

Hevenor, John W. *Which Side Are You on?: The Harlan County Coal Miners, 1931–39*. Urbana. Ill.: University of Illinois Press, 1978.

Hill, Christopher. *Lenin and the Russian Revolution*. London: Penguin, 1971.

Holton, Sandra Stanley. *Feminism and Democracy: Women's Suffrage and Reform Politics in Britain, 1900–1918*. Cambridge University Press, 2003.

Horton, Aimee Isgrig. *The Highlander Folk School, 1932–1961*. Toronto: Catalyst Centre, 2002.

Horton, Myles, and Dale Jacobs, ed. *Myles Horton Reader: Education for Social Change*. Knoxville: University of Tennessee Press, 2003.

House of Commons Committee on Housing in Greater London. *Housing in Greater London*. HMSO, 1965.

Hull, N. E. H., and Peter Charles Hoffer. *Roe V. Wade: The Abortion Rights Controversy in American History*. Lawrence: University Press of Kansas, 2001.

Hulme, Derick. *The Political Olympics: Moscow, Afghanistan, and the 1980 U.S. Boycott*. New York: Praeger Publishers, December 30, 1990.

Human Rights Watch. "Human Rights Watch." <http://www.hrw.org/> (accessed on July 19, 2006).

Human Rights Watch. "World AIDS Day: Human Rights Watch Calls for Increased Support, Protections for Global AIDS Activists." December 1, 2005. <http://hrw.org/english/docs/2005/12/01/global12114_txt.htm> (accessed May 30, 2006).

Hutt, Michael ed. *Himalyan People's War: Nepal's Maoist Rebellion*. Bloomington: Indiana University Press, 2004.

Institute for Anarchist Studies. <http://www.anarchist-studies.org> (accessed May 25, 2006).

International Forum on Globalization (IFG). "Globalization." <http://www.ifg.org/analysis.htm> (accessed June 1, 2006).

International Monetary Fund (IMF). "Globalization: A Framework for IMF Involvement." March 2002 <http://www.imf.org/external/np/exr/ib/2002/031502.htm> (accessed June 1, 2006).

International Olympic Committee. "Olympic Charter." August 2004. <http://multimedia.olympic.org/pdf/en_report_122.pdf> (accessed May 17, 2006).

Internet Modern History Sourcebook. "Fordham University." <http://www.fordham.edu/halsall/mod/modsbook.html> (accessed on July 19, 2006).

Jenkins, Roy. *Churchill*. London: Macmillan, 2001.

Johnson, Allen S. *A Prologue to Revolution: The Political Career of George Grenville*. Lanham, Md.: University Press of America, 1997.

Jones, David J.V. *Chartism and the Chartists*. London: Allen Lane, 1975.

Jurist Legal News Archiva. "Guantanamo." <http://jurist.law.pitt.edu/currentawareness/guantanamo.php> (accessed May 16, 2006).

Justicia: U.S. Supreme Court Center. "Roe v. Wade. 410 U.S. 113 (1973)." <http://supreme.justia.com/us/410/113/case.html> (accessed May 17, 2006).

Kadragic, Alma. *Globalization and Human Rights*. Philadelphia, PA: Chelsea House, 2006.

Kahn, Alfred J. *Family Change and Family Policies in Great Britain, Canada New Zealand, and the United States*. Clarendon Press, 1997.

Kaplan, Lawrence, F., and W. Kristol. *The War over Iraq: Saddam's Tyranny and America's Mission*. New York: Encounter Books, 2003.

Kaufman, Burton I. *The Presidency of James Earl Carter, Jr*. Lawrence: University Press of Kansas, 1993.

Kersaudy, Francois. *Norway 1940*. Lincoln: University of Nebraska Press, 1998.

Kinsman, Gary. *The Regulation of Desire: Homo and Hetero Sexualities in Canada*. Montreal: Black Rose Books, 1996.

Knock, Thomas J. *To End All Wars: Woodrow Wilson and the Quest for a New World Order*. Princeton: Princeton University, 1995.

Kobler, John. *Ardent Spirits: The Rise and Fall of Prohibition*. New York: G. P. Putnam's, 1973.

Kornbluh, Joyce L., ed. *Rebel Voices: An IWW Anthology*. Ann Arbor: University of Michigan Press, 1968.

Kornbluh, Peter. *The Pinochet File: A Declassified Dossier on Atrocity and Accountability*. New York: New Press, 2004.

Kotkin, Steven. *Armagadden Averted: The Soviet Collapse 1970–2000*. Oxford, U.K.: Oxford University Press, 2000.

Krepinevich, Andrew F., Jr. *The Army and Vietnam*. Baltimore: Johns Hopkins University Press, 1986.

Kuhn, Maggie. *No Stone Unturned: The Life and Times of Maggie Kuhn*. New York: Ballantine Books, 1991.

Kush, Christopher. *The One-Hour Activist: The 15 Most Powerful Actions You Can Take to Fight for the Issues and Candidates You Care About*. Jossey-Bass, 2004.

Kyvig, David E. *Daily Life in the United States, 1920–1940*. Chicago: Ivan R. Dee, 2004.

La Botz, Dan. *César Chávez and la Causa*. New York: Pearson Longman, 2006.

Labor and Labor Movements. "American Sociological Association." <http://www.bgsu.edu/departments/soc/prof/mason/ASA/> (accessed on July 19, 2006).

Lacey, Fred. *Memphis Workers Fight: The City Sanitation Workers' Strike*. Boston: New England Free Press, 1969.

Lacquer, Walter. *A History of Zionism*. New York: MJF Books, 1972.

Lampe, Gregory P. *Frederick Douglass, Freedom's Voice, 1818–1845*. East Lansing, Mich.: Michigan State University Press, 1998.

Lane, Harlan. *When the Mind Hears: A History of the Deaf*. New York: Vintage Press, 1989.

Le Blanc, Paul. *A Short History of the U.S. Working Class*. New York: Humanity Books, 1999.

Legal Information Institute, Cornell University. "Code of Federal Regulations." <http://www4.law.cornell.edu/cfr/> (accessed on July 19, 2006).

Lemert, Charles C. *Deadly Worlds: The Emotional Costs of Globalization*. Lanham, MD: Rowman and Littlefield Publishers, 2006.

Leuchtenburg, William E. *The Supreme Court Reborn: The Court Revolution in the Age of Roosevelt*. New York: Oxford University Press, 1995.

Lewis, William C., Jr., ed. *Margaret Chase Smith: Declaration of Conscience*. (American National Biography, Scribner Encyclopedia of American Lives.) New York: Doubleday, 1972.

Libby, Ronald T. *Eco-wars: Political Campaigns and Social Movements*. New York: Columbia University Press, 1998.

Library of Congress. "Library of Congress Online Catalog." <http://catalog.loc.gov/cgi-bin/Pwebrecon.cgi?DB=local&PAGE=First> (accessed on July 19, 2006).

Library of Congress. "Woody Guthrie and the Archive of American Folk Song: Correspondence 1940–1950." <http://memory.loc.gov/ammem/wwghtml/wwghome.html> (accessed May 25, 2006).

Liliuokalani, Queen of Hawaii. *Hawaii's Story by Hawaii's Queen*. Rutland, Vt.: C.E. Tuttle Co., 1964.

Lisio, Donald J. *The President and Protest: Hoover, MacArthur, and the Bonus Riot*. New York: Fordham University Press, 1994.

Lloyd-George, Robert. *David and Winston*. London: John Murray, 2005.

Love, James. *Remuneration Guidelines for Non-voluntary use of a Patent on Medical Technologies. TCM Series No. 18*. World Health Organization, 2005.

Mahatma Gandhi Foundation. "The Salt March." <http://www.saltmarch.org.in> (accessed May 22, 2006).

Making of America. "Cornell University." <http://cdl.library.cornell.edu/moa/> (accessed on July 19, 2006).

Mamdani, Mahmood. *Good Muslim, Bad Muslim: America, the Cold War, and the Roots of Terror*. New York: Pantheon, 2004.

Mann, Chris. *Hitler's Artic War: The German Campaign in Norway, Finland and the USSR 1940–45*. New York: Thomas Dunne Books, 2003.

Manso, Peter. *Brando: The Biography*. New York: Hyperion, 1994.

Margaret Chase Smith Policy Center, The University of Maine. "Biography: Margaret Chase Smith (1897–1995)." <http://www.umaine.edu/mcsc/AboutUs/Bio.htm> (accessed May 22, 2006).

Marples., David R,. *The Collapse of the Soviet Union 1985–1991*. Harlow, U.K.: Longman, 2004.

Marsh, Margaret S. *Anarchist Women, 1870–1920*. Philadelphia, Penn.: Temple University Press, 1981.

Martin, Bradley K. *Under the Loving Care of the Fatherly Leader: North Korea and the Kim Dynasty*. New York: St. Martin's Press, 2004.

McCartney, John T. *Black Power Ideologies: An Essay in African-American Political Thought*. Philadelphia: Temple University Press, 2006.

McCauley, Martin. *Russia, America and the Cold War, 1949–1991*. 2nd ed. New York: Longman, 2004.

McDarrah, Fred. *Anarchy, Protest, and Rebellion: And the Counterculture that Changed America*. New York: Thunder's Mouth Press, 2003.

McDonald, Kevin. *Global Movements: Action and Culture*. Malden, MA: Blackwell Publishing, 2006.

McKay, Ernest A. *Against Wilson and War, 1914–1917*. Malabar, Fla.: Krieger, 1996.

Meier, August, and Elliott M. Rudwick. *CORE: A Study in the Civil Rights Movement, 1942–1968*. New York: Oxford University Press, 1973.

Migration Policy Institute. "US in Focus." <http://www.migrationinformation.org/USfocus/> (accessed June 1, 2006).

Milani, Mohsen M. *The Making of Iran's Islamic Revolution: From Monarchy to Islamic Republic*. Boulder, CO: Westview Press, 1994.

Miller, M., ed. *The Russian Revolution: The Essential Readings*. Oxford University Press, 2001.

Ministry of Home Affairs, Government of India. "History: Milestones in Indian History." <http://mha.nic.in/his3.htm> (accessed May 22, 2006).

Moïse, Edwin E. *Tonkin Gulf and the Escalation of the Vietnam War*. Chapel Hill: University of North Carolina Press, 1996.

Montgomery Bus Boycott. "They Changed the World: The Story of the Montgomery Bus Boycott." <http://www.montgomeryboycott.com/> (accessed June 5, 2006).

Morgan, Iwan W. *Nixon*. London: Oxford University Press, 2002.

Morgan, Robin. *Going Too Far: The Personal Chronicle of a Feminist*. New York: Vintage Books, 1978.

Morgan, Ted. *Reds: McCarthyism in Twentieth-century America*. New York: Random House, 2003.

Moritz, Theresa and Albert Moritz. *The World's Most Dangerous Woman: A New Biography of Emma Goldman*. Vancouver: Subway, 2001.

Morrison, Joan, and Robert K. Morrison. *From Camelot to Kent State: The Sixties Experience in the Words of Those Who Lived It*. Oxford University Press, U.S.A., 2001.

Morto, Alexander. *The Roots of Mexican Labor Migration*. Westport, Conn.: Praeger Publishers, 1994.

Murolo, Priscilla and A. B. Chitty. *From the Folks Who Brought You the Weekend: A Short, Illustrated History of Labor in the United States*. New York: New Press, 2001.

Nardo, Don, ed. *The Great Depression*. San Diego, Calif.: Greenhaven Press, 2000.

National Archives and Records Administration. "National Commission on Terrorist Attacks Upon the United States." September 20, 2004. <http://www.9-11commission.gov/> (accessed May 24, 2006).

National Archives and Records Administration. "The Formation of Political Parties: The Alien and Sedition Acts." <http://www.archives.gov/exhibits/treasures_of_congress/page_5.html#> (accessed June 1, 2006).

National Archives. "Teaching With Documents: Telegram from Senator Joseph McCarthy to President Harry S. Truman." <http://www.archives.gov/education/lessons/mccarthy-telegram/> (accessed May 25, 2006).

National Commission of Independent Self-Governing Trade Union. "Solidarity Web Site.". <http://www.solidarnosc.org.pl/eng1.htm> (accessed May 24, 2006).

National Commission on Terrorist Attacks. *The 9/11 Commission Report: Final Report of the National Commission on Terrorist Attacks Upon the United States*. New York: W.W. Norton, 2003.

National Film Board of Canada. "Web of War." July 1, 2005. <http://www.nfb.ca/trouverunfilm/> (accessed May 20, 2006).

National Lawyers' Guild. "The Assault on Free Speech, Public Assembly, and Dissent." <http://www.nlg.org/resources/DissentBookWeb.pdf> (accessed May 24, 2006).

National Research Council of the National Academies. *Science, Medicine, and Animals*. Washington, D.C.: National Academies Press, 2004.

National Security Archive Electronic Briefing Book No.16. "Tiananmen Square, 1989." <http://www.gwu.edu/~nsarchiv/NSAEBB/NSAEBB16/> (accessed April 30, 2006).

National Security Archive, George Washington University. "Tonkin Gulf Intelligence "Skewed" According to Official History and Intercepts." December 1, 2005. <http://www.gwu.edu/~nsarchiv/NSAEBB/

NSAEBB132/press20051201.htm> (accessed May 18, 2006).

Nelson, Gaylord, with Susan Campbell, and Paul Wozniak. *Beyond Earth Day: Fulfilling the Promise*. Madison, WI: University of Wisconsin Press, 1992.

Nelson, Jill. *Police Brutality: An Anthology*. New York: W. W. Norton, 2001.

Nelson, Samuel P. *Beyond the First Amendment : The Politics of Free Speech and Pluralism*. Johns Hopkins University Press, 2005.

New Deal Network. <http://newdeal.feri.org/> (accessed June 3, 2006).

Ngai, Mai. *Impossible Subjects: Illegal Aliens and the Making of Modern America*. Princeton University Press, 2004.

NICHD - National Institute of Child Health and Human Development. "NICHD - National Institute of Child Health and Human Development." <http://www.nichd.nih.gov> (accessed on July 19, 2006).

Niven, Bill. *Facing the Nazi Past: United Germany and the Legacy of the Third Reich*. New York: Routledge, 2002.

Nobel Prize Committee. "Nobel Peace Prize, 1989." April 1, 2005. <http://www.nobelprize.org/peace/laureates/1989/index.html> (accessed May 26, 2006).

North Atlantic Treaty Organization (NATO). "London Declaration." <http://www.nato.int/docu/basictxt/b900706a.htm> (accessed May 25, 2006).

Northrup, Herbert R. and Amie D. Thornton. *The Federal Government as Employer: The Federal Labor Relations Authority and the PATCO Challenge*. Philadelphia: Wharton School, University of Pennsylvania, 1986.

Notable American Unitarians. "Frank Gannett: Newspaper Publisher, 1876–1957." <www.harvardsquarelibrary.org/unitarians/gannett.html> (accessed May 19, 2006).

Oates, Stephen. *Let the Trumpet Sound: The Life of Martin Luther King, Jr*. New York: New American Library, 1985.

Office of Global Health Affairs. "Office of Global Health Affairs." <http://www.globalhealth.gov> (accessed on July 19, 2006).

Ogban, Jeffrey Ogbonna Green. *Black Power: Radical Politics and African American Identity*. Baltimore: Johns Hopkins University Press, 2004.

Olson, James S. and Randy Roberts. *Where the Domino Fell: America and Vietnam, 1945–1995*. New York: St. Martin's Press, 1996.

Operation Rescue/Operation Save America. <http://www.operationsaveamerica.org/> (accessed May 17, 2006).

Ostrow, Scott A. *Guide to Judging the Military: Air Force, Army, Coast Guard, Marine Corps, Navy*. Lawrenceville, N.J.: ARCO, 2003.

Oxfam GB. "Drug Companies vs. Brazil: The Threat to Public Health." May 2001. <http://www.oxfam.org.uk/

what_we_do/issues/health/papers.htm> (accessed May 14, 2006).

Oxfam GB. "Public Health at Risk." April 2006. <http://www.oxfam.org.uk/what_we_do/issues/health/papers.htm> (accessed May 14, 2006).

Oxford University Press. "The Theory, Practice, and Influence of Thoreau's Civil Disobedience." August 7, 2003. <http://www.wellesley.edu/Peace/Rosenwald/thoreau.html> (accessed May 15, 2006).

Partridge, Elizabeth. *This Land Was Made for You and Me: The Life and Songs of Woody Guthrie*. New York: Viking, 2002.

Pemberton, William E. *Exit with Honor: The Life and Presidency of Ronald Reagan*. Armonk, NY: M.E. Sharpe, 1998.

PEW Hispanic Center. "Size and Characteristics of the Unauthorized Migrant Population in the U.S." <http://pewhispanic.org/reports/report.php?ReportID=61> (accessed May 25, 2006).

Pew Initiative on Food and Biotechnology. "Fact Sheet: Genetically Modified Crops in the United States." 2004. <http://pewagbiotech.org/resources/factsheets/display.php3?FactsheetID=2> (accessed May 29, 2006).

Pickering, Paul A., and Alex Tyrell. *The People's Bread; A History of the Anti-Corn Law League*. Leicester: Leicester University Press, 2000.

Pierce, Richard B. *Polite Protest: The Political Economy Of Race In Indianapolis, 1920–1970*. Indiana University Press, 2005.

Pipes, Richard. *Russia Under the Old Regime*. London: Penguin, 1995.

Powaski, Ronald E. *The Cold War: The United States and the Soviet Union, 1917–1991*. New York: Oxford University Press, 1998.

Powers, Mary G and Macisco, John J. Jr. and Center for Migration Studies. *The Immigration Experience in the United States: Policy Implications*. Center for Migration Studies, 1994.

Reagan Foundation. "Tear Down This Wall." June 12, 1987. <http://www.reaganfoundation.org/reagan/speeches/wall.asp> (accessed May 24, 2006).

Record, Jeffrey. *Dark Victory: America's Second War Against Iraq*. Annapolis, Md.: Naval Institute Press, 2004.

Reed, Roy. *Faubus: The Life and Times of an American Prodigal*. Fayetteville: University of Arkansas Press, 1997.

Reed, T. V. *The Art of Protest*. Minneapolis: University of Minnesota Press, 2005.

Reef, Catherine. *Working in America*. New York: Facts on File, 2000.

Reeves, Richard. *President Reagan: The Triumph of Imagination*. New York: Simon and Schuster, 2005.

Reporters sans frontières. "Why We Are Boycotting Beijing 2008?" 2001. <http://www.rsf.org/rubrique.php3?id_rubrique=174> (accessed May 17, 2006).

Republic of Korea. Ministry of Unification. <http://unikorea.go.kr/index.jsp> (accessed May 21, 2006).

Resource Information Service. "homelesspages." <http://www.homelesspages.org.uk/index.asp> (accessed June 3, 2006).

Risen, James and Judy L. Thomas. *Wrath of Angels: The American Abortion War*. New York: Basic Books, 1998.

Rising-Moore, Carl and Becky Oberg. *Freedom Underground: Protesting the Iraq War in America*. New York: Chamberlain Bros., 2004.

Robinson, J.H., ed. *Readings in European History*. Boston: Ginn, 1906.

Rosebraugh, Craig. *Burning Rage of a Dying Planet: Speaking for the Earth Liberation Front*. New York: Lantern Books, 2004.

Rosen, Ruth. *The World Split Open: How the Modern Women's Movement Changed America*. New York: Viking Penguin, 2000.

Rosenblatt, Roger. *Coming Apart: A Memoir of the Harvard Wars of 1969*. Little Brown and Company, 1997.

Ross, Becki. *The House that Jill Built: A Lesbian Nation in Formation*. Toronto: University of Toronto Press, 1995.

Rothschild, Joseph, and Nancy M. Wingfield. *Return to Diversity: A Political History of East Central Europe Since World War II*. 3rd edition. New York: Oxford University Press, 1999.

Ruse, Michael, and David Castle, eds. *Genetically Modified Foods: Debating Biotechnology*. Amherst, N.Y.: Prometheus Books, 2002.

Saar, Erik and Viveca Novak. *Inside the Wire: A Military Intelligence Soldier's Eyewitness Account of Life at Guantanamo*. New York: Penguin Press, 2005.

Sachar, Howard M. *A History of Israel: From the Rise of Zionism to Our Time*. New York: Alfred A. Knopf, 1996.

Sacher, H. M. *A History of Israel*. New York: Alfred Knopf, 1979.

Saville, John. *1848: The British State and the Chartist Movement*. New York: Cambridge University Press, 1987.

Sayer, John William. *Ghost Dancing the Law: The Wounded Knee Trials*. Cambridge, MA: Harvard University Press, 1997.

Scheffler, Judith A., ed. *Wall Tappings (2nd edition)*. New York: Feminist Press, City University of New York, 2002.

Schlesinger, Arthur. *The Colonial Merchants and the American Revolution*. New York: Atheneum, 1968.

Schlissel, Lillian. *Conscience in America: A Documentary History of Conscientious Objection in America, 1757–1967*. New York: Dutton, 1968.

Schultz, John. *Chicago Conspiracy Trial*. New York: Da Capo, 1993.

Schwartz, Ronald David. *Circle of Protest: Political Ritual in the Tibetan Uprising*. New York: Columbia University Press, 1994.

Scotch, Richard. *From Good Will to Civil Rights: Transforming Federal Disability Policy*. Philadelphia: Temple University Press, 2001.

Sedition Act of 1798. Available at: University of Oklahoma College of Law. "A Chronology of U.S, Historical Documents: The Sedition Act of 1798." <http://www.law.ou.edu/ushistory/sedact.shtml> (accessed June 3, 2006).

Selucky, Radoslav. *Czechoslovakia: The Plan that Failed*. London: Nelson, 1970.

Sherman, Janann. *No Place for a Woman: A Life of Senator Margaret Chase Smith*. New Brunswick, N.J.: Rutgers University Press, 2000.

Shilts, Randy, and William Greider. *And the Band Played On: Politics, People, and the AIDS Epidemic*. New York: Stonewall Inn Editions, 2000.

Shostak, Arthur B. and David Skocik. *The Air Controllers' Controversy: Lessons from the PATCO Strike*. New York: Human Science Press, 1986.

Sierra Club. "Year in Review: Contract On America's Environment." <http://www.sierraclub.org/planet/199412/yir-contract.asp> (accessed May 26, 2006).

Simon Wiesenthal Center. "Simon Wiesenthal Center." <http://www.wiesenthal.com> (accessed on July 19, 2006).

Sinclair, Andrew. *Prohibition: The Era of Excess*. Boston: Little Brown, 1962.

Small, Melvin. *The Presidency of Richard Nixon*. Lawrence: University Press of Kansas, 1999.

Smith, Paul Chaat and Robert Allen Warrior. *Like a Hurricane: The American Indian Movement from Alcatraz to Wounded Knee*. New York: New Press, 1996.

Smith, W.H.C. *Second Empire and Commune: France, 1848–1871*. New York: Longman, 1996.

Social Science Information Gateway. "SOSIG." <http://www.sosig.ac.uk/> (accessed on July 19, 2006).

Social Sciences Virtual Library. "Digilogical." <http://www.dialogical.net/socialsciences/index.html> (accessed on July 19, 2006).

SocioWeb. "Blairworks." <http://www.socioweb.com/> (accessed on July 19, 2006).

Solinger, Rickie, ed. *Abortion Wars: A Half Century of Struggle 1950–2000*. Berkley: University of California Press, 2000.

Solomon, Gerald B. *The NATO Enlargement Debate, 1990–1997*. Washington, D.C.: Center for Strategic and International Studies/Praeger Publishers, 1998.

Southern Poverty Law Center. "Southern Poverty Law Center." <http://www.splcenter.org/> (accessed on July 19, 2006).

Southern, Eileen. *The Music of Black Americans: A History*. New York: W. W. Norton, 1997.

Spitz, Robert Stephen. *Barefoot in Babylon: The Creation of the Woodstock Music Festival*. New York: Viking Press, 1979.

Stanton, Mary. *From Selma to Sorrow: The Life and Death of Viola Liuzzo*. Athens, Ga.: University of Georgia Press, 1998.

Stewart, James Brewer. *Holy Warriors: The Abolitionists and American Slavery*. New York: Hill and Wang, 1976.

Stone, Geoffrey R. *Perilous Times: Free Speech in Wartime from the Sedition Act of 1798 to the War on Terrorism*. New York: W.W. Norton, 2004.

Stone, Geoffrey R. *Perilous Times: Free Speech in Wartime: From the Sedition Act of 1798 to the War on Terrorism*. New York: W.W. Norton, 2005.

Students United for a Responsible Global Environment (SURGE) <http://surgenetwork.org/> (accessed June 1, 2006).

Suh, Dae-Sook. *Kim Il Sung*. New York: Columbia University Press, 1995.

Tackach, James. *Uncle Tom's Cabin: Indictment of Slavery*. San Diego: Lucent Books, 2000.

Tacke, Charlotte, ed. *1848: Memory and Oblivion in Europe*. New York: Lang, 2000.

Tate, Merze. *The United States and the Hawaiian Kingdom: A Political History*. New Haven, Conn.: Yale University Press, 1965.

Taylor, Paul F. *Bloody Harlan: The United Mine Workers of America in Harlan County, Kentucky, 1931–1941*. Lanham, Md.: University Press of America, 1990.

Thapa, Deepak, and Bandita Sijaputi. *A Kingdom Under Siege: Nepal's Maoist Insurgency, 1996 to 2004*. London: Zed Books, 2004.

Thomas. "Library of Congress." <http://thomas.loc.gov/> (accessed on July 19, 2006).

Thompson, Bill. *The Soviet Union Under Brezhnev: 1964–82*. New York: Longman, 2003.

Thompson, Dorothy. *The Chartists: Popular Politics in the Industrial Revolution*. London: Temple Smith, 1984.

Thompson, Paul. *The Terror Timeline: Year by Year, Day by Day, Minute by Minute: A Comprehensive Chronicle of the Road to 9/11—and America's Response*. New York: Regan Books, 2004.

Thomson, David. *Marlon Brando*. New York: DK, 2003.

Tikkun. "On Limits of Compassion for Israeli Settlers in Gaza: A Jewish Perspective (by Uri Avnery)." 2005. <http://www.tikkun.org/rabbi_lerner/

Uri%20Avnery%20on%20Gush%20Settlers> (accessed May 23, 2006).

Timerman, Jacobo. *Chile: Death in the South*. New York: Knopf, 1987.

Tomaszewski, Irene, ed. *I am First a Human Being: The Letters of Krystyna Wituska*. Quebec City: Vehicule Press, 1997.

Tomaszewski, Irene, ed. *Inside a Gestapo Prison: The Letters of Krystyna Wituska 1942–1944*. Detroit, Michigan: Wayne State University Press, 2006.

Tonge, Jonathan. *Northern Ireland, Conflict and Change*. New York, N.Y.: Longman, 2002.

Topmiller, Robert J. *The Lotus Unleashed: The Buddhist Peace Movement in South Vietnam, 1964–1966*. University of Kentucky Press, 2002.

Touraine, A. *The May Movement: Revolt and Reform: May 1968—the Student Rebellion and Workers' Strikes—the Birth of a Social Movement*. Random House, 1971.

Trudeau Centre for Peace and Conflict Studies, U. of Toronto. "Environmental Scarcities, State Capacity and Civil Violence: The Case of Indonesia." May, 1997. <http://www.library.utoronto.ca/pcs/state/indon/indon3.htm> (accessed May 26, 2006).

Tygiel, Jules. *Baseball's Great Experiment: Jackie Robinson and His Legacy*. New York: Oxford University Press, 1997.

U.S. Census Bureau. "United States Census Bureau." <http://www.census.gov> (accessed on July 19, 2006).

U.S. Department of education. "Joint Letter from Secretary Paige and Secretary Rumsfeld." October 9, 2002. <http://www.ed.gov/policy/gen/guid/fpco/hottopics/ht10-09-02c.html> (accessed May 29, 2006).

U.S. Department of Justice. "Granting Pardon for Violations of the Selective Service Act, August 4, 1964 to March 28, 1973." January 21, 1977. <http://www.usdoj.gov/pardon/carter_proclamation.htm> (accessed May 31, 2006).

U.S. Department of Justice. "Guidance Regarding the Use of Race By Federal Law Enforcement Agencies." June 2003. <http://www.usdoj.gov/crt/split/documents/guidance_on_race.htm> (accessed May 10, 2006).

U.S. Department of Labor. "Compensation from before World War I through the Great Depression." 2001. <http://www.bls.gov/opub/cwc/cm20030124ar03p1.htm> (accessed June 3, 2006).

U.S. Department of State. "Report on the Taliban's war on women." November 17, 2001. <http://www.state.gov/g/drl/rls/6185.htm> (accessed May 15, 2006).

U.S. Government Printing Office. "Executive Sessions of the Senate Permanent Subcommittee on Investigations of the Committee on Government Operations." January 2003. <http://a257.g.akamaitech.net/7/257/2422/06amay20030700/www.gpo.gov/congress/senate/mccarthy/83869.html> (accessed May 25, 2006).

U.S. House of Representatives. "The United States House of Representatives." <http://www.house.gov/> (accessed on July 19, 2006).

U.S. House of Representatives. "Contract With America." <http://www.house.gov/house/Contract/CONTRACT.html> (accessed May 26, 2006).

U.S. Legal Forms, Inc. "Police Brutality Law and Legal Definition." <http://www.uslegalforms.com/legaldefinitions/police-brutality> (accessed May 10, 2006).

U.S. National Archives and Records Administration. "Teaching With Documents: Court Documents Related to Martin Luther King Jr., and Memphis Sanitation Workers." <http://www.archives.gov/education/lessons/memphis-v-mlk/> (accessed June 2, 2006).

U.S. National Archives and Records Administration. "Teaching with Documents: FDR's First Inaugural Address." <http://www.archives.gov/education/lessons/fdr-inaugural/> (accessed June 2, 2006).

U.S. National Park Service. "Historic Places of the Civil Rights Movement: We Shall Overcome." <http://www.cr.nps.gov/nR/travel/civilrights/index.htm> (accessed May 20, 2006).

U.S. Naval Institute. "The Secret Side of the Tonkin Gulf Incident (by Dale Andradé and Kenneth Conboy)." August, 1999. <http://www.usni.org/navalhistory/articles99/nhandrade.htm> (accessed May 18, 2006).

U.S. Senate. "The United States Senate." <http://www.senate.gov/> (accessed on July 19, 2006).

U.S. Senate. "Margaret Chase Smith: A Declaration of Conscience, June 1, 1950." <http://www.senate.gov/artandhistory/history/common/generic/Speeches_Smith_Declaration.htm> (accessed May 22, 2006).

U.S. Sentencing Commission. "Final Report on the Impact of United States V. Booker on Federal Sentencing." March 2006. <http://www.ussc.gov/booker_report/Booker_Report.pdf> (accessed May 21, 2006).

U.S. Sentencing Commission. "United States v. Booker:" January 12, 2005. <http://www.ussc.gov/Blakely/04-104.pdf> (accessed May 15, 2006).

UC Berkeley Library. "Anti Viet Nam War Protests, 1969." <http://lib.berkeley.edu.MRC/pacificaviet/#1969> (accessed June 2, 2006).

UNAIDS. *2006 Report on the Global AIDS Epidemic*. Geneva: Switzerland: UNAIDS, 2006.

UNAIDS. *AIDS Epidemic Update—December, 2005*. Geneva: Switzerland: UNAIDS, 2005.

UNAIDS. "UNAIDS Research." <http://www.unaids.org/en/Issues/Research/default.asp> (accessed on July 19, 2006).

United Farm Workers. "History." <http://www.ufw.org/> (accessed May 9, 2006).

United Kingdom Parliament. "House of Commons Hansard Debates, July 17, 1990." <http://www.publication.parliament.uk/pa/cm198990/cmhansard/1990-07–17/Orals-1.html> (accessed May 26, 2006).

United Nations Office of the High Commissioner for Human Rights. "United Nations." <http://www.ohchr.org/english/> (accessed on July 19, 2006).

United Nations Program on HIV/AIDS. "2006 Report on the Global AIDS Epidemic." <http://www.unaids.org/en/HIV_data/2006GlobalReport/default.asp> (accessed June 2, 2006).

United Nations. "Kyoto Protocol to the United Nations Framework on Climate Change." December 11, 1997. <http://unfccc.int/resource/docs/convkp/kpeng.html> (accessed May 16, 2006).

University of Missouri-Kansas City Law School. "Famous American Trials: 'The Chicago Seven' Trial—1969–1970" <http://www.law.umkc.edu/faculty/projects/ftrials/Chicago7/Account.html> (accessed May 25, 2006).

University of Oregon. "Little Rock,1957: An Overview." <http://www.uoregon.edu/~jbloom/race/overview.htm> (accessed May 21, 2006).

University of Ulster. "Conflict Archive on the Internet; Northern Ireland Conflict, Politics and Society." <http://cain.ulst.ac.uk/index.html> (accessed June 3, 2006).

University of Virginia. Institute for Advanced Technology in the Humanities. "Resistance to Revolution." <http://www.iath.virginia.edu/seminar/unit1/mob.html> (accessed May 24, 2006).

University of Washington. "The Cold War and Red Scare in Washington State." <http://www.washington.edu/uwired/outreach/cspn/curcan/main.html> (accessed May 25, 2006).

Vasil, Raj. *Governing Singapore: A History of National Development and Democracy.* Eastern University Press, 2004.

Victoria University Library at the University of Toronto. "Icons of Revolution." May, 1998. <http://library.vicu.utoronto.ca/exhibitions/posters/> (accessed May 21, 2006).

Virtual Campus of Public Health. "Virtual Campus of Public Health." <http://www.campusvirtualsp.org/eng/index.html> (accessed on July 19, 2006).

Vizentini, Paulo, and Marianne Wiesebron. *Free Trade for the Americas?: The United States' Push for the FTAA Agreement.* New York: Zed Books, 2004.

Wallace, Patricia Ward. *Politics of Conscience: A Biography of Margaret Chase Smith.* Westport, Conn.: Praeger, 1995.

Washington Post. "The Viet Nam Protests: When Worlds Collided." 2000 <http://www.washingtonpost.com/wp-srv/local/2000/vietnam092799.htm> (accessed June 2, 2006).

Wayne State University, Walter P. Reuther Library. "Walking Buzzards." <http://www.reuther.wayne.edu/MAN/2Memphis.htm> (accessed June 5, 2006).

We Shall Overcome: Historic Places of the Civil Rights Movement. "Selma-to-Montgomery March." <http://www.cr.nps.gov/nr/travel/civilrights/sitelist1.htm> (accessed June 3, 2006).

Weber, Thomas. *On the Salt March: The Historiography of Gandhi's March to Dandi.* New York: HarperCollins Publishers India, 1997.

Weddington, Sarah. *A Question of Choice.* New York: Penguin, 1993.

Wells, Tom. *The War Within: America's Battle Over Vietnam.* New York: Henry Holt, 1994.

Wexler, Sanford. *The Civil Rights Movement.* New York: Facts on File, 1999.

Weyler, Rex. *Greenpeace: How a Group of Journalists, Ecologists, and Visionaries Changed the World.* Emmaus, Penn.: Rodale, 2004.

Whelpton, John. *A History of Nepal.* London: Cambridge University Press, 2004.

White House. "White House Office of Communications." <http://www.whitehouse.gov/news/> (accessed on July 19, 2006).

Wiener, Jon, ed. *Conspiracy in the Streets: The Extraordinary Trial of the Chicago Eight.* New York: New Press, 2006.

Williams, Juan. *Eyes on the Prize: America's Civil Rights Years, 1954–1965.* New York: Viking, 1987.

Winters, Paul A. *The Civil Rights Movement.* San Diego, Calif.: Greenhaven Press, 2000.

Winters, Paul A., editor. *The Civil Rights Movement.* San Diego, Calif.: Greenhaven, 2000.

Woods, Ngaire. *The Globalizers: The IMF, the World Bank, and Their Borrowers.* Ithaca, NY: Cornell University Press, 2006.

Woodstock Preservation Archives. "Statement on the Historical and Cultural Significance of the 1969 Woodstock Festival Site." September 25, 2001. <http://www.woodstockpreservation.org:81/archmat/FinalSigState.pdf> (accessed May 26, 2006).

Woody Guthrie Foundation and Archives. "Wood Guthrie: Biography." <http://www.woodyguthrie.org/biography.htm> (accessed May 25, 2006).

Wooley, Bryan. *When the Morning Comes.* Lexington, Ky.: University Press of Kentucky, 1975.

Workman, Dave P. *Peta Files: The Dark Side of the Animal Rights Movement.* Bellevue, Wash.: Merril Press, 2003.

World Bank (WB). <http://www.worldbank.org/> (accessed June 1, 2006).

World Bank and UNAIDS. *Responding to HIV/AIDS Crisis: Lessons from Global Best Practices.* Geneva: Switzerland: The World Bank, 2005.

World Bank. "HIV/AIDS in Africa—Regional Brief." <http://web.worldbank.org/WBSITE/EXTERNAL/ COUNTRIES/AFRICAEXT/EXTAFRHEANUTPOP/ EXTAFRREGTOPHIVAIDS/0,contentMDK:20411613~ menuPK:717155~pagePK: 34004173~piPK:34003707~the SitePK: 717148,00.html> (accessed May 31, 2006).

World War One Document Archive. "The Sedition Act, 1918." <http://www.gwpda.org/1918/usspy.html> (accessed May 18, 2006).

Wynn, Neil A. *From Progressivism to Prosperity: World War I and American Society*. Holmes & Meier, 1986.

Yell, Mitchell L. *The Law and Special Education*. Upper Saddle River, N.J.: Merrill, 1998.

Yew, Lee Kuan. *From Third World to First: The Singapore Story: 1965–2000*. New York: HarperCollins, 2000.

Young, Alfred F. *The Shoemaker and the Tea Party: Memory and the American Revolution*. Boston, Mass.: Beacon Press, 2000.

Zakin, Susan. *Coyotes and Town Dogs: Earth First! and the Environmental Movement*. Tucson: University of Arizona Press, 2002.

Zirkel, Perry A. *Section 504: Student Issues, Legal Requirements, and Practical Recommendations*. Bloomington, Ind.: Phi Delta Kappa Educational Foundation, 2005.

Zukin, Sharon. *Point of Purchase: How Shopping Changed America*. New York: Routledge, 2004.

Index

Boldface indicates a primary source.
Italics indicates an illustration on the page.